Not Irish Enough

Not Irish Enough

An Anglo-Irish Family's Three Centuries in Ireland

Sara Day

NEW ACADEMIA PUBLISHING

Washington, DC

Printed in the United States of America

Library of Congress Control Number: 2021913474
ISBN 978-1-7348659-7-4 paperback (alk. paper)
ISBN 978-1-9558353-6-7 hardcover

New Academia Publishing, 4401-A Connecticut Ave. NW, #236,
Washington, DC 20008
info@newacademia.com - www.newacademia.com

To my father Michael William Henry Head (1912-1970),
whose Irish stories inspired this book.

Contents

Illustrations

Acknowledgments

It was my brother, Patrick Head, who gave me the original idea to pursue our vanishing family story, although he has often joked that he had a pamphlet in mind, not a tome! But I had spent my career working on large and challenging projects and I came to see that this one deserved no less of an effort. A project as ambitious as this would not have been possible without the help of a great many people in Ireland, the U.K. and the U.S.A. However, the historical and genealogical groundwork for this book began in the main and specialized reading rooms of the Library of Congress, where I had been a senior writer-researcher-curator-editor in the exhibits and publication offices.

During four research trips to Ireland, first to Waterford City and North Tipperary, then back to North Tipperary, then two more in Dublin's archives, I met many local historians and archivists, beginning with Donal Moore, Waterford City archivist, who threw more light on the civic roles of Michael Head and his two sons in the late seventeenth century. In North Tipperary, Kevin Griffin spent several hours guiding me, my mother, and first cousin through the former Derry Castle lands along Lough Derg, the Heads' first estate in that troubled county. Griffin's book on the history and traditions of the parish of Ballina/Boher has been of continuing importance to my research on the Heads of Derry Castle and dispossessed previous owners, as well as other Anglo-Irish families in the area. At Ashley Park, a successor to the house and estate owned for three generations by the junior branch of the Head family and a popular event venue today, I was introduced to Daniel Grace, an extremely knowledgeable and prolific historian of the parish of Monsea & Killodiernan and North Tipperary whose many publications and guidance have been of inestimable value to me for twenty years.

On a second research trip, local historian Nancy Murphy began to help me track down family graves and inscriptions, while Danny allowed me to copy the copious Head family deeds from the late seventeenth century until 1825, which had been copied for a title search by the subsequent owners of Ashley Park. These provided the essential pathway for my book. Capt. Donald Swan, the owner of Modreeny in Cloughjordan, the other onetime family property still in existence, showed us around the house and the Charlie Swan Equestrian Centre there, named after and run by his son, the champion National Hunt jockey and trainer. For my cousin, Barbara Bowers, a passionate devotee of horse racing, a true "Protestant with a horse," this was the high point of that trip. Barbara became my partner during my first research trip to Dublin, assisting me in archival research in the National Library of Ireland and Register of Deeds.

On our first visit to the former Head estate of Derrylahan Park in the parish of Lorrha and Dorrha, we were warmly greeted by Felim Kennedy, who lives in a wooden house on his land in front of the ruins of the house burned by the IRA in 1921. Felim introduced us to ninety-year-old Maureen "Betty" Perry, whose mother was a Head of Carrig, at Dooley's Hotel in Birr. She gave me historical materials relating to her branch of the family. On a second visit to the area, this time with my husband, we stayed at Somerset, John and Vera O'Meara's house on lands adjacent to the former Head property where the O'Mearas had farmed for generations. That night, warmed by an outstanding Jameson whiskey and a peat fire, they shared their family archive with us. Vera copied materials of interest for me in Birr while I spent a long afternoon copying by hand a curiously revealing 1892 deed in the muniments room of Birr Castle, with the permission of the earl and countess of Rosse, whose ancestors were wellknown to two generations of Heads of nearby Derrylahan.

From the purely local, my research began widening with the help and encouragement of Rolf and Magda Loeber, Dutch academics based in Pittsburgh, who spent decades researching and collecting Irish historical and literary materials during many extended visits to Ireland. Anne Burnham, my Irish-born friend of many years, introduced me to them and they invited me to spend a couple of days in their archives. Rolf brought relevant materials to my attention, sending me further information later, before his untimely death. He was working at the time on a book with Anne Burnham's editorial assistance. Anne would become one of my two primary editors. Her innate knowledge of Ireland and its history saved me from many a pitfall as I struggled to tell a rather different version from the one she was taught at school in Ireland, while her eye for consistency, repetition, style, and tone makes her an outstanding editor. After an interruption of several years researching and writing another book, I collected a considerable library of books related to my focus and benefitted from the extraordinary genealogical and historical riches to be found through search engines and online resources such as Findmypast.com and Irishnewsarchive.com.

At this point, two others with deep ties to Lorrha parish, military researcher and enthusiast Gerard O'Meara and local historian David Broderick, reached out to me. Both of them have been a tremendous help with research on the last Head proprietor of Derrylahan, my grandfather Colonel Charles O. Head. For his book *Lorrha People in the Great War*, Ger included a great deal of historical information about the family from my grandfather's autobiography *No Great Shakes* and his own research. David Broderick of Lorrha got in touch with me as he was working on a ten-year project to research Derrylahan Park and the Head family, culminating in a popular powerpoint presentation "Bringing the Matter to a Head." I was able to lead him to the Heads' subsequent home in the U.K., which he visited. David has become another source of local research, always generous with his responses, including photographs. He told me about a blog, "Family History," which appeared to feature photographs and information about my grandfather's parents and his siblings at Derrylahan. This blog is constantly reinforced with new postings by writer and genealogist Nicola Jennings, who turned out to be a fifth cousin several times removed. Nicola has been an unequaled resource on family history, confirming and extending stories that I had thought might be apocryphal. While I was getting nowhere on the Head family's fifth estate in North Tipperary, I was referred to Tim Boland's article on the Heads of Ballyquiveen, allowing me to include information I had been challenged to find on my own and which further reflected the effects of agrarian rebellion on County Tipperary landlords. Noel Monteith who grew up on the farm assigned to his father by the Irish Land Commission after Charles Head's land was compulsorily purchased in the 1920s, has provided me with information about that division, including his annotations to a map of the former estate. Pat Smith, a Monteith family member, provided the names of the eight original Land Commission awardees.

While I worked in the publishing office of the Library of Congress, my colleague Margaret (Peggy) Wagner enjoyed hearing stories about the Heads of Derrylahan as told me by my father, who spent his first nine years there until the burning. By a stroke of good luck, I met her again following her retirement from a remarkable thirty-five-year career, and she asked me if I had managed to write "that book." Knowing she was expert in World War I history, I had brought a copy of my WWI chapter. To my surprise and delight, this consummate historian and editor offered to read other chapters and edit them, with particular focus on the historical context, which was as important to my conception of the book as the details of the family's three centuries in Ireland. An outstanding fact checker, cross-questioner, and believer in clarity of expression, she made vast improvements to my earlier drafts—a perfect balance with Anne Burnham's many valued and nuanced suggestions. More recently, I acquired the perspective of two biographer friends, Jennifer Cockburn and Avis Bohlen, who read and critiqued all chapters while I did the same for theirs. Likewise, Danny Grace read several chapters and offered corrections and suggestions. I would also like to thank many other literary friends who read parts of this book at various stages, including my longtime friend and colleague Linda Osborne, Rick and Judy Gilmore, Mary Kopper, and Joanna Woods. My cousins Barbara Bowers, Robin Dean (since deceased), and Victoria Wilson sent me photographs, letters, handwritten memoirs, and unpublished manuscripts left to them by their mothers, all of which added to the few family archives and photographs that survived a second house fire in England, now mostly held for the next generation by my brother. Thad Garrett tracked down a number of hard-to-find articles and made the two excellent maps of Ireland and County Tipperary featured in this book. Dodge-Chrome, a local digital printing service, made high-resolution scans of many old photographs in my possession.

In March 2020, I reached out to the eminent Irish historian and biographer Roy Foster for advice about finding a publisher for my book. I had been a longtime admirer of his many books and was particularly inspired by his iconoclastic *The Irish Story: Telling Tales and Making it Up in Ireland*. Confined as we were to our homes by the COVID pandemic, we began an e-mail correspondence during which I began to view him as a mentor. He and others encouraged me to extend this history through Brexit in my epilogue, and he subsequently read that and several chapters for which he expressed an enthusiasm that buoyed me through the final push. Through it all, my husband, Stephen Day, my man for all seasons, accompanied me to Co. Tipperary and subsequently published an amusing short story "Extreme Spousal Support: Tracing Irish Ancestors." Along with many helpful editorial suggestions, he was abidingly patient and supportive during my years of effort and preoccupation with *Not Irish Enough*. I could not have done it without him. He also allowed me to co-opt his ancestor Col. Robert Phair (Phayre) to lead my way through chapters 3 thru 5. Last, but not least, I was delighted when the publisher of my previous book, Anna Lawton of New Academia Publishing in Washington, DC, agreed to publish this book. The index was compiled by Amron Gravett of Wild Clover Book Services.

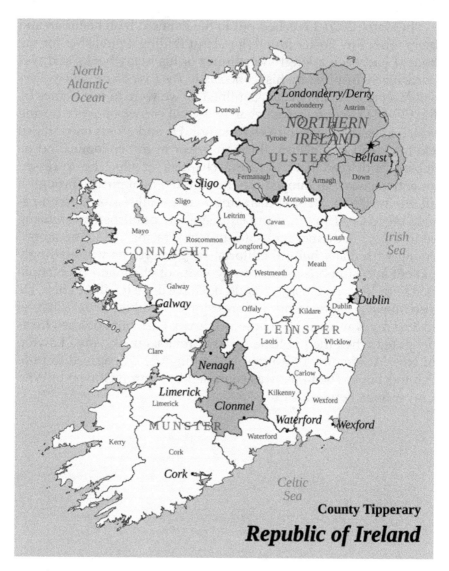

1. Map of the Republic of Ireland and Northern Ireland, showing the four provinces, Ulster, Connacht, Leinster, and Munster, counties, and major cities, and highlighting County Tipperary and the capitals of its North and South Ridings, Nenagh and Clonmel. The map was adapted by Thad Garrett from "County Tipperary in Ireland" by O'Dea (Own work) [CC-BY-SA-3.0], via Wikimedia Commons. Available at https://commons.wikimedia.org/wiki/File:County_Tipperary_in_Ireland.svg.

Introduction

Three Hundred Years in Ireland,
but not Irish Enough

History forgets the losers.
—Roy Foster, *The Irish Story* (2002).[1]

My experience of Irish landlords is entirely the opposite of
the picture that is usually painted of them...The Irish land
agitation was a perfectly natural, though hardly moral,
struggle on the part of the tenants to get possession of their
land, and an equally natural endeavour by the landlords to
retain their property. The champions of the tenants' side,
with their own ends in view, placed no limit on the defa-
mation they poured on the heads of the landlords; the latter
had only the rights of property and Parliamentary sanction
as their blunt and almost worn-out defensive weapons. But
as a class they deserve rescue from the infamy with which
they have been overwhelmed.
—Lt. Col. Charles O. Head, *No Great Shakes* (1943).[2]

Of the many stories my father told me about growing up with his
family in County Tipperary, Ireland, the one that made the deepest
impression was of the night the IRA burned Derrylahan Park, his
family's home. The IRA's real target, however, was my grandfather,
Charles Head, a twice retired British army officer, local justice of the
peace, and outspoken Unionist—for Ireland's continued inclusion
in the United Kingdom—whom they had failed to assassinate two
weeks earlier and who had already wisely departed for England.
The burning of Derrylahan occurred just days before a truce ended
the Anglo-Irish War on July 11, 1921. During those last weeks, a
number of others in the area of Birr—six miles away in Co. Offaly,

then known as King's County—were murdered, or executed as spies and informers by the IRA, and other houses belonging to Anglo-Irish landlords were torched.

My grandparents obviously thought that the best chance for saving their property was for my grandfather to leave Ireland until peace was restored. Women and children were generally not targeted during this conflict or the civil war which followed. About seventy-six such houses were burned during what the Irish termed the War of Independence (1919-1921), mostly in Munster, the conflict's heartland; approximately 199 more were reduced to smoldering ruins during the subsequent Irish Civil War (1922-1923), including many of outstanding architectural merit, along with priceless collections of paintings, furniture, *objets d'art*, and family and estate documents. Many of the owners, like my grandparents, had fled to England before or after the Free State of Ireland was inaugurated in 1922.

My grandfather left a vivid account of those final years in Ireland in his memoir published in 1943—which he self-deprecatingly titled *No Great Shakes!* It was one of the few family accounts that were available when I became curious about my family history. By then, my father was long dead, as was an older sister, who would have had her own fascinating story to tell about the dramatic conclusion to her Irish childhood (the oldest sister was away at boarding school). However, forty years after the burning, she and her sister wrote accounts of their childhoods at Derrylahan. Most family documents were lost—either due to family problems in the late nineteenth-century, in the Derrylahan fire, or in a later, accidental one in England. So over the years I read my grandfather's book repeatedly until I found I had more questions than answers. What had my father's family done to deserve being burned out of their home?

My grandfather lived a good part of his youth serving the British Empire overseas, an extended absence from his very troubled birthplace that may have sheltered him from the realities of political changes there. While he devoted a final chapter to his view of Irish history, including the long fight for the right to self-government from a parliament in Dublin, I found it to be inadequate and judgmental. He was a talented writer (this was not his only book), and a man of upright character and strong opinions who had endured embittering experiences in the country he loved. Were his opinions fair or merely reflective of his prejudices? Sometimes I suspected that he chose to generalize and explain away the realities of Ireland's nineteenth-century agrarian unrest and terrorism, most of which he did not experience directly (he was born in 1869). Irish lawyer and prolific author Terence de Vere White, in an entire chapter, "The Unknown Unionist," of his 1972 book *The Anglo-Irish*, roundly mocked Charles Head as a regular Colonel Blimp for his particular view of Irish history, quoting him so copiously that I couldn't help wondering if he had acquired permission from the publisher: "The gods he [Colonel Head] worshipped were not the gods of Ireland," declared White. "Patriotism meant love of England. Duty meant duty to England; loyalty, loyalty to the King of England."[3] The reality was, as he made clear in his autobiography, my grandfather felt both British and Irish, a sentiment shared by a great many of his Anglo-Irish tribe.

Certain that White had his own prejudices and detecting inaccuracies in his account of my grandfather and his antecedents, I decided to pursue my own research into the three hundred years during which the Head family flourished or floundered in Ireland. In doing so, while sometimes sympathizing with my grandfather's strong views, I came to understand his selective memory or "convenient amnesia," as I termed it. He was indeed a man of his time, tribe, politics, and class, a thorough-going Tory. My quest became far more than family history: the family was no longer the sole subject but a device to shed light on a comparatively neglected aspect of Irish history, the experience of the Anglo-Irish lesser landlords, rather than the more chronicled aristocrats.

My father died in 1970 when I was only twenty-six, but I never forgot the colorful and humorous stories he told me of his childhood in Northern Tipperary. With early retirement from the Library of Congress in Washington, DC—where I had honed my research and writing skills on many historical projects resulting in books and exhibitions—my opportunity came to measure his stories and my grandfather's published memoir against my own research into a broader history. They say that every author writes in an effort to discover, understand, and come to terms with something they need

to know, and I am no exception. The Anglo-Irish side of my ancestral history (and that of my husband) obsesses me. Not surprisingly, I find myself viewing it with an ambivalence born of family
pride, loyalty, honor, and love—countered by the terrible history of
invasion, land grabbing, abuse, murder, famine, and poverty that
have marked Irish history for the last millennium.

County Tipperary has been called Ireland's "premier county"
because of its fiercely nationalist history: "where Tipperary leads,
Ireland follows," so the saying went, and, following independence,
Ireland's history was more often told from a nationalist point of
view. In his iconoclastic book *The Irish Story: Telling Tales and Making
It Up in Ireland*, historian Roy Foster examines how and why the key
moments of Ireland's past—the 1798 Rising, the Famine, the Celtic Revival, the Easter 1916 Rising, and the 1960s-1990s Troubles—
have been worked into a shifting, politicized, and sentimentalized
narrative, a "story of Ireland" which often demonizes Anglo-Irish
Protestant landowners, such as the Head family, as Unionists who
remained loyal to the United Kingdom as well as, perhaps more de-
servedly, the British government. He explains that the function of
studying and teaching this "specifically oriented" version of Irish
history in the predominantly Catholic school system "was to stress
the continuity of the separatist tradition...as well as implicitly (or
indeed explicitly) to stress the fact that British rule in Ireland was
always an undesirable and undesired imposition, taking the form
of oppression and exploitation of a people struggling to be free."
Professional historians at both the historically Catholic University
College Dublin, and the historically Protestant Trinity College began rejecting the nationalist bias from about 1940 onward.[4]

Some contemporary historians have thrown down a gauntlet
to the descendants of those who were marginalized in Ireland
following its independence to recount and analyze their stories
and add them to the general historical pool.[5] The challenge for
scions of these families, among whom I belong, is not to forge an
alienating body of self-justifications but to provide well-researched
and reasoned counterweights to many one-sided histories. While
books that present a more balanced or nuanced history have been
welcomed by professional and academic historians, they have
too often been dismissed as revisionist by those wedded to the

"everything British was bad" mantra—again, a convenient amnesia. Apparently, "revisionist" first became a term of abuse during the sectarian and political terrorism in Northern Ireland, when historians who rejected physical force republicanism were accused of being part of a political movement. I have been astonished and somewhat intimidated by the fury with which some of the so-called revisionist histories have been attacked on certain Irish websites. But the Anglo-Irish are "no petty people," as William Butler Yeats argued in the Senate of the Dáil (Irish Parliament) in 1925, and their lesser-known stories deserve to emerge to enrich the complicated tapestry of Irish history.

Ironically, my first voyage of discovery to Ireland in search of the Head family of Waterford City and Co. Tipperary began just three weeks after the terrors of 9/11. I came close to postponing plans that had involved months of work and years of anticipation. I flew out of an almost deserted Washington Dulles airport on an almost empty plane, away from my adopted country, which was now shocked and devastated by vicious terrorist acts, to the country of my father's birth, where terrorism had driven him from his home. In Waterford, I searched for records of the Heads, who were shipping merchants, aldermen, and mayors there before acquiring land in Co. Tipperary at the end of the seventeenth century. In North Tipperary, I visited the ruins and remaining houses built or occupied in the eighteenth and nineteenth centuries by various branches of this once and still respected and prolific family. Despite the touchiness of my topic, I encountered extraordinary generosity and warmth from area residents, particularly from local historians, who led me to several priceless family stories and documents.

On a subsequent trip to North Tipperary, and probably resulting from the questions I was asking, I found that, for the first time, my grandfather's memoir was being read by local historians (probably in photocopied form since it is hard to find an original copy). These historians have taken on the task of unearthing and publishing segments of the history of the mostly long-departed Anglo-Irish Protestant landowning families of the region. The much-published local historian Daniel Grace, who has been extraordinarily helpful to me for twenty years, has written that "Land League propaganda appears to have tarred all landlords with the same brush. Recent studies have shown that only a minority of landlords actively exploited their tenantry."[6] Such local research has contributed to the Connacht Landed Estates Project, a database hosted by University College, Galway, and funded by the Irish Council for Research in the Humanities and Social Sciences, containing brief descriptions of estates and the families associated with them in the provinces of Munster and Connacht. Historian Terence Dooley, director of the Centre for the Study of Historic Irish Houses and Estates at Maynooth University, Co. Kildare, and the author of numerous studies on the subject, has been a major resource for this book.

Most of the records of over seven hundred years of British involvement in Ireland and of documents important for genealogical research were destroyed in the 1922 firebombing of the Irish Public Record Office in Dublin during the Irish Civil War. Historians and genealogists are thus faced with an extraordinary challenge. But, gradually, supplementary source material, including the papers of some of the landed families, has been entering the archives. These and the rich reserves of newspapers, memoirs, and fiction are being mined by historians and literary scholars. During two further trips to Ireland, I spent time in Dublin at the National Library, the National Archives, and the Registry of Deeds, in all of which I found considerable documentary evidence of the Heads' trajectory in Ireland. However, a major roadblock and frustration is that the voluminous and essential records of the Irish Land Commission remain closed to historians and researchers.

Our family's tenure in North Tipperary began in 1696 when shipping merchant John Head, the oldest son of a two-time Protestant mayor of Waterford during an extremely troubled period in English and Irish history and soon to be mayor himself, acquired the nearly 1,200-acre land grant on scenic Lough Derg on the Shannon River through marriage to the daughter and sole heir of one of the Cromwellian officers compensated with land forfeited from Irish rebels. Thus began the Head tradition of marrying advantageously—for land, money, or social and political connection—benefiting as did so many others of the eighteenth-century Protestant Ascendancy in Ireland after penal laws ensured land ownership, political power, and religious domination for members of the Anglican Church of Ireland. He and the next two generations of Heads at Derry Castle on Lough Derg increased the acreage and worked hard to improve the productivity of what had been largely marginal land.[7] Over time, the estate became seriously encumbered with the cost of dowries for numerous daughters and setting up younger sons in professions while incomes fell dramatically with the drop in the market for agricultural products to feed vast standing armies following the end of the Napoleonic Wars. Added to the general malaise were all too frequent failed harvests due to bad weather, poor land, the population explosion among the already impoverished small farmers and laborers, and insidious violence by agrarian protestors, particularly in Munster. The 3,000-acre Derry Castle estate was one of thousands that foundered in bankruptcy around the time of Ireland's Great Potato Famine in the mid-nineteenth century. Many thousands of desperately poor laborers and tenant farmers and their families were evicted from these failed estates, and many of those who were evicted starved or were forced to emigrate.

As with many such landlord families, some of the Heads and their relations, unable to adapt to their changed circumstances, descended into poverty and obscurity. Yet, throughout these troubled times, the more enterprising persisted and succeeded in Ireland, as professionals, through more advantageous marriages, or by adjusting to changes in land ownership and national politics. The sale of thousands of bankrupt estates in the wake of the Famine through the Encumbered Estates Court, for example, allowed my great-grandfather, a descendant of a junior branch of the family, to rise phoenix-like with a far larger estate—the ill-fated Derrylahan Park—a large family, and some prominence in county affairs before the tide of history turned against him and his ilk.

In 1902, some fourteen years after his father's death, my grandfather, along with his younger brother, secured a mortgage to buy back from the Court of Chancery what remained of the estate, control of which their feckless, alcoholic, and bankrupt oldest brother had been forced to relinquish by his father's trustees and in the face of the Gladstonian land acts. Despite the angry invective and the reality of the land wars, the many years that Charles Head spent overseas with the British army in India, China, and South Africa had filled him with nostalgia for his childhood home. By the time he was called back into active service in 1914, he had turned his eight hundred neglected acres into a successful working farm. Indeed, Charles Head's was another short-lived and ill-fated attempt to hold on to a share of that most disputed commodity, Irish land.

I have many friends and acquaintances, as well as a beloved daughter-in-law, in America who are proud of and curious about their descent from Irish Catholic immigrants. I'm well aware of the deep animosity that endures in some quarters in Ireland and the United States toward Britain and the former Anglo-Irish Protestant landlords, particularly during the potato famine of 1845-1849, the suppression of various patriotic rebellions against British rule, and mass evictions for nonpayment of rent. This has often given me pause, but my own curiosity has spurred me on in pursuing my family's Irish story as part of the fabric of the Anglo-Irish tribe. The Heads were never more than what academics refer to as "minor gentry," denoting the size of their estates, but they or their kin seemed to make enough colorful appearances in local and national history that their experiences and perspectives are revealing of an alternative or lesser-known aspect of Ascendancy life and its demise. I hope my account will provide further links of understanding across a long and bitter divide, humanizing those for whom those halcyon years in Ireland did not end well.

Sara Day
Washington, D.C.
2021

Chapter 1

Derrylahan: The Big House Burns, but Memories Endure

Is it height—in this country of otherwise low buildings—that got these Anglo-Irish houses their 'big' name? Or have they been called 'big' with a slight inflection—that of hostility, irony? One may call a man 'big' with just that inflection because he seems to think the hell of himself.

—Elizabeth Bowen, "The Big House" in *The Mulberry Tree* (1986).[1]

When the big curtains caught fire and the flames climbed into the sky, it was a glorious sight.

—Anonymous IRA participant in the burning of Derrylahan

"ANOTHER MANSION BURNED. Derrylahan Reduced to Ashes. Col. Head "Too Friendly with the English." So ran the headline of the *King's County Chronicle*, a Unionist newspaper, on July 7, 1921. It was the only announcement of that atrocity in the press. Five days earlier, at 2 a.m. on Saturday, July 2, 1921, Margery Head, two of the young Head children, and the few women servants who lived in the house were rudely awakened by loud banging on the doors. With Colonel Head away in England—after narrowly escaping an IRA assassination squad on his land in mid-June—eight-year-old Michael was the only male in the house that night. Ten-year-old Grace was there but the elder daughter Betty was away at boarding school.

It must have occurred to my grandparents that failure to execute the Colonel might result in further attempts on their safety. However, the couple presumed, or perhaps hoped, that calm would be restored once the truce ending the Irish War of Independence (1919-1921) was signed, which appeared to be imminent. Margery

Head, a strong and courageous woman, could have joined her husband with the children but she did not want to leave their only home unoccupied, which would have left it vulnerable to pillage or arson. The remote Victorian stone house had no telephone and the family car had been left in nearby Birr for repairs, leaving just a pony and trap for transportation. Considering its remoteness and the constant threat of terrorist acts, it is surprising that one of the male staff was not asked to spend nights in the house. There had been at least three nighttime raids of the house by the IRA looking for arms, armed men were seen drilling in the park, and two young Protestants had just been executed by the IRA on their family farm on the other side of Birr before their farmhouse was burned. The Heads' Protestant chauffeur and the Catholic gamekeeper shared a cottage about half a mile from the house. However, if either of these men had been in the house, it would have made no difference to the outcome and might have resulted in more murders.

"About twenty men, it seemed, arrived at about 2 a.m. and ordered everybody in the house to get out, as their intention was to burn it," my grandfather wrote some twenty years later. Betty described what she had been told: The men "had already stolen thirty gallons of petrol from a neighbour which they poured everywhere and when they struck a match it virtually exploded. There was no time to save anything much and those in the house had to sit outside in their nightclothes." "My wife besought, implored and finally offered to purchase at high price the salvation of the house, but without the slightest effect," my grandfather continued. "She then asked time to pack some clothes, and was given five minutes, but on their expiry, nobody would carry down her trunk, and she could not do it herself, so she lost all her clothing except the night attire she wore." When one of the men appeared from the house with a small Minimax fire extinguisher wondering what it was for, she snatched it from him, crashed it into action, and turned it full in the leader's face. It is surprising he didn't shoot her. One of the men grabbed the extinguisher, and she was thrown to the ground with such force that she suffered a fractured rib, all this while her terrified children, who were being held under armed guard, watched. Finally, with the house ablaze, the arsonists left. The kitchen wing of the house was the only part left relatively intact.

The flames were seen as far away as Birr, but there was no real hope of dousing the fire. In the wake of a two-month-long drought that unusually hot summer, there was no water close enough for a chain of buckets. The gamekeeper and chauffeur smashed the windows furthest away from the fire and threw out as much of the remaining furniture as they could. Forty years later, my grandmother penned some very brief notes about the burning of their house to her daughter Grace: "Keeper and chauffeur save all possible. Kindly cook removes our food! And kindly parlour maid saves the silver. These brave deeds happen whilst the house is flaming and floors crashing…the house becomes a shell." "Some proportion of these articles were not collected by us again," reported my grandfather. "In a very few hours the home we all loved was a pitiful ruin. The feelings of the waifs on that lovely summer morning cannot be described, nor the exhaustion they endured before they found another roof to shelter them. A few days later my wife and children joined me in England."[2] According to local folklore, they tried to seek shelter with another "Big House" family in the area but, fearing they would meet the same fate, the owners refused to take them in.[3] Instead, a horse and cart carried them slowly into Birr where they could stay with relatives.

2. Derrylahan Park. Lorrha, County Tipperary after the burning by the IRA during the night of July 1-2, 1921. Birr Historical Society.

Derrylahan Park was the scene of the happy, carefree childhood of just two generations of Head family children before its burning in July 1921. Formerly Walshpark, the estate of a branch of the Walshes, the prolific and widespread Old English Catholic family, it was purchased through the Encumbered Estates Court in 1859 by my great-grandfather William Henry Head, the descendant of a numerous family resident in North Tipperary since the late seventeenth century. He proceeded to tear down the Walsh's undistinguished and, in his eyes, old-fashioned Georgian house and commission the renowned Dublin architect Sir Thomas Newenham Deane to design the high Victorian mansion with the most modern of amenities, along with farm buildings, gatehouse, and smaller but well-appointed stone houses for his staff. The house, built of brick and faced with cut stone, was deliberately located at the end of a mile-long drive from the nearest road.

My grandfather, Charles Head, born in 1869, spent the first eight years of his life at Derrylahan, along with numerous brothers and sisters, before leaving for boarding school.[4] Charles remembered the estate as a delightful place for children: "A large variety of wild life abounded in it, especially wild-fowl and butterflies," he wrote years after leaving Ireland. "Wild fruits such as strawberries, raspberries, gooseberries, barberries and blackberries grew in abundance in their season, and could be made the objects of short expeditions for their gathering. Old bits of ruins cropped up all over the place, useful for exploring and picnics. All sorts of tree-freaks lent themselves to the construction of miniature cabins in the Swiss Family Robinson style. The cottages on the estate could always be drawn for a glass of milk or slice of home-made bread."

When Charles was a child, the prosperous Derrylahan estate comprised the demesne and "Pleasure Ground" surrounding the house and, beyond that, extensive lands let to tenant farmers, a total of 2,300 acres.[5] Charles's oldest brother, William (Willie) Edward Head inherited Derrylahan on the death of their father in 1888. The estate was to be held in trust until he turned twenty-five in April 1889. Charles, the third son, had left Ireland for military training in England at age sixteen and was now a young officer with the Royal Horse Artillery, stationed in Devon. As a result of Willie's profligacy and bankruptcy and the Irish land wars and land acts of the late nineteenth century, most of the farms were sold to the tenants and the house was rented. Years of living abroad heightened Charles's nostalgia for his childhood at Derrylahan and, in 1901, he decided to buy back, with a mortgage from his mother and bachelor younger brother, the neglected mansion and what was left of the equally neglected land. The estate on which Charles Head's children spent the early part of their childhood was greatly reduced from their grandfather's time. Yet 800 acres seemed vast to them.[6] Following his early retirement from the British Army, Charles Head turned his acreage into a working farm. His English wife, an heiress to a fine brewery fortune, was able to provide the funds needed to return the house and gardens to the show place they had been.

The Heads' three children, Betty, Grace, and Mike, were born in 1909, 1911, and 1912, so that the memories that Betty and Grace wrote down forty years after they left Ireland ran from about midway through WWI up to, but not including, the burning of their home in July 1921. Both women echoed their father in writing lyrically about the flora and fauna and natural beauty of the Derrylahan grounds and the nearby bog. The "Pleasure Ground," as it was called in Ireland, contained the shrubberies and rare trees that W. H. Head had planted. There was a wide gravel sweep to the front door on the north side of the house with rough grass beyond it that became a golden mass of daffodils in the spring. On the south and east sides of the house were lawns, flower beds, and a tennis court, and on the west end was the kitchen with its backyard. Like other Irish houses, the stables or farmyards were about half a mile from the house. About a quarter of a mile from the house, there was a walled two-acre kitchen garden with numerous varieties of fruit and vegetables. Both black and white grapes grew in the greenhouse and, on both sides of the center path were beds of St. Brigid anemones which made a multi-colored carpet in the spring.

Derrylahan had two large and beautiful oak woods as well as the bog, so it was a veritable paradise for wildlife. The bog was a favorite place for dragonflies, moths, and butterflies and such beautiful birds as the curlew, nightjar, and yellow wagtail. The whole estate was a paradise of wildflowers. There were bee orchids beside the avenue, and primroses, violets, bluebells, and wood anemones grew everywhere. Near the ruins of the old house was an avenue of beech trees with a carpet of snowdrops, and there were yet more snowdrops under a chestnut tree near the house. In Victorian times, a railway briefly ran through the Park and a large patch of columbines grew where the track had been removed. "Anyone who has ever been to Ireland in the spring must remember the gorse which is more golden than anywhere else and smells so sweet," noted Betty.

"In the soft fruit season," Betty recalled, "the garden was kept locked and we were only allowed in for ten minutes a day. We would rush to get a rhubarb leaf and then fill it as full of fruit as we could in the time. However, it didn't really matter as we could climb over the wall—much to the gardener's wrath. There were so many apples that sheets were tied to the trees and the apples were shaken into them. The apple loft was up a back staircase out of the scullery and the gardener slept next door." Fruit was the equivalent of today's children's passion for sweets (candy). "My brother once had a very bad tummy ache in the middle of the night," Betty

3.   Two Edwardian fairies, Betty and Grace, among the daffodils at Derrylahan, ca. 1914. Head family.

remembered, "and when asked if he had eaten much fruit replied, 'Not so much as usual—only 7 apples and 6 pears.' Of course we had no telephone and, as the avenue was a mile long and we were five miles from Birr, getting help in an emergency was very difficult. The groom was roused out of bed and sent post haste in the dogcart to Birr for the doctor, who came and dealt with the crisis."

All was perfection for those adventurous, outdoors-loving sisters except for one fly in the ointment, their difficult and grimly authoritarian English nurses; in fact, Grace, who was a free-spirited, taxing child, was reputed to have had one nurse who drank methylated spirits and drugged her "so that she had peace for her drunken orgies." Things improved greatly, recalled Grace, when their brother Michael was born in 1912. "He had a wonderful Irish nursery maid called Susie who was only sixteen when she came to us. She took over from the trained nurses and made our nursery world heaven." My father told me many stories about Susie whom he loved dearly and would not forget. I would see her influence in endearing habits such as leaving a small square of toast on the side of his plate "for the starving Irish." I'm sure he knew that Susie was memorializing the terrible potato famine but I don't remember him explaining that to me. Perhaps my father also inherited Susie's love of singing favorite Irish songs like "It's a long way to Tipperary" (remembered today as a World War I song) and the traditional Irish song "With a shillelagh under me arm and a twinkle in me eye, I'll be off to Tipperary in the morning." As a young man, he would accompany himself with his squeezebox (concertina) but he was forced to leave that on the beach at Dunkirk during the 1940 evacuation.

Most of Grace and Betty's memories began after their father was recalled into the British Army at the outbreak of the Great War. He was away for almost the entire four years so that their mother was left to run the farm and household (see Chapter 18). Betty remembered that her mother had "very little help in the house and the farm to run" during the war, and thus allowed the children "a glorious amount of freedom." Betty and Grace played most often with the children of the older groom, Tommy and Sissie Rathwell, "but my brother was too young for our games," at least at first. Immediately after breakfast, they waited outside their friends' cottage in the farmyard, intrigued to hear the whole family saying their prayers together. In the meantime, the sisters kept a wary eye on a large and threatening tom turkey in the yard. In April, they discarded shoes and stockings like all the village children and went barefoot until the autumn. "After a time, the soles of our feet hardened like leather and we could even cross stubble fields if we ran. On cold days, we would paddle in mud as it seemed to make our legs warmer when it dried." Their favorite place to play was in the hayloft, even though they were forbidden to do so because "the animals did not like the taste of the hay afterward!" Sometimes they put blocks of wood across the loft and laid hay over them so that they could crawl around in the tunnels they made. It was extremely hot and, as Betty wrote, "...if the roof had fallen in, we could have suffocated."

As the girls got older, governesses came and went in rapid succession and only one of them had any control over them: "...much to their wrath, we spent most of our free time with the maids or workmen." They did lessons in the morning and were taken for walks after lunch. "At one period," presumably after the war, "my sister and I did French and music with a tutor. We were so frightened of him that we persuaded our governess to sit in the room throughout the lessons and then he didn't hit our knuckles with the ruler." Their younger brother Mike also provided some relief. He had turned the housemaid's pantry upstairs into a workshop where he hammered away all day, singing at the top of his voice: "[E]very time Mike passed the door he banged on it with a hammer. The tutor always rushed out but by then Mike was well out of reach."

"Mike and Grace were great tree climbers," Betty remembered. "There were some big fir trees in the pleasure grounds and they would climb up...and then slide down on the outside of the branches." Grace was a tomboy from an early age. "You, Grace," her mother wrote her formidable middle-aged daughter in 1961, "were an independent character, indifferent to nurses or elder sister when, aged four, striding across a large bush-covered park, half a mile between you and the pram [in which the nursemaid was pushing baby Michael], equally adventurous doing heroic climbing stunts, which you teach the groom's young boy (much against his parents' wishes). The garden wall is only 1 foot wide and quite 14 feet in height and this you run along, regardless."

"Haymaking in the summer was the best time of all," remembered Betty. "Sometimes I sat on the driver's lap while the hay cutter went round and round, pulled by a white pony and a black horse." Betty also loved the month of June when the turf was being cut by men using long-handled spades. This was a lengthy process. In addition to the turf cut for Derrylahan, each of the men on the farm was allocated a patch of bog where they cut their own turf, and some of the neighboring farmers had the right to part of the Heads' turf bank. "There is nothing so glorious as the bog," Betty recalled with enthusiasm. "I went there a lot. The wildness of it and the lovely peaty smell to which is added that of bog myrtle and heather. It is covered with a little plant called Sundew which catches flies on its sticky leaves and there is also pretty, multi-colored bog cotton or sphagnum moss."

There was always great merriment when the corn was being threshed. "We had our own machine in a barn. It was run by a petrol engine which also worked the circular saw. The circular saw was a horrible thing and a spaniel was very badly cut from going under it when it was running. However, she was none the worse once the wound healed." Everyone rushed about carrying full sacks of corn, pushing sheaves into the machine, and removing straw. Dust everywhere got into eyes and throat, and the dogs had great sport chasing rats and mice. The children roasted apples on the threshing machine, which they thoroughly enjoyed despite the oily taste. "This was an even more hilarious time," remembered Betty, "as the maids brought the men's dinners from the house and everyone had a romp. I remember the laundry maid being rolled in the heap of barley chaff which must have been most painful." When the harvest was in, they had a harvest home dance, just one of a succession of neighborhood harvest dances attended by everyone from miles around. "The dances were all 'sets'—rather like Scottish Dancing— and the music came from a piano accordion. We were only allowed to remain until midnight and the evening did not really warm up until later. No one went to bed and the dancing went on until it was time for the maids to get the early morning tea." Another festive marker was the big Christmas tree that was erected for the children on the estate.

"No place in Ireland could exist without horses and, as my father had been a Royal Horse Gunner, we had various horses beside the work horses," Betty explained. "There was a racehorse called Enniscorthy who produced a foal each year. She was practically impossible to catch and I think her foals all went to the army in the war." They had a pony that was too big and difficult to stop and two donkeys "we bought from the tinkers for ten shillings each," which refused to move at all. They gave up their Model T Ford during World War I after the chauffeur joined the army and bought a smart new trap and a pony called Rose. "Horses in those days were completely terrified of traffic," Betty remembered. "Once my mother and I left Birr at a gallop and once I went to a point-to-point with the maids and, when leaving, the pony reared, the shafts broke and we all landed in the mud." As Betty was at the back of the trap, she was squashed by the cook and was the muddiest of all. They borrowed a trap for the journey home. "When shopping in Birr, we stayed in the pony trap or dogcart and shouted for the shop keepers to come out to take the orders. The horses or ponies were much too wild to leave unattended."

"In Ireland," remembered Betty, "fairs were held in the streets of the market towns, and the filth and confusion were unbelievable. The streets were jammed solid with donkey carts and cattle. Although the actual buying and selling took place early, everyone adjourned to the pubs afterwards. As there were no cattle trucks, the poor animals were not led or driven to stables or fields until all hours. I could never understand how they could wait in the street all day without getting mixed up or wandering off. There never seemed to be anyone looking after them. We kept mostly bullocks with a few thoroughbred Herefords and enough cows to provide milk for the house and farmhands. We made our own butter and had delicious soda bread and scones made from the buttermilk." There was always great excitement if the "extremely bad tempered" Hereford bull escaped from the paddock of which he was the sole occupant. The paddock was the old walled garden where the old house used to be. The children loved throwing a ball into the bull's paddock and running to retrieve it before they were chased! One day, Betty went to Birr station with her mother to collect a new young bull she had bought. "When we got to the station we found he'd broken out of the railway truck and all the porters had shut themselves into the goods shed. It was left to my indomitable Mother to deal with the bull. She and one of our men cornered him in the end but he was always very savage."

Margery's children shared her dislike of parties: "at children's parties we stood together and refused to join in at first, though things improved somewhat after tea," Betty remembered. Unlike his reserved wife, however, Colonel Head enjoyed social life and sporting before the war and during the brief period after he returned home in January 1919, especially bridge, polo, foxhunting, and tennis. He bought ponies very cheaply from farmers, trained them to play polo, and sold them in Dublin, where he often played himself. He had always loved hunting but the local fox hunt tended to avoid Derrylahan, because the foxes always charged straight across the bog, where horses and riders would get bogged down. When their parents gave tennis parties, the children were sent to have tea with the gamekeeper and chauffeur—two bachelors who "did for themselves" in their little cottage: "They certainly made very good soda bread!"

Picnics were popular. Sometimes they picnicked on the shores of Lough Derg. "On one occasion, my sister and I were paddling and we both fell in so our return journey was very cold and clammy." Sometimes they picnicked on Knockshegowna, otherwise known as Fairy Hill, which they could see from the house and is supposedly haunted. In summer, they usually went to the seaside at Bray, just south of Dublin in Co. Wicklow. Once, when returning from the beach, they found their boarding house had burned to the ground with all their belongings. Seaside resorts were not crowded in those days, however, so they found another boarding house quite easily.

Betty explained that their grandparents lived in London so they thought London *was* England as that was the only English place they ever visited. "Their London house had a garden at the back where we met the children from surrounding houses. We soon took possession of their dolls' prams and expensive toys. Their nannies were quite amazed at meeting such savages from the bog, speaking with such pronounced brogues." Grace recalled a particularly naughty episode when Margery brought several of her Irish servants with them to London. "They were completely off the bog and had never even seen a large town, much less a city like London. They were much more trouble to Mummy, I should imagine, than we were. We took them out for a walk one day, or perhaps they took us. There was a dense fog. We said we knew the way home and promptly left them. I think a kindly London policeman came to the rescue."

As World War I was drawing to an end in 1918, the IRA "became troublesome," Betty recalled, among other things, raiding the big houses to secure arms—and the Head house was not spared. My grandfather described in his memoir the repeated acts of terrorism in the neighborhood in the final months before he was forced to flee to safety after a failed attempt to assassinate him. My grandmother was told that a dozen militant IRA members, who were holed up in a former priest's house rented to sympathizers, were seen drilling at dusk in the parkland. It must have been terrifying. Aware of the increasing danger, Margery Head had sent the best furniture, household wares, and clothing for storage in Birr. Even the children felt the rising tension. Grace remembered that she and her brother buried their favorite toys in a metal box. However, they grew so bored that they dug them up the day before the burning—only to lose them all.

It was Grace who placed these frightening encounters with the IRA in proportion to what they all recalled as an enchanted childhood. "Children have a way of accepting whatever comes their way as far more ordinary than their elders ever imagine. Therefore the fact that for two years or more of our lives we lived in an atmosphere of what today might be called gangsterism and revolutionism [terrorism] was only part of our daily existence—combined with highly entertaining Irish servants, gorgeous places to play, trees to climb, the farm to wander over and acres and acres of bog to explore. No television could ever replace the servants' hall tales of hounds that attacked children and combs that were dropped on the bog by banshees and must not be touched. A little old woman we knew of, who lived under a railway bridge in a house of sacks, came out on moonlit nights and danced on the gravel before our windows. We'd look out and see her in her tatters with her hair flying."

The stories my father told me before his early death were largely focused on his eccentric relations rather than the details and context for the burning of his Irish home. If he told me more, it was only those stories that remained with me, but they were colorful enough to fuel my passion to learn more. He must have been aware of the accounts that his older sisters wrote about their childhood forty years after the family left Ireland but, if he wrote anything himself, it did not survive. It was an experience in New York in early 1965, described at the beginning of the next chapter, that began to raise my consciousness of the enduring Irish Catholic bitterness against the usurpers who became known as the Anglo-Irish Protestants.

Chapter 2

Behind It All:
Religion, Land, and Colonization

The stories I was told when I was a child gave me no sense of context or the long troubled Anglo-Irish history. When I arrived in New York City from England with a friend on the first *Queen Mary* in 1964, I was an inadequately educated at the time, naïve but adventurous and sensitive twenty-year-old, aware only that my father had spent the first part of his childhood in Ireland and the family house had been burned "by the IRA." The following March, my friend and I were invited to a St. Patrick's Day ball by a pair of young Irish Americans. I innocently revealed to my dance partner that I was a daughter of the Anglo-Irish landed gentry. I had no idea how reviled they were by him and his associates. Worse, I was a descendant of one of the despised officers who were compensated for their loyalty to the Cromwellian Parliamentarians with generous grants of land wrested from rebellious Catholics of Gaelic and Anglo-Norman descent. I do not think I was aware of that at the time. I pinned the British naval crown brooch I had just been given for my twenty-first birthday to my favorite emerald green velvet ball gown—if ever there was a badge of my Unionist antecedents that was it. I thus became exhibit A to the Irish American nationalist elite as my handsome but bitterly unchivalrous date (whom I never saw again) paraded me around the dance floor. Since, in my youthful vanity, I had not worn my glasses despite my severe myopia, I could only sense the mockery and antipathy that surrounded me that evening.

This experience points up the then still prevailing opinion that, in the gentry or English county class I was born into, it was considered best not to educate daughters into university level but to "finish" them in advance of marriage! Ignorance was bliss, or certainly more socially acceptable: men don't like bluestockings, dear, at least not our kind! And how awkward to have a biddable daughter or wife turn into an overly curious interrogator. For me, forever curious and hungry for knowledge, higher education and a stimulating career had to wait until my permanent residency in the United States with an equally progressive partner. It was decades before I came to understand the dark and complicated history between England and Ireland and the strength of Irish American support, first for Irish independence, then for reunification of the two Irelands that were created in 1921. As I was to discover, the deep-rooted problems between Britain and Ireland, which peaked in the Anglo-Irish war for Irish independence of 1919-21, went far beyond religion and land to issues of political and economic power, social class, bigotry, and a visceral rejection by the Irish of imperial domination and colonial dependency. To put it baldly, Ireland was England's first colony.

The first wave of conquerors and settlers from England, Anglo-Norman Catholic adventurers, invaded and settled Gaelic Ireland during King Henry II's reign in the twelfth century. These "Old English," as they came to be called in Ireland, soon intermarried with the Gaelic Irish (also long Catholic) adopting their customs and language and becoming, as is often said, "more Irish than the Irish."[1] In the face of constant push-back by Gaelic chieftains, however, the area directly controlled by England's royalty (distinct from the lands held by the "Old English") shrank during the fifteenth century to what became the four eastern counties of Louth, Meath, Dublin, and Kildare. In order to protect the lives and property of the remaining "faithful lieges of the lord king" (under a statute enacted in 1488), and to enforce the use of the English language and culture in this district, a fortified earthen rampart known as the Pale was built to enclose it, leaving half Meath and half Kildare on the outside, hence the term "beyond the pale."

Within the Pale, an English governor, or lord deputy, representing the English monarch, presided over a small royal court in Dublin. A standing crown army defended the Pale against attacks by dispossessed Irish. Poyning's Law (1495) tightened English control over the loyal counties by requiring the lord deputy in Ireland to apply for a license to hold parliament and to submit all bills to the English king and his council for approval. Among the Anglo-Norman or Old English community, the FitzGerald earls of Kildare and the Butler earls of Ormond were the most overbearing. It became obvious, as they battled each other for the prerogative to protect English interests, that the FitzGerald faction was the more powerful of the two. Thus Henry VII and Henry VIII each successively appointed the ruling earls of Kildare to be their representatives in Ireland, further consolidating the power of that family. In 1541, Henry VIII and his successors were declared to be kings rather than lords of Ireland, a constitutional change that was ratified by the Irish Parliament that June. From then on, Old English and Gaelic lords had the opportunity to surrender their titles and receive regrants of English titles, bringing them and their supporters under the full protection of the law.[2]

With the sixteenth-century Protestant Reformation and King Henry VIII's subsequent establishment of the Protestant Church of England—a move continued by his short-lived son Edward VI, and reinforced when Elizabeth I succeeded to the throne in 1558—the first of many rebellions against English Protestant monarchs occurred in Catholic Ireland. In 1579, the Old English noblemen Gerald Fitzgerald, 14th earl of Desmond, in the southwestern province of Munster, and James Eustace, viscount Baltinglass, in the Pale, revolted on the basis that Queen Elizabeth was not a legitimate ruler of Ireland because she was, from the Catholic point of view, the illegitimate child of an adulterous liaison with Anne Boleyn. Pope Pius V had issued a Bull in 1570 that excommunicated Queen Elizabeth and freed all her subjects from allegiance to her. In this charged atmosphere, the Catholic Mary, Queen of Scots—who was raised in France and was briefly married to the French Dauphin—posed a double threat to Queen Elizabeth.

Not surprisingly, English Protestants developed a hatred for the Papacy and its allies, especially Spain and France. They feared that a still-Catholic Ireland would become a strategic threat to the security of England and argued that Irish-born Catholics should not hold government positions in Ireland. By the 1580s, eight thousand English soldiers were dispersed across all four of the country's provinces: Ulster, Connaught, Leinster, and Munster. The greatest concentration was in the province of Munster (spread through the modern counties of Cork, Kerry, Limerick, and Tipperary), where they were fighting forces loyal to the earl of Desmond, one of the Fitzgeralds. Following the latter's defeat and Desmond's assassination in 1583, Desmond's lands, and those of his ally, James Eustace, 3rd viscount Baltinglass, were confiscated and subsequently allocated to "undertakers." These were the soldiers and officials serving in Ireland, along with merchants, courtiers, and wealthy recruits from England, loyal to the Protestant crown, who undertook to import tenants from England to work their new lands. A total of almost 300,000 acres was consigned to new owners, a process that became known as the Plantation of Munster.[3] The focus of settlement on Desmond's lands was along the fruitful south bank of the Shannon River. In 1585, the first member of the Otway family in Ireland, John Otway, received a grant of Castle Otway, Co. Tipperary, by patent. The Otways would become part of the wider kin network of the Head family in Northern Tipperary.

That same year, 1585, Hugh O'Neill, the last of the high kings of Ulster and now 2nd earl of Tyrone, raised an army in Ulster against the lord deputy, and declared himself a champion of the Counter-Reformation. He and his confederate chiefs were supported by Catholic Spain. Fearing effective encirclement by Spain, Queen Elizabeth and her advisors ordered a greatly increased level of expenditure in Ireland and increased the English army presence there to 21,000 men. The Catholic threat to English Protestantism lessened with the beheading of Mary, Queen of Scots in 1587 and England's defeat of the Spanish Armada seeking to invade the British Isles the following year.

As that threat receded, Queen Elizabeth, with the help of the Dublin Corporation and Adam Loftus, the Protestant archbishop of Dublin, founded Trinity College, Dublin, in 1592. The object was to provide Ireland with a well-trained Protestant priesthood, as well versed in theology as were their Catholic rivals. Queen Elizabeth expressed the hope that it would educate all Irish youth but, because it was firmly Protestant and modeled on a Cambridge college, its students were largely Protestant and New English. The first three provosts were puritan in their outlook, ensuring that the college remained a bastion of Calvinist theology and trained a regular supply of Church of England clergy. This ambition became almost impossible to achieve, however, during the political and religious upheavals of the seventeenth century.[4] Hugh O'Neill, meanwhile, continued to conspire with Catholic Spain and called on the Irish nobles in Munster to make war on the English—efforts resulting in the Nine Years War or Tyrone's Rebellion (1594-1603). In 1598, an army led by an agent of O'Neill, supported by local Catholics determined to reclaim their land, dramatically overthrew the Protestant settlement in Munster. Survivors of this first plantation of Munster fled to England. However, in December 1601, at Kinsale on the southern Ireland coast near Cork, an army under Charles Blount, Lord Mountjoy, lord deputy of Ireland, defeated O'Neill's Irish army and the four thousand well-equipped soldiers Philip III of Spain had sent to support O'Neill's Catholic forces. O'Neill hunkered down in his Ulster heartlands but agreed to Mountjoy's conciliatory terms in March 1603, a few days after the death of Queen Elizabeth I.

The principals hurried to England to win favor at court with the new king, James I of England and VI of Scotland, who horrified O'Neill's opponents by granting him a royal pardon. However, the foiled Catholic Guy Fawkes plot to blow up the Houses of Parliament when James was to be present for the opening ceremony on November 5, 1605, made it impossible for the principally Catholic Old English community in Ireland to claim that Catholicism was just a private affair. England now stationed garrisons, which were commanded or run by Protestants, strategically throughout Ireland. The Act of Supremacy of 1537 had established the key tenet of the Reformation, that the King rather than the Pope was the supreme head of the church in England and Ireland. In 1560, a second Act of Supremacy prescribed an oath of supremacy which required renouncing all foreign jurisdictions for all officeholders and clergymen in Ireland. The writing was now on the wall and, in 1607, the Ulster nobles Hugh O'Neill, earl of Tyrone, and Rory O'Donnell, who had been created earl of Tyrconnell, fled Ireland with their wives, families, and retainers—the so-called "Flight of the Earls." The earls and their associates were charged with high treason and their lands were declared forfeit to the Crown.[5] Ulster, like Virginia, would become an obvious choice for an English Protestant settlement.

From 1609 on, James I launched the Ulster plantation: most of the vast sweep of land in counties Armagh, Cavan, Donegal, Fermanagh, Tyrone, and Coleraine was confiscated and granted at low rents to English and Lowland Scots in portions of one to two thousand acres. On January 28, 1610, agreement was reached between the Irish privy council and the City of London for the plantation of lands within the county of Londonderry, the old County Coleraine. The colonists were to let the land to Protestant tenants. Native Irish who had assisted the state during the Nine Years War were to be moved to segregated areas while the rights of freeholders or Gaelic nobles involved in revolts were deliberately ignored. The Old English (Norman Old English, Catholic, and loyal to the crown) and Gaelic lords were insecure about their own lands in view of these New English Protestant plantations.

By 1630, about 6,500 adult English and Scottish males had settled in the Ulster counties escheated to the crown following the Flight of the Earls, and distinct English, Scottish, and Irish localities were emerging.[6] A violent confrontation between former and current Catholic landowners, on one hand, and the English and Scottish Protestant settlers, on the other, was becoming inevitable.

Chapter 3

Civil War:
England, Scotland, and Ireland, 1641–49

The '1641 Ulster massacres' mean as much to the Protestant tradition as Cromwell's 'atrocities' at Drogheda in 1649 do to Catholic popular culture.
—Jane H. Ohlmeyer, editor, *Ireland from Independence to Occupation* (1995).[1]

In October 1641, Irish Catholic landowners in Ulster led by Sir Phelim O'Neill took advantage of the fact that King Charles I and his Parliament were at loggerheads and rose in a ferocious rebellion against religious discrimination and English and Scottish Protestant land-grabbing. Intending first to seize Dublin, they ultimately spread the rebellion throughout Ireland.[2] Appalling atrocities were committed on both sides.

Historian J. C. Beckett published a brief but dramatic account of this rising in 1966: "Many English settlers were slaughtered in the first heat of the rising ; others, after being held as prisoners for a time, were deliberately murdered, sometimes by scores together. Thousands more, driven from their homes, plundered of their goods, stripped almost naked, were left to find their way to some place of refuge, or to perish in the attempt." He explained that this excessive violence arose from the undisciplined fury of the Irish over endless grievances rather than a policy set by their leaders. "But in popular propaganda the cruelties inflicted on the settlers, dwelt upon and exaggerated, became irrefutable proof of a preconceived plan to massacre the entire Protestant population; and they amply account for the horror with which Protestants throughout the British Isles looked upon the rebellion and all connected with it."[3]

At the time of the rebellion, English writers put the Protestant victims at over 100,000. William Petty, in his Irish survey of the 1650s, estimated the death toll at around 30,000. Both of these were gross exaggerations. Close examination of the depositions of the Protestant refugees collected in 1642 suggests that about four thousand settlers were killed directly and as many as 12,000 may have died of causes related to disease or privation after being expelled from their homes.[4] But, as Nicholas Canny has asserted, "a detailed narrative of the course of events in the months immediately following its outbreak is still lacking, as is an identification of those individuals who led the disturbances, besides Phelim O'Neill, and those social groups that were engaged in action in various parts of the country. Only a close study of the 1641 depositions held by Trinity College, Dublin Library—witness testimonies mainly by Protestants, but also by some Catholics, from all social backgrounds—can reveal this information."[5]

One of the murdered settlers at Carrickfergus was a Rev. John Head. Shortly thereafter, in Mallow, Co. Cork, the Rev. Emmanuel Phair and his son Robert Phair (later Phayre), maternal ancestors of my husband, lost property and livelihoods.[6] Both the Reverends Head and Phair had come to Ireland from England after receiving their clerical degrees from Oxford University in the early seventeenth century. Although the Rev. John Head of Carrickfergus was the first recorded Protestant Head in Ireland, he cannot have been the father of my ancestor Michael Head and his brother and sister, John and Mary Head, all of whom were born around that time. In fact, it seems certain that the widow and infant son of the Rev. John Head of Carrickfergus managed to escape to England in 1641 after much suffering. His son, who attended Oxford like his father, became the notorious scatological writer Richard Head![7] But when the rebellion broke out in Munster, the Phairs' wealthy relative, William Jephson (later major-general), raised a troop of horse which Robert Phair joined at age twenty-two, as conjectured by historian and archivist William Welpy based on related evidence.[8]

Nicholas Canny claims that "the fount of the disturbances in Munster was in Co. Tipperary." On December 13, 1641, the rebels, led by the Catholic noblemen and gentry of the county, "gained access to the episcopal centre of Cashel," and soon thereafter held "all the considerable towns of the county"—Cashel, Clonmel, and Fethard. They robbed all the Protestant settlers in these communities, murdered some of them, stripped the survivors of their clothes, and sent most of them on the road to Waterford to get passage to England. The priests in Tipperary and elsewhere insisted on the religious justification of the war while the Tipperary gentry had usurped the authority of the marquess of Ormond. They now set up an army to pursue the insurrection further in the province of Munster and beyond.[9]

In the wake of the uprising in Ulster, the Long Parliament in Westminster passed in February 1642 "An Act for the speedy and effectual reducing of the rebels in His Majesty's Kingdom in Ireland," which King Charles I approved. By this act, confiscated Irish rebels' land would be awarded to those who "adventured" the money to suppress the rebellion. One of these was William Wade, a London merchant who invested £600 according to the list of original investors who lent the money in the expectation of being paid in Irish land.[10] It is possible that he was the father of Capt. Samuel Wade who had his claim to lands in Co. Tipperary confirmed by Charles II in 1670, the very same lands that passed to the Head family through marriage in 1696. The parliament in Dublin appointed Sir Charles Coote—who had first arrived in Ireland as an officer in General Mountjoy's army—governor of Dublin and commissioned him to raise a regiment to put down the rebellion. Coote has been accused by historians of killing innocent civilians during his advance south to secure Co. Wicklow and of calling for the massacre of all Catholics. The burning of farms and villages by Coote's soldiers to destroy the logistical resources of the insurgents intensified the hatred of the Irish population toward the Protestant government.[11] After Coote was killed in battle in May 1642, he was succeeded by his oldest son, also Sir Charles Coote, who would play a role in the ascendancy of the Heads.

In May 1642, Old English and native Gaelic Catholics combined to form the Catholic Confederacy, which established an independent assembly in Kilkenny. Although they insisted they were loyal to the crown, they were determined to secure religious freedom and a role in the Irish parliament. This new confederacy was opposed by Old

English Royalists led by James Butler, 12th earl of Ormond, who had been brought up a Protestant in a Catholic family. Both the Irish Catholic rebellion and the English response to it were complicated by the outbreak of the first English Civil War when King Charles I raised his standard at Nottingham on August 22, 1642, initiating a bloody contest with Parliament. Now Ormond, who had been the leader of the Royalist forces in Ireland up to this point, found himself in opposition to Parliament and firmly on the King's side. With the Ulster uprising on the verge of collapse due to inadequate leadership, Owen Roe O'Neill, a nephew of Hugh O'Neill and a veteran of the Irish regiment in Spanish Flanders, returned to Ireland and was appointed general by an Ulster Irish assembly to succeed Sir Phelim O'Neill. He appeared to be on the brink of success as the Catholic rebellion spread all over Ireland.[12]

Fearing that they would lose their lands otherwise, the Old English wanted a speedy conclusion to the war. While King Charles ordered Ormond to negotiate terms with the Confederacy, the Gaelic Irish, led by O'Neill—and the papal nuncio Cardinal Giovanni Rinuccini when he arrived in 1645—insisted on the restoration of confiscated lands and full recognition of Catholicism. The Irish Gaelic aristocrat Murrough O'Brien, Lord Inchiquin, a Protestant despite his descent from the ancient royal house of Munster, led the Protestant army, which was loyal to King Charles at that time. In January 1644, King Charles appointed Ormond lord-lieutenant of Ireland. Ormond's family connections gave him useful leverage in negotiations with the Confederate Catholics, although he staunchly upheld the Protestant interest in the first Ormond peace in 1646.[13] He would prove to be tenaciously loyal to Charles.

When the king refused to grant Inchiquin the lord presidency of Munster, the ruthlessly ambitious warrior abandoned the royalist cause in 1644 and declared for Parliament. Young Robert Phair joined Inchiquin's forces at this point and was promoted to lieutenant-colonel two years later. After winning a strategic battle in Cork, Inchiquin proceeded to expel Catholics from the city and county. He also seized the ports of Youghal and Kinsale as well as Cashel in southern Tipperary, burning, looting and slaughtering Catholics as he went.[14] In January 1645, Parliament rewarded Inchiquin with the lord presidency of Munster, which the king had refused him.

The English Civil War seemed to be over when, in June 1647, the Parliamentary army under Oliver Cromwell captured the king in Northamptonshire, but Charles temporarily escaped captivity in November. That year, Ormond surrendered Dublin and other towns under his command to parliamentary troops under Col. Michael Jones, who had landed near Dublin. Ormond now left Ireland to join the young Prince Charles Stuart on the Continent as one of his closest advisors. In the wake of capturing major towns from the Confederates in Munster, with the exception of Limerick, Clonmel, and Waterford, Inchiquin began negotiations with the Confederates in February 1648. But he had become dissatisfied with his treatment by Parliament and was preparing to change sides yet again. In April, he declared once again for the king. Robert Phair is recorded for the first time in the journal of the House of Lords after refusing, along with Sir William Fenton and Major Nicholas Pourdon (ancestor of the Purdons related later to the Heads of Derry Castle), to join the Royalist uprising within Inchiquin's army. Parliament agreed in May that these officers and others, including Lord Broghill's children, would be exchanged for Inchiquin's eighteen-year-old son who was being held hostage in London following his father's defection to the royalist cause. Capt. William Penn (later Adm. Sir William Penn, father of the founder of Pennsylvania) carried young Inchiquin to Ireland in his ship *Assurance* and returned to England with the exchanged prisoners in May 1648.[15]

Since Parliament's negotiations with the King had broken down, the civil war resumed in England until August 1648 when Oliver Cromwell defeated Scottish Royalists at Preston, Lancashire, and invaded Scotland. In late September, the earl of Ormond returned from temporary self-exile with Prince Charles in France. His apology and renewed fidelity to the king resulted in his appointment as the king's lord-lieutenant in Ireland.

The outbreak of England's second civil war convinced the king's more ruthless antagonists that no peace could be made while he was alive. On November 20, 1648, Parliament's New Model Army laid before the House of Commons their demands that the king, who was again in captivity, be brought to trial. In early December, the army occupied Westminster. Col. Thomas Pride, acting on the orders of the army council, carried out what came to be called Pride's Purge, forcibly expelling from Parliament 143 members (mostly Presbyterians) on the grounds that they were royalist sympathizers. The remaining Rump Parliament, which was completely under army control, then ordered the trial of Charles I.

Once the king—who persisted in his claim that no court had jurisdiction over a monarch— was found guilty and convicted of treason against England by the high court of justice specially created by the rump House of Commons on January 27, 1649, fifty-nine parliamentary commissioners signed the warrant of January 29 for his execution. It was addressed to Col. Francis Hacker, Col. Hercules Huncks, and Lt. Col. Robert Phair. They were directed to see that the king was put to death by the "severing of his head from his body" between the hours of ten in the morning and five in the afternoon the next day.[16] Hacker was the only one of the three to sign this order, the other two refused. Nonetheless, all three of these officers were arrested as regicides on the restoration of Charles II.

Thomas Herbert, appointed as Charles's attendant by Parliament early in 1648, slept on a pallet at the king's bedside at St. James's Palace during his last night. Even though he was in the pay of Parliament, Herbert "was much trusted and loyal to the King." But now, between nine and ten on January 30, Col. Hacker knocked on the door and was visibly trembling as he told the king that it was time to go to the palace of Whitehall. Col. Matthew Tomlinson, who had been ordered by the Army Council on December 23 to take charge of the king at St. James's Palace, and Dr. William Juxon, bishop of London, walked on either side of the king, with Herbert following behind. Two companies of infantry (halberdiers), including Col. Phair, quickly surrounded them, drums beating continuously. The king passed from the hall to the scaffold, draped in black, through a window that had been enlarged for the purpose. The executioner and his assistant were masked and disguised beyond recognition. Also on the scaffold were Bishop Juxon, whom the king had asked to offer him the last rites, Col. Tomlinson, and Col. Hacker, several soldiers on guard, and two or three shorthand writers. Herbert remained inside the palace, having begged to be excused the pain of being a witness.[17] It was very cold, and Charles had dressed in two shirts so that he would not shiver and give the impression of fear.

There was a long delay before the actual execution because the House of Commons was rushing through a vital piece of legislation making it illegal for anyone to proclaim a new king and proclaiming themselves to be the true representatives of the people. It was nearly two o'clock in the afternoon before Hacker knocked for the last time on the door of the room where the king, Juxon, and Herbert had been kept waiting. Before the axe fell, Charles spoke briefly from notes, attesting to his innocence, saying that he saw his execution as God's judgment on him, and declaring he had forgiven the world. With one blow, the executioner severed his head from his body. A seventeen-year-old boy a long way off saw the axe fall and heard from the crowd "such a groan as I never heard before, and desire I may never hear again."[18]

Six days later, Charles II was proclaimed king of England, Scotland, and Ireland by the Scots but Parliament appointed an executive council of state on February 13, and formally abolished the monarchy on March 19 and the House of Lords two days later. On March 30, Parliament approved Oliver Cromwell as commander-in-chief of the New Model Army to reconquer Ireland as well as appointing him civil and military governor of Ireland.

Chapter 4

Cromwell and the Protectorate, 1649-59

Cromwellian settlers: "...the dregs of each base trade, who range themselves as snugly in the houses of the noblest chiefs, as proud and genteel as sons of gentlemen."
— *The Poems of David O'Bruadair, 1625-1698*

At last Parliament could confront seriously the longstanding and complex Catholic and Royalist rebellion in Ireland. In April 1649, lots were drawn to select those regiments of the standing army that would go to Ireland under Oliver Cromwell's command. These included four horse regiments (one of them under the command of Henry Ireton, Cromwell's son-in-law), five troops of dragoons, and four regiments of foot. In addition to these, six newer regiments of the New Model Army were formed, one of which was under the command of Robert Phair, now a full colonel. One of the officers in Phair's regiment (formed from Kentish troops who had previously served in Ireland) was a certain Henry Prittie whose descendants would be linked by marriage, land use, and politics to descendants of the Head family in Northern Tipperary.

In May 1649, the Committee for Irish Affairs reported to the House of Commons on Irish Arrears, including the considerable back pay (some £11,625) that was owed to certain officers, among them then Lieutenant Colonel Phare [sic], who was owed £836.[1] On May 19, Parliament declared England a "Commonwealth." But how was Parliament going to fund this potentially ruinously expensive Irish expedition? The answer became a principal cause of the conflict in Ireland for three hundred years.

On August 15, Cromwell landed near Dublin with thirty-five ships, the only time he ever left the British mainland. His son-in-law

Henry Ireton followed two days later with seventy-seven ships bound for the south. Others followed.[2] After heavily defeating Ormond at Rathmines, just outside Dublin, on August 2, and taking almost two thousand prisoners, Lt. Gen. Michael Jones had since succeeded in driving all Catholics out of Dublin so that Cromwell was "most heroically entertained" by the Protestants who remained. He told the vast numbers of Protestants who came to see him that his mission, his crusade even, was "to restore them all to their just liberty and property," and to support them in their "great work against the barborous and blood-thirsty Irish, for the propagating of the Gospel of Christ, the establishing of truth and peace and restoring that bleeding nation to its former peace and tranquility." Those who supported him in this effort would find "favour and protection from the English Parliament." He was loudly cheered for this oration.[3]

Intent on pursuing Ormond, who was heading north with his depleted troops, Cromwell ordered the advance on Drogheda, Co. Louth, which had fallen to the Royalists in July. Thirty miles up the coast from Dublin, that important trading town was and is located on a strategic bridging point of the River Boyne. Both the northern and southern sectors of the town, which was divided by the river, were protected by imposing walls. The lofty steeple of St. Mary's Church, which was virtually embedded in the south-eastern corner of the wall, provided a deadly vantage point for firing on any enemy approaching from the south. By the time Cromwell's troops arrived at Drogheda, Ormond had fallen back but he had deputed the garrison's commander, English royalist Sir Arthur Aston, with about two thousand men, to hold off Cromwell as long as possible from marauding further north. When, on September 10, Aston refused Cromwell's official summons to surrender, still hoping that Ormond would send reinforcements, Cromwell gave the order to attack.[4] Cannon balls from eleven siege guns mounted on a hill south of the town began to crumble the walls. Assaulted from without, Aston also could not be sure of loyalties within the town which, even within families, were seriously divided. For example, Aston turned his own grandmother and her relations out of the town when he discovered that these ladies had plotted to betray Drogheda (Ormond later gave them sanctuary).

The rules of war with regard to siege were well known, once walls had been breached no quarter could be demanded. Even so, as Aston informed Ormond, his men "were unanimous in their resolution to perish rather than deliver up the place." The Cromwellian cannonade knocked down the church steeple and the tower at the corner of the wall but the brave defenders beat back the first attempted assault. On a second attempt, seven or eight thousand men of the Cromwellian army poured through the walls and Cromwell, infuriated by the repeated refusal to surrender, ordered all the defenders to be put to the sword. Aston himself was beaten to death with his own wooden leg.[5] According to historian J. C. Beckett, "Almost the entire garrison and such recusant clergy as could be found were put to death, and no doubt many of the townspeople perished also; but there seems to be no foundation for later stories of an indiscriminate slaughter of the whole civilian population."[6] There was no doubt that Cromwell's Protestant troops were filled with a sense of revenge for the atrocities committed in the 1641 uprising. Cromwell gave no direct orders for the massacre of the civilian inhabitants but, as he declared in his report to Parliament: "This is a righteous judgement of God upon these barbarous wretches, who have imbrued their hands in so much innocent blood…it will tend to prevent the effusion of blood for the future, which are satisfactory grounds to such actions, which otherwise cannot but work remorse and regret."[7]

Somewhere between two and four thousand people died at Drogheda. The massacre frightened many lesser garrisons, such as Dundalk and Trim, into peaceful submission while forces under Sir Charles Coote secured Ulster and Connaught. As historian Antonia Fraser put it, "what should have rightfully been the Curse of England became the Curse of Cromwell."[8] Perhaps unfairly, therefore, the Curse of Cromwell grew in Ireland from the Drogheda massacre on, blackening his name through Irish history for over three hundred years, in fact until this day in many Catholic quarters.

Ormond retreated with his remaining royalist forces to the Confederate capital of Kilkenny, having abandoned the principal garrisons guarding the northwestern approaches to Dublin. Thus, before pursuing rebel forces in the south, Cromwell called in on Dublin where Mrs. Cromwell was settling in, fully intending "to

enjoy…the title and command of Vicereine, if the plan [the subjuga-
tion of Ireland] succeeds," according to the Venetian Ambassador.[9]

As Cromwell's New Model Army marched south to capture
major ports in the provinces of Leinster and Munster, it was accompanied by twenty ships with supplies and siege artillery. Wexford
was the first objective since it was the potential main port of entry
for Royalist support from France and Spain. It was also the base for
a fleet of Confederate privateers who raided English Parliamentary
shipping and contributed ten percent of their plunder to the Confederate government in Kilkenny. The army of 6,000 men camped
on the bank of the Slaney River estuary opposite the town of Wexford, hunkering down in terrible weather and beset by dysentery.
Cromwell dispatched his friend Lt. Gen. Michael Jones to capture
Rosslare fort, which guarded the harbor. The fort immediately ca-
pitulated, and now supply ships could enter the harbor. But, after
negotiations with the Royalist commander in Wexford for an orderly surrender broke down, Cromwell ordered an assault that destroyed both town and harbor. Parliamentary soldiers broke ranks
and ran amok, killing and looting. According to historian Tom Reilly, the massacre of fifteen hundred Catholics, particularly priests,
after the fall of Wexford on October 11 may have been worse than
at Drogheda.[10] This was quite apart from the estimated nearly two
thousand Irish soldiers that died, according to Cromwell's own report.

The capitulation of Cork, Cromwell's next target, was a result
of an astute move he had made in London earlier that year. Roger
Boyle, lord Broghill, was a powerful Protestant landowner in the
South of Ireland and the brother of the earl of Cork who was in exile
in England for his earlier support of King Charles. Broghill was
on the verge of raising troops to support the Royalist cause when
Cromwell met him in London and convinced him to side instead
with the Protestants against the Irish Catholic army.[11] After receiving
news on October 16 that the English members of the garrison in
Cork and the English inhabitants had risen in revolt against the Irish
governor and troops (an action that caused Inchiquin to lose all but
two hundred of his foot soldiers), Cromwell ordered Cols. Blake
and Phair to assist Broghill in stirring the Munster garrisons into
revolt.[12] Cromwell wrote to the speaker of the English parliament

on November 14 that he had subsequently dispatched Colonel Phair along with nearly five hundred foot soldiers and £1,500 to Cork. When their ship was blown off course into Dungarvan harbor, nearby in Co. Waterford, Phair decided to march overland to capture Youghal. He was accompanied by Lord Broghill and Sir William Fenton into the town, where they "were received with all the real demonstrations of gladness an overjoyed people were capable of." Phair then left two hundred men of his regiment of foot to garrison the town and marched with the remainder overland to Cork where they were met with no resistance. Cromwell appointed Fenton, Blake and Phair "Commissioners for a temporary management of affairs there."[13]

Cromwell besieged Catholic Waterford next but the appalling weather that had drenched his troops and sickened them with dysentery during the siege of Wexford continued, forcing him to raise the siege on December 2 and march to winter quarters at Youghal while Phair remained at Cork. Gen. Michael Jones succumbed to the prevailing sickness in Youghal, a great loss to Cromwell despite unsubstantiated rumors that he had poisoned him out of jealousy.[14] Cromwell himself suffered through several miserable bouts of sickness while in Ireland. Historians suspect that he contracted a form of malaria and it was this that eventually contributed to his death.[15] Parliament recalled Cromwell to England in January 1650, but either this summons failed to reach him or he chose to ignore it—he was determined to take advantage of an incredibly mild January to prepare for resuming military operations in February. Ridding Ormond influence from the castle garrisons and towns of Co. Tipperary was his first objective. He offered generous terms to the garrison of Fethard under the command of Lt. Col. Pierce Butler (a name that would reoccur in the Head family story 140 years later) and to the town of Cashel. From Fethard he wrote urgently to Phair, now military governor of Cork, "Haste, Haste, we are in the verie bowels of Tippary…many places take up our men, wherefore I must needs be earnest with you to speare us what you can. If you can send two Companies more of yor Regimte to Mayallo (Mallow) do it. If not one at least…" followed by a P.S., "Sr. if you thinke that we draw you too low in men, whilest we are in acc'on, I presume you are in no danger, however, I desire you would make this use of it, to ridd the Towne of Corke of suspitious and ill-affected persons as fast as you can." He signed off, "Salute all my Friends with you... Pray for us. I rest, your loving friend. O Cromwell."[16]

Cromwell encountered some resistance from the Tipperary town of Cahir before its governor, Capt. George Matthews, Ormond's half-brother, surrendered. Clonmel, which since December had been under the governorship of Ulsterman Hugh Dubh O'Neill, nephew of Owen Roe O'Neill, was the last target of Cromwell's campaign in Tipperary. O'Neill mounted such a fierce defense that Cromwell summoned Broghill and his forces to assist. The brilliant O'Neill laid a trap for the attacking forces once the wall was breached, resulting in the massacre of a thousand parliamentary soldiers. The battle raged for hours before Cromwell realized he could not secure Clonmel and ordered a retreat to the camp to begin a siege. When a delegation from the town, led by the mayor, approached the camp to negotiate terms for surrender, Cromwell failed to realize that this was a cover for crafty O'Neill and his army to escape through the south gate and head for Waterford.[17] Finally, Cromwell turned his attention to Kilkenny, where the Ormond family's magnificent castle dominated the town. Negotiations for surrender were fruitless for a time as Sir Walter Butler demanded the same favorable terms Cromwell had given to other towns. Cromwell refused but he allowed a compromise which protected the townspeople from sacking and allowed Butler's men to march away free, with enough arms to protect themselves from the Irish brigands, called Tories, who were now pillaging everyone.[18]

Cromwell's presence was now urgently required in England. He sailed from Youghal harbor in May 1650 to face a Scottish royalist army led by the late king's heir, newly crowned King Charles II of Scotland. After Cromwell's forces defeated his at Worcester on September 3, 1651, young Charles escaped to France, followed two months later by the ever-loyal Ormond. In the meantime, Cromwell's son-in-law Henry Ireton continued the Irish campaign. When Ireton took Waterford in August 1650, he disbanded the council and placed the city under military rule (see chapter 6). Limerick, under the military command of Hugh Dubh O'Neill, surrendered to Ireton in October 1651 after a long and bitter siege; however, two thousand soldiers of Cromwell's New Model Army were killed and

Ireton died of the plague that was raging in the city. In January 1652, O'Neill was transported to London in the same ship that carried Ireton's coffin.[19] Galway surrendered to the Cromwellians under Sir Charles Coote in April 1652, the last major Irish city to fall.[20]

Charles Fleetwood succeeded Henry Ireton as commander-in-chief in Ireland in July 1652. He had recently married Ireton's widow, thus becoming Cromwell's replacement son-in-law. He proceeded to ruthlessly carry out the parliamentary policies of land confiscation and reallocation and the persecution of Catholic priests and transplantation of Ulster Presbyterians. That year, Parliament enacted an Act for the Settling of Ireland by which the claims of "adventurers" (mostly London merchants and tradesmen) who had loaned money for the military campaign in Ireland, and arrears of pay due to soldiers, were to be met by the confiscation and redistribution of vast tracts of Irish land in the provinces of Munster, Leinster, and Ulster. Those considered to be most guilty, including 105 named rebels, were subject to execution, banishment, and transportation to the West Indies, while others who had not demonstrated "constant good affection" to parliament were subject to forfeiture and transportation to Connaught (the counties of Galway, Roscommon, Mayo or Clare), thus the famous watchword "To hell or Connacht," as it was spelled at that time.

As military governor of Cork, Robert Phair was responsible for the control and well-being of the citizens of Cork, both civil and military. Among the citizens were thousands of idle English soldiers, most of whom had received no pay for several months, in addition to the surrendered Irish soldiers. In October 1652, Phair was given license to commandeer shipping in Cork harbor "for the transportation of Irish soldiers," as were the governors of Wexford, Waterford, Youghal, and Kinsale. Thousands of Irish soldiers were shipped to Europe where they joined the French and Spanish armies. In July 1654, Cromwell wrote to the king of Spain on behalf of Colonel Phair, Lord Broghill, and Major Peter Wallis, requesting that Spain fulfill its side of the bargain struck regarding these additional soldiers. The three officers had not received the agreed twenty-four Spanish pieces of eight for each of three thousand men landed nearly two years before. Cromwell also wrote on Phair's behalf to the Prince of Condé in France, requesting payment for three thousand Irish soldiers transported to Flanders. The financial loss was calculated at £2,933.4s.1d, for which Phair was allocated land in Co. Cork. That same year, the endless wars involving England, France, and Spain were causing renewed concern so the Irish Committee ordered Phair to send no more Irishmen to Spain or Flanders but "to transport them to the Caribbean where their military strength would be less of a danger to England."[21]

In September 1653, the "Barebone's Parliament" passed the Act of Satisfaction (Cromwell had expelled the "rump" of the Long Parliament for trying to make itself permanent). That December, an Instrument of Government made Oliver Cromwell lord protector of the Commonwealth. Sir William Petty, physician-general to Cromwell's army in Ireland, secured the contract the following year to chart Ireland, an enormous task which became known as the Down Survey. This led to the Civil Survey and Book of Distribution (1654-55) of the land forfeited in the ten counties designated as resources from which to pay the state's debts—Antrim, Armagh, Down, Meath, Westmeath, King's County, Queen's County, Tipperary, Limerick, and Waterford. One half of the baronies in each county were set aside to satisfy the claims of merchant adventurers, the other allocated to meeting army arrears. Munster counties were to meet 30.5 percent of the claims.[22]

The Cromwellian land settlement was the greatest early modern transformation in Irish land ownership, creating an estate system which lasted, with minor adjustments, until the late nineteenth century. John P. Prendergast's pioneer and classic study of this system, *The Cromwellian Settlement of Ireland* (1865), coincided with the emergence of the Irish land question as a contentious political issue. His experiences as an Irish land agent and historian made him an advocate of tenant right and a supporter of the early land reformers in Ireland.[23] The massive settlement effort began with the Civil Survey, a Cromwellian document which surveyed the extent and nature of land and its ownership as a prelude to confiscation from owners who had not shown support for the Parliamentary cause during the 1641-49 Irish rebellion. Since over 70 percent of Tipperary's area was affected, much of it Butler property, it had the highest percentage of any county in Ireland.[24] Of its land reserved for division between 204 adventurers and the army, army officers and privates drew grants in Upper Ormond, Lower Ormond, Owney and Arra, Kilnamanagh, Kilnalongurty, and Slieveardagh, all Old Irish areas. Many of the privates sold their minute grants to their officers, such as Lt. John Otway, who purchased debentures or lands in Upper Ormond from soldiers in the 1650s and 1660s, with the price usually less than half the amount owed in pay or in debentures. Senior officers such as Abbott, Finch, Prittie, and Sadleir came to own large estates in the three baronies of the northwest of the county.[25] Col. Henry Prittie was granted Dunalley Castle and 5,900 acres, while the more junior Capt. Samuel Wade was given a total of 1,197 acres in various parishes and Edward Worth, lord bishop of Killaloe, 1,162 acres.

Wade's substantial grants in the impoverished parishes of Templekelly and Kilmastulla (Ballina/Boher Parish today), within the Barony of Owney and Arra on the west border of Northern Tipperary, included many lands formerly owned by the O'Briens, the rebellious Gaelic Mac I Brien clan long resident in the area. The grants crossed several townlands between the shores of Lough Derg (the largest lake on the Shannon River which divides Counties Tipperary and Clare) and a low range of the Arra Mountains (hills) behind.[26] The lands ran from just north of the village of Ballina at the bottom of the lake for several miles north (with what came to be regarded as a romantic view across the lake to the Clare hills). They were, however, of very mixed quality, from arable, woodland, and boggy land to undeveloped mountainous and rocky wasteland with little in the way of boundaries, cultivation, or habitation.[27]

On the eight hundred acres of the Cahirconner (Derry Demesne) and Ryninch lands, as described in the Civil Survey, "stands a little castle with a little bawne about it in an island in ye Shannon, it wants repair, & a thatch house within the bawne." This tower house was Cahirconnor or Derrycastle, inherited by Protestant Bishop Murtagh O'Brien of Killaloe, one of the O'Briens of Arra, in the late sixteenth century. Besides Cahirconner and Ryninch (800 acres), other townlands included Derry (102 acres, totally waste), Shesiraghkele (the name derived from the Irish for ploughland) or Derry/Coolbawn (88 acres) and lands further east in Grange (7), Legane (163), Cottoone (183, a forgotten name but encompassing parts of Newtown, Killary, and Englishtown), and Common (in commonage) to Roran further east (31).[28]

The lands' inhabitants were mostly "Irish Papists" in 1640 (described that way in the Civil Survey) but the 1659 Census lists John Walker, Gent, as occupying the Derry and Cahirconnor lands (possibly a tenant of Samuel Wade) on which lived fourteen Englishmen and just eight Irishmen, an indication that many had been transported to lands to the west of the Shannon River. Those sentenced to be transported were the upper classes—the landlords, landowners, and gentry of the planted counties. However, the actual transplantation was a mess: most dispossessed landlords never went to Connaught and those that did usually found the land promised was not there when they arrived. The "common people" were too valuable as laborers and cultivators to be expelled. The same census, although probably unreliable, gives the population of the Barony of Owney and Arra as 1,224 people, of which 235 were English, and 989 Irish, while the population of the Ballina-Boher parish was 182 Irish and 50 English, a ratio of almost four to one.[29]

Less clear is whether Wade's 212 acres of Rathone (renamed later Ashley Park by Wade's great-grandson John Head) in the parish of Monsea-Killodiernan, part of the great Norman manor of Nenagh in the Barony of Lower Ormond during the Middle Ages, were part of his Cromwellian grant or acquired by him subsequently. In any case, they were confirmed to him in 1678 (see chapter 5). In 1640, according to the Down Survey, the Gaelic O'Kennedys were the leading landowners in the parish. The Rathone lands were owned by the Norman Old English Grace family. All the landowners in the parish were Catholics with the exception of Elizabeth Butler, countess of Ormond, who was Protestant.[30]

The Tipperary countryside had been devastated by the years of warfare and attention was now given to restoring agriculture and the economy. A council of trade was set up by the parliamentary commissioners in 1655, and encouragement was given to manufacturers. That year, Cols. Henry Prittie and Daniel Abbott were awarded the lead and silver mine in the Slieveardagh Mountains (more accurately hills) in Tipperary. The mine was exempted from the excise and Abbott brought over workmen from England since skilled labor was not available locally.[31] By 1657, other ironworks in Ireland included Sir Charles Coote's ironworks in Queen's County, which was employing sixty families, while Robert Phair launched the Enniscorthy ironworks on his land in Co. Wexford. Despite the swarms of beggars roaming the Irish countryside, thousands of whom were transported to the West Indies, the economy was beginning to recover.[32]

Fleetwood was replaced in July 1655 by Henry Cromwell who treated the Baptist officers under his command with suspicion due to their political and religious radicalism. Quakers, whose converts included Richard Lawrence, former military governor of Waterford (ca. 1650-51), and Robert Phair, military governor of Cork, moved into the gap. Lawrence, whose main patron had been Fleetwood, responded to a critique of Fleetwood's intent to banish all Catholics in Ireland to the west of the Shannon River, with his virulently anti-catholic work *The interest of England in the Irish transportation stated*. He argued that the transplantation policy was essential to secure Ireland from further catholic rebellions. When these Nonconformist Protestant groups opposed the protectorate, Henry Cromwell began to cultivate the former Anglicans of Cork led by Dr. Edward Worth, dean of Cork since 1646 (and the future bishop of Killaloe), and the Scottish Presbyterians of Ulster.[33] Dr. Worth's clerical party consisted of members of Protestant settler families and ministers who had been educated in Ireland. He and his collaborators had close contact with the Munster gentry, including the Boyle family and Broghill. Worth established a Cork association of ministers in 1657 whose principal function was to ordain ministers. But Worth's ultimate aim was the erection of a national Protestant church to which adherence would be demanded. Uniformity, not toleration, was his overriding concern.[34] Since Baptists and Quakers were protected by Munster's military governors, it was essential to restore the province's government to civilians. Worth backed the campaign to restore municipal charters.

Within a year of Henry Cromwell's arrival, municipal corporations had been restored, permitting a fruitful alliance between civilian magistrates, who enforced religious order, and the clergy who preached obedience to the existing social and political order. Edward Worth and Henry Cromwell were eager to introduce pragmatic presbyterianism into other parts of Ireland beyond Ulster. They wanted to check religious unorthodoxy, to propagate the Gospel, and to restore the clergy to their legal rights, including tithes.[35]

But the Presbyterians wanted to impose their theocratic system of church government throughout Ireland, and that Cromwell could not accept. He felt less confident about the Presbyterians' loyalty than that of the Munster Protestants. It was the Presbyterians who posed the main threat of Protestant dissent from the re-established Church of Ireland after 1660, a major problem since the Scots in Ireland numbered around 80,000 by this time. However, the How Acts of Uniformity of 1663 and 1666 attempted to establish uniformity within the Church of Ireland by excluding Presbyterians and those with Presbyterian sympathies. It did so by requiring episcopal ordination of clergy and an undertaking from ministers not merely to use the revised Book of Common Prayer but also to give public assent to it.[36]

Oliver Cromwell died on September 3, 1658 at the age of 59. His body was hastily buried in Westminster Abbey and his funeral on November 23 was very elaborate. Dignitaries and ambassadors from far and wide attended and thousands of mourners followed the open chariot with his wax effigy. During his final moments, when he was almost incoherent, he allegedly chose his son Richard in preference to the more suitable Henry as his successor. Richard would last just seven months and twenty-eight days as Protector.[37] Henry Cromwell was recalled to London in June 1659 and his carefully built alliance with conservative clergy and settlers in Ireland was overthrown. Conservatives were replaced in the commission of peace by Quakers and Baptists.[38] Ireland's government was entrusted to political and religious radicals. This radical alliance suited Colonel Phair's advanced republican and dissenting beliefs. On August 16, 1658, following the death of his first wife, he had married Elizabeth Herbert, daughter of Charles I's last attendant Thomas Herbert, at St. Werburgh's, Dublin—an alliance that would turn out to be his salvation.

Chapter 5

Restoration and Settlement: Backing the Right Horse

Charles [II] dared not alienate the Irish Cromwellians at a time when his throne was still insecure, when Scotland was full of unrest, and when even in England there were powerful discontented elements ready at every opportunity to conspire against him. Inclination led him to favour the Roman Catholics, but prudence compelled him to side with the Protestants.

—J. C. Beckett, *The Making of Modern Ireland 1603-1923* (1966)

At this point, in December 1659, the regiment of Old Settlers led by Sir Charles Coote was stationed at Drogheda, north of Dublin. According to a census taken about that time, Ensign John Head was a junior officer in Major George Peppard or Pepper's company, numbering forty-two men. He was listed as one of the tituladoes—men of title—in Drogheda.[1] Assuming that an ensign would be about nineteen or twenty, this could place John Head's birth date around 1639 and, therefore, much too young to have been a member of Cromwell's invading force in 1649. George Pepper, however, came to Ireland that year as a captain of a company in Henry Ireton's regiment of foot, later under the command of General Fleetwood.

On December 13, 1659, a group of officers under Sir Theophilus Jones and Sir Hardress Waller, senior officer in Ireland, backed by gentry of old Protestant stock, captured Dublin Castle in the name of parliament and deposed Edmund Ludlow (the English republican commander-in-chief of the army in Ireland) and the civil administration in a *coup d'etat*. Jones, who was the younger brother of Cromwell's friend, the late Lt. Gen. Michael Jones, had fallen out of favor with the Commonwealth government. A little more than a week after the coup in Dublin, the number of garrisons—including Col. Phair's at Cork—which had declared support was judged sufficient to assure success and the council of officers requested Broghill and Coote to join them in Dublin with a view to establishing a provisional government operating through the authority vested in Maj. Gen. Hardress Waller. Waller and the council of officers then proceeded to require Protestant officials of the counties, cities, and principal boroughs to elect representatives to meet in Dublin on January 24, 1660, "to consult and deliberate, do and consent to such things as shall be found necessary for the good of the Publick, and the service of the Parliament, to whose pleasure all is to be submitted."[2]

But the coup was a sham. Its leaders, with the exception of Hardress Waller, were preparing to receive the king once the excluded members of the English parliament were reinstated. Coote and Lord Broghill, both of whom were former royalists, soon made contact with Charles II of Scotland, son of the late Charles I, who was in exile with his court in Brussels, and declared themselves leaders in the effort to restore him to the throne. Naturally, there was some opposition. Ludlow had returned to Ireland and, believing that some of the garrison commanders in the south and southeast, including Colonel Phair in Cork, would only accept orders from their commander in chief or parliament, encouraged them to defy the authority of the council in Dublin. The council brought articles of impeachment against Ludlow while army officers and garrison commanders in his faction were to be court martialed and removed from command. Sir Hardress Waller, as one of the regicides, had every reason to fear a monarchical restoration. With his confederates, he seized Dublin Castle again on February 15, 1660, denouncing the council of officers as "Rebels and traytors"; but he got little support and had to surrender to Sir Charles Coote a few days later.[3]

The council of officers formally adopted a declaration on February 16 calling for a full and free parliament through admission of the excluded members and new elections to fill vacant seats following principles that would disqualify those who had assisted the king or rebelled against parliament. It was prefaced by a denunciation of the calamitous effects on religion, freedom, prosperity and national reputation "of a few inconsiderable persons of annabaptistical and other fanattique spirits" and hoped that a "happy settlement" would restore the orthodox Protestant ministers to their accustomed rights, supported by their tithes. The soldiers and Dublin council then endorsed the declaration and the officers in Dublin subsequently dispersed to their commands in the country to secure the widespread adoption of the declaration. On February 25, the mayor and council of Drogheda concurred with the printed declaration, with its fifty-five signatories, including Major Peppard and Ensign John Head, and entered it into their council book.[4]

As one of the council of officers who moved to wrest control away from religious radicals who were taking over the Irish government as the Cromwellian era drew to an end, John Head was well-placed to benefit from subsequent events. Somewhere in his circle were his brother Michael, who also became known as "captain," and their sister Mary. Michael Head was the forebear of the large family which is the principal subject of this book.

On March 2, a convention opened in Dublin to shepherd the country through the uncertainties following the collapse of the Commonwealth. It was dominated by Henry Cromwell's former allies, 137 of the so-called Protestant Substantial Settlers, whose main aim was to secure their own interests. The members pledged support for the army, repudiated the tyranny of the Rump Parliament, asserted the right of Ireland to have its own parliament and to tax itself, and claimed that Ireland was not bound by acts emanating from the English parliament. They proposed a learned, preaching Protestant ministry organized on a parochial basis and supported by tithe, but there was to be no tolerance for extremists such as Quakers, Baptists, Sectaries or Independents.[5] On March 16, the Long Parliament dissolved itself and Coote and Broghill, having received royalist overtures, managed to convince the majority that their interests would best be served by restoring the monarchy.

Charles II was proclaimed king in London on May 8 and in Dublin on May 14, 1660, and the Westminster Parliament ordered the restoration of Anglicanism and the arrest of all surviving regicides. Col. Robert Phair, who refused to recognize the Restoration, was arrested on May 18 in Co. Cork and sent under a guard of fifty troopers to Dublin, and thence to the Tower of London on June 13.[6] The Dublin Convention was adjourned when news arrived that Charles II had landed at Dover. The king entered London on his thirtieth birthday. Principally anxious to have confirmed all grants of forfeited land and leases made since 1653, the Irish Convention then sent Broghill and Coote to lay certain requests before the king. As historian J. C. Beckett put it, these were: "the appointment of a chief governor and council; calling a parliament of Protestant peers and commoners; issuing a general pardon and indemnity to all the Protestants of Ireland, on terms to be fixed by parliament; preparation of an act of attainder; preparation of an act for the settling of estates; and restoration of forfeited glebes and tithes to the clergy."[7] Their almost complete success is recorded in the king's gracious declaration of November 30, 1660, confirming the land title of Cromwellian soldiers and Adventurers and restoring "innocent papists" to their estates. This was confirmed in the Act of Settlement of 1662. In September 1660, King Charles rewarded Broghill and Coote with earldoms.

Justice caught up with the surviving regicides who had failed to escape the country. On October 19, Col. Francis Hacker was hanged, one of ten who suffered the extreme penalty; Col. Huncks had saved himself by giving evidence against Hacker and Col. Axtell. Sir Hardress Waller was imprisoned for life (he died in 1666). On November 2, Robert Phair petitioned the new king for release of his estate from sequestration, so that he might return to his family in Ireland: "his estate being sequestered, he can hardly subsist." The request was returned "not to be released." By December, he was allowed the liberty of the Tower, where he had now been imprisoned for six months, "on his word not to depart thence."[8] However, it suited Charles II to accept Sir Thomas Herbert's claim for a pardon, creating him a baronet and overlooking Phair's crime because he was Herbert's son-in-law.

On January 30, 1661, exactly twelve years after the execution of Charles I, the bodies of Oliver Cromwell, Henry Ireton, and John Bradshaw were disinterred from Westminster Abbey and exposed all day on the gallows at Tyburn. At sunset, the bodies were taken down and buried in the common pit below the gibbet. The heads were cut off and exposed on the top of Westminster Hall.[9] In 1662,

Robert Phair was granted permission to leave the Tower and remain in Sir Thomas Herbert's house in London for three months to allow him to recover his health. On June 22, the Court at Hampton Court ordered that Phair should be released from prison and must give sufficient security to allow him to appear at Dublin to swear fealty before James, now duke of Ormond and newly appointed lord-lieutenant of Ireland by Charles. Phair then returned to his family at his home near Cork City.[10]

In the interim before Ormond returned to Dublin, Ireland was governed by lords justices, including Sir Maurice Eustace, the new lord chancellor; Lord Broghill, now earl of Orrery; and Sir Charles Coote, now earl of Mountrath. All three belonged to families established in Ireland before the wars, and Eustace was inclined to favour the older Protestant settlers; but Orrery and Mountrath "were directly interested in maintaining the Cromwellian settlement of land and property."[11]

Seven commissioners, forming a "court of claims," were appointed to administer the provisions of the 1662 Act of Settlement under the terms of the Book of Survey and Distribution. Charles II's promise to restore the titles of any Catholics who were innocent of involvement in the Irish Rebellion proved very difficult—**there simply wasn't enough land to go round.** For instance, Leap Castle in King's County (Offaly), formerly the stronghold of the O'Carrolls of Ely, which, under James I, had been officially planted by Protestants in 1620, had passed into the Darby family by marriage. The O'Carrolls appealed to the duke of Ormond to restore their lands. Ormond allowed them to take the Leap Castle demesne back again in 1664, but it was restored to the Darbys in 1667.[12] According to Beckett, "Charles dared not alienate the Irish Cromwellians at a time when his throne was still insecure, when Scotland was full of unrest, and when even in England there were powerful discontented elements ready at every opportunity to conspire against him. Inclination led him to favour the Roman Catholics, but prudence compelled him to side with the Protestants." At the end of the Restoration period, Irish Catholics owned about one-fifth of the land compared with three-fifths in 1641.[13]

Ensign John Head appeared again in Major George Pepper's 1661 and 1665 petitions to the Claims Court on behalf of soldiers in his company who had not been paid their debentures, the land owed them for service in the Irish army. George Pepper had been granted lands in Co. Meath in 1656 but John Head seems to have sold his debenture for £41 and 7 shillings instead of land. Pepper claimed that "all of said Debentures were for money due for service in Ireland...That lands were set out in satisfaction of the said Debentures with the said George Pepper's own company in Col. Fleetwood's Regiment in the year 1656 in the Co. of Meath and Barony of Duleek at 12 pence per acre...All of which lands were set in the year 1659 at the yearly rent of £300..." An addendum stated that "Capt. George Pepper is in possession of all lands claimed 7th May 1659 except 150 acres sold by the Claimant unto Lord Bishop of Killaloe in Julianstown, Co. Meath, near Drogheda."[14] George Pepper's sister Susannah was married to Edward Worth, who succeeded to the episcopacy as bishop of Killaloe in 1660; however, Susannah Worth had converted to quakerism in Kinsale in 1655. Described as an "adroit political player" during the religious conflicts of the 1640s and 1650s, Edward Worth nonetheless emerged at the restoration of Charles II with his reputation for loyalty to the English crown apparently unquestioned. The Peppers were yet another family, like the Otways, Darbys, and Pritties, which became closely associated with the Heads in Co. Tipperary.[15]

Between 1660 and 1662, about two thousand clergymen were "ejected" from their livings in the Irish Protestant Church for refusing to conform to the restoration of Anglicanism—the 1662 Act of Uniformity required the Book of Common Prayer to be used everywhere—and this may have provided the opportunity for John Head to qualify for ordination. He may have had the support of Edward Worth. There is no record of how or where he studied for the ministry. According to the 1666-67 Hearth Money records of the tax imposed on hearths, or chimneys, to supplement the royal income for the barony of Lower Ormond, however, a John and William Head had separate residences with one hearth each at Ballycommon, in the parish of Monsea, northwest of Nenagh, in northern Co. Tipperary. One year earlier, only William Head was listed in the parish of Monsea. The village of Ballycommon was a few miles from Lough Derg where Capt. Samuel Wade's residence at Derry also had just one hearth. Close study of the Hearth Money records for Co. Tipperary show that the Lower Ormond and Owney and Arra baronies were still heavily populated with Irish, for whom the tax must have added to their misery.

It appears that most of the Cromwellian profiteers had either left or had not taken up residence. An important exception was former colonel, now esquire, Thomas Sadleir, who, as sheriff of Co. Tipperary at that time, was appointed to levy and collect the Hearth Tax. Sadleir had settled at Kilnahalagh (which his patent stated will "henceforth and forever be known as Sopwell") in MacEgan castle, a fine four-storey tower house, which, according to the Hearth Tax record, had six hearths, which required him to pay 12 shillings. Examples of those who would become important resident landowners in the Nenagh region but were not yet listed were Henry Prittie and Edward Worth.[16] Daniel Grace, a leading historian of Northern Tipperary, found no evidence that John and William Head of Ballycommon were antecedents of John Head, the future owner of Ashley Park near Nenagh.[17] He is correct. John Head of Ashley Park was in fact descended from Michael Head of Waterford. If, as seems likely, however, this was the Rev. John Head, Michael Head's brother, then he brought up his three sons—John, Thomas, and George—in Ballycommon. The three brothers were first cousins of Michael's son John who acquired the Derrycastle lands through his marriage to Elizabeth Wade in 1696.

I suggest that William Head was the first of this particular Protestant family in Ireland, who may have arrived around 1620, and that he was the father of John, Michael, and Mary Head (see below). There has to be an explanation of why Michael Head was so well-connected to major beneficiaries of land grants in Northern Tipperary even before his son's marriage to Elizabeth Wade. The Reverend Head's son, George Head, Esq., lived in Borrisokane, according to his 1725 will. George's son was another Rev. John Head, born in Kilworth, Co. Cork, educated in Waterford and at Trinity College, Dublin (TCD), who died young in 1730 as Church of Ireland curate in Borrisokane. Thus, a branch of the Heads was well-established in Northern Tipperary before the Waterford Heads established themselves at Derry.

Following the Restoration, nonconformist extremists, such as Robert Phair and other former parliamentary officers, were unwilling to accept the return of episcopacy. In mid-April, 1663, the duke of Ormond heard of a revived plot to seize Dublin Castle and take him hostage. That June, seventy Presbyterian plotters were arrested and, on June 25, four of these were tried for high treason, and three of them were hanged, drawn and quartered in Dublin. Phair, a strong Commonwealth man, who had been allowed to return to his estates in Co. Cork and Wexford, was implicated in the abortive plot in 1666 but was not arrested. There had been an extraordinary change in his religious opinions. In about 1660, when they were in London, he and his wife became disciples of the self-proclaimed prophet Ludovick Muggleton, who claimed to have a divine mission.[18]

That same year, 1666, Michael Head, who was probably already a shipping merchant with links to London, was married in Dublin to Grace Collins. She died after giving birth to their son John, and Michael was remarried the following year to Elizabeth Hunt. Also in Dublin, Mary Head, Michael and John's sister, married a Mr. Higgins. He was likely to have been the Toby Higgins who was also named in George Peppard's (Pepper) 1665 claim. The Higginses stayed on in Dublin but Michael Head and his family, now including a second son Thomas, moved from Dublin to Waterford around 1670. Their fortunes in Waterford are described in the following three chapters.

Chapter 6

Waterford's Protestant Council: Michael Head, Merchant and Mayor

Waterford, like other wealthy Irish port cities, such as Dublin, the capital, and the other major Munster ports, Cork and Limerick, became a seedbed and microcosm of ascendant Protestant power in the second half of the seventeenth century following the Cromwellian conquest. Having moved from Dublin to Waterford with his young family in about 1670, Michael Head, ambitious and increasingly well connected beyond the confines of the city, spent the remainder of his adult life there, establishing himself as a successful trader and merchant and rising rapidly through the ranks of the Waterford Corporation to senior alderman, two one-year terms as mayor, and finally justice of the peace. To understand the still-medieval city and its displaced Catholic hierarchy, it is necessary to understand the culture and history that preceded his arrival there.

Seventeenth-century Waterford was the largest city in Munster with the advantage of a fine natural harbor on the south side of the River Suir—large ships could approach its quays even at low tide. Initially a Viking settlement second only to Dublin in importance, it was the principal point of entry for the Anglo-Norman invaders of the twelfth century. The walled city was, like Dublin, English in character and appearance. The river Suir separates Co. Waterford from counties Tipperary and Kilkenny to the north and from Co. Wexford on the east. Waterford City is near the estuary of two other navigable rivers, the Nore and the Barrow. Together they formed what was at that time the most important river system in the country, enabling the transportation of local beef, pork, and butter from the rich farming counties of Waterford, Tipperary, Kilkenny, and Carlow. Cork and Limerick were Munster's two other major ports at that time, but Waterford had particularly close trading ties with Bristol, England's principal trading port, sending a fleet there every July for St. James's fair. It also had a continental trade, especially with France and Spain.

Waterford's guild system and corporation council were modeled on Dublin's. However, as the Counter-Reformation raged in Waterford during the reign of James I, its Catholic Old English administration was in chaos over the refusal of several elected mayors to swear the oath of supremacy to the king. The government even revoked the city's charter in 1618 and it was not restored until after the accession of King Charles I. In 1626, Charles granted the city a new charter, known as the Great Charter, for a corporation or common council whose provisions ruled the city until the mid-nineteenth century.[1] The new Corporation of Waterford consisted of the mayor, two sheriffs, a recorder, eighteen aldermen, and nineteen assistants or common councilmen. The mayor was chosen for a one-year term from among the aldermen by the sitting mayor and council and, at the same time, two sheriffs were chosen from among the common councilmen. The mayor presided in the city courts; he was a justice of the peace for the city and, together with the council, sanctioned the making of by-laws by the city's craft guilds. He was also the admiral of the port of Waterford with jurisdiction over the tidal area of the three rivers. Even so, the citizens had the power to remove the mayor from office for misdemeanors, although this was rarely done.

When it came to political and economic clout, the Corporation exercised the power of making freemen at will; by the charter, all sons, sons-in-law, and apprentices of freemen after seven years of service were entitled to their freedom. A mayor during his tenure could also nominate freemen. Freemen were the largest category of electors and their other important privileges included the right to reduced rates of customs and tolls in the city and the right to vote in parliamentary elections. The Waterford Corporation had jurisdiction over an area beyond the city walls, including interests in several townships.[2] It claimed river rights north to Carrick-on-Suir and the right of appointment and tithes for parishes in south Kilkenny and east Waterford.[3] Senior aldermen had the right to purchase impropriate tithes—tithes awarded to a lay person—in those parishes which, in essence, provided them an annuity from ten percent of all the produce of the land. Michael Head would in due course take full advantage of that right.

After Cromwell's failure to capture Waterford in 1649, the city garrison was finally overcome on August 10, 1650, by a dragoon regiment under the command of Col. Thomas Sadler [Sadleir]. The Cromwellians threw Archibald Adair, the Catholic bishop of Waterford, out of his palace and Gen. Henry Ireton took possession of it. The soldiers than quartered themselves in the large nave of Waterford's eleventh-century Christ Church cathedral, where dinner was prepared and served, while Capt. William Bolton, wearing jackboots, climbed to the pulpit and harangued the troops. Between 1651 and 1656 the corporation was dissolved by Henry Ireton and the city was placed under military law and administered by commissioners. The soldiers caused severe damage to the cathedral and other Waterford churches. Most of the officers were Nonconformists, particularly Baptists, who were not only virulently anti-Catholic but also dissented from the established Anglican Church. Capt. Samuel Wade, whose daughter would marry Michael Head's oldest son in 1696, helped found Waterford City's Baptist church in the early 1650s, where he himself preached.[4] In fact, the Baptists were so successful in military circles that their ranks included twelve military governors in 1655.[5] Col. Thomas Sadleir, who became governor of Galway, was one of these, Col. Henry Prittie was another.[6]

In 1661, a petition for restitution lodged by the dean and chapter of Christ Church Cathedral, as well as depositions made to the Irish House of Lords (meeting for the first time in many years following the Restoration), provided evidence of the damage, most notably to the ancient cathedral. Major Andrew Rickards and William Bolton, a former captain of dragoons in Col. Henry Prittie's regiment, both then Waterford commissioners, testified as witnesses in Dublin and Waterford about the removal and sale of "ancient ecclesiastical furniture, tombs, sepulchral brasses, organs and bells," which caused particular indignation. Rickards saw two brass eagles and two tall brass candlesticks from the cathedral "sould by the authority of Collonel Saddler [sic], Capt. Wade, Capt. Halsey and some others who were then commissioners" and the broken pipes of "ye great paire of organs" among the plunder awaiting shipment abroad at the custom house. He also testified that the "steeple house" had a narrow escape from the "calculating rapacity" of the same Samuel Wade, who told the Cromwellian commissioners that "they might have seven hundred pounds for its materials" by demolishing rather than repairing it.[7]

Waterford's corporation was restored in 1655 but it was now an exclusively Protestant body. Both Bristol merchant Thomas Noble and John Heaven, a skinner, settled in Waterford and played leading roles on the city's council. The restored Corporation of Waterford continued in the medieval tradition of the guild and tithe system. Trade and craft guilds were mutual aid and regulatory associations of merchants or craftsmen in towns and cities. Guilds monopolized trade and industry in their areas, controlled entry into trades and crafts through apprenticeships, and insisted on common standards of workmanship. Guild membership, the key to a successful career in city politics, was originally obtained through completion of an apprenticeship or through being the son of a guild member.[8]

Michael Head was a member of the Hammermen guild, which included goldsmiths, silversmiths, and watch makers. The guild was given a charter of incorporation by Waterford Corporation in 1657.[9] There are a number of possible reasons why Michael Head was a member of the Hammermen but none of them had anything to do with smithery. He might have been the son of a guild member in Dublin (the posited William Head?), one of two women he married in Dublin might have been the daughter of a guild member there, or, as a former army officer who became a merchant, he might have been awarded membership. In the last case, he would have had to have been a trader for some time before his name first appears in the *Council Books of the Corporation of Waterford* in August 1670.[10]

With the restoration of Charles II in 1660 and the restoration of the Anglican Church of Ireland, nonconformist extremists, such as Robert Phair, were unwilling to accept the return of episcopacy (see chapter 5). It was only with the approach of Charles's coronation in April 1663 that Mayor William Bolton began reacting to the rumors of a threatened insurrection by former soldiers in the province of Munster. Bolton reported to Sir George Lane, secretary to the lord-lieutenant, the duke of Ormond, that the soldiers in Waterford were murmuring about an imminent Presbyterian uprising to be followed by the replacement of the earl of Orrery, the former Lord Broghill, as lord president of Munster. Orrery was second only to the duke of Ormond in terms of his power and influence in Ireland. The chief cause of discontent among the soldier-settlers was the widespread fear that they would lose some or all of their estates in the process of land distribution that was fully underway following passage of the Act of Settlement. The attempt to indemnify Catholics who could prove that they had played no part in the 1641 rebellion or its aftermath was almost certainly responsible for the revival of a virulent strain of anti-Catholicism among the Protestant population in the early 1660s.[11]

It was in this context that Bolton laid down a series of strict rules for all guild members and freemen of the city. On November 26, 1662, the council ordered that "all persons claymeing any freedome in this city take the oath of supremacy [acknowledging the king's authority in things spiritual as well as temporal] within fifteene days" and that all members of the council living within five miles of the city take the oath by "Friday next." Then followed an extensive list of names, headed by the mayor and aldermen and including members of several guilds, all of whom immediately took the oath. On December 10, a number of aldermen and common councilmen who had not yet taken the oath were fined by the sheriff receiver. The inevitable discrimination against Catholics followed a few days later: "if any merchants, shopkeepers, artificers, or tradesmen shall presume to take any apprentice from and after the 28th day of this instant December that is not educated in the Protestant religion and confirmed therein by ecclesiasticall [authority]," they will be fined by the council.[12]

Already, on November 18, leading Irish Catholic merchants sent a petition to Ormond against the harsh penalties they were facing. As merchants with the title and right as freemen of the city, they had been advancing "his majesties revenue" since his "happy restauracion" "by venturing abroad." They were recognized as freemen deserving of all the privileges granted to the city "until that William Bolton, now mayor, seeming to take notice of them as persons uncapeable of those priviledges, hath and doth dayly force them to pay strangers duties for their goods." Dublin Castle commanded the mayor to answer those complaints but Bolton, who claimed that he did not see this petition until the end of December, eventually replied to the complainants "that they have noe just title or right to freedoms in Waterford or other of his majesties corporacions in Ireland, for that they are not Protestants nor will take the oath of supremacy nor bee of any office that may bee useful to his majestie and his Protestant subjects. That they have not, as they alledge, bin looked upon as freemen since his majesties happy restauracion…"[13]

The town clerk, rather than backing down, next ordered on January 6, 1663, that the oath of supremacy must be taken before the mayor by all members of guilds. On April 8, 1663, two weeks before the royal coronation, "the papists and phannatiques [protestant nonconformists] were warned out of this citty and an order to that purpose received from the lord president of Munster." As for the coronation day itself, the council ordered the day before that it be kept "with all befitting solemnity, and that the councell meete at the Guildhall att nyne of the clock in the morning, and the severall guilds to goe from there orderly to church," accompanied by music and flower-bedecked children from the free school, and that bonfires be lit in front of all councilmen's houses.[14]

Six years later, in 1669, when William Bolton was again elected by the council to serve as mayor, he refused to appear, demonstrating utter contempt for the mayor and council, and then left the city. This caused "great disturbance and prejudice…to the honor and authority of this citty." The council book from 1663 to 1669 is patchy, to say the least, so it offers no explanation of his actions. However, he had received confirmation of the historic Faithlegg castle and land grant in the Court of Claims in 1667 so, having no further interest in civic involvement, he had apparently turned his attention to the power of landownership. He had achieved the traditional social climb from city to county and was cutting his links with "trade." Bolton was ordered to pay a fine of twenty pounds sterling and the current mayor, John Heaven, the merchant alderman who had moved to Waterford from Bristol, agreed to serve another year.[15]

The council then had the devil's own problems with Bolton who had evidently come to blows with members of the first Heaven administration. The entry for February 26, 1670, summarizes the renegade alderman's damaging actions. He had evidently accused the city and its magistracy of grave scandals in articles to the lord-lieutenant, all "contrary to his oath and duety as a member of this board." The mayor and council now suspended the unscrupulous Bolton from his aldermanship and from acting in any public office within the city to which that title had entitled him. They gave him one month to appear before the council and explain himself or be expelled altogether from the council. Expanding on this indictment ten days later, the Heaven administration announced they had good proof that Bolton had written "a most factious and seditious letter" to the grand jury of Waterford County during the last quarter session, endeavoring to win their favor and turn them against the mayor and council with the intent of drawing them into his party and "thereby to overturn the government of this citty." In effect, he had been trying to remove the council's powers to appoint its magistrates and, having failed to appear in his own defense, the council had decided to dismiss him from being an alderman, strike him off the roll of freemen, and would proceed to elect another alderman in his place.[16] As Cromwellian land grantees climbed into gentry status, their power base became the county grand juries and the Irish Parliament.

Perhaps as part of a reshuffle resulting from the turmoil caused by Bolton's insurrection, Michael Head and Edward Collins, who was likely to have been the brother of Head's first wife, Grace Collins, and three other young men were summoned to appear before the next council for the first time in August 1670. On June 22, 1671, "Michael Head, merchant, appeared before the mayor and council and was admitted and sworn a freeman of this citty." The fact that neither Edward Collins nor Michael Head was a freeman of Waterford before 1671 seems to indicate that they were new to the city. They appear to have gained their freedom through the 1671 Ordinance, "New Ruyles and Orders for the Regulation of Corporations in Ireland." Upon payment of 20 pounds, the following were to be admitted as freemen: "all foreigners, strangers and aliens, as well

others as Protestants, who are or shall be merchants, traders, arti-
sans, artificers, seamen or otherwise skilled and exercised in any
mystery, craft, or trade or in working or making of any manufacture, or in the art of navigation, then residing and inhabiting within the city of [in this case Waterford], or who should at any time
thereafter come into the city with intent and resolution to inhabit,
reside and dwell..." Since the Catholic merchant families had lost
political control, there was a need to restock the major ports with
politically reliable and preferably English merchants and traders of
the Protestant faith to ensure English control. Michael Head now
began a rapid ascent to civic power and wealth.

In his chapter on "Municipal Life in the time of Charles II," Edmund Downey remarked on the amazing burdens which "the City
Fathers of Waterford carried on their shoulders" more than two
centuries before publication of his *Story of Waterford* (1914). These
included administering the property of the Corporation and the affairs of the city generally; looking after and regulating the entire
business of the port—collection of customs, dues payable by ships,
and dues levied on imports and exports; providing accommodation for troops and maintaining the walls, forts and gates of the city
in good repair; overseeing and repairing the Court House, prisons,
and all public buildings under their jurisdiction; conserving and
distributing water supplies; supervising various city guilds and
charities; keeping a watch on those who had freedom of the city and
upholding their privileges; currying favor with Dublin Castle and
placating the English Court when that seemed necessary; administering the finances of the Church, including numerous repairs,
especially to Christ Church Cathedral; bestowing advowsons—the
right to recommend or appoint a member of the Anglican clergy for
a vacant benefice—and other privileges.[17]

The duke of Ormond had been largely responsible for encouraging
Irish commerce, industry, learning, and religious tolerance and he
had vehemently opposed the 1667 Importation Act prohibiting the
importation of Irish cattle into England. But his Irish policy had
made him powerful enemies at court and, in March 1669, they persuaded Charles II to remove him from office as lord-lieutenant.
Despite Ormond's removal, his influence on commerce and reli-

gious tolerance continued for a while. On June 25, 1672, during the Waterford mayoralty of Thomas Bolton (William Bolton's brother), Michael Head, Richard Seay, and William Dennis junior were elected common councilmen and just two weeks later, on July 8, Head and Seay were elected sheriffs for the ensuing year. Their actions while in office indicated a more tolerant attitude toward Catholics during a period of increased commercial prosperity.[18] This reflects the passage in England that year of the Declaration of Indulgence, presaging the relaxation of Irish laws that excluded Catholics from towns, the Irish bar, and certain local offices and by the provision of a small royal bounty to Presbyterian ministers. During their first council meeting, Head and Seay and their new colleagues voted to approve the inherited right of Irish Catholic merchant Nicholas Porter to the freedom of the city. One of the five Catholics who swore oaths to Porter's eligibility was Richard Fitzgerald, who would become mayor in the Jacobite Council of 1688-90.[19]

Considering the demanding responsibilities of sheriffs, it is astonishing to see how often Head was absent from council meetings, most likely due to his trading activities. There are many instances in the council books of members being fined or voted off the council for absenteeism but this fate never befell Head. For example, according to the council book entry for October 2, 1669, since aldermen John Lapp and John Houghton had left Waterford with their families and failed to attend council for the past four years, they were now dismissed from the council. Head was never absent for more than a few weeks at a time. On October 1, 1670, it was noted that Alderman Sir Thomas Dancer, who had served as mayor and justice of the peace for Waterford, "hath removed himselfe, family, and concernes from the citty and discontinued his attendance at this board for some yeares past, he bee and is hereby removed from being a member of this board." The Dancers were among the earliest to settle in Co. Tipperary following the Act of Settlement. A later Sir Thomas Dancer was a neighbor of William Henry Head in Modreeny in the mid-nineteenth century.[20]

Despite his absences, the council minutes show many examples of Michael Head's growing reputation for probity and reliability. When the council became aware that numerous counterfeits were being circulated of the copper tokens stamped by silversmith

Edward Russell and distributed in 1667—to be used by the poor to buy goods, since there were insufficient small silver coins in circulation at that time—Sheriffs Head and Seay were called on, along with the mayor and four aldermen, including the disgraced Alderman William Bolton, to lend money to be exchanged for the tokens. All tokens, both original and fake, were to be turned in on November 22, 1672 in exchange for the same value of coins by the sheriffs.

In March 1673, Michael Head, Mayor Henry Aland, and the city recorder were asked to go to the assizes in Kilkenny on behalf of the corporation to attend the trial of a case brought against the city about disputed property. The council subsequently voted in June that Alderman Andrew Rickards and Sheriff Michael Head attend the assizes for a different trial on July 18. This must have happened, judging by Head's absence for much of that month. As a senior alderman, Rickards was benefitting from acquiring impropriate tithes under the control of the Waterford council. His acquisition of the Brickinsmill parish tithes in October 1672 would become one of numerous charges of corruption brought against him in 1680. Tithes controlled by the Waterford council were a frequent and important concern. Impropriation of tithe, which was intended to support clergymen in the conduct of their duties, was a consequence of the granting of the lands of the dissolved monasteries to laymen after the Reformation.

On April 27, 1674, Joseph Osborne, Michael Head, and Richard Seay were elected aldermen by majority vote. It had been less than two years since Head had first become a common councilman in June 1672. Head and Seay then took the oaths of allegiance and supremacy "and desired further time to consider of the short oath in the rules." Michael Head was absent for the next five sessions, and he was still a common councilman when he next appeared on June 22. That day, he and Richard Seay "took the short oath in the rules against takeing armes against the king, etc. and also the oath of aldermen, they having taken the oathes of allegiance and supremacy at the time of their election to the office of aldermen." [21] A week later, they took their seats as aldermen for the first time. Then Aldermen Cooper, Head, Seay, and councilmen Hitchin, Marriott,

Osborne, and Collins were sworn free of the staple. The Irish staple emerged in the thirteenth century as a regulatory body to govern the trade in basic or staple goods such as wool and hides. However, the staple's importance as a trade regulatory body had declined by this time and it became a means by which loans could be raised and spare capital ventured in relative security.[22]

Alderman Joseph Ivie was sworn in as mayor on October 1, 1674. After a strong start, Ivie and the council suffered a degree of verbal abuse during the later months of his mayoralty. It appeared that his youth and inexperience made it hard for him to control a fractious council as well as the trade and craftspeople of the city. Perhaps most serious was his confrontation with Joseph Osborne who, as recorded on April 16, 1675, "hath misbehaved himself in his carriage and expressions to Mr Mayor and hath disobeyed his commands and the order of this board for pulling down of his penthouse incroached on High Street, and hath rescued a prisoner from the constable to whom he was committed by Mr. Mayor, and other threat'ning expressions appearing by several despositions…" Apparently Osborne had that day shouted a final insult as he was leaving, saying he was "glad to bee ridd of a pack of fooles or knaves, meaning this council."[23] The council then proceeded to consider Osborne's offenses, all of them contrary to his oaths as a freeman and member of the council, and ordered that he be removed as a member.

Despite his absence from the meeting on June 29, 1675, Michael Head was unanimously elected to serve as the next mayor and Nathaniel Marriott and Edward Collins were elected sheriffs. Michael Head was apparently just as young (in his early thirties) as the beleaguered Joseph Ivie but had succeeded in establishing a reputation for competence and trustworthiness in just five years of council service. One of the first actions of his council was to assure former mayor Joseph Ivie that the council would indemnify him for any suit that might be brought against him by former alderman Joseph Osborne. Michael Head and his sheriffs were sworn into office on September 29 before the deputy mayor, Thomas Christmas, esq., Richard Stephen, the recorder, and the rest of the council and attending citizens. Head's was a businesslike mayoralty, with considerable disbursements for salary and repairs to and decisions about such city buildings as the hospital. However, the final entry of his term in office indicates that the council had been so lax in its spending controls for some time that "the state of the revenue hath and doth remaine in an uncertain condicion and is much suspected to bee greatly impaired." The council then threatened severe punishment for any sheriff receiver, auditor, or anyone else involved in handling the city's revenue found to have allowed disbursement without receiving prior permission and warrant from the mayor and council.[24] Head had been an auditor of the city accounts from November 1674 during Joseph Ivie's mayoralty.

Judging by his frequent absences from council meetings the year following his mayoralty—there is no record of him ever being chastised by other members for these absences—Michael Head was again bent on extending his trading activities. He was absent for the duke of Ormond's official visit to the city on August 27, 1677 (the duke had been officially reinstated to the lord lieutenancy that year) and also for the swearing in of the next mayor in late September. The wool trade seems to have been brisk in 1678, and Alderman Head was one of the traders granted licenses to export wool from the port of Waterford on payment of £20 each.[25]

In the meantime, Charles II had continued to assure the grants made to many of the Cromwellian soldiers and adventurers. Samuel Wade was one of twenty-three of the "most humble and obliged servants," mostly Cromwellians, who signed an address drawn up at Nenagh and presented to Ireland's lord-lieutenant, James Butler, the first duke of Ormond, in March 1670. The address was to thank Ormond for "appearing for the English interest in time of their unexpected danger and preventing those dangerous endeavours which struck at the foundations of us all in these parts."[26] Wade indicated that he had taken up residence on his Derry Castle lands and was anxious to have them made secure by royal approval following the restoration of Charles II. As for his Rathone lands, an 1824 certified copy of the original deed, shows that the King granted on July 30, 1678 "by Letters Patent to Samuel Wade Junior, his heirs and Assigns for ever," the 154 acres of profitable plantation land of Rathone and a further 58 acres still in dispute, as well as 59 acres of profitable plantation land in Knockoland and Drumniscart lying in the Barony of Lower Ormond, County of Tipperary, together with all "singular Castles Mannors Messuages, Forts, Mills, Houses, cottages, Bawnes Buildings Barnes Stables Gardens Orchards Lands tenements woods underwoods Meadows Pastures Feedings, Tuffs, Furzes heathes boggs Loughes Mountains Comons & Comons of Pasture Moores Marches Water Watercourse flashings eares Quaries, etc."[27] These lands would become the Ashley Park estate of a first junior branch of the Derry Castle Heads.

Anti-Catholicism became rife once again that summer, 1678, with the discovery of the publication by Titus Oates in England of details of the so-called Popish Plot, revelations which were ultimately found to be phony (Oates was subsequently known as "Titus the Liar"). Oliver Plunkett, the bishop of Armagh, was caught up in these rumors. He was arrested for alleged conspiracy with the French against the English government and was taken to England and hanged, drawn, and quartered in 1681. In November, all Catholic merchants were ordered by the lord-lieutenant and his council in Dublin to be expelled from six cities, including Waterford. The Catholic bishop of Waterford had to flee from the city after being accused of complicity in the "Plot," and, in October 1680, a warrant was issued for the arrest of Robert Power, dean of Waterford, and for Richard Power, earl of Tyrone.[28] He had previously been indicted twice at the Waterford assizes for a treasonable conspiracy. Brought to England, Tyrone was locked up in Gatehouse Prison following his impeachment by the House of Commons. Titus Oates's fabrication caused some thity-five people to be executed before inconsistencies in his testimony led to his conviction for perjury and imprisonment.

After the plot was discredited, Tyrone was allowed to return to Ireland. He may already have been a neighbor of Michael Head in the village of Gurteen, across the River Suir in Co. Kilkenny. Protestants in England and Ireland never ceased to worry that Irish Catholics were conspiring with the Catholic superpowers of Europe, especially France, to destroy the Protestant interest in Britain. Everyone assumed that, lacking a legitimate heir, Charles II would be succeeded in due course by his Catholic brother, the duke of York. An opposition group of peers, members of parliament and local politicians emerged which was intent on preventing the perceived threat of popery and arbitrary government on the lines of Louis XIV of France, whom they knew to have expansionist ambitions. They sought to protect the Protestant religion and secure the liberties of English people. Above all, they sought to exclude the duke of York from the succession through an Exclusion Bill. This group came to be called Whigs. Their opponents, who sought to preserve the hereditary succession, came to be called Tories.[29]

The Waterford council increased security, agreeing with chief constable Michael Brown that a convenient room would be provided for the use of officers of the main guard and that the garrison be allowed to use the old market house near the Key [Quay] gate as a guardhouse until the market was brought back within the city walls. A cavalry patrol was ordered to keep watch every night until further notice, and the council also ordered Brown to bring a list of men in the parish who were English and fit to be sworn as constables to replace the Irish petty constables. Also, during this highly charged council meeting, Patrick Moore, an apprentice to Michael Head, was admitted to city freedom.

During 1680, Michael Head was frequently asked, as a city surveyor and auditor, to lead investigations into one or another problem and report back with proposed solutions. In July, there was the first evidence of a major scandal when senior alderman Thomas Christmas accused Alderman Andrew Rickards of criminal misuse of Corporation property and funds. This was all the more astonishing because Rickards was a major in the Cromwellian regiment that captured Waterford in 1650, a mayor during the Cromwellian commission period and again following the restoration of the Corporation, a prosperous draper and, above all, another of the Corporation auditors. On July 10, Christmas brought no less than ten charges against Rickards. He accused him of cheating the Council in connection with house property, rents, tithes, and cash belonging to the civic authorities.

The council met on September 9 to consider Rickards' voluminous response to these charges. To the charge of stealing £6 of public money and pretending he had been robbed of it, Rickards declared that the money had been stolen by Alderman Head's brother-in-law (probably Thomas Hunt), who apparently worked as an assistant in Rickards' draper's shop. Rickards alleged that the money had been found at Head's house and Rickards agreed to Elizabeth Head's request that he allow her brother to remain with her that night and he would return the money the next day. However, the bird had flown by then. Michael Head assured Rickards that he would get the money from his relative and pay it back. When Rickards returned home, he claimed that he found that his shop had been ransacked and that £80 and a large quantity of "Cambrick, Hollands, Stockings, Gold and Silver Buttons, and Silks to the value of £200" were also missing. Rickards concluded that "for his word sake," when he discovered his great loss and because of the high esteem he had for Head and his wife, he would not make any further search for the thief. This all sounds unlikely.

Alderman Christmas then repeated all the various charges he had made and endeavored to substantiate them with documentary proof. When the council assembled on September 23, it solemnly declared that all the charges against Alderman Andrew Rickards had been duly proved. Six days later, the council found that Rickards' conduct was scandalous, dishonorable, mercenary and deceitful, and they ordered that he be suspended from office until he gave satisfaction to the council.[30] They asserted that his actions were "against common honesty and justice or the trust reposed in him by this corporacion or contrary to his oathes and duty of a freeman and member of the common council of the citty and county of the citty aforesaid and one of the auditors of the corporaction accounts…"[31] There is no record of how Rickards' serious accusations against Michael Head's brother-in-law were handled.

On March 28, 1681, Charles II dissolved Parliament to block passage of the earl of Shaftesbury's Exclusion Act (which would prevent the duke of York from becoming king). Charles declared that he would rule without parliament to the end of his reign. Ireland then followed England in sending a series of loyal addresses to the crown. Beginning with Dublin's, there were 44 in all during the spring and summer of 1682. Waterford's began in orotund and sugary fashion:

> Most gracious and dread sovereign, wee your majesties most loyal, most faithfull, and most obedient subjects, the mayor, sheriffs, and citizens of his majesties citty of

Waterford in common council assembled, acknowledge our utter detestacion of all those malevolent practices and seditious machinacions which have been of late drawn into practice by some mutinous and ill designing persons...wee are and shall bee ever ready on all occasions to second with our lives and fortunes for the defence and preservacion of your majesties royal person and prerogative and the lawfull descent of the imperial crowne of these realms in the lineall and lawfull course of it, and of the true Protestant religion and government as it is now established by law, both in church and state, against all combinacions and confedracyes and associacions whatsoever which shalbee contrived and entered into by any papists or sectaries or other factious disturbers of the publique peace, of what profession or denominacion soever they bee..."[32]

The Protestant leaders in Ireland knew which side their bread was buttered on. In the early 1680s, the Irish economy was showing signs of recovery. The longer the land settlement remained unchallenged, the more willing the new owners were to invest in their property and make improvements. Trade picked up, despite temporary setbacks during intermittent wars between England and the Dutch Republic and restrictions placed on the Irish economy by the English. The Navigation Act of 1671 forbade the direct import into Ireland of sugar, tobacco, and other named colonial products but proved fairly easy to evade. The 1671 Cattle Act, on the other hand, despite prohibiting a profitable export trade to England of Irish livestock, beef, pork, and bacon, stimulated a diversification of the Irish agricultural economy into salt beef, butter and sheep, and helped promote an expansion of trade with the Continent and the colonies.[33] There was a dramatic rise in receipts from customs and excise and the population began to grow. The customs inward and outward for 1681 was £14,826. According to Downey, this was a very large sum.[34]

Michael Head was deeply involved as a leading trader and shipping merchant. It is known that he was related to Joshua Head, a master grocer of considerable means in London. The most likely cause of Head's frequent absences over the years was that these cousins were also linked by trading, that Michael Head was delivering Irish commodities to London and returning with goods from Joshua's enterprise. There is also evidence that Michael and, in due course, his son John added Leghorn in Italy to their route after it became a free port in 1675. Trade there was largely controlled by Jewish merchants, and its governor had a monopoly on salt and brandy. These were listed as commodities on one of the Heads' ships when it was impounded in Limerick harbor in 1704 (see chapter 8). Trading in the Mediterranean was a dangerous undertaking at the height of the Barbary slave trade in the sixteenth and seventeenth centuries. Barbary and Turkish pirates captured hundreds of thousands of Europeans and sold them as slaves in North Africa and the Ottoman Empire. Thus, when news arrived in March 1682 that Frances Knowles, a Waterford merchant, member of the council, and former sheriff, had been captured and sold into slavery with the Turks, the council called for volunteers to raise the money to redeem him. The next time Mr. Knowles was mentioned in the council record was when he was reinstated as a common council member in 1690. He had obviously fallen on hard times, since he petitioned the council for support and, following his death, the council voted to support his widow.[35]

In the wake of the discovery in the late spring and summer of 1683 of the Rye House Plot—a plan by opposition leaders in England to assassinate Charles II and his brother and heir James, duke of York—the government cracked down with a series of state trials and other repressive measures. Despite the fact that the government failed to find any evidence of an Irish dimension, the Waterford council again felt a need on July 29 to send a loyalty address and thanks to God for preserving the lives of the royal brothers "from the seditious and horred designes of rebellious and profligate wretches," and declared an abhorrence "of all traitorous and wicked conspiracies" against the King's "person or government." They acknowledged "the blessings of peace, prosperity, and happiness and the exercise of the true Protestant religion established by law" that they enjoyed under Charles II's government, "according to the fundamental lawes of these kingdoms." The addresses of 1683, like those of 1682, represented mainly the views of the Protestant ruling elite in town and country, rallying behind the crown and succession, as did their Tory-Anglican counterparts in England. In December 1683, the Waterford council voted to bar anyone from a seat on the council who was not a communicant in the established [Anglican] church.[36] There was no way of knowing that King Charles would be dead two years later and that all too soon the Protestant ascendancy would be severely challenged under the rule of his Catholic heir James II.

In the meantime, two former Cromwellian soldiers of nonconformist belief and early and late blood links to the Heads departed the scene. Col. Robert Phair (Phayre) died on September 19, 1682, of an apparent stroke at the age of sixty-two. The following year, Capt. Samuel Wade died, possibly at Derry, although he also lived comfortably in Waterford according to various mentions of his garden there in the Waterford Corporation records. His young and only child, Elizabeth, was his sole heir. She would become the wife of Michael Head's older son John in 1696 (see chapter 8). In 1684, Michael would be elected mayor for the second time.

Chapter 7

Waterford's Jacobite Council

Shortly after he became mayor again on September 29, 1684, Michael Head conferred freedom of the city on Capt. Richard Coote, which was subsequently confirmed by the council.[1] These are the only mentions of Richard Coote in the Waterford Corporation records. If he was in fact Richard Coote, later first lord of Bellomont (1636-1700), as seems likely, he was a Protestant nephew of Sir Charles Coote, earl of Mountrath, and his subsequent absence would be explained by his decision, following the accession of pro-Catholic James II the following year, to move to the Continent, where he served as a captain of horse in the Dutch army. He was one of the first to join William of Orange in the Glorious Revolution of 1688 that brought William III and Mary II to the throne. Michael Head's action indicates a continuing bond between the Heads and the Cootes—Mayor Michael Head's brother John Head was a junior officer in the Old English force led by Sir Charles Coote when Dublin Castle was captured in December 1659 (see chapter 5).[2]

In late November, Mayor Head had to contend with the troublesome former mayor, William Fuller. Apparently, Fuller had admitted his guilt in casting a slur on his fellow councilors. Angered that the Waterford corporation had replaced him as master of the St. Stephen's leper house, Fuller had submitted articles to the government in Dublin accusing "Mr Mayor Head, Mr Recorder Bolton, Aldermen Richard Seay and Richard Mabanke, or any of them," of being against the church and government. The Waterford council now voted to petition the lord-lieutenant and his council for a hearing so that they could vindicate themselves. In January 1685, the council in Waterford ordered Fuller to give up his master's seal and any lepers' documents he was holding to the new master,

Alderman William Denis, and suspended him from the council until they had received a ruling from Dublin confirming the city's right to make that appointment.[3]

This local dispute paled in comparison to the scale of the problems that were to follow the unexpected death of King Charles II on February 6, 1685. Succession now passed to his fifty-one-year-old Catholic brother, James, duke of York, as James II of England and Ireland and James VII of Scotland. Within hours, the new king made a reassuring speech to his privy council saying he would *preserve* the Protestant religion. This was published in the official government newspaper the *London Gazette* and widely disseminated. The Anglican clergy read it from their pulpits. For a while, James calmed fears by making few changes in Charles's government.[4]

Just three days after King Charles's death, on February 6, 1685, Henry Prittie of Kilboy near Nenagh, Co. Tipperary, conveyed to his trustees, Michael Head of Waterford, Thomas Sadleir of Ballingarry, and Charles Alcock of Powerstown, both in County Tipperary, 3,642 acres of his lands in the Barony of Owney and Arra in County Tipperary. This was an evident attempt to shield Prittie's substantial land grant from a reversal of policy by James II. It began "This Indenture made the Ninth day of February in the reign of our Sovereign Lord Charles Annos Dom 1685" but "Charles" was deleted and replaced with "James." It then described the lands in great detail plus all the buildings, orchards, gardens, woods, water courses, mines, and minerals. Rents from all these properties were also to revert to the trustees "& their heirs forever." Unfortunately, the signature page for this important document is missing.[5]

This raises once again the question of how Michael Head came to be so trusted by Henry Prittie. Both Thomas Sadleir and Henry Prittie were officers in Cromwell's army with strong connections to Waterford, but Michael Head was a generation younger. Head might have met and impressed Prittie in Co. Tipperary if he visited his brother John there in the 1660s, or the connection may have been made through Col. Thomas Sadleir, Capt. Samuel Wade's commander when Waterford was captured by the Cromwellians in 1650, who would become high sheriff of Co. Tipperary.

Perhaps it was Charles's action in recalling the first duke of Ormond to England just a few days before his death that impelled

Cromwellian grantees like Henry Prittie to attempt legal measures to shelter their lands. Ormond's moderate rule had ushered in a period of considerable economic prosperity and reassured those who had consolidated their land grants through the claims courts. Protestant Ireland now fell into a state of profound anxiety while Roman Catholic Ireland was understandably euphoric. The minority Protestants, who held 80 percent of Irish land, feared that state policies would change, and that "they would lose power, privilege, property, and support from England." The Roman Catholics, on the other hand, had hopes that they would recover what they had lost as a result of the events between 1641 and 1653, or even earlier with the Ulster Plantation. Protestant fears of betrayal not only created a loss of confidence so that the economy suffered but exacerbated the siege mentality that already existed.

James now turned to his old friend Richard Talbot to help him run Irish affairs and gave him command of Ormond's infantry regiment. In June 1685, the king promoted Talbot to the peerage with the titles baron of Talbotstown, viscount Baltinglass, and earl of Tyrconnell. Although he remained in England for the time being, Tyrconnell began to influence a new direction in Irish policy, immediately taking over responsibility for military affairs in Ireland. He was determined to restore the political and military power of the Old English Catholics and aimed to break or seriously modify the Restoration land settlement. Even though that act had restored some of the Catholic estates, Talbot blamed Ormond for the bad deal the Catholics received. But, as historian Tim Harris has pointed out, those Catholics who had managed to regain their land at the Restoration, or purchased land from the Cromwellian settlers, or who had profited from trade under Charles II, were likely to have been just as alarmed about the actions of James and Tyrconnell as were the Protestants.[6]

With so much at stake, the Waterford council had hastened on March 4, 1685 to approve the final wording of a loyalty address to James: "To his most excellent majesty James the Second of England, Scotland, France, and Ireland king, defender of the faith etc. Most dread soveraign, wee the mayor, recorder, sheriffs, and citizens of your majesties antient and loyal citty of Waterford in your kingdom of Ireland in our common councell assembled, and having duly lamented the death of our late soveraign your majesties dear brother of everblessed memory, do as truly rejoice at your majesties quiet and peaceable possessing your lawfull and hereditary throne, beseeching God that your majesty and your rightfull heires may long and long reign over us therein." Mirroring their words to Charles II just four years before, they assured their new king that they would be prepared to give their lives and fortunes in his defense and offered their "most humble and hearty thankes for the most gracious assurance your majesty has been pleased to give us in your declaracion of protecting us in the injoyment of those things that are most dear unto us." The address was signed by Mayor Michael Head and the entire Waterford council. All the important local dignitaries, dressed in their official regalia, would have been involved in proclaiming the new king. In April, the mayor was charged with deciding on the solemnities to be followed on coronation day, April 23, 1685. However, no description of these ceremonies was recorded.[7]

According to historian Herman Murtagh, at this time "Protestants were strongest in Waterford city where it was estimated they formed half the population of about 5,000."[8] But the far smaller Protestant community in the town of Borrisokane in heavily Catholic northern Tipperary was alarmed on June 21 by a rumor that there was to be a "rising...of the Irish" and that all the Protestants "should have their throats cut by them." The Protestants kept watch that night, marching through the streets armed with swords, staves or guns in self-defense. Concerned about what appeared to be "disorderly and suspicious meetings of the disaffected," the government ordered the judges to prosecute the Protestants for "a riotous and seditious unlawful assembly." Ten of the activists were found guilty and more than fifty others were convicted for spreading the report.[9] Borrisokane was to become the home of the descendants of Michael Head's brother John.

That month, James's English parliament tightened its control over the Irish economy by reviving the Navigation Act, which prevented Ireland from trading directly with the North American colonies. Other acts forbade the importation of certain Irish products, such as tallow and hide, into England. Facing these economic uncertainties, Michael Head's second mayoralty principally focused on controlling the city's revenue through stringent accounting, managing its buildings and infrastructure, and updating the valuation and management of the city's tithes. On June 22, it was confirmed that the city's tithes for the Kilkenny parish of Kilkilliheen (Kilculliheen), Rathpatrick, and Portnescully had been let for one year to various council members by public cant (auction), with the city paying the proxies and the new tenants advancing half a year's rent.[10]

When Louis XIV intensified the persecution of the Huguenots in France in October 1685 by revoking the Edict of Nantes—Henry IV's 1598 guarantee of toleration—British and Irish Protestants were even more terrified. The fact that this coincided with James's accession to the English throne convinced them that he was making plans in secret with French Catholics. The following spring, the duke of Savoy (a client of Louis XIV) invaded Piedmont in Northern Italy and, together with his French allies, massacred some eight to ten thousand Protestants (the vast majority women, children, and old people), selling into slavery those who managed to escape with their lives, increasing the growing apprehension of British and Irish Protestants.[11]

Michael Head was succeeded as mayor by William Goodrick in September 1685 but, on January 22, 1686, as one of the five senior aldermen, Head was sworn in as justice of the peace of Waterford City and the county at large, the first of many members of the Head family to be given this responsibility. He was now one of the local judicial officials who conducted the quarter-sessions or assizes, which tried all cases except treason, murder, felonies punishable by penal servitude for life, and felonies of a political or rebellious nature. The justices of the peace also promoted an "out of session" jurisdiction known as the petty sessions to deal with offenses of a summary nature.

As Michael Head was absorbed by these duties, Tyrconnell was rapidly remodeling the military in Ireland, dismissing Protestant officers and men, and replacing them with Roman Catholics. The same policy was followed in many branches of administration: Roman Catholics were appointed as judges, admitted to corporations, and even given seats on the privy council. Lord Clarendon, an Anglican and brother-in-law of the king, who had succeeded

Ormond as lord lieutenant, could do little to allay the alarm among Protestants and, by the summer of 1686, many were leaving Ireland for England and elsewhere. Most of these refugees were merchants who felt that their capital would be safer in England but many were dismissed officers who took their skills and grievances to Prince William of Orange in Holland, who would, within three years, become King of England.[12]

Greatly influenced by the arrogant, hot-tempered, and violently argumentative Tyrconnell, who arrived in Ireland in June 1686 as commander-in-chief of the Irish army, Lord-Lieutenant Clarendon informed the principal municipal corporations that the oath of supremacy was no longer to be required of persons seeking the freedom of the city. In addition, Catholics were to be permitted to enjoy some share of the ordinary municipal privileges. On August 23, several Catholic merchants, including Nicholas and Richard Fitzgerald, were sworn freemen of Waterford City. Lord Clarendon visited the city in September and was presented with the city freedom in a golden box. On that same day, a long list of Old English Catholics, including Francis, the lord archbishop of Dublin, and several knights and gentlemen, were awarded freedom of the city.[13]

On October 21, council members were ordered to agree on a method to raise money for the support of the new Catholic officers and soldiers of the garrison. Five senior Protestant aldermen who had served as mayor, including Michael Head, and five of the local Catholic merchants newly re-granted freedom, Richard Fitzgerald, Edward Browne, Nicholas Porter, Martin Walsh, and Nicholas Lee, were charged with raising money from residents of Trinity Parish. In November, freedom of the city was granted to an astonishing number of Catholic petitioners, including two deans and the twelve officers of the garrison. The Protestant council was hanging on by a thread and the burdens of supporting the garrison were weighing on its members.[14]

Not all the Irish cities were as compliant as Waterford. For instance, the new Catholic officers and soldiers were ill received by the populace in Derry, Dublin, and Kilkenny. There were frequent conflicts over quarters. Protestant clergyman William King later complained that the Catholic troops never paid a farthing for meat and drink, and that they extorted "vast Sums of Mony" from Protestant innkeepers. With the exception of Dublin, they were quartered in private as well as public quarters. Originating in counties Waterford and Cork, rumors of planned uprisings by English Protestants or Irish Catholics increased in the autumn of 1686. However, as in Borrisokane, the government directed local JPs to prosecute anyone who maliciously spread rumors and that helped quieten local fears.[15]

Clarendon was recalled in January 1687 and Tyrconnell arrived in Dublin on February 6 to replace him, although with the lesser title of lord deputy.[16] Although Tyrconnell began by attempting to calm fears with a proclamation issued on February 21 that promised to protect "all his Majesties Subjects...of what Perswasion in Religion or Degree in their just Rights and Properties due to them by Law, and in the free Exercise of their Religion," as long as they remained loyal to the King, many municipal authorities were not convinced.[17] The Waterford council, for example, reacted by awarding freedom of the city to ten young Protestant men, many of them sons of long-standing council members. One of them was John Head, Michael's older son. On March 1, a further eight well-connected and reliable young Protestants were awarded city freedom. Annual tithes were awarded on April 1 for the following year as usual to Protestant aldermen, including the parish of Rathpatrick to Michael Head and two other parishes to an apparently rehabilitated Major Rickards.[18]

Actions like these showed that the municipal authorities in Waterford, Dublin, and elsewhere were in no great haste to comply with Tyrconnell's orders. The result of their obstructionist policy was the issuing of writs of *quo warranto* in 1687, requiring them to show by what authority they held their office and that they had exercised its powers according to its charter. On April 2, the Waterford council concluded that Mayor Goodrick, Alderman Head, Sheriff Smith, and a Mr. Taylor, or any three of them, should take the city charter to Clonmel to get the advice of counsel there "about the present affaires of this corporacion," specifically about threats from the Dublin government to remove the city's charter. On April 6, it was decided that Mayor Goodrick, Aldermen Denis and Barker, Sheriff Smith and the town clerk should travel to Dublin the next day, there to employ an attorney and retain counsel to aid them in defending the city against removal of its charter. In the meantime, four additional Protestants were sworn freedom of the city.[19]

Despite these councillors' best efforts, Waterford's Protestant charter was declared null and void by the Court of Exchequer, as were most of the other city charters. The following March (1688), new charters were issued appointing the members and officials of all corporations by name. Séamus Pender, editor of the *Council Books of the Corporation of Waterford*, estimated that about two-thirds of the members of these new corporations were Catholics. In Dublin, however, although the new lord mayor and sheriffs were Catholics, fifteen of the forty-eight burgesses were Protestants, as were ten of the twenty-four aldermen.[20] For the remaining months of Goodrick's mayoralty, the Waterford council worked tirelessly to pin down rents, leases, and civic appointments to Protestant council members, other municipal authorities, or senior Anglican clergy. On June 29, 1687, David Lloyd was elected mayor for the following year while, during the same meeting, it was agreed that past, present, and future mayors, aldermen, and council members and their wives and children could be buried in Christ Church Cathedral at no charge.[21]

David Lloyd's pre-Jacobite mayoralty was of short duration, September 29, 1687 to late March 1688. James II's harsh suppressions of England's municipal corporations, including the dismissal of the most obstinate officials and forcible garrisoning of the most recalcitrant towns, raised a new wave of anxiety in Protestant Ireland. The Waterford council sped up attempts to tighten its reins on power. On January 14, 1688, the rectory, parsonage, and tithes of Rathpatrick were awarded once again to Alderman Michael Head for twenty-one years while the city auditors decided to pay the former receiver the 40 shillings that Major Rickards still owed him. The tithes of two other parishes were awarded to Alderman Christmas and those of Portnescully to Alderman Head, all for 21 years. On January 24, more tithes were demised to current aldermen, among whom were former mayors Goodrick and Head. Head was awarded the rectory, etc., for Kilkilliheen (Kilculliheen). Council meetings in February were largely taken up with deciding on payments to the many workers repairing Christ Church and its Lady Chapel and St. John's Bridge.[22]

James II granted a new charter to Waterford on March 22, 1688, with the obvious intent of converting the council to majority

Catholic control. Michael Head was absent from the final meetings in March before the Jacobite council members took their seats. The tension caused by the new charter is reflected in the old council's decision to securely lock all the previously kept council books, sheriffs' accounts and city papers into a chest to be kept by Mayor Lloyd and Aldermen Christmas and Clayton and stored at Mayor Lloyd's house.[23] Under the new charter, Richard Fitzgerald was to become mayor and his twenty-four aldermen would be dominated by formerly disenfranchised Catholics, including such Old English noblemen as Richard Power, earl of Tyrone (lord-lieutenant of the county and city of Waterford), Sir Stephen Rice and a number of Catholic gentry, as well as merchants. However, four former Protestant mayors, Thomas Christmas, Michael Head, Richard Seay, and William Fuller, would remain among the aldermen on the Jacobite council.[24] Presumably, they had been favorable to the principle of toleration or perhaps they still considered James to be their rightful king, although Britain was now (or soon would be) embroiled in the "Glorious Revolution" that would remove him. Thereafter, with one interesting exception, to be described later, Michael Head vanishes from the historical record until the restoration of the Protestant council in Waterford in July 1690.

Meanwhile, James's actions in ordering seven Anglican bishops to the Tower of London for refusing to order the reading of his Declaration of Indulgence (suspending by royal authority all penal laws against Catholics and dissenters, issued on April 4, 1687) in churches under their control brought Protestant resistance in England almost to boiling point. That point was reached with the birth on June 10, 1688 of an heir, James Francis Edward, to James II's second wife, Mary of Modena. James's two Protestant daughters by his first marriage, Mary (who was married to Europe's Protestant champion, William of Orange-Nassau) and Anne, were now supplanted in the succession. William of Orange had his own claim to the British crown as the posthumous only child of Willem II and his queen Mary, the eldest daughter of Charles I. The news of a Catholic heir was received with widespread rejoicing in Catholic Ireland. The mayors of recently purged Dublin and Limerick splurged on claret and wine to celebrate the prince's birth. However, just twenty days later, on June 30, five English peers and two commoners sent an invitation to James's son-in-law and nephew, William, Prince of Orange, to invade England by force. William was strongly motivated by his recognition that Louis XIV represented a serious threat to the Netherlands.

William landed at Torbay, Devon, on November 5 with an army of 15,000 men. On December 11, James withdrew from London, intending only to retire temporarily to France. A Convention of Lords Spiritual and Temporal, and Commons assembled at Westminster and, on February 13, 1689, published a declaration that James had abdicated the government. Two months later, a Convention of the Scottish Estates made a similar declaration. William and Mary were proclaimed king and queen of England in London and Westminster on February 13, and shortly thereafter in the rest of the kingdom. This news was greeted throughout Britain with bonfires and demonstrations of thanksgiving for the country's deliverance from popery.

Matters were quite different in Ireland. Following James's flight in December and subsequent "abdication" from the English throne, Tyrconnell had raised an army approaching 45,000 men, made up overwhelmingly of Catholics. On February 22, William and Mary, promising Catholics freedom of worship, formally offered financial compensation to those in Ireland who laid down their arms; those who continued in arms would be declared traitors. Tyrconnell responded by declaring that the armed associations in Ulster and Sligo supporting the new monarchs were treasonous and sent Richard Hamilton with 2,500 men to defeat the rebels. This was effectively a declaration of war.[25]

Seeing Ireland as a receptive staging ground for recapturing his crown, James landed at Kinsale to "great rejoicing" on March 12, accompanied by the French ambassador, French military experts, and Jacobean officers. James was the first king of England to visit Ireland since Richard II in 1399. When Tyrconnell greeted the king, he was rewarded with a dukedom. The day after James arrived in Dublin, he issued a proclamation summoning parliament and another declaring that henceforth all subjects of his kingdom of Ireland should "enjoy the free exercise of their religion." He knew he had to avoid promoting arbitrary government and popery after being thrown out for those reasons in his other two kingdoms. In April, the same month William and Mary were crowned, James's forces advanced against the city of Londonderry (today's Derry), which had declared for the Protestant monarchs, and placed that city under siege. After fifteen weeks of great suffering by the citizens, the siege was lifted when the Jacobite army broke camp and retreated south.[26]

The so-called "Patriot Parliament" that assembled on May 7 was seventy members short of its quota, the Ulster counties of Donegal, Fermanagh, and Londonderry and a number of boroughs having refused to make returns. It was also overwhelmingly Catholic, including only six Protestants. Alderman Nicholas FitzGerald and John Porter, the recorder or borough judge, represented Waterford. The earl of Tyrone sat in the House of Lords. Hugh Gore, the Protestant bishop of Waterford and Lismore, unlike many of his brethren, had remained in Ireland, but he was aged and infirm, and evidently did not take his seat.[27] The first measure passed was an act recognizing James's "Just and Most Undoubted Rights" to his "Imperial Crown"; another placed the entire Irish military under the overall command of the king. A generous measure for liberty of conscience did away with all the penal laws enacted to enforce acceptance of the established Anglican Church, except for the Act of Uniformity. In addition, Catholics would not henceforth be required to pay tithes to Protestant ministers; instead, the monies should be invested in their own clergy.[28]

Inevitably, land settlement was the most controversial issue. Supporters of repealing the acts of settlement and explanation emphasized the injustice of the land settlement under Charles II. Many who were innocent of rebellion had never had their claims heard, others had been declared rebels only because their lands were located in rebel territory, and even those found innocent seldom succeeded in reclaiming their estates. This was because all land apparently available for compensation was appropriated by aristocrats like Ormond, Anglesey, Orrery and Mountrath (Coote). James reluctantly agreed to pass an act giving the landholders of 1641 or their heirs the right to recover their property, and a special court of claims was to be established for determining individuals' rights. Those who had rebelled against James would also forfeit their lands, and these would be used to compensate "New Interest" purchasers. The measure was further enforced by an act of attainder against Protestants, listing 2,470 individuals who were to be declared traitors, in effect virtually every Protestant of substance, if they did not return to allegiance with James by a certain date. The Williamite response was to outlaw by judicial procedure for high treason a corresponding number of Jame's more prominent Irish supporters, including approximately one hundred with Waterford addresses But the 1689 legislation overturning the Protestant ascendancy in land ownership and securing greater independence for Ireland was only a revolution on paper. Its outcome would depend on the war.[29]

In his article on Jacobite Waterford, Herman Murtagh listed the fifty Irish Williamites with Waterford addresses attainted by the Jacobite parliament in 1689.[30] Oddly, Michael Head was not on this list, whereas the other former Waterford mayors who had remained on the Jacobite council were. Head lived in the nearby village of Gurteen, across the river from the city, but many other listed individuals lived outside the city. The question of whether or not Head was a Jacobite loyalist is raised again by his official appointment to raise money for the Jacobite army. In the face of the continuous reinforcement of the Williamite army in Ireland, James issued a commission on April 10, 1690 "according to the ancient custom of this Kingdom used in time of danger," for raising £20,000 per month for three months "on personal estates and the benefit of trade and traffic" from the major cities and all the counties of Ireland. This was for the support of the greatly enlarged Irish army. Local commissioners were charged with raising stipulated amounts. Catholic commissioners for the City of Waterford were to raise £1,262 12s.9d each month. For the County and City of Waterford, "The Mayor, Recorder, and Sheriffs, *pro temp*, Richard Fitz-Gerald, Michael Porter, Michael Head, and James White, Esqs" were placed in charge. Their portion for three months was £382 12s 3d.[31] Michael Head appears to have been the only Protestant Waterford commissioner charged with raising funds for the Irish army. However, he was not listed either for Waterford county or city as being outlawed for high treason in the Irish courts, 1690-1, nor was he on the list of

Jacobites with Waterford addresses pardoned under the articles of Limerick and Galway.[32] Apparently his agility at moving between camps without recrimination equaled his brother's (see chapter 5).

The showdown between James and his son-in-law took place less than three months later. William landed at Carrickfergus on June 20 with a fleet of about thirty vessels, while James was still in Dublin. William's markedly international Protestant armies— English, Irish, Scottish, Dutch, Danish, and Huguenot—numbered about 35,000 men. The vastly outnumbered Jacobite army—including Irish Catholics from the garrison at Drogheda, reinforced by 6,500 French troops sent by King Louis XIV—chose the River Boyne as the best defense against the Williamites' progress toward Dublin. Though it was not an overwhelming victory for the Williamites, the Battle of the Boyne (July 1, 1690) did cause the Jacobite army to lose its nerve, as well as its guns and all its baggage as it retreated in disarray. Drogheda surrendered the following day. When he saw his men give way, James made haste for Dublin where, at an emergency meeting with his privy council, he announced that, since his army was unreliable and had "basely fled the scene of battle and left the spoil to his enemies," he was "never more determined to head an Irish army" but was resolved to "shift for myself, as should they." Leaving Tyrconnell in command, James fled, eventually arriving in France, where he remained for the rest of his life as a pensioner of Louis XIV, forever despised by the Irish.[33]

Meanwhile, Patrick Sarsfield led the remainder of the Irish army to Limerick, and most of the civilian members of the Jacobite administration in Dublin followed him there. There was temporary anarchy in Dublin until William made a triumphal entry into the capital on July 5. The former mayor and aldermen were present at the welcoming ceremony in St. Patrick's Cathedral, and Protestants celebrated in the streets.[34] Though not the decisive encounter of the war, the Battle of the Boyne is celebrated each year as the charter of Ulster Protestants' religious and political liberties. It also represented, for William's European allies, a devastating defeat for expansionist Louis XIV.

When the Jacobite government withdrew from Dublin, eleven Protestant aldermen who had been displaced by Tyrconnell in 1687 stepped up "to revive the magistracy and take up the exercise of it."

They successfully petitioned William to approve their action and authorize them to elect other members to fill the city government quota. The restored corporation then passed an act disenfranchising Catholic freemen.[35] On July 20, Waterford City was summoned to surrender by 300 Williamite cavalry, backed up the next day by five regiments of foot and fourteen guns. With seventeen guns in the city, the Jacobite governor appeared to be preparing a defense. However, he had been ordered by Tyrconnell to capitulate and Jacobites in the city had already placed their most valuable goods on three French ships prepared to sail from Duncannon. The 1,500-man garrison, consisting of Tyrone's regiment and two others, was poorly clothed and armed, and the city's fortifications were weak. The earl of Tyrone was one of the Jacobite emissaries who negotiated the city's capitulation and, on July 25, the garrison marched out with their arms, having received a safe conduct to the nearest friendly garrison. Tyrone was then imprisoned in the Tower of London where he died at the end of October.[36]

The pre-1688 corporation was restored in Waterford city on July 28, and David Lloyd served diligently as mayor in extremely challenging circumstances until late September 1693. Former Protestant mayors Head and Seay and Capt. Thomas Christmas, who had served on the Jacobite council, were restored as aldermen, while formerly disgraced Andrew Rickards was nominated by William III to resume membership as an alderman. In the meantime, a battalion of English troops garrisoned the city. On August 7, the restored clergy and corporation of Waterford composed the standard loyalty address to King William and Queen Mary.

As the war raged on, two regiments of Danish infantry were billeted in the city for their winter quarters with their German commander, the duke of Würtemberg-Neustadt. The Danes' pay was in arrears and, in January 1691, the soldiers began robbing people in public and swearing they would plunder the city. When the corporation voted about £320 to Würtemberg for the subsistence of his men the situation was eased.[37] Alderman Head was one of the council members "bound for payment of the said sum to bee taken up at interest at three monethes end with interest and to have the corporacion seal to save them harmless." It must have been a considerable relief to the townspeople when the Danes departed in May 1691.[38]

On July 12, the Williamite army defeated Patrick Sarsfield's Irish forces at Aughrim. During this most disastrous battle in Irish history—and the decisive battle of this war—7,000 Irish soldiers were killed and another 450 were taken prisoner, compared to about 2,000 Williamite casualties. Galway surrendered on July 21 and Tyrconnell died following a stroke in mid-August. Limerick surrendered on October 3, and, on that same date, the warring parties signed the Treaty of Limerick, ending the war. A French fleet which had arrived to relieve that city sailed away with about 5,000 Irish Catholic troops; a further 6,000 sailed later in ships provided by the English government.[39] The Jacobites succeeded in negotiating terms that were reasonably fair, including religious toleration for Catholics and safeguards for their persons and property, but an angry backlash in the remaining years of the century resulted in a reinstitution of the penal laws against Catholics and nonconformists and the beginning of the Protestant ascendancy that brought Michael Head's descendants to County Tipperary.

Chapter 8

A Tortuous Fight for County Tipperary Land

The bitterness over the Treaty of Limerick epitomized the two cultures left confronting each other in Ireland amid the debris of William's war. One was Catholic, French-connected, romantically Jacobite (despite the Stuarts' dismal record in Ireland) and temperamentally Gaelic (despite the Old English leadership of the Jacobite cause)... [The other was] triumphalist Protestantism and the governing caste that took as its watchword Protestant 'Ascendancy'.
—Roy Foster, *Modern Ireland*, 152.

Waterford City was badly damaged by the Williamite war, both physically and economically. In the absence of any records of the Jacobite council, it is impossible to know how the citizens managed to subsist but, throughout the 1690s, the restored Protestant council recorded countless initiatives to repair the damaged city and quay, to rebuild city finances, to support the poor, and to advance observance of the Protestant religion. A public notice issued by the city in June 1692 attempted to enforce observance of "the Lord's Day" by "forbearing all manner of manuall labours, gameings, playes, reveling, swearing, cursing, unnecessary walking abroad or to publick places except the church, and all other undue and prophane practices on said day." In March 1693, the city sought both to increase the Protestant population and attract industry by providing accommodation at low rents for fifty French Huguenot families so that they could pursue linen manufactory.[1]

With Protestants returned to control of national and local government, many of the most prominent merchants and Cromwellian grantees sought to solidify their claims on Irish land and the increased social status that went with it. As Bruce Elliott has reported in his study of the Protestants of North Tipperary, "Some of the Cromwellian colonels and a number of lesser officers settled upon their new estates in North Tipperary and became the ancestors of such landed gentry of later centuries as the Sadleirs, Pritties, Otways, Poes, Gasons, Abbotts, Andrewses, Cambies, Tolers, Breretons, Wallers, and Atkinsons."[2] But first the senior merchants of Waterford reestablished their claims on Waterford tithes and property. A rent roll of the Corporation for 1693 confirmed Michael Head's control of the Kilkenny parishes of Rathpatrick, Portnescully and Kilkillihin and awarded the parish of Lisduggan to his son John for £5 15s., plus the same in yearly rent. John's good friend John Lapp [Jr.] was awarded two small parks and a garden plot as well as the late Captain Wade's garden. In October, three ministers petitioned to fill livings under the control of Waterford council members. One of these, the Rev. John Congrove, Congreve, or Congrave, was recommended to the bishop of Ossory for the vicarage of Portnescully.[3]

In the same rent roll, it was Andrew Rickards' executors, not the man himself, who were confirmed for "the hither part of Gibbit hill" and various other properties in Waterford.[4] Rickards had lived a colorful life and was already established as a member of the gentry with his property of Dangan Spidoge (Davidstown) in Co. Kilkenny. But his blood line would enter the highest ranks of the old Irish aristocracy. On December 13, 1692, Rickards' daughter Anne married James Power (de la Poer), who succeeded his older brother the following year to become the third earl of Tyrone. Richard Power, the first earl, had been pardoned after his death in order to save his estate for his Protestant eldest son who had supported William. James Power, however, had been in Waterford's Catholic garrison at the time of the city's capitulation in 1690. After submitting to William, he was granted a pardon in 1697, allowing him to inherit the family property. James and Anne's only child Katherine Power married Sir Marcus Beresford who eventually was made the earl of Tyrone.[5] Together they carried out much of the remodeling of the house and grounds of the Power family estate of Curraghmore at Portlaw, Co. Waterford. Their grandson George was made the first marquess of Waterford in 1789. Curraghmore remains one of the most important great houses of Ireland.

The Heads' route to land ownership through marriage was more tortuous. Michael Head's older son John rose through the council ranks in the 1690s: both John Head and his friend John Lambe were elected to the council and then as sheriffs in 1693 (John Head as first sheriff). John Head became an alderman in December 1697 and mayor in 1700. In August 1696, John married Elizabeth, sole heir of the late Capt. Samuel Wade, but continued his father's mercantile activities as a shipowner in the later 1690s, trading between Waterford, London, Dublin, and Leghorn, Italy.[6] The deed of annuity, or marriage settlement, for his future wife dated July 22, 1692 was submitted in evidence during an intense legal battle with Dublin banker Elnathan Lumm, to whom John was heavily indebted after suffering severe losses at sea. The deed and the dispute are explained later in this chapter.

Much of 1694 was devoted to repairing the damage to the city caused by the Jacobite occupation. Priorities included the fortified walls, the piers of the quay, and the great dock itself before the customhouse could be cleared and likewise repaired. Sheriff John Head was on a committee established to decide on the best method for achieving this work, along with Mayor Francis Barker, several senior aldermen, and three council members.[7] These men were also ordered to "treat with the gentlemen of the county of Waterford about the new courthouse and county goal, and report the proposals."[8] A great deal of attention was given to lowering and fixing rents and leases on multiple properties owned by the corporation, imposing fines when necessary, and generally putting the city's ruined finances in order.

On December 28 that year, Queen Mary died from smallpox. The Jacobites considered her death to be divine retribution ("honour thy father") but she was widely mourned in Britain. Her funeral service at Westminster Abbey was the first of any royal attended by both houses of parliament and the great English composer Henry Purcell wrote his "Music for the Funeral of Queen Mary" in her honor. A month later, the city of Waterford sent an orotund address to King William on the death of his consort.[9] Michael Head was absent for much of 1695 until he returned to the council meeting on June 29. John Head disappeared once his father returned to the council meetings, extended absences which surely indicated their overseas trading activities. By now they were, more than likely, consolidating the trading routes of ships either owned by them or under their control.

Ireland lay in "the Line of Trade" and thus English control was essential to guarantee the safety of English shipping.[10] On July 11, 1695, the council recommended Richard Christmas, alderman and mayor elect, and Anthony Suxbury, councilor at law and Waterford's recorder, to represent Waterford in a new Irish Parliament (Suxbury had also represented Waterford in the brief 1692 parliament). For whatever reason, John Head unsuccessfully petitioned against Suxbury as a representative.[11] But the war had left a bitter legacy of hardening attitudes and intensification of hatreds. Under the virulently anti-Catholic lord deputy Henry, Lord Capel, this parliament enacted the first of the Williamite penal laws in 1695. Catholics were prohibited from educating their children either at home or abroad, joining the army, bearing arms, or owning a horse worth more than five pounds. They were also forbidden from participating in public life, including having posts in parliament or government offices. Two years later, the Banishment Act exiled "all popish Archbishops, bishops, vicars general, deans, Jesuits, monks, friars and all other regular popish clergy & all papists exercising ecclesiastical jurisdiction." Even so, around one thousand priests were given permission to remain in Ireland.

In addition to all the other lands Michael Head had acquired during his quarter century in Waterford, with the August 1696 marriage of his son John to Elizabeth Wade he secured the richest prize for his heirs, Samuel Wade's County Tipperary land grant. Elizabeth was still a minor and likely under Michael's guardianship, although she later revealed that there had been considerable negotiations on the marriage settlement with her own family.[12] Much can be construed from the testimony she gave to the lawyers preparing to argue in 1704 about the legality of a premarital deed of separate maintenance or jointure. The 1692 deed they were referencing placed rents from the lands and demised premises of Rochestown in Co. Kilkenny in trust for Elizabeth and any future children for ninety-nine years, said trust administered by two executors, Abraham Smith and John Lapp, friends of the Heads on the Waterford council, and the heirs of those executors. Elizabeth Head testified at that time that her relations and friends would not have allowed her to marry John Head without this agreement of support.

Ironically, the lands in the baronies of Upper and Lower Ormond that Elizabeth Wade brought to the marriage were among those that had been most devastated by the Williamite wars because they were so close to the seat of war in Limerick. Land values slumped, a large arrear of rents had arisen as a result of the wartime devastation, and there was a general scarcity of money. The few tenants who had remained on the land were impoverished. Tenants who had fled the country during the war found their lands lying waste when they returned.[13] The impossibility of demanding rental payments on the Wade-Head land must have contributed to the severe financial problems the couple faced within a few years of their marriage.

Following his marriage, John Head became even more active in civic affairs, serving as an alderman from 1697. Ever the enterprising merchant, he also invested in infrastructure for the family trading business. As part of the disposition of properties controlled by the council, he was awarded the annual rental of the herring houses (for the storage of smoked herring) "on ground near Gooses gate" for thirty-one years "and he is to keep and leave in repair all that he builds on the premises." He proceeded to build what was probably a warehouse.[14] It's not known how many ships he owned and the exact nature of his losses at sea but the debt he accrued certainly equaled the value of a merchant ship and its cargo. Council records show that Michael and John Head had associates and employees in their trading enterprise and on the council. Caleb Wade, who may have been a nephew of Capt. Samuel Wade, and was an employee of Michael Head, was elected to the council in June 1697 and sheriff in 1699. Michael's younger son Thomas was sworn into freedom of the city on December 12, 1699. While he would only rise to be sheriff in 1710, he became a successful merchant in his own right with property in Co. Kilkenny. Patrick Moore was a merchant and former apprentice of Michael Head who had become a common councilman in 1682. He was granted permission in August 1698 to build a slip "by St. Johns bridge in the wast over against the mill, and that any others have like liberty on either side of the river…the builders to be free of waterbayliffes fees…"[15] All these men were consistently described as merchants but, in the meantime, Michael Head's great-nephew John Head, son of "gentleman" George of Borrisokane, entered Trinity College Dublin in February 1697 in preparation for the ministry like his grandfather. He was the first of a great many Heads to attend TCD.

In 1700, an Act of Resumption was introduced and carried by the opposition in the British House of Commons to revoke William III's grants of forfeited estates in Ireland and to sell the resumed estates to defray army arrears and allied military expenses incurred during the Williamite war. William had granted a vast amount of forfeited land to his mistress, Elizabeth Villiers, to military commanders such as the Dutch nobleman Godert de Ginkell—who was entrusted with the conduct of the war in Ireland after William III returned to England and rewarded with the title of 1st earl of Athlone—and to other favorites and advisers. Opposition fury at such profligacy during a period of strained national finances was the visible evidence of a deeper struggle for primacy between parliament and monarch, a struggle which resulted in humiliation and defeat for the king when, after a successful passage through parliament, the resumption act cancelled the royal grants. The forfeited estates were auctioned or sold at thirteen times the annual rent.

Among those listed as claimants for forfeited estates in the barony of Ormondy in Tipperary was Nicholas Toler, ancestor of the Toler family who became closely related to one of John Head's grandsons. Deeds for one estate acquired by Toler were witnessed by Irish Catholics, while a £300 mortgage on another was witnessed by Henry Prittie and two other Protestants. John Otway was listed for a debt of £300 from Thady O'Meara of Lisanisky in 1681.[16] The Tolers, Pritties, and Otways were all among the families that intermarried with the Heads in the eighteenth-century Ascendancy period, contributing to the built up feelings of dispossession and frustration by the former Catholic landowners (see chapter 9).
Burdened by debt, John Head wrote increasingly anxious letters from March to October 1702 to banker Elnathan Lumm in Dublin.[17] By this time, John's wife Elizabeth was mother to four young children, Michael, Samuel, Elizabeth, and Grace.

Elnathan Lumm vs. John and Elizabeth Head

Elnathan Lumm was one of the chief bankers of Dublin and an MP in the Irish Parliaments of 1692 and 1695. He was commended by a contemporary as a man of high integrity and good estate (his wife was an heir of the Cromwellian colonel Peter Purefoy whose estate was in King's County, today's Co. Offaly), and was known to be punctual and honest in his dealings. The first of John Head's surviving letters to Elnathan Lumm was dated March 9, 1702, the day after the ailing King William died and Princess Anne of Denmark succeeded her cousin and brother-in-law as Queen Anne. John was obviously under pressure regarding a debt of some £900, a huge sum at that time. His handwriting is extraordinarily difficult to decipher: "It is hard to be so threatened…whether he will comply or not I can't tell but if he does not I hope by May 1…in the meantime I am willing to do what is reasonable to secure…I don't think it's reasonable to hand him deeds lying against and for the same debt…"

On September 9, John responded to Lumm's letter advising that he had received the draft deed John sent him—probably the lease made between John and Elizabeth Head and Lumm on August 27 for the lands of Ballyhane and other townlands in the Barony of Lower Ormondy, Co. Tipperary for the sum of £900. These amounted to 689 acres of profitable land and 152 acres of unprofitable land and a further 298 acres of Derry and the 271 associated lands of Rathone.[18] On October 10, he referred to the Kilkenny lands formerly purchased by his father and settled on him at marriage. These must have been the lands in Rochestown, County Kilkenny described in the possibly bogus marriage settlement of 1692. He repeated his intention, "god willing," to clear his debt to Lumm "in 6 months," and concluded that he would "do anything for your security and satisfaction…nothing more desired by your most humble servant John Head." In his letter four days later, he mentioned having made over four small parcels of wine he had purchased to a Mr. Portland and tried to differentiate these from the security he had offered Lumm. The final letter, dated October 21, attempted to reassure Lumm that the lands he had proposed as security were "under no other Incumbrances." He continued to insist that he intended to clear his debt in a matter of months.

John's business affairs must have gone from bad to worse because he began to lean heavily on his father to bail him out. In mid-March, 1703, Caleb Wade arrived in Limerick on behalf of his employer Michael Head bearing a bill of sale to prove that John Head had sold his 180-ton ship the *Queen Anne*, with its full load of 1,000 bushels of salt and all its tackle and furnishings, to his father for the familiar sum of £900. Wade explained that he had come to take over command of the ship since its master had died a week or so earlier. He swore that the bill of sale was not a sham account: £800 principle and the remainder as interest.

It seems that Lumm had had the ship impounded in Limerick harbor for "Outlawry." This was the legal process that deprived a person of the protection of the law, forfeiting his goods and chattels and the power to seek any redress in any court beyond attempting to reverse the outlawry by writ of error. Wade said that the Limerick sheriffs moved so fast that they would not allow Dublin merchant William Cairnes, who was loading the ship on the account of William Brown of London, the three days needed "to send old Mr. Head notice to make his defence" and produce a letter formerly written to the late master. A jury decided that the ship was John Head's property and prevented her being loaded. With much persuasion by Wade, the sheriffs had now promised to allow loading but said they must wait for Lumm's agreement. Wade begged Lumm to write to him in Waterford and assured him that he had nothing to do with this matter beyond his monthly pay and his wish to serve "my old master Mr. Michael Head." He informed Lumm that he had ordered the payment of £100 bail for the ship in the meantime.[19]

On March 20, Michael Head wrote to his friend Michael Lincoln in Waterford after consulting with Lincoln's father-in-law, counsellor at law John Porter, "about the grat wrong done him in Limerick." Porter, a Catholic, was the city's former recorder, or judge, and member for Waterford of the Patriot Parliament, a useful friendship made perhaps during Michael Head's service on the Jacobite council. Michael Head explained that he had already paid "several greate sums of monny" for his son, including the £800 with principle to Edmond Forstall of Gurteens, his son's representative and another Catholic.[20] He explained that John had taken the step of selling the galley *Queen Anne* to him for that sum only after Elnathan Lumm failed to respond to his October 1 offer of the same ship and a parcel of wine as security for his debt. It seems that Lumm did not reject the offer in writing until January 20, when John had already sold the galley to his father. Michael now asked Lincoln to enter bail, as Caleb Wade had requested, and effect an order for the ship to proceed on her voyage and for William Cairns to load the ship. John Porter also wrote to Michael Lincoln to explain the sequence of events as Michael Head had explained them to him. Porter said he had personally witnessed the signing of the bill of sale on January 7; however, he added to the murkiness surrounding the entire dispute by saying that this document was only drawn up after John received Lumm's refusal. Copies of these letters were sent to Lumm, which must have further convinced the savvy Dublin banker that a Waterford cabal was acting against him.

Unfortunately for the highly respected Michael Head, his son's troubles carried over to him. In 1703 or 1704, articles of agreement were drafted between Michael Head and Elnathan Lumm to resolve Lumm's further attempt to seize the *Queen Anne* in Limerick harbor for John Head's still unpaid debt. The *Queen Anne* was contracted to sail from Limerick to Leghorn in Italy and then to the Port of London, and a considerable part of the cargo due to be delivered in Leghorn was ready to be loaded. But John Head still owed at least £600 to Lumm. If Lumm would allow the ship to sail to Leghorn, then Michael Head would pay Lumm the proceeds of any insurance claim that might arise and, if it was allowed to finish its full voyage to London, then Michael Head and his executors would pay "600 pds of Lawfull Money of England at ye end of 40 days next after ye sd Ship or Vessel shall arrive in ye Port of London aforesaid towards satisfaction of ye debt" owed by John Head. It should then be allowed to sail on to Dublin. On the reverse of this draft document is the following: "And in case ye sd EL shall for himself make any insurance of ye said ship for ye sd whole intended Voyage That whatsoever shall be recovered in case of ye miscarriage of ye said ship over and above ye ? and charges about such Insurance shall be applyed towards paymt of ye sd debt due by ye said John Head." The insurance document for 1703/1704 is addressed to Mr. John Head of Waterford for the *Queen Anne*'s voyage to London, which would have been forfeit if the ship matter was not resolved in his favor, but it does not mention either Lumm or Michael Head. In September 1703, John Lambe was elected mayor but his term seems to have been completed by John Lapp. Both men were intimately involved in John Head's attempts to hold onto his Tipperary lands.

In January 1705, the long-smoldering dispute was brought as a bill to the High Court of Chancery by Elnathan Lumm. He claimed that John Head had granted and conveyed to him by a deed dated August 26, 1702, the lands of Ballyhagh etc., in Co. Tipperary subject to redemption on payment of the sum of £900 and interest at the rate of £10 a year and that the deed had specified that his mortgage on the said Tipperary lands gave him the right to claim the lands if the debt remained unpaid. This seems to indicate that Lumm was never interested in the offer of the *Queen Anne*, only in the Tipperary lands. However, John and Elizabeth Head's friend, Waterford merchant John Lapp, had countered with a "Trespass in Ejectment for Recovery" of the mortgaged lands in the Palatinate Court of Tipperary on the basis that he and the late Abraham Smith owned the title to these lands for 99 years through the 1692 indenture for the marital support of Elizabeth Wade. Lumm further stated that the same John Lapp was the subscribing witness to the 1702 mortgage for the Tipperary lands. So what were the terms of this disputed deed of jointure? A copy of this deed, supposedly dated July 26, 1692 (a year before Lapp was elected to the council), was delivered to the lawyers on January 23, 1704, by John Head and signed and sealed by witnesses, including Henry Prittie's wife Elizabeth and her brother Charles Alcock of Powerstown. It specified that "rents, Issues and Profitts" of the Rochestown lands in Co. Kilkenny, which were intended for the support of Elizabeth and any children, should not be threatened by any business misfortunes suffered by John Head. [21]

Elizabeth Head's fascinating testimony reveals so much about the powerlessness of married women when it came to property rights, even if the property was brought by her to the marriage. She testified to her memory that the 1692 treaty of marriage conveyed the mortgage of the Kilkenny lands purchased by Michael Head to trustees for the use of John Head for life and to Elizabeth Head and their heirs for jointure (the support of a widow and her children following her husband's death). She insisted that she and her relatives would not have agreed to her marriage without this jointure. She also said that, at the time of her marriage, she "was Seized of Lands of Inheritance of £300 per annum value and being then under age was not Capable to make any settlement thereof and that it was for that reason other Lands belonging to the said John Heads father were Admitted for her Joynture and not her owne Estate."[22] Elizabeth confessed that she joined in the 1702 deed of mortgage to Mr. Lumm at the "Instance and Importunity of her Husband who promised to redeem the said Mortgage in Six Months after but was prevented by great losses he sustained at sea." She said that she was a subscribing witness but was "a stranger to" the contents. It seems from this that the losses at sea were in addition to those he had sustained previously. She said that John Head was "in Good Condition" at the time he persuaded her to join in the 1702 mortgage on the Tipperary lands (obviously that was not the case), and she hoped that she would not now be deprived of the 1692 deed of jointure since she had nothing else for the support of herself and four children as her own estate was encumbered by other creditors.

Having laid out this immensely complicated case to his counsels, Solicitor-General Sir Theobald Butler and Justice Richard Nutley of the Queen's Bench, Lumm asked their opinion on whether he should submit another bill to attempt to get a settlement from Elizabeth Head.[23] Nutley responded on January 21, 1705, that he was of the opinion that the 1692 deed appointing John Lapp and Abraham Smith as trustees was fraudulent despite Mrs. Head having sworn it was made before her marriage. The two counsels also argued that it was not a valid trust since it left John Head to collect rents and receive profits from the Kilkenny lands (i.e., treat the lands as his own) until the trustees should take it away from him if he were to get into difficulty. Moreover, Lapp and Elizabeth Head were witnesses to Lumm's mortgage on the Tipperary lands and yet never informed him at that time of the previous conveyance. Butler seemed to think Lumm could make these arguments in a new bill in the High Court of Chancery while Nutley advised Lumm to submit a new bill in the chancery court of the Palatinate Court of Tipperary.

Although Lumm seemed to have a strong case against John Head and his enabler John Lapp, there are no further documents in the Lumm Papers. If the case was being prosecuted further, either in Chancery or the Tipperary Palatinate Court, the records of both were transferred later to the Public Record Office in the Four Courts Building and lost, along with 800 years of documents, when that building was firebombed in 1922. Palatine jurisdiction was a seventeenth-century term applied to major medieval seigniorial jurisdictions that included all or most of the pleas and prerogatives that were reserved elsewhere to the crown. The palatine lord, in this case the duke of Ormond, issued writs in his own name and appointed justices to determine pleas in his court. This, the last major palatinate court, was abolished in 1716 (see below).[24]

In any case, the matter must have ended with Lumm's death in 1708. The terms of his will, which was dated April 12, 1708, and probated in 1715, show Lumm to have been very controlling of his wife and family, quite typical of the era. He left generous sums to his wife, two daughters, and two sons. However, he stipulated that, should his wife choose to remarry, everything he had left her, a substantial portion of which may have come from her own Purefoy inheritance, would be null and void. What he had left to his daughters would be null and void if they married without their mother's advice and consent. The terms of his partnership with his oldest son Purefoy Lumm would be null and void if he did not meet the terms of his will. He was obviously very fond of his youngest son Thomas, who was only fourteen at the time. He left him a generous legacy, including selling two properties if there was insufficient money to pay for his support and education, and told his oldest son to apprentice his brother and then take him into the banking business. Most revealingly as it pertains to the dispute with the Heads, he mentioned that the "times and uncertainty" would make it difficult to collect his debts, so he wanted certain properties to be sold to support his family, if necessary.[25]

That year, 1708, the Registry of Deeds in Dublin was established as a repository of records of land transactions such as leases, conveyances and mortgages, together with wills and marriage settlements where they pertained to land. It was intended to restrict the possibility of land passing into the hands of Catholics.[26]

On April 19, 1709, Michael Head registered a deed lease, release and conveyance dated February 24-25, 1709, of his townlands and villages of Gurteen, Killinurry, and Farnoghe in the barony of Ida, Co. Kilkenny. He declared that he had more recently purchased a retrenched 208-acre part of Farnoghe commonly called Tory Hill which should be settled the same way. His trustees were Richard Christmas and the Rev. Alexander Alcock, gentlemen merchants of Waterford, and John Jackson, gentleman, of Portnescully, Co. Kilkenny.[27] Note the new emphasis on the "gentlemen" status. But Michael Head's will, which was registered on May 20, 1709, and proved by the Protestant Consistorial Court on May 7, 1711, identified him as "Alderman of Waterford." Unfortunately, as the prerogative will of a wealthy Protestant, it was lodged in the Public Records Office in Dublin and lost with all the other records there.

Fortunately, Michael's will was recorded as a memorial at the Register of Deeds. He was to be buried in the Cathedral Church in Waterford. His beneficiaries were listed as "Son John Head a merchant suffering loss," John's wife Elizabeth, grandchildren Michael and Samuel, Elizabeth and Grace Head, second son Thomas Head, his brother John Head, and his cousin Mary Hunt (probably his wife's niece). His trustees were instructed to pay all testamentary costs and funeral expenses out of the townlands of Woodstock and Castle Mitchell in the Barony of Riban and Nara, Co. Kildare, formerly demised by the late earl of Kildare to Daniel Hutchinson, Dublin merchant, then to Michael Head. Other lands owned or leased by Michael in Co. Waterford and Co. Kilkenny were also listed. The residue was to go to his younger son Thomas Head and his grandson Michael Head.[28] Thomas Head of Headsgrove, Co. Kilkenny, married Mary Congreve, daughter of the late Rev. John Congreve, vicar of the parish of Portnescully, Co. Kilkenny, on April 13, 1711. Since that parish was impropriate to the corporation of Waterford and the tithes were held for some time by Thomas's father, the connection is obvious. The marriage was childless.[29] (see chapter 9).

With the death of Michael Head, alderman and shipping merchant, the family turned its attention to establishing itself in Northern Tipperary. Although Michael's older son, John, began to focus on improving the Derry Castle lands, he continued his entrepreneurial activities in Waterford until the end of his life. His younger brother, Thomas, continued to expand his trading activities in Kilkenny and Waterford. Gentry status for the Waterford branch of the Head family occurred only when young Michael Head, grandson of the Waterford Michael, consolidated the title to the Derry Castle lands for himself and his male heirs. Gentry status came sooner to the first John Head and his son through their positions as Anglican clergymen in Co. Tipperary.

Chapter 9

Ascendancy:
Social, Economic, and Political Ambition

Alderman Michael Head had long sought to raise his family's status, as did so many others of his striving, self-made merchant class. His close friendship and alliance with those who had received Cromwellian land grants ultimately paid off, but the prize was delayed and nearly lost due to his older son's serious financial difficulties. It was Alderman Head's grandson and namesake who would build on his grandfather's hard-earned wealth and his Trinity College, Dublin education in the law to establish the family's rise into the resident gentry of Northern Tipperary.

While John and Elizabeth Head fought to hold onto their right to the Derry Castle lands, the family's longtime allies, Col. Henry Prittie and his heirs, added to their original land grant through marriages to heiresses of other leading "new settler" estates in the northern part of County Tipperary. Their successes on that score placed them well ahead in the race for land, status, and political power in the first part of what became known as the Protestant Ascendancy (1690-1790). In 1702, Henry Prittie of Kilboy, grandson of the Cromwellian colonel, married Elizabeth, daughter of and heiress to James Harrison of Cloughjordan, son of another Cromwellian colonel. Through this marriage, the already sizeable Prittie estate of 3,600 acres acquired a further 900 acres. Merging these estates greatly benefited the Prittie family since they gained in freeholder strength in an area already well planted with rural Protestants. In the next two generations, each of the heirs to the Prittie estate married heiresses: Deborah Bayly in 1736 and Catherine Sadleir in 1766.[1] By that time, a third Michael Head had married into the Prittie family.

As a result of the seventeenth-century land settlements, the three northern baronies of Co. Tipperary—Upper Ormond, Lower

Ormond, and Owney and Arra—had a large proportion of Protestant tenants. The towns with the highest Protestant population in the region were Birr, Borrisokane, and Cloughjordan. The last two were built by Protestant landlords who employed many of the local inhabitants, both Catholic and Protestant, on their estates. However, landowners in Owney and Arra, where the Derry Castle lands were mostly located, had difficulty attracting Protestant tenants until the 1740s due, historian Thomas Power says, to its "unattractive aspect."[2] These lands were "unattractive" not only because they had been laid waste during the two sieges of Limerick (1690 and 1691), causing many tenants to leave or become impoverished, they were also mountainous, rocky, sparsely populated, and marginal compared to the richer agricultural lands of the Vale of Tipperary in the Ormond baronies. It would take a great deal of work to attract suitable tenants and make those lands profitable.

The Derry lands were located where the River Shannon, Ireland's longest river, widens into Lough Derg north of the village of Ballina, located at its foot. The cathedral town of Killaloe is located across a short bridge from Ballina that connects Co. Tipperary to Co. Clare. The eastern portion of the Church of Ireland diocese of Killaloe matched almost exactly the lands described as Northern Tipperary, which would be recognized as a separate legal jurisdiction in the nineteenth century. Killaloe's history long preceded the arrival of Anglo-Irish settlers. It was the birthplace of Brian Boru, who ruled from there as high king of Ireland from 1002 to 1014. Fourteen miles downstream, the medieval center of Limerick stands at the head of the wide Shannon estuary that flows into the Atlantic Ocean. By the eighteenth century, with the opening of canal systems throughout Ireland, Limerick harbor, where John Head's loaded ship had been impounded by the authorities, established itself as Ireland's premier commercial port on the western side of the country.

Protestant England was roiled once again with religious conflict following the death in 1714 of Queen Anne. Since all of her many children died before reaching adulthood (her sole surviving child, William, duke of Gloucester, died at the age of eleven on July 30, 1700), the 1701 Act of Succession had settled the succession of the

English throne on the Protestant House of Hanover following exclusion of about fifty Catholics higher in line. The 1707 Act of Union
with Scotland (as the treaty said, England and Scotland were now
"United into One Kingdom by the Name of Great Britain") restated
the Act of Settlement banning Roman Catholics from succeeding to
the throne. Scotland was justifiably feared for its continuing support for the Catholic Stuart dynasty and its powerful ally France.

The accession to the British throne of the Elector of Hanover as
King George I ushered in a Whig regime which set about prosecuting members of the 1710-1714 Tory ministry for financial irregular-
ities. Tory leader Henry St. John, viscount Bolingbroke, who had
charge of the 1701 bill for securing the Protestant succession, was
dismissed from office. Bolingbroke subsequently supported the
Jacobite rebellion of 1715 which sought to overthrow the new king
in favor of James II's son, James Francis Edward Stuart, the Old
Pretender. The uprising was badly botched and ended at the Battle
of Preston in November 1715. With the death of Louis XIV, James
Stuart's cousin and major sponsor, the cause was lost and James
Stuart sailed away from Scotland in February 1716. Louis XV, the
new French king, wanted peace with Britain and refused to endorse
further Stuart schemes — at least at that time.

As a result of his suspected role in the Jacobite rising of 1715,
the second duke of Ormond was attainted for high treason, his annual pension of £5,000 was withdrawn, and a £10,000 reward offered for his capture. His vast estate, mostly in Co. Tipperary, was
forfeited to the Crown, enabling a number of families to extend or
consolidate their lands, including grantees under the acts of settlement.[3] Ormond's Palatinate Court of Tipperary was abolished in
1716, eleven years after Elnathan Lumm's solicitor advised him to
sue John and Elizabeth Head for fraud in that court (see chapter 8).
All proceedings in the Court of Record of the County of Tipperary
were to be removed into the Court of Common Pleas in Dublin,
and all proceedings in the Court of Chancery of Tipperary into the
High Court of Chancery.[4] John Head's loyal trustee John Lapp died
in 1714, the year that saw the renewed political/religious turmoil in
England.

In the midst of this latest turmoil, the Heads were honing a
plan to secure the Derry Castle lands for the family. Michael Head,

described as "son and heir of John, Waterford city, Esq.," entered Trinity College Dublin in 1715 and was admitted to the Irish Bar from the Middle Temple on June 15, 1717.[5] Young Michael's legal knowledge would enable him to secure the Wade-Head lands at last, with considerable help from the lands' longtime trustees, the Prittie family.

The ruling Protestants in Ireland were beginning to seek more than provincial power when, in 1719, the English Parliament enacted the Declaratory Act, stating that it had a full right to legislate for Ireland. This brought immediate criticism and realization of the limitations to the Irish Protestants' power and social position. Famed essayist/satirist Jonathan Swift, dean of St. Patrick's Cathedral in Dublin from 1713 to 1745, bitterly criticized English rule and challenged the right of the English parliament to legislate for Ireland. A second Declaratory Act (1720) abolished the Irish Lords' right of appellate jurisdiction, further defining Ireland's status as a dependent kingdom. Swift's campaigning pamphlet against the import of English manufactures (1720), and subsequently against the royal grant of a minting patent for halfpence to William Wood— led to Swift's deduction that "government without the consent of the governed is the very definition of slavery."[6] He declared that the English parliament had no more right to make laws for Ireland than the Irish Parliament had to make laws for England. Protests like this fueled a rising Irish Protestant Patriot movement.

Meanwhile, the Irish Parliament, which now exclusively represented Protestant propertied classes, had internal religious conflicts and ethnic animosities to cope with. An estimated 50,000 families had moved from Scotland to Ulster between the 1690s and 1715, bringing the number of Presbyterians and other Nonconformists roughly equal to the number of Episcopalians in Ireland. These newcomers were not land speculators but energetic traders and farmers whose accrued wealth within one generation, especially through the linen trade, made them even more unpopular with the Protestants of the Anglican Church of Ireland such as Swift.[7] The Irish Parliament passed a limited Toleration Act (1719), introduced by opponents of Presbyterians to forestall anything more generous. Although it exempted Protestant dissenters from the restrictions imposed by the Act of Uniformity (1666), which had long proved to be inoperable in any case, they remained liable to pay tithes and subject to the authority of the Anglican ecclesiastical courts. It also precluded nonconformist ministers from serving on juries and in parish or ward offices but allowed them to hire deputies.

The methods by which the Head family secured and built on their land holdings through the law and marital alliances can be traced through major deeds registered in the first half of the eighteenth century.[8] In 1721, Thomas Head, John Head's half-brother and a successful merchant, was apparently settling his affairs. In July, he leased Headsgrove, his mansion house and 180 acres at Maddenstown, in the Barony of Iverk, Co. Kilkenny, for 999 years to Col. Henry Ponsonby of Woodstown, Co. Waterford for £325 and a yearly rent of £100.[9] That December, 1721, the Waterford and Kilkenny trustees of the late Michael Head of Waterford and his sons Thomas and John Head entered a tripartite deed in the Registry of Deeds to secure the remaining half of Michael Head's half portion of the "Lordship Towns and Lands of Woodstock" and Castle Mitchell in the Barony of Riban and Nara, Co. Kildare, after payment of funeral expenses, debts and legacies. The trustees would have the discretionary power to provide John Head "with necessarys during life," provided they expended no more than £30 per annum. John said he would only need £15 per annum. It was agreed that one quarter of the remaining years of Michael Head's half portion of those lands would now go to Thomas and one quarter to John's son, Michael's namesake grandson.[10]

Two years later, Thomas Head left his estate to his cousin Thomas, second son of the Rev. John Head of Borrisokane, Tipperary; to his nephew Michael, "oldest son of my brother John Head"; to Samuel Head, "second son of ditto;" and other relations. Thomas was to be buried in the Cathedral Church of Waterford, near his father and mother.[11] Then, in 1725, Henry Prittie and Charles Carr, bishop of Killaloe, were named as trustees in the marriage deed of John Head's surviving daughter Grace to Arthur Burdett, eldest son and heir apparent of the Rev. John Burdett, dean of Clonfert. Grace was to have a marriage portion of £1,500 secured by mortgages of £400 on her grandfather's lands in Co. Kilkenny and £1,100 by a mortgage on 520 acres of the Owney and Arra lands in Co. Tipperary.[12]

With John Head's creditors continuing to circle as he fell ever more deeply into debt, he was in no position to defend his wife's right to the Tipperary lands. His son Michael proceeded to turn his knowledge of the law towards resolving the situation, as can be seen in a 45-page tripartite deed of 1727. This massively comprehensive and repetitive deed "in trust to Henry Prittie and Charles [Carr], Lord Bishop of Killaloe by John Head of Derry and Elizabeth Head alias Wade his wife and Michael Head of Dublin, son and heir apparent of said John Head" was drawn up "to prevent any threat or action to the lands." Michael Head also appointed as secondary trustees his law school friend Arthur Dawson of Castle Dawson, Co. Londonderry, and William Sumner, a public notary.

Dawson and Sumner's task was to settle John Head's enormous debts, which now amounted to £3,000 (today's equivalent of £708,000), though there was no mention of Elnathan Lumm or his executors in the list of creditors included on the deed. John had apparently accumulated these further debts while engaging in land speculation. In addition to the lands in Co. Kilkenny deeded to John by his father (the questionable 1692 deed is cited), John had been leasing additional lands in Co. Tipperary.[13] Dawson and Sumner were charged with raising £4,000 altogether, of which £1,000 would go to Michael for his use. A considerable portion of this deed enforced Michael's inheritance right as the eldest son and the inheritance rights by primogeniture of his as yet unborn male heirs in order of their birth. If Elizabeth (Wade) Head were to outlive John, then she should "have hold and enjoy during her natural life the dwelling house of Derry and the demesne thereto belonging" as well as an annuity of £200 payable from the rents.[14]

The heir to Derry Castle was approaching his mid-thirties and it was time for him to marry. There is a mystery about the origin of his chosen bride, probably unsolvable because there is no surviving documentation, beyond a genealogical notification that marriage articles for Michael Head of Derry Castle to Mary O'Neill were drawn up on January 19, 1733-34. Michael's friend Arthur Dawson had married Jane O'Neill of Shane's Castle on Lough Neagh in County Antrim, the ancestral home of the O'Neillship of Ulster, raising the intriguing possibility that Michael's wife, identified in *Burke's Landed Gentry of Ireland* as "Mary, daughter of O'Neill," was

Jane's sister. Indeed, Jane and a Mary O'Neill were daughters of Charles O'Neill, while their brother John O'Neill, later viscount O'Neill, inherited Shane's Castle. But *Burke's Peerage of the United Kingdom* (1911) listed Mary O'Neill's husband as Robert Burrowes of Ballybrittas, County Kildare, *not* Michael Head. Jane's husband, the well-connected Arthur Dawson, represented his home county of Londonderry in the Irish Parliament for many years and was made a baron of the Irish Exchequer in 1741. He was described by artist and bluestocking Mary Delany, renowned for her "paper mosaicks" and her lively correspondence, as "a very clever, sensible man."[15] He and his wife Jane were childless but Michael and his mysterious Mary O'Neill (described in one source as "an English lady") had two sons, the standard Michael (Henry) and John (Edward).[16]

A year earlier, there was another marriage in Tipperary that would have long-term consequences for Head family fortunes. Daniel Armiger Toler of Beechwood married Letitia Otway, daughter of Thomas Otway of Otway Castle. The first of their six daughters was born in 1734. Phoebe Toler, the youngest, would marry John Edward Head, the younger of Michael and Mary's two sons. From then on, the upwardly mobile Tolers became important benefactors of the junior branch of the Head family. Of the Toler sons who would enter the historical record, Daniel was born in 1739 and John Toler, the future notorious justice (see the next several chapters), was born December 3, 1745. Another son, Otway Toler, who was born in 1751, never entered history but must have done well materially since he willed a comfortable property to his nephew, Lt. Col. Michael Head of Ashley Park, John and Phoebe Head's only son.[17]

John Head, "the merchant suffering loss," remained the entrepreneurial risk-taker, establishing a glass-making business in his sixties on his late father's property at Gurteen, two miles from Waterford. A notice in the *Dublin Journal* in May 1729 gave "notice that The Glasshouse near Waterford is now at work, where all persons may be supplied with all sorts of flint glass, double and single, also garden glasses, vials and other green glass ware. Sold at reasonable rates by Joseph Harris at Waterford, Merchant." In November 1731, the same journal advertised that "The Glass-house near Waterford belonging to John Head, Esqr. has been at work for some time where all gentlemen or others may be supplied with bottles, with or without marks, or at the warehouse in Waterford. There will also soon be made there best London crown & other glass windows & sold at reasonable rates." This manufacturing business would have met with the approval and perhaps incurred the support of the highly influential Dublin Society, founded in 1731 to promote manufactures and the useful arts and representing the tradition of experimental, improving landlordism.[18]

John Head managed the glasshouse for eight years before his death on October 31, 1739 at the age of seventy-two. Unfortunately, this predecessor of the famous Waterford glass company died with its owner. John left the glasshouse lands in his will to Arthur Dawson, the man who had apparently succeeded in settling his debts; to John, younger son of Michael and Mary; and to his daughter-in-law, Mary O'Neill Head. In February 1740, Michael Henry Head of Derry advertised in the same *Dublin Journal*, "To be let for a term of years the glass house at Gurteens and 21 acres of land, with a good quay and slips, warehouse, sheds and a malt house, situated close to the River Suir." He added "There are several materials belonging to the glass works to be disposed of with the said premises, as pots, iron tools, a large parcel of ingredients for crown glass, kelp, etc."[19]

The timing of this advertisement was unfortunate. A devastating famine in Ireland between 1739 and 1741 killed one third of the population of one and a half million. Tipperary was particularly devastated by the collapse of the wool trade since sheep-farming was the dominant economic activity there. Historian Patrick C. Power claimed that "this catastrophe, greater than the so-called Great Famine of 1847, was caused by a frost which hit the crops first in 1739. The peak-point of death was in May 1741."[20] Protestant emigration from Ireland following this famine was said to amount to about 12,000 annually from Ulster alone. Perhaps this agricultural disaster contributed to the early death of Michael Head of Derry Castle, who must have worn himself out in his attempts to improve his formerly marginal land and survive the agricultural disaster. He died in 1749, just ten years after his father, leaving his widow Mary and their young sons. Since the boys' uncle, Samuel Head, had moved to nearby Castlelough on Lough Derg following his marriage to a widow, a daughter of the bishop of Meath, it seems likely that he became their guardian, particularly following their mother's death in about 1760.[21]

Britain was embroiled in a series of European-wide wars from 1740 to 1763, part of the continuing struggle between Britain and France that started in 1689 and would last until the final defeat of Napoleon in 1815. In 1743, war broke out between these perennial antagonists as part of the larger War of the Austrian Succession. The Jacobite threat returned yet again when English Tories asked the French foreign minister for help in a Stuart restoration. Plans for an invasion by French soldiers were kept secret from "The Old Pretender," living in splendor at his jacobite court in Rome. Still a loyal supporter of James, the seventy-eight-year-old second duke of Ormond toured England, ostensibly in search of horses in his role as Louise XV's master of horse, but really to gauge the health of jacobitism there. Acting on behalf of his father, Charles Stuart ("Bonnie Prince Charlie") lost the support of Louis XV for an invasion but borrowed 40,000 livres from a Parisian banker to purchase arms. Lord Clare, the commander of the Irish brigade of the French army, introduced Charles to Irish ship owners who agreed to help get him to Scotland with money, volunteers, and arms.

Charles Stuart landed in Scotland in July 1745. When "the Young Pretender" and his Jacobite forces reached Edinburgh in September, he was received by a cheering crowd of twenty thousand. On September 18, his father was declared King James VIII of Scotland with Charles as his regent. Charles held court at Holyrood Palace for five weeks. Although, after crossing into England, the jacobites captured Carlisle on November 18 and Preston on November 26, Charles was outvoted in his determination to march on to London. Following a series of battles in retreat to Scotland, the jacobite forces were finally defeated at the Battle of Culloden on April 16, 1746, ending any hope of a jacobite restoration.

The War of the Austrian Succession concluded with the Treaty of Aix-la-Chapelle in 1748 but conflict erupted again in 1756 with the Seven Years' War. This war arose out of the attempt by the Austrian Habsburgs to win back the rich province of Silesia, which had been wrested from them by Frederick the Great of Prussia. It also involved overseas colonial struggles for control of India and North America (the French and Indian War, 1754-63). Following James Stuart's death in 1766, the pope refused to recognize Charles's claim to the British and Irish thrones and gradually switched his support to the Hanoverian dynasty, a decision which led to the gradual relaxation of the penal laws in Britain and Ireland.

While the military skills of France and Spain were augmented by those of exiled Irish Catholic soldiers, the British army officer corps was filled with the sons of the Irish Protestant landed gentry from the eighteenth century on. As the great historian Cecil Woodham-Smith put it: "It is a curious contradiction, not very often remembered by England, that for many generations the private soldiers of the British Army were largely Irish; the Irish have natural endowments for war, courage, daring, love of excitement and conflict; Macaulay described Ireland as 'an inexhaustible nursery of the finest soldiers'."[22] In the preface to his book *Napoleon and Wellington*, my grandfather Col. Charles Head agreed with Macaulay:

> We lived in Ireland, the nursery of so many British soldiers in former days. At the end of the eighteenth century the Irish gentry were a flourishing community... Large families were the rule, and every household contributed most of its younger sons to one or other branch of His Majesty's forces. In my much later time every house still had a portrait of a red- or blue-coated warrior adorning its walls and regarded with pride by the family. Descendants of the Old Cromwellian and Elizabethan settlers, adulterated but little with native Celtic blood, but their intelligence and energies sharpened by the nature of their lives and their association with a keen-witted people, they were great fighting material, and contributed beyond proportion to their numbers to the officer class of the British army. And it was not only the mansions and halls of Ireland that provided the cannon-fodder that was wanted, the cottages and cabins of the countryside sent their men and lads in crowds to the colours."[23]

Young Michael Henry Head and John Edward Head both joined Dragoon regiments within a year of each other: In 1759, Michael

Henry Head was a lieutenant in Honywood's Dragoons, the 11th Regiment of Dragoons, which became the 11th Light Dragoons in 1775. John E. Head was listed in *Gentleman's Magazine* of March 4, 1760 as commander in the 14th Regiment of Dragoons (later the 14th Light Dragoons).[24] There is no record of where or how long they served, and it is likely they were militia rather than regular officers sent to Munster to crush the Whiteboys (see below). Unlike most of the sons of the Anglo-Irish gentry in the eighteenth and early nineteenth centuries, neither brother was registered at TCD. They both seem to have retired from the army to farm and manage their respective estates following their marriages. But their brief service gave them skills to join Irish volunteer regiments in the face of further threats from France once it allied itself in 1778 with the American colonists' war for independence (see chapter 10).

Ireland had enjoyed peace at home since the late seventeenth century but, "From the middle of the [eighteenth] century onward," as historian J. C. Beckett described it, "agrarian unrest was endemic over much of Munster and Leinster. Bands of 'Whiteboys' as they were commonly called, scoured the countryside by night, houghing [maiming] cattle, destroying property, attacking and torturing those who had incurred their displeasure." Beckett traced the origin of this "campaign of terrorism" to the action of certain Anglo-Irish landlords who had evicted tenants in order to amalgamate their holdings into large and more profitable grazing farms.[25] According to Roy Foster, "Landlord enterprise and investment were notably high in the 1740s and 1750s, reflecting the fact that rent-rolls had doubled from the mid-1740s; financially, mid-Georgian Ireland was an era of landlord prosperity."[26] From 1758, when free importation of cattle into Britain was granted for five years, huge areas of land were turned over to pasture. Especially in previously peaceful southern Tipperary, whole villages were swept away, commons were enclosed, and peasants were evicted. Not surprisingly, the Whiteboys, a secret Catholic agrarian society, so-called because they sported white cockades and wore white shirts over their clothes, reacted forcefully against exorbitant rents, known as "rack-rents," the detested tithe system for the support of the Protestant Church of Ireland clergy, excessive priests' dues, evictions, and other oppressive acts by targeting landlords, and were greatly feared.[27]

Father Nicholas Sheehy, a Catholic priest for parishes in the area of Clonmel on the border of Counties Tipperary and Waterford, spoke out against the penal laws, the eviction of poor tenants by Anglo-Irish landlords, the elimination of common land by enclosure, and compulsory tithes, beliefs which led him into conflict with local Protestant leaders. Their accusations led to his trial in Dublin for conspiracy against the state. Following his acquittal, a more serious charge of involvement in the disappearance or murder of an informer led to a second trial, this time for high treason. He requested that this also take place in Dublin, but, following a second acquittal there in February 1766, he was immediately rearrested for murder. On March 12, 1766, Sheehy was tried at Clonmel before a grand jury selected by Tipperary's high sheriff Daniel Toler for being an accessory to the murder of John Bridge. The evidence against him was believed to have been fabricated by local Anglo-Irish landowners and an Anglican priest. He was convicted and sentenced to be hanged, drawn, and quartered three days later. Others who were accused were also executed, including a cousin of the priest.[28]

In his final speech, Sheehy claimed he was being put to death for a crime which had never been committed. The murder victim was alleged to be in Cork after the date of the "crime" and was thought to have emigrated to Newfoundland. Penal laws against Catholics, and especially Catholic priests, were now reinforced by right-wing members of the April 1766 grand jury at Clonmel, including Daniel and John Toler.[29] A Rev. John Hewetson of Suirville, Co. Kilkenny, former tutor to the Toler brothers, was closely associated with proceedings there. Thought by many to be an informant, he was called by later generations "Whiteboy Hewetson." Sheehy's trial and execution inflamed nationalist opinion and had a great effect on Dublin-born British statesman and philosopher Edmund Burke.

In the midst of this agrarian violence in the extreme south of the county, the Head brothers married into the politically ambitious Prittie and Toler families. In 1761, Michael Henry Head became engaged to Margaret, the sixth daughter of the latest Henry Prittie, who was elected to represent Co. Tipperary in the Irish Parliament in May that year, marking the successful entry of the family into county representation.[30] A complex marriage settlement, called "A Memorial of Indented Deeds of Lease and Release bearing date 16 & 17 June 1761," is primarily a creation of trustees by Michael Henry Head, and it demonstrates the growing links between the leading landowners of the western baronies of Northern Tipperary.[31] Margaret Prittie's marriage portion of £2,000 would be secured by her father to their neighbors Anthony Parker and John Bayly. Head granted in trust to his uncle Samuel Head and to Robert Snow and their heirs and assigns for one year his considerable acreage in the barony of Owney and Arra in Co. Tipperary and lesser acreage in Co. Waterford, the City and County of Limerick, and Co. Kilkenny. This memorial was signed by Michael Henry Head and one of the witnesses was his cousin George Head.[32] Two days later, the same terms were drawn up to secure Margaret Prittie's £2,000 marriage portion plus a further £1,300 of Michael Henry Head's own money.[33] Within two or three years, Michael Henry Head's younger brother, John Edward Head, married Phoebe Toler, a younger daughter of Daniel Toler of Beechwood and Letitia Otway, formerly of Otway Castle, further cementing the marital bonds of Northern Tipperary landowners.[34] As mentioned above, Daniel Toler was high sheriff of Co. Tipperary in 1766. His oldest son, also Daniel, and his youngest son John (born 1745), later the earl of Norbury, were members of the grand jury in the April 1766 assizes against the Whiteboys in Co. Tipperary.

After Samuel Head died childless in 1764, there was a dispute over the ownership of the Rathone lands north of Nenagh.[35] It seems Samuel had entered into a number of mortgages to various parties in order to raise money for his own use and may also have arranged to convey the Rathone lands to George Burdett, his sister's son, following his death. Final settlement was made when Samuel's nephew, Michael Henry Head of Derry Castle, paid off the aggrieved mortgagees and acquired the Rathone and Drumniscart lands in February 1765.[36] At some point after this, Michael let those lands to his younger brother John, subject to a head rent to himself and his heirs.

The last ties to trade of the Head family in Ireland ended with Samuel's death. Despite using the Co. Tipperary lands to raise money, he was apparently a successful Dublin merchant who was made freeman of Waterford in 1725, the same year as his brother Michael. Samuel had considerable business interests in Bordeaux, France, most likely in the wine trade. According to historian Brian Murphy, "Many Irish people settled in Bordeaux and formed mercantile groups to take advantage of the fact that return cargoes were available, thus creating a situation where Irish trade with France exceeded that with Britain... By 1773, there were 43 Irish merchant firms established in Bordeaux." Catholics now dominated the merchant class, carrying on the bulk of the country's trade, making fortunes, and gaining influence. Their domination of the eighteenth-century mercantile class can be explained by the exclusion of Catholics from land ownership and by the Ascendancy's snobbish contempt for trade.[37]

Having been given life tenure of the Rathone lands by his older brother, John E. Head apparently left the army/militia and, between 1765 and 1770, built a house on the north shore of Lough Ourna for his growing family, an heir, yet another Michael Head, a future general, born in 1769, and four daughters, Letitia, Mary, Phoebe, and Catherine. The house, which he renamed Ashley Park, is marked on a 1777 road map and is mentioned in a late-eighteenth-century guide book: "Half a mile to the left of the road [Nenagh to Portumna], pleasantly situated near a fine lough, is Ashley Park, the seat of Mr. Head."[38] The fact that he was able to build this house, for which no illustrations or plans survive, even though he was found on the list of Co. Tipperary freeholders in 1775 as having only "a small fortune," indicates that he was receiving financial benefits from his marriage into the ascendant Toler family. John began to establish new tenants on the Ashley Park lands but, despite all his efforts to improve his land, the small estate would continue to accrue encumbrances, leading to acrimonious legal battles fifty years later.[39]

By 1777, there were 184 gentlemen's seats in Co. Tipperary. In Northern Tipperary, the Otways at Templederry, the Sadleirs at Sopwell Hall, and the Tolers at Beechwood had built new residences in mid-century.[40] This reflected the long and dramatic rise in rental incomes. Fine and sometimes very grand country houses were being built all over Ireland during this period. Builder-landlords commissioned architects to design traditional Irish Georgian style houses that reflected their prosperity and standing, while sparing no expense on the decoration of the interiors, particularly plasterwork. At the same time, a notably sophisticated standard was achieved in the Irish manufacture of silver, glass, jewelry, and furniture. These activities provided unprecedented employment for craftsmen of all types and for laborers who worked to lay out the demesnes encircling most of these houses. The Ascendancy built obsessively to convince themselves not only that that they had arrived but also that they would remain.[41]

Lesser landlords like the Head brothers benefited socially and materially from their marital ties to more prosperous and politically powerful families. In 1766, Margaret Head's brother Henry Prittie married Catherine Sadleir, daughter and co-heiress of Francis Sadleir of Sopwell Hall, descendant of the Cromwellian soldier, military governor of Waterford, and sheriff of Co. Tipperary; his sisters married other local landowners, such as Michael Henry Head of Derry Castle.[42] Historian Thomas P. Power described the importance of these links in his magisterial study, *Land, Politics and Society in Eighteenth-Century Tipperary*: "These alliances formed the basis of a unified gentry and cohesive landed class in the northern part of the county. They served to elevate the Prittie family to a leadership position based on family ties and, by extension, command of freeholders, which were most numerous in the area before 1793."[43] According to one source, Michael Henry Head served as high sheriff of Co. Tipperary in 1772, but *Burke's Landed Gentry* listed another Prittie son-in-law, Peter Holmes, as high sheriff for that year. The high sheriff was the senior law officer of a county. Annually appointed, he also had ceremonial and administrative functions, including presiding over the assizes and executing high court writs.[44]

Michael Henry Head of Derry continued close ties with the Burdetts, entering into a one-year lease on August 2, 1771, with his second cousin, Arthur Burdett, lieutenant in the Fourth Regiment of Horse, for the undivided half share of three towns and lands in King's County and for the town and lands of Bunclody in County Wexford with its flour mills, all belonging to the Hon. Barry Barry of the City of Dublin. The number of landowning members of the Irish Parliament with connections to the Head family are apparent in the rolls of the "Knights, Citizens and Burgesses" assembled for the fifth session of the Irish Parliament in October 1775. Barry Barry was MP for Co. Cavan in 1775; Arthur Dawson for Newtown in Co. Clare (Dawson died in 1775); John O'Neill for Randalstown in Co. Antrim; Henry Prittie for Gowran in Co. Kilkenny; Peter Holmes for Banagher in King's County; and Thomas Pepper for Kells in Co. Meath. Other MPs whose descendants would become connected to or associated with the Heads were the Hon. Pierce Butler for Killsleagh in Co. Clare; the Hon. Lt. Col. Arthur Browne, who was succeeded as MP for Gowran by Henry Prittie; Hugh Massy for Co. Limerick; and David La Touche the Younger for Longford in Co. Londonderry. La Touche, grandson of a Huguenot officer in the army of William of Orange, became the founder of the first Bank of Ireland in 1783.[45]

In the parliamentary elections of 1776, Henry Prittie was elected MP for Co. Tipperary. A poll book for that election shows that the bulk of support for Henry Prittie and Daniel Toler (Phoebe Toler Head's oldest brother) came from the leading Protestant landowners and freeholders of the north of the county. Prittie's support came from 95 freeholders on his estate, which was worth £5,000 a year [£8,000 per historian Miriam Lambe] supplemented by marriage links and connections. In the eighteenth century, voting in county elections in Ireland was restricted to owners or leaseholders of at least a forty-shilling freehold, i.e., property worth forty shillings after payment of rent or other charges. Leases perfected for the lifetime of three named individuals qualified as freeholds for voting purposes. Forty-shilling freeholders were generally Protestant: Catholics could not vote at elections between 1728 and 1793, nor could anyone married to a Catholic, leading many Catholic members of religiously mixed marriages to convert.[46] Henry Prittie's brothers-in-law Thomas Otway (£2,000 per annum in rental fees), Peter Holmes (£5,000), Michael Henry Head (£1,000-2,000), and Matthew Bunbury (£2,000 but already deeply in debt) were important landowners who could vouch for the votes of their freeholders.[47] Deficient in wealth and freeholders, however, Daniel Toler, who was not elected in 1776 but succeeded Prittie as MP for Co. Tipperary in 1783, was dependent on the second preference votes of Prittie and his connections. "Prittie's victory and Toler's good showing signaled a shift to the north [from the south of the county] in the leadership of the Protestant political community compared to the 1760s," according to Power. A rare manuscript in the Dunalley Papers illustrates a political inventory or poll book drawn up by the Prittie connections in preparation for the 1776 election.[48]

The Toler brother who became the most influential and notorious, however, was John Toler, who was elected MP for Tralee in Co. Kerry in the 1776 election. He graduated with a B.A. from TCD in 1761, an M.A. in 1766, and was called to the Irish bar in 1770. A droll character, his exploits and disruptive behavior in the Irish Parliament were recorded by his fellow MPs and members of the Bar, Jonah Barrington, Richard Lalor Sheil, and John Philpot Curran. He liked to boast that he commenced his legal career with £50 in cash and a brace of silver hair-trigger pistols which was all that his dying father could give him as a younger son. "Now, Jack," said his father, "with these be always ready to keep up the credit of the family and the character of an Irish gentleman." "Both at the Bar and in Parliament," Barrington reported, "Toler was noted for his duels as readily as in a debate." Barrington also noted that "he had more readiness of repartee than any man I ever knew" and his "extreme good temper was a great advantage."[49] His career as he rose from judge to solicitor-general (1789-98) to attorney-general (1798-99), and to chief justice of the Irish Common Pleas (1800-1827) was greatly controversial in his time (he became known as "the hanging judge," partly with reference to his sentencing to death of insurrectionists in 1798 and Robert Emmet in 1803). But John and Phoebe Head's children, particularly their only son Michael, benefited from his connections and his generosity. Despite his dismal reputation among Irish Catholics and nationalists, his generosity both to his tenants and his friends was frequently noted by his contemporaries. How to confront and assess history's extremely negative judgment of this man who, according to many of his contemporaries, so callously judged others?[50]

In October 1777, Michael Head of Derry Castle hosted famed agricultural economist and writer Arthur Young who was making his second tour of Ireland, this time a sweep through the center of the country from Dublin to Mitchelstown in Co. Cork. Young was interested in the improvements made by Irish landlords to agricultural practices on their estates. He traveled in his own four-wheel chaise with three horses and two servants on roads that were often extremely challenging. Before he arrived at Derry, Young stayed with Michael Head's brother-in-law Peter Holmes at Johnstown House.[51] Holmes gathered in a group of well-informed local landowners, who provided the Englishman with a raft of details about farming and the state of the economy in the barony of Lower Ormond. Young was told that the poor were much better off than they had been, "for their land and cabins are not charged to them *by gentlemen* [Young's italics] higher than they were 30 years back, while all they sell bears double the price. Potatoes are rather more cultivated and eaten than twenty years ago and are managed better." Young learned that there were no "white boys" in the baronies of Northern Tipperary, "nor any riots that last longer than a drunken bout at a fair." However, the latest Whiteboy outbreak in southeastern Co. Tipperary had only been brought under control the year before. The proximity of Holmes's estate to the Shannon River with its abundant waterfowl and swarming fish added considerably to the pleasures of life for the gentry and a better diet than endless potatoes for the cottiers or laboring class, if they were granted the right to fish (there were extreme penalties for poaching).

Young was horrified by the suffering of the poor in many of the less prosperous areas, placing the blame squarely on the shoulders of rack-renting landlords and middlemen (entrepreneurs who rented large acreage from landowners and sublet it for shorter periods at higher rents).[52] Despite the testimony from landlords like Holmes that the poor were much better off than they used to be, Young described their "cabbins," particularly in regions such as Connaught, as "the most miserable looking hovels that can well be conceived: they generally consist of only one room: mud kneaded with straw is the common materials of the walls." They had no windows to allow light in and smoke out. He reported that "some are thatched with straw, potatoe stalks, or with heath, others only covered with sods of turf cut from a grass field." Furniture was often sparse and the family slept on straw, sometimes along with their precious livestock. Although improving landlords in more prosperous areas

were increasingly building stone cottages for their tenants and laborers, Young concluded that many small farmers who were better
off chose to remain in their cabins according to the "customs and
inclinations of the people."[53]

Following his stay with Peter Holmes, Young traveled south,
perhaps at Holmes's suggestion, to call on Michael Head for four
days at Derry Castle on Lough Derg. As Young was pulling up in
front of Head's spacious house overlooking the Lough, his host
told him that he was just about to dine with his neighbor and friend
Anthony Parker, descendant of Capt. John Parker, who was granted 1,242 acres in the barony of Owney and Arra in 1667. Young
jumped at the chance since he had heard that Parker's father, who
was high sheriff of Co. Tipperary in 1740, had made a "fine mountain improvement" more than thirty years before. This mountainous land of 40 acres covered in furze and heather was worth very
little when the improvements began. A regime of ploughing, mar-
ling, and sewing alternate crops of oats, wheat, and oats again, produced perfect pasturage for sheep. Parker's house in his demesne of
Castlelough was so close to the Lough that its waters often lapped
against it. Parker, according to Young, was married to a Miss Massy
(Amy Massy was actually his mother). They had four sons and six
daughters.

The Parker and Head families must have been extraordinarily compatible; their friendship would endure through at least two
more generations. Michael Head and Anthony Parker had both
married in 1761, the year that Parker was high sheriff for Co. Limerick (he was later high sheriff for Co. Tipperary in 1768), and their
marriages produced large families. Michael and Margaret would
eventually have three sons, including an heir, Michael Prittie Head,
born in 1770, and ten daughters! "Within 15 years," wrote Arthur
Young, "this gentleman [Michael Head] has improved Derry so
much, that those who had only seen it before, would find it almost a new creation. He has built a handsome stone-house, on the
slope of the hill rising from the Shannon, and backed by some fine
woods, which unite with many old hedges well planted to form a
woodland scene, beautiful in the contrast to the bright expanse of
the noble river below."[54] He continued, "It is a singular demesne, a
stripe of very beautiful ground, reaching two miles along the banks

of the river, which forms his fence on one side with a wall on the other." Soaring behind the whole was one of the hills of the Arra Mountain range. Lough Derg, a two-mile-wide section of the Shannon River, bent around either side of the Derry demesne providing views from the house to the west and north and to the cultivated lands rising almost to the mountain tops on the Clare side of the Lough. Head was reclaiming land from Lough Derg, had 400 head of sheep which brought him an annual profit of £221, and there were 60 skilled workers quarrying high quality slate in the hills behind the demesne to be shipped via the Shannon "to distant parts of the kingdom."

Michael Head told Young that his grandfather was the first in the area to use shelly marle as manure on the light gravelly soil, another example of John Head's lifelong entrepreneurship. The shells of fresh-water mollusks are much valued by farmers as a source of carbonate of lime. Michael reported that the marle was dredged up from the bottom of the Shannon by men John Head brought in from Dublin who were used to raising ballast. Michael always laid ten boatloads of sixty bushels each on each acre of his land, thus reclaiming much bad land for tillage with considerable profit. Crops of oats, bere (barley), wheat, and English barley were rotated "as long as the land will yield" and fields allowed to lie fallow until they had recovered. Head informed Young that the rent on average was fifteen shillings per annum for profitable land and one shilling for mountain. Since his land was about half profitable and half mountainous, the average rent was eight shillings. Rents had about doubled in the last twenty years.

While estates were generally large in the area, the farms were all small, none above 300 to 400 acres (although that was large for Ireland generally at that time), and many were taken in partnership by three to five families. Leases were given to Protestants for three lifetimes. Cottiers [poor cottagers] provided the labor on most of the estates in the region. Commoners used horses to plough their land while gentlemen used four oxen. For five pence a day year-round, each cottier family was given a cabin and an acre of land, a cow, as many pigs as they could rear, and some poultry. Women earned extra money by spinning and helping with the harvest. Young interviewed a poor cottier and persuaded him to list his expenses and receipts, including rent, tithes, hearth money, hay for his two cows, wool for weaving clothes, tools, etc. He found that all were well able to read and write and took care in keeping accounts. Head said that the cottiers' circumstances were better than they were twenty years earlier, despite reporting earlier that rents had risen during that period. This must have been due to greater productivity and income. While there was no regular system of cattle-grazing in the Barony of Owney and Arra, all the gentlemen raised cattle in their demesnes while the ordinary farmers kept a few of each breed of cattle. These farmers did not have large flocks of sheep, rather they kept a few breeding ewes and sold lambs and two-year-old ewes and pigs at market in Limerick.[55] Shooting wild-fowl and fishing brought in extra income for all and were valued sport for gentlemen.

Young took his leave of Michael Head after four very agreeable days and traveled through Castle Connell to spend the night in an inn at Limerick.

Running through all accounts of resident Ascendancy landlords was their great love of their estates and the considerable investments they made in their demesnes, not just in terms of money, but in design, taste, imagination, and energy. Like Michael Henry Head and Peter Holmes, and with few exceptions, they made intense efforts to improve agricultural productivity and the lives of their workers and tenants. But prosperous times could not last forever. The age of revolution with its wars and insurrection—the American Revolution, the French Revolution, the Irish insurrection of 1798, and many others, even including the Industrial Revolution—would produce a harshly different reality. While the Head dynasty seemed to be well established in Northern Tipperary, the huge costs of providing marriage settlements for all those daughters and establishing younger sons in socially acceptable professions, plus the costs of house building, demesne embellishment, and other personal costs was a dangerous burden passed on to the next generation of owners of these estates.

4. "English Protestantes striped naked & turned into the mountains in the frost, etc." Woodcut from *The Teares of Ireland* by James Cranford, London, 1642. An example of English propagandist art which, according to later historians, exaggerated the incidence of Catholic rebels stripping Protestants naked to humiliate them during the Irish rising of 1641.
©British Library Board. General Reference Collection G.5557.

Cromwell taking Drogheda by Storm.

5. Cromwell taking Drogheda by Storm, 1649. "The '1641 Ulster massacres' mean as much to the Protestant tradition as Cromwell's 'atrocities' at Drogheda in 1649 do to Catholic popular culture." Engraving by Barlow, published 1750.
National Army Museum, London.

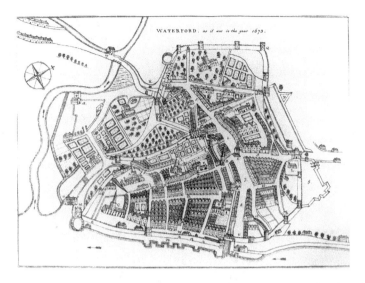

6.   Map of the City of Waterford, 1673, from H. H. Ryland, *History, Topography and Antiquities of the County and City of Waterford* (Kilkenny, 1824). The map was made two years before Michael Head's first mayoralty and shows the medieval city walls with its towers, forts, and gates largely in place. A. marks Christ Church Cathedral.

7.   View of Waterford. Oil on canvas by William van der Hagen, 1726. Large ships could approach Waterford's quays even in low tide. By 1726, Christ Church Cathedral had been rebuilt and many of the Cromwellian officers had long since moved to their land grants in the rich agricultural lands beyond the city.
Both Museum of Treasures, Waterford.

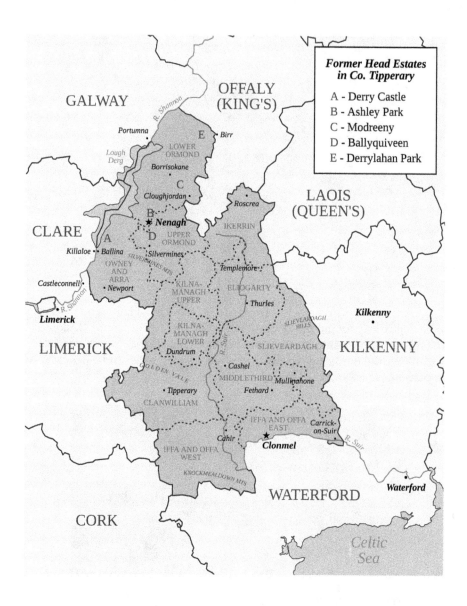

8. Map of County Tipperary with the locations of the former Head family estates in North Tipperary, and the baronies, towns, rivers, and mountains mentioned in the text.

The map was also adapted by Thad Garrett from "County Tipperary in Ireland," by O'Dea, etc.

9. Phoebe Toler Head (ca. 1737-1804). Undated oil on canvas by unknown artist, in the style of Sir Peter Lely. Phoebe was a sister of John Toler, later Lord Norbury, and mother of Col. Michael Head, commander of the 13th Light Dragoons during the Peninsular War, and four daughters.
Head family.

10. The Irish House of Commons. Oil on canvas by Francis Wheatley, 1780. It was painted to commemorate an address by Henry Grattan who spoke passionaely for a motion that "the people of Ireland are of right an independent nation and ought only to be bound by the King, Lords and Commons of Ireland." John Toler is at the extreme left, fourth row, next to two men wearing hats. Henry Grattan is standing in the front row on the right. The Protestant Ascendancy parliament was known as Grattan's Parliament.
Bridgeman Images, with permission of Leeds Museums and Galleries, Lotherton Hall.

11. Trinity College, Dublin. Print by James Malton, 1793. Founded in 1592 by Queen Elizabeth I, Trinity College was the university of the Protestant ascendancy for much of its history.

12. View of the Custom House. Print by James Malton, 1793.
Building began on the beautiful Custom House on the River Liffey in 1781 from a design by architect James Gandon, who was also working on the King's Inn and Four Courts buildings at that time. The Custom House was destroyed by fire on May 25, 1921 by units of the Dublin IRA.
Both National Library of Ireland.

Chapter 10

Revolution, the Irish Parliament, and the 1798 Rebellion

I am now to address a free people...Ireland is now a nation.
—Henry Grattan, Speaker of the Irish House of Commons,
  April 16, 1782.

What have you got in your hand? A green bough. Where
did it first grow? In America. Where did it bud? In France.
Where are you going to plant it? In the crown of Great
Britain.
—From the catechism of the United Irishmen.

The Age of Revolution forced the beginning of the long decline
of Protestant Ascendancy in Ireland. Following the outbreak of
rebellion in the North American colonies in 1775, four thousand
English regular army troops stationed in Ireland were withdrawn
and shipped to America. The next year, twenty-two new peers were
created by the Irish government for their support of this and other
government measures.[1] When France and Spain became allies of
the American colonies in 1778, and with troop strength in Ireland
reduced dramatically, there were renewed fears of French invasion,
a perennial fear that foreigner invaders would use Ireland as a back
door to invading England itself. With government approval and
under the overall command of the earl of Charlemont, the so-called
Irish Patriots formed a national volunteer force, drawn from the
urban and rural middle classes and led by Protestant gentry and
aristocrats, to defend the island from invasion and from growing
nationalist unrest. The mainly landlord officers of these independent Volunteer regiments soon realized their potential for political
influence, particularly parliamentary reform.

In March 1776, in the wake of the brutal November 1775 murder of a magistrate, Ambrose Power of Barretstown, in southern Tipperary, a revised and extended Whiteboy Act increased the number of felonies that incurred the death penalty and thus the power of the local magistrates. Ambrose Power was a member of the grand jury in 1766 that sentenced to death for murder on highly suspect evidence the anti-tithe protester Father Nicholas Sheehy (a cherished Tipperary martyr to this day) and he had recently apprehended the Whiteboy leader William Mackey at Fethard fair. The Roscrea Blues under the command of Col. Laurence Parsons was the first of the Co. Tipperary Volunteer corps formed to oppose the Whiteboys. Two more were mustered in May under the command of Benjamin Bunbury and Col. Sir Cornwallis Maude. In July, the two companies of the Nenagh Volunteers were formed under Peter Holmes and another under Sir John Carden at Templemore by the end of the year.

Far more Volunteer corps mustered in Northern Tipperary in 1779. The three companies of Col. Henry Prittie's Ormond Union wore uniforms of scarlet, faced white, with silver epaulets and white buttons. Col. George Stoney led the Burraskane (Borrisokane) Volunteers, with Major Thomas Stoney and Lt. Anthony Stoney as his subordinate officers. A large corps of officers— including Major Simon Pepper, Capt. John Head, and Lt. James Otway—supported Col. Daniel Toler in his command of four companies of the Ormond Independents, a battalion of light infantry. They were outfitted in scarlet faced in black, with silver epaulets and wings. Col. Thomas Otway was in command of the Castle Otway Volunteers.[2] According to W. E. H. Lecky, the great Anglo-Irish historian of the eighteenth century in England and Ireland, nearly the entire resident landed gentry took part in the Volunteer regiments, for whom the uniforms were all manufactured in Ireland, while ladies gave Volunteer rank precedence in society.[3]

Many of the officers of the Irish Volunteers were members of the Lords or Commons, and they used the Volunteers' new-found power to influence Parliament and to pressure the English government, particularly on free trade. Lord Charlemont led the Patriots in the Irish House of Lords, closely allied with Col. Henry Grattan and Lt. Col. Henry Flood in the House of Commons. Grattan and

Flood commanded the Dublin Independent Volunteers. In April 1780, Henry Grattan made an initially unsuccessful bid to persuade the Irish House of Commons to vote for an Irish Declaration of Independence. Its failure was due to the Crown's effective control of the majority in Parliament through the system of patronage and newly created seats. As it became clear that England was losing the war in America, the Volunteers were increasingly militant. Political Protestants, while remaining loyal to the English connection, had long resented England's stranglehold over the country's economic and political life. The Irish Parliament was unable to initiate its own legislation and was corrupted by government pensions in the gift of an Irish executive appointed by London. All this offended Protestant national pride.[4] In addition, historian Roy Foster cites local resentment against pressure from England to mitigate the laws against Catholics and argues that the strong links between Ulster and America "reinforced the current of radical anti-government feeling in that province." Irish unrest was suddenly manifest at all levels, and the beleaguered British government had to make some kind of response. One result was the policy of relaxing penal laws against Catholics.[5]

When the Volunteer regiments met in convention at Dungannon, Co. Tyrone, in February 1782 to agitate for Irish parliamentary independence, Henry Prittie, commander of the Ormond Union and brother-in-law of Michael Henry Head of Derry Castle, came out strongly for Henry Grattan's resolutions favoring an independent Irish Parliament and parliamentary reform. The Whig party, which opposed a strong monarchy and was supported by the great aristocratic families, took power back from the Tories in England that year and, in December, they granted parliamentary independence to Ireland. In the meantime, Henry Prittie influenced the Tipperary grand jurors who controlled local government. He and Daniel Toler, John Head's brother-in-law, were elected to parliament without a contest in July 1783. At the time, Prittie and Toler and their allies among the Northern Tipperary gentry considered themselves to be Irish Patriots seeking parliamentary reform and legislative independence from the parliament in Westminster, but their views would change.

Under the leadership of Henry Flood and Frederick Hervey,

bishop of Derry, a second Volunteer National Convention met in Dublin between November 10 and December 2, 1783 and drew up a detailed parliamentary reform plan. Col. Daniel Toler was one of the Volunteer delegates from Co. Tipperary. The main criticism of the electoral and parliamentary system was that it was not representative, even in a Protestant context. No fewer than 234 out of three hundred members sat for "close" boroughs where the return of members was wholly under the control of a single patron; the rest were elected on a narrow, property-based franchise.[6] At the extreme of corruption, patrons in several boroughs with only thirteen or fewer voters nominated over two hundred MPs. Co. Tipperary was home to 119,706 inhabitants but they were predominantly Catholic and unable to vote because of the penal laws. Few other than Grattan seemed to see the contradiction of fighting for Irish parliamentary rights while excluding the majority of the Irish people. Patrons dominated each of Tipperary's three freeman boroughs of Cashel, Clonmel, and Fethard. Co. Wexford's boroughs were overwhelmingly described as "venal, decayed and rotten." On the other hand, the County of the City of Waterford had forty thousand inhabitants and one thousand electors, both freemen and freeholders, "one half of whom are *foreigners*."[7] Despite this rampant corruption, the Irish House of Commons rejected bills based on the reform principles by large majorities in November 1783 and March 1784. Votes of thanks were passed to Toler, Prittie, and another Co. Tipperary landowner and MP Thomas Barton for voting with the minority.[8]

In the middle of this struggle for parliamentary control, thirteen-year-old Michael Head, only son of John Head of Ashley Park, entered TCD in December 1782, so that he was in Dublin during the period of pride and prosperity coinciding with what became known as "Grattan's Parliament." The city's population grew rapidly and its wealthier residents, many of whom were members of parliament, spread into elegant squares and stately terraces. The most important architect in Dublin during this time was James Gandon who was designing buildings such as the Custom House, the Kings Inn, and the Four Courts. Gandon was also responsible for the extensions to Parliament House, the world's first purpose-built two-chamber parliament house, on which construction had begun in 1729.

Dublin's grace and grandeur were replicated in other Irish cities, including Waterford, Limerick, and Cork. Many of the wealthiest of Ireland's Anglo-Irish Ascendancy were drawn to sessions of parliament in Dublin, which also coincided with the Irish social season, not by accident! The lord-lieutenant presided over state balls and drawing rooms in Dublin Castle, while leading peers flocked to their enormous and richly decorated town houses around Merion, Mountjoy, and Fitzwilliam Squares. It was a particularly interesting time for the teenager, when two of his Toler uncles must have provided access to or insights into the height of Ascendancy political power and culture in the Irish capital. He may even have resided with one of them. While Michael Head did not receive his B.A. until 1788, he was appointed to a cornetcy in the 12th Light Dragoons on December 3, 1785, aged sixteen. Like most young Protestant Irishmen of the period, he joined the army through influential relations, in his case the Toler family, which purchased a cavalry commission for him. He was to serve by successive steps in the 8th, 12th and 13th Light Dragoons.

In 1788, King George III fell ill with the first of his bouts of insanity, and the Westminster parliament debated about whether to appoint a regent. The Irish parliament upset Westminster by claiming the right to appoint a separate regent. The king recovered before any of this could happen but Prime Minister William Pitt the Younger began to consider whether a full union between England and Ireland was necessary, particularly after the outbreak of the French Revolution in 1789. Republican ideas began to circulate in Ireland, with its close political, commercial, and social links with France. The first declared principle of the French Revolution held particular meaning for Irish Catholics and Presbyterians. It proclaimed the abolition of every kind of religious disqualification and it swept away the whole system of tithes. Presbyterians in Belfast celebrated the fall of the Bastille, and there were signs that there was a resurgence of political "volunteering," which made Dublin Castle nervous. Theobald Wolfe Tone, a young Protestant barrister, published a brilliant pamphlet arguing for parliamentary reform, which he believed could happen if Protestant radicals and Irish Catholics cooperated. He was invited to Belfast, where he and a group of northern liberals, including his close friend Thomas Russell, established the Society of United Irishmen in October 1791. Just a month later, Tone and Russell traveled to Dublin to establish a branch with militant populist Napper Tandy as secretary. In contrast to the limited reforms advocated by the opposition in Parliament, the Society aimed at radical changes that would entitle all men to vote irrespective of religion, class, or property, bringing freedom and equality for everyone—except women, of course.

The British government, having learned painfully from the revolution in America the importance of securing the allegiance of discontented factions, had begun to remove the penal law restrictions against Catholics by relief acts in 1778 and 1782, providing they swore an oath of allegiance. Catholics could now bequeath land to a single heir but without the rights attached to freehold (1778), while the 1782 act allowed them to buy land and removed most of the restrictions affecting Catholic education and the Catholic clergy. Following the French Revolution, the British government enacted further legislation to prevent any alliance between Catholics and radical Presbyterians, including the Relief Act of 1792, allowing Catholics to practice law, and the Relief Act of 1793, giving Catholics the right to vote and to hold most civil and military offices. The violent anti-Catholic rhetoric of the second bill's opponents and the resentment of Protestants to this perceived betrayal by the British government contributed significantly to the growth of religious conflict. The bill was far more threatening to those in authority, including landowners, representing as it did a threat to the status quo of political power if the franchise were to be extended to Catholics and the dominant Protestant voice in Parliament weakened. Catholics, however, remained barred from sitting in Parliament or serving as lord-lieutenant, chief-secretary or chancellor of the exchequer. They could not be king's counsel, judges or governors, sheriffs or sub-sheriffs, and could not hold higher military rank than colonel.[9] Caught between the two sides, Grattan began to lose support in the Irish House of Commons.

In February 1792, Daniel Toler (Tipperary county MP), John Toler (solicitor-general), Peter Holmes (MP for Kilmallock, Co. Limerick), and nearly all Northern Tipperary landowners spoke against the Catholic Relief Bill introduced that month, whereas

Tipperary landowners who welcomed the measure tended to be in the south of the county. According to Lecky, John Toler "placed the Government opposition to the admission of Catholics to Parliament on the highest possible ground." As John Toler put it, "He [The Roman Catholic] has no right to demand it, nor have the Crown and Parliament, who are but trustees for its preservation, a right to alienate what has been confided to them as a trust."[10] Bigotry of all kinds began to raise its ugly head. That same month, a provocative allusion in debate by Solicitor-General John Toler to Napper Tandy's physical ugliness provoked Tandy, son of a Dublin ironmonger and member of the Dublin Corporation, into challenging Toler to a duel. This was treated by the House of Commons as a breach of a member's privilege, and a speaker's warrant was issued for Tandy's arrest, which he managed to elude till its validity expired on the prorogation of Parliament. Tandy then took proceedings against the lord-lieutenant for issuing a proclamation for his arrest. Although the action failed, it increased Tandy's popularity among his supporters and his expenses were paid by the Society of the United Irishmen. That spring, Wolf Tone, a Protestant, became secretary of the Catholic Committee, further underscoring the United Irishmen's support and the growing unease among liberal Protestants with the discrimination of Catholics in civic life.

On October 3, 1792, there was a "very numerous" meeting of the Protestant gentry, clergy, and freeholders at Nenagh. They drew up a declaration to the two county MPs Daniel Toler and John Bagwell, to support the constitution and to "vigorously oppose all attempts at innovation or alteration in Church and State." Sixty of the principal gentry signed the address as did "near 600 freeholders," or about two-fifths of all the county's freeholders.[11] It was reported in November that a number of large landowners in Lower Ormond, including Toler and Prittie, were forcing their Catholic tenants to sign the Nenagh address. Nonetheless, influenced by the United Irishmen's motions for reform, the Irish government passed the Catholic Relief Acts in 1792 and 1793, granting Catholic 40-shilling freeholders the right to vote and opening up a wide range of civil and military offices to Catholics, including ability to serve on the county's grand jury. In March 1793, the first Catholic in the county was chosen as a justice of the peace, and one of the county's chief Catholics, James Scully of Kilfeacle, was made a magistrate through the recommendation of John Bagwell, who was sheriff in that vital year. In the summer assizes of 1793, four Catholics were on the grand jury.[12] Granting votes to Catholic forty-shilling freeholders had an unfortunate consequence, however, since it gave an additional impulse to landlords to subdivide their land in order to multiply the votes they could command.

As this struggle for Catholic relief was taking place in Ireland, republican France declared war on Great Britain on February 1, 1793, retaliating after Britain expelled the French ambassador following the January 21 execution of King Louis XVI. Britain had begun military preparations in late 1792, declaring that war was inevitable unless France gave up its conquests in Belgium and Holland that threatened British trade. The United Irishmen's address to the Volunteers to take up arms again in defense of Ireland and their rights, to push ahead with parliamentary reform and full Catholic emancipation, and to gather again in convention in Dungannon was now seen by Dublin Castle as verging on treason. From the beginning of the war, Prime Minister William Pitt and other leaders in Westminster presumed that Ireland was a high priority in revolutionary France's plans to destabilize England. In every war with the French since the 1690s there had been invasion scares. The immediate concern was to prevent Ireland from becoming a seat of dissatisfaction which the French could exploit—but how to defend the island when so many regular troops had been withdrawn to fight in the war? The 1793 act had restored the right to Catholics to bear arms, and this opened the way to enlist Catholics in an armed militia, a paid, non-regular, home defense force raised in each county.

From late 1793 to early 1795, Michael Head of Ashley Park served as a subaltern (Capt. Lt.) in the 12th Light Dragoons. The great dynastic powers of Europe (Austria, Prussia, Great Britain, Spain, Sardinia, and the Netherlands) were united in trying to reverse the outcome of the French Revolution and restore the French monarchy. The 12th Light Dragoons left Ireland in 1793 to aid Adm. Sir Samuel Hood at the siege of Toulon, where a young Capt. Napoleon Bonaparte began to make his name.[13] Since Toulon was already abandoned by the English, a single squadron of the regiment then participated in driving the French from the island of Corsica while the rest of the regiment sailed to Italy and landed at Civitavecchia. There the conduct of the officers and men so impressed Pope Pius VI that he wrote a letter of commendation to Sir John Coxe Hippisley (an English MP, who was at that time conducting negotiations with the Vatican), stating that he wished to present a gold medal to each of the twelve officers, including Gen. Sir James Steuart and Col. Sir James Erskine.[14] Later, three of the junior officers, Capt. Lt. Michael Head, Lt. the Hon. Pierce Butler, and Capt. Robert Browne, were presented to the Pope, and this is the scene shown in the huge history painting by James Northcote in the collections of the Victoria and Albert Museum. In 1796, French troops commanded by Bonaparte invaded Italy, defeated the papal troops, and occupied the Papal States. Having refused to renounce his temporal powers, Pius was taken prisoner two years later and transported to France. He died in Valence in August 1799.

The government in Ireland proceeded to suppress any form of radicalism and the Society of United Irishman became a secret, radical organization, intent on establishing a republic by revolutionary methods and therefore treasonable in the eyes of the government. Wolfe Tone went to France to enlist that country's military support in establishing an Irish republic. In the meantime, Grattan's bill for complete Catholic emancipation was defeated in May 1795. While Peter Holmes, Tipperary's high sheriff for 1795, could not make up his mind, John Head's brother-in-law, archconservative MP and solicitor-general John Toler, was one of those who spoke out strongly against it. "He spoke for above two hours, and left the question without an attempt to argue it, but concluded with a vehement assertion that the bill could not be carried without the repeal of the bill of rights, the breach of the coronation oath and of the compact between the two countries, according to a witness."[15] He was rewarded with a title for his wife, who was created a peeress of Ireland in her own right in 1797 as baroness Norwood of Knockalton, Co. Tipperary. The overreaction of the loyalists during the crisis atmosphere preceding the anticipated rebellion was based on their conviction that the Catholics were drawing up titles to estates they had formerly owned, to which they believed the French would reinstate them. Insecurity about land tenure was a constant for Protestant landlords.

That year, the Protestant Orange Order and the Catholic Defenders, a far more dangerous anti-Protestant rural secret society fueled emotionally by resistance to tithes, rising taxes, and claims for land redistribution, were founded in County Armagh during a period of Protestant-Catholic sectarian conflict over land. The Orange Order, a Masonic-style brotherhood, was sworn to maintain the Protestant Ascendancy and established order of Crown, Church, and Constitution, while the Defenders came to represent all Catholic-linked agrarian movements across Ireland. Militant loyalism and revolutionary republicanism gained forces rapidly.

Wolfe Tone's first attempt to land with a forty-three-ship French fleet at Bantry Bay in West Cork with 14,500 French soldiers in December 1796 was unsuccessful due to a raging snowstorm—but this was just the beginning of efforts to engage the French in military engagements in Ireland.[16] According to historian Marianne Elliott, however, the Bantry Bay effort under Gen. Louis Lazare Hoche was a disaster for France. "Never again would France mount preparations to help Ireland on a scale equal to that of 1796, and Hoche had already transferred his attention to the Rhine in an all-out race to secure peace with Austria before Bonaparte could do so through his Italian campaign."[17]

The 12th Dragoon Guards returned to England in 1795 and the regiment was used to suppress a food riot in Nottingham. In 1797, 1798, and 1799, Michael Head served with the regiment in Portugal under General Steuart. He was present at the landing of the British troops at Minorca in November 1798 and at the siege and capitulation of Ciudadella, resulting in the capture of Minorca from Spain as a British naval base for the duration of the war. At this time, he was aide-de-camp to Col. Sir James St. Clair-Erskine (previously Erskine) whose brilliant military and political career was no doubt important to Michael Head's advancement.[18] On July 19, 1799, Michael Head "obtained a Majority in the 8th Light Dragoons" and the following June, he transferred to the 13th Light Dragoons as a lieutenant-colonel.

While the situation in Europe and Ireland reached new levels of warfare, rebellion, and violence, the older of the female cousins in the Head family of Northern Tipperary began to make the marriages that were expected of daughters of the landed gentry. The first to marry was John and Phoebe Head's daughter Letitia. In 1785, she married John Armstrong Drought of Lettybrook in Queen's County. Articles of Agreement for their marriage were drawn up on March 11, 1785. Letitia's marriage portion was £2,000 and her fiancé conveyed certain lands and judgement debts in order to secure an annual jointure for her of £200 yearly should she survive him and to provide for any children. They would have five daughters and three sons. All three sons rose to some distinction in Queen's County leadership, the law or the military.[19] John Head's other three daughters all married after the death of their mother in 1804.

Then there were the marriages of the long roster of daughters of Michael and Margaret Head of Derry Castle, each one adding to the crippling burden of encumbrances on that estate. In 1788, Maria married Cornet William Gore of the 14th Dragoons, a son of the bishop of Limerick; Deborah, the eldest daughter, married in 1793 Major William Casaubon Purdon, late 4th Horse, of Tinerana across Lough Derg in Co. Clare. Their son Simon Purdon was to figure dramatically in one of the most colorful and tragic episodes of the Heads' story when the consequences of the ruinous dowry system hit home (see chapter 14). Two more of the Derry daughters married in 1795: Catherine married the Rev. Frederick Eyre Trench and Grace the Hon. Robert Leeson, half-brother of the Earl of Milltown.[20] Margaret-Anne Head married a cousin, the Rev. John Burdett, in 1802. Like their cousin Letitia, both Catherine and Margaret-Anne produced large Ascendancy families. Of two younger Derry Castle sisters who married in the early nineteenth century, Louisa, who married barrister Thomas Forde of Seaforde, Co. Down, became the mother of yet another very large family.

As this roster indicates, the Protestant landed gentry continued to consolidate economic and political power through marital alliances. Further consolidation of their voting power came from joining an irregular political cabal when they were named freemen of cities in which they did not live. For example, by the second half of the eighteenth century, a corrupt oligarchy of Ascendancy families gained political power in Limerick City. "They retained power by granting the freedom of the city, and with it the right to vote in parliamentary elections, to their friends and supporters living outside the city. Hundreds of men living in counties Limerick, Clare, and elsewhere in Ireland were admitted as freemen during the period from 1760 to about 1819. At the same time, admittance was denied to legitimate Limerick merchants and tradesmen who were legally entitled to the franchise by virtue of birth, marriage, or apprenticeship; only those who pledged their vote to the ruling party were given their certificate of freedom."[21] Michael Henry Head of Derry Castle, a deputy lieutenant of Co. Tipperary at the time, and his son and heir Michael Prittie Head became freemen on September 27, 1794. A number of Parsons of Parsonstown (Birr), King's County, Henry Prittie of Kilboy, a number of Purdons of Co. Clare, etc., are on those extensive lists but absolutely no Catholics.

Insurrection in County Tipperary

Meanwhile, sedition was in the air in Co. Tipperary and across Ireland generally. Tipperary's predominantly Catholic militia of 764 men, constituted in 1793 and recruited from all over the country, was serving in Londonderry in the north of Ireland in 1797, where the spirit of rebellion was very strong. It was commanded by Col. John Bagwell of Clonmel, one of the county's MPs. Militia units from other counties served in Tipperary. Before long, the Tipperary and Kerry militia admitted they were "United," reflecting the seditious and nationalistic nature of those counties. Col. Bagwell oversaw the court-martial of the Tipperary militia after an informer clarified the extent of its infiltration and conspiracy by United Irishmen and Defenders. Perhaps for that reason, the regiment saw no active service in rebel areas during the 1798 rebellion; however Tipperary militiamen on their way home carried the separatist message with them.[22]

Realizing that the landlords had little confidence in the reliability of the militia, the government encouraged them in 1796 to mobilize predominantly Protestant yeomanry regiments as a strong and loyal back-up force for the militia and the standing army. Again, the yeomanry corps were mostly under landlord command, numbering 30,000 by 1797, and some groups were composed almost entirely of Orange lodges. That fueled the extraordinary viciousness that characterized the full-scale rebellion in 1798. Yeomanry corps, both cavalry and infantry, were raised across Co. Tipperary, one of the most notable being the Castle Otway Cavalry raised by Cooke Otway. A number of the Volunteers of the 1770s and 1780s joined up.[23] By this time, John and Michael Henry Head were in their sixties and undoubtedly worried about the security of their properties and safety of their families. Like many of the Tipperary landlords, they probably had their houses barricaded. Yeomanry corps in their area provided some confidence while just over 3,300 rank and file soldiers of the regular army were stationed at that time in the three baronies of northern Tipperary.

Nenagh, just five miles from John and Phoebe Head's Ashley Park property, was an important United Irish center from 1792 on. If John Head was a magistrate, as Michael Henry Head of Derry certainly was, then they regularly heard evidence against citizens who had been sworn into the United Irishmen. The leader of the Nenagh group of United men was Hervey Montmorency Morres, a descendant of the Anglo-Norman DeMarisco family which was associated with Tipperary from the late 12th century. He was born in Rathnaleen Castle, near Nenagh, in 1767 and had already had a long military career on the Continent. He returned in 1795 to live at Knockalton but became disgusted with the harsh tactics of the military authorities and joined the United Irishmen Society in 1796. He became a close friend of the idealistic Lord Edward Fitzgerald, a son of the duke of Leinster and cousin of Whig Prime Minister Charles James Fox, and they were among the very few leaders within the society who had military experience.

In May 1797, Michael Henry Head of Derry's brother-in-law Peter Holmes of Johnstown, whose large landholdings included the town of Nenagh (formerly owned by the dukes of Ormond), wrote to the chief-secretary at Dublin Castle that he was anxious to get the high sheriff of Co. Tipperary to call a meeting of the grand jury, of which he was a member. Holmes and his father-in-law Henry Prittie were opposed to any further concessions to Catholics. But, following the death in the summer of 1796 of Daniel Toler, who was equally opposed to further Catholic concessions, pro-Catholic

Francis Mathew, who inherited his father's title as the earl of Landaff the following year, was elected to fill his place, and Colonel Bagwell, who had espoused the Catholic cause since 1792, was returned to office.

Adjacent King's was the most restive county as 1798 began. Big houses there had been raided for arms and, on one estate, fifty ash trees were cut down by gangs to make handles for pikes, the principal weapon of the angry peasantry.[24] Harsh retaliation by the authorities began when Col. Richard Mansergh St. George, a veteran of the American War of Independence and a hardline Co. Cork magistrate, and his agent and host Jaspar Uniacke were brutally assassinated by a gang armed with pikes, pitchforks, and scythes at Uniacke's home in the mountainous area between Cork and Tipperary in February 1798: "While they were lighting him to his bedroom, a gang of men appeared on the landing. Mrs. Uniacke was flung over the staircase down to the hall, her husband was stabbed and thrown down beside her, while Col. St. George was hacked to death with a rusty scythe." After that, before the rising in Wexford, a stream of murders took place. Near Parsonstown in King's County, Mr. Dooling was shot dead in front of his wife, Sir Henry Manix was killed in his garden, while Mr. John Daragh of Eagle Hill, Kildare, was shot in the stomach."[25] Thomas Judkin Fitzgerald, who was born a Uniacke, was the high sheriff and chief magistrate of Co. Tipperary for 1798, and he became determined to do everything in his power—far too much as it turned out—to avenge his relative and put down the growing rebellion.

In March, raids to secure weapons increased, and Judkin Fitzgerald estimated that, by the end of the month, the "disturbers" held between three and four hundred firearms. Sir John Carden of Templemore, a military man and capable estate manager, had reacted to rumors that a general attack on the town of Templemore, which his father had laid out, was imminent. He placed his garrison of dragoons and the entire neighborhood on alert but the attack never materialized. In March, Carden wrote a desperate letter to the lord-lieutenant, Lord Camden: "This country is now so bad that it should be declared in a state of absolute rebellion. Every house for a considerable distance around this placed was robbed of its arms last night, and the insolence of the people is astonishing. They look upon their plan as on the eve of being accomplished."[26]

With episodes of serious violence on the rise, including two important pitched battles in the south of the county, Fitzgerald called a special meeting of all the county magistrates at Cashel on March 27. On the strength of reports by Fitzgerald, Carden, and others, Dublin Castle decided on March 30 to impose martial law on the south of Ireland on April 2.[27] On April 6, the military commander of the Cashel area ordered those who had robbed arms to surrender them within ten days. As a result, a priest made nine hundred men in his parish assemble and lay down their arms, ask forgiveness, and take the oath of allegiance, the first of several such instances. The bishop of Killaloe on the Tipperary/Clare border near the Derry Castle estate claimed that fifteen hundred pikes had been seized by the rebels in his area.[28]

Fear of raids for arms by gangs of United Irishmen and by the Defenders resulted in many landlords and families closing up their houses and fleeing to the towns. Fitzgerald reacted by issuing a proclamation on April 20 ordering the gentry who had fled, many of whom were magistrates reluctant to risk their lives, to return to their residences within twenty-four hours. Rather too dramatically, since he insulted male landowners by issuing the order in a broadside, he cited the example of brave Mrs. Deborah Bunbury, née Prittie, of Kilfeacle, Margaret Head's sister, who had repulsed an arms raid on her house with the sole help of two manservants.[29] He called her a widow but she was in fact estranged from her feckless husband, who was living the high life in London.

By mid-May, local and government authorities felt that order had been restored in Co. Tipperary. Meanwhile, the government, acting on a report by an informer, arrested at their secret meeting place in Dublin sixteen leaders of the Leinster Directory of the United Irishmen. Of the leaders in that area, only the charismatic Ascendancy peer Lord Edward Fitzgerald remained at large. But the man who had seen himself as the military commander of the insurgent forces was captured and mortally wounded in Dublin on May 19. When the remainder of the United Irishmen leaders decided to go ahead with the rebellion in Kildare and surrounding counties, emissaries were sent from King's County to raise their supporters in Ormond, but they could find no support in Northern Tipperary. Judkin Fitzgerald's brutal and unorthodox methods in ordering the flogging of suspects and forcing disarmament in Co. Tipperary were now antagonizing many Protestants but few made public protests. Many of the Catholic bishops and priests spoke out against the United Irishmen on the basis that the French revolution that inspired them was virulently anti-clerical. Judkin Fitzgerald turned his attention to suspected insurgents in the south of Co. Tipperary as the insurgency reached its bloody climax against the British army, the militias, and the yeomanry at Vinegar Hill, near Enniscorthy, Co. Wexford on June 21. Tipperary's planned role in the rebellion was foiled, but Judkin Fitzgerald's brutal tactics left a festering resentment.

In June 1798, Gen. Charles Cornwallis, 1st marquess Cornwallis, commander of British forces during the American War of Independence and subsequently governor of India, was appointed lord-lieutenant of Ireland and commander-in-chief of the Royal Irish Army. His appointment, which had been discussed as early as 1797, was made in response to the outbreak in late May of the Irish rebellion and was greeted unfavorably by the Irish elite. They preferred his predecessor Lord Camden, and suspected Cornwallis had liberal sympathies with the predominantly Catholic rebels. However, he struck up a good working relationship with Lord Castlereagh, whom he had appointed as chief-secretary for Ireland. In his combined role, Cornwallis oversaw the defeat of both the Irish rebels and a French invasion force led by Gen. Jean Humbert that landed in Connacht in August 1798. Panicked by the landing and the subsequent British defeat at the Battle of Castlebar, Pitt despatched thousands of reinforcements to Ireland, swelling British forces there to 60,000. The French invaders were defeated and forced to surrender at the Battle of Ballinamuck, after which Cornwallis ordered the execution by lot of a number of Irish rebels. Having been found on board a captured ship—part of a small French insurgent-affiliated expedition that landed at Ballina, Co. Mayo, in August—Wolfe Tone committed suicide on the morning that his sentence to be hanged, drawn, and quartered was to be carried out. He was to join the tradition of Irish nationalist "martyrology" that inspired the continuing resistance. It has been estimated that, by the end of the summer, the death toll on both sides, from various causes, was 30,000, the most violent episode in Irish history since the seventeenth century.[30] During the fall, Cornwallis secured government control over most of the island, and organized the suppression of the remaining supporters of the United Irish movement.

As attorney-general for Ireland from 1798 to 1799, John Toler was responsible for the prosecution of those involved in the insurrection. Toler carried out his duties with notorious severity, as in the case of lawyers and United Irishmen John and Henry Sheares, the sons of a member of Parliament, who were hanged, drawn, and quartered for their revolutionary involvement. The assizes at which Toler was present were invariably followed by wholesale executions, but the presiding judge at the Sheares trial was Hugh Carleton, 1st viscount Carleton. Toler was by no means the only senior judge who earned notoriety for the severity of their judgments, but the *Dictionary of National Biography* asserts that "his [Toler's] indifference to human suffering…disgusted even those who thought the occasion called for firmness on the part of the government."

An oft-quoted source on Toler is Richard Lalor Shiel's *Sketches of the Irish Bar*:

> In the year 1798, Lord Norbury [who was then plain John Toler] was his Majesty's Solicitor-General [sic, Attorney-General]. His services to Government had been hitherto confined to the display of ferocious rhetoric in the House of Commons, of which I have quoted a specimen. The civil disturbances of the country offered a new field to his genius, and afforded him an opportunity of accumulating his claims upon the gratitude of the Crown, which could not have found a more zealous and, I will even add, a more useful servant during the rebellion…To strike terror into the people was the great object to be attained, and Lord Norbury had many qualifications for the purpose. He stood in a court of justice, not only as the servant of his sovereign, but as the representative, in some measure, of the powerful Cromwellian aristocracy to which his family belonged, and in whose prejudices and passions he himself vehemently participated. His whole bearing and aspect breathed a

turbulent spirit of domination. His voice was deep and big; and in despite of the ludicrous associations connected with his character, when it rolled the denunciations of infuriated power through the court, derived from the terrible intimations which it conveyed, an awful and appalling character. He did not, indeed, cease to utter absurdity, but his orations were fraught with a kind of truculent bombast—a sort of sanguinary 'fee, fa, fum,' while the dilation of his nostrils, and the fierceness of his look, expressed if I may say so, the scent of a traitor's blood."[31]

It is hardly surprising that no modern historian has come to the defense of this publicly feared and apparently destested man, despite his private reputation for generosity to his friends, relations, tenants, and servants.

In the wake of the Irish insurrection, English morale was greatly boosted by Horatio Nelson's victory over the French navy in the Battle of the Nile on August 1, 1798, and, by the following month, the insurrection was generally considered to be over. A constitutional union between Ireland and England seemed like a logical consequence of the insurrection, although English politicians such as William Pitt had been arguing for the idea since the 1780s in the face of the intractability of the Irish Parliament. It now came to pass with extraordinary speed. Both Henry Prittie and John Toler were rewarded for their support but Henry Grattan and Lord Charlemont were fiercely opposed to the Union.

Chapter 11

Union, the Napoleonic Threat, and the Emmet Uprising

Mr. Emmet...You have avowed and endeavoured to vindicate principles totally subversive of the government, totally subversive of the tranquillity, well-being and happiness of that country which gave you birth, and you have broached treason the most abominable.
—Lord Norbury, September 19, 1803.

Let no man write my epitaph...When my country takes her place among the nations of the earth, then shall my character be vindicated."
—Robert Emmet, speech from the dock, September 19, 1803.

In the wake of the 1798 insurrection, British Prime Minister William Pitt the Younger and Lord Cornwallis, the new lord-lieutenant for Ireland, actively promoted bringing Ireland into the British Union of England, Scotland, and Wales, with a single parliament at Westminster, to prevent Ireland becoming a steppingstone for French invasions. Indeed, Napoleon Bonaparte, now first consul of France, planned to land in Ireland in 1800, but that was before his attention turned to driving the Austrians out of northern Italy (Battle of Marengo, June 14, 1800), and crushing the Austrians and Bavarians at Hohenlinden, Bavaria. In the subsequent peace treaty, Austria accepted French control up to the Rhine and French puppet republics in northern Italy and the Netherlands. After the British defeated the French army at Alexandria, Egypt in 1801, the Treaty of Amiens (March 1802) temporarily ended hostilities between the French Republic and Great Britain and martial law, which had been in effect in Ireland during the conflict, was subsequently suspended. But the Treaty of Amiens would not remain in effect for long.

Pitt and his team in Dublin used bribery, bullying, and the promise of peerages to persuade the Dublin parliament to vote itself out of existence. The Marquess Cornwallis found the process quite distasteful. "My occupation is now of the most unpleasant nature," he wrote, "negotiating and jobbing with the most corrupt people under heaven. I despise and hate myself every hour for engaging in such dirty work, and am supported only by the reflection that without an Union the British Empire must be dissolved."[1] The *Oxford Companion to Irish History*, however, mentions that "Modern accounts suggest the exchange of patronage for parliamentary support remained within the limits of 18th-century convention, and emphasize the extent to which both sides engaged, through pamphleteering, petitions, and public meetings, in a competition for public opinion as well as parliamentary votes."[2]

The terms of union, drawn up entirely by the British government, were quite generous: Ireland was offered broad representation in the Westminster Parliament with four bishops and twenty-eight representative peers in the House of Lords and one hundred MPs in the House of Commons; the Episcopalian churches of England and Ireland were to be united as an established church, and Ireland was to contribute to the expenses of the United Kingdom in the proportion of two to fifteen, i.e., two-seventeenths of the whole. There would be free trade between the two countries, with certain exceptions.[3] According to historian Patrick Geoghegan, Pitt saw Union as elevating "Ireland to the center of British empire building at a time of great insecurity." Opponents of the union saw it "as a cynical alliance designed to tie Ireland to Britain, and destroy the privileges that had been won in 1782."[4]

Desperate to assure the allegiance of Ireland at this dangerous time, Pitt, in his public speeches, encouraged Irish Catholics to expect that passage of an act of union would bring long-sought goals: Catholic emancipation, confirming the right of all male Catholics to vote and to own land; the commutation of the hated tithes that supported the Protestant clergy; and public funding of the Catholic clergy. As a result, Catholics across the country and in predominantly Catholic Co. Tipperary came out strongly in favor of the Union. But Henry Grattan and the most prominent of a mixed group of government officials were violently opposed as self-declared "patriots" defending their independent parliament. They feared that direct rule from London could not be trusted to maintain Protestant supremacy.[5] Members of the parliament in Dublin—representing the Irish Protestant aristocracy and leading gentry—were jealous of their political, economic, and cultural heritage and furious at the prospect of being transferred to London. And the Irish bar feared losing its enormous influence in parliament if legislators were removed across the Irish Sea.

Among the anti-Unionists in Co. Tipperary were John and Michael Head of Ashley Park and James Otway of Prior Park and a number of other landlords, both Protestant and Catholic, who signed an anti-union petition in February 1799. On March 14, during the week when the court of assizes met, the opposition group led by Lord Lismore and the Hon. Francis Mathew, asked the sheriff, Francis Hely-Hutchinson, with forty-eight others, to call a county meeting to consider the matter. However, the move was blocked by a counter-requisition supported by Catholics and signed by 192 men. Anti-unionists like the Heads and Otway, who were early in the field, appear to have been brushed aside when their names were published. The two MPs for North Tipperary initially opposed the Act of Union but were persuaded to vote for it.[6] On August 1, 1800, the Irish and English Parliaments passed the Act of Union, creating the United Kingdom of Great Britain and Ireland, and it took effect in January 1801.

Following the vote, members of Co. Tipperary's leading gentry who supported the Union received a high proportion of new peerages. Among others, Henry Prittie, brother-in-law of Michael Henry Head of Derry Castle, was created Baron Dunalley, and John Toler, brother-in-law of John Head of Ashley Park, became Baron Norbury.[7] Earlier that month, Toler was appointed chief justice of the Court of Common Pleas, an appointment he held for nearly twenty-seven years, during which he became known as "the hanging judge." The formidable and violently anti-Catholic John Fitzgibbon, Lord Clare, lord chancellor of Ireland from 1789 until his death in 1802, considered Toler to be unfit for the bench: "Make him a bishop, or even an archbishop," he is reported to have said, "but not a chief justice."[8]

Unlike Pitt, George III was strongly opposed to Catholic

emancipation, believing that this would violate his coronation oath to protect the established Protestant Church of England. Unable to change the king's views, Pitt resigned on February 16, 1801 and Cornwallis did likewise, returning to England. Pitt returned to power in 1804, by which time conduct of the war against Napoleon overrode any other concern. Pitt's promises to secure suffrage for Catholic men were not addressed or were turned aside, a neglect that had grave consequences.

What was not swept aside by the Act of Union was the continuation of a separate Irish administration. The first lord-lieutenant or viceroy to take office in Ireland after enactment of the union legislation was Philip Yorke, earl of Hardwicke, who arrived in Dublin in early April 1801. The Act of Union had extinguished the viceroy's legislative powers, but he was now to audit and inspect Ireland's military and civil establishments and demand an accounting from the Treasury and other offices. He was instructed to protect the established Church, to "promote trade and manufactures," and "to encourage Protestant citizens to establish manufactures in Irish cities." King George III believed that some of the eighteenth-century viceroys had conducted themselves like "quacks" by engaging in "all matters from not knowing the magnitude of the undertaking," thus enabling some people "in that uncivilised land" to manipulate viceroys and to profit from their ignorance of Irish affairs. Thomas Pelham, the ambitious British secretary of state for home affairs, now expected to see Ireland reduced to the status of an English county, particularly with regard to patronage. Hardwicke and Pelham struggled acrimoniously for control of Irish affairs until Hardwicke's brother succeeded Pelham, allowing Hardwicke a freer hand. The king declared the patronage binge over, saying that it should be "clearly understood that the union had closed the reign of Irish jobs." Ironically, passage of the Act of Union had been facilitated by the most liberal dispensation of titles, places, and pensions ever recorded in Ireland.[9]

Closure of the Irish Parliament and removal of Irish MPs to London had a devastating impact on Georgian Dublin. From one of the most elegant and sophisticated capitals in Europe, second only to London in the British Isles, it began a long decline. Without its own parliament, it could no longer draw hundreds of peers and bishops, along with their thousands of servants. While many still came to Dublin for the Social Season, where the lord-lieutenant hosted debutantes' balls, state balls, and drawing rooms from January until St. Patrick's Day (March 17) every year, many found them less appealing than in the days when they could sit in parliament for a session in College Green. Many of the leading peers, including the duke of Leinster and Viscount Powerscourt, almost immediately sold their palatial Dublin townhouses, Powerscourt House and Leinster House. Though many still flocked to Dublin every social season, many no longer bothered, or went to London. The loss of their revenue and that of their extensive staff hurt the Dublin economy severely. In 1808, David Digues La Touche, founder of the Bank of Ireland, acquired the Parliament House as the bank's new headquarters.

Revocation of martial law following the Treaty of Amiens, the short-lived truce between Britain and France, encouraged Dublin republicans to recommence harassing the loyalist community. On July 14, 1802, as republicans celebrated Bastille Day with huge bonfires, they clashed with loyalists at King William's equestrian statue at College Green. That October, young Robert Emmet, who would become the most iconic of Ireland's nationalist heroes and martyrs, returned to Dublin after two years abroad, including in Paris, where he had been avidly seeking support for Irish independence from Bonaparte and other leaders of the French consulate.[10] Emmet now assumed the role of chief military strategist of the United Irishmen. He and his associates hoped that war between Britain and France would be resumed within months. The following year, Emmet inherited £2,000 from his late father. He invested it and donations from well-laced sympathizers in setting up depots for stockpiling and manufacturing weaponry.

The United Irishmen initially expected to cooperate with British-based republicans led by Col. Edward Despard, but Despard was arrested. On February 21, 1803, Despard and his United Irish conspirators were sentenced to be hanged, drawn, and quartered in Southwark, London, for high treason for their plan to assassinate King George III. Despard's sentence was commuted to hanging and beheading since it was feared that the more draconian punishment might spark public dissent. He was executed in front of a crowd of at least 20,000 spectators.

Both Emmet and Despard were from Irish Protestant gentry families. The prosperous, well-connected Emmets had long ties to Co. Tipperary. Robert Emmet's father Robert was born there in 1729 and became the state physician of Ireland and, ironically, the man responsible for the health of King George III in the unlikely event of a royal visit to Dublin. Robert was the youngest of three extraordinary sons. His brilliant oldest brother, Christopher Temple Emmet, had been called to the Irish Bar at the astonishingly early age of twenty but died seven years later, in 1788, a year after he had been elevated to king's counsel. The next brother, Thomas Addis Emmet, trained as both a doctor and a barrister, was a member of the United Irishmen's executive directory, and had played a key role in shaping its ideology. At age fifteen, Robert entered TCD. Although he was a brilliant student and orator, he was expelled along with eighteen other students in 1798 for seditious activities.

Colonel Despard was the youngest of six surviving brothers in a Protestant D'Espard family of Huguenot descent, which had fled France two hundred years earlier. The oldest son inherited the family estate near Mountrath in Queen's County while all the others became British army officers. Despard had become friends with young Horatio Nelson when he was posted with his regiment to Jamaica in 1772. Three decades later, Nelson was a character witness for Despard at his trial, speaking of his "honorable and heroic actions" in the Caribbean. But the white slave owners of the Caribbean claimed that Despard was a traitor not only to his nation but to his race, since he had married a local woman and championed the rights of freed slaves. He returned to London to answer these allegations and dedicated himself to political reform.[11] Four years after Edward Despard was executed, John Head's daughter Mary would marry one of his brothers, Francis Despard, at Ashley Park.

In May 1803, Britain was once again at war with France, facing a powerful army led by a military genius, the "first consul for life" who would soon proclaim himself Emperor Napoleon. The French had occupied Hanoverian territories in Germany and fears of a

French invasion of Britain were running high—as were fears that France would inspire rebellion in Ireland, fears that were not unfounded. In Dublin, a stash of rebel gunpowder ignited accidentally on July 16 and destroyed the Patrick Street depot, forcing the hand of the rebel leadership. Emmet backed those who argued for an immediate insurrection in the hope that the French would sail to their aid without delay, bringing much needed muskets. His gamble proved unwise. Fatally, neither the French nor the muskets made an appearance. Cells of heavily armed men in private houses in Dublin prepared to attack Dublin Castle and other complexes on July 23, while thousands of rank-and-file followers from Kildare and Dublin were told to mass in Thomas Street to await final instructions at 6.00 p.m. Remarkably, no government troops were deployed despite a series of ill-disciplined attacks on army officers, magistrates, and loyalists earlier in the evening. The viceroy and Dublin Castle administration were highly criticized for this later and subsequent failures to prevent or adequately prosecute this latest insurgency.

Late that evening, Emmet marched with two hundred men toward the Castle but, in a tragic coincidence, Viscount Kilwarden, chief justice of the King's Bench for Ireland, his daughter, and his clergyman nephew, the Rev. Richard Wolfe, had decided to leave their suburban residence to take refuge in the Castle at that point. As they tried to move through the mob on Thomas Street, Kilwarden and his nephew were pulled from their carriage and piked to death. Kilwarden's daughter was allowed to escape to the Castle. Emmet did not witness this gruesome assault. With his small advance group of only about a dozen men, including six from Co. Kildare who had not lost faith in him or the plan of the rebellion, Emmet had left Thomas Street and was last seen marching toward the Castle and attempting to rally supporters to the cause among the crowds lining the streets. When this had little effect, he became convinced that the plan had gone wrong and gave the order to cancel the attack on the Castle. Apparently, he had decided it was best to regroup, formulate a better plan, and fight another day. Realizing the cause was lost, he left the scene and headed for shelter in the Wicklow Mountains south of Dublin. He was horrified when he heard that Kilwarden had been murdered.

On July 28, the Westminster Parliament rushed through emergency legislation permitting the imposition of martial law and suspension of habeas corpus in Ireland. There were mass arrests in Kildare, Wicklow, and County Dublin, filling regional jails, while the magistrates in the provinces were encouraged to smash the United Irish infrastructure using the carte blanche of martial law.[12] On August 25, after Emmet had moved to Harold's Cross, Dublin, to be near Sarah Curran, his fiancée—with whom he had hoped to escape to America—he was betrayed, arrested, and imprisoned.[13] His brother Thomas Addis Emmet, who brokered the United Irish alliance with France in 1803, sailed for America in October 1804 and established a lucrative legal practice in New York. Embittered by France's failure once again to support their Irish allies, Thomas Emmet later convinced himself that "Bonaparte was the worst enemy Ireland ever had."

Chief Justice Norbury and Robert Emmet: The Trial

John Toler, now Lord Norbury, and his fellow justices and the authorities at Dublin Castle were so enraged by Kilwarden's brutal murder that they were determined to punish Emmet for the crime, even though he was not there when it happened. Irish and British officials saw Emmet as a traitor, and perhaps as an instigator of the rebellion, and that was enough. For more than twelve hours on September 19 the packed courthouse at Green Street in Dublin heard clear evidence of Emmet's complicity in the insurrection of July 23. There was never any doubt about the outcome. The new attorney-general, Standish O'Grady, was in charge of the case. The counsel for the crown included William Plunket and four other barristers. Emmet was represented by the liberal barristers Peter Burrowes and Leonard MacNally (MacNally was later unmasked as a spy for the government). With considerable hyperbole, O'Grady presented overwhelming evidence for two and a half hours, arguing that the prisoner was an extremist who had "encompassed and imagined the death of the king, formed an alliance with the king's enemies, and had attempted to wage war against the crown."[14] Plunket, who had been a close friend of Thomas Addis Emmet at university, launched a brilliant but vitriolic two-hour attack on Robert's character and plans, for which Thomas never forgave him. As far as Plunket was concerned, Ireland was not capable of surviving "as an independent country for a year" without Britain's support. He argued that "God and nature have made the two countries essential to each other, let them cling to each other to the end of time, and their united affection and loyalty will be proof against the machinations of the world." The lord-lieutenant, Lord Hardwicke, who, as a devout Protestant, was sympathetic to Emmet, admiring him as a "perfect enthusiast," was anxious that the young man should "have a fair chance of being brought to a proper temper of mind before his death." But, as he wrote to his brother, "It is universally admitted that a more complete case of treason was never stated in a court of justice. [Emmet] produced no witnesses and made no defence."[15] The prosecution presented nineteen witnesses throughout the day.

Lord Norbury now gave his final speech to the twelve-man jury, which lasted one hour. He summarized all of the written evidence along with his own observations, reminding the jury of its duty: "If you have a doubt, you should acquit him. If you do not... you should find him guilty." The jury needed only a few minutes to reach its verdict. Now all that remained was the sentence to be declared. But first the clerk read the indictment of three counts for high treason, concluding with the standard question to the prisoner: "What have you, therefore, now to say, why judgement of death and execution should not be awarded against you according to law?"

In his famous speech from the dock—he was denied the time to prepare a text, although he had some notes—Emmet mounted a spellbinding defense of his character, determined to "unmanacle his reputation," as he put it. He was also keen to assert that he was not an agent of France: "I am charged with being an emissary of France, for the purpose of inciting insurrection in the country and then delivering it over to a foreign enemy. It is false! I did not wish to join this country with France..." He insisted that the rebellion was entirely for the cause of Irish liberty. At that moment Robert's brother Thomas was in Paris negotiating with the French, and Robert revealed to the courtroom that the French would not be allowed to land unless certain assurances that Ireland would be able to govern itself were received in advance. He cited the American

War of Independence as the model. "God forbid that I should ever see my country under the hands of a foreign power," he continued, explaining that he would not barter victory over the British for tyranny under the French. The behavior of France toward smaller nations was abhorrent to Emmet.

Norbury, scandalized by Emmet's pronouncement that "Our object was to effect a separation from England," interrupted numerous times. He warned Emmet that he was making "an avowal of dreadful treason...which I do believe has astonished your audience." Instead of being intimidated by the older man, Emmet launched into a savage critique of the British administration in Ireland. Norbury again interrupted when Emmet tried to give a complete account of the rebellion's objectives. According to historian and Emmet biographer Patrick Geoghegan, Norbury's antipathy threw Emmet's carefully thought-out structure into disarray. Now he turned to a justification of his right to speak: "You, my lord, are a judge. I am the supposed culprit. I am a man—you are a man also. By a revolution of power we might change places, though we could never change character." An exasperated Norbury thundered, "If you have anything to urge in point of law, you will be heard; but what you have hitherto said, confirms and justifies the verdict of the jury." Emmet returned to his role in the conspiracy, depicting himself as the sole organizer in an effort to spare the lives of other leaders. He attacked Norbury once again: "If I stand at the bar of this court and dare not vindicate my character, *what a farce is your justice!* If I stand at this bar and dare not vindicate my character, *how dare you calumniate it?*" Emmet denied that even Dublin Castle could "torture" any reference from his proclamation to infer that he was in favor of "barbarity and debasement."

Norbury now reminded Emmet that he was stretching the patience of the court and had no right to demand time to justify his actions: "Mr. Emmet...You have avowed and endeavoured to vindicate principles totally subversive of the government, totally subversive of the tranquility, well-being and happiness of that country which gave you birth, and you have broached treason the most abominable." In a patronizing attempt to elicit some expression of remorse, Norbury referred admiringly to Emmet's deceased father and oldest brother, the brilliant young barrister. "You, sir, had the honour to be a gentleman by birth, and your father filled a respectable station under the government...You had an eldest brother whom death snatched away...He left you a proud example to follow."

It was now almost 10.30 p.m. and the trial had begun at 9.30 a.m. Emmet, who had been standing throughout, was exhausted, and he began to conclude his address with the most famous and quoted passage of his entire speech:

> I have not been allowed to vindicate my character. I have but one request to ask at my departure from this world: it is *the charity of its silence*. Let no man write my epitaph; for as no man who knows my motives dares now vindicate them, let not prejudice or ignorance asperse them. Let them rest in obscurity and peace: my memory be left in oblivion and my tomb remain uninscribed, until other times and other men can do justice to my character. When my country takes her place among the nations of the earth, then, and not till then, let my epitaph be written. I have done.[16]

Norbury then sentenced Emmet to be hanged and beheaded for high treason, and Emmet bowed his head. According to one tradition, Norbury was so moved by the pathos of the scene and Emmet's final remarks that he burst into tears. While this seems to counter all the accusations of callousness made by his later critics, it also underscores his innate sympathy for a young man of his own class and education, a man of the Anglo-Irish elite.

Emmet's trial was preceded by the trials of fourteen tradesmen who had been arrested with pikes in their hands. All except two were found guilty and executed the day after their convictions. Four others were tried and executed later. While Emmet awaited execution in Kilmainham Jail that last night, he was apparently asked if he favored a French invasion. He replied with much vehemence, "I execrate the French, they are only actuated by a thirst for carnage and spoil, and I consider Bonaparte as the most savage tyrant by whom the word was ever disgraced." He also wrote to the chief-secretary William Wickham that he had hoped, if allowed "to proceed with my vindication, not only to have acknowledged the delicacy with which I feel with gratitude, that I have been personally treated; but also to have done the most public justice to the mildness of the present administration of this country, and at the same time to have acquitted them... of any charge of remissness in not having previously detected a conspiracy..."[17] The sentence was carried out the next day in front of a huge crowd on a specially constructed scaffold on Thomas Street. The United Irish Society ceased to exist as a formal organization in 1806.

In her book timed for the bicentenary of Emmet's trial and execution, historian Marianne Elliott traced "The Making of a Legend," demonstrating how Robert Emmet became the central figure in "the romantic drama of Irish history." As she put it, "the sentimental detail is remembered, the uncomfortable forgotten." Emmet's patriotic sacrifice, his courage, his gentility, and his unconsummated love for Sarah Curran were deeply affecting to Romantics like Thomas Moore, Robert Southey, Samuel Coleridge, and Percy Bysshe Shelley. On the other hand, Daniel O'Connell, another nationalist hero, was brutal in his assessment of the planning and execution of Emmet's rebellion when asked to reflect on it in 1842:

> There never was a more rash or foolish enthusiast. At the head of eighty men, armed only with pikes, he waged war on the most powerful government in the world, and the end of the mad fiasco was the murder of the best of the Irish judges, Lord Kilwarden, a really good and excellent man. His nephew, Wolfe, who happened to be in the carriage with him, was also murdered; for this murder, even if it stood alone, Emmet deserved to be hanged.[18]

Nonetheless, Thomas Madden Emmet's descendants in America made Robert Emmet an icon there, helping to energize the bitter anti-Englishness of developing Irish American nationalism. Emmet inspired the Fenian or Irish Republican Brotherhood of the mid-nineteenth century. Between 1898 and 1915, Thomas M.'s grandson, Dr. Thomas A. Emmet, published privately a stream of books arguing English tyranny in Ireland. There was saturation coverage of the rebellion and trial in the U.S. and Irish press and popular journals for the 1903 centennial and for years afterward, all in the form of romantic idealization. Seventy-four plays were devoted to Emmet in Ireland and America, particularly during the centenary decades of his birth and execution. Dr. Emmet launched an intense search for Robert Emmet's body but his grave has never been found—adding greatly to the Emmet mystique.

Patrick Pearse, architect of the 1916 Easter Rising, who revered Emmet, gave a famous speech at the Emmet Commemoration in the Academy of Music, Brooklyn in 1914. He acknowledged that "No failure, judged as the world judges such things, was ever more complete, more pathetic than Emmet's." "And yet," he argued, "he has left us a prouder memory than the memory of Brian victorious at Clontarf or of Owen Roe victorious at Benburb. It is the memory of a sacrifice Christ-like in its perfection." He concluded, "A traitor? No, but a true man. O my brothers, this was one of the truest men that ever lived. This was one of the bravest spirits that Ireland has ever nurtured. This man was faithful even unto the ignominy of the gallows, dying that his people might live, even as Christ died. Be assured that such a death always means a redemption."[19] Pearse carried the banner of Emmet's call for redemption to the Easter Rising two years later. In 2003, Ireland and the Irish in America celebrated their national hero in a year-long series of festivities, including at the statue of Emmet by Jerome Connor erected near the Irish Embassy in Washington, D.C., in 1966.

As for Norbury, his conduct of the trial, according to Patrick Geoghegan, closely followed the dictates of the law. Marianne Elliott believes that it was a fair trial. The exoneration of Norbury's conduct by United Irishman William St. John Mason, Emmet's first cousin, has been ignored and "the hanging judge" remains an arch villain in the Emmet patriotic legend.[20] Norbury was particularly reviled by Daniel O'Connell and his disciples during the battle for Catholic emancipation in the 1820s (see chapter 12). By the time of the 1903 centenary, according to Elliott, "Lord Norbury was deemed 'one of the most loathed of all names in modern Irish history...a descendant of the Cromwellian planters,' a 'Pontius Pilate' to the sacrificial Emmet. Popular legend had him dying without issue and drowning in the bath."[21]

As Irish officers and soldiers joined their counterparts in the British Army in the long-drawn-out battle against Napoleon's forces on the battlefields of Europe, life continued much as usual for the Head family, although marked by the death of John Head's wife. Phoebe Toler Head, youngest sister of John Toler, Lord Norbury, died at Ashley Park on September 30, 1804. She was buried in the church-yard of Castletown-Arra Parish on the shores of Lough Derg where the Heads of Derry Castle were traditionally buried. Her relation-ship with her brothers was of great benefit to her own family and, as the mother of a serving officer, she had no reason to be anything but proud of her brother's sentencing of Robert Emmet. John Head was now left arranging the marriage settlements for their four still unmarried children, including his officer son, and with increasing worries about the viability of maintaining his small estate with his limited resources.

A deed of defeasance dated January 7, 1807, shows that John was in debt to his brother-in-law, Otway Toler of Modreeny, and that these debts needed to be paid to secure the £3,000 marriage set-tlement owed for his daughter Mary's marriage to Frances Green Despard of Swanderry in Queen's County, captain in the Queens Co. Militia and a brother of Col. Edward Despard, whom the Brit-ish had executed for treason. This was the first sign of John Head's financial problems. Mary Head married Francis Despard two days later at Ashley Park. Four months after that, Otway Toler died, leav-ing his Modreeny property to his nephew Lt. Col. Michael Head.

On October 24, 1808, while stationed in England, thirty-nine-year-old Michael Head married twenty-seven-year-old Elizabeth Ravenscroft, the eldest daughter of Edward Ravenscroft of Port-land Place, London, a wealthy director of the East India Company, at Topsham Church, Exeter. The marriage license was registered in the names of Edward Ravenscroft and Lt. Col. James Thewles of the 4th Dragoon Guards, another member of the Irish landed gen-try and husband of Elizabeth's sister Frances. Edward Ravenscroft paid £8,000 (a huge sum) to Michael Head as marriage portion in return for collateral to support her if Michael should predecease her.[22] That year, Lt.-Colonel Head's eighteen-year-old nephew, John-Head Drought, joined the 13th Light Dragoons as a cornet [today's second lieutenant]. Drought would serve throughout the Peninsular War, at Waterloo, and at the capture of Paris.

Michael and Elizabeth's only child, William Henry Head, was born on September 8, 1809, in Twickenham, London. Earlier that year, the 13th Light Dragoons had been ordered from their stations in the West Country to locations near Hampton Court to prepare for embarkation to Portugal. This, therefore, seems the most likely period when Michael Head served as aide-de-camp to William Henry, duke of Clarence (the future King William IV), at Bushy House in Bushy Park in southwest London.[23] Exceedingly proud of his own warrior sons by the actress Dorothy [Dora] Jordan (with whom he lived happily for years before his 1811 marriage to Princess Adelaide of Sax-Meiningen) and always keen to demonstrate his support for the forces fighting Napoleon, the duke graciously agreed to be godfather to Michael Head's baby son, a fact that is commemorated by the engraving on the duke's baptismal gift of a pair of solid silver candlesticks. This explains the names given to the baby, a break from the traditional Michael or John. The candlesticks, later embellished with branches by a descendant, remain in the family.

William Pitt had returned to the premiership in May 1804, but he paid greatest attention to the Napoleonic threat for the remaining months left to him before his death in January 1806. The month he returned as prime minister, the Code Napoleon—a clearly written pan-European set of laws replacing a patchwork of feudal laws—went into force on the Continent. This came into force in May 1804. At the end of that same year, Napoleon was crowned emperor of France. Meanwhile, as an expert in finance who also served as chancellor of the exchequer, Pitt was able to muster Britain's superior industrial and financial resources to combat France. Though Britain's population of 16 million was barely half of France's 30 million, the British were able to subsidize a large proportion of the approximately 450,000 Austrian and Russian soldiers, who also opposed the French. With the assistance of Britain's well-organized business sector, the Royal Navy was able to vastly increase in size. In October 1805, it also achieved a transforming victory when a fleet under Admiral Horatio Nelson defeated a fleet of French and Spanish ships at Trafalgar, a triumph that established Britain as master of the seas for a century.

Although Napoleon achieved a stunning victory against Austria and Russia at Austerlitz (December 2, 1805), he subsequently made a series of mistakes. Hoping to isolate Britain economically by cutting off its trade with its ally Portugal, he invaded the Iberian peninsula, dethroned Spain's King Charles V, and replaced him with his own brother, Joseph Bonaparte, in 1808. This led to a mass revolt and guerilla warfare in Spain. During the course of the ensuing Peninsular War (1808-1814), the Spanish guerillas, aided by British troops under Wellington and their Portuguese allies, would drive the French out of the Iberian peninsula and eventually invade southern France. While large numbers of his troops were tied down in Spain, Napoleon made his fatal decision to invade Russia in 1812.

The last of the British merchants and their families in Portugal sailed home in February 1809, just ahead of Marshall Jean-de-Dieu Soult's devastating sacking of the port of Oporto. A year later, in early February 1810, the 13th Light Dragoons received the order to embark for service in Portugal. Boarding ship on March 5, they finally left from Portsmouth on March 14 and reached Lisbon on March 28. Attached to Maj. Gen. Sir Rowland Hill's division, along with four regiments of Portuguese cavalry under Lt. Col. Loftus Otway, another Anglo-Irish neighbor and distant relative of the Heads, the 13th had its first experience of bivouacking in July and crossed the Tagus River in August at Villa Valhe.[24] Lt. Col. Head took over command in June when the regiment's commander, Colonel Bolton, was promoted to major-general. Head was promoted to full colonel by brevet on July 25, probably following the highly successful outcome of a skirmish between a troop of the regiment and a French cavalry troop.[25]

For the next six months, beginning in September, the regiment suffered from the less glamorous afflictions of war—sickness, insufficient food and water, exhaustion, and boredom. After an exhausting 40-mile march north from their unhealthy camp site near Escalos de Cima, the regiment was held in reserve to "observe and check the movements of the enemy's cavalry" during the battle of Busaco (September 27).[26] Throughout October, the regiment joined all the other British/Portuguese troops as they marched south toward Lisbon, drawing Marshall André Masséna's army on to Wellington's defensive lines at Torres Vedras. The land there had been stripped bare of supplies and the French were expected to starve, but Masséna moved north to Santarem and fortified his position. The 13th marched north to Chamusca and wintered there from November 21, 1810 to March 10, 1811. They would soon be engaged in the battle that would make them both notorious and highly admired and enter Col. Michael Head's name into the contest of military reputation.

Campo Mayor, March 25, 1811

My grandfather considered his cavalry officer grandfather to be the ancestor in whom he could take some historical pride "as his name appears with creditable distinction in Napier's *Peninsular War*." Charles Head's account of the role of the 13th Light Dragoons in the Battle of Campo Mayor is incorrect in some respects.[27] But then he did not have the advantage of Ian Fletcher's meticulous revisionist account in an entire chapter of his *Galloping at Everything: The British Cavalry in the Peninsular War and at Waterloo 1808-15: A Reappraisal*. As Fletcher writes, "so controversial was Campo Mayor that it provoked a furious row between the two central characters, Robert Ballard Long and William Carr Beresford, as well as a most vitriolic correspondence which continued between the supporters of both men long after the war had ended." "Campo Mayor," he claims, "represents everything that is wrong with the way in which the British cavalry have been misrepresented in the Peninsula, owing to the failure on the part of successive historians to come up with anything other than flawed research."[28] Fighting words!

Marshall Soult was besieging Badajoz, in March 1811, when Wellington dispatched Gen. William Beresford with a force of about 18,000 men to relieve this strategically important border fortress between Spain and Portugal. Beresford's cavalry, including the 13th, was commanded by Brigadier General Long. Before Beresford got anywhere near the fortress, however, it fell to the French. Wellington ordered Beresford to continue south to attack Soult with a strict warning to keep a tight hold on his cavalry unless there was a favorable opportunity for attack. As Beresford's army approached the poorly defended town of Campo Mayor, he saw its French garrison taking off toward Badajoz. Long was sent with the light cavalry to cut off the French retreat, drive off their cavalry, and hold up the French infantry long enough for the British infantry and artillery to arrive on the scene.

Long later claimed that he asked Beresford if he should attack and, despite Wellington's warning, Beresford immediately detached Long with the five troops of the 13th Light Dragoons and the five weak squadrons of Loftus Otway's Portuguese cavalry to "turn and gain the rear of the town." From atop a ridge to the east of the town, Colonel Head was watching the French move slowly along the road when he was joined by Long who said, "Colonel Head, there's your enemy. Attack him," adding, "and now, Colonel, the heavy brigade are coming up on your rear, and, if you have an opportunity give a good account of these fellows." Head replied simply, "By gad, sir, I will."[29] That is the only quote directly attributed to Head throughout his service in Portugal.

The commander of the French 26th Dragoons, seeing the 13th forming to charge, turned his cavalry to charge too, both sides giving a great cheer as they did so. The two cavalry units crashed into each other and then wheeled around for a second charge. At this point, sabers were drawn and it became a furious melée of man-on-man combats between the two and half squadrons of the 13th Light Dragoons and the three squadrons of the 26th Dragoons. One of the 13th's officers later wrote: "The 13th behaved most nobly. I saw so many instances of individual bravery, as raised my opinion of mankind in general many degrees. The French certainly are fine and brave soldiers, but the superiority of our English horses, and more particularly the superiority of swordsmanship our fellows showed, decided every contest in our favour..."[30] During the fight, Corp. William Logan cut down one of the French dragoons, whereupon the 26th's commanding officer, Colonel Chamorin, engaged him in single combat to exact revenge for his slain countryman. Logan quickly got the better of the French officer, cutting him about the face and knocking his helmet off. Then he brought down his saber with a mighty blow, splitting Chamorin's skull completely open and exposing the brain.[31]

Scattered in all directions, the French dragoons took off along the road to Badajoz, hotly pursued for ten miles by the 13th, followed at first by Long at the head of the Portuguese squadrons, and then by Otway with his two squadrons. Having stopped to make sure the heavy brigade was following, Long discovered, to his astonishment, that they had moved off the battlefield—he later discovered that this was at the suggestion of one of Beresford's aides. Beresford then ordered the heavy brigade to halt, having been incorrectly informed by one of Long's aides that the 13th had been taken prisoner. The real problem was that neither Beresford nor Long was able to see what had actually happened. In fact, Head and the 13th Light Dragoons caught up with the section of the French convoy drawing sixteen heavy guns as well as mules, a number of wagons and immense quantities of stores, baggage of all descriptions, provisions, and horses—the entire camp equipage which had left Campo Mayor for Badajoz early that morning. The gunners and drivers surrendered without a fight and were sabered when they tried to escape. Troopers then mounted the mules to bring the guns back to Campo Mayor. In the meantime, Head rallied the 13th, some of whom had been wounded by artillery fire from Fort San Christobal as they approached the bridge across the Guadiana river to Badajoz.

At this point, Head must have wondered what had happened to the heavy brigade. His men were exhausted and their horses blown. Halfway back along the road, he met Lieutenant Holmes of the 13th who had been wounded during the first charge and had not taken part in the pursuit. Holmes told Head that the French hussars and infantry were approaching him and there were no Allied infantry or cavalry to give him support. A second messenger told him that the French cavalry had regained their arms and horses and were heading toward him. Head had no option but to order his men to abandon the guns and the rest of the captured convoy and ride back to the Allied lines. The French could not believe their luck. A force of two thousand infantry and one cavalry regiment were sent out from Badajoz to assist in bringing the guns back inside the town.[32]

The historian of the 13th records that Head was received with "coldness and somewhat bitter sarcasm" by Beresford, even though the men were "particular friends."[33] When Wellington received Beresford's misleading report of the battle, placing primary blame on the regiment and omitting the fact that he and Long had failed to send back-up, Wellington was so enraged that he issued a strong reprimand to Head and the 13th:

I wish you would call together the Officers of the dragoons and point out to them the mischiefs which must result from the disorder of the troops in action. The undisciplined ardour of the 13th [Light] dragoons, and 1st regiment of Portuguese cavalry, is not of the description of determined bravery and steadfastness of soldiers confident in their discipline and their Officers. Their conduct was that of a rabble, galloping as fast as their horses could carry them over a plain, after an enemy to whom they could do no mischief when they were broken; and the pursuit had continued for a limited distance, and sacrificing substantial advantages, and all the objects of your operation, by their want of discipline...If the 13th [Light] dragoons are again guilty of this conduct I shall take their horses from them, and send the Officers and men to do duty at Lisbon.

Wellington concluded this damning reprimand by praising the conduct of Col. De Grey and the heavy brigade, which had stood by doing nothing, illustrating how little Wellington knew of the true facts. He also issued a General Order which again censured the 13th "for their impetuosity" and want of discipline, although he did give the regiment credit for its "bravery and resolution."[34]

Stung by the tone and content of the rebuke and its obvious misrepresentations, the regiment's officers wrote a letter containing the full and true facts of their exploit. Signed by them all, it was given first to Long who passed it on to Wellington. Wellington read it, said if he had known the true facts, he never would have issued the rebuke but, characteristically, refused to withdraw it. Long read out Wellington's General Order censuring their conduct to all the regiment's officers but went on to say that he would never allow it to be entered in the regiment's Orderly Book. "I cannot find words to express my admiration of your gallantry on that occasion," he told them, "your discipline was most conspicuous; in short, gentlemen, the 13th Dragoons have gained such a laurel on that day as will never fade."[35] Meanwhile, the army sided with the 13th, feeling that they had been treated unfairly with the various reprimands. As Napier wrote, "the unsparing admiration of the whole army consoled them."

On April 16, 1811, Long and the 13th Light Dragoons—still under Head's command although his name is no longer mentioned—with the Portuguese cavalry, this time supported by heavy cavalry, met a French cavalry force at the village of Los Santos. When the French cavalry panicked and bolted, the British cavalry pursued them for ten miles, cutting down any stragglers. Long returned to Los Santos with his cavalry and over 150 prisoners. This time Beresford was able to see what was happening and allowed the heavy brigade to move forward. He also commended Long on the affair, passing this on to Wellington in his report. How different to the Campo Mayor failures.

By the end of 1811, Wellington replaced Beresford with Maj. Gen. Sir Rowland Hill as overall commander of the Allied army. After the battles and skirmishes involving the cavalry in 1811, the Allied army never returned to the wide-open undulating plains south of the Guadiana River, one of the few regions in the Peninsula where the cavalry could operate effectively, resulting in a long period of relative inactivity. In 1812, the 13th was moved to the 2nd Cavalry Division D under Long and continued there through 1813, even after Long returned to England. In 1813, Colonel Head became too ill to continue his grueling command in Portugal. Charles Head recalled being told by his father that his grandfather endured one three-week period without removing his riding boots; it was hardly surprising that he was a martyr to gout for the rest of his life. He was invalided home on June 4 having been promoted to major general.[36] Colonel Head was officially succeeded in command on July 4 by Lt. Col. Sir Patrick Doherty, another Irishman, who commanded the regiment at Waterloo in 1815. Michael Head was never again in active service, although he remained on the army's rolls.

When William Napier, historian of the Peninsular War and a veteran of that campaign himself, criticized Beresford's handling of the Campo Mayor affair in his third volume in 1828, a stream of pamphlets under the titles *Strictures* and *Further Strictures* was issued by supporters of both Beresford and Long, angrily refuting the charges made against their heroes. Napier answered their accusations in his *Justification of his History of the Peninsular War in Reply to the Further Strictures*, in which he provided his sources word for word. Then Beresford himself hit back in his *Refutation of Napier's Justifications of His Third Volume*, angrily dismissing those sources. The pamphlet war, amounting to over 750 pages of debate, lasted from 1831 to 1840. Specifically to what passed between him and Head back at the camp, Beresford wrote:

> In my brief observations to Colonel Head, the points mentioned with disapprobation were, the thoughtlessness evinced in the pursuit, and, as I then understood to be the case, the unmilitary and irregular manner in which it had been conducted. The courage of the troops was admitted, and most assuredly was not censured...After reading the evidence of Colonel Doyle, Sir L. Otway and Sir Henry Watson, on the pursuit of the 13th Light Dragoons, I am convinced that I was misinformed by General Long with respect to the disorder and irregularity that were said to have attended it...[and] I cannot coincide in the unqualified admiration which it has drawn forth from the historian...I had in General Long a most bitter, but secret enemy, who in his private letters maligned my conduct on every occasion...[37]

Colonel Head, by then promoted to lieutenant general, died in December 1827, too soon to learn of Napier's vindication of his and the 13th's actions, and the subsequent recriminations and counter-recriminations. According to his son, he "had preserved bitter memories of the incident." Sir John Fortescue, historian of the British Army, was to write in 1899: "Of the performance of the Thirteenth, who did not exceed two hundred men, in defeating twice or thrice their number single-handed, it is difficult to speak too highly. Indeed, I know of nothing finer in the history of the British cavalry...if he [Colonel Head] had been supported and his trophies had been secured, the action would no doubt have become a classic in the annals of cavalry."[38] Fortescue must have been referring to the number of the men of the 13th who were actually involved in this incident. His judgment must have given enormous pleasure to my grandfather and his youngest brother, regular army officers who were serving in India and the Boer War respectively at that time. However, it did not end there. Sir Charles Oman published his 7-volume *History of the Peninsular War* in 1902. In volume IV, he took the opposite view to Napier on the 13th Light Dragoons, failing to note that Wellington eventually withdrew his reprimand and giving all credit to Beresford for subsequently capturing Badajoz intact.[39] No wonder this episode and its aftermath are still being examined and argued by military historians today.

As usual, there were a great number of Irishmen involved in this particular incident and the later dispute. A high proportion of the 13th Light Dragoons was Irish, as were Beresford, Otway, Napier, and probably Holmes. Beresford was the illegitimate son of George de la Poer Beresford, earl of Tyrone and afterward 1st marquess of Waterford in the peerage of Ireland. Thus Beresford was the great-great-great grandson of Andrew Rickards, the one-time nemesis of Mayor Michael Head of Waterford (see chapter 6).[40]

During his absence in Portugal, there were a number of family occurrences in England and Ireland that might normally have required Colonel Head's attendance. His cousin, Michael Henry Head of Derry Castle, died on May 11, 1812 and, on Christmas Eve that year, young Phoebe Head was the third of John and Phoebe Head's daughters to marry at Ashley Park. Her groom was the Hon. Eyre Massy, a fifty-four-year-old widower with five daughters. Phoebe produced yet another daughter, Phoebe Letitia, and, at some point that year, John Head, now in his mid-seventies, married Maria Brookman, widow of Capt. William Brookman of the 11th Regiment and mother of a daughter.

The following years were to bring increasing headaches and financial problems for the Heads of Derry Castle and Ashley Park and untold numbers of other landlords, as well as their tenants and dependents—early harbingers of Ireland's infamous nineteenth-century "Troubles."

Chapter 12

Landlord Troubles and Catholic Emancipation

That county [Tipperary] is by far the most troublesome county in Ireland—and my firm belief is that the turbulence has become habitual, that it arises out of sheer wickedness—encouraged by the apathy of one set of magistrates and the help and connivance of another."
—Home Secretary Sir Robert Peel to Lord Francis Leveson-Gower, chief-secretary for Ireland, August 14, 1829.

While Colonel Head was fighting in the Napoleonic Wars, the gentry families of Co. Tipperary, including his relations, were increasingly under fire on ideological and economic fronts. Col. Head's uncle, the senior Michael Head of the family, who had been the proprietor of the Derry Castle estate since his father's death in 1749, was feeling the stress of financial pressures and rural disturbances before his own death in 1812. Michael Henry Head left a raft of encumbrances on his estate from supporting the debts of his apparently rambunctious oldest son, while setting up two younger sons and ten daughters in professions and advantageous marriages—and probably from expenditures on his demesne and estate way beyond the income it provided.

The two oldest sons, Michael Prittie (M. P.) Head and Henry Aldborough Head, both served in the 7th Light Dragoon Guards, another glamorous and expensive cavalry regiment. Michael retired early as a captain to support what seems to have been an irregular family and to play a role in county magistracy and Whig politics both before and after he inherited the estate. There is a mystery about Michael Prittie Head that may be impossible to solve. By this time, 1812, he was the father of six children, a son, Michael Henry, and five daughters, and yet there appears to be no record of his marriage before the first child was born in 1790 when he was only twenty years old. According to local lore, Michael Prittie Head was a strikingly handsome man, deserving the allusions of his middle name. But who was the mother of his children? Was she a beautiful local Catholic girl, perhaps even a servant, who was never accepted by his family? His only recorded marriage, to Mary Butler, a child-less divorced woman, did not take place until August 5, 1817, when his children were mostly grown.[1] This marriage was solemnized in Portpatrick on the west coast of Scotland, rather than at Derry Cas-tle or in Limerick, possibly a clandestine marriage away from his family.[2] Portpatrick is only 21 miles from the town of Donaghadee, Co. Down, on the Irish coast. The question of the legitimacy of Mi-chael Prittie Head's children would be raised in the 1837 Chancery Court case "Biggs v. Head and Others" (see chapter 13)."[3]

Of M. P. Head's two younger brothers, Henry Aldborough Head rose to lieut.-colonel and moved to County Antrim at some point following his marriage in 1808 to a daughter of Samuel de la Cherois Crommelin of Carrowdore Castle, Co. Down, establishing a branch of the Head family in Ulster.[4] The third son, John, was set for the ministry, like the first John Head in the seventeenth century. He graduated from TCD in 1804, was ordained into the Church of Ireland (C of I) in 1807, and from that year until his death at an advanced age in 1871 was perpetual curate of the Church of Balli-naclough, south of Nenagh. He would become an important and colorful figure as Dean of the Killaloe diocese of the C of I during the entire span of its devolution as Ireland's state religion. He mar-ried Susan Darby, a daughter of one of the long line of Protestant proprietors of Leap Castle in King's County (Offaly), on the bor-der with Tipperary. Their large family and many descendants re-mained in Co. Tipperary and elsewhere in Ireland or emigrated to Canada or Australia.

Michael Henry Head's heir, M. P. Head, who seems to have owed his father a considerable amount of money in the form of bonds, was evidently a far more liberal and politically involved character than others in his family. He was in fact a member of the reforming Whig Party (later the Liberal Party) favorable to the ide-als of the American and French Revolutions, as was his cousin, the

Hon. Francis Aldborough (F. A.) Prittie, younger brother of the 2nd lord Dunalley.[5] After the Catholic Relief Act of 1793 gave qualified Catholics the franchise, the large Catholic vote served to unite two major politically liberal interests in the county. F. A. Prittie led those interests in the north of the county and they were led in the south by Francis Mathew, who succeeded his father as viscount Landaff in 1806. Both men represented the county at Westminster, Mathew as an Irish representative peer in the House of Lords.

Before he succeeded to the Derry Castle estate, M. P. Head may have been persuaded by the serious rural disturbances that broke out in Co. Tipperary in 1807 to ally himself with other Tipperary landowners sympathetic to the Catholics agitating to replace the loathed tithe system, the single most radicalizing element of Protestant Ascendancy rule. John Poe, the high sheriff of Co. Tipperary that year, chaired a meeting of the "Noblemen, Gentry, and Freeholders of the County Tipperary, assembled by a Public Notice" at Cashel on Saturday, August 22, 1807. Among the several resolutions unanimously agreed to, three were moved by George Lidwell of Dromard, the previous high sheriff, and seconded by M. P. Head. One of them resolved "That from our local knowledge of the very heavy burdens imposed on the lower orders of the people by the present system of Tithes, we are confident that the abolition of Tithes, and the substitution of some other less exceptionable provision for the Clergy, would powerfully tend to promote tranquility, extend industry, and effect a co-operation of all classes against the common enemy."[6]

The "common enemy" was undoubtedly France. These Tipperary voters believed that "a Peaceable and legitimate pursuit...and a strict preservation of the good order and quiet now subsiding in this our country, will best tend to the speedy and satisfactory accomplishment of the abolition of Tithes." M. P. Head was one of a three-man committee appointed to collect information and assist the Co. Tipperary representatives in the united Westminster Parliament to achieve their objective.[7] On January 20, 1808, the *Clonmel Herald* published a declaration proclaimed by "the undersigned Protestant Noblemen, Gentlemen, and Freeholders of the County Tipperary, actuated at all times by cordial goodwill towards our Catholic countrymen and impressed by the wisdom and necessity of uniting all classes in the common defence of this crisis." Declaring that they "publicly and unequivocally" felt "no repugnance whatever to the measure of imparting to the Catholics of these realms an equal and full enjoyment of all the civil and military privileges, franchises, and advantages of our happy Constitution, upon equal terms with their fellow subjects, of what religious persuasion whatsoever," they concluded that they saw "no good cause for prolonging the restraints and disabilities which the Catholics suffer under the existing laws."

This declaration was signed by seven noblemen, the two liberal MPs for Co. Tipperary, and forty-four gentry and freeholders, including "Michael Head" (presumably Michael Prittie Head rather than his father, Michael Henry Head, whose politics are not known but liable to have followed those of his Tory nephew, the 2nd lord Dunalley). But nothing was achieved at this point and the quest to abolish the tithe system and achieve Catholic emancipation continued to fester into popular rebellion before resolution under the leadership of Daniel O'Connell.[8] O'Connell, who was born into a wealthy Catholic family in Co. Kerry, studied at Catholic schools in France, and was admitted to London's Lincoln's Inn in 1794, transferring to Dublin's King's Inn two years later. A brilliant barrister by training and a skilled radical politician by instinct, he rose to the leadership in 1808 of the Catholic Committee lobbying the Westminster Parliament.

In April, 1811, "a most representative meeting of independent & enlightened Protestants of the county of Tipperary" was held in Thurles with the aim of petitioning Parliament "to remove the penal and disabling statutes, which aggrieve and degrade the Roman Catholics of these realms adhering to the faith of their forefathers."[9] M. P. Head was among a large number of these liberal Protestants who signed this petition as the Westminster parliament was debating Henry Grattan's Catholic Emancipation bill; however, the upper echelons of the Irish Protestant government were vehemently against it.[10] The bill was dropped in May 1813 after the clause allowing Catholics to sit in parliament at Westminster—led by the Tory party from 1807-1826— was rejected in the Commons by just four votes.

Throughout 1811 and early 1812, Tipperary, Waterford, Kilkenny, and Limerick were terrorized by local factions, each of them bent on forcing lower rents and regulating tithes—and, in the process, destroying anyone who disagreed with them. Those who took lands at higher rent or paid the tithe faced murder or mutilation, while the gentry faced night raids for arms, mutilation of cattle, and destruction of property. "Faction fighting," stimulated by recreational violence and more seriously by class and religious conflict, reputedly began in Tipperary in 1805, and quickly spread all over Ireland. These fights between opposing factions of small farmers and laborers usually took place at fairs or other meeting places where there was copious alcohol, much of it illicitly produced. The usual talk of cattle and the weather was soon overtaken by fiery anticipation of the organized fighting about to take place. Opposing factions like the Caravats and the Shanavests, the "three year olds" and the "four year olds," the Black Hens and the Magpies, the Dingers and the Dowsers fought with long, specially prepared and polished sticks of oak, ash, holly, or blackthorn, the latter called an alpeen or shillelagh. A far more vicious weapon was the "loaded butt" whose stump end was hollowed out and filled with lead. Not surprisingly, deaths and serious injuries were commonplace as strong, inflamed Irishmen wielded these weapons against each other. Landlords tended to ignore faction fighting and even encourage it, believing it was preferable to see the Irish fighting among themselves than against the government. Civil authorities and the Catholic Church made serious efforts to stop the practice, with varying success, until Daniel O'Connell provided many of these fighters with a common cause in the 1820s.

Local banditti, who simply stole without any political aims, added to the disorder in the disturbed areas, including Co. Tipperary. In 1813, Robert Peel, the Tory MP for Cashel and a young and passionate defender of the English and, therefore, Irish Protestant constitution, arrived in Dublin to assume the office of chief-secretary for Ireland.[11] Peel shortly became convinced that the traditional system of local leadership by country gentlemen had broken down, that too many of the local magistrates were corrupt, partisan, incompetent, or "supine with timidity." Such timidity was hardly surprising, since magistrates lived with the fear that attacking local insurrectionary forces could result in violent reprisals; having their crops destroyed, their trees cut down, their fences leveled, and their livestock wounded or driven off, or, worst of all, death for themselves and perhaps their families. In January 1813, the Tipperary magistrates met at Fethard to work out a plan of action against the current disturbances, but the meeting was thinly attended and accomplished nothing.[12]

At the same time, the regular army that generally policed the country had been severely reduced as men were dispatched to oppose Napoleon's armies and serve in the War of 1812 against the United States. The militia, which remained in Ireland and was dominated by Catholics, was considered to be unreliable, while the presence of a predominantly Protestant volunteer yeomanry was too often inflammatory to the Catholic rural population, and prone to having its arms stolen by rebels. By May 1812, the Irish government faced the reality that London, influenced by the need for rigid economy after the ruinous costs of the Napoleonic Wars, had decided to limit the peacetime military establishment in Ireland to fewer than 30,000 men and disband the militia. The government in Ireland had to compete with the demands for occupation forces in France and British commitments elsewhere.

By early winter of 1813, the relationship between the Irish government at Dublin Castle and the magistrates in the disturbed areas had deteriorated into mutual distrust. The government in Ireland, which again feared a revolution if France decided to "provide assistance" to the disaffected, belatedly investigated the magistracy in 1815. The findings were both embarrassing and shocking: of 4,175 magistrates listed for Ireland, 557 were dead (perhaps the recently deceased Michael Henry Head was among them), 1,355 were no longer resident in Ireland, and were no longer acting as magistrates, leaving only 1,952 for the whole country.[13] With new reports of a possible major uprising, Peel and Attorney-General William Saurin argued for a bill to create a new civil police force in Ireland, to be called the Peace Preservation Force (PPF). The bill, which was passed at Westminster in July 1814, was extremely unpopular with the resident magistrates. Under the bill's provisions, a county's lord-lieutenant could appoint an outside chief magistrate and an "extraordinary" establishment of police (a clerk, a chief constable, and up to fifty sub-constables to be chosen from discharged soldiers and militia men) to any disturbed area, with salaries and costs of operation to be paid for out of local rates as long as the force was needed. Later that month, parliament passed another bill reenacting the Insurrection Act for three years, for emergency use only. This act imposed a sunset-to-sunrise curfew and summary justice for lawbreakers.

Tipperary was the scene of the first attempt to apply the Peace Preservation Act. A series of exceptionally violent outrages there in the spring of 1814 had culminated in the assassination of a "Mr. Long," one of the more active Tipperary magistrates. In mid-September, when the lord-lieutenant proclaimed the barony of Middlethird around Cashel to be in a state of disturbance, it received a force of twenty ex-cavalry sergeants under the direction of the barony's chief magistrate, Richard Willcocks. When this decision sparked a storm of criticism among them, forty magistrates assembled at Cashel and asked the Irish government to apply the Insurrection Act. At that time, Peel was absent on the Continent—he had challenged Daniel O'Connell to a duel after a series of insults from the pugilistic Irishman. The duel was aborted and Peel made it clear to the Tipperary magistrates on his return that their request was refused due to insufficient evidence.[14]

This was the state of the county when John Head's son, the other Michael Head, newly promoted major general, returned to Ashley Park with his wife Elizabeth and five-year-old William Henry around 1814 bearing the badges and honors of warfare and the polish of cosmopolitan society. He had been away from home for most of his adult life. Now, at age forty-six, and with his health permanently damaged by the rigors of the Peninsular War, he must have been dismayed by the dangerous state of affairs in Co. Tipperary as well as the reality of his own and his father John Head's diminished financial resources. His mother, Phoebe Toler Head, had died in 1804 so that his father, a minor landowner in comparison to his older brother, Michael Head of Derry Castle, had less recourse to the Toler family for help with his tangled financial affairs. John Head's daughters' marriage settlements, the weddings, and the ruinous expenses of a cavalry officer son on active duty, required extravagant outlays and were charged to the small Ashley Park estate or on credit. But a principal complicating factor in John Head's private and financial affairs was that, in 1811, at the age of seventy-four, he took as his second wife a young widow, Maria Brookman, of no fortune or social connections but who was ambitious for herself and her young daughter. A clash between his heir and his pushy new wife was inevitable.

On June 15, 1815, Allied forces under Wellington dealt Napoleon a final blow, defeating his army at the battle of Waterloo. This ended more than two decades of intermittent combat between France and the European powers, but peace had some unfortunate consequences. Landowners and strong farmers had flourished during the Napoleonic Wars by supplying the armies with horses, cattle, sheep, and grain. Agricultural economist Arthur Young considered that Irish rents had doubled in twenty-five years, and they rose again until the end of the Napoleonic Wars—encouraging extravagant spending by landlords. After Waterloo, however, the inflationary bubble burst. Rents were no longer rising, and all over the country they were in arrears and becoming increasingly difficult to collect, even on well-managed estates. The most extravagant gamblers and spendthrifts became spectacularly bankrupt, while many small or moderate landowners, among them John Head of Ashley Park, were in serious financial trouble. It never occurred to gentlemen to save, and they began to suffer from a lack of easily available funds.[15]

Tipperary was one of the southern counties that experienced a disastrously high growth of the Catholic rural population through the first half of the century. The Catholic population in North Tipperary was, by the end of the Napoleonic wars, nearly twelve times as numerous as the Protestant population. This presaged disaster, for it accelerated subdivision of holdings and increased reliance on potatoes, producing deepening misery for the Irish poor, at least one-third of whom were dependent on the crop.[16] Moreover, in several Irish counties, those who relied on the potato for subsistence—generally those at the bottom of the socioeconomic scale—were aggrieved by the tithe on potatoes; Catholic smallholders had to give part of their crop to the local Protestant clergy.[17]

While peace was restored following a brief application of the Peace Preservation Act in the South Tipperary barony of Clanwilliam after the assassination of an influential magistrate in late 1815, peasants faced the potential of famine the following year. Rain and floods at harvest time ruined the potato, hay, and grain crops leading to soaring food prices and heavy unemployment. Experts now believe that the "year without summer," which affected the whole of Europe, was caused by the eruption of Tambora volcano on Sumbaraw Island, Indonesia, in April 1815. Throughout Ireland, farmers struggled as harvests failed. Then, partial failure of the potato crop in 1817 and a typhus epidemic threatened the rural poor with starvation. Drought and another typhus epidemic followed in 1819. Through all of these life-threatening problems, the government at Dublin Castle and Westminster dispensed considerable funds to prevent disaster.

In the midst of this chaos and misery, John Head was struggling to sort out his personal finances as his health was failing. A tripartite deed of settlement dated April 27, 1815 confirms that his son, the general, had returned home to Ashley Park with his family. Subsequent deeds indicate that the general and his stepmother did not get on. To resolve this problem, John Head placed his property of Rockview in trust with the understanding that he and his wife Maria would live there for the rest of their lives. Through the terms of the deed, he hoped to secure from his remaining capital of £2,500 and his lands of Ballythomas and Drumniscart a £300 annuity for Maria, in half-yearly payments from his death, and a £130 annuity for his still unmarried youngest daughter Catherine after payment of his wife's annuity.[18]

The 1815 deed jumped the gun over the Rockview property since, in his will dated February 25, 1816, John described himself as "late of Ashley Park but now of Nenagh in the County of Tipperary Esq." He seems to have known he was mortally ill as he sought to guarantee the regular payment of the annuity to Maria, "his dearly beloved wife," and declared that he had entered into an agreement with the trustees for the repurchase of the Rockview lands and had paid part of the purchase price. As soon as he or his wife had paid the remainder, the property was to be hers and her descendants' as well as all his household furniture, cars, carriages, and stock following his death.[19] He confirmed that his son was indebted to him for a bond of £1,000 and that this should be repaid with interest to his wife. John Head died less than a year later in January 1817, but the will was not decreed by the Court of Prerogative Wills to Maria Head until July 16, 1822.[20]

Ashley Park would soon be lost to the Heads, and the Derry Castle estate was also floundering in debt as hard times continued. In October 1819, the *Dublin Evening Post* announced that considerable lands in Cos. Waterford and Kilkenny belonging to Michael Prittie Head of Derry Castle but originally acquired by his ancestor Michael Head of Waterford City, as well as 900 acres of County Tipperary land, were to be sold "for the purpose of Paying off Incumbrances."[21] Interested parties were to contact Michael P. Head at Derry Castle or his brothers-in-law Thomas Forde and William Gore in Dublin. Losing these lands must have reduced the number of M. P. Head's freeholders and, therefore, the political clout he had exercised, but he was legally and morally required to meet the demands and needs of his father's and his own large families. Just the year before, on October 1, 1818, M. P. Head took over the chair at a general meeting of the "Friends of the Independence of the County of Tipperary," a Whig party organization whose secret committee had secured ample funds to defray the expenses of a politically independent candidate for the county. The Friends of Independence were now "earnestly requested to prepare their Freeholders for Registry with as much care and as little delay as possible."[22]

Not all the Heads were facing a loss of status due to financial problems, at least at this stage. Gen. Michael Head's nephew, John-Head Drought, was high sheriff of King's County in 1821 and gave that county's welcoming speech to Great Britain's new king George IV when he visited Dublin that year.[23] The king and the new lord-lieutenant, the marquess of Wellesley, were presented with loyal addresses by Catholic representatives.[24] But the brief period of good will following the king's visit ended in October 1821 with a series of events that led to a two-year period of almost uninterrupted agrarian outrage.

The latest wave of famine lasted over four harvest years (September 1819-August 1823), so that the basic causes for agrarian unrest seem to have been economic, due to increased cost of food, starvation, and the landlords' determination to continue collecting the high rents that their tenants could no longer pay. At the same time, the Protestant clergy and other tithe holders were determined to resist efforts to lower or ban the collecting of tithes that supported them. The unusually wet autumn of 1821 caused much of the Irish potato crop to rot in the ground; by the following May (1822), Clare, Cork, Mayo, Limerick, Kerry, Roscommon, and Sligo were faced with famine. Once again, the government acted to provide relief for famine victims; considerable sums of money were allocated, primarily to provide employment for those unable to buy food.[25] Some, however, were unimpressed by the grants and subscriptions coming from Great Britain. The Irish author Henry Stratford Persse reported to his sons in February 1822, "English generosity has interposed and sent relief, and what relief is it? Some of the food that, in our poverty early this season, we were obliged to send away, even though we knew we would want it in the spring." As historian Paul Bew has noted, this was the beginning of the argument that Ireland should not export food during a famine.[26]

It was at this point that M. P. Head built an impressive new mansion on his Derry Castle demesne to replace the stone house built by his father.[27] During a partial famine, public works provided extensive employment throughout the south and west of Ireland. Head might have wished to provide employment to his own tenants in the hope that it would avert starvation and local violence. A contemporary description of the new house, which was burned in 1872, indicated a fortress-like façade. This was not surprising since most landlords felt threatened during this troubled time, their houses often had steel shutters affixed to the windows and the landlords themselves were heavily protected by armed guards when they traveled. Whether or not Head's decision to build a large new house was for altruistic reasons, it may have exacerbated the class division that was inherent in all landlord-tenant relations, a social divide which was not only based on economic differences but also on cultural and religious inheritance. There was an unbridgeable economic gap between the carefully laid out and groomed landlord demesnes and the humble cabins of the small farmers and laborers.[28]

Concurrent with the latest wave of famine and agricultural disturbances, the ongoing battle for Catholic emancipation became even more insistent under the leadership of Daniel O'Connell and a group of fellow barristers. In 1823, O'Connell created the Catholic Association as a pressure group against the British government. The following year, O'Connell and the Catholic Church established the Catholic Rent of a penny a month, payable by all who subscribed to the Catholic Association program, to raise funds to help finance the Catholic Association's efforts. The Catholic Association comprised a mixture of merchant, professional, and landowning Catholics. Although some of the gentry were relatively conservative, O'Connell held an enormous influence over the Society and largely dictated the policies it pursued. While it was radical in its approach to winning Catholic emancipation, it also seemed to be extremely loyal to the Crown and thus more likely to gain the support of MPs in Westminster. Association-sponsored rallies and marches achieved impressive results, as did the mobilization of the Catholic forty-shilling freeholders at election time. In the meantime, the Church of Ireland rector at Borrisokane, where two members of the Head family had been rectors in the past, reported that 681 parishioners (small farmers and tradesmen) had departed for North America. Many more would follow.[29]

All too aware of religious and economic tensions between the Catholics and Protestants in Munster, M. P. Head had been advocating tithe reform and, presumably, Catholic emancipation for many years. However, the law-and-order Toler side of the Head family was against these measures. John and Michael Head of Ashley Park had both voted against the Union, perhaps wary of the carrot of Catholic emancipation made by the British government; the general was certainly a Tory under the influence of his uncle, John Toler, Lord Norbury. Bolstered by long-lasting Tory governments at Westminster and the Castle, the seat of Irish government, Norbury was still chief justice of the court of common pleas and, as an ultra-Tory and virulent opponent of Catholic emancipation, he was a thorn in the side of its proponents. His greatest adversary, O'Connell, deemed him "an especial object of abhorrence." Although he found Toler "a *pretty* gentleman at the Bar," he thought him ridiculous as a judge; after the aging Toler became "cruelly deaf," O'Connell took to referring to him as "the thing."[30] As one of Norbury's counsel (counselors at law), whom Irish Catholics nicknamed "Counsellor," O'Connell later was appalled by the chaotic manner in which Norbury ran his court.

The contemporary biographer and dictionary compiler John Gorton noted that Norbury was "chiefly known from his reputation for wit and drollery." Although many puns and jokes were wrongly attributed to him, "It is a matter of history that the court of common pleas of Dublin was frequently thronged with idlers attracted by the amusement which was to be found in the humorous conduct of its proceedings. The spirit of the judge naturally extended itself to the counsel...who played against each other, and occasionally involved the court in such a clamour, that it was difficult to determine whether the exclamations of the parties, the protestations of the witnesses, the cries of the counsel, the laughter of the audience, or the Stentorian voice of the chief justice predominated." After a trial closed, Norbury's delivery of his charge was an exhibition in itself. Seeming at first to favor the defendant, he then proclaimed the fatal "but,'" claiming to enter more deeply into the case while "flinging his judicial robe half aside, and sometimes casting off his wig, starting from his seat, and throwing off a wild harangue" in which "little law, method, or argument could be discovered." He also threw in anecdotes from his early life, various jests, and "sarcastic allusions to any of the counsel who had endeavoured to check him during the trial" as well as very well delivered quotations from Milton and Shakespeare.[31] In her 1977 paper for the *Dublin Historical Record*, Moira Lysaght was generally acid in her characterization of Toler. However, as she wrote, "He was a man made up of strange contradictions: his jovial appearance and manner, as well as his reputation for being a benevolent landlord, and a kindly master, are at such variance with his conduct in the administration of law that he would qualify for an additional title—the Irish 'Jekyll and Hyde.'"[32]

No wonder the competent and politically radical Daniel O'Connell became determined to unseat this increasingly incompetent but still powerful member of the Protestant Ascendancy. Norbury's position eventually became untenable, even to his strongest supporters, especially with the British government's aim of establishing a better relationship with the Catholic majority. The discovery in 1822 of a letter written to him by William Saurin, the attorney-general for Ireland and a bigoted opponent of religious toleration, further tainted Norbury's reputation. In the missive, Saurin urged Norbury to use his influence with the Irish Protestant gentry who made up local juries against the Catholics. At Daniel O'Connell's instigation, the case of Saurin's letter was brought before the Westminster parliament. Saurin, who owned considerable lands in Co. Tipperary and whom O'Connell called "our mortal enemy," was dismissed from his post. But Norbury survived the Saurin scandal as well as an 1825 petition drawn up by O'Connell, which called for his removal on the grounds of him falling asleep during a murder trial and later being unable to present any account of the evidence given.[33]

While Toler succeeded in remaining chief justice, Ireland endured another murderous uprising associated with a possibly mythical figure called Capt. Rock. The agrarian rebellion of 1821-24 began in Co. Limerick with the harsh and insensitive behavior of magistrate Alexander Hoskins. After his popular and "magnificently indulgent" predecessor was fired for incompetence, Hoskins was imported from London in 1818 as chief agent for absentee landlord Viscount Courtenay's grossly mismanaged 34,000-acre estate. Although he lacked any previous land agency experience in Ireland, Hoskins was apparently instructed to raise the current income of the property and to lower the appallingly large arrears that had accumulated.[34] He immediately increased the annual rent by as much as 40 percent and canceled the generous abatements on rents granted between 1814 and 1818. The estate lands were centered on Newcastle, near the Limerick border with Co. Kerry, and Hoskins doubled the rents on the lands adjacent to the town. These were "the principal means of support to the inhabitants of a town perfectly insulated and totally destitute of trade or business."[35] Lastly, he attempted to collect arrears from defaulting tenants. In the meantime, he and his son and daughter took up residence in "The Castle" in Newcastle, where Hoskins proceeded to pursue a wildly extravagant gentry lifestyle.

When the abused tenants, especially the substantial middlemen, often Protestants—some of whom were relatives of the previous agent—began protesting, they were harshly punished or intimidated by Hoskins. There were multiple failed attempts to assassinate him but it was his son Thomas who was fatally shot. A blacksmith, Patrick (Paddy) Dillane, who took the lead in this and other fatal shootings of men thought to be allied with Hoskins, was reputedly the first "Captain Rock."[36] The rebels lit signal fires on hilltops to communicate and celebrate the killing of their detested enemy. By the end of October, four or five thousand troops under the command of Maj. Gen. Sir John Lambert were stationed in the town of Newcastle near the Kerry border.

The vicious infection spread to Co. Tipperary when, in the early morning of November 19, 1821, local "Whiteboys" in search of weapons burned the thatched house and outbuildings of wealthy farmer Edmund O'Shea near Mullinahone. Sixteen people, including seven family members, five of them children, six male laborers, and three female servants, perished in the fire. In fact, it may have been Rockites (followers of the aforementioned Capt. Rock) from Co. Limerick who were the perpetrators as they traveled up the Shannon toward Nenagh. Within two weeks, other Limerick Rockites, a striking number of whom were very young men, began to post notices in the area of Cashel, Cahir, and Clonmel "demanding large reductions in tithe rates, forbidding the payment of tithe arrears, and setting forth an approved scale of rents." This area became the cockpit of agrarian activities once again. However, there was generally little Rockite unrest where the Heads had their lands, in the baronies of Upper Ormond, Lower Ormond, and Owney and Arra, which were separated from the rest of Tipperary by a chain of mountains.[37]

There were exceptions. In parts of Northern Tipperary, the presence of Orange Order lodges stimulated a militant Catholic reaction in the form of Ribbon lodges or committees based in the towns. A local Protestant minister reported that Rockites using a sectarian oath were mobilizing recruits around Ballingarry between Borrisokane and Birr.[38] On January 25, 1822, the Catholic *Dublin Evening Post* reported from Nenagh, "This town is in a dreadful state at present" following a mortal confrontation between Catholic townspeople and a corps of largely Protestant yeomen. "We would only impress upon the government the necessity of disbanding the corps. Nenagh, containing nearly 7,000 inhabitants, was one of the most peaceable in the kingdom, till arms were put into the hands of these people. If we are to have the insurrection act, let it be executed by the regular military."[39]

The insurrection act introduced in February 1822 again required a sunset-to-sunrise curfew and summary justice for lawbreakers, of whom about 330 a year were being transported to Australia for seven years. A general revision of the magistracy was also under way. In May, according to a Lady Spencer, "13 magistrates 'with [Francis A.] Prittie at their head' applied repeatedly to the Irish government for military assistance under the terms of the Insurrection Act without success, whereupon Prittie wrote to the Castle and threatened that if immediate attention was not shown to the application...he would bring the case before Parliament; upon which he was instantly attended to and obtained the relief the district required."[40] On May 22, 1822, the *Freeman's Journal* reported, "General Michael Head has been appointed a Justice of the Peace for the County of Tipperary." As a senior military officer, General Head's authority was needed. Whatever the state of his private affairs, he was clearly not a bankrupt since this would have disqualified him as a magistrate. It is likely that both his liberal cousin, Francis Prittie, and his conservative uncle, John Toler, regarded him as a Tory bulwark on the Tipperary magistracy. According to historian Victoria Crossman, "On a number of occasions over the course of the century the inactivity of local magistrates coupled with doubts about their efficiency and reliability led to the appointment of military officers to the commission. This was done in counties placed under emergency powers in 1822 and 1833, and during the Fenian outbreak."[41]

In August 1823, a special session under the insurrection act was held at Nenagh to hear the complaint of attorney-at-law Gleeson against the Nenagh police for the rough way in which he was arrested and treated for being out after curfew. Among the magistrates on the bench were Major-General Head, Sir Robert Waller, Lord Dunalley, Anthony Parker, and Thomas Ryder Pepper.[42] General Head also served on the grand jury at the Clonmel assizes on March 24, 1824.[43] Michael Prittie Head, however, seems to have resigned or been removed from his commission as justice of the peace, perhaps due to his Whig sympathies. It is notable how many of these magistrates were descendants of the original Cromwellian land grantees. It was evidently a commonplace at that time that the peasantry traced a belief that the land was rightfully theirs back to the seventeenth-century Protestant land settlement of Tipperary and that they "know even the individuals who are descended from the soldiers of Cromwell."[44] Many threatening notices that were posted by Rockites predicted the demise of the Protestantism espoused by these descendants.

Over the two and a half years of the rural insurrection, there were ninety murders in six southern counties, all attributed to the Rockites who brutally terrorized across classes—attacking landlords, magistrates, informers, and wealthy Catholic farmers. Up to a thousand victims may have been badly beaten or injured. A special commission in Cork charged two hundred men with Rockite or similar Whiteboy activity but just fifteen were hanged. Daniel O'Connell defended many of the accused, winning many reprieves or reductions in sentences and becoming a hero to the small farmers and laborers who were the principal perpetrators.

In the meantime, various decrees for the sale of Ashley Park appear to support my grandfather Charles Head's understanding that his grandfather and family remained at Ashley Park until its sale or rent. Ten days after the Court of Prerogative Wills confirmed for Maria Head the validity of her late husband's will, *Saunder's News-Letter* of Dublin published a July 20, 1822 High Court of Chancery decree for renting Ashley Park for three years while a chancery case was under consideration. Maj. Gen. Michael Head was the plaintiff, while his brother-in-law, the Hon. Eyre Massey, and others were defendants. The dwelling house, offices, garden, and demesne lands of Ashley Park, containing about 115 acres, as well as five acres of the Drumniscart lands, were to be let to the highest and fairest bidder. Maria Head was living in Dublin at that time. On January 30, 1824, *Freeman's Journal* reported the marriage of Maria's daughter Jane Brookman, described as "step-sister to Major-General Head of Ashley Park, County Tipperary," to John Kirwan Esq., eldest son of Francis Kirwan of Glann, Co. Galway.[45] It is unlikely that General Head attended this marriage.

Several editions of the *Dublin Evening Post* that June announced that William Henn, one of the Masters of the Court of Chancery, would on June 11 "set up and sell by Public Cant the Town and Lands of Ashley Park." Henn reported that the house and offices were in perfect repair and the demesne lands were highly ornamented with Plantations and fully grown timber "and fit for the reception of any Nobleman or Gentleman who may become the Purchaser."[46] Ashley Park house and related lands were sold to George Guy Atkinson of South Park by deed of conveyance on August 27, 1824.[47] Gen. Michael Head and his family then moved to Modreeny, an estate that had been willed to him by an uncle, Otway Toler, in 1808. William Henry Head was about fifteen years old and apparently never forgot his happy boyhood at Ashley Park.

The hard work and canny politics of Daniel O'Connell were beginning to gather fruit. In 1825, the Catholic Association achieved its first parliamentary electoral victory in Waterford by using priests to canvas every freeholder. The Association's candidate, Villiers Stuart, was a liberal Protestant landlord like Michael Prittie Head (who had only recently divested his Waterford lands). However, the election descended into sectarianism when Stuart's opponents, the Tory Beresford family, were denounced as "Orange bloodsuckers," enemies and exploiters of the Catholic people, and bigots. The election was conducted in an orderly fashion, but Protestants in Waterford, who had been able to call the constituency their own since 1690, were now on the defensive.[48] This must have resonated with the Head family: not only were they descended from seventeenth-century Protestant mayors of Waterford City, but Gen. Michael Head's nemesis at the battle of Campo Mayor was William Carr Beresford, illegitimate son of the 1st marquess of Waterford (see chapter 11).

On May 27, 1825, Michael Head was promoted to lieutenant general. The following July, his son William Henry, now sixteen, entered TCD as a *Socii Comitate* or Fellow Commoner—a designation for sons of the wealthy who, in return for double fees, were allowed to complete the college course in three years instead of four. Although William Henry did not get his B.A. until 1830, he was an outstanding student, winning a gold medal for Classics. He was called to the Irish Bar in 1833. He later told his son Charles that his father was extremely tough and mean about funding his college education and living costs in Dublin. However, funds may have been limited since the general was permitted to sell his army commission five months after his son entered TCD.

By 1827, Co. Tipperary was in an anarchic state once again following the murder of a land agent, execution of the assailant, and the subsequent assassination of a brother of the person who identified the killer. The magistrates in Clonmel twice that year petitioned the Irish administration for reimplementation of the insurrection act, calling the county in October "a vast depot of arms."[49] Home Secretary Robert Peel speculated once again that the magistrates were the weak link in the administrative chain. In August 1829, he wrote to the new Tory chief- secretary, Lord Francis Leveson-Gower, "That county is by far the most troublesome county in Ireland — and my firm belief is that the turbulence has become habitual, that it arises out of sheer wickedness — encouraged by the apathy of one set of magistrates and the help and connivance of another."[50] The turbulence and his ruined health proved too much for Lt. Gen. Michael Head, JP. He died, reputedly from gout but more likely from something like phlebitis, at the end of 1827.[51] His gravestone in Modreeny churchyard reads, "Underneath lieth the body of Michael Head Esquire of Modreeny, a Lieutenant General in His Majesty's Service. Who after a lingering illness departed this life on 11th of December 1827 aged 61. His afflicted widow has caused this stone to be erected over the precious remains of one of the best of husbands." Gen. Head's will, leaving his estate to his only son, was proved on May 22, 1829.[52]

Several months before General Head's death, on May 22, 1827, the new British prime minister, George Canning, advised King George IV on the progress of negotiations whose chief object was to obtain the resignation of John Toler, Lord Norbury, the man whose lofty position had contributed a good deal to his nephew's success: "It is obvious that Lord Norbury knows the full value of that retirement, & is resolved to make the best market of it that he can." Canning, who favored Catholic emancipation, was desperate to establish the prominent Irish lawyer and Whig politician Lord

William Plunket as chief justice of common pleas before the Irish chancellorship became vacant. In that way, Plunket would be well positioned to succeed as Lord Chancellor, which he did in 1830. "Lord Norbury," Canning wrote, "old as he is, is in robust health; & may yet set the Government at defiance for many years...Lord Norbury's incapacity is of that doubtful & desultory sort, which it would be very difficult to establish by satisfactory proof—to his prejudice—in any inquiry that must precede a Bill [to remove him]; while on the other hand it is such as exposes, by his continuance on the Bench, the administration of publick justice in Ireland to ridicule & contempt."[53] Toler was finally induced to resign as chief justice of the court of common pleas later in 1827, when the Whigs returned to power, and compensated with a pension of £3,046 a year and an earldom. Daniel O'Connell, who had been trying to have him ousted for years, remarked that "he was bought off the bench by a most shameful traffic." Canning died on August 8, 1827, and he was succeeded as prime minister by the duke of Wellington, an anti-Catholic Tory.

On July 5, 1828, Daniel O'Connell was elected to the Westminster Parliament for Co. Clare, achieving an overwhelming victory (2,057 to 982) against the Tory government candidate, William Vesey Fitzgerald. Although Fitzgerald was a supporter of Catholic emancipation and personally popular, O'Connell had reminded the Catholic Association that they had resolved to oppose any member or resolution of the current Tory government. Before emancipation, a Catholic could not sit in Parliament, but he could run for election. O'Connell was elected with the votes of the forty-shilling freeholder cottiers whose loyalty he had won during the disturbances in Munster and who were again shepherded to the polls by their priests. This was a shock to the landlords of Co. Clare who were accustomed to controlling their tenants' votes. It was particularly shocking to landlords who had generally supported their tenants during famines by reducing rents and through acts of charity. As expected, O'Connell was barred from taking his seat by the required oath of allegiance. However, Wellington, the new prime minister, and Sir Robert Peel, leader of the House of Commons, saw that, if O'Connell were not allowed to take his seat, there would be revolution in Ireland. This led directly to passage of the Catholic Relief Act of 1829.

There were, in fact, many mass meetings in support of O'Connell following his election. One of the most impressive took place on Sept. 28, 1828, when ten thousand men marched in battle array decorated with the insignia of rebellion at Killaloe, on the western bank of the River Shannon across the bridge from Ballina, the village nearest Derry Castle. Among the noisily cheering "mob," as the Protestant press would call these Catholic crowds, there were some who proclaimed O'Connell to be their king. The crowd was mostly orderly, but a roving band of three hundred men ordered sixty potato pickers off the lands of Nathaniel Barton at Grange, near Killaloe, and burned the house of Patrick Regan in the Glen of Aherlow: both were Protestants. If they did not stop such violent behavior, O'Connell told the organizers of such mass meetings, they would lose the support of the Catholic Association.[54]

The Hon. Francis Prittie, MP, Henry Grattan, MP, and Michael Prittie Head were among the noblemen, members of parliament, and "gentlemen of other ranks" who signed a "Declaration of Protestants in Favour of A Final and Conciliatory Adjustment of the Catholic Question." They felt "called upon...to declare the conviction we entertain, that the disqualifying laws which affect his Majesty's Roman Catholic Subjects are productive of consequences prejudicial in the highest degree to the interests of Ireland, and the Empire to which she is united ...they are a primary cause of her poverty and wretchedness, and the source of those political discontents and religious animosities that distract the country, endanger the safety of its institutions, and are destructive alike of social happiness and national prosperity."[55] After the Catholic Relief Act was passed with the begrudging support of King George IV on March 24, 1829, the Catholic Association ceased to exist. Now, without renouncing their religious faith, Catholics could sit in parliament and become members of corporations, and they were eligible for most of the higher civil and military offices from which they had been excluded. Still closed to them, however, were the positions of regent, lord-lieutenant, and lord chancellor in the Irish government in Dublin.[56] In the wake of the Catholic Relief bill, the Tory government in England tried to minimize its impact by discontinuing the voting privileges of the 40-shilling freeholders and raising the bar for the franchise to £10.

On August 24, 1829, the *Tipperary Free Press* reported the "Undisputed Return of Mr. O'Connell." The high sheriff for Co. Clare, Simon George Purdon, stood at the center of the hustings in the Ennis Courthouse with O'Connell at his right, wearing the dress of the Repeal [of the Union] Association. Purdon called out, "A reasonable time having elapsed, is it your wish that Daniel O'Connell Esq. should be returned as a Knight of the Shire to represent you in Parliament?" Following cries of "yes, yes," Purdon continued, "Such being your wish, I now declare Daniel O'Connell Esq. duly elected as a Knight of the Shire to represent you in Parliament." The immense cheering and waving of hats and handkerchiefs carried outside the courthouse and throughout the town.

Chapter 13

Tithe Wars, Breach of Promise, Murder, and Mayhem

In the second quarter of the nineteenth century political power in Ireland began to ebb away from the Protestant ascendancy and to seep into the hands of a clerically dominated Catholic middle class. This slow tortuous process of change was accomplished in a climate hostile to interdenominational goodwill—religion was one aspect of the Irish Question and not the Question itself: which in essence was the presence of a privileged, garrisoned minority within an impoverished ethnically dissimilar, majority society struggling for control of its own destiny.
—Thomas McGrath, "Interdenominational Relations in pre-famine Tipperary," in *Tipperary: History and Society*, 282.

Irish property must support Irish poverty.
—Anon.

After the short-lived Tory administration of the duke of Wellington and Sir Robert Peel, the Whig Party under the 2nd earl Grey returned to full power in 1831. That summer, on July 27, the high Tory, ultra-Protestant, and much derided earl of Norbury died at last at the age of eighty-six, maintaining his reputation as a wag to the end. Learning that his neighbor Lord Erne was dying and knowing that he himself was on his death bed, he called his man-servant, saying, "James, run around to Lord Erne and tell him with my compliments that it will be a dead-heat between us."[1]

For Daniel O'Connell, Norbury's most determined enemy, however, the decade of the 1830s was his heyday as he devoted himself to parliamentary politics in Westminster and allied himself with the reform agenda of Whig governments under prime ministers Lord Grey and Lord Melbourne. Having achieved Catholic emancipation, his next target was repeal of the Act of Union, thus returning to Dublin an Irish parliament for the Irish people. Since this objective received little support from Westminster or the government bureaucracy in Dublin, he turned his attention to tithe reform and reform of the Church of Ireland. This must have pleased Michael Prittie Head, the Whig member of the family. With the return of a Whig government at Westminster, he regained his commission, taking the oaths that entitled him to continue as JP for Co. Tipperary in January 1832.[2] However, Head's financial affairs were too dire by now for much political involvement, particularly as he realized how his troubles had impacted his family's status and financial wellbeing.

Tipperary continued to lead the country in incidents of unrest and violence. Despite Daniel O'Connell and the Catholic Association's success in taming much of the faction fighting that preceded the push for Catholic emancipation, fights broke out again following the news that the Catholic Relief Act had passed. Following a riot or faction fight the evening of a fair in Borrisokane on June 27, 1829, where two men were shot and killed by a police constable and twenty-one others were seriously injured, four more were shot dead in a funeral cortege for one of the deceased. This was too much for the many more of the local Protestant families who decided to emigrate. Two months earlier, on April 21, there was a faction fight on the bridge between Ballina and Killaloe, a few miles from the Derry Castle estate. The mob went berserk at the police's rough treatment of the fighters and stormed the military barracks in Killaloe, wrecking it. Three local small farmers were shot and killed by the police.[3] Among the local gentry and magistrates present at the inquest were Richard Ponsonby, bishop of Killaloe, and Capt. [Michael Henry] Head of Derry Castle. Police Sergeant Browne was initially found guilty of willful murder but was acquitted that August at Clonmel. That month, O'Connell was returned to the Westminster Parliament as MP for Co. Clare in an election presided over by High Sheriff Simon George Purdon.

Richard Ponsonby, a member of the influential Irish Whig

branch of the Ponsonby family (the family was of Cromwellian stock), was still bishop of Killaloe when forty-seven-year-old Rev. John Head, third son of Michael Head of Derry Castle and brother of its then proprietor Michael Prittie Head, was installed as dean of Killaloe. Bishop Ponsonby's tenure at Killaloe was brief, from March 1828 to September 1831, when he became bishop of Derry, but, while they were there, Simon George Purdon, John Head's nephew, became friendly with the well-connected and wealthy Ponsonby family, including four daughters (see below). Bishop Ponsonby was succeeded by the Hon. Edmund Knox, brother of the earl of Ranfurly, but John Head remained in the influential position of dean until his death in 1871, while retaining his parish of Ballinaclough, where he had been rector since 1807.

Although Killaloe was not one of the largest and richest dioceses in the Church of Ireland, Dean Head would have been kept busy even if these had not been such troubled times.[4] Surviving records from the late eighteenth century indicate that the diocese of Killaloe and Kilfenora had 138 parishes, 50 benefices of approximately two parishes each, and 38 churches. Its total landholdings were 7,528 acres, of which 6,795 were profitable. Incomes of bishops and deans were based on rental and tithes from these lands. The dean had inspecting and presiding power over the chapter of the cathedral and was required to preach not only in the cathedral but in other churches of the same diocese from which he received any income. He convened chapter meetings and presided over the chapter's business transactions. In theory, he was to visit all churches within his jurisdiction at least once every three years and was directly responsible for the spiritual welfare of the diocesan parishes. Deans and provosts were addressed as "Very Reverend."[5]

John Head's tenure as dean of Killaloe was fraught from the beginning with the Tithe Wars (1830-34), continued through reforms of the Church of Ireland (1833 and 1838) and the horrendous suffering during the Irish potato famine of 1845-47, and ended with his death shortly after the disestablishment of the Church as the state religion.[6] Unfortunately, the records of the Church of Ireland were lost in the firebombing of the Public Records wing of the Four Courts Building in Dublin in 1922 so that it is virtually impossible to trace his administrative and pastoral role in these traumatic affairs.

He also controlled or acquired three townlands in his parish so that he was both a landlord and a tithe-holder. Thus he was often a target of the rural outrages that are occasionally referenced in local newspapers. He appears to have been a tolerant and hardworking clergyman and landlord, beloved by the Catholic rural poor for his leadership in local relief committees.

Under the Whig government, electoral reforms received a boost with the 1832 Representation of the People (Ireland) Act, commonly known as the Irish Reform Act. It was the first decisive blow aimed at so-called rotten boroughs with very small electorates that nonetheless could send two elected burgesses to Westminster as members of parliament. These could be used by a landed patron to gain unrepresentative influence within the unreformed House of Commons. The Irish boroughs were now given a more uniform franchise. In addition to those who qualified under the previous rules, all occupiers of property worth at least £10 and resident freemen by birth or servitude became electors. The freemen were members of trade guilds, either because they had inherited membership or because they had served an apprenticeship to become members. For almost a century from the mid-seventeenth century, the Heads had considerable electoral powers as members of trade guilds and as corporation burgesses in Waterford. After moving to Co. Tipperary, some of them were freemen of Waterford and Limerick cities, although not resident there. This corrupt practice was ended with passage of the Parliamentary Boundaries (Ireland) Act of 1832, which passed the same day as the Irish Reform Act and settled and described "the Limits of Cities Towns and Boroughs in Ireland in so far as respects the Election of Members to serve in Parliament."[7]

Drastically reduced political clout aside, matters were already going from bad to worse for the Heads at Derry Castle. The estate was under the control of the Court of Chancery and creditors, including family members whose jointures depended on the estate, brought increasing numbers of suits against Michael Prittie Head, making his last years miserable.[8] Unable to raise the dowries that were essential to securing appropriate marriages for his four surviving daughters (Maria had died in 1818) or a marriage settlement for his only son, they seemed destined to remain unmarried. But two members of the younger generation of Heads, William Henry Head and Henry Darby Head, were determined to continue the family's landlord tradition. Following the death of his father in December 1827, nineteen-year-old William Henry assumed the burden of finalizing the sale of Drumniscart, the last disputed part of the Ashley Park estate, to George Atkinson, and settling with those who had a claim on it, including William Casaubon Purdon of Tinerana, father of Simon George Purdon.[9] He also inherited his father's dispute with his brother-in-law, the Hon. Eyre Massey, and others over the lands of Chastrytane which evolved into his dispute with two cousins, Arthur Burdett and Phoebe Massey, over the same lands.[10] The most dramatic evidence of the toll sorting out the Ashley Park mess took on him and on family relationships was that he later omitted from the genealogical information he compiled about his family the names of his four aunts, Letitia Drought, Mary Despard, Phoebe Massey, and Catherine Sheffield Cassan, their husbands and families, as well as his grandfather's second wife Maria Head. The omission of John Head's daughters and second wife continued in all entries pertaining to the Heads in *Burke's Landed Gentry of Ireland*, even though William Henry sustained a relationship with some Massey descendants.[11]

William Henry was, therefore, cutting his legal teeth while still an undergraduate at Trinity College. In early November 1833, several Irish newspapers reported on the latest class of law graduates: "On Saturday the Court of Chancery was extremely crowded by ladies, who were anxious to see young barristers called to the bar," including twenty-four-year-old "William Henry Head, Esq., only son of Lieutenant General Michael Head of Modreeny, County Tipperary."[12] The duke of Clarence, William Henry's godfather, succeeded his brother as King William IV on June 30, 1830. Although the king must have had numerous and mostly forgotten godchildren, the connection certainly gave a luster to William Henry Head's ambitions and pretensions. After he was called to the Irish Bar, he would use his knowledge of the law to bring about his return to larger landownership while beginning to serve as a reliable and knowledgeable magistrate at a time when county magistrates were under even more intense criticism by the Westminster and Dublin governments. His cousin Henry Darby Head, eldest son of the

Rev. John Head and called to the Irish Bar in 1842, followed a similar route at his father's Ballyquiveen estate near Nenagh and on grand juries starting in the 1840s. But the other barrister in the family, Samuel, oldest son of the landless Henry Aldborough Head, stayed on in Dublin after being called to the Bar in 1839. Three of William Henry's uncles-in-law were justices of the peace at this time: John Armstrong Drought for King's County and Stephen Sheffield Cassan and Francis Despard for Queen's County, although the disputes over the Ashley Park estate had ruptured any chance of a relationship with them.

Young William Henry lived with his mother at the elegant Georgian Modreeny house near Cloughjordan, one of the earliest Protestant settlements in Northern Tipperary. There he raised cattle on the small estate's excellent pastureland. Elizabeth Head's father, · the wealthy retired East India Company director Edward Ravenscroft, had died in London in 1828 but his will indicates that he left his estate primarily to his second wife, Emma Ravenscroft, who lived another twenty years.[13] However, Elizabeth's generous marriage jointure guaranteed their comfortable life in Modreeny even before her son's business acumen became apparent.

In the meantime, having completed his year as high sheriff of Co. Clare, Simon George Purdon remained active in a number of county leadership roles, presuming that he would inherit the family estate of Tinerana on the Clare side of Lough Derg upon the death of his elderly father.[14] The Heads' connection with the Purdon family began in 1793, when forty-one-year-old Major William Casaubon Purdon of the 7th Dragoon Guards married Deborah, eldest daughter of Michael and Margaret Head and sister of Michael Prittie Head. In addition to their son Simon George, born in 1797, they would have a second son and several daughters. The family grew up at Tinerana House, which was built in about 1775, roughly the same time as the original Georgian houses at Derry Castle and Ashley Park.

Simon George was evidently an intelligent, dashing, and eligible young man. He was educated at Winchester, one of the finest public schools in England, and Oxford University, and was a cornet by purchase in the soon-to-be disbanded 19th Regiment of Light Dragoons. Two years later, in 1824, he served as an *attaché* at the

British Embassy in Sweden under Lord Vesey Fitzgerald, another Clare landlord. Simon's long, ill-starred love affair with Henrietta Head—or Henrie, as he called her—began when the two met after Simon returned from Sweden in late 1824 or early 1825.[15] He was twenty-seven or twenty-eight and she was just eighteen. Apparently, he fell madly in love with the accomplished and sheltered young woman and spent a great deal of time at Derry Castle, where he was warmly welcomed by the genteel, liberal, and somewhat unworldly Head family. The elder Purdons, on the other hand, did not socialize with the Heads; in fact, Deborah Purdon apparently had no contact with her brother, an unexplained rift which most likely had to do with threats to her jointure or her disapproval of his irregular marriages. Nonetheless, M. P. Head apparently thought of his nephew as a son-in-law-in-waiting.

The Head sisters were all well-educated and musical, but Henrietta was the beauty and her father's favorite. Simon wrote her adoring letters during the eighteen months he was in London on estate business in 1827 and 1828 (he sold many of his properties in the Irish and English enclaves of Limerick City that year) and sent her sheet music and other gifts, including his portrait. By this time, it was all too clear that the Derry Castle estate was in severe difficulties, and Simon tried but failed to get a substantial loan for his uncle while he was in London. Although his father never prevented Simon George from paying almost daily visits to Derry Castle, he began to make it clear that he did not favor a marriage with Henrietta, his son's first cousin, and that he expected him to make a better match. The Tinerana estate was encumbered and much was expected of him to maintain the family's high status. Serving as high sheriff of Co. Clare in 1829 was not a bad start. In 1833, Lord Vesey Fitzgerald, who, after succeeding to his mother's Irish peerage the year before, was then lord-lieutenant of Co. Clare and colonel of the Clare militia, appointed Simon George Purdon a captain of that regiment.

Like M. P. Head, Simon Purdon would become one of the more liberal landlords and undoubtedly shared with him a determination to see the end of the hated tithe system. Protestants in Tipperary represented an estimated 4.4 percent of the county's population, while

Catholics comprised an overwhelming 95.6 percent of the population in 1831.[16] Small wonder that Catholics bitterly resented having to pay tithes for the support of Anglican ministers. Emboldened by the passage of Catholic emancipation, Catholic tenant farmers began withholding the tithes they were obliged to pay to the vicar of the local Church of Ireland parish. Protestant clergymen were insulted and branded as the worst enemies of the people by priests and agitators, attacked, and even murdered. Tithes were collected by tithe collectors or clergymen at the point of bayonets, peasants were shot down and bayoneted by the hated Irish constabulary, and they in turn were stoned and pitchforked by peasants. While Parliament had declared that the tithe system needed reform, the Anglican Church insisted that tithes must be collected in the meantime. Tithe resistors had one apparent victory in Carrickshock in Co. Kilkenny in December 1831. Four tithe resistors were killed but thirteen police constables were stoned to death while packed together in a narrow lane.

The list of tithe defaulters in Co. Tipperary crossed every class, and included aristocrats, magistrates, attorneys, gentlemen, and officers, and even two members of parliament, most pertinently Timothy Carroll, a Nenagh coroner. The vast majority, however, were ordinary people. The mass meetings of the anti-tithe movement and written and verbal threats succeeded in cutting off payments to Church of Ireland clergymen, the only source of income for some of them. Defaulters hid their livestock during daylight, locked the animals up after dark, and boycotted sales of livestock taken from tithe resistors. Secret agrarian societies reappeared and began brutal retributions against those who failed to comply with their orders to resist tithe collection as well as the collection of rents.[17] The government at this point ceased all attempts to collect tithe arrears, which amounted to one million pounds for the years 1831, 1832, and 1833.[18]

Not surprisingly, large numbers of Protestants were again emigrating from Ireland, as reported by *Dublin University Magazine* in July 1834. The Protestants, claimed the magazine, were the very portion of the population which was "all on the side of England, and of property, and of law." They were men "orderly, steady, industrious, loyal and religious" who "as a body, had no superiors in their class of any nation in the world." The government was busily conceding to "clamor, turbulence, and threats."[19] This period, 1830-1834, saw the largest outflow of Protestant emigrants. The parish of Modreeny was a particularly large exporter of Protestants to Canada. There were about 250 Protestant families living in William Henry Head's parish in 1831, of which about 100 families emigrated at this time.[20]

Daniel O'Connell continued to upset Irish Protestant Tories and confirmed their worst fears by demanding repeal of the Act of Union and restoration of the Irish parliament. In no way would such a parliament resemble the purely Protestant Ascendancy assembly that had been dissolved in 1800, for it would now be dominated by Irish Catholics of many different backgrounds. Fortunately for the Tories, there was little enthusiasm for repeal in Ireland or in Westminster. However, O'Connell demanded further reforms from the new Whig government, and the Anglican Church made a popular target for those who felt its privileged position in Ireland was unconscionable. The Church of Ireland had more archbishops, bishops, deans and chapters, and parochial clergy than could possibly be deemed necessary. The Irish Church Temporalities Act of 1833 abolished ten Sees, and the remaining twelve were reduced and even taxed. This was just a first and, from the point of view of its opponents, inadequate step and it became a prelude to the disestablishment of the Church of Ireland later in the century.[21]

The Lichfield House Compact, signed in February 1835, was an agreement among the Whig government, the Irish Repeal party led by O'Connell, and the radicals to act as one body against the Conservative party. O'Connell agreed to suspend the demand for repeal of the Union, disestablishment of the Church of Ireland, and parliamentary reform in return for reduction of tithes, municipal reform in Ireland, and the appointment of men with liberal sympathies to Irish public office.[22] The Whigs defeated the Tories under Sir Robert Peel at the polls, and Lord Melbourne became prime minister. That summer, Thomas Drummond appeared at Dublin Castle as under-secretary to chief-secretary Lord Morpeth and lord-lieutenant Lord Mulgrave, both Whig politicians. The Scottish-born administrator and reformer had previously worked on the ordnance survey in Ireland and had been moved at that time by the poverty and miseries of the people and the injustices and misrule he observed. This hard-working liberal official now became the virtual governor of Ireland.

Convinced that the rural magistrates' pernicious control over the selection of county constables had made the constables a partisan body, Drummond began by organizing an effective police force under an inspector-general employed by the government in Dublin. Peel's old force had been infiltrated by members of the divisive Orange Order, which was now dissolved. Most of the senior officers of this new paramilitary force had army experience and were now made stipendiary magistrates. But the force itself was composed chiefly of Irish peasants who had to submit to an oath that precluded membership of political or secret societies, and from voting in elections. Drummond ordered them to prevent faction fights by suppressing fairs that were notorious for their disorder, and to put down agrarian outrages. These new police, however, were not to be used to "levy tithe or to collect rent by distress" while parliament was preparing to reform or abolish the tithe system. Drummond's liberal administration calmed the country for a while but bitterly antagonized many of the uncompensated rural magistrates by placing legally qualified stipendiary magistrates over them and removing their rights to appoint constables and sub-constables.

On February 1, 1836, William Casaubon Purdon died at Tinerana aged eighty-three. His wife, the former Deborah Head, had died eighteen months earlier. With Simon George Purdon's succession to the proprietorship of Tinerana following his parents' deaths, it would seem on the surface that there was no further barrier to his marrying Henrietta Head. Instead, he hastened to Dublin to make arrangements with the bishop of Derry for the settlement preceding his intended marriage to the bishop's daughter, Louisa Elizabeth Ponsonby. M. P. Head heard rumors of these plans from his friends Lord Bloomfield and Peter Holmes. On April 6, Simon George wrote to Henrietta's father from Dublin, explaining that his father had previously expressed disapproval of marriage to Henrietta because of the close blood relationship between them and, a few days before his death, "exacted a promise from me that what he then required would be explicitly obeyed." He implored his uncle to allow him to break off his engagement. Both Michael and Henrietta wrote back but were shocked by the arrogance and cold-heartedness of Purdon's response to his uncle. Broken-hearted by the shaming of his daughter, Michael Prittie Head died on July 27, two months after the abrupt and painful ending of her long relationship with his nephew. Simon George Purdon married Louisa Elizabeth Ponsonby on August 11.[23]

A week or so before his cousin's death, William Henry Head, whose address was given as "Headsboro," sat on the grand jury at the Co. Tipperary summer assizes in Clonmel, perhaps for the first time. Among the large attendance of Co. Tipperary magistrates were Michael Prittie Head's neighbor, close friend, and trustee Peter Holmes as well as a member of the Prittie family. Reflecting customary protocol, Chief Justice John Doherty, journeying from Kilkenny, entered the town accompanied by the high sheriff and an escort of the 3rd Light Dragoons. He told the grand jury, "Some of the petitions contained cases of the most revolting and atrocious circumstances, which, it should be stated generally arose out of the ejectments of the tenantry."[24] This indictment of Co. Tipperary landlord practices would soon be taken up by Drummond in an angry exchange with senior Tipperary magistrates.

Capt. Michael Henry Head, now the beleaguered proprietor of the Derry Castle estate, brought two important cases in defense of his family and the estate in 1837. The first was *Biggs v. Head and Others* brought before Master of the Rolls Sir Michael O'Loghlen in the court of chancery on May 3.[25] O'Loghlen was the first Catholic appointed to the Bench since 1688, at a time when the Dublin administration was trying to remove about one-third of the existing Protestant magistracy. This case, on behalf of Michael Henry Head, devisee (beneficiary), and Mary Head, widow and executrix, was "to restrain Henry Staines from further prosecuting this cause, as solicitor for the plaintiff [Biggs], and from supplying the plaintiff with any evidences, papers, vouchers, or documents, which he acquired as family solicitor for Michael Prittie Head." As mentioned in the previous chapter, it was asserted that legacies charged on the estates of Michael Prittie Head, were given by the will to his wife and "illegitimate children," that his wife was sole executrix, and that persons named Anthony Parker and Peter Holmes were trustees in the will for the purpose of paying off the legacies so charged.[26] For the first time, the extent of the encumbrances on the Derry Castle estate was stated as exceeding £30,000, an enormous sum ($3.6 million today) which had involved M. P. Head in several law suits from 1827 until his death. During those nine years, Staines acted as Head's confidential solicitor, and several hundred letters had passed between them. At the family's request, Staines had traveled to Derry Castle following M. P. Head's death to consult with the family about how best to proceed under his will, and how to make arrangements with the creditors "so as to extricate the property from the expensive litigation in which it was involved."[27] He was allowed to take a copy of the will and other documents away with him.

According to a report in the *Dublin Morning Register* of May 9, 1837, William Henry Head, also a beneficiary of the will, made application to Justice O'Loghlen on the *Biggs v. Head* case with the same purpose as Michael Henry Head. According to this report, Staines had acted for both Biggs and Michael Prittie Head but, when he failed to negotiate a solution to Head's financial problems, Head negotiated with another Dublin solicitor, David Daly, for the loan of the sum he needed and to act as his solicitor. Following M. P. Head's death, Staines went back to Biggs and refiled the original *Biggs v. Head* case, apparently using Head's unproven final will. Staines claimed he had used an earlier will from another creditor's case but comparison of the two wills demonstrated his culpability. Sir Michael O'Loghlen granted William Henry's application with costs, citing various decisions at law and in equity where solicitors were restrained from acting under similar circumstances. This case is still used today as a precedent in rules governing the retention of a solicitor.[28] Quite a triumph for young William Henry Head! But were the Head siblings at Derry Castle really illegitimate and was this another reason for the Purdon parents' rejection? Despite strenuous efforts, I have been unable to find an answer.

The second case, the notorious breach of promise suit brought by Michael Henry Head on behalf of his sister Henrietta against their cousin Simon George Purdon, is further proof of just how desperate the Heads were. Most middle- and upper-class families were reluctant in the nineteenth century to use breach of promise actions since they led to wide publicity and often mockery, scrutinizing intimate personal matters, as they tended to do. This was repugnant to the family feeling of the period, especially where young women were concerned. Neither the plaintiff nor the defendant could be called to testify until the law was changed in 1869. However, this does not explain why none of Henrietta's three sisters or their stepmother was called as a witness. For a family whose debts already amounted to £30,000, the burden of the costs of this trial must have been tremendous. Counsel for Henrietta included five barristers, of whom at least three were king's counselors, as well as David Daly, acting as agent.[29] Simon George Purdon's counsel included two KCs and three other barristers as well as an agent. The case took place in the Court of Common Pleas in Dublin on June 14, 1837 before Chief Justice Doherty and was covered by twenty-three Irish newspapers, some of them in extraordinary detail.

"It being generally known that the trial of this case was fixed for yesterday," began the reporter for *Freeman's Journal*, "the interest to witness it was so general and so intense, that on the opening of the doors, at a few minutes past ten o'clock, the rush into the body of the court and galleries was tremendous, and in a short time every part was crowded to excess; so crammed was the outer bar that several of its members resorted to the galleries for accommodation. We understood the Bishop of Derry, father-in-law of the defendant, to be present in court." How the bishop's presence must have distressed Michael Henry Head and any other members of the Head family who were present. As an advocate for his Derry Castle cousins, it is likely that these included William Henry Head of Modreeny. But how many others of this large family divided by debts were there to support their distressed kin?

Mr. West, KC, opened the pleadings, stating that damages sought by the plaintiff were £20,000 (an enormous and unrealistic sum, two-thirds of the encumbrances on the Derry Castle estate). The plaintiff had nine counts in the declaration, six containing pleas of general promises to marry and three to marry after the death of the defendant's father. The defendant "pleaded the general issue and the statute of limitations."

Edward Litton, KC, set the tenor with an impassioned state-ment. He painted Henrietta as a trusting and somewhat naïve young woman swept off her feet by her sophisticated and worldly older cousin who took full advantage of the welcome he always received as a relative at Derry Castle. Well educated and accom-plished, she had been brought up in "that state of finish which makes the mind and the heart peculiarly susceptible to attention, and peculiarly susceptible to injury and insult." Evidently a beauty, she was the third daughter and the favorite "of the late Mr. Michael Head, well known as a gentleman of fortune and station in this country, of an ancient and honourable family of wealth and rank in the district in which he lived, and which family were admired, caressed and respected by all who knew them."

Litton then read out a number of letters that Purdon wrote Henrietta while he was in London in 1827, to the prurient delight of some and distaste of others in the crowded courtroom. No doubt Litton had selected those in which Purdon referred to her again and again as "my own dearest, dearest little wife," "BELOVED AND ADORED HENRIE," "the only being on earth in whose society I feel happy." He begged her to save herself for him and not accept any other suitors, which she apparently obeyed faithfully, although knowing that almost insuperable difficulties faced them. Not the least of these, although never alluded to by Litton, was the fact that there was no dowry for her or any of her sisters. Another problem was their too close blood relationship.

In a letter dated May 19, 1827, Purdon wrote, "How I hate the word *if*, my adored wife, in any way alluding to our longed for union, and yet you always make use of it; for instance, you even say, *if* we are married. My own Henrie, we *will* be married…Hurry, consult your own heart, and look at the difficulties that surround all chance of an open union, perhaps for years, and if you love me with half the enthusiasm that I doat [sic] on you, you will promise me with all your heart and soul." An undated letter shows that he was trying to persuade her to agree to a private union without his father's full consent: "No power on earth shall part us or prevent it. Nothing but death of yourself can or shall prevent it. It may be de-layed, but sooner or later we shall be one in the eyes of the world as we are at this moment in the eyes of the Almighty…Dearest love, I have often asked you—partly in joke, partly in earnest—to consent to a private union. Will you, my beloved girl, promise me that it shall be as soon as an opportunity arrives?"

Henrietta apparently refused to agree to a clandestine and dishonorable connection which would mean they would have to live on his meager annual allowance of £250 and risk his relationship with his father. Simon George's response appeared to indicate that his father was not as serious a problem as she feared, at least not at that point: "I am not angry with you for not promising at once to accede to my request, because I valued your reason for not doing so; but, my adored wife, be assured that you are mistaken in supposing that anything horrible, or in any way that could injure my father's health, or shorten his days, could arise from his knowledge of our union…I cannot or will not exist without your dearest love."

And so the "perhaps for years" that Purdon dreaded came to pass, and Henrietta thought she remained engaged to him as he continued to visit her and her family over the years, until his father's death, when the visits stopped altogether. Litton, of course, made much of the arrogance and cruelty of the letters Purdon wrote Michael P. Head and Henrietta after they heard about his engagement to Miss Ponsonby. But his April 6 letter from Dublin to "My dear uncle" was pleading. Purdon confirmed the reports of his intention to marry Miss Ponsonby and explained that his father had insisted that he must not marry Henrietta, "stating he was decidedly averse to my making connection with so near a relative; and, also, without any thing to assist in paying off my sister's charges on the Clare property." Believing that his son was deceiving him, the old man exacted a promise from him a few days before his death that he obey his wishes. "I now implore you to acquit me, and believe me that I am not such as I may seem. I know Henrietta is generous, and she will at once acquit me, and say I am free." He said that his sister was the only one aware of what had passed between him and his father.

A month after his April 6 letter from Dublin, Simon George wrote to Michael P. Head a deeply hurtful letter from Tinerana: "Sir, As your information is so very authentic it is quite unnecessary for me to add to it, neither do I hold myself bound to answer you, or any other man, what should be my own concern. I am sure the

Bishop of Derry will be most happy to hear from you any circumstance relative to what you call my engagement with your daughter. You may furnish him with it as soon as possible, and follow up any proceedings you think advisable, as my resolve cannot be shaken." The next day, he wrote to Henrietta: "Could I let his curse rest on me with his last breath, and are you the woman who would require me to do so? I did not think you were, till I received your father's letters; and did I not tell you on the first occasion he [his father] spoke to me, that I feared it would be again renewed and if so it would be final. It has been so…I did expect that I could have still been to you and all, a brother. But that has not been allowed me by your father, nay, I may say yourself…I am still, however, and ever shall be, Your well wisher, S. G. Purdon."

Litton declared that he did not believe "that the defendant's father ever exacted such a promise from him." He called Purdon's letter "the coldest, the most cruel, the most unfeeling, and most heartless insult that could be offered towards an unfortunate and injured woman," and stated his belief that Purdon's correspondence had contributed to Michael Prittie Head's death. "Ah! I might almost have said that the marriage equipage and the funeral procession moved on together," Litton said, "and that the marriage festival and rejoicings were witnessed by this unhappy and heart-broken family while they wept over the tomb of their lamented father." Attributing Purdon's conduct to "the cursed spirit of ambition" to become "connected with the daughter of the Bishop of Derry, who is connected with Lord Grey," he argued at great length for the jury to affirm the innocence and purity of the plaintiff.[30] "You are called upon to give such a verdict as shall throw a shield, a panoply round the happiness, the feelings, and the honor of this high and respectable family." *The Clonmel Advertiser* reported that his powerful speech was loudly applauded.

Michael Henry Head was the first witness called to prove the circumstances of the long courtship. He identified some music and superbly bound books given by the defendant to his sister and declared that "The defendant always said that he could not marry my sister till the death of his father." Cross-examined by Mr. Bennett, he calmly testified that he frequently carried notes from their cousin to his sister. Miss Edwards, the Head daughters' former English governess, who now lived in London, testified that Purdon had told her about his feelings for Henrietta when he was in London in 1827. Henry Brewster Darley, William Casaubon Purdon's land agent, testified that the Clare property was only worth £2,700 a year in rent roll, not the £5,000 that Litton claimed, and was also considerably encumbered, requiring interest payments of £1,100 a year. It was stated that the late Mr. Purdon left the remainder of the Limerick properties to his younger children.

When attorney Bennett rose to make the defendant's case to the jury, he begged them not to be swayed by Litton's eloquence. He said that Mr. Litton had asked him to produce the letters that the plaintiff had written to the defendant but Simon George had refused to hand them over, instructing him "to say there was nothing written in them but the dictates of a pure and innocent female."[31] Bennett argued there was little proof of most of Litton's allegations and the jury should be careful not to go so far as to take the Purdon family's property away from them, particularly since Simon George Purdon was likely to be starting a family! He also denigrated the use of Purdon's correspondence in a public court—precipitating a heated exchange with Litton—and assailed the sordid motives attributed to his client: "God knows whether the speculation in the way of ambition would turn out a good one or not, for some politicians there are who say that the Whigs will very shortly be out (great laughter)."[32] He believed his client's story that his father forbade the alliance and noted the paucity of witnesses for the plaintiff. Again, he referred to the letters his client had "written so long back as nearly ten years ago. God help many of us if every letter we wrote in our youth was to be thus produced against us (laughter)." Although Michael Henry Head "certainly gave his evidence like a high-minded gentleman...his evidence went to show that moderate damages only should be given."[33]

Thereafter, Chief Justice Doherty admonished the jury "to banish from your minds every feeling of passion or prejudice, and devote yourselves altogether to the facts of the case as they have appeared before you." He had found this case to be "one of the most distressing in character, both from its intrinsic nature, and the station the parties hold in society—I am not sure it is not one of the most melancholy that has fallen within my experience..." The jury retired for about ten minutes' deliberation and returned a verdict of three thousand pounds damages, and six-pence costs.

Although the judgment of £3,000 was a fraction of the damages requested, it was, according to one study, by far the highest awarded in breach of promise cases involving people from the Co. Limerick area in the 1830s.[34] The costs of the trial must have whittled away a chunk of that. But Henrietta's honor was intact and Simon George Purdon's status as a leading landowner and magistrate in Co. Limerick seems to have been unaffected. One English newspaper, *The Suffolk Chronicle*, suggested that the £3,000 awarded by the jury "may serve to obtain for her a better husband."[35] In fact, on January 22, 1838, Henrietta, now age thirty-one, married thirty-three-year-old Henry Parsons, son of Richard Parsons, formerly of Cragbeg, Co. Limerick, in Kilmastulla Church, not far from Derry Castle. Presumably, Henry Parsons was one of the large, long-established Parsons family whose senior member was the earl of Rosse of Birr Castle but it can hardly have been a match to equal the life that she might have had as the wife of Simon George Purdon. Sadly, Henrietta's first child, a boy, was stillborn at Derry Castle in December 1838. Her second child, a daughter born in Limerick, appears to have survived infancy, but there are no records of her after that, nor evidence that the marriage endured.[36] In due course, two of Henrietta's sisters would marry widowers, another route to avoiding despised spinsterhood and one that seemed to waive the need for dowries.

Despite the scandalous trial, county honors and duties continued to fall to the proprietor of Tinerana. On the very day of the trial and in subsequent issues, the *Limerick Chronicle* announced the stakes for the Ennis Races that August. Simon George Purdon was to be one of the stewards. The following year, he was a steward for the brand new Loch Derg Yacht Club and a deputy lieutenant for Co. Clare. One month after the trial, his wife had given birth to a son and heir, the first of their ten children.

An indented deed of mortgage, signed on November 4, 1837, might have guaranteed some financial security for M. P. Head's legatees. Michael Henry Head had appointed David Daly, the family solicitor, as a trustee for the estate in April, just before the breach of promise trial. On November 4, Michael Head, David Daly, John Daly (presumably David's brother), Mary Head, as executrix of M. P. Head's will, and sisters Caroline, Emily, Henrietta, and Margaret Head signed the deed. This granted certain estate lands to John Daly for £13,000 "in satisfaction of Incumbrances affecting said lands," thus removing the 5 percent per annum interest charges to give priority to the jointure of £500 willed by M. P. Head to his widow, and the legacies of £3,000 for each of the daughters. And so the sell-off of Derry Castle lands continued.

Passage of the Tithe Act of 1838 removed the burden of tithe from the majority of Catholic landholders, and the Irish government abandoned all efforts to collect arrears. Tithe was now converted into a rent charge payable by landlords at three-quarters of the original amount due. Landlords could recover the sums from tenants who could in turn recover them from sub-tenants while the poorest classes of tenants were excluded from payment. However, this made the nonpayment of rent far riskier since a landlord could either evict or refuse to renew a lease. Thus, violence continued in the face of rising incidents of eviction for nonpayment of rent. This problem was particularly severe in the countryside to the south and west of the Shannon River in Cos. Clare, Limerick, and Kerry. But Co. Tipperary was the most violent of all, with 190 violent crimes in Tipperary between 1836 and 1838, while Co. Limerick had just 76.[37]

In April 1838, Francis Wayland, son of a Tipperary landlord, was fatally wounded and an innocent passerby, Austin Cooper, was shot dead with a blunderbuss. One of the four perpetrators was also shot dead, another escaped, and two (William Hickey and William Walsh) were brought to trial by a special commission in January 1839 and sentenced to death. Ironically, a blunderbuss belonging to Michael Head was stolen that year, seemingly a minor crime but indicative of the constant search for arms by rural agitators and a symbol for landlords of the threats against them.[38] Once again, Tipperary magistrates, including on this occasion Lords Glengall, Lismore, and thirty others, pleaded in a letter to the Irish government for more stringent legislation for the suppression of crime. They claimed that "neither life nor property was safe" and that no one could be brought to justice because of the intimidation of juries. Strongly backed by chief-secretary Viscount Morpeth, under-secretary Drummond replied dismissively on May 22 on behalf of the lord-lieutenant, Lord Mulgrave, who became the marquess of Normanby that year: "His Excellency conceives that it may become matter of serious question whether the proprietors of the soil are not in many instances attempting too rapidly to retrace their steps…the number of ejectments in 1837 is not less than double the number in 1833." He followed with the famous admonishment, "Property has its duties as well as its rights" and that "to the neglect of these duties, in time past, is mainly to be ascribed that diseased state of society in which such crimes take their rise." Drummond's letter was so critical of the landlords that the lord-lieutenant of Tipperary, the Earl of Donoughmore, refused to print it.[39]

It was Drummond's view that the Tipperary landlords had allowed smallholders to multiply on their lands because it was presumed that they would vote for their landlords, a presumption that was smashed by O'Connell in the 1828 Clare by-election. Following the abolition of the franchise for 40-shilling freeholders—raising the entry level for voting to ten pounds—landlords, according to Drummond, began pushing for the consolidation of farms, a policy in line with current economic thinking. The doubled eviction rate in Tipperary inevitably caused feelings of deep hatred in the countryside. A furious Lord Glengall raged at this government view of agrarian outrage. "The murders in consequence of landletting," he roared, "arose not from quarrels between landlord and tenant, but between tenant and tenant fighting for land."[40]

The recently launched conservative Protestant newspaper, *The Nenagh Guardian*, reported in August 1838 that Daniel O'Connell had returned to Ireland. "With the news of his ill-omened arrival comes the first thunders of the cannon, announcing the commencement of a campaign, which is to end in what is vaguely called, 'Full Justice to Ireland,' or a 'Repeal of the Union.'" O'Connell's first visit on arrival was apparently to Under-Secretary Drummond at Dublin Castle. The same newspaper reported on August 11 that the Irish Metropolitan Conservative Society of Dublin had resolved to petition the Queen for the removal of Lord Normanby as lord-lieutenant. Since his arrival, these Protestant academics wrote, "the government of this country has been managed on principles perfectly new and unprecedented; and in a spirit directly opposed to the administration of preceding governments of Ireland, no matter to what political party they may have belonged..." From their point of view, previous administrations had managed to keep in check the almost constant factional attempts to rouse the mass of Roman Catholic peasantry into revolt against and separation from England. They believed that Lord Normanby's arrival as lord-lieutenant had introduced a dangerous new principle into the administration of the Irish government, namely "of consulting solely the wishes of the anti-English faction, and especially of the Romish Priesthood, who, of late years, since the establishment of Maynooth College, have been most fearful patrons and supporters of disaffection." In the area of patronage, the Whig government "has conferred all places, as they became vacant, upon the members or creatures of the anti-English faction." The result of appointments of Catholics to judgeships, they felt, was that "laws have not been enforced to suppress crime; relatives of those on trial have been allowed on juries," while factional laws were now overruling established law through terrifying threats and deeds of retribution to anyone who disobeyed: "Fathers of families have been murdered in the noon day, in the sight of multitudes of lookers on; and yet no one has been brought to justice for the crime."[41]

It was not until the summer of 1839 that Normanby and Drummond were summoned to testify before the House of Lords Committee on the State of Crime in Ireland. By that time, attacks on landlords had increased exponentially. In mid-October 1838, Johnston Stoney of Emil Castle, Cloughjordan, a neighbor of William Henry Head, was traveling to a dinner party given by George Garvey, JP, and had just passed Lord Bloomfield's gate when he was shot at with a blunderbuss loaded with slugs and buttons. Twelve slugs and one button hit him in the arm and leg, but not fatally. Previously, George Wayland, father of the young man who had been wounded in April 1838, but was still clinging to life, had received a second notice "threatening destruction to every member of his family if the persons now in custody for the murder of Mr. [Austin] Cooper are not set at liberty."[42] A special commission led by Judge Burton was due to try these men for murder in January 1839.

In the midst of this unrest and attempting to alleviate it, Whig reforms for Ireland continued. The Irish Poor Relief Act of 1838 divided the country into 130 poor law unions to administer aid to the destitute and disabled. Each union was controlled by a board of governors, and poor rates were levied on local property to pay for the relief provided. Co. Tipperary was divided into the North and South Ridings that year, with Nenagh designated the administrative capital of the North Riding. A new county jail, courthouse, and Catholic chapel were built and three new streets added. From 1843 on, the summer assizes for North Tipperary were held in the new Nenagh Courthouse. The Nenagh poor law union, with 89,874 inhabitants in 1841, was the most populous union in Co. Tipperary and the seventeenth largest in the country.[43] The elected poor law guardians reflected the composition of the religious denominations in the administrative districts, with Catholics controlling the poor law guardians and responsible for dispensaries, fever hospitals, and workhouses. William Henry Head was elected by Cloughjordan voters to be a guardian for the Nenagh Union in March 1840.[44]

The Municipal Corporation (Ireland) Act of 1840 led to a major reform of local government. Prior to the passing of the act, there were sixty-eight borough corporations in Ireland; many of them were ineffective, some virtually defunct, and none of them in any way representative of their populations. The Act dissolved all but ten of the corporations and stripped guilds of their civic role. All but one, the guild of goldsmiths, was rapidly disbanded. Among the reformed corporations were Waterford City and County and Limerick City and County, which had been controlled by Protestants (including early members of the Head family) since the seventeenth century. Naturally, Protestants saw these reforms as another sign of the general advancement of the majority Catholics in administrative institutions in Ireland after emancipation. In the first elections held under this act in Waterford in October 1842, the Protestant establishment was overwhelmingly defeated. Thomas Meagher, a merchant like the seventeenth-century Heads, became Waterford's first Catholic mayor since that century.[45]

The fate of the Derry Castle estate remained in the hands of the Court of Chancery in Dublin. On August 1, 1838, the Court announced its intention to let to the highest bidder considerable lands of the estate that had fallen out of lease, including all except 50 acres of the demesne and the mansion, offices, gardens, and plantations. These had gone into receivership the previous February. "Proposals in writing, under £20, yearly rent (Post Paid) will be received by the Receiver for the Master's Approbation." David Daly was solicitor for the receiver.[46] On August 18, the same newspaper reported the sale of the Droughtsville estates in King's County. Thus, another estate in the wider Head kinship was in severe difficulties even before the cataclysm of the potato famine.

A far more affluent King's County landlord, a first cousin of William Henry Head, seemed to be flourishing, however. Hector John Toler, the 2nd earl of Norbury, owned 26,720 acres in six counties with 654 tenants, of which the largest estate was in Co. Tipperary. He had chosen to live on his 3,598-acre estate of Durrow Abby, near Tullamore, King's County (Offaly today), which his father had purchased from an impoverished landlord in 1815. The tenants were in wretched condition but their good-natured new landlord had apparently made large expenditures and was profusely generous, raising the 156 tenants to "comfortable independence." He was also building a splendid new residence at the cost of £20,000, on which 200 to 800 people were employed.[47] However, his land agent, George Garvey, was unpopular with the tenants, having put some of them out of their houses for nonpayment of rent. It has long been deemed possible that mistaken identity contributed to a tragedy that began on January 3, 1839.[48]

On that date, Lord Norbury's Scottish land steward, Adam Saunderson, was outside with Lord Norbury and standing about nine feet behind him when he heard the report of a gun and saw gun smoke rising from the hedge which skirted the plantation. He saw a man on the other side of the hedge bend down and then run as hard as he could to get out of the ditch in which he had been concealed. Saunderson followed him for about twenty yards but returned when he heard Norbury calling out. Catching him as he fell, he carried him to one of the lodges and told the women there to assist "his lordship" while he ran to the Abbey to get help. Norbury's son-in-law, Vandeleur Stewart, was there and together they helped bring the severely wounded and weakened man to the Abbey. Two doctors were immediately sent for and they found that Norbury had six wounds from a blunderbuss loaded with swan shot (a very heavy load). The wounds proved fatal, after forty-three hours of what *The Spectator* newspaper characterized as extreme suffering. An autopsy revealed that two of the shot had torn through his breast bone, lodging bone and cloth in his lungs, which increased his agony.[49]

Some 150 landlords from the region—almost certainly William Henry Head among them—attended the funeral at the Durrow Abbey church, despite the fact that the Night of the Big Wind on January 6, the worst storm in Ireland for centuries, caused immense damage and uprooted hundreds of trees making many roads unpassable. Many sent regrets that they were unable to get there. One hundred of Lord Norbury's attendants and workmen walked two by two in front of the hearse which was drawn by six horses and accompanied by ten domestics, five on each side. In order to emphasize the horror engendered by this murder and the disgust felt that the assassin was being concealed, the family and gentry refused to permit the tenants to carry the coffin to the grave, as was the usual custom. Instead, the coffin was carried mostly by magistrates, twelve at a time, including the lord-lieutenant of King's County, William Parsons, Lord Oxmantown (heir to the earl of Rosse of Birr Castle), and Lord Charleville.

On January 10, Lord Oxmantown called a meeting of the King's County magistrates in Tullamore to settle steps to be taken following the murder of their neighbor and friend.[50] Oxmantown began his passionate and emotional speech by praising the late Lord Norbury's many good qualities as a man and as a landlord who "never interfered in politics." Asking what motivated "this diabolical outrage," Oxmantown launched unwisely into a catalog of accusations that would produce a storm of criticism from the liberal press. "It is part of an extensive conspiracy or combination to effect that by assassination which they dare not attempt by open rebellion ("hear hear" from the assembly), virtually to wrest the property from the proprietors, by abolishing rent—in fact to secure for themselves the privilege of holding their farms without paying rent, and to effect this by assassinating the landlord who may venture to assert his right by ejectment (hear)." He continued, "It is evident that a conspiracy so wicked could not exist, except amongst a peasantry in the highest degree demoralized." He further declared that it had become impossible to bring a criminal to justice in King's County, an opinion obviously shared by the majority of his fellow magistrates, who responded with cheers.

At a time when the average Irish peasant had seemed, from Oxmantown's point of view, content and attached to his landlord, he had been happy to support Catholic emancipation, he said. He never regretted his vote on that question because he considered it to be just. However, he had recently become "grievously disappointed." Since the Irish Catholics gained political power, and with the encouragement of priests and agitators, the landlord had been "calumniated and vilified, was represented as a foe instead of a friend, and every art [was] made use of to excite the worst passions against him (hear again)."

After describing attempts on the lives of several other landlords, including Johnston Stoney, John-Head Drought, and Francis Biddulph (Drought was a first cousin and Biddulph the father of William Henry Head's future wife), Oxmantown suggested that they call on the Irish government "to propose to Parliament immediately on its assembly, an efficient *arms act*" and vigorous measures to repress agitation. He hoped that angry feelings would subside in future years but was not hopeful that the present Government would act "based upon the proceedings in another County." In fact, the special commission in Clonmel that had been charged with trying the assassins of Austin Cooper and Francis Wayland was conducted with complete justice by Judge Burton and the prisoners were found guilty and subsequently executed.

Oxmantown appointed a committee to prepare resolutions.[51] When the committee returned, Capt. Chidley Coote said that, having come from another county [Tipperary] where unchecked outrages had resulted in a special commission, "If the system of outrage was allowed to progress," it was the poor people who were the principal victims: "the rich had good houses over their heads, they had arms in their hands; but the poor man who lived in the thatched cottage was most exposed and most ultimately he the sufferer from the wild code" of the last years.

Lord Charleville read out a letter from a former magistrate now living in Dublin, begging him not to be carried away with passionate party retribution. This occurrence, he wrote, had already been seized on by the English and Irish press "and turned to the vilest purpose of party warfare...and this before a single fact has been elicited, calculated to throw the least light upon the cause or the author of the crime...Government, priests, demagogues, people, [are] all involved in one common accusation." "As to the people," commented Charleville, "they surely derive no benefit for the murder; they, to the contrary, will, in every way, suffer by the heavy calamity which had deprived them of a generous benefactor." Lord Charleville then spoke of his special friendship with Lord Norbury who had dined with him the evening before his murder. "The Government of Ireland," he continued, "in permitting the existence of the Precursor Society, and allowing them to indulge in such language as was used by Mr. O'Connell at their meeting about the very time Lord Norbury was shot, in permitting the language of abuse against landlords of the country, has produced the worst consequences."[52]

The first of the resolutions placed much of the blame on Under-Secretary Drummond, whose insulting response to the magistrates of Tipperary "has had the unfortunate effect of increasing the animosities entertained against the owners of the soil, by the occupants who now consider themselves the sole arbiters of the law." Robert Cassidy, a Catholic magistrate, then rose to say he did not agree with that resolution: "I didn't come here to hear the government of the country and the religion I profess assailed, and the people of the country arraigned as the perpetrators, or, at least, abettors of murder...I came here to record my sense of the atrocity that has been committed, and by all means to bring the perpetrators of that foul crime to justice." Nicholas Fitzsimon, another Catholic and MP for the county, included in his remarks his "hope that you would not have said to the people of this country they were attempting to effect that by assassination which they were unable to do by open rebellion." Protestant landlord Henry Trench of Congor Park also dissented.

As had been predicted, the liberal press was enraged by Oxmantown's and Charleville's speeches. On January 23, the nationalist *Freeman's Journal* published "The Murder of Lord Norbury and the Calumnies of Lords Oxmantown and Charleville." It began, "We have read the Tullamore proceeding with disgust greater than we can easily express. The occasion was one which demanded another tone of deliberation, and another strain of speech and resolution." The writer targeted three libelous accusations made by Lord Oxmantown, the first against the conspiratorial Irish Catholic peasantry, the second against their priests: "Here is a moan because of a rupture between the Catholic tenant and the Protestant landlord, and how does the Protestant landlord set about mending the rent? He charges a recent most hideous deed of blood upon the whole body of the rural population, and in nearly as distinct terms brands the ministers of their religion as instigators of the crime." The third libelous attack was made upon the Irish government: "Lord Oxmantown proposes to apply for protection to the Castle, insolently adding that he expects neither support nor sympathy. This man is the lord lieutenant of his county—how long will he be suffered to retain that office?"

The author remarked that Drummond's so-called insult would not have offended the landlords so much if they had indeed been attending to the duties of property. He praised "the speeches of two or three liberal gentlemen whose voices were heard upon this occasion," and continued:

[Men such as these, however, have considerable] "influence at meetings of magistrates in Ireland. It is the curse and plague of that country to possess a landed aristocracy infected with a religious bigotry the most benighted, and a fell hostility to every government that cherishes a kindly feeling towards the people...They are conspirators against themselves; their own murderers, and the assassins of the public quiet. It is only justice to the unfortunate Lord Norbury to state that he was honourably distinguished, as all accounts concur in bearing witness, from the aristocratic horde with which he was associated. He was no slanderer of the people, their faith, and their priesthood; he was no ranting assailant of the Queen's government at county meetings or Orange gatherings. The darkest mystery envelopes his horrid fate, which we sincerely trust the exertions of the executive and the temptations of the large rewards offered may speedily enable us to penetrate.

But, although numerous suspects were arrested, they were all subsequently released for lack of evidence, and the mystery was never solved.

Lord Normanby relinquished his post as lord-lieutenant of Ireland when he was recalled to London in March 1839 to become home secretary in Melbourne's administration. Lord Oxmantown, who had earned a first-class honors degree at Magdalen College, Oxford, and pursued his passion for astronomy on his return to King's County, succeeded his father as earl of Rosse in 1841, and built the largest reflecting telescope in the world at that time in the gardens of Birr Castle. He remained lord lieutenant of King's County until his death in 1867. In the House of Lords on July 19, 1839, Lord Brougham presented a Report from the Committee on the State of Crime in Ireland based on testimony from a number of witnesses, including Lord Normanby and Thomas Drummond. Normanby said he was anxious as early as possible to give the best explanation that he could of any acts of his which might be called into question. Thomas Drummond died, possibly from overwork on Irish affairs, in Dublin in April 1840. His funeral "was attended by almost every person of importance in the state or city and the whole populace joined in the procession." A statue was erected by public subscription in Dublin's City Hall. The obvious needs for reform would lead to the Devon Commission appointed by Tory prime minister Sir Robert Peel in 1841 to research the problems with land leases. William Henry Head would give extensive testimony to this commission. Meanwhile, the outrages continued, and Daniel O'Connell began his "monster" repeal meetings to which hundreds of thousands of Catholic farmers and laborers flocked to hear their charismatic leader.

Chapter 14

Repeal, Bankruptcy, and the Great Famine

If these were ordinary times, I would admit the rule, that every country is bound to support its own poor. As long as Ireland was not affected with a peculiar calamity she did so. I now object to that doctrine, because Ireland has been visited with the most afflicting dispensation that has befallen any country; and I think it is not too much to say, that it is a national fate, and that all should come forward to avert it as a national calamity.
—William Henry Head, speech, Nenagh, Co. Tipperary, January 24, 1847.

Daniel O'Connell was certain that self-government was the route to curing Ireland's ills, but when a Tory government under Sir Robert Peel took office in August 1841, the prospect of gaining repeal of the Act of Union through the Westminster Parliament seemed to diminish. Believing that some kind of extra-parliamentary pressure was needed, and having concluded his term as mayor of Dublin, O'Connell and his aides switched their tactics for repealing the act and restoring the Irish Parliament in Dublin by staging a series of open-air meetings in the three southern provinces that would attract large audiences. O'Connell explained that these "monster meetings" were not to convince Irish nationalists "but to convince our enemies—to convince the British statesmen...I want to make all Europe and America know it—I want to make England feel her weakness if she refuses to give the justice we require—the restoration of our domestic parliament."[1] During a six-month period in 1843, the O'Connellites organized more than thirty repeal gatherings. Some of the sites chosen were intended to highlight Ireland's

Celtic past and thereby to awaken in the people a renewed sense of Irish history and culture.

On May 25, 1843, O'Connell spoke to the great repeal meeting for North Tipperary on Grange Hill, one and a half miles from Nenagh. "From five o'clock in the morning the people began to pour in from the neighbouring districts and there were steamers plying the Connaught shore of the Shannon to Dromineer in which thousands were conveyed to join in this great assembly. An estimated 400,000 people came to hear the Liberator's speech at 2.30 p.m. after his triumphal procession from Thurles through Nenagh," claimed Young Ireland's newspaper, *The Nation*.[2] The conservative *Nenagh Guardian* was more restrained, estimating in its full coverage that 100,000 persons gathered on the ground, while O'Connell himself claimed that the numbers there exceeded those at any previous meeting.[3] Many of those who attended joined a procession from Nenagh to Grange, led by a band and men of various trades with all their regalia, which passed under two symbolically decorated triumphal arches mounted at crossroads for the occasion.

After he climbed onto the large platform erected for the occasion—which proved to be dangerously unstable—O'Connell began to speak in his magnificent ringing voice. "You came here to give Peel and Wellington to understand that it is your fixed determination that Ireland will be governed by the Irish and for the Irish." "Yes, yes," roared the crowd, as he continued to whip up patriotic fervor: "That you are tired of Saxon misrule," O'Connell went on, "that those who call you aliens in blood and aliens in language are enemies," and, he added, "The Union was taken from us by bribery and corruption, and even some of the gentlemen of Tipperary were connected with it."[4] Among the many promises he made that day were the elimination of tithe, compensation to tenants for improvements they made to their land, and fixity of tenure: "the landlord should give leases of 21 years, or larger if he pleases." Many Catholic priests and the Roman Catholic bishop of Killaloe were active participants in the meeting and the festive dinner in Temperance Hall that night. Even though the crowds at this and all the other monster meetings were remarkably disciplined and well-behaved, the government in Dublin retaliated by dismissing eight Catholic magistrates.[5]

Despite their crowd-pleasing entertainments and excitement, topped by O'Connell's flamboyantly inspirational speeches, the monster meetings failed to achieve their objective. British government and public opinion remained steadfastly opposed to granting self-government to Ireland in any form: it was deemed to threaten the existence of the United Kingdom and its empire. The Peel government banned, at the last minute, the monster meeting scheduled for October 8 on the fields of Clontarf near Dublin, symbolically chosen as it was where Irish king Brian Boru defeated a Viking army in 1014. O'Connell—a lifelong pacifist and constitutionalist—then canceled the meeting and ordered the massive crowds to go home. Nevertheless, he and eight of his associates were charged with unlawfully trying to alter the government and the constitution. After a lengthy trial before a packed jury, they were found guilty, fined, and sent to Dublin's Richmond Prison for up to a year. Their early release in September 1844 was gained by an appeal to the House of Lords in Westminster. With his health failing and following a schism with the more radical Young Irelanders, O'Connell never regained his momentum, and the repeal effort sputtered out in the trauma of the potato famine. O'Connell died, brokenhearted, in Rome in 1847, but his ideas endured through later nationalist movements.

While the repeal movement waxed and waned, the last of the Head family proprietors of the Derry Castle estate were in no shape to improve the circumstances of the many hundreds of extremely impoverished people eking out an existence on their lands. Like many others in Ireland, the estate had been in terminal financial condition for years. An advertisement for the sale of Derry Castle in the *Dublin Evening Post* of August 20, 1840 was seriously misleading, claiming that the estate was not only free of middlemen, having only yearly tenants, but "use of spirituous liquors is unknown throughout this vast district, the necessary consequence is a total absence of POLITICAL DIFFERENCES OR DISTURBANCES of any kind." If there was any truth to this, it may have been due to Father Theobald Mathew's temperance movement which was at its height, just before the Great Famine of 1845-49.[6] On September 10, 1840, the *Cheltenham Chronicle* reported the result of that year's highly publicized auction, held at Dublin's fashionable Gresham Hotel: "The sale of this splendid property has made a considerable sensation in the moneyed world," the report began. So much so that George Robins, the most famous auctioneer of his day in England, had been summoned to Dublin to conduct the sale. The rooms were crowded long before the auction began. Using his considerable eloquence to whip up excitement and competition, Robins insisted that the property was free of political turmoil and "that scourge of Irish property, the middle men, who it is pretty generally known, are the pests who take the farms at low rents in order to re-let them to the industrious class beyond their value." The property was knocked down for 70,000 guineas; however, even though Mr. Guinness, "our wealthy townsman (and the best brewer of porter in Europe)," was thought to be the purchaser, neither he nor anyone else came through with a firm offer at that time.[7]

Far from the region being "undisturbed," the *London Times* repeated the *Nenagh Guardian*'s assessment of reality the following year. The unsettled districts of northern Tipperary were being patrolled nightly by the 17th Lancers and a party of the Irish Constabulary, while other neighborhoods, including one very close to the Heads' former estate of Ashley Park, were occupied by detachments of the 20th Regiment. A dispute over encroachment of property had led to the murder of two farmers. This local paper continued to report endless heinous crimes from 1841 to 1845. Some involved issues with landlords, but more often, as previously stated, they stemmed from friction between tenants, nearly all of them over disputed land.

On May 19, 1841, an "improving" landlord, Robert Hall, a seventy-year-old Dublin merchant who had purchased his property between Cloughjordan and Borrisokane in 1828, was stalked and shot dead by two assassins on a tenant's farm, where he was investigating a report of burning land. According to Daniel Grace, Hall had "paid premiums to tenants who ploughed their land before Christmas, sowed turnips and other green crops, or laid down good quality grasses and clovers. He brought best quality seeds from Dublin and sold them to his tenantry at cost price. He built comfortable houses for his laborers and 'gave constant employment to a great number of persons.'" Even so, from the impressions of landlord William Steuart Trench of Sopwell Hall, who happened on the murder scene on his way to the Borrisokane petty sessions, Hall was disliked by the local peasantry for various reasons: "…on the faces of the peasantry could be plainly seen an expression of triumphant satisfaction."[8] One of the assassins was subsequently hanged after the other turned Queen's evidence. His accomplice, a farmer, was charged with conspiracy to murder, but acquitted at the assizes for lack of evidence. The *Nenagh Guardian* alleged in August that "In no district, shire or county in the kingdom is there more crime perpetrated with impunity than in this far-famed and celebrated county." The newspaper attributed this lawlessness to the laws to "the Rockite [violent agrarian movement] code of plunder of fire-arms, and carrying out the Captain's legislative functions by threats and intimidation," thus deterring witnesses from coming forward to give evidence.[9]

During this troubled period, William Henry Head, ever a supporter of British-Irish union, served on grand juries at the Clonmel and Nenagh Assizes before he was appointed a justice of the peace for Co. Tipperary by the lord chancellor of Ireland in March 1842 at the age of thirty-three.[10] He was probably present at a meeting of magistrates in April 1842 called to address "the very alarming state of the northern part of Co. Tipperary, as evidenced by the numerous outrages perpetrated within the last fortnight." As so often before, the magistrates sent a strongly worded dispatch to the executive government in Dublin asking for prompt measures to "afford protection for the lives and properties of the peaceable and well-disposed inhabitants of the disturbed districts."[11]

As an example of the increasing difficulty of convicting criminals in northern Tipperary, William Henry Head was one of two magistrates who indicted a laborer, Michael Leonard, for "willful and corrupt perjury" at Borrisokane in late 1842. According to Head, they had taken the testimony of the severely beaten young man at his home, where he named the men who assaulted him. However, after three weeks recovering, the evidently intimidated victim said he was mistaken in identifying his assailants. He was convicted for perjury at Nenagh in early 1843. The punishment levied after his conviction was harsh, one month in jail and then transportation for seven years—better perhaps than losing his life to his assailants.[12] The new Nenagh Courthouse was ready for the summer 1843 assizes at a cost of £7,000 but the magistrates were increasingly frustrated in the face of intimidation of victims and witnesses. The lawlessness and the resulting paranoia continued.

Following the 1838 Poor Law Act (see chapter 13), relief for the poor was financed by local poor law rates that were levied on occupiers of land valued at four pounds and over. The intention was to save money by doing away with outdoor relief and the provision of public works for the unemployed during periods of hardship. Relief was to be offered only in the local workhouse and only as a last resort. Each poor law union was supervised by a board of guardians.[13] William Henry Head was one of thirty-four members elected in 1842 to the Nenagh Board of Guardians—by Cloughjordan ratepayers in his case. "Each of the guardians considered it his primary duty to keep down the poor rate in his particular division—especially as he himself was usually one of the largest payers," claimed Grace, somewhat sarcastically. He also noted that, while two Catholic members who lived nearby had almost perfect attendance, Head only attended six of forty-seven meetings between March 31, 1842 and February 1843. Grace acknowledged that distance could have been the reason, while guardians also had their own business affairs to attend to.[14] Richard Uniacke Bayly, Dean John Head's son-in-law, who lived far closer to Nenagh and became the most active of the Poor Law Guardians, acknowledged that the business of the guardians was complex and time-consuming.

Minor gentry he may have been, but William Henry Head was earning a reputation for rational thinking and probity. On August 16, 1844, in the grand jury room of the Nenagh Courthouse, he testified before the Devon Commission appointed by Sir Robert Peel to inquire into the occupation of land in Ireland. Peel established the commission as part of his attempt to balance his uncompromising rejection of repeal with measures of moderate reform, yet, to many in Ireland, its efforts were defeated by one major flaw. As Daniel O'Connell put it, "It is perfectly one-sided, all landlords and no tenants."[15]

Parts of Head's testimony have been quoted by historians, from Tipperary-based Daniel Grace to Canadian scholar Bruce Elliott.[16]

As Elliott explained the area's troubles: "The economic situation in North Tipperary was made worse by the peculiar social structure of the area. The resident gentry in the most fertile part of the region were gentlemen of moderate means and small estates who were themselves adversely affected by the economic troubles of the early nineteenth century. The uncertainty of rents forced many of them to seek economic survival by enlarging their demesne farms and converting tillage to more pastoral uses." This was certainly the strategy of William Henry Head, a so-called "improving landlord" like the earlier Michael Heads of Derry Castle. Elliott assessed that the number of tenant evictions in Co. Tipperary "proportional to population was greater than in any other county but Kerry." W. H. Head and other landed gentry devoted their properties primarily to stock rearing. "These practices," which derived from the economic uncertainty of the landlords, "drove tenants and labourers from the lands that could best support them," claimed Elliott in his well-regarded 1988 study, "and were major contributory causes of the distress of the common people."[17]

Asked by the Devon commissioners what he thought was the cause of the high level of agrarian outrages in his district, Head responded in part: "The district is dotted over with small landowners in the upper classes [among whom I include myself], who are generally anxious for the possession of land. This tends to bring them into collision with the lower orders, and there is a struggle between them for the land itself, and this circumstance may have helped to have raised a feeling of hostility between them." "[I]t is certainly unfortunate," he continued, "that...the lower classes should see, in most of those opposed to them in the competition for land, persons of a different religion from themselves." He affirmed that consolidating smallholdings into larger farms was another problem, leaving the rural poor huddled together in certain spots, far too numerous "to be supported by the land they occupy." They labored under the double evil of too little land and lack of employment on the lands of others. His own experience was that he could get any number of laborers he wanted any day for eight pence a day.[18] However, experienced laborers from neighboring estates were much preferred over the most impoverished and less experienced "cottier" laborers. While not wanting to lay the blame on any one class, Head did not think the outrages were perpetrated by the lowest class of landless or almost landless people; more generally they resulted from disputes between small farmers who used their servant boys to perpetrate the crimes. In his considered opinion, "It is a sort of intimidating system...Every serious crime, generally speaking, can be traced to the tenure of land."[19]

Whatever the reasons for their alleged criminal activity, the reality was the situation of the rural poor by the early 1840s was dire. Despite multiple warnings, chronic over-population and subdivision of land had continued unabated to the point where 45 percent of holdings were of less than five acres. Those of less than an acre were not even considered, so hundreds of thousands of very small patches were not counted. Enough potatoes could be grown on an acre and a half to support a family of four or five for twelve months, whereas the cultivation of grain required far more land, equipment, and knowledge of tillage. Potatoes needed little cultivation, being simply earthed up by spade from trenches, and could be grown at the edges of bogs or on the mountainside where farm equipment could not be used. Mixed with milk or buttermilk, they made a scientifically healthy and nutritious diet. Poor people also fed them to their pigs, if they had any. Pig-raising, so essential to their subsistence economy (it was commonly said that "the pig paid the rent") declined drastically when there was a lack of potatoes. Thus a bloated, closely-packed and impoverished population, living in appalling conditions, three-quarters of whose laborers were unemployed, was dependent on the potato for survival.[20] It is important to stress, however, that social stratification was far more complex than is popularly assumed. As Grace has emphasized, there were gradations in all classes. Some laborers, particularly those in landlord employment, were sure of regular work and remuneration and it was generally agreed that landlords treated their workers better than the farmers did.[21]

The Devon Commission, which had visited every part of Ireland and examined 1,100 witnesses, published its report in February 1845. It repeated the findings of the 1841 census that Ireland's population had exploded from six million to more than eight million, making it the most densely populated country in Europe. According to Cecil Woodham-Smith in her brilliant, if rather nationalistic, 1962 bestseller *The Great Hunger: Ireland 1845-1849*, the report stated that the principal cause of Irish misery was the bad relations between landlord and tenant. "Ireland was a conquered country, the Irish peasant a dispossessed man, his landlord an alien conqueror. There was no paternalism, such as existed in England, no hereditary loyalty or feudal tie." She tempered this harsh assessment with the observation that there were some landlords who were notable exceptions, "whose names survive and are regarded with affection in Ireland today."[22] In other words, all was not black and white. Many individual landlords indeed did care for their tenants, sometimes to the point of bankruptcy. The report's most important recommendation was that outgoing tenants should be compensated for any improvements they had made. A bill to effectuate this was introduced in June 1845 but was withdrawn at that time. This was the beginning of this author's understandable quest for evidence that W. H. Head was one of the "good landlords" still remembered for acts of charity.

Efforts at various reforms were nonetheless continuing. In order to ease the burden on the grand juries in the Nenagh assizes, justices of the peace in Lorrha and Cloughjordan, among others, applied to have more petty sessions set up at the local level. William Henry Head was among the five magistrates in the parish of Modreeny applying for petty sessions in Cloughjordan.[23] At the same time, on the eve of the potato famine, the government and landlords were embracing an effort to improve Ireland's rural economy by building an ambitious network of railways to connect the major farming areas with the island's principal ports. W. H. Head was a patron of the completion of the Galway and Kilkenny line to connect the ports of Galway and Waterford with a proposed branch line to Killaloe and Nenagh. Other local patrons included his cousin, John Head, dean of Killaloe, their Bayly cousins—John Bayly, a landlord who was then high sheriff of County Tipperary, and his brother and agent Richard Uniacke Bayly—and Simon George Purdon, former fiancé of Henrietta Head. Newspapers at this time were full of plans and prospectuses.

Concurrent with the Devon Commission, the long-drawn-out drama of the Derry Castle estate came to a climax. Initially, it was purchased in May 1844 for £38,000, half the amount apparently offered by Mr. Guinness four years earlier. On August 13, it was resold for £39,500 to Francis Spaight, Esq., of Limerick, the sale presided over by Thomas Goold, master of the court of chancery. The principal creditor this time was Dublin barrister Richard Beere, a member of a Tipperary landed family. Spaight acquired 3,000 Irish acres of land, the mansion house, and offices "on the most picturesque and frequented part of the Upper Shannon, near Killaloe."[24] Once all the documents had been signed and the money paid out to numerous other creditors, including many Head relations, it was agreed that the Head family would move out in early April 1845.

Local legend has it that Henrietta or one of her sisters fell down dead from grief and shock on the steps of the mansion as the family was leaving on April 3, 1845. In reality, it was their stepmother who succumbed to her grief. Mary Head, widow of Michael Prittie Head, died at the age of seventy-three on April 5, 1845 at Castletown Rectory. "Deep affliction, and an almost unprecedented reverse of fortune, preyed on the heart of this venerable lady, who survived just two days after quitting an abode which in other times had been to her one of life and joy," according to the *Tipperary Vindicator*.[25] Perhaps Mary Head, in no psychological or physical shape to make that move, had accepted an invitation to stay with the Rev. Standish Grady Parker, the most recent heir to the Parker family's Castletown and Castlelough estates. Neighbors and close friends of the Derry Castle Heads since the eighteenth century, the highly regarded Parker family had built the Protestant rectory and church on their land, where Michael Prittie Head and a teenage daughter were buried.[26]

As for the siblings, Henrietta was already living in Limerick with her husband, although she may have been at the mansion to support her family that day. Michael Henry, Caroline, Emily, and Margaret Head moved to Castle Connell, Co. Limerick, on the Shannon River south of Derry Castle. This picturesque and once fashionable spa town, where many family friends had large houses, is eleven miles from Limerick City and close to the boundaries with counties Clare and Tipperary. An end note to the Heads' 150-year tenure at Derry Castle came with the announcement of the death, on January 3, 1846, of Mary Vaughan, former housekeeper to Capt. Michael Henry Head, his father, and grandfather, at the remarkable age of one hundred and fifteen. "It was she who lighted the first fire in the splendid mansion of Derry Castle on its completion. This extraordinary woman could up to twelve months ago see to thread the finest needle."[27] How many of the joys and dramas of the Heads of Derry Castle must she have witnessed but did not record.

It cannot have taken long for Francis Spaight, a successful businessman, to discover the reality of what he had purchased. The Spaights were timber, corn, and coal importers from Canada and the owners of a fleet of steamers out of Limerick that conveyed cargo and passengers around the world. When he bought the estate, the number of tenants, laborers, and servants numbered about 1,200, "including widows and poor persons under a nominal rent which they had not paid for years."[28] The situation was far worse than it appeared. It seemed as if the Heads had mismanaged the estate, whether out of sheer incompetence or benevolence toward the Catholic tenantry, reflecting M. P. Head's lifelong liberal politics. Even as late as September 1842, the Heads were regarded as one of the "families of distinction in the neighbourhood." Michael Henry Head and the women of his family were identified this way when they all attended a dinner to celebrate the roughly seven hundred men "employed in the stupendous work now in active and permanent operation at the Imperial Slate Company's Quarries" near Killaloe, as the *Nenagh Guardian* described them that year.[29] Michael Henry Head served at the Nenagh quarter assizes more than once in 1844. In the wake of this latest family humiliation and the striking contrast in the way the new owner of the Derry Castle estate began addressing its appalling condition, it seems logical that young William Henry Head of Modreeny would develop into a hard-headed businessman, as a son later described him, determined to avoid his cousins' fate.

On August 5, 1845, one year after purchasing the estate, Spaight launched an attempt to execute 190 decrees and attachments for arrears of rent against defaulting tenants. The deputy sheriff of Tipperary, accompanied by fifty Royal Irish Constabulary and fifty soldiers of the 1st Royals stationed at Killaloe, marched to the section of the Derry Castle estate where the offenders lived. There they found every house locked up and barricaded and not a single head of cattle on the land nor any human to be seen, except for a few urchins acting as scouts. When the sheriff knocked on doors, the occupants refused to open them. The party was forced to retire from the scene.[30] The *Nenagh Guardian* was severely critical of "the folly of permitting tenants to run into large arrear…The more arrears a tenant owes, the less inclined he is to pay, and the longer he holds, or is permitted to hold the land, the less inclined he is to give it up." Meanwhile, claimed the editorial, the tenants take what they can out of the land without making any improvements, thus leaving the land worth one-third of its original value.[31] "This is always the result of a mistaken indulgence, or a want of proper resolution and determination on the part of a Landlord or Agent, to obtain his rights—for he is ultimately obliged to do at last what he should have done at first." However, five days later, the same newspaper emphasized that "The indulgent Landlord who has so kindly and considerately suffered these arrears to accumulate, is *no other than the Court of Chancery*, and the active Agent in the proceedings is Mr. David Daly, the Receiver under the Courts, and the Law Agent of one of the Creditors of the Estate before its sale." The *Nenagh Guardian* article made clear that "The Tipperary Landlords do not, therefore, deserve the strong censure…expressed in the *Evening Packet*," failing to acknowledge its own critical statements.[32]

Spaight continued to be frustrated in his efforts to collect overdue rent. After he advertised the upcoming auction of the produce of five fields of wheat, two of oats, and some hay seized by the receiver and overseen by seven bailiffs, the tenants harvested and hid the crops overnight, "not a straw was left."[33] But a considerable number of the tenants were law-abiding and eager to please their new landlord. Four hundred men and women assembled one morning to dig his potatoes and were then treated to a meal and dancing—the favorite Irish diversion from general misery—in two halls on the estate until the following morning. Only a week earlier, however, the *Nenagh Guardian* had reported that "the awful plague," the potato blight, had appeared in the Nenagh neighborhood following torrential rains in advance of the harvest. A sub-inspector intimated in late October, however, that potatoes planted in moor or boggy soil were comparatively safe. Richard Uniacke Bayly reported that "the rich lands have suffered most, particularly lea fields."[34]

Though Francis Spaight was temporarily stymied in his efforts to make his purchase profitable, two years later the devastating potato famine would provide a drastic solution.

Tensions between landlords and tenants remained high. In November 1845, Patrick Clarke, an extensive landowner and formerly a member of a Dublin firm of solicitors and land agents, was shot and killed on his own demesne. Clarke, another "improving" landlord, had intervened to prevent a dispute over crops between a tenant and the tenant's two sons. The following month, the magistrates of Northern Tipperary, under the chairmanship of Lord Dunalley, sent an address to the British Public, in which they described Mr. Clarke's murder, commenting that: "Generally...no attempt is made by the surrounding peasantry to arrest the murderer, and subsequent information can rarely be obtained in furtherance of the ends of justice...Englishmen...can have no idea of the terrible influence which the constant dread of impending assassination exercises over the mind." The magistrates claimed that in their jurisdiction, between August 1844 and February 1845, there had been sixteen murders, sixteen attempted murders, and fifty-two cases of firing into houses, robberies of arms, grievous assaults, and threatening notices. Once again, they called for a modified insurrection act to be implemented by the government when it was felt to be necessary. They also asked for a new law imposing a fine on any district where a murder or attempted murder should occur, with the proceeds payable to the victim or his survivors. William Henry Head was among the signatories to this appeal.[35]

Novelist Maria Edgeworth wrote of the Clarke case, "This system of picking out landlords for vengeance is worse than open rebellion...It appears to be the system of the leagued people to show that no landlord's nor agent's life, let him be ever so good, can be safe unless he gives up possession of his land, either for the present rent, whatever it may be, or in short, to give up rents altogether. It would soon come to *that* if the first demand were granted."[36] By the following spring, the potato blight would replace terrorist acts by the peasantry with death by starvation and disease. The potato famine temporarily broke the insurgent spirit of the landless and small farmers.

In August 1845, the blight that had ravaged the potato crop in North America reached England. When, in October, potatoes were due to be dug out of the ground in Ireland, terrifying reports began to flow into the governments in Dublin and London. At first, the potatoes looked healthy but, within a few days, the storage pits became a stinking black mass. Thus, Francis Spaight's tenants appeared to have dug a splendid crop for him and celebrated long and hard at his expense before reality struck. The British government sent scientists to Dublin to determine if something edible could be salvaged from the diseased potatoes. They returned home three weeks later, having published volumes of useless and almost incomprehensible suggestions. Meanwhile, the abundant Irish oat harvest continued to be exported despite the probability that it would be needed to help feed those who were dependent on the potato.

Apart from dispatching the "men of science," the British Government had taken no steps to confront the growing disaster. On October 28, the Dublin Corporation called the first of a series of meetings resulting in a deputation to the lord-lieutenant, Lord Heytesbury, to urge him to adopt measures "to avert calamity." Daniel O'Connell, a member of this large deputation, drew up proposals calling for immediately stopping the export of corn and provisions, throwing open the ports for free import of food, rice, and Indian corn from the colonies, and setting up relief organizations and employment on public works. The deputation proposed that the costs of the measures be met by levying a ten per cent tax on the rents collected by resident landlords, and between twenty to fifty percent on rents collected by the agents of absentee landlords. Their proposals received a cold reception. But, in the meantime, Robert Peel had made the momentous decision to repeal the protectionist Corn Laws so grain could be freely imported to feed those in Ireland who had been relying solely on the potato. Forced to ally himself with Whigs and radicals to achieve this long-debated reform, he infuriated the landlords in his own party. On November 9 or 10, without waiting for Treasury sanction, Peel "secretly" ordered £100,000 to be spent on purchasing Indian corn (maize) in the United States and shipping that vital food to Ireland.[37]

Peel appointed a relief commission consisting of some of the ablest and most influential members of the Irish administration under the chairmanship of Sir Randolph Routh, officer in charge of the commissariat department of the army. Charles Edward Trevelyan, permanent secretary at the Treasury, had overall responsibility for guiding and implementing the government relief policy. Although the British government made this attempt to alleviate the situation, in subsequent decades nationalists would place much of the blame for what followed entirely on Trevelyan.[38] But it should not be forgotten that he was a civil servant implementing a policy decided by his political masters. The relief commissioners proceeded to form committees of local landowners or their agents, magistrates, clergy (both Catholic and Protestant), and important residents. These committees were to buy food for resale to distressed people or even provide food free in urgent cases. Local employment schemes such as roadbuilding were to be organized and the landlords were encouraged to increase employment on their estates. But this relief program was affected by a major flaw, similar to the one that undermined the Devon Commission: the onus for relief was placed heavily on Irish landlords, many of whom were already on the verge of bankruptcy due to existing encumbrances and debts and now the crippling effect of both poor law taxes and non-payment of rents.

Six magistrates, under the chairmanship of Richard Uniacke Bayly, attended an explanatory session at the Nenagh courthouse in February 1846 and agreed to apply to the Irish Board of Works for £4,000 to employ local men on twenty-two public works. Sixteen projects were approved, including laying new lines of road, lowering hills, or filling hollows on existing roads. The Lower Ormond sessions on March 2, chaired by Jonathan P. Walsh of Walsh Park, Lorrha, applied for a further eighty-one works at a proposed cost of £9,926, of which twenty-two were sanctioned.[39] The Public Works (Ireland) Act was passed in March 1846 but works in the most distressed areas were slow to get underway, apparently a deliberate ploy by Trevelyan and the British Treasury to postpone assistance for as long as possible. Daniel Grace drew up a map of the Nenagh Union showing the percentage of unemployed laborers in each electoral division during the spring of 1846. Unemployment was among the worst in areas where the Heads had owned or still owned estates: Castletown, 75 percent; Templekelly, 50 percent; Borrisokane, 66.6 percent; and Cloughjordan, 75 percent.[40]

In April, local landlords began informing Dublin Castle of anguished crowds gathering around their houses demanding relief. Caleb Going of Traverston reported that individuals in a crowd of two hundred warned him that, unless they got work at once, "they would be driven to desperation." Going begged the authorities to begin relief work at once. Jonathan P. Walsh wrote of "the sudden appearance of large assembled bodies of the distressed poor marching through this district of the country." His house had been surrounded by a mob estimated at seven hundred people. Walsh warned "that the people will not remain quiet much longer under their extreme distressed estate" and attacked the board of works for "their very long delays" in opening operations in Lower Ormond." Thomas Brereton, a resident magistrate of Portumna, Co. Galway, reported that three hundred men had visited several gentlemen's houses in the parish of Lorrha and Dorrha demanding food or employment. Brereton described their leader, Anthony Moylan, as "a great agitator" who had attended repeal meetings all over the country.[41] In late April, a disconcerted Richard Uniacke Bayly, secretary of the Ballinaclough & Kilkeary committee, wrote, "I am sorry to say some landlords have not contributed to our funds." However, Father Michael Scanlan, parish priest of Ballygibbon, praised the generosity of several landlords, mentioning in particular the absentee marquis of Ormond, Nicholas Biddulph of Congor, and the Falkiner family.[42]

On April 29, a meeting was held at the courthouse in Borrisokane for the purpose of appointing a baronial relief committee for Lower Ormond, and subcommittees for its districts and parishes. Thomas Sadleir of Ballinderry Park, who was tireless in his efforts to help the starving poor, proposed that Fr. Scanlan be asked to act as secretary. As proposed by Nicholas Biddulph, a committee was appointed for the barony. It included magistrates Thomas Sadleir, Jonathan W. Walsh, William H. Head, Charles Atkinson, William S. Trench, Thomas G. Stoney, and others; clergy, including Dean John Head and activist priests such as Frs. Nolan and Scanlan; landed proprietors; and poor law guardians.[43]

The *Tipperary Vindicator* had reported on April 10 that "the tide of emigration has been seldom, if ever, so strong as at the present moment. From the ports of Cork, Waterford, Limerick, Dublin, Sligo, Galway, etc., hundreds...are quitting their native shores, determined to trust their fortunes to the protection of Providence in other and more favoured climes. From the North Riding of Tipperary, and more particularly from the baronies of Upper and Lower Ormond, the number of emigrants is extraordinary." But the majority of these were relatively comfortable farmers who could sell their land and thus afford to emigrate.

Twenty-two relief districts were formed in northwest Tipperary during the late spring and early summer of 1846, of which at least fifteen were based on Church of Ireland (Protestant) parishes. According to Grace, the Catholic clergy were probably the most important members of local committees due to their knowledge of and influence over the lives of their parishioners. The first task was to raise funds by voluntary subscription. "Every resident and non-resident landlord was expected to contribute as liberally as his means allowed," and the committees often published the names of subscribers and amounts contributed in the local press. Grace compiled a table showing that the majority of subscriptions paid to rural committees came from members of the landed gentry, while certain rectors and parish priests also made generous contributions. Of the 82 percent from the gentry and clergy, Henry Prittie, Lord Dunally contributed approximately half.[44] The *Tipperary Vindicator* published several reports on the setting up of relief commissions in Northern Tipperary parishes, specifically in Modreeny. There was some talk of dividing that parish in two but it was decided that the Rev. Frederick Trench, Church of Ireland minister at Cloughjordan, had been conducting effective charitable operations there for many years. Subscription lists for Modreeny included £40 from the lord-lieutenant (equivalent to $5,000 today), £10 from Lord Dunalley, £5 each from Fr. Scanlan and the marquis of Ormond, and £4 from William H. Head. Lord Dunalley gave £40 to Cloughjordan while the Rev. Trench and Fr. Scanlan gave £5 each.[45] Some landlords, such as Dunalley, had lands in several parishes and would be contributing to several different committees.

The bitter acrimony over repeal of the Corn Laws was a disaster for famine-struck Ireland, since it caused that crisis to slip into the background in Westminster with the false sense that the issue had been taken care of. Even more serious, was the popular theory of *laissez faire* espoused by the Whigs, who returned to power when Peel's government fell in June 1846. Even in the face of the unfolding disaster, Lord John Russell's new government decided not to buy any more food, and instead let private enterprise supply the market. They failed to take into consideration that private enterprise in the food and provision trade in Ireland was largely undeveloped. Fully two-thirds of the Irish population depended on agriculture, and many who did so survived on subsistence farming, making them dangerously vulnerable to crop failures. Large numbers, particularly in the west and southwest, hardly *purchased* any food at all. They grew potatoes and lived on them. Government meal depots closed in mid-August, and committees were now forced to purchase supplies on the open market at inflated prices. The numbers employed on public works in Northwest Tipperary peaked at 18,946 during the week ending August 1.

The national potato yield per acre in 1846 was disastrous. Richard U. Bayly wrote on September 12, "Potatoes in general are not fit for use and there is scarcely a field where a labourer could dig more than a few stone in a day's work."[46] When blight struck again that autumn, there was no food to distribute and relief was limited to a hugely over-subscribed second phase of public works (October 1846 to June 1847). In the new scheme, the full cost of the works was to be borne by local taxation, throwing an enormous financial burden on Irish ratepayers, particularly the already financially precarious landlords. The *Nenagh Guardian* predicted that "it will be a dead weight upon their properties for ten years or more, which many of them will be totally unable to bear."[47] Meanwhile, British Treasury Secretary Trevelyan refused to allow the export of grains to be halted, despite Randolph Routh's unsuccessful suggestion that the export of higher-priced grains be prohibited.[48] This was one of Trevelyan's worst mistakes, providing some substance to the later nationalist charge that the British government was prepared to allow a large proportion of the Irish people to starve.[49]

Although Indian corn was available for purchase in Nenagh, its cost was prohibitive and the poor lacked the money to buy it and the means to process it. That autumn, a number of local committees, particularly Nenagh, were supplied with a total of 52 tons of whole meal at cost by landlords Lancelot Bayly of Bayly Farm, Ballina-clough, and Wills C. Bennett of Riverston, Nenagh. Their generosity allowed the committees to sell it to the poor at 1s. 10d. (twenty-two pence) per stone, 25 percent cheaper than the price demanded by Nenagh merchants. Those lucky enough to be employed on public works earned just eight or ten pence a day. The parish priest for Ballina & Boher praised Francis Spaight for employing about three hundred persons on his property, including some of the tenants, every day that the weather allowed. Spaight apparently paid them every week. The previous winter, he had distributed one hundred tons of Indian meal, and Mrs. Spaight had given large quantities of food, blankets, clothing, and money to the district's poor.[50] Several local landlords took out large loans for improvements to their properties, such as drainage schemes, thus providing employment. Some, like Sir Edward Waller and Thomas G. Stoney, expended so much that it contributed to their bankruptcies in 1850 and 1851.

But the winter of 1846-47 happened to be the worst in living memory, and starving people were searching desperately for food. Funds collected by the Nenagh committee fell by over 20 percent: Modreeny, William Henry Head's parish, fell by 35 percent, while Monsea, including the Heads' former estate Ashley Park, fell by as much as over 80 percent, all reflective of the increasing insolvency of local estates. "A Monsea Correspondent" informed the *Tipperary Vindicator*, "Nothing can exceed the misery to which the population of this once most wealthy parish is reduced."[51] Voluntary groups, such as the Quakers, established soup kitchens, but they were woefully inadequate. People were now dying of starvation, exposure, or diseases, including typhus and dysentery. By January 1847, the government conceded that the system was not working and decided on a new policy of feeding the destitute directly from soup kitchens. The *Tipperary Vindicator* confirmed that local committees were overwhelmed by the growing distress: "The labours of relief committees are wholly inoperative, without funds, without resources, with nothing to cheer the gloomy prospect of those who have devoted themselves to the task of seeing after the unparalleled wants of the poor."[52]

Ireland and Northern Tipperary call for Help

On January 14, 1847, five hundred leading Irishmen from all walks of life, including twenty-six Irish MPs met under the banner of the Irish parliamentary party in Dublin's Rotunda Hospital and agreed on a number of resolutions. Deeply critical of the policies of the British government, including the fact that massive amounts of food were being exported from the country, they agreed that the famine was an imperial disaster and recommended that relief committees be allowed to sell food under cost to the destitute.[53] Ten days later, the landowners, clergy, and gentry of North Tipperary met in Nenagh's courthouse for the same purpose. "The Conservative, the Whig, the Old Ireland, the Young Ireland, the Protestant and Roman Catholic parties seemed all fused into one body; having in view but one object, and seemingly united in one determination, and all seemed as if animated with but one feeling...'Justice for Ireland,'" reported the *King's County Chronicle*, a landlord newspaper, in its January 27 issue. Among those in attendance were the high sheriff John Trant, in the chair; Nicholas V. Maher, one of the county's MPs; the most active of the magistrates, including Thomas G. Stoney, Henry Prittie, Edward Waller, J. R. Minnitt, William H. Head, Jonathan W. Walsh, George Garvey (land agent to the Rosses of Birr Castle and the Toler family), George Atkinson, Thomas Sadleir, Richard Uniacke Bayly, and Caleb Going. Dean Head was among the many Protestant clergymen, while the numerous Catholic priests included the Revs. A. Nolan and M. Scanlan. Many of the merchants and shopkeepers of Nenagh were there too.

The meeting was called to consider "the present distressed state of Ireland, and to petition Parliament to adopt speedily such remedial measures as the calamitous condition of the country so imperatively requires." Maher wanted the basis of the meeting to be the proposals adopted by the meeting in Dublin.[54] "Would to God that a similar meeting had been held 30 years ago (hear, hear). There is a party at last established in Ireland, determined that the people shall not starve...the object of this meeting is to avert the misery if possible." He continued, "I must say that the present Government have committed a great error, by the non-interference with public enterprise, assisted by their lectures on political economy (hear, hear)."

In seconding Maher's resolution, Bayly, in his role as chairman of the board of guardians and member of a number of relief committees, emphasized "that the Destitution was very great. In the workhouse of the Nenagh Union, there are 300 paupers more than it had originally been built for." If the state of these people, many of whom were employed in public works, was so bad, "how horrifying must be the condition of those who have no employment, or who are unable to labour." He rejoiced that the North Riding of Tipperary was the first county in Ireland to back the resolution of the great National meeting in Dublin.

The Rev. Scanlan proposed the next resolution after giving an impassioned speech against the government for its doctrines of political economy. He was "deeply impressed with the necessity of all Irishmen uniting together for the safety of Ireland; and that not only all parties, but all classes, should cordially cooperate mutually to assist and protect each other." This resolution was seconded enthusiastically by Head. In his usual businesslike manner, he urged that the meeting should imitate the conduct of the Dublin meeting "by not indulging in long speeches, but to act practically upon the occasion," and continued:

> I think it peculiarly incumbent on all classes of Irishmen in this country to unite (hear, hear). The gentlemen of the country, those who are resident at least, are doing as much as can be expected from them (hear, hear). If these were ordinary times, I would admit the rule, that every country is bound to support its own poor. As long as Ireland was not affected with a peculiar calamity she did so. I now object to that doctrine, because Ireland has been visited with the most afflicting dispensation that has befallen any country; and I think it is not too much to say, that it is a national fate, and that all should come forward to avert it as a national calamity (hear, hear and cheers).

Head referred to inferences made by the *London Times* that the landed classes were only uniting then because property was being affected, "as if nothing else could affect them. I think it fair ground for them [the landlords] to unite if they find their property and the property of all classes injured. Property is not to be ridiculed in this manner…It was interference with property that caused the revolution of America (hear, hear and cheers). It was a small taxation that called forth a Hampden to the field (hear, hear and great cheering)." According to the newspaper account, he resumed his seat amid loud cheering.[55]

The Nenagh meeting resulted in a petition that was addressed "To the Right Hon. The Lords Spiritual and Temporal in Parliament Assembled" from the assembled clergy, gentry, and landowners of the County of Tipperary. Even though the two countries were presently united by the "monstrous anomaly of the same constitution, and equally entitled to the same just laws, the same wise government, and the same fostering care," England was constantly advancing in unparalleled prosperity, wealth, and power while Ireland remained the poorest, with the lowest level of economic progress, of any nation in Europe. The petitioners believed that disparity was not "entirely attributable to any defect in the natural character of the Irish people, but that it has been the fruit of a long course of neglect, as well as of ignorant and partial legislation on the part of the British Government, for which it owes this country, not only redress, but reparation." Moreover, the petition continued, "since the prorogation of Parliament, we conceive that the comforts and lives of the Irish people have been sacrificed to meet the sordid and selfish views of the English and foreign traders; and that, at a time when famine was abroad in the land, not only was there no check put upon the exportation of corn, but a positive refusal was given by Government to the most reasonable request on the behalf of starving men, that stores should be established throughout the country with the view of bringing down the market prices to the level of the poor men's means."

The petitioners earnestly called on the next session of Parliament to consider the present lamentable state of Ireland, paying attention "to the appalling fact that thousands in Ireland are at this moment starving, and millions on the eve of famine; and that unless the most prompt and effective measures are taken to feed this famishing multitude," there will be the direst consequences. "Many thousands of the poorer classes, who have hitherto obtained a scanty and precarious subsistence by conacre potatoes, are now left without any future means of subsistence ...[and] unless provision is made for the future livelihood of this very large and very destitute class, the land in this country will be burdened beyond what any land can be."[56] "We are persuaded," the petition concluded, "that the real interests, as well as the honour and character of the whole nation, will be served by such just, generous, and enlightened policy as may not only meet the present fearful visitation, but may render Ireland a credit instead of a reproach, as well as a constant source of embarrassment, difficulty, and danger." Dean Head proposed that copies of the petition be entrusted to Lord Hawarden for presentation in the house of lords, and to the Right Hon. Henry Labouchere, chief-secretary for Ireland, in the house of commons.[57]

When Queen Victoria opened Parliament on January 19, 1847, she began her speech by expressing her deepest concern for Ireland. During lengthy parliamentary debates about Russell's relief policies early in 1847, forty-three Irish MPs and sixty-four Irish peers signed a petition claiming their willingness "to submit to any charge" necessary to further extend workhouse accommodation but urging the retention of the workhouse test of destitution for the able-bodied poor. However, former lord chancellor Lord Brougham, while eulogizing the exemplary patience of the Irish people in the face of an unprecedented calamity, nonetheless cautioned the government to take care that the Irish people did not latch onto the idea that they would be permanently supported out of the public revenue. Any measures taken should be temporary, and they should understand that this temporary assistance must be repaid. [58] The Irish parliamentary party collapsed into warring factions when faced with varied reaction to the Whigs' Irish relief bill, which proposed the establishment of soup kitchens in the place of public works (the act, passed in February, became known as "the Soup Kitchen Act").

The British press, particularly the *London Times*, increasingly vilified Irish landlords and the Irish land system. The perceived predatory character of Irish landlordism was widely attributed in England to the deep financial indebtedness of many Irish landlords without discussion of the burdens of taxes and poor law rates. *The Times* sneered at the Irish landlord as "the old original pauper of Ireland" and "the grandfather of all destitute persons." In addition to the resentment already felt toward them in Britain for their perceived dumping of evicted pauper tenants on the shores of England, Scotland, and Wales, the Irish landlords and their representatives at Westminster were now seen as greedy, clamoring petitioners.[59] Determined to increase the burden on Irish landlords, British parliamentarians amended the Poor Law Act in June 1847 (see below).

On February 13, 1847, the *Tipperary Vindicator* reported, "The severity of the weather is almost unexampled. The cold is intense, accompanied by dense fog. Ice covers the rivers and streams. The sufferings of the poor are really terrible. God in his mercy help them!" Meanwhile, the Irish board of works issued instructions in March that public works should start to be scaled down. The conservative *Nenagh Guardian* was horrified that upwards of 2,500 laborers from the three baronies of the Nenagh Union would be "sent upon the world to perish." The newspaper pointed out that there was no employment in agricultural labor because farmers "have neither seed to crop, nor food nor money to give for the labour of others." It protested that, despite the appointment of sixty-four inspectors of "the soup brigade," there was "not one drop of soup as yet for the destitute," and it savagely condemned the Whig administration for its callous policy toward Ireland. The same newspaper reported sarcastically on April 24 that seven weeks after passage of the Temporary Relief or "Soup Kitchen" Act, the relief commission had succeeded in distributing fourteen tons of paper but not one ounce of food. "Perhaps our rulers are only trying the experiment of how long an Irishman can live without eating." In fact, the distribution of food did not commence in the Nenagh Union until May 6. The soup kitchens were by far the most effective of all the relief programs, but the poor loathed the indignity of having to line up with soup bowls.[60]

Although the potato crop was free of blight that summer and quantities were coming to the Nenagh market, the acreage planted that year was only about 10 percent of the usual pre-famine crop. Nenagh's poor law union estimated that acreage devoted to potatoes had fallen from 14,035 in 1846 to just 2,342 in 1847. Diseases such as typhus and dysentery were now raging in the Nenagh workhouse and among the population still living in their cabins. Nevertheless, dwellings were being knocked down at an alarming rate following large-scale evictions, particularly in the area ringed by Nenagh, Cloughjordan, and Borrisokane.

Disease was not confined to the poorer classes. Caroline Head died at Beech Lawn in Castle Connell quite suddenly on April 8, more than likely from disease. Her obituary noted that "In every relation of life she won the affection and esteem of all who knew her, and her loss will be long and deeply deplored by her sorrowing relatives and friends." A little more than two months later, on June 24, Capt. Michael Henry Head, last Head proprietor of the Derry Castle estate, also died at Castle Connell.[61] No cause of death was given for either of the siblings but, as Cecil Woodham-Smith noted, "Among the upper classes the percentage of those who caught fever and died was high; in Cavan, upper-class mortality was estimated at 66 percent…in almost every district in Ireland mortality among the upper-classes was reported to be proportionately higher than among the poor."[62]

Despite Ireland's troubles, the Heads' successor at Derry Castle was determined to put his newly acquired property on a more secure financial footing, including, as he testified to the Select Committee of the House of Lords on Colonization from Ireland, clearing the "dead weight," as he put it, of impoverished cottiers and consolidating their smallholdings into larger farms. Spaight wisely decided not to resort to large-scale eviction, realizing that there "would have been open Rebellion in the country and no Safety for Life to myself or any Member of my Family."

As he was engaged in the passenger trade, his solution was to offer free passage and provisions to those willing to emigrate, and the value of two pounds on landing, providing the tenants "tumbled," that is, pulled down, their cabins on the Derry estate. He made the offer only to entire families and said he had "got rid of crime and distress for 3 pounds, 10 shillings a head."[63] "From the Derrycastle & Burgess Estate, Killaloe," announced the *Limerick Reporter* in April, "100 poor families, averaging 500 persons, gladly surrendered their small holdings to the proprietor Francis Spaight…and set off for America in the *Jane Black*, where they are to be landed free of charge, with the intention of setting up in Canada as farm labourers. Others from Derry Castle traveled in the *Albion*

(60 passengers) and still more in the *Horatio* (40)."[64] Spaight said in his testimony that the entire scheme cost him about £5,000. He freely admitted that he could not have unburdened himself of his impoverished tenants so easily were it not for the recent crisis. Cottiers had previously clung limpet-like to their small plots, but failure of the potato crop rendered the land almost valueless to them. He testified that his former tenants had written such enthusiastic reports of their success "that they have induced Hundreds of others to make Application to go out, and in consequence I shall have 710 going from me this year."[65] By 1848, Spaight had reduced the population of the Derry Castle estate by approximately 50 percent. Local folklore is harsh on Spaight, although some of the stories are too lurid to be credible. The fact is that he saved many lives and gave impoverished peasants an escape to a land where brains, hard work, and good luck might offer better prospects —but did he learn how many of them died en route and on arrival?

The reality of passage on emigrant ships and arrival in the new world was cruel. Cecil Woodham-Smith and American writer John Kelly have described the horrors awaiting these and thousands of other Irish immigrants in Canada, where "intelligent officials and citizens apprehensively awaited the immigration which would fall on them as soon as the St. Lawrence was clear of ice." The U.S. had taken temporary steps to prevent the landing of poor immigrants in its ports and, despite rumors of the desperate conditions in Ireland, the Canadian government had received no official warning of what to expect. The ice on the St. Lawrence was unusually thick that year, and the first vessel from Ireland did not arrive until May 17. A week later, masses of "coffin ships" were lined up for two miles along the St. Lawrence to land their sick and dying passengers at Quebec. A fever hospital was set up on Grosse-Isle in the St. Lawrence, but it proved to be totally inadequate.

Both Woodham-Smith and Kelly vividly described the horrific conditions on Grosse Isle. Kelly reported that Francis Spaight's ship, the *Jane Black*, arrived at Grosse Isle from Limerick on May 20 with thirteen dead and twenty fever and dysentery cases. "Many of her sick would die within days," Kelly wrote. He claimed that 5,294 Irish emigrants died on the island. A Celtic cross there records the disaster. Its inscription in Gaelic reads, "Thousands of the children of Gael were lost on this island/While fleeing from the foreign tyrannical laws and an/artificial famine in the years 1847-8. God bless them. God save Ireland."[66]

The draconian Poor Law Extension Act of June 1847 marked a major shift in British government policy with respect to famine distress in Ireland. Under the new act, Irish property owners and tenants would henceforth bear the full burden of fiscal responsibility for relief, which was to be administered solely by the Irish poor-law system. For the first time, the poor-law authorities were allowed to extend relief to destitute persons without necessarily obliging them to become inmates of a workhouse. In the case of the able-bodied, this outdoor relief was to be made available only under the most stringent conditions, mainly where insufficient accommodation existed within the workhouses. The act embodied the principle popular in Britain that "Irish property must support Irish poverty," without recognizing the backbreaking burden this placed on economically distressed landlords.

While British government ministers, many British MPs and a wide section of the British public and press considered the poor law amendment as a long overdue measure of popular justice and genuine benevolence toward Ireland, British financial self-interest was well-served by the new law. What few in Britain seemed to realize, however, was the potential impact of the notorious Gregory or quarter-acreage clause, which decreed that any family living on more than a quarter of an acre would not be eligible for public assistance.[67] The clause encouraged and facilitated wholesale clearances of impoverished tenants from many estates with the excuse that they would now be eligible for relief, and greatly raised mortality rates in those districts of the south and west where most evictions were concentrated. The 1847 eviction rate for Co. Tipperary was the highest in Ireland, 7.9 percent for that year alone.

Following the general election in July, a large number of radical Whigs entered parliament, reflecting middle-class industrial and commercial hostility toward large government expenditure on Irish relief. The immediate result was closure of the soup kitchens in September. Local boards of guardians launched outdoor relief instead, distributing raw Indian meal at designated centers within each poor law union under the direction of relief officers.[68] For the first time, Jonathan Walsh of Walsh Park, obviously under extreme pressure, joined the increasing corps of evicting landlords. In September, he evicted three families, comprising twenty-six people, from the lands of Curragh and had their houses torn down. One of those evicted was suffering from fever and on September 10 another man, named Duffy, "died on the side of the road in the greatest misery."[69] However, according to Lorrha author Gerard O'Meara, the Walsh family is remembered in the parish as being generous landlords: "During the 1840s they sold potatoes in Birr and Nenagh with the intention of lowering prices and so assist people affected by the Great Famine."[70]

Other North Tipperary landlords, like the Walshes, continued to provide relief to their tenants. Even Irish nationalist and author John Mitchel praised the generosity of many resident landlords: "Irish landlords, sir, are not all monsters of cruelty...The resident landlords and their families, did, in many cases, devote themselves to the task of saving their poor people alive..."[71] Robert Leeson, a relative of the Derry Castle Heads, was praised by his tenants at Ballyanny and Grange for "his true spirit of the most charitable and humane feelings" in forgiving them all arrears of rent due. He was also employing twenty-five men on drainage at Ballyanny. At a meeting of the Nenagh board of poor law guardians, Nicholas Biddulph, future father-in-law of William Henry Head, described the sorry state of his parish of Ardcroney: "I am sorry to say destitution is alarmingly on the increase...I know many families who have no means of supporting themselves...and must commit plunder. Yesterday a number of persons came to me and told me they were starving, they could procure neither employment nor food. Lamenting their condition, I gave them some meal."[72] As November approached, the *London Times* described "gloomy forebodings of another season of distress but little inferior in intensity to those of the past two years."[73]

On November 2, 1847, Major Denis Mahon of Strokestown, Co. Roscommon, was shot dead in his open carriage as he returned from a meeting devoted to keeping the local workhouse open. He had inherited a devastatingly mismanaged estate on which rents were £30,000 in arrears, rates had not been paid for some years, and the land had become divided and subdivided. Mahon, a humane man who was generally well thought of, was faced with a massive destitute tenantry. At first, he offered work and free passage to Canada to the poorest of his tenants—eight hundred tenants accepted his offer. In the spring of 1847, he spent £14,000 to charter two ships, provisioning them generously. Typhus took a terrible toll during the long voyage to Quebec—one ship was reported to have lost over 260 passengers. Still, the crisis on Mahon's land worsened and he was forced to evict the remaining three thousand tenants. Amidst intense local resentment, Mahon fell out with the local priest, who was wrongly alleged to have denounced him from the altar, saying that the landlord was "worse than Cromwell—and yet he lives." This libel was repeated in the House of Lords and the British press, reminiscent of the allegations made against the local priest following the assassination of the 2nd earl of Norbury in 1839 (chapter 13). This dramatic episode contributed to the growing alienation of the Catholic clergy and hierarchy from the British government and the British political world in general. Seventeen Irish Catholic bishops expressed their "fierce anger" and bitter resentment in a March 1848 statement to Pope Pius IX about British accusations that Catholic priests were inciting and conniving at assassination.[74]

Major Mahon was the only large landowner to be assassinated during the potato famine, a fatal result from both inheriting an estate in appalling condition and political fallout largely beyond his control—a fate Spaight had been wise enough to predict and successfully avoid through similar assisted emigration for his poorest tenants. In contrast, the attempted assassination of land agent Richard Uniacke Bayly, a genuine hero of the relief efforts in the Nenagh region, produced an outcry of sympathy for Bayly in the local and national press, both Catholic and Protestant, and in the House of Lords.

"Atrocious Attempt to Assassinate Richard Uniacke Bayly, Esq., J.P" was the headline in the short-lived nationalist newspaper, the *Tipperary Vindicator*. According to testimony at the series of trials held in late January 1848, Bayly and his young brother-in-law

Michael Head, youngest son of Dean John Head, were attacked late in the afternoon on Saturday, November 13, 1847, while driving home in a horse-drawn gig to Ballinaclough from Nenagh, where Bayly had an office for the receipt of rents. A twelve-year-old boy was running alongside for company. The assailants, who were lying in wait behind a wall at a crossroads, called out "halt" and simultaneously fired a shot from what proved to be a blunderbuss. The charge passed through Head's hat and struck Bayly on the right side of his face, severely damaging his teeth, jawbone, and neck. After Bayly dropped the reins and slumped into Head's arms, Head, with the help of the boy, managed to bring the bolting horse under control about a hundred yards up the road. He carried his bleeding brother-in-law into a house and drove furiously back to Nenagh to fetch medical assistance while the boy was dispatched to fetch the police.[75]

When Dr. O'Neil Quin arrived half an hour later, Bayly was still conscious but weakening from severe hemorrhaging. Quin agreed to Bayly's request that he be carried home, where two other doctors joined Quin in a frantic but seemingly hopeless attempt to staunch their patient's bleeding. The following evening, Michael Head hastened to Dublin to bring back the surgeon general, James W. Cusack, "one of the most eminent medical men in Ireland." Cusack arrived the next day to find his patient close to death. He operated at once and succeeded in tying the carotid artery, a remarkable surgical feat for the time. Bayly hovered between life and death for the next few days, then made an astonishing recovery. By the middle of December, he was pronounced to be out of danger. Shortly before Christmas, the *Nenagh Guardian* reported that a bonfire had been lit at the Market Cross in Nenagh "to express delight at the recovery of Richard U. Bayly."

As Grace has affirmed, Bayly was "one of the best known and most respected figures in North Tipperary and was highly thought of by the authorities at Dublin Castle. He was a prominent landowner and land agent, an active magistrate, chairman of the Nenagh board of guardians and, in the words of the *Nenagh Guardian*, "the head and front of all our charitable institutions," including the chairmanship of Nenagh Fever Hospital, the Nenagh Loan Fund, the Nenagh Gas Company, and the North

Tipperary Farming Society. The nationalist *Tipperary Vindicator*, while reminding readers that Bayly was undoubtedly a high conservative and a leader of his party in the northern portion of the county, admitted that he was universally considered to be a man of judgment, tact, and discrimination: "...we never heard that his partisanship partook of personal offensiveness, or that his labours to confer benefit on the great mass of the population were tinged by sectarian animosity. He was indefatigable as chairman of the Nenagh Union, as Chairman of the Finance Committee, and in doing all in his power to provide employment for the people."[76]

The delay in granting outdoor relief to the able-bodied had led to an outburst of anger against the poor law guardians. Fearful for their own lives, two elected guardians of the poor law union, Michael Hawley of Cloughjordan and Edward Biggs of Terryglass, resigned at the December board meeting. Edward Biggs explained that "the relieving officer for the district, or his deputy, was exciting the people and throwing odium on the guardians for the manner in which they were administering relief."[77] Thomas Sadleir of Ballinderry Park, Borrisokane, an ex-officio member, told the board meeting that "the people have a very ferocious feeling in my neighbourhood against the guardians; really their distress is so frightful that I cannot blame them." The previous Sunday, Sadleir and two other ex-officio guardians, Nicholas Biddulph of Congor and George Atkinson of Ashley Park, had been placarded on the chapel gates at Ardcroney as "starvers of the poor."

Bayly, however, was targeted for murder not for his leadership in relief efforts but for his work as a land agent. It was not an isolated incident but rather part of a serious upsurge in violent crime during the second half of 1847. Compared to the same period in 1846, homicides had increased by 50 percent, firings at people and into homes by 100 percent, and robberies of arms by 150 percent. Three-quarters of these crimes had been committed in the three neighboring counties of Clare, Limerick, and Tipperary. The Home Secretary read from the local constabulary report when referring to the Bayly attack in Parliament: "To demand the payment of rent, to take legal proceedings for the payment of arrears, is to hear a sentence of death passed in deliberate convention." After extensive investigations of eviction incidents on several estates for which

Bayly was agent, it was found that John Daly, a tenant farmer on the estate of absentee landlord Thomas T. Rowley, who was facing eviction after he and other tenants failed to pay rent for three years, had hatched the plot with several co-conspirators. Four men, armed and primed with whiskey, had lain in wait for Bayly in the fading light. Following several trials before the special commission in Clonmel, during which Michael Head testified, John Daly and another of the assailants were hanged, and more than two others who had abetted in the attempt were transported for life or ordered out of the country. It was judged that the chief informant, William Dwyer, would need constant police protection after his release from jail, and he was granted free passage to America.

As for Bayly, he became agent for the large Hawarden estate at Dundrum in South Tipperary and moved there in 1850 with his wife, the only daughter of Dean John Head, with whom he had a large family. Some years later, he moved to Co. Cork, where he had inherited an estate from a Uniacke relation. When he retired as land agent for the Hawarden estate after twenty-five years, he received glowing tributes from the tenantry "for his considerate, impartial and honourable management" of that estate." He lived to the age of eighty-two, despite his painfully disfiguring injuries.[78]

Although large tracts of potatoes were sown in the surrounding districts of Nenagh in April 1848, hopes were dashed when blight reappeared that summer. Captain Darley, the poor law inspector of Nenagh union, warned the commissioners in Dublin in August that "the potato crop throughout the entire of this union is irreparably damaged...From many fields the most offensive smell arises, clearly proving that putrefaction is going forward."[79] In September, the poor law commissioners launched a large effort to appoint temporary inspectors to oversee different unions. Among these inspectors was the dauntless Richard Uniacke Bayly, who had resigned as chairman of the Nenagh poor law union in the wake of his injuries.[80] In late February 1849, Capt. John Armstrong Drought, a cousin of William Henry Head, arrived as poor law inspector at the Nenagh union. He introduced large-scale "remunerative work," using the paupers' free labor to produce commodities useful for the workhouse. With the return of a large and healthy harvest of potatoes that summer, one thousand men left the workhouse in the hope of finding harvest employment. Their hopes were realized. The potato blight was over at last.

Henrietta Head's one-time fiancé, Simon George Purdon of Tinerana in Co. Clare, was among many landlords seriously contemplating selling up and leaving the country but changed his mind. He and other landlords continued to fight to save their properties from the crippling poor rate with increasing evictions for nonpayment of rent and in a desperate attempt to turn their land over to pasturage. As a correspondent for the *Illustrated London News* put it, "The system intended to relieve the poor, by making the landlords responsible for their welfare, has at once made it the interest and therefore the duty of landlords to get rid of them."[81] But it was too late to save thousands of severely indebted landlords from their remorseless creditors and steps had to be taken to help them sell their properties. The Encumbered Estates Court was established for that purpose in 1849.

Chapter 15

"Phoenix":
Challenging Fate in Tipperary

The Irish landlords had suffered severely during the famine...by the end of 1849, the tenants looked as though they had just come out of their graves while the landlords looked as if they were just entering theirs.
—John E. Pomfret, *The Struggle for Land in Ireland*, 43.

Each of these family homes, with its stables and farm and gardens deep in trees at the end of long avenues is an island—and, like an island, a world.
—Elizabeth Bowen, *Bowen's Court*, 19.

From the point of view of their critics in England, there could be no improvement in Irish agriculture as long as large acreages remained in the hands of impoverished proprietors. In July 1849, Parliament created the Encumbered Estates Court for the purpose of selling out the properties of indebted landlords. Establishing title to bankrupt estates through the Court of Chancery had often taken decades and was very expensive, as the Derry Castle story showed. The new act aimed to free the land of legal barriers, such as family settlements, entail, and complicated titles.[1] Every creditor was permitted to enter a bid for an encumbered estate, and the final purchaser was granted an indefeasible title by the court. All claims were discharged except for those recorded in the deed and the leases held by occupying tenants. Within a year, twelve hundred petitions for sales of estates had been lodged with the court and, over the next thirty years, an estimated 25 percent, or five million acres, changed hands, the biggest transfers taking place in the early 1850s.[2] Unfortunately, the old landlords received a fraction of what their estates were really worth because of this vast dumping of land on the market. According to J. S. Donnelly, Jr., while landed property had sold in Ireland for an average of twenty to twenty-five years' purchase of current rents in the 1830s, prices realized in the 1850s were as low as ten to fifteen years' purchase.[3] The timing of the Derrylahan sale may have been fortunate for the Head family.

By the fall of 1857, the court had disposed of more than three thousand estates. British government authorities hoped that Englishmen would purchase the estates, but, to their surprise, over 90 per cent of the eight thousand purchasers were Irishmen, including professionals and successful merchants. Among these Irishmen was William Henry Head, who, in late 1851 or early 1852, began to increase his landholdings through the Encumbered Estates Court with the purchase of the principal division of the lands of Redwood, the fine estate belonging to the late Major Bloomfield in the parish of Lorrha.[4] This seemed to indicate that Head came through the famine years solvent and with money to spare, which again raises questions about his record during those years. On the other hand, his mother is likely to have received a considerable legacy following the death of her stepmother Emma Ravenscroft in August 1848, as specified in her father's will.[5]

Details of Head's Redwood acquisition as well as his Modreeny lands are recorded, along with the names of his various tenants, in the voluminous papers of Griffith's Valuation at the National Archives of Ireland. This survey, carried out between 1848 and 1865, involved the detailed valuation of every taxable piece of agricultural or built property in Ireland. The person in economic occupation of the property was responsible for paying local taxation (county and poor law taxes) based on Griffith's. The only exceptions were tenants whose holding was valued at less than £5 annually, in which case their landlord was liable for the tax. This was a powerful incentive for landlords to rid themselves of smaller tenants in any way they could, contributing to the wave of evictions throughout the second half of the nineteenth century. The peasants soon realized that, even though the new landlords were often more active and made more improvements in the land, many were considerably less indulgent to their tenants than their predecessors, determined as they were to extract the full value of the land. The new proprietors managed their estates far more vigorously, actively opposing subdivision and subletting and dealing a final blow to the middleman system that the famine had done so much to end.

William Henry was not the only member of the Head family to take advantage of the Encumbered Estates Court. Dean Head of Ballinaclough and Simon George Purdon of Tinerana sold over 500 acres they co-owned, located in the barony of Clanwilliam, Co. Limerick, through the Court in 1853.[6] Castletown on Lough Derg, formerly a Parker family property, was also sold through the Court. Meanwhile, William Henry's cousin Henry Darby Head, equally well trained in Irish law, increased his father Dean Head's landholdings south of Nenagh to 941 acres and built the impressive Ballyquiveen House during the 1850s.[7]

One of the most important of the Northern Tipperary estates brought to the Encumbered Estates Court was Castle Otway, which the well-connected Otways, who were among the wider kin of the Head family, had owned for centuries. The Otway estates were encumbered, as Derry Castle had been, by family loyalties in the form of annuities and dowries, all of which were charges on the land and had to be listed. The sales prospectus, which was illustrated with fine lithographs of the two main residencies, Lissenhall House and Castle Otway, described it as "one of the finest places in the North Riding of Tipperary...The country about is thickly studded with gentlemen's residences" and "The estate...is occupied by a respectable and industrious class of tenantry." Offered at auction by the Court on behalf of Capt. Robert Jocelyn Otway, the intent was to sell only sufficient properties to settle outstanding accounts with tradesmen. Thus, Lissenhall House was sold to its sitting tenant, but Castle Otway itself was withdrawn prior to the auction in December 1853.[8] The Encumbered Estates Court was succeeded in 1858 by the Landed Estates Court that handled both unencumbered and partially encumbered estates.

The 1850s to the late 1870s were boom years for Irish landlords and farmers. Due to foreign competition, the price of grain fell steadily and soon reached a point where Irish farmers considered it to be unprofitable. However, the price of livestock and of graziers' produce was rising so that landlords hastened to complete the conversion of tilled land into pasture. As William Henry Head's land at Modreeny had long been under pasture, together with land he rented from Lord Dunalley, he made a great deal of money from cattle-farming for export, particularly during the Crimean War (1853-1856), between Russia and a coalition that included Britain.[9]

An account of an accident that befell William Henry in October 1853, the very month that Britain entered the war, demonstrates his closeness to the family of a neighbor and fellow magistrate, the well-regarded Nicholas Biddulph of Congor. He had been paying a visit to the Biddulphs and, while driving in the tax-cart past their demesne wall, he raised his hat in salute to the young ladies walking in the grounds. Either the shadow of his hat or a sense that the reins had been relaxed caused Head's spirited horse to plunge violently and "break its knees." Head was thrown with great force to the road where he lay unconscious for some time. Some neighboring workmen helped him to his feet and, although he was badly hurt, he managed to remount his tax cart and proceed to Modreeny where he made a full recovery, presumably through the devoted ministrations of his elderly mother.[10] One of those young ladies would become his wife.

Five years later, in August 1858, the lord-lieutenant for Ireland approved the appointment of William Henry Head to be a deputy lieutenant for County Tipperary in the place of the late earl of Glengall.[11] His fortunes were rising rapidly. Attracted by its shooting and cattle-raising capabilities, he was already negotiating for the purchase of the bankrupt Walsh Park in the parishes of Lorrha and Dorrha in the far north of Northern Tipperary near Parsonstown (Birr), King's County (Offaly). This 1,323-acre estate, which had been advertised for sale in April 1857, belonged to the late Jonathan W. Walsh, a fellow magistrate and probably Head's friend and creditor.[12] The fatal drain of tenant problems during the famine—which led to some horrifying evictions of whole families on Walsh's estate—added to the unsupportable encumbrances on the estate (he was the oldest child of a very large family). These forced his son and heir, John Adams Walsh, who later emigrated to Canada, to bring Walsh Park to the Encumbered Estates Court. As mentioned, Head already owned adjoining lands from the former Redwood estate.

In late October 1858, forty-nine-year-old William Henry Head Esq., now D.L. (deputy lieutenant), arrived at Quinn's Hotel in Bray on the coast south of Dublin, perhaps to consider it as a possible honeymoon hotel with his very young fiancé, Isabella Biddulph of Congor Park. With the coming of the railway, Bray had grown into Ireland's largest seaside resort. Hotels and extensive residential terraces now stood in the vicinity of the seafront, and a railway entrepreneur developed the town's Turkish baths in an extravagant Moorish style.

William Henry Head, now aged fifty, and Isabella Biddulph, not quite twenty, were married on January 5, 1860, in Congor Church by seventy-eight-year-old Dean John Head with the assistance of the Rev. John La Touche and Rev. Mr. Falkiner, incumbent of the parish. William Henry's cousin, John Massy of Stagdale Lodge, attended the wedding. Isabella's mother was the daughter of banker William La Touche of Fitzwilliam Square, Dublin. Their ancestor was David La Touche, founder of the Bank of Ireland in the eighteenth-century, whose Huguenot ancestors came to Ireland as linen manufacturers in the seventeenth century. Her father, Nicholas Biddulph, a descendant of a junior branch of the Biddulphs of Rathrobin, King's County (Offaly), owned 74 acres near Borrisokane and larger acreage in King's County. In terms of property and social position in the county, Isabella might have been thought to have married well, despite her groom's age. At the same time, it was now announced that a Mr. William Hodgins of Cloughjordan had concluded the purchase of Walsh Park in trust for William Henry Head for £12,000.[13]

As young Isabella Head embarked on marriage to a wealthy older man, it seems appropriate to consider advantages she would have in a century with generally limited roles for upper class women. As social historian Terence Dooley put it, "They rarely inherited estates; they had no political influence in the sense that they could not vote or enter parliament; and they were confined to the role of mistress of the household and maid-servants, hostess or occasionally philanthropist." However, the marriage settlements of women like Isabella, which guaranteed them a separate income, meant that they enjoyed much greater liberty than unmarried women of their own class. In Isabella's case, she was the only one of her many sisters to marry. This was not uncommon in the case where landlords like Michael Prittie Head of Derry Castle were so encumbered by debt that they were unable to provide dowries for their daughters. Private roles for single and married women of their gentry class meant that finding a record of their interests and activities remains challenging in the absence of letters or diaries. However, with the explosion in family history available online, some of those private records are becoming known.[14]

William Henry had spurned living in the Walsh's Georgian house, which he considered to be too close to the road (not gentlemanly enough!). Instead, he commissioned leading Dublin architect Sir Thomas Newenham Deane to design a high Victorian house to be built at a cost of £6,640 on a site a mile into his new demesne. Snobbery aside, it is likely that the old house was dilapidated and the Heads preferred a house with modern conveniences. As Charles Head recalled, "The new house was of limestone, every bit of which had to be carted up a rough lane across a bog to be deposited in place. A great quantity of ornamental cut stone was procured from a quarry fifty miles from the scene, and brought by road to the building."[15] This was evidently used to face the brick building. In reporting the sudden death of a young farmer in early June 1863, *King's County Chronicle* provided the information that "during the week he was engaged drawing bricks with a horse and cart from Gallen for the mansion now in process of erection for William Henry Head, Esq., D.L."[16]

In an admiring announcement, the *Nenagh Guardian* proclaimed: "This new house in Derrylahan Park is a very pretty structure, built in the Gothic style, with high pitched roofs and pointed gables, crowned with beautiful finials. It has been erected from a design by Sir. Thomas Deane & Son, architects of several other much-admired mansions in this part of the country, among them the new castle at Portumna. There has also been completed a beautiful lodge and entrance gate. An extensive range of stabling and farmyard are in course of erection. The total cost is estimated at £20,000. The name of W. H. Head, Esq., D.L., stands prominent among the landlords of Co. Tipperary. The numbers of men he has employed are not even all his own tenantry, but those on adjoining estates also. His conduct and consideration for the poor afford an example worthy of attention."[17]

In 1867, following the demolition of the old Georgian house, Head, always the practical businessman, offered the building materials for sale by auction, organized in parcels of differing sizes.[18] According to his son Charles, William Henry "spent the rest of his life making a park of his estate." Head also set about letting the farms on his lands. For instance, in March 1862, he advertised 75 acres of excellent tillage and pasture lands of Lissernane in the parish of Dorrha, five miles from Parsonstown (Birr). Proposals were to be addressed to him at Derrylahan Park or to his land agent John Exshaw in Borrisokane.[19] Head further extended his lands through renting. In February 1865, he rented 135 acres of the lands of Ballyduff as a representative of Patrick Meara, who had also been the caretaker of the Lissernane lands, for a yearly rent of £82.[20] He purchased those lands in 1874. The Meara or O'Meara family continued as tenants and then purchasers of the Ballyduff farm.

In late July 1862, when Head attended the summer assizes at Nenagh, his address was given as Derrylahan Park, although his address was still given as Modreeny in the 1862 edition of *Thom's Directory* for Tipperary. As an indication of the continuing domination of the landed gentry, that directory listed twenty-nine deputy lieutenants and no less than 209 magistrates for the county. While *Thom's* was out of date on the change of address, the rapidly growing Head family had certainly moved to Derrylahan Park from Modreeny by 1864, since William's eighty-nine-year-old mother, the former Elizabeth Ravenscroft of London, died there on April 1, 1864 (she was buried with her long-deceased husband, the general, in the churchyard at Modreeny). Exactly a week later, the Heads' first son and heir, William Edward, was born in the house he would eventually inherit. Following the birth of several daughters and a second son (John Henry), Charles Octavius, the eighth child, as his middle name indicates (his father was a Latin scholar), was born there in June 1869. Three more children would follow him, including the last, Michael Ravenscroft Head, born in 1880 when his father was seventy-one.

While the Heads settled into peaceful family life in rural Ireland, the American Civil War (1861-1865) tore apart all certainties in the country that had offered a new life for so many Irish people forced to emigrate. Irish Americans were fighting on both sides but far more on the Union side, probably more than 140,000. The war had devastating effects on the interlinked economies of other countries, particularly Britain. For example, when the North blockaded Southern ports, raw cotton was prevented from reaching the manufacturing towns of Lancashire, forcing most of the cotton mills to shut down. By the beginning of 1862, soup kitchens were being set up there. By the end of that year, one third of the population of the cotton-milling town of Blackburn was dependent on assistance from relief committees. William H. Head, a newly minted deputy lieutenant, was one of five members of the Head family in a long list of "inhabitants of the North Riding" of Co. Tipperary who appealed to the county's high sheriff in late October 1862 to convene a meeting "for the purpose of considering the GREAT DISTRESS now prevailing in LANCASHIRE and adopting means to alleviate the same."[21] Among these petitioners were two family members who had earned genuine local respect for their tireless efforts during the Irish Famine, John Head, dean of Killaloe, and the dean's son-in-law Richard U. Bayly. The *London Times* reported on December 15 that remittances were flowing in from all over the country and elsewhere to the relief committees in Lancashire, including presumably from the Irish landlords who had been lumped as one and branded as evil by the British public just fifteen years earlier. The tremendous efforts to avoid death and disease in Lancashire were in striking contrast to the Irish potato famine when a million people died of hunger and disease, millions more were evicted from their homes and forced into workhouses or to emigrate, and thousands of landlords descended into bankruptcy.

By now, William H. Head could well afford to support charitable causes as he continued to make considerable profits from exporting cattle that he raised on his extensive pasture lands at Modreeny and Derrylahan. All this was threatened when a false alarm was raised in September 1865 by a priest in Donegal, who wrote to several Dublin newspapers alleging that there had been an outbreak of dreaded rinderpest or cattle plague in his district. Hugh Ferguson, the best-known veterinarian in the country, eventually confirmed that it was not rinderpest but "only the ordinary murrain." But in 1865 there had already been an order preventing the export of cattle from England to Ireland: more than 25,000 animals had died or been slaughtered in England, with an estimated loss to the economy of over £5 million. In January and February 1866, further orders were published in Ireland prohibiting anyone from going to England or Scotland with cattle, appointing inspectors to disinfect everyone entering Ireland from abroad, allowing inspectors to examine areas thought to be infected, and empowering them to slaughter any cattle they determined were infected. Not surprisingly, cattle dealers and owners, including William H. Head, expressed considerable doubt about the actual incidence of disease and the draconian measures taken. Professor George Brown, chief of the Veterinary Department and the official responsible for dealing with animal diseases, was called in and confirmed a significant number of cases of murrain near Lisburn in Co. Antrim, despite the prohibition of imports from Britain. Stringent measures were taken and the murrain was stamped out in Ireland within three months.[22]

William Head had taken an activist position, serving on the cattle plague committee in Dublin and attending its meeting in Dublin's Mansion House in June 1866. According to the *Freeman's Journal*, Head was highly skeptical about the seriousness of this rumored outbreak. He declared that he had never seen his considerable stock of cattle in better condition and regretted that the widespread panic was causing great injury to the country (and to himself!). He therefore proposed that the committee should do everything in their power to allay the alarm. They could do useful work in watching for incidents of the disease; but all the bulletins and reports seemed calculated to make the people of other countries imagine that the plague was raging in Ireland while, in his opinion, Ireland deserved a clean bill of health. It was unfortunate, he said, that a tax was imposed on exporters of cattle [from Ireland]. Not only did that lead to depreciation in the value of stock but it inhibited Englishmen from purchasing Ireland-bred cattle. His strongly expressed opinions were greeted with applause. Edward Purdon, the committee's secretary, then announced that an application had already been made to the government to have the tax on the exportation of cattle removed.[23]

Despite the apparent calm in Ireland at that time, the Fenian revolutionary movement had come to a head in 1865 with the trial for high treason of the most prominent organizers of an anti-government plot. This secret revolutionary society had been organized around 1858 in Ireland and the United States to achieve Irish independence from England by force. Following the abortive Young Ireland uprising of 1848, led by William Smith O'Brien, and including both Catholic and Protestant revolutionaries, many of them graduates of Trinity College, vast numbers of embittered young Irishmen emigrated or were transported to the United States, Australia, South America, and Canada, where they redoubled their agitation against England. One of those embittered emigrants, former Young Irelander John O'Mahony, was the organizer of the movement in the United States, and it was he who gave the society its name, the Fenian Brotherhood. It was also known variously as the Fenian Society, Irish Republican Brotherhood, and Irish-American Brotherhood.[24] By the end of the Civil War, John O'Mahony held the rank of colonel of the 69th Regiment of the New York State Militia, a Fenian regiment. Irish involvement in the war gave rise in the short term to the Fenian raids into Canada and military experience for thousands of Irish American officers for possible Fenian activities in Ireland and England. Between 1866 and 1871, the Fenian Brotherhood raided British army forts, customs posts, and other targets in Canada to bring pressure on the United Kingdom to withdraw from Ireland.

In Ireland, the Catholic Church had pushed back on Fenian activities when, in a pastoral pronouncement, Cardinal Paul Cullen, archibishop of Dublin, the first Irish cardinal, condemned the Fenian newspaper, *The Irish People*—started by Fenian organizer James Stephens—for its radical socialism, which advocated the seizure of all privately-owned property and the extermination of both the gentry and the Catholic clergy! The trial of the Fenian leaders began on November 27, 1865. The judge, former member of parliament, solicitor-general, and attorney-general William Keogh, was highly unpopular with Irish Catholics. They saw him as having betrayed his own principles and compared him to the infamous hanging judges Jeffrey and Norbury. Irish nationalists considered the jury to be composed of supporters of English rule hostile to the Irish revolutionaries. Not surprisingly, the four principals, James Stephens, John O'Leary, Thomas Clarke Luby, and Jeremiah O'Donovan Rossa, were found guilty, and their sentences were extremely severe—twenty years of penal servitude at Dublin's Richmond Prison for three of them, while O'Donovan Rossa, business manager of the suppressed Fenian newspaper *The Irish People*, was sentenced to penal servitude for life at Pentonville Prison in England.

Once again, William H. Head warned of the dangers of panic among the resident rural gentry, this time in the face of Fenian threats. On December 12, 1866, the *King's County Chronicle* republished his December 4 letter to the *Nenagh Guardian* in which he questioned that newspaper's publication of alarmist letters "with anonymous signatures," which he saw as "eminently calculated to have that effect...Undue and exaggerated alarm in this matter may have effects almost as disastrous as *actual conflict*." While admitting that he had no insight into the threats posed or the authorities' intentions, he could not bring himself to believe "that the great body of the Roman Catholic middle classes, tradesmen, farmers, etc., with their respected clergy, would not readily range themselves, if called on, on the side of order with their Protestant fellow countrymen, for the protection of life and property," or that the "labouring classes" would turn on their employers without provocation. The legislature could hardly address needed reforms if it was preoccupied above all else with public safety.

The Fenian movement continued with a brief uprising in Co. Kerry in February 1867, followed by an attempt at national insurrection. The rebellion in Ireland never got off the ground due to poor planning. However, the execution of the "Manchester Martyrs" in November 1867 prompted a partial reconciliation between the Catholic Church and Fenianism and there was a groundswell of popular sympathy for the Fenian movement in Ireland. Following O'Donovan Rossa's release from prison and exile under an 1870 amnesty agreement, he emigrated to the United States, where he organized the first ever bombings by Irish republicans of English cities; this so-called "dynamite campaign" was largely funded by Irish immigrants in the States.

During March 1867, William Spaight of Derry Castle, who had

succeeded his father, received a report that the Fenians were going to attack his house. According to the *Limerick Chronicle*, seventy brave members of his tenantry arrived fully armed "to protect their humane, good landlord from insult or injury," while several of the Spaights' gentry friends provided true Irish hospitality to the defenders.[25] It seems that the attack never took place. In July of the previous year, however, the *Nenagh Guardian* reported that an unoccupied house on William Henry Head's Ballyduff lands had been "maliciously levelled a few nights ago." The former occupant had emigrated, and the motive for that wanton destruction seems to have been to prevent Head putting another of his workmen into the house. Predictably supportive of landlords, the *Guardian* felt this was a shabby way to treat "an obliging neighbor and a good employer."[26]

In the general election of November 1868, the Liberals won a majority of 112 seats over the Conservatives led by Benjamin Disraeli, and William Ewart Gladstone became prime minister for the first time. Ironically, Gladstone's decision to pacify Ireland by legislating on issues pressed by the Fenians' main opponents, Catholic moderate nationalists inspired by Cardinal Cullen, resulted in the disestablishment of the Irish Protestant Church (1869) and the First Land Act (1870). Landlords were now nervous about the probable consequences of the first attempt by the British parliament to intervene in the Irish land question on the side of the tenants. Perhaps this threat accounted for Head's decision to offer Modreeny for sale through the Landed Estates Court in 1869 on the basis that it would be impossible to cope with challenges on two separate estates. Just as likely were the mounting expenses of his large family and his passion for embellishing his new demesne. Perhaps not coincidentally, William Spaight also announced the sale of 1,451 of his 4,597 acres in Owney and Arra, Curravillier, Legane, and more, which did not include the Derry Castle mansion, in the same June 7, 1869, edition of *Allnut's*.[27]

William Henry Head's Modreeny estate was sold in three lots. The commodious mansion house was on lot 1 with extensive outbuildings and an excellent walled vegetable garden. A trout stream ran through the well-planted pleasure grounds, which also included the ruins of an ancient Norman castle or tower house. The lands of Modreeny (lot 2) and Ballyhasty (3) were all of prime quality and in pasture for a long time. The timber was beautiful and valuable, including a large oak wood. The prospectus concluded: "Modreeny is situated in a highly improved locality, one mile from the Market and Post Town of Cloughjordan, a Station on the Parsonstown and Nenagh branch of the Great Southern and Western Railway between Nenagh and Roscrea, thus affording rapid communication with Dublin and Limerick. The Parish Church adjoins the demesne. The poor-rates are nominal."[28] The first lot, the demesne of 242 acres with the mansion-house, was sold to a Mr. Mitchell, an agent, for £6,050; Mitchell also purchased the second and third lots for £900 each. George Whitfield, JP, was the actual purchaser.[29] It must have been a hard decision to sell this beautiful and productive estate, which would become, at least when I visited it in 2001, Charlie Swan Racing.[30]

The monopoly of Protestant power and privilege suffered another major blow in Ireland with the Disestablishment Act of 1869. In fact, many historians believe that, together, the Disestablishment Act and the First Land Act of 1870 placed the writing symbolically on the wall for the end of the Protestant landlord ascendancy. The Irish Catholic Church had made it clear to British liberal politicians that Ireland would not be tranquil until the Established Church of Ireland was removed as a grievance, as spelled out in strongly worded letters released by Archbishop Paul Cullen's National Association from 1864 to 1868. The National Association also sought the redistribution of land in Ireland and state aid to denominational schools. But the church issue was the priority, and the association worked in tandem with English and Scottish dissenters to obtain legislation through their Liberation Society. Once Gladstone, as the Liberal Party leader, became convinced of the necessity of disestablishment, despite attempts by bishops of the Irish church and Conservative politicians to significantly extend the reforms of the 1830s, there was no stopping him. As prime minister from 1868, he could pass a disestablishment bill any way he wanted, and he began to draft it himself. He had hoped for discussions with leaders of the Irish Church, but Archbishop Richard Chevenix Trench of Dublin refused to negotiate a compromise, a grave mistake.

Intense debates on the disestablishment bill in the Commons and Lords and between the two houses lasted for months, but when the bill received the royal assent on July 26, 1869, the battle was over. The Disestablishment of the Irish Church Act of 1869 decreed that the Church of Ireland would cease to be the state church as of January 1, 1871. It then became a voluntary body, thus breaking apart the Anglican churches in Ireland and England. The aged Dean John Head of Killaloe requested that his name be added to the Declaration of the Central Protestant Defence Association which was established in opposition to the disestablishment act. Since the people of Ireland had contributed to the grossly over-endowed Irish church, most of its secular properties were seized and vested in church commissioners, who were to liquidate the assets and re-distribute the funds as specified in the legislation. The Representative Church Body was established to receive ownership of church buildings, glebes, and schoolhouses, and existing ministers were protected by compensatory lifetime annuities. About a thousand clergymen chose to retire and were given lump-sum payments. At the same time, the British Government's *Regium donum* to the Presbyterian church, dating from the early eighteenth century, and the annual state subvention to Maynooth Seminary for Catholics, were discontinued.[31] The two institutions were compensated for their losses, however, with generous payments from the former assets of the church. Gladstone calculated that, when those sums were deducted, £7-8 million would be available to relieve distress in Ireland.

After 1871, Irish landlords played a significant role in the governance of the Irish Protestant Church at all levels. According to historian W. E. Vaughan, the general synod became "the largest regular gathering of Irish gentry in Dublin since 1800."[32] When local elections were held for lay delegates to the Church Synod following passage of the disestablishment act, William Henry Head was elected for Dorrha parish. However, he was not among the 417 laymen selected to attend the first general synod in Dublin, and he did not attend either the August or September 1871 Killaloe synods. Among family members and associates who did attend were his cousins Henry Darby Head and the Rev. Jonathan Head, sons of Dean John Head, who died that June; his brother-in-law Nicholas Biddulph;

and his land agent John Exshaw. Perhaps William Henry regarded Biddulph and Exshaw as representing his views; Exshaw's father had been a well-regarded Church of Ireland minister.[33]

Not surprisingly, Charles O. Head, who shared the landlords' disdain for Gladstone, expressed a jaundiced view of these events in his 1943 autobiography: "In 1869," he wrote, "Gladstone, the constitutional purist, made another little rift in [the Union]. With his three *corps d'armées*, the Scottish Presbyterians, the Welsh Nonconformists and Irish Roman Catholics, and his guerilla troops, the English High Church party sniping from a flank, he disestablished the Irish Church…[the disestablishment] had a cogent influence in uniting these strange allies, and thus giving Gladstone a Parliamentary majority to enable him to oust the presumptuous and hated Disraeli from office." He felt that the British government should have provided a concession to the Irish Protestants to balance the advantage given the Irish Catholics by, for instance, reducing the number of Irish representatives in the House of Commons as a *quid pro quo* for the levelling of the Irish Church.[34] Both major British political parties sought support from the influential Irish home rule block of MPs over the following decades, and that block was an important factor in legislative triumphs against Irish landlords.

Gladstone now turned his attention to landlord-tenant relations in Ireland and elsewhere in Europe to devise a scheme of regulation. The chief-secretary for Ireland, Chichester Parkinson-Fortescue, suggested that the Ulster Custom of security of tenure for tenants ought to be protected by law and that a yearly tenant not enjoying this protection should be entitled to compensation from his landlord if he was evicted. The Ulster Custom, giving the tenant the option of renewal upon the termination of a lease, was established in the seventeenth century to attract tenants or settlers. The Landlord and Tenant Act of 1870 gave it the force of law. The vast majority of tenants who did not enjoy that protection, however, were given increased security by compensation for improvements made to a farm if they surrendered their lease as well as compensation for "disturbance" damages (for tenants evicted for causes other than non-payment of rent). Perhaps predictably, Charles Head's opinion of Gladstone's first land act was that it "introduced that fatal condition, dual ownership, into the relations of landlord and tenant, and made farms liable to a periodic revision of rents, which naturally encouraged the Irish farmer to depreciate the value of his holding…and started Irish agitation flaming."[35]

Death of John Head, Dean of Killaloe

The death of the Rev. John Head, dean of Killaloe, in June 1871, five months after the disestablishment act went into effect, seemed to mark the end of an era and produced an outpouring of affection and respect across religion and class for the liberal and tolerant old man. The *Nenagh Guardian* referred to the eighty-nine-year-old as the "Good Samaritan" who quietly helped those in need. It quoted a weeping tenant at his funeral, "Better there could not be; so good indeed, that were there a nation of such landlords, Ireland's Home Rule would be complete." He had been perpetual curate of Ballinaclough for sixty-four years, from 1807 until his death, and dean of Killaloe from 1830-1871. Some amusing stories have been told about Dean Head. It was said that some of his sermons were sometimes as long as two and half hours. Once, when he was very old, he fainted in the pulpit and was carried into the vestry. The congregation thanked heaven for the shortening of his sermon and were preparing to leave when he appeared and said, "Oh! my friends, don't go yet, I have not finished my discourse."[36]

The turnout for the funeral was extraordinary. A cortège of tenants from nearby family estates, wearing white scarves and bands, walked ahead of the coffin, while eight of his tenants from Shragh and Barnagore earnestly entreated and won the honor of carrying the coffin of their beloved landlord halfway to the church. Behind the hearse, walked his large family—including four sons (Henry Darby Head, JP, Rev. Jonathan C. Head, who succeeded his father as rector of the Ballinaclough parish, Michael Head, and Capt. Edward Head); his grandsons; his nephew Dr. Henry Haswell Head of Fitzwilliam Square, Dublin; his son-in-law and daughter, Richard and Harriet Uniacke Bayly; and several other relations, including his cousin Lord Dunalley. They were followed by clergy of all denominations, medical men, and solicitors, and a vast number of gentry, farmers, servants, and peasantry. Between one and two hundred carriages, cars, and saddled horses brought up the rear for as far as the eye could see. Dean John Head's coffin was laid in a grave next to his long-departed wife (the former Susannah Darby of Leap Castle) under a symbolic cypress tree in a quiet corner of the churchyard, where it can be seen today.[37]

But where were the Heads of Derrylahan? Just eleven years earlier, Dean John had conducted the marriage of William Henry and Isabella. What could have happened since? Distance cannot have been the reason for their absence because Capt. Edward Head, one of the dean's four surviving sons, traveled from his land near Derrylahan at Carrig, where his many children would become close to the Derrylahan children. It is possible that Isabella, who seems to have been perennially pregnant, had suffered a miscarriage or perhaps they were no longer close to the Derry Castle Heads. After all, William Henry was a trusted legal counsel to the discredited last Head proprietors of Derry Castle—there must have been bitter wrangling by the wider family over what remained after creditors were paid. There may have been a falling out over William Henry Head's presumptuous assumption of the Head family's entry in *Burke's Landed Gentry of Ireland*. While acknowledging Henry Haswell Head, M.D., grandson of Michael Head of Derry Castle, as "senior representative of Head of Derry Castle," William Henry now placed his junior branch at the head of the remaining landed members of the family in Co. Tipperary—indeed, as a deputy lieutenant for the county, he was now the most prominent member of the family locally. His absence at the funeral must have been noted by the impressive number of his friends and associates among the Tipperary gentry who attended.[38]

Apart from the demands of his large family, William Henry was preoccupied at the time with the great blow he had been dealt as he was laying out his new demesne. The Landed Estates Court had ordered the sale of part of the lands of Sharragh on Head's and Henry Trench's properties to the Parsonstown and Portumna Railway Company, against which these landlords made an unsuccessful joint petition in 1871. The Birr-Portumna railway proceeded to lay its track right across his demesne, partly through an ugly cutting, and separating his new house from the main road, necessitating two lodges and pairs of gates on the avenues. The infrequent trains were a considerable annoyance to this man who loved nature and scenery above all and spent the rest of his life embellishing his parkland with specimen trees. Ironically, the company soon failed and the line became derelict, resulting in desperate fights by local farmers for the abandoned rail for the building of barns and sheds.[39]

On the morning of April 18, 1872, the Derry Castle mansion, which was for many older locals still the symbol of the Head family, was totally destroyed by a fire in which two local youths lost their lives. The *Belfast News-Letter* claimed that ill-feeling had been generated against William Spaight because of a lawsuit he had brought to prevent fishing in the river from Dromineer to Parteen, near O'Brien's Bridge, which had long been regarded as a public right. Other sources, such as the *King's County Chronicle*, claimed that the burning was linked to local agrarian agitation and the struggle to have the demesne divided.[40] The *Limerick Chronicle* reported that September that William Spaight had received £5,000 from his insurance company and that the rebuilding of the mansion would begin the following year. It never did. According to his 1889 obituary, he continued to live in a less pretentious house in the grounds.

The following month, in his role as a magistrate at the Lorrha petty sessions, William H. Head summoned Bigo Coulehan of Ross for cutting turf illegally on his bog. Head's steward had discovered that Coulehan and his men were cutting more than he had a right to. Landlord and tenant agreed to compromise over a long-standing agreement. A small case like this would most likely be mediated today before reaching a court but what makes it interesting is that the other magistrate presiding with Head that day was most likely a professional magistrate.[41] As Vaughan has noted, landlords across Ireland were seeing their local powers slipping away in the face of reforms to the judicial system and the enforcement of law and order. In the eighteenth century and well into the nineteenth, landlords had controlled the magistracy and grand juries. While they were still given lavish marks of respect by the constabulary (JPs were saluted and arms were presented to the county lieutenants and deputy lieutenants), they did not control them. They had little control over promotions and postings, the government determined the numbers and distribution of the forces, and they were paid by the Treasury. Landlords were no longer completely independent as magistrates, watched over as they were by paid career magistrates and the constabulary, who were only too quick to report any shortcomings to Dublin Castle. Several landlords were removed from their commission as justices of the peace or threatened with removal.

The landlords were restricted in two ways: at petty sessions by stipendiary magistrates and at the quarter sessions by the assistant barristers, who were professional lawyers and who usually presided. Sub-sheriffs and their bailiffs enforced the administration of estates. Even more galling was the fact that the stipendiaries and constabulary secured the prestigious positions that were formerly theirs. The constabulary assumed the uniforms, military bearing, and airs and graces that were previously the prerogative of the army and militia, while the paid stipendiaries were given extra powers, eventually becoming known as resident magistrates (or RMs), the title that the gentry had used to differentiate themselves from paid magistrates.[42]

Ironically, in view of the Derry Castle arson and the severe troubles that would resume before the end of the decade, a meeting was called in March 1873 to discuss reducing the extra police forces that had been summoned in the face of recent agrarian disturbances. In 1871, the Protection of Life and Property (Ireland) Act had effectively suspended habeas corpus. W. H. Head, D.L., who obviously felt well in control of matters on his own property, now expressed his opinion that "the tranquility at present existing in the riding was unmistakable, and any prophesies as to its non-continuance were certain to prove false and unfounded" William Spaight, despite the burning of his home, supported withdrawal of extra police: "If the spirit of crime and outrage were rife in the county a police barrack within every mile could not prevent the commission of crime."[43] While they almost certainly had the lifting of the police tax at the front of their minds, the incidence of area crimes against landlords and their servants accounted for only one quarter of the total at this time. Family disputes among tenants' families, however, accounted for 32 percent, and disputes between tenants and subtenants accounted for most of the rest. Between the famine and the land war, only two landlords of the first rank were assassinated: the despised Lord Leitrim in Co. Donegal in 1878 and the earl of Mayo in 1872.

But there was a wave of threatening letters with crude drawings of coffins and pseudonyms, the most common agrarian outrage, between October 1869 and May 1870.[44]

Charles O. Head claimed in his memoir that the Heads never had any tenant problems on their Derrylahan estate during his father's lifetime, but he was only three and six years old in 1872 and 1875, when the only documented disputes with one particular tenant occurred. William O'Meara had been evicted for nonpayment of rent to W. H. Head and another man in April 1872. O'Meara claimed that he had exceeded the arrears in rent of £21 with improvements to the land, and he was allowed to stay.[45] There are differing accounts of what happened in late September 1875. The day after the seizure of the same O'Meara's crops for rent (or restraining of Meara's cattle for the same purpose), this tenant made an apparent threat on the life of the Heads' land agent, John Exshaw, a justice of the peace and active guardian in the Borrisokane workhouse. Exshaw was driving past O'Meara or Meara's house with his son when he was met by a man who said that O'Meara wished to speak to him. Exshaw saw O'Meara struggling with his wife, presumably over the gun he was carrying, and then running across the field with the gun in his right hand shouting something like "stop." The elder Exshaw whipped up his horse to get out of range, but his son saw O'Meara raise the gun to his shoulder and appear to cock it. Exshaw swore to the special investigative session convened in the Lorrha courthouse and presided over by Thomas Butler Stoney that O'Meara had intended to shoot him with his licensed double-barreled gun. The defense argued that the gun found by the police was an old single-barreled gun. The case was forwarded for trial to the Nenagh Assizes.[46]

There was an interesting sequel to this incident. The Irish Nationalist newspaper *Dublin Weekly Nation* took issue in 1878 with the number of times English newspapers had "inflated or invented" reports of atrocities, including attempted assassinations, in Ireland. It reported that the editor of the *Daily Express* had admitted the week before that John Exshaw, who was reported to have been "shot at" by a man "said to have had a gun 'in his hand'...while altercating with Mr. Exshaw," had now declared "that nothing of the kind had occurred."[47]

Derrylahan Park: An Enchanted Childhood

In Northern Tipperary and across most of Ireland during this generally peaceful and relatively prosperous interlude, landlord families continued to live in secluded comfort, separated from the realities and struggles of those less fortunate, most of whom were Catholic. Charles Head, eighth child of William Henry and Isabella Head, provided a picture of his own happy childhood with numerous brothers and sisters at Derrylahan Park (see chapter 1) when he saw the delight his own children took in it several decades later. He particularly recalled the large variety of wildlife and wild fruits. The siblings explored and enjoyed picnics in ruins scattered across the park and built miniature cabins in misshapen trees, while the hospitable cottagers on the estate were always ready to provide glasses of milk or slices of home-made bread. "The first eight years of my life were passed agreeably in these surroundings."[48]

What Charles failed to mention was that three of his little sisters, born within three years of each other (1863-65), died during his early childhood. Catherine Mary died on July 10, 1873 aged ten, Maria Isabel died on October 18, 1875, also at the age of ten, and Frances Henrietta, always known as Fanny, died aged twelve on July 18, 1876. This must have had a deeply saddening effect on the entire family. A year later, eight-year-old Charles and his older brother John Henry were sent away to boarding school in Bray, the spa town long favored for holidays by their parents. Charles's characterizations of his father give some sense of his attitude to his sons' schooling. William Henry was entirely unlike his strict martinet of a father, Gen. Michael Head, who seems to have had little sympathy with his son's "shy, diffident, sentimental, poetical" nature and his delight in classical studies and literature. Thus he "took few pains to alleviate the harsh conditions that were then prevalent in scholastic life, or to relieve them with kindly intervals of recreation. Some hardness of disposition was consequently engendered in the boy, which manifested itself more particularly when our turn came for school life." It is not known where Charles's oldest brother, Willie, was educated. Perhaps, as heir to the estate, he was tutored at home or perhaps he had been expelled from boarding school. His mother would indicate years later that he had always been difficult and intemperate.

The school holidays "were a perpetual joy," wrote Charles. "There were ponies and donkeys to be ridden, but our chief delight was in shooting and fishing. A grouse moor, or bog as it was called, lay within half a mile of the house, and on the Twelfth we'd get our twelve to fifteen brace with a couple of Irish setters to help us. The bog was of great extent, most of it belonging to us, but the rest of it was a sort of no-man's-land on which we encroached when it pleased us. We would be out at 5 a.m. on the opening day, to forestall any stray sportsman who might have an idea of indulging himself with a shot on the unclaimed portions of the bog, and we would get back to breakfast about 10 a.m. fairly exhausted with our bog-trotting."

When Charles was a child, the Derrylahan estate comprised the demesne and parkland surrounding the house and extensive lands let to tenant farmers for a total of 2,300 acres.[49] However, unlike the lakeside and mountainous Derry Castle estate or the pasturelands of Ashley Park or Modreeny, a good percentage of Derrylahan's lands consisted of peat bog. In fact, Ireland's raised or peat bogs are found mostly in the Shannon River basin of Central Ireland. At the end of the last Ice Age, much of central Ireland was covered by shallow lakes left behind by the melting ice. Over thousands of years, the partially decomposed remains of dead plants, particularly Sphagnum mosses, accumulated in these waterlogged areas. Before they began to be exploited commercially for peat in the mid-twentieth century, raised bogs had an average depth of between 24 and 30 feet. When the young Heads were roaming the bog on their land and beyond, peat was cut for fuel by hand. Again and again, two generations of Head memoirists recall the bog's natural splendors and mystique.

Charles, who may have inherited his more sociable character from his mother, although he says little or nothing about her in his memoir, remembered with particular fondness two men employed by his father with whom he spent a great deal of time as a child. The first was the butler, "an ardent Irish Nationalist. I would sit for hours in his pantry listening to his tales of the wrongs of Ireland and the greatness of her past history." Despite his beliefs, this man was cheery and good-natured "without a spark of bitterness or ill-feeling towards Irish landlords." He did all the light carpentering and plumbing jobs around the house and, in his considerable free time, "he would ramble about the place, collecting butterflies, of which he made a large collection, all preserved and set up by himself in a case of his own making." He would get up at crack of dawn to fish in a stream three miles away and bring his catch back in time for the family's breakfast.

The other man was the gamekeeper, "a fervid Orangeman. Strolling about the place with him or sitting in his cottage, I learnt all about the 'prentice boys, Lord Antrim and King William 'of glorious, pious and immortal memory.' His scorn for the 'papishes' was immeasurable, and yet he got on quite well with all the other people on the place, even with the Nationalist butler. He always shot with us, generally beginning when we had finished, and landing his bird some seventy yards away with his self-loaded special cartridges. At snipe or any sort of rough shooting he was the best shot I've ever seen, and his instinctive knowledge of the ways of game was profound. He was a terror to poachers, a ruthless exterminator of vermin; and, while we had him, our head of game expanded in the most gratifying manner."

Charles liked all the people on the place, including the coachman who taught him to ride on the ponies or carriage-horses. They always treated him with the greatest kindness, but he considered their relative positions were permanent: "I never contemplated the extirpation of the landlord-class with all its consequences and alterations of feelings." The ten to a dozen workmen on the place were paid about ten shillings weekly, with a few extras, such as turf, milk, grazing, etc. While recognizing later that the reformer would cry "Shame," these men seemed quite happy to him as a child. They were big strong fellows, "very different to the C3 population [the lowest grade of fitness by military standards] of English towns, who live on substitutes and artificial food. Our men throve on potatoes, bread, bacon and cabbage. From time to time one of them would emigrate, no doubt to reinforce the great army of British haters abroad, but the bitterness in their hearts would be aimed at the British Government, to which they attributed all their sorrow, and not at the Irish landlords whom they knew, and on the whole, thoroughly respected. 'The great man, the grand man, the raal ould Irish gentleman' was always an object of general esteem in Ireland," in Charles's opinion.[50] Social historians largely agree with this appraisal, always citing exceptions, of course.

William Henry Head, however, "was by no means a typical specimen of his class," according to Charles. "Reserved, studious, scholarly and rigidly self-disciplined, he differed entirely from his fellow-squires and mixed but little in their society or in any other. I never knew him as anything but an old man, with the habits and manners of past ages. He was a *laudator temporis acti* if ever there was one, and was intolerant and scornful of all our new-fashioned ways, though heaven knows they weren't very advanced. Though on our shooting days the advantages of our breech-loaders were so obvious, nothing would induce him to abandon his old muzzle-loader, not even the accidental firing away of his ramrod one day and the time it cost us to find it again. He dropped all his relations and all his early friends, and lived the life of a recluse, buried in his place."

William Henry abhorred fox hunting and all other equine sports, unlike his third and fourth sons, Charles and Michael, who became outstanding competitive riders and polo-players. Those two sons would become career army officers and Charles explained the childhood influences on him. "From my earliest childhood I was brought into touch with the great war era which marked the close of the eighteenth and the beginning of the nineteenth centuries. My father, a man of peace who abhorred war, was a fervid admirer of Napoleon, and decorated nearly every room of his house with pictures, busts, and plaques of the Emperor in all his well-known poses. How my parent reconciled his ultra-peaceful ideas with Napoleon's warlike character I never discovered. Of Wellington we had not a trace, and his name was only mentioned with cold disapproval." And yet William Henry posed for a studio photograph wearing his father's cavalry officer's uniform in 1864, perhaps at the suggestion of his wife.

Charles recalled that some of the children were taken twice annually to visit their mother's large family, the Biddulphs of Congor, who lived thirteen miles away. "I can still in memory," he wrote, "hear the old carriage-horses pounding along the muddy or dusty road, and the wheels crunching on the sheets of stones with which the roads were repaired." Referring to Anglo-Irish snobbery, he noted that "All Irish households with any pretensions to social rank kept their carriages and pairs with coachmen and cockades complete. We always had a pair of big brown horses that could jog along steadily at about ten miles an hour. With their silver-mounted crested harness they made a good show and provided us with a very reliable mode of conveyance for a circle of some fifteen-mile radius. Beyond that was an unknown and untouched world." Two Biddulph brothers were fleet surgeons in the navy and two others were army officers and all enchanted their young nephews and nieces with colorful stories about far-off places, no doubt influencing Charles's own choice of a career. He always admired the uniforms and bearing of the soldiers stationed at the barracks in Birr.

Anglo-Irish Protestant gentry families like the Biddulphs and the Heads were often as large as Irish Catholic families. But the Anglo-Irish, like the British, were ruled by primogeniture, the common law that the oldest son inherited the estate, invariably with all its crushing entailments, while younger sons were placed in the British services, the clergy, law, land agency, or medicine (the career chosen for the second son, John Henry). As for the girls, their assigned role in life was to make as advantageous a marriage as possible, hopefully with the bonus of land or inherited wealth. (Indeed, that was the summa of my father's ambitions for me!)

"No doubt we were a snobbish community," Charles admitted:

The landed gentry looked down on the townsfolk, though many of the latter were of their own stock and breeding. And even among the landed classes there were grades of distinction, measured by acreage, family antiquity or aristocratic connection. Great pains were taken to assert local social superiority, and pedigrees and family connections were rated as matters of great importance, especially by our women. Any old bit of ruin on an estate entitled the place to be called a castle, or, better still, an abbey, though the dwelling-house itself might be a very commonplace building of comparatively recent erection. A drive or approach was always an avenue, though no trees may have bordered it; and it would be made winding through the park, doubling or trebling the distance required to reach the road, so as to give the impression of great spaciousness. Ponds or pools were always lakes, and streams were rivers. Entrance gates and lodges were imposing affairs; and the pillars of field gates were substantial stone structures that may now be seen standing forlorn in the fences with an old bedstead or plough filling the gap between them.

Perhaps it was not considered manly for an army officer to say much about the women of his family. Certainly, Charles's failure to say anything at all about his mother beyond her family connections is striking to a modern reader and in stark contrast to all that he wrote about his father. A bride's social connections, or even better a large dowry, particularly if it included land, were always important to the Irish landlord class (note that Charles says that it was the women who made much of so-called grades of distinction). In reality, though, there is evidence that William Henry sincerely loved and admired his wife, whom he called Issy, and greatly depended on her steadfast character. She reigned over a very large household, including the eleven children she bore over twenty years and the army of nurses, governesses, tutors, and domestic servants that were hired to take care of them.

While Charles and his siblings spent their childhoods sheltered from reality in an oasis of comfort and security, two decades of relative prosperity and calm were drawing to an end. Three years of severe economic depression began in 1873 when a world-wide industrial boom came to an end. British industry began to flood the Irish market with cheap surplus stock and prices fell. Irish industry was devastated, and many workers were paid off as industries closed down. Skilled craftsmen found themselves sliding into the casual labor market. It was a time of crisis in the cities and towns but the situation in the countryside was even worse. Starting in 1877, there were three successive bad harvests, the worst being that of 1879.The failure of the potato and oats crops in the west brought many communities to the edge of famine. At the same time, low yields were accompanied by falling prices due to the arrival in Europe by ocean steamer of grain imports from the vast new wheat lands of North America. The result was the land war of 1879-82.[51]

Chapter 16

Land Wars and the End of Landlordism

Why then should we carry on a hopeless bankrupt business, flaying tenants alive and eternally plunged in scalding water ourselves, merely for the benefit of some firm of London usurers who are safe out of range of a blunderbuss or boycott?
—Members of the Irish Landlords Convention, 1890s

Three bad harvests in a row between 1877 and 1879 brought two decades of relative prosperity in rural Ireland to an end and the return of rural agitation.[1] Tenant-farmers and landlord-farmers suddenly saw the value of their agricultural produce decline by 36 percent, the value of their crops by 50 percent and the value of their livestock by around 36 percent. In October 1879, Michael Davitt founded the Land League, a union of large and small farmers and shopkeepers dedicated to forcing rent reductions and fighting evictions. Nationalist Protestant landlord and member of Parliament Charles Stewart Parnell soon led the league, which he used to support his long battle for the return of a parliament to Dublin, particularly after the sympathetic William Gladstone returned to power.

Michael Davitt was born in Co. Mayo at the height of the Great Famine. He and his poor farming family were evicted from their home in 1850 due to arrears in rent. They managed to settle in Lancashire, where young Davitt lost an arm in a factory accident. He then received a good education in a Methodist school and, having developed an interest in Irish history and a deep hatred for landlords, he became an organizer for the Irish Republican Brotherhood in the North of England, which led to his 1870 conviction for gun-running and sentencing to fifteen years of penal servitude.

In April 1879, following his conditional release in 1877, Davitt launched a renewal of agricultural agitation at a hugely attended meeting in Irishtown, Co. Mayo, which he could not personally attend because of the risk of being rearrested.[2] With the active support of Charles Stewart Parnell, he then made plans for a vast campaign to force reductions in rents, exploiting growing discontent by welding the open and secret wings of nationalist politics: Fenianism, Irish-American politics, and the Home Rulers.

Parnell, a handsome and rather aloof Anglo-Irish Protestant landowner with encumbered estates in Co. Wicklow, built on the patriotic tradition of the eighteenth-century Anglo-Irish Protestant politician Henry Grattan, but he and his activist sisters inherited anti-British hostility from their American mother (Delia Tudor Stewart was the daughter of Admiral Charles Stewart, a naval hero of the War of 1812).[3] After he was elected as a young Home Rule MP for Co. Meath in 1875, his fight at Westminster for Irish home rule won the Fenians' admiration. When Davitt's Land League of Mayo was superseded by the Irish National Land League in October 1879, Parnell became its president and Davitt one of its secretaries. Its slogan was **"the land for the people."** In December 1879, Parnell left for the U.S. to seek financial support for the Irish Land League. Meanwhile, the Land War began in earnest with organized resistance to evictions, the fight for reductions in rents, and aiding the work of relief agencies. Between 1879 and 1882, 11,215 families were evicted, 11,320 outrages were recorded, of which 7,035 were threatening letters, and the Land Act of 1881 was passed.

Parnell hurried home from the U.S. to campaign in the March-April 1880 general election that returned Gladstone and the Liberal Party to office. Of the twenty-one new Nationalist MPs, nineteen were Parnell supporters, allowing him to make a successful challenge for leadership of the Home Rule Party in May. In a September 1880 speech in Ennis, Co. Clare, Parnell proposed a nonviolent approach to censuring tenants who took farms where another tenant had been evicted. "What are you going to do to a tenant who bids for land from which a neighbor has been evicted? Kill him? No, you must show him on the roadside when you meet him, you must show him in the streets of the town, you must show him at the shop counter, you must show him in the fair and in the market place and even in the house of worship by leaving him alone, by putting him into a **moral Coventry**, by isolating him from his kind as if he were a leper of old—you must show him your detestation of the crime he has committed."[4]

The Land League's subsequent campaign of ostracism soon acquired the name of its first major victim. Capt. Charles Boycott was the agent of an absentee landlord, Lord Erne, who lived in Lough Mask House, near Ballinrobe in County Mayo. As harvests had been poor that year, 1880, Lord Erne offered his tenants a 10 percent reduction in their rents. In September, protesting tenants demanded a 25 percent reduction, which Lord Erne refused. Capt. Boycott then attempted to evict eleven tenants from the estate. Although Parnell's speech did not refer to land agents or landlords, the tactic of ostracism was first applied to Boycott when the alarm was raised about the evictions. Boycott soon found himself isolated. His workers stopped work in the fields and stables, as well as in Lord Erne's house, local businessmen stopped trading with him, and the local postman refused to deliver mail. When Boycott was unable to hire anyone to harvest crops on the estate, fifty members of the Protestant Orange Order from Counties Cavan and Monaghan volunteered to do the work. So great was the fear of violence—despite the local Land League leaders' promise there would be none—the volunteers were escorted to and from the estate by one thousand policemen and soldiers. No violence occurred, and the measures taken to prevent it ended up costing far more than the harvest was worth. The "boycott" continued after the harvest, and Capt. Boycott soon left Ireland.

Within weeks, Boycott's name was everywhere. *New-York Tribune* reporter James Redpath first wrote of the boycott in the international press. "Boycott" was used by *The Times* in November 1880 as a term for organized isolation, and the *Daily News* wrote on December 13, 1880: "Already the stoutest-hearted are yielding on every side to the dread of being 'Boycotted.'"[5] The land league soon turned its attention to other landlords who refused to lower rents to the level they demanded which was essentially that the rents be reduced to Griffith's valuation, which was based on 1849-51 prices. By the late 1870s, this was perhaps as much as 33 percent below the real letting value of land.[6]

Henry Darby Head of Ballyquiveen was among those landlords in North Tipperary whose experiences with or in the face of boycotting tactics were liberally recorded in the local press. In 1830, the year that the Rev. John Head became dean of Killaloe, the family acquired the Ballinaclough townlands of Coolagh, Ballyquiveen, and Shragh. Further lands were added through the years at Ballylisheen, Barnagore, and Happygrove. The size of the Head holdings had increased from six acres in 1830 to 941 in 1876, probably as a result of Dean Head's Church of Ireland privileges and his son's legal expertise in acquiring bankrupt properties through the Encumbered Estates Court. Henry Darby Head, a graduate in law from Trinity College Dublin, built Ballyquiveen House in the 1850s. Inside an imposing façade of ten windows and a sturdy front door, a grand staircase rose from the main hall, around which pitch pine paneled doors with decorative architrave led to high-ceilinged rooms. A standard mile-long avenue led from the gatehouse through a small demesne to the house.

Tim Boland, whose grandfather purchased the Coolagh property and house from Henry Darby Head's heir John Prittie Head in 1888, published an account of the confrontation between Henry Darby Head, his tenants, and the local land league in his "The Head Family of Ballinaclough." Boland's subtitle, "Where love and respect gave way to Boycott and Eviction," recalls the contrast between this locally despised landlord and his revered father, the Rt. Rev. John Head.[7] Locals had become enraged against the Heads when Michael Meara, a tenant of Henry Darby Head, addressed the board of guardians at Nenagh Workhouse in March 1880. He stated that he had twenty arable acres and ten acres of mountain pasture at Barnagore. Having requested relief outside of the workhouse for himself and his family, he explained that his £60 income had been used to pay one and a half year's rent and £6 on a bank loan. He had nothing left but the price of a bag of Indian meal. He also sold his only cow to settle his rent bill. He and his family, which included new-born twins, were living on "spring water and meal." He was granted "relief for a month according to his requirements." Although his landlord, Henry Head, and Head's brother, Nenagh land agent Michael Head, were present as members of the board, they apparently avoided getting involved in this case, which must have enraged the Meara family's friends and supporters. A few months later, Meara vacated his farm and emigrated. That December, Father Lynch, president of the Silvermines and Ballinaclough branch of the land league, encouraged his congregation to join the local land league which met every Sunday in Silvermines.

Efforts by the land league to reach agreement on rent were successful on most local estates but broke down in the case of Henry Head's land. At a meeting on March 9, 1881, the tenants offered to pay either Griffith's valuation or the rents that had existed in 1870.[8] Henry Darby Head argued that he had not increased the Barnagore rents since 1870, but Father Glynn of Killeen alleged that Head had doubled rents on taking over the estate in 1871 following his father's death. Head then offered a rent decrease of 20 percent, which seemed entirely reasonable in comparison to other agreements, but was rejected by his tenants. They left the meeting without paying any rent. It is probable that Henry D. Head, like most landlords, felt that his level of indebtedness would have brought ruin to himself if he reduced rent even further. But land league propaganda was relentless.

On June 29, the following notice of boycott was posted at Ballinaclough Chapel and at Mr. Head's entrance gates at Ballyquiveen: "The men of Barnagore are to be turned out of their homes because they will not betray the Land League and pay rack rents. Will not Tipperary men stand by them and give up all communication with the tyrant, or sell to the tyrant, or work for the tyrant. Every servant not a traitor will today leave his house." Notices posted at Dolla and Templederry carried this message: "Men of Tipperary! Will you allow the Barnagore tyrant to crush your brothers? NO!! No more legalised robbery. Let every man do his duty. Boycott the tyrant. God save the people."

The boycott was immediately obeyed. All Head's servants left Ballyquiveen House, resulting in Henry Head and his family "having to perform all the menial duties necessary for his establishment, even to milking the cows." The *Nenagh Guardian* reported that "some of Mr. Head's servants, who had been in his employment since they were children and whose parents had been in the employment of Dean Head left the house weeping." Unable to acquire supplies in Nenagh, Head was forced to order them from Limerick and Dublin. The *Nenagh Guardian* menacingly suggested that his forced outsourcing of supplies could be voluntarily followed by the other landed gentry of the area, thus putting the livelihood of the Nenagh traders at risk. The Silvermines and Ballinaclough land league responded with the following motion: "That we condemn the actions of those, who in any way assist rack-renting landlords, whether they be shopkeepers, traders, professional men or others, and we call upon all true friends of the cause to withdraw their support from such parties, and to let them live by the rack-renter if they can."

Rather than submit to the pressure being exerted on him, Head proceeded to employ six "emergency" men to handle the work on his estate and obtained a personal bodyguard of four police officers. Father Glynn condemned Head's treatment of his "wretched tenants" and mocked his "emergency six" and his "guard of honour." On August 1, 1881, one month after the boycott commenced, John Baker and James Kealy, agents of the county sheriff, protected by fifty members of the 64th Regiment, and fifty members of the constabulary, went to Barnagore, where they evicted Thomas, Patrick, and Michael Ryan, along with their families. Each tenant owed one year's rent, increased by approximately 50 percent when "fees" and "costs" were added. Notices were posted at the farm entrances and at Dolla that the farms would be sold at Nenagh courthouse on the following Tuesday. In March 1883, two more Barnagore tenants were evicted on the instructions of Henry Head. Perhaps succumbing to the stress, Henry Darby Head died on May 1, 1884, aged sixty-six years. He was buried in the family plot in Ballinaclough Cemetery on the following Monday morning at 8 o'clock. Tim Boland thought it was unlikely that the Barnagore tenants were pall bearers as many of them had been for his father just thirteen years before! Henry's son John Prittie Head inherited the Ballyquiveen estate and a raft of problems.

As long as William Henry Head lived, the Derrylahan estate seems to have avoided the worst of such confrontations with the land league. Whether or not William Henry's son, Charles, became aware of the boycotting of his cousin Henry Darby Head at the time (he was away at school when those events took place), he was only too aware of the obloquy poured on Irish landlords as a class throughout his lifetime. "My experience of Irish landlords is entirely the opposite of the picture that is usually painted of them," he would write:

> Some particular estates, for peculiar reasons, would be specially selected for agrarian agitation, and its owner held up to execration in the Press and Parliament as an inhuman monster, but there was never a great amount of fire behind all this smoke, and the luckless proprietor was usually as blameless and honest a member of society as the owner of any description of property in the United Kingdom. The Irish land agitation was a perfectly natural, though hardly moral, struggle on the part of the tenants to get possession of their land, and an equally natural endeavour by the landlords to retain their property. The champions of the tenants' side, with their own ends in view, placed no limit on the defamation they poured on the heads of the landlords; the latter had only the rights of property and Parliamentary sanction as their blunt and almost worn-out defensive weapons. But as a class they deserve rescue from the infamy with which they have been overwhelmed."[9]

In August 1881, Gladstone introduced the New Land Act, which gave statutory recognition to the "Three F's"—free sale, freedom of contract, and fixity of tenure, a long-standing rallying cry for Irish tenants, thus threatening to undermine the strength of the Home Rule cause and its leader by defusing rural agitation. The Irish Land Commission was established under the terms of the 1881 Land Act as "a body corporate and a court of record, with the powers, rights and privileges of the High Court relating to matters within its jurisdiction." Thus it began life as a rent-fixing body and it was considered to be a stabilizing force in agrarian society during the turbulent Land War years.[10] Sub-commissioners were empowered to hold land courts to adjudicate a fair rent between landlord and tenant with the aim of lowering rents by an average of 20 percent.

As could be predicted, the conservative *Nenagh Guardian* railed against the act, claiming that decisions being made by sub-commissioners in Northern Tipperary and King's County were "castigating the landlords...If they had been the servants of the League they could not have done much more. No wonder the farmers have rushed en masse to the Land Court [in Dublin]...No wonder that [they] are exultant." The Irish Land Act, concluded the newspaper, "threatens to be even more revolutionary in its consequences than anyone predicted it would be."[11] Large landowners, such as Lord Dunalley and the Earl of Rosse, could afford expert defense against hardline decisions, while many lesser landlords, who could least afford it, saw their rents reduced to the point where it was almost impossible to make a profit. Despite the precipitous reduction in landlords' income, Daniel Grace claimed that "No farmer was *permanently* evicted from his holding" in the parish of Monsea-Killodiernan north of Nenagh during the land war years.[12] The greater alliance of substantial farmer, smallholder, and cottier which had sustained the League and Parnell's leadership began to collapse as the beneficiaries of the new legislation accepted its terms and those excluded continued to seek redress. According to historian Alvin Jackson, "Gladstone's Land Act may therefore be seen as a kind of demolition ball, sweeping away the intricate but fragile architecture of the Irish National Land League."[13]

On October 13, 1881, after a bitter public exchange with Gladstone, Parnell was arrested on suspicion of "treasonable activities," including appearing to subvert the new land legislation. Five days later, Parnell and his lieutenants issued the "No-Rent Manifesto," calling for a national rent strike. Two days after that, the government, after interning the leaders, moved to outlaw the league itself. Parnell and the league leadership were incarcerated in Kilmainham Jail. Without Parnell's leadership, the league was beset by local vendettas and violent criminal activity, including attempted murder. On April 19, 1882, the *Dublin Daily Express* reported that the town and district of Borrisokane had been "liberally posted with 'No Rent' manifestoes...One was posted on the Courthouse door, where the Sub-Commissioners were to sit, warning people to avoid the landlord's court. On all the farms which they were to visit a manifesto was displayed. On a police barrack door another copy was posted, and on the gate of Mr. Exshaw, agent to Mr. David Clarke, landlord of Borrisokane [and perhaps still the agent of William Henry Head], a threatening notice was posted."[14] Exshaw had testified on behalf of David Clarke, JP, apparently an absentee land-lord who came over from London to hear his cases.

Just a few days later, Gladstone and Parnell reached an agreement expressed in the "Kilmainham Treaty" of April 25, 1882. Parnell agreed to withdraw the "No-Rent Manifesto" and undertook to move against agrarian crime, while the government promised to address the two constituencies excluded from the benefits of the 1881 Land Act—those with rent arrears and leaseholders. There was a great demonstration in the parish of Monsea-Killodiernan not far from Nenagh on May 3 to celebrate the release of Parnell and other land league leaders from Kilmainham jail the previous day.[15] As a result of this crisis, Parnell increased his stock with both the government and the agrarian radicals, providing him with political leverage over both. The Land Act was consequently amended to protect tenants in arrears.[16]

The Kilmainham Treaty was swiftly followed by one of the most shocking crimes of the late Victorian era, the Phoenix Park murders. The murder of the chief-secretary for Ireland, Lord Frederick Cavendish, and the under-secretary, T. H. Burke, on May 6, 1882, the day they arrived in Ireland, by revolutionary nationalists of the bloody but marginal "Invincibles" sect inspired a backlash that Parnell used to reconstruct the national movement along more conservative lines. On May 6, Parnell denounced the crime with utmost vehemence and sincerity, according to historian D. George Boyce.[17] In January 1883, seventeen Invincibles were arrested and five were later executed. The organization subsequently collapsed in Ireland. Parnell now renamed the Land League the Irish National League and moved to secure the support of the Catholic hierarchy for the Home Rule campaign.

In the midst of this general tumult, there appeared to be little or no tenant agitation at Derrylahan, where the older Head children were growing up fast. Elizabeth Phoebe (Bessie) Head, the eldest of the four surviving daughters, married the Rev. George Bennett, a Church of England minister, in 1882 when she was twenty-one. She would have three children and spend many years in England. It was a typical marriage for the daughter of a comparatively small landowner. As Terence Dooley noted in his social history of so-called Big House families (in which he focuses mainly on aristocrats with large estates), geographical barriers had broken down during the Victorian era but social barriers remained. Thus "daughters of untitled landowners from small to middling sized estate backgrounds do not seem to have been eagerly sought by peers or their sons as only twelve out of a sample of 72 on whom information was available married into the peerage. The proportion of younger sons who were upwardly mobile was even smaller... Many of these younger sons and daughters married children of army officers or clergymen who were one generation removed from estate ownership."[18]

Two of Bessie's sisters, Isabella and Anna, married army officers. Like her older sister, Isabella (Bella) seems to have met her future husband in England. In 1889, at the age of nineteen, Bella married twenty-one-year-old George Dundas of the Bedfordshire Regiment, fourth son of Adam Dundas of Dundas, the 27th Dundas of Dundas of Inchgarvie, Scotland. The youngest daughter, Anna Septima (Annie) was twenty-six and the family was in markedly reduced circumstances in 1899 when she married George Langtry MacLaine, Jr., a thirty-four-year-old Ulster lawyer and former army officer whom she may have met through the Co. Down branch of the Head family. They would have two sons. Michael Ravenscroft (Raven) Head was born on May 12, 1880, sixteen years after his oldest brother Willie, seven years after his sister Annie and eight years before his father's death. He seems to have been his mother's favorite.

A letter that Willie Head wrote his fourteen-year-old sister Bella early one morning, perhaps during the winter of 1884, when she was in London with her younger sister Annie, shows he was fond of his sisters. The nineteen-year-old envied the good time Bella seemed to be having in London and wished he could join her there for a week, "however I have not collected enough brass yet." He was trying to do that by breeding rabbits: "I have just come in from the Rabbits so my hands are nearly off me with the cold it froze very hard last night we may soon begin to look out for skating." Was he being kept short of funds by his parents? A typical landlord's son, he wrote of a shooting party the previous week: "we got 20 brace Rabbits and 15 brace Rock Pheasants besides other things.

Lord Hastings wants me to go 'shoot' with him next week but I do not think I will go." His horse had been having "the strangles" and he had the vet over three times the week before. "I am going to ride him for the 1st time today he will be very fresh, however I am not like you, do not tumble off when the <u>horse</u> turns round," he teased her, telling her she should get some riding lessons while she was in London, as Bessie had done when she was there.[19] Ironically, Willie's serious mental problems were later attributed to falls off his horse that resulted in head injuries. His somewhat condescending reference to his sister Georgie collecting "disgusting mushrooms" every day with Miss Bain, and wondering what on earth they did with them, raises the question of why she was at home at the age of sixteen with a governess, or was she a nurse-companion? Family lore has it that Georgiana was simple-minded, perhaps to justify her fall from grace seventeen years later (see chapter 17).

As the heir to the estate, Willie was expected to remain in Ireland. What to do with a son and heir who seems not to have shown any intellectual promise and, according to his mother, was always intemperate? As mentioned previously, it's not known where William Edward (Willie) Head was educated, whereas the next two sons were sent away to boarding school. He must have been a disappointment to his scholarly father. If so, his father's worst fears would be realized. William Henry Head may have turned to a relative like Henry Haswell Head who, with his connections through both of his wives to high-level influence in Co. Down, could have helped secure the commission for Willie in 1885 as a gentleman lieutenant in the 4th Brigade of the North Irish Division of the Irish Militia based at Carrickfergus Castle near Belfast, Co. Antrim.[20] On August 17 the following year, William Edward Head married Mary Katherine Johns, eldest daughter of Thomas Digby Johns of Rosebrook, Co. Antrim, a lawyer and the town clerk of Carrickfergus, at St. Nicholas Church, Carrickfergus.[21]

The brothers born on either side of Georgiana (Georgie), John Henry and Charles Octavius, were sent away to boarding school in Bray. Charles, who was two and a half years younger than John, described the school in his memoir. Bray School was "owned and managed by a kindly old English lady, Miss Haynes, who had a very capable Irishman to do the teaching for her. He was almost entirely a self-educated man, who by perseverance and hard work had gained a degree at one of the minor Irish University Colleges; and a man of strong, upright character, sympathetic and a very practical teacher." Charles flourished academically during his eight years at the school. His and John's intermediate exam results were published in *Freeman's Journal*.[22] He was a prize winner in 1881, won honors in nine subjects and an exhibition, or scholarship, valued at £15 for three years in 1882, when he was in the Junior Grade (the sole winner of an exhibition at the age of thirteen), while John Henry earned honors in four subjects and the 3rd class prize awarded in books, valued at £1.

Charles was clever and ambitious, but he was the third son and was intended for the army. "Before I was fourteen I had got to the top of the school," he wrote almost sixty years later, "and as it seemed to be unable to raise my education to any higher level, I proposed to my parents that I should be sent to an English Public School, but their response was negative. It was indicated to me that what had been good enough for my father was good enough for me, and the differences in travelling conditions between his epoch and mine did not invalidate the precedent. Besides I was to go to Woolwich as soon as I was sixteen, so it was not worthwhile going to another school for only two years!" He wrote that he forgot much of what he had learned during the next eighteen months under a new and incompetent headmaster. His frustration over his parents' response was still palpable in his old age. Instead, he was sent to a "crammer" in Dublin, "a hateful time" of short-term intensive study to prepare for the entrance exam to the Royal Military Academy, Woolwich, known as the "Shop." He passed into Woolwich when he was two months over sixteen, "raw, green, undeveloped and unsophisticated for my age."[23]

There was a footnote to the Heads of Derry Castle at this time. On December 19, 1884, Emily Sheffield Cassan died at Harmony Lodge, Castle Connell, near Limerick. She had been a widow for twenty-three years and was the last of Michael Prittie Head's children. Her sister Henrietta Parsons had died in Dublin in 1879, long estranged from her husband, or widowed, and having lost both her children as infants. She outlived her first cousin and former fiancé, Simon George Purdon of Tinerana, by seventeen years (see chapter

13 for her 1837 breach of promise suit against him). Purdon, a respected landlord, and his wife Louisa had six sons and four daughters but, due to the deaths without heirs of their sons, the Tinerana estate devolved to two daughters who soon sold it. A sad ending all round to two families and their estates facing each other across beautiful Lough Derg.[24]

With the Conservative party briefly back in power in 1885, Lord Ashbourne, lord chancellor of Ireland under Prime Minister Lord Salisbury, introduced an Irish land purchase bill. What became known as the Ashbourne Land Act stimulated tenant interest in purchase as it allowed the tenant to obtain the full purchase price from the Irish Land Commission established by Gladstone in 1881, lowered the annuity to 4 percent, and extended the repayment period to 49 years.[25] The purchase price was advanced to the landlord in cash. At about the same time, however, the Conservative lord-lieutenant, Lord Carnarvon, told Parnell that the Conservative party, inspired chiefly by Lord Randolph Churchill, wanted to set up an aristocratic, class-bound home rule, with the Westminster Parliament still in authority. When Parnell appeared to agree with this approach, his nationalist lieutenants began to accuse him of pontifical rule, of never forgetting that he came from "the conquering race in Ireland," and that he wanted the Irish gentry to emerge as the natural leaders of the people.[26]

The general election of 1885 was the first held under the 1884 Reform Act that extended the right to vote to the agricultural laboring class of Ireland: from 1885 on, a landlord in the south and west had little or no chance of winning a parliamentary seat. Not surprisingly, considering the new electorate, the Liberals won 335 seats, the Conservatives 249, and the Home Rulers 86. Parnell could keep either party out of office, and Gladstone now announced his own and the Liberal party's conversion to Irish home rule. But Joseph Chamberlain, a self-made businessman from Birmingham and a radical Liberal, opposed home rule because he believed it threatened to end the Union; an Irish parliament, with an Irish executive, was self-government of a very different order to the kind of local bodies he envisaged. Chamberlain desired a "federal" or "home rule" all-round arrangement of how the U.K.

was constituted. Another sticking point was the kind of men who would rule Ireland under Home Rule. "If agitation and threat had helped bring Parnell to power in Ireland," historian Boyce has written, "its lessons, or apparent lessons, were not lost on many in England: they saw crypto-Fenians, agrarian terrorists, and violent nationalists as clearly unfit to rule Ireland."[27] Chamberlain resigned from Gladstone's third government in 1886 in opposition to Irish home rule.

Gladstone's Home Rule bill was defeated on June 8, 1886, by 343 votes to 313. Following its defeat, Gladstone asked for and was granted the dissolution of Parliament. In the ensuing general election in July, he and his bill suffered a total rejection by the English electorate, putting the anti-Home-Rule Conservatives and Unionists into power that August for almost twenty uninterrupted years.[28] Col. Edward Saunderson, a Unionist landlord and Orangeman and the author of *Two Irelands; Or Loyalty versus Treason* (1884), was elected for North Armagh and became leader of the Irish Unionist parliamentary party. In May 1886, Saunderson identified "85 reasons why this House should not consent to this [Home Rule] Bill. They are not abstract, but concrete reasons—and they are to be found sitting below the gangway opposite," pointing to the home rule supporters.[29] Saunderson also assured the House of Commons that the Southern Unionists were very anxious to live "in our own native land...we are Irishmen as the tenants are...we love our nation as much as they do."[30]

As Home Rule consolidated its electoral hold on nationalist Ireland during the 1880s, opinion among the Protestant Unionists also hardened. Opposition became increasingly militant in the northeast, where Unionists were firmly entrenched. At the same time, influential voices called for "special treatment" for the Ulster Unionists in any Home Rule settlement. They were the only Unionist group in Ireland whose geographical cohesion as an almost self-contained Protestant society, ranging from landowners and businessmen to tenant farmers and industrial and agricultural laborers, made them a formidable political force.[31] Colonel Saunderson, whose daughter would marry the eldest son of Dr. Henry Haswell Head of Dublin in 1892, organized Ulster resistance to Home Rule and brought Lord Randolph Churchill to Belfast as a supporter of the Unionist cause. Saunderson was leader of the Parliamentary Unionists in 1888 and of the Irish Unionist Alliance in 1891. Alvin Jackson, his biographer, considered Saunderson to be "the single most significant figure in the early development of organized Unionism in Ireland" but "Saunderson's failings had massive repercussions."[32]

Despite impressive Unionist efforts, Unionism in the southern provinces remained a minority movement partly due to the imbalance in the religions of the population. In 1911, for instance, there were only some 256,699 Protestants scattered among a Roman Catholic population of 2,551,854. Unionists there, even though they tended to represent the tip of the social pyramid, could barely rely upon returning three members to parliament, whereas Ulster Unionists could usually count on winning half of the parliamentary representation of that province.[33] The Irish Loyal and Patriotic Union (ILPU), the southern unionist organization, had its first annual general meeting in January 1886. Founded in 1885 to resist the Nationalist movement, its immediate object was to support maintaining the Union between Ireland and Great Britain in the forthcoming general election. The Rev. J. H. Jellett, provost of Trinity College, Dublin (TCD), gave a speech urging electoral and registration work by unionists. Despite this and other ILPU efforts, the delayed election was a great Nationalist victory, although there was a significant swing toward the Conservatives in Great Britain.

Among the organizations representing landlord and Unionist interests, the Irish Landlords Convention (ILC), founded in 1886 and composed of members drawn from all strata of the landlord class, concentrated on landlords with mortgage difficulties. Its executive committee called on the British government to compensate Irish landlords for losses they sustained after 1881 as a result of land legislation. They asked for advances to "pay off mortgages and family charges" and for "the incidence of certain public charges, rates and taxes" to be readjusted. Their pleas fell on deaf ears. British politicians were increasingly becoming aware of the need to woo the expanding electorate, leading them to sympathize more with the masses than the besieged landlord minority. By the 1890s, members of the Convention had become frustrated enough in their quest to do something for the plight of encumbered landlords to ask; "Why then should we carry on a hopeless bankrupt business, flaying tenants alive and eternally plunged in scalding waters ourselves, merely for the benefit of some firm of London usurers who are safe out of range of blunderbuss or boycotter?"[34]

As Unionist and landlord resistance became increasingly organized, Parnell pursued a moderate and conciliatory policy on land purchase, still hoping to retain a significant landlord presence under home rule. He opposed any ideas that jeopardized the newfound respectability of the home rule movement and constitutional nationalism. When William O'Brien, a political lieutenant, launched a renewed land agitation, the Plan of Campaign, to compel landlords to lower rents through a process of collective bargaining with their tenants, Parnell deftly sidestepped, announcing that he was recovering from serious illness.[35] In November 1886, when the National League violently attacked the most notorious absentee landlord of his generation, the marquess of Clanricarde, who tried to evict all tenants who resisted him on his Co. Galway estate, Parnell likewise disassociated himself from this controversy. After Parnell sought Vatican assistance to suppress clergymen involved in the Plan of Campaign, Pope Leo XIII condemned the Plan and all clerical involvement in it. In March 1887, however, the London *Times* began publishing a series of articles, "Parnellism and Crime," in which Home Rule League leaders were accused of being involved in murder and outrage during the land war. This prompted the government to set up a Special Commission in September 1888 to investigate the charges made against Parnell and the Home Rule Party. Parnell's name was fully cleared.[36]

The month the first *Times* article appeared, Conservative prime minister Lord Salisbury appointed his nephew, Arthur Balfour, as chief-secretary of Ireland. Balfour made his intentions clear from the beginning of his tenure and is thought to have declared, rather undiplomatically, "I shall be as relentless as Cromwell in enforcing obedience to the law, but, at the same time, I shall be as radical as any reformer in redressing grievances and especially in removing every cause of complaint in regard to the land." Balfour's likening his rule to Cromwell almost guaranteed raising nationalists' backs and anger. That July (1887) he secured the tough Criminal Law and Procedure (Ireland) Act, a permanent measure aimed at preventing boycotting, intimidation, unlawful assembly, and organization of conspiracies against the payment of rents. It gave resident magistrates in districts proclaimed under the act powers of investigation and summary jurisdiction and empowered the lord-lieutenants to suppress subversive organizations.[37] Hundreds of people were imprisoned, including over twenty MPs. Among the Irish MPs sentenced to prison and hard labor were Parnellites John Redmond, a member of parliament since 1881 (five weeks for a strong and inflammatory speech in support of tenant farmers), and his brother Willie Redmond, "the *enfant terrible* of Irish politics" (three months for resisting a tenant's eviction). Trial by jury was abolished, the National League was declared illegal, and Balfour sent armed police and soldiers to evict tenants, using battering rams against small cottages after days-long sieges.

Balfour, however, is also associated with the conscious Conservative policy of constructive unionism, or "killing Home Rule with kindness." His principal contribution toward confronting the continuing arguments over land reform was the establishment of the Congested Districts Board as part of the Purchase of Land Act of 1891. Politicians and humanitarians had drawn attention to the grave social problems caused by uneconomic holdings in the counties of Donegal, Mayo, Galway, Clare, and Kerry, where one million people struggled to survive. The Board was invested with extensive powers to encourage agriculture and industry in these western coastal parts of the country as well as to provide assistance to those who wished to emigrate.[38]

During this troubled time in Ireland, Charles Head was among the Royal Military Academy cadets brought from Woolwich on June 20, 1887 to swell the number of troops for Queen Victoria's Jubilee parade on the road outside Buckingham Palace. A great admirer of the Queen, he never forgot this one opportunity to see her in person—a little old lady dressed in black—as her carriage passed him on its way to Westminster Abbey. In July, he graduated ninth in the Artillery section from Woolwich and won the riding prize. After receiving his commission at just over eighteen, making him the youngest officer in the army for the next six months, he joined one of the two field batteries of the Royal Horse Artillery stationed in Exeter. "Socially Exeter was a most enjoyable place," he wrote. "The people around were more than kind to us boys, and treated us with a hospitality which could not have been exceeded. I made some excellent friends there..." He appreciated the fact that one of the captains who lived in the officer's mess with six subalterns, including himself, "managed it with such economy that our mess-bills rarely exceeded seven or eight pounds a month; a fact which, as none of us were wealthy, was a great benefit to us all." Charles's parental allowance was just £100 a year and the pay of second lieu-tenants a mere five shillings and seven pence a month. He very much admired the charm and strong personality of his major's en-ergetic wife. "She was one of my earliest and greatest friends, and, though not much older than myself, as my major's wife, she, quite naturally, mothered me," he wrote, noting that, after her husband's death, she became a suffragette and, during the Great War, joined "a heroic band of hospital nurses, who proceeded to the Balkans, and devoted themselves to the suffering Roumanians and Serbi-ans." Never strong, she soon died from her exertions.

Charles was less impressed by the military value of the two bat-teries: "the guns were muzzle-loaders, then out of date in continen-tal armies, and soon to be superseded in our own." Even worse, discipline was bad. His second colonel there proved to be a humor-less martinet, whose petty ways made him very unpopular with his subordinates. Despite this serious fly in the ointment, there was plenty of time for riding: "almost every afternoon three or four of us used to sally forth on our battery horses in search of fences to jump, and turf for a gallop," no easy thing in Devonshire. His accounts of his years in Devonshire and elsewhere during his army career are filled with humorous anecdotes, providing a lively social history of his times, even down to a description of the strict protocol covering uniforms and civilian attire at the time. When it came time to move the batteries to Aldershot in 1891, he described the pleasures of the various stops they made on the long march from Devon. Always one to note attractive women, he wrote, "At Reading a beautiful barmaid ogled me seductively, but I fled abashed."

Things were far from carefree at home in Ireland. On October 18, 1888, William Henry Head died of asphyxia, aged seventy-eight.

He had been in poor health for some time, as noted in a letter he sent to his wife in late 1886, which ended with a postscript in which he said, "I was not well enough" to spend much time with a neighbor who had stopped by—just enough time to "read a few verses."[39] A couple of his own poems, "The Fox Hunt" and "A Summer Excursion," were found with this letter. "My dearest Issy," he began. "Not much occasion to write perhaps. Without any wish to exaggerate, I may say I could not have had a worse night than last. I can do very badly without you, but of course I don't wish to control your movements of which you are best judge…I thought close carriage best to send…I suppose it would be too much to hope for any reasonable change in yr mother but hoping to see you back with best love, Your affectionate husband, Will H. Head."

Asphyxia, which might have been caused by congestive heart failure, is a long drawn out and agonizing way to die. He cannot have been well enough to attend his oldest son's wedding in Carrickfergus, Co. Antrim, that August. Bitterly antagonistic to Gladstone's Irish policies, particularly the land acts that had begun whittling away much of what he had built at Derrylahan, he was according to his son Charles, relieved to be leaving the scene.

> For a long time he held Gladstone in high esteem, for his earnestness, eloquence, orderliness and classical erudition, but when that statesman began meddling with the relations of landlord and tenant in Ireland, a subject which he was ill-qualified to handle, and in which he produced dire confusion and difficulty, my father's regard for him rapidly altered into dislike and contempt. Before he died, he saw the introduction in Parliament of a Bill for Home Rule, in his mind an utterly impracticable project, of which the very thought of its enactment reconciled him to his approaching departure to another world."[40]

William Henry's friend and father-in-law, Nicholas Biddulph, also died in 1888. He was succeeded by his oldest son, Lt. Col. Francis Edward Biddulph, the only child of Nicholas's first marriage and the second trustee of William Henry's will, after his half-sister Isabella. Isabella Head and Francis E. Biddulph were to hold the estate in trust for young William Edward Head until he turned twenty-five, on April 8, 1889. By an indenture dated eleven days later, on April 19, Willie elected to take possession of the Derrylahan mansion during his mother's lifetime in return for a £100 annuity, payable to her in equal half-yearly instalments.

Young William Edward Head, unstable, poorly educated, and probably dangerously rebellious against his aged father's coldly dutiful standards, could not have been less equipped to deal with the prevailing social and economic climate in Ireland. There had been a sharp decline in the selling value of landed estates from 1879 on, Irish land was no longer regarded as safe collateral, and mortgagees panicked during the land war, beginning to call in their loans as landlords temporarily defaulted, closing all avenues of borrowing to the latter.[41] Family lore describes Derrylahan with Willie at the helm as the scene of wild parties and debaucheries. Willie drank to excess, ran up debts, secured two different mortgages on the Derrylahan and Ballyduff properties in 1891 from money-lender Thomas Joyce of Dublin for enormous loans, pawned treasures from the house, and failed to pay his mother's annuities.[42] Joyce assigned these mortgages to Dublin solicitor John A. French. By 1892, Willie had ruined his health as well as his fortune. His mother and uncle sent him to the exclusive and very expensive St. Ann's Hydropathic and Turkish Baths in Blarney, Co. Cork, where they hoped the healthy regimen, with its prohibition of any stronger beverage than pure water, would turn him away from heavy drinking. St. Ann's boasted a circulating library, a reading room, covered tennis courts, three grass tennis courts, a theatre, an American bowling alley, a billiard room for ladies and gentlemen, and access to trout-fishing and fox-hunting—hardly a punishment, apart from the absence of alcohol!

Solicitor John A. French, who was earning a ruthless reputation for gaining control of properties when interest payments were not made, had evidently forced foreclosure in court. Isabella Head then presented a petition for the sale of the Derrylahan and Ballyduff properties to the Land Judge's Court in respect of her arrears and an absolute order for sale was made. But Willie remained in control of the property and its income stream, posing significant financial risks to both his mother and the lender. Something had to be done and, with Willie more or less incarcerated at St. Ann's, there was no better opportunity. With the estate now in receivership in the Chancery Division of the High Court of Justice, Willie was forced, on April 1, 1892, to sign a receivership deed between himself, his mother, who was then living at 50 Upper Leeson Street, Dublin, and land agent Toler R. Garvey of Parsonstown (Birr).[43] Willie signed and sealed the deed in the presence of the chaplain and resident physician of St. Ann's Hill.

By the terms of the deed, Willie was required to appoint Toler Garvey to act as receiver over the rents and profits of his estate, to negotiate fair rents with the tenants and manage the sale to such tenants of their holdings under the terms of the "several land acts now in force in Ireland for such purposes or any acts extending or Amending the same."[44] Garvey was also to let the Derrylahan mansion house, with its gardens and pleasure grounds, shooting and fishing rights, for up to five years, to manage and superintend the management of the property, and pay all bills and taxes out of receipts, deducting 5 percent for his expenses and trouble. The indenture listed all the tenant farmers with their annual rents. As a further example of his ne'er-do-well character and irresponsibility, Willie seems also to have turned over the £200 annuity due to his wife Mary Katherine per their 1886 marriage settlement to solicitor French. When faced with his own financial problems a few years later, having retired from the army and commuted his pension to set himself up in farming his land, Col. Francis Biddulph approached the same notorious money-lender for loans at the same exorbitant rate of 60 percent. When Biddulph went bankrupt in 1898, Joyce gained control of his property, St. Kilda's near Birr, and the Biddulphs were evicted by bailiffs, causing severe distress to the family.[45]

Unfortunately, Willie's bankruptcy was only the beginning of the embarrassment and damage caused by the heir to the family of one of the most respected landlords in North Tipperary, William Henry Head, D.L. Willie was probably already estranged from his poor young wife. In the meantime, his youngest siblings, Annie and Raven (Michael), were presumably living with their mother in Dublin, where John Henry was studying medicine at Trinity College. Charles was now stationed at Aldershot, England, far enough away to escape the scandal at Derrylahan but no doubt extremely upset to hear all the bad news from his family.

The Heads were not the only family suffering public embarrass-ment. The sensational divorce case brought by Parnell's longtime collaborator in the Home Rule Party, Capt. William H. O'Shea, against his wife Katharine (Kitty) on grounds of adultery with Par-nell came to trial on November 15-16, 1890. As long as it had suited him, O'Shea had hypocritically turned a blind eye to her longtime relationship with Parnell, who now advised Kitty not to contest the divorce. O'Shea won custody of the children, including her two daughters by Parnell. Parnell managed to hold onto leadership of the Home Rule party in the wake of the divorce, but Gladstone was informed by a large proportion of his Nonconformist supporters that Parnell's continued leadership of the Irish party would mean the loss of the next election and putting off the Home Rule bill until he was no longer around to dictate it. Then Timothy Healy, one of Parnell's longtime Catholic lieutenants, virulently attacked Par-nell and Katharine O'Shea in meetings and in the press. Broken by stress, Parnell died on October 6, 1891 aged forty-five, only three and a half months after marrying Kitty. The bitterness, which did not end with Parnell's death, resulted in a dramatic split within his party. Parnell's vacant seat of Cork City fell to an opponent but, on December 31, 1891, Parnellite John Redmond defeated Michael Davitt in the Waterford City by-election and assumed the leader-ship of the minority Parnellite rump of the Irish Parliamentary Par-ty (IPP). The larger anti-Parnellite group formed the Irish Nation-al Federation (INF) under John Dillon. But Parnell never lost his high standing with ordinary people, who referred to him as "the uncrowned king of Ireland." Families were split by being for or against him, while the Catholic Church denounced him.[46]

Lord Salisbury's Conservative government fell in July 1892, and the general election a month later brought Gladstone and the Lib-eral party back into office with a very slim majority of forty. The Westminster parliament and the majority of the British people were now firmly Unionist. Even so, Gladstone remained determined to reintroduce a Home Rule bill. A great Unionist Convention was held in Dublin that summer with delegates filling two halls. The chairman, Lord Fingall, was supported on the platform by more than a hundred other notables, including the duke of Leinster and Lords Mayo, Dunsany, Emly, Ventry, Massy, and Cloncurry. A few days before the Dublin convention, the Ulster Unionists held a convention in Belfast, presided over by the duke of Abercorn. The Ulster Unionist movement, which was becoming increasingly independent of the movement in the rest of Ireland, returned sixteen members of parliament, including Colonel Saunderson, compared to the paltry three from the southern provinces.[47] In King's County (Offaly), for instance, William Henry Head's former neighbor, William T. Trench, JP, ran unsuccessfully as a Unionist for the Birr seat in the 1892 election.[48] Trench succeeded William Henry as a deputy lieutenant for Co. Tipperary that June—while William Edward Head, JP, was being dried out in Co. Cork!

The senior branch of the Head family was increasingly drawn into the Ulster Unionist movement, particularly following the marriages of two children of Dr. Henry Haswell Head, JP (whose first and second wives were both from prominent Co. Down families) into leading Ulster landowning and political families. Henry Nugent Head, an officer in The Cameronians, who had been educated at Harrow, Trinity College Dublin, and Cambridge, married Rosa Saunderson, daughter of Col. Edward Saunderson, at Saunderson's Co. Cavan estate in 1892. Three years later, Henry Nugent Head's sister Edith Grace married Robert Perceval-Maxwell, of Finnebrogue House, Downpatrick, another prominent Co. Down family. The Maxwells had long been leaders in Ulster politics.[49]

Equally Unionist in its politics was the large family of Dean John Head's fourth son, Capt. Edward Head, who had retired from the 89th Foot at the early age of thirty. He and his family lived in cramped and increasingly impoverished circumstances at Carrig Cottage on 91 acres near Derrylahan. Capt. Edward lived the life of a country gentleman "gone to seed," who was not above poaching on his neighbors' property and made his long-suffering wife miserable with temper tantrums, according to a granddaughter. Yet Edward's temperament and the family's straitened circumstances did not put too great a damper on family life. Edward's youngest daughter Gracie loved dancing, riding, friendship, and poetry, had several suitors—but hated cleaning the house! She and her siblings were popular and went to many balls, tennis tournaments, and other amusements in Birr. According to her diary, she flirted with her distant cousin Charlie Head when he was home for Christmas in 1892, sending him violets on December 21 while he sent her "a lovely box of sweets" two days later. [50]

The Edward Heads were just a few among many less prosperous descendants of the Protestant landowning class who found employment and opportunity through emigration, work in the new political order, and marriage to Roman Catholics. The oldest son had a good job with the Land Commission, another worked for the Nenagh Council as an inspector of roads, and yet another emigrated to Australia, never to be heard from again. The second son, Edward Francis (b. 1853), was the most successful, having emigrated to Canada in 1881 after training as an architect and engineer at a cousin's firm in London for nine years.[51] He became a sought-after designer of grain elevators in Manitoba. His oldest daughter, Ethel "Annie" Head, spent several months visiting relatives in Ireland in 1910-11 and later wrote an account of those visits and of the "Irish Branch" of the Head family (see chapter 17).[52]

Gladstone's second Home Rule bill of 1893 was designed to secure Irish control over Irish affairs while assuring the equality of Scotland and Wales. The preamble to the bill affirmed the supremacy of the Westminster parliament in its control of imperial affairs. Unlike the 1886 bill, the lord-lieutenant would now be assisted by an executive committee of the Irish privy council, and he would have the right to apply or withhold the royal assent to Irish legislation. The lord-lieutenant could be a Catholic, but his term of office was fixed at six years. The proposed Irish legislature was now to be bicameral, but Irish representation at Westminster was proposed to be reduced to eighty. The bill passed in the House of Commons in September 1893 but was thrown out by the House of Lords, thus essentially ending its consideration. Gladstone retired from the Liberal leadership in 1894.[53]

In the meantime, one dissolute young Unionist and JP, William E. Head, declared himself to be not one jot interested in Home Rule when he turned up penniless in Chicago in late October 1893. By November 4, 1893, both Ireland, via the *Sligo Champion* and Chicago via the *Chicago Herald* knew that the great Illinois city was "host" to, as a *Herald* headline stated, "An Irish Magistrate in Trouble."

The following story recounts the troubles that a certain "Captain William [Joseph *sic*] Edward Head" told a local journalist while he was the penniless guest of the Harrison Street Police Station there.

It is hard to know if Willie Head told a cock and bull story, or whether the reporter, who was perhaps an Irishman himself, embellished the facts. The reporter evidently took to "the Captain," as so many seemed to do. He thought him "a good-natured looking man of about 50 years" (in fact he was twenty-nine). The captain told him that he had recently married a rich lady from Belfast (he married Mary Katherine Johns seven years earlier and there is no evidence that she was rich) and that he took advantage of this new-found fortune by accepting an invitation from his former gamekeeper, who "had a great regard for the 'master,'" to join him in Tacoma, Washington, where he had made good, for a hunting adventure. The captain said he had had to let his gamekeeper go in the face of the reduction of his rent rolls by the land league in 1881 (his father was still alive at that time and is unlikely to have done any such thing). Also, he claimed to have "been in Australia before Parnell's time on a 'lark' and that it would be better than a spin with the Birr beagles to tear after bears in Takoma."

Be that as it may, the reporter, while admiring Head's "great good humour" about his situation, had fun with his uncomfortable status as an Irish landlord, a military man, and a JP, penniless and defenseless in a town where he knew there were "280,000 Celts." "He had heard terrible tales of the 'American Irish' and of their hatred of the 'loyal minority' who vote for Lord Salisbury and shout for the queen." So what brought Willie Head to this low point so far from home? He said that he had arrived in Boston from Queenstown, Ireland (Dún Laoghaire today), on September 21 (1893) and traveled by train to Washington, D.C. There he was "fleeced, gulled, humbugged, relieved of £500 [$2,500 today]" and his pocket watch. Is it likely that he was carrying that much cash? Knowing Willie's proclivities, this disaster happened when he was stone drunk. He must have used his considerable Irish charm to persuade the manager of the National Hotel to allow him to remain there, bed and board free, for three weeks while the police searched for the thieves. He even managed to convince the British ambassador to personally lend him £50, and purchase a return train ticket to Takoma, Washington, via Chicago. He previously shipped all his trunks, guns, and valuables to Takoma—another likely story!

Willie arrived in Chicago having gone through the ambassador's money—there must have been a bar on the train! When he asked "hangers on" at the station where he should go for the next part of his long journey, he was persuaded to sell the return stub of his ticket for $4 with which he paid for a hotel room. He presented himself at the Grand Central station the next morning, only to be told that he would have to pay $8 to replace the missing return ticket. Not knowing which way to turn, "[H]e strolled into the Harrison Street station at 4 o'clock yesterday afternoon," wrote the unnamed reporter. No wonder Willie felt threatened. That particular police station was in one of the roughest and most dangerous parts of Chicago at the time. More than that, he feared that "the first man he might appeal to for assistance might be John Finnerty [sic] himself!"[54]

Willie told his story to the astonished police officers, saying that "if he could get 40 cents to telegraph to Washington he could get plenty of money." Another unlikely proposition! Police Captain Hartnett supplied him with the cash for the telegraph. To whom did Willie address it? Surely not the British ambassador! The story ended with the policemen responding to Willie's practiced blarney by giving "the huntsman" supper and making up a bed for him in one of the jail cells where "he went to sleep behind the bars with as much comfort and composure as if no misfortune had befallen him." He did remark, though, that "he had little doubt but many a Land Leaguer whom he had sent to jail would shout for glory to see him behind bars."!

It is not known if Willie ever got to Takoma and exactly when he returned to Ireland. Within six years, however, he would be taken to court and imprisoned as a habitual drunkard and fraudster, not a surprising outcome to his increasingly irresponsible and dissolute life.

While Willie wandered, tensions were rising among Irish Nationalists. Following Parnell's death, the division and tensions between Parnellites and anti-Parnellites in the Home Rule movement grew ever more intense. John Redmond continued as leader of the minority Parnellite rump, while John Dillon was more Parnellite than Parnell, seeking to maintain a centralized party machine on the model of the National League and remaining loyal to the Liberal alliance. Meantime, anti-Parnellite T. M. Healy annexed parts of the Parnellite constituency, in particular the substantial farming interest together with the Catholic Church, unencumbered by the Liberal Party. The warfare between Healy and Dillon came to a head in 1895 when Healy was voted off all his leaderships in the Irish Parliamentary Party, although he remained the "enemy within" for years.[55]

Political nationalism might have been going nowhere, but Irish cultural nationalism was giving Irish Catholics and Protestants a new sense of their own history, traditions, and culture in a revolt against homogenizing Anglicism. In 1884, Michael Cusack founded the Gaelic Athletic Association (GAA), which excluded from membership policemen, soldiers, and other people associated with "Britishness" and those who played "foreign games," particularly "disgusting cricket"! In 1892, TCD academic Douglas Hyde wrote a manifesto called "On the Necessity for De-Anglicising the Irish People," in which he argued that Ireland should follow its own traditions in language, literature, and dress. The following year, he helped found the Gaelic League (Conradh na Gaeilge) to encourage the preservation of Irish culture. William Butler Yeats was the dominating figure of what became known as the Irish literary renaissance, gathering around him a following of the most creative figures at the turn of the century: Lady Gregory, George Moore, and J. M. Synge, all Anglo-Irish. A new generation of Irish republicans (including Patrick Pearse, Éamon de Valera, Michael Collins, and Ernest Blythe), became politicized through their involvement in the Gaelic League. By 1898, the League had fifty-eight branches, 200 by 1901, 600 by 1903, and 900 by 1906, playing an increasingly significant part in widening and strengthening Irish consciousness and enforcing the teaching of Irish in 3,000 schools.[56]

Charles Head, now a captain, was stationed at Clonmel, Co.Tipperary, between 1895 and 1897, allowing him to make frequent visits to Derrylahan. What he saw there must have distressed him deeply. While he and the rest of his family would have been heartened by the Unionist (formerly Conservative) party's triumph in the 1895 elections, his older brother had abandoned the house (which was usually rented) and the estate, while the tenanted land was being sold off or let to those who farmed it. Toler Garvey, agent and receiver for the Derrylahan estate, oversaw the dismantlement of the impressive estate assembled by the late William Henry Head, placing an advertisement to let 300 acres of Derrylahan's demesne land in November 1897 and, four months later, charging W. N. Biddulph, a Birr auctioneer, to let by auction at Derrylahan Park various grazing lands for the following eleven months.[57] Meanwhile, the Irish nationalist press, particularly the local *Midland Tribune*, was increasingly vicious in its attacks on the landlord class and British rule. Perhaps Charles was relieved when he received orders to depart for India, where he spent the next four years as third in command of B Battery of the Royal Horse Artillery. Soon after his departure, the Local Government Act of 1898 replaced grand juries with democratically elected county and district councils, supervised by the Local Government Board, effectively destroying the power of the Ascendancy in local politics (see next chapter). Anglo-Irish noblewoman and poet Maria La Touche expressed the prevailing Ascendancy view of local government when she wrote of it: "Giving us Local Government is very like giving Nursery Government to the two youngest and most quarrelsome of the babies."[58]

13. The Presentation of British Officers to Pope Pius VI, 1794. Oil on canvas by James Northcote, R.A., 1800.

Capt. Lt. Michael Head is standing at left with the sword, Lt. the Hon. Pierce Butler next to him, and Capt. Robert Browne kneeling. After slipping gold medals over their heads, the Pope took Capt. Browne's helmet in his hands and expressed the wish "that Heaven would enable the cause of truth and religion to triumph over injustice and infidelity." Pope Pius VI was captured by Napoleon's forces in 1798 and imprisoned in Valence, France, where he died the following year.

©Victoria and Albert Museum, London. Given by Richard Browne Clayton, 1863.

14. "Murder of Lord Kilwarden," engraving by George Cruikshank from *History of the Irish Rebellion in 1798* by W. H. Maxwell (London, 1854 edition).
Arthur Wolfe, 1st viscount Kilwarden, lord chief justice of Ireland, and his nephew were murdered on the streets of Dublin by Robert Emmet's rebels on the night of July 23, 1803. This historical work justified England's iron suppression of the rebels, whom Cruikshank consistently depicted as a brutal, savage, angry, and destructive mob rather than patriots fighting for independence.
Classic Image, Alamy Stock Photo.

ROBERT EMMET AND NORBURY.

15.   Robert Emmet and Norbury. Chromolithograph from a supplement of *The Weekly Freeman*, December 13, 1902.

No portraits or likenesses of Robert Emmet were made during his lifetime. In this highly dramatized illustration made to honor the centenary of the Emmet uprising, Emmet, with a noticeably Napoleonic profile and stance, is shown giving his famous speech from the dock directed at John Toler, Lord Norbury, chief justice of the Court of Common Pleas, who sentenced young Emmet to death for treason.

National Library of Ireland.

16.   Major-General Michael Head (1769-1827). Oil on canvas, possibly from the studio of James Northcote, undated.

Col. Michael Head commanded the 13th Light Dragoons during the Peninsular War, most notably at the Battle of Campo Mayor. The painting was damaged by fire, either at Derrylahan, July 1921, or Hinton Hall, Shropshire, 1950.

Head family.

17.   Daniel O'Connell making a speech at the first "monster meeting" at Trim, Co. Meath, Ireland, March 19, 1843. Two months later, on May 25, he would speak at the great repeal meeting in North Tipperary.
Historical Images Archive, Alamy Stock Photo

18.   Modreeny, Cloughjordan, Co. Tipperary, the onetime home of Lt. Gen. Michael Head and his son William Henry Head, who sold the estate in 1869 some years after moving to Derrylahan Park. Modreeny was built ca. 1790 by Otway Toler and willed to his nephew, then Lt. Col. Michael Head, following his death in 1807.
Head family.

19. Derrylahan Park, newly built. Photoprint, ca. 1862. William Henry Head commissioned leading Irish architect Sir Thomas N. Deane to design the fashionable Gothic style house which was built at the cost of £6,640 on a site a mile into his new demesne. The total cost of the gatehouse, stabling and farm buildings was £20,000.

Head family.

20. William Henry Head (1809-1888), a studio photograph taken late in life, ca. 1880.
Head family.

21. Isabella Biddulph Head (1840-1911).
Courtesy of Nicola Jennings.

22a, 22b, 22c, 22d. Four of William H. and Isabella Head's ten children: John Henry (1866-1912), Charles Octavius (1869-1952), Michael Ravenscroft (1880-1950), and Francis Henrietta (1862-1876). Fanny, who died of consumption, was the third daughter to die in childhood.
All courtesy of Nicola Jennings.

23. Gladstone and the Land League. Unknown author.
Liberal Prime Minister William Gladstone's Land Act of 1881 was an attempt to solve the problem of the tenant-farmers and to end eviction and violence. It largely succeeded but was seen by its opponents as appeasement to the Land League.
Public domain, Wikimedia Commons.

24. William Edward Head (1864-1945), aged nineteen.
Willie, who inherited Derrylahan Park on his father's death in 1888 and legal control of the estate the following year, was feckless, dissolute, and temperamentally incapable of managing the estate or of negotiating the legal requirements of the Land Acts.
Courtesy of Nicola Jennings.

Chapter 17

Scandal, Army Service, and a Third Home Rule Bill

We, Irishmen, of the King's County, representing many separate interests and sharing a common desire for the welfare of our country, hereby declare our unalterable determination to uphold the Legislative Union between Great Britain and Ireland. We protest against the Home Rule Bill at present before Parliament upon the following grounds...
—Speech by Major Charles Head at meeting of King's County Unionists in Birr, King's County, late June 1912.

Birr, still called Parsonstown by some dyed-in-the-wool Unionists, was the town closest to Derrylahan and considered by the Head family and their like to be a social and cultural oasis. The local Catholic population, however, was increasingly antagonistic to displays of social elitism. The *Midland Tribune*, Birr's recently established newspaper, took up the voice of the disaffected, making its position *vis à vis* the British monarchy and local landlord society more than abundantly clear as the century drew to a close. As it reminded its readers in May 1897, the newspaper was launched to champion the Nationalist cause at a time when "the land question was the burning topic of the hour." Tacking the Land League colors to its mast, the paper forcefully attacked the 1888 Irish Coercion Act, "speaking out when a tenant's interests were threatened," while never fearing the consequences from landlord interests (which were just as roundly represented by the *King's County Chronicle*).

On June 22, 1897, the sixty-year reign of Queen Victoria was commemorated with great ceremony across the British Empire. Predictably, the nationalist *Tribune* excoriated the loyalist Jubilee Committee preparations in Birr and reported the counter-demonstrations organized by local nationalists. The earl of Rosse, evidently not wanting to inflame local feelings, held aloof from helping the Jubilee Committee in any way, and the paper reported that "the children of the Convent schools and of the Workhouse schools refused to take part in them."[1] In fact, "Birr Nationalists draped the monument to the Manchester Martyrs in black, with 'Murdered in the Record Reign' printed in large red letters across the shroud, and at ten o'clock at night removed the drapery with ringing cheers for [the martyrs] to the lively strains of 'God Save Ireland.' Thus ended Jubilee Day in Birr."[2] A week later, the paper castigated the *King's County Chronicle* for describing Birr as the "Model Town," along with "a bungling tissue of lies which would lead the stranger to believe that the inhabitants had planned a small war to celebrate the Jubilee."

The *Tribune* mocked such exclusive and, to the nationalists, excluding, annual events as the Parsonstown Horticultural Show in August: "'Parsonstown' is a super-select suburb on the outskirts of Birr. The cultured residents so dread rubbing skirts with the 'populace' that they take every precaution to ensure privacy for their public gatherings. Had it not been that the strains of a brass band floated through the open doorway now and again, you would never have suspected anything unusual was going on in the hall—least of all such a fashionable assemblage as a flower show."[3] This and occasional balls in Oxmantown Hall were just the kind of entertainments that the impoverished but socially active young Heads of Carrig Cottage participated in.

By September, when the duke and duchess of York sailed up the Shannon in drenching rain from Killaloe to Banagher—where they were met by the earl of Rosse who took them to the railway station in his carriage—the *Tribune* was firing with all its guns. It mocked the one-sided reception given the royals and claimed that "The Royal tour has proved conclusively that outside of Dublin, Unionists and Castle flunkeys are a very small factor in the population... The attempt to get up anything approaching a popular display was a miserable failure. The Conservatives had the cheering all to themselves."[4]

The final blow to the political power of the landlord class in Ireland came with passage of the Local Government of Ireland Bill the following year. Its long and immensely contentious progress through the House of Commons was handled by the chief-secretary for Ireland Gerald Balfour, who was, like his brother Arthur, a nephew of the Conservative prime minister Lord Salisbury. The bill followed the revolutionary principle of replacing nominated bodies, such as the grand juries and poor law guardians, with popularly elected urban and rural council members (urban councils already in existence were retained).[5] The grand juries (in Tipperary's case, composed of twenty-three large landowners nominated by the high sheriff, who in turn was appointed by the lord-lieutenant) had run the local government of each county. County councils would now take over their powers for supervising roads and bridges, courthouses, lunatic asylums, fever hospitals, and county infirmaries.[6] Stripped of their local government functions, the only powers retained by the grand juries were the spring and summer assizes where it was decided whether the accused should be indicted before judge and jury. An elected board of guardians would remain in charge of poor relief. Rural district councils (RDC) now took over the role of the nominated poor law guardians, acting as the sole tax-collecting authority and controlling housing, water and sewerage, public health, and compulsory education.

Hundreds of electors turned out to decide between the grand jurors and farmers, unionists and nationalists who had put forward their names for election to the seven area divisions of the new North Tipperary County Council. Several members of the former grand jury, including the Hon. Cosby G. Trench of Sopwell Hall, Anthony Parker of Castletown, William T. Trench of Redwood House, Lorrha, and Charles Tuthill of Portroe, submitted their names for election. Within weeks, six more large landowners, all of whom had been high sheriffs of County Tipperary, including Henry O'Callaghan Prittie, 4th baron Dunalley of Kilboy, offered their services.[7]

Although they were barred from elective position, local priests played a major role in encouraging the candidacy of Catholic farmers they deemed worthy to run and in judging whether the landlords had dealt fairly enough with their tenants to deserve election. The electoral odds in predominantly Catholic North Tipperary were clearly stacked against the landlords. But Anthony Parker, gentleman farmer of Castlelough and most recent scion of the Parker family, close friends for three generations of the Derry Castle Heads, was an exception. He had confirmed his candidature "not as a politician nor as a nominee of any party for I owe allegiance to none but simply as an independent Irishman and a neighbour who has lived his life among you in Duharrow." The Rev. William Marrinan, the Catholic parish priest of Portroe, then published a powerful endorsement of Parker in the *Midland Tribune*: "Long ago has he given evidence of his sympathy with tenant farmers of Ireland. At the landlords' convention in the early days of agitation, he proposed compulsory sale to all tenants at Griffith's valuation. To his own tenants on the estate he has given a rebate of twenty per cent less than the Land Courts rents." He went on to describe the spacious cottages Parker had built for his tenants and the generous amount of fuel he had provided them in an area lacking bogs. In short, "if all landlords were like him there would be little need for agitation."[8]

Parker won a council seat for the Derrycastle division and was subsequently appointed chairman of the council's finance committee but, in the six other divisions, nationalist-farmer votes swamped unionist landlord support. The ignominious routing of Lord Dunalley with just four votes could be explained by his ill-timed eviction of one of his tenants a month before polling day. Some former poor law guardians did better in the elections for the rural district councils; however, Thomas Armstrong Drought, JP, a cousin of William Henry Head, and the earl of Rosse were soundly beaten by nationalist farmer candidates in the Birr division.[9]

William E. (Willie) Head, having resigned his commission of the peace, was not among the landlords who assembled for the last meeting of the grand jury in the Nenagh courthouse on February 27, 1899. In fact, his chronic alcoholism soon brought him before the law. At the Nenagh quarter sessions that fall, "Capt. William Edward Head, late of Derrylahan, Parsonstown, surrendered to his bail and pleaded guilty to a charge of having obtained money by false pretences from James McGrath, publican, Garrykennedy, Nenagh, by means of a bogus cheque." His solicitor said his client had pleaded guilty, and he called on Dr. Myles of Birr and Head's uncle, the Rev. William Nicholas Biddulph, to testify that the prisoner had received two serious fractures of the skull, in 1889 and 1891, which rendered him insane when he was drinking. Willie, whose address was given as Shannon Vail, was discharged on entering into a bond to spend a year in the Kingswood Park Retreat near Bristol, England.[10]

Neither of Willie's army officer brothers was in the country at the time of this disgrace. Nineteen-year-old Michael Ravenscroft Head had spent just one year at the Royal Military College, Sandhurst as a gentleman cadet when he received a commission in August 1899 as 2nd Lieut. in the 5th Dragoon Guards to replace a recently deceased young officer. He joined the regiment in Natal, South Africa, where it had been shipped from Lucknow, India, in anticipation of the Second Boer War (Oct 1899 to May 1902) and was present at the bloody battle and siege of Ladysmith. He was awarded the King's South Africa Medal in October 1902 and spent four more years stationed in South Africa.

The bitter hostility of the Boers' fight for independence invoked almost hysterical anti-British feeling in Ireland. "Irish Transvaal committees" were set up to mobilize support for the Boers, who were depicted as fellow sufferers under British domination, and to dissuade young Irishmen from joining up to fight them. In fact, 28,000 Irishmen served honorably in the British Army in the Boer War while nationalist John MacBride, later executed for his part in the 1916 Easter Rising, organized the Irish Transvaal Brigade of around 300 men. The new county councils reveled in voting addresses of congratulation to the president of the Transvaal, Paul Kruger—who went into voluntary exile as Britain's victory became certain. On his return from the War, Gracie Head's brother, another Michael Head, was mocked by the new Nenagh county council for having deserted his post as a surveyor of roads to participate in this "despised imperialist war" and was forced to take a qualifying exam for his sinecure as assistant road surveyor, which he failed.[11] The impetus for this action came from the fledgling radical nationalist Sinn Féin party (called Cumann na Gaedheal at that point) founded by Arthur Griffith, which "tried to discourage recruitment for the British forces and the police by counselling local authorities not to give jobs to men who had served in them."[12]

Capt. Charles Head was stationed with B Battery of the Royal Horse Artillery at Bellary (Balari), India, when the South African War broke out.[13] "Of course, like everyone else, I tried hard to get to the scene of operations, but, with no major to command the battery, all my efforts were unavailing," he wrote four decades later. "There was nothing to do but watch the club telegrams which at the beginning only related a mournful procession of disasters. News of the relief of Kimberly, Ladysmith, and Mafeking made being posted there seem less urgent."[14] And so Charles continued in India and was transferred from Balari to Umballa (Ambala) to command an Artillery battery, again in the absence of a major.[15] The weather was unbearably hot and, with all the British cavalry and infantry gone to South Africa, the station was dull and empty. However, Charles also acted as brigade commander since, as he mentioned somewhat sarcastically, the colonel preferred the cooler climes of Simla in the Himalayan foothills in the summer.

In November 1899, when the Boxer Rebellion broke out in China, Charles was ordered as captain to another Horse Artillery battery stationed at Lucknow, which was now requisitioned to join the Indian expeditionary force raised to quell the uprising. Always eager for action, he lost no time in hurrying there. "The Boxer rebellion, as it was termed," wrote Charles four decades later, "was a perfectly natural, but utterly hopeless, effort on the part of a few patriotic and enterprising Chinamen to relieve their country of foreign interference with its Government, and, if possible, to restore to it those extensive territories and valuable ports of which various foreign nations had deprived it." Russia had annexed a large tract of Manchuria, Port Arthur, and the Liaotung Peninsula and Germany had taken over Kiao Chiao (Tsingtao, today's Qingdao) and considerable land surrounding it.[16] "We ourselves had, perhaps, made good our claim to Hong-Kong, but our seizure of Wei-hai-wei was only an eye-washing counter-blast to Russia's grab of Port Arthur, and had little justification either in morality or material value."[17] An Eight-Nation alliance sent a total of 20,000 troops to put down the Boxer Rebellion. Empress Dowager Cixi belatedly supported the Boxers with an Imperial Decree declaring war on the foreign powers. Diplomats, foreign civilians, and soldiers, as well as Chinese Christians in the Legation Quarter of Peking (Beijing) were placed under siege by the Imperial Army of China and the Boxers for 55 days. But the allied forces defeated the Imperial army, and captured Beijing on August 14, 1900.

Charles's battery arrived at the mouth of the Pei-ho River almost at the same time as the relief of the legations at Beijing was achieved, so there was little use for their services.[18] During two expeditions made by his battery in pursuit of vanished rebels, Charles enjoyed watching Chinese laborers gathering in a tall and magnificent harvest of millet, where women chose to hide as the mounted foreign soldiers approached their villages. Charles's sympathy was entirely with the Chinese whom he found to be "attractive, hard-working, honest, and good-tempered." While the Boxers had guns and rifles, few of them knew how to use them; and their favored weapon was "a long monstrosity, which it took two men to carry, one shooting it off the other's shoulders." Charles would bring one of those monster guns and other Chinese treasures back to Ireland with him but argued defensively against the frequent later accusations that the foreign soldiers looted ruthlessly: "Looting was strictly forbidden in the [British] army, and we got few opportunities of breaking the regulations, had we desired to do so! In our expeditions, the pawn-shops, where the local inhabitants had deposited their winter clothes and the surplus of their silver ornaments, was usually taken possession of officially, as a prize of war, and its contents distributed to us gratis or by auction." As a result, he brought a haul of handsome female garments home with him to the delight of the women in his family and social circle.

The foreign armies stayed on in China through that winter and the following summer. "At winter's close," recalled Charles, "we moved north from Tientsin to Shan-hai-kwan, a place on the sea, where that wonderful architectural work, the great wall of China, starts for its 2,000-mile stretch round the old Chinese dominion..." but whose "antiquity is now desecrated by a gap allowing passage to the Nieuchwang railway." As soon as the battery arrived there, Charles was granted a two-month leave to travel in Japan.[19]

Back in Shan-hai-kwan, Charles had some amusing experiences, one involving a humorless German officer on horseback and what he thought egotistically was a murderous assault on him by a mule, failing to realize that the animal had amorous intents on his horse. Tragically, the German shot the mule dead. Charles and his British fellow officers felt increasingly alienated from the Germans following other untoward incidents but now became better acquainted with the Russians. After the Russian artillery officers sent a polite invitation to lunch with them in their tents, three very stout field officers with long beards and in full uniform and decorations greeted them. "When nearly filled to the full capacity of sobriety with liquid refreshment, caviar sandwiches and other Muscovite delicacies," Charles wrote, "we were ushered into another tent for the real business of the day, the meal itself...After two very substantial courses, the Russian Colonel intimated to my major and myself that we should now return to the anteroom." There, "to our surprise and embarrassment we found that apartment now tenanted by three enormous Russian ladies, painted, scented and lightly draped, reclining on three divans and acknowledging our intrusion by smiles of welcome." The two British officers were introduced "to two of the voluptuous beauties," the third evidently reserved for the Russian colonel. "But again the British appetite failed," and, after making a few belabored compliments in tortured French, they managed to explain that they hadn't yet eaten enough. The Russian colonel led them back to the dining tent and took two of his compatriots back with him to enjoy a rather different course in the ante-room for the next fifteen minutes!

After returning to their less interesting but comfortable home base in Lucknow that November, Charles soon heard with considerable relief that his much longed for home leave was granted after nearly four years in India.

Perhaps Charles was unaware that his mother was coping with another scandalous family drama during the final months of his first long tour of duty in India. This problem had nothing to do with Willie who was, at the time, imprisoned at the Ennis Inebriates Reformatory in Co. Clare for "habitual drunkenness and fraud." According to family lore, thirty-three-year-old Georgiana (Georgie) had borne a child out of wedlock and this proves to be the case. Nicola Jennings, a distant cousin in Dublin who is descended from the Biddulphs and has done much research on the linked families, had heard from a direct descendant still living near Bristol that Georgiana gave birth to a daughter, Georgiana May Head, at 23 Southwell Street, Bristol, on May 1, 1901. According to the 1901 census for England, Georgie's mother Isabella Head was renting a house in Bristol that year, specifically at nearby 6 Normantown Road in the Bristol suburb of Clifton. Also in the house was twenty-two-year-old Emma Marshall, "living on own means" like Isabella, and a cook/domestic servant, all born in Ireland. Georgie's baby was immediately put up for adoption by a local family and Georgie seems to have been placed in protective care in private homes from that point on.[20] Although this seems harsh by modern standards, Georgiana, if she had been Catholic or from a lower social class in morally conservative Ireland, might have been confined to a Magdalene Laundry, the notorious prison-like workhouses for so-called "fallen women." These were originally founded in 1767 by Anglicans for Protestant women and later taken on by Catholic orders.

So that was the family situation when Charles arrived home for Christmas that year, staying with his mother at her home in Moors Park, Birr (adjacent to Crinkill Barracks, which might explain Georgiana's apparent indiscretion with a soldier). According to the 1901 census, Derrylahan Park, listed in the Court of Chancery, was then rented to a forty-four-year-old Catholic farmer, Daniel Brereton, who lived there alone with two young sisters, described as domestic servants. Five of the six other houses on the property were occupied by laborers or servants. Perhaps propelled by a determination to restore family honor and position, Charles began the process of purchasing out of bankruptcy what remained of the Derrylahan estate after much of the land had been mortgaged to moneylender Thomas Joyce and then Dublin solicitor John A. French—parts of which were sold to tenants thru the Land Acts (see chapter 16). The Court of Chancery had published "A final notice to claimants and incumbrances" on the estate of William E. Head, with Isabella E. Head as petitioner.[21] Two months after Charles rejoined B Battery at Lucknow, India, in March 1902, the Hon. John Ross, land judge of the chancery division of Ireland's high court of justice, conveyed the mansion house and the 803-acre demesne of Derrylahan to Charles after he received a mortgage from his mother Isabella Head and his uncle Col. F. E. Biddulph of Dalkey, Co. Dublin. The mortgage allowed him to pay £6,500 to his brother William E. Head. Charles then received a further mortgage on May 14, 1902 on the property from Isabella and his brother Michael Ravenscroft Head, "then serving with HM Field Force in Africa." At this point, he granted the mansion house and 103 acres to his mother and uncle, the first mortgagers.[22] Since Isabella was then living in Bristol and returned to live in Birr, the mansion house may have continued to be rented.

Charles played a great deal of polo during his nine months back in Lucknow, breaking up the summer heat with weeklong visits to the neighboring hill station of Naini Tal, where his mother's uncle, the governor of the North West Provinces, Sir James La Touche, accommodated him at Government House. At the end of the hot weather, Charles was delighted when the battery was ordered home to England. He took a short leave in the state of Rajasthan, first in Jodhpur, where he played polo with Maharajah Sir Pertab Singh, among other Indian luminaries, and then to Bikaner, where he was royally entertained to dinner by the Maharajah and his staff. He made the tactless mistake, he admitted, of beating the Maharajah at billiards after dinner.

After Charles returned to Ipswich, England, with the battery in December 1902, he looked forward to spending a pleasant time there. However, promoted to major at last, he was posted to South Africa with orders to depart in a month. This prospect held no appeal for him: the war was over, he was "run down and debilitated" after years in India, and he thought that life in South Africa would not be entertaining. On appeal, he was allowed five months of leave before departure, some of which he spent at Derrylahan. He described the estate of about five hundred acres of grassland and some five hundred acres of woodland, moor and bog as being in "a deplorable condition of neglect; drains were choked, fences broken down, overgrown or removed altogether, land covered with weeds, great fallen trees were lying about haphazard; and to give it its final stamp of chaotic squalor, the great storm of February 1903, just after I took possession, swept over it and flattened out some thousands more of its best trees. I was paying it a fleeting visit just then, and as I lay in bed, with the house rocking and swaying, I could hear my property outside tumbling and crashing like the sounds heard later on the Somme battlefield. The sight next morning from my window was a dismal one; the biggest trees on the lawn were not only flat, but they had brought up several tons of earth on their roots, leaving holes like the largest shell-craters; and a whole wood had fallen across one of the drives, cutting off the stables and farm buildings from the house."[23]

That January, the Irish Land Conference, established to promote a voluntary land purchase scheme, published its 1902-1903 report of its attempts to bridge the gulf between what landlords would accept and what tenants would offer. As they announced, "...the landowners who have not hitherto sold are, as a body, resolved not to part with their estates on terms under which, in addition to the loss already incurred, their present incomes would be substantially reduced."[24] The Wyndham Land Act of August 1903 was based on the recommendations of that report, laying down financial parameters by which an agreement between landlord and tenant would be automatically approved by the Land Commission. The act appealed to the farmers because it guaranteed annual repayments of loans given to purchase their land, lower than existing rents, and to the landlords because it gave a 12 per cent government bonus on the sale price of an entire estate, ensured payment in cash, and allowed them to retain on favorable terms demesne farms not mortgaged to the Land Commission. The result was that the majority of small farmers became the owners of their own holdings within a decade. Although Charles Head had purchased what remained of the Derrylahan property some months earlier, the terms of the Land Act providing for purchase of entire estates with loans repayable over 68½ years seems to gibe with knowledge in the family that the loan was not yet paid off when the house was burned in 1921. Charles evidently saw himself in the role of gentleman farmer and felt, correctly, that he had purchased legitimate title to his land.

Willie Head, whose profligacy and bankruptcy led to the deterioration of the former showplace, was now in even deeper trouble. In early 1902, when his brother Charles was home on leave, Willie was an inmate at the Ennis Inebriates Reformatory in Co. Clare. He had been incarcerated there in 1900."[25] The history taken upon his admission repeated the earlier testimony of his appearance before the court in Nenagh, that he had had a fall from his horse about ten years earlier which "injured his brain, and that since then he was subject to delusions, especially when he was drinking." These delusions were described as generally running on his social position "imagining still to be the owner of Derrylahan & on the large sums of money he is possessed of." According to his mother, "he has always been of the most intemperate habits." At nearly 6 feet, Willie weighed just 142 pounds on admission but was 156 pounds when he was released on bail on September 29 that year, 1902. His estranged wife, Mary Katherine, had died at her mother's home in Dublin ten days earlier, on September 19.

Willie's mother, acting as his guardian, reported to the Ennis Reformatory on October 28 that her son was "going on well and to my knowledge has never tasted any spirits whatever." A month later, she reported that her son "is all right so far. It is a little hard on him sometimes when he sees others taking drink in house but his will is getting stronger."[26] But, as primary beneficiary to his late wife's will, which was probated in November, Willie may have had access to her small estate, allowing him to spend time in Dublin. There, on February 14, 1903, he was imprisoned for public drunkenness in Dublin's Mountjoy Prison for seven days with a 10 shilling fine, resulting in his being recommitted to the Ennis Reformatory for "false pretences and being a habitual drunkard." Since Charles never mentioned any of his siblings by name in his memoir, it is impossible to know whether he gave any support to his brother, now a petty criminal but listed in the prison register as "gentleman."

It seems that Willie Head was an early pawn in a new experiment for treating alcoholism in Ireland. According to author and historian Conor Reidy, some commentators believed at the beginning of the twentieth century that "between 60 and 80 percent of crime there was alcohol related." The Inebriates Act of 1898 was passed to allow treatment in an inebriate reformatory rather than imprisonment in certain cases of drunkenness and alcohol-related crime. If the reformatories were operated by the state or by local government, or another appropriate corporate body, they were known as certified reformatories (thus, in 1899, a state institution, the Ennis Inebriates Reformatory, was opened in Co. Clare in a former prison complex). It was thought that "less than two years cannot be considered sufficiently long to secure hopeful results in any but exceptionally mild cases of inebriety."[27] The regimen at the reformatory was, of course, total abstinence from alcoholic beverages for a minimum of eighteen months. The mandated regimen also included plenty of fresh air, wholesome food, physical exercise, and hard work, which, for men, meant a choice of carpentry, shoemaking, tailoring, gardening, and chopping firewood—but there was absolutely no science-based or medical treatment for prisoners' addiction to alcohol.[28]

Following his release in 1904, Willie married Dora Clarke, whose sister was married to one of Isabella's brothers, the Rev. William N. Biddulph, who had testified to the cause of his nephew's insane actions when drunk. His mother reported the following April that Willie "is very steady and never touches drink, he seems very happy with…his wife." He also enjoyed gardening, an avocation that may have begun when he was in prison. Willie reported annually after that, starting in 1906, when he said he "was never better and have not the slightest desire for strong waters of any sort."[29] But he continued what was probably a lifelong struggle with alcoholism, always supported by his steadfast second wife. According to the 1911 census, they were then living in Knocklahard, Ballinrobe, Co. Mayo with their twelve-year-old niece Georgina Biddulph (sadly, the niece died of tuberculosis four years later). They remained married until his death in 1945.

As he had feared, Charles's months in South Africa, at Bloemfontein and Kroonstad, were spent in training and gun practice with the 76th Battery at a terrible time of year weather-wise on the South African veldt; however he was proud of the battery's progress and accomplishments during his time with them.[30] His brother Michael, however, spent several more years in South Africa, where, now a captain, he was the winner of the Beresford Cup in April 1906 as a member of the 5th Dragoon Guards' polo team. This was the most important South African polo tournament.[31]

Charles's new station was in Cahir, Co. Tipperary, which enabled him to spend much of his time over the next four years, while he waited for battery command, in restoring Derrylahan "after some years of neglect and mismanagement." He wrote lyrically about his love of the place:

It is a hard nature which is not stirred and attracted by old associations. To me it was a never-ending source of pleasure to wander round the old scenes of childish exploits, and dream of the light-hearted days when existence in a certain sphere seemed to be a natural right of which nothing could deprive one, and which required no effort of one's own to maintain. Naturally my cherished memories were mostly of a sporting nature. The little fence that I used to jump backwards and forwards about twenty times on a long-suffering pony, the furze bush from under which I blew with my single-barrel muzzle-loader an unsuspecting woodcock, the stream from which I extracted small trout with an enticing worm, they all appealed to me clamorously, and bade me remain with them for the rest of my natural term on earth.

He had achieved his ambition of buying back his family home, but he still had a long and impatient wait to achieve his other ambition, to command a battery of the Royal Horse Artillery. As he said, promotion had been very rapid during the South African War—as it was for his brother Michael—but then promotions were locked down again, and he had to wait four years at Cahir for news that he would command a battery in India: "even at the last moment I had considerable doubt as to whether I'd accept it, but having waited so long I decided to do so, with a mental reservation of terminating my connection with it at the end of the two years which I still had to serve to qualify for a modified pension."[32] As always, Charles took every opportunity while in Ireland to compete in steeplechases, to hunt, and to play polo. In 1905, he won the 8th Division RFA (Royal Field Artillery) Point to Point Race on his horse West Briton in the heavy weight race. This was also probably the time when he went around the country finding and buying back family treasures that Willie had pawned, including the engraved silver candlesticks that the duke of Clarence—later King William IV—gave to his godson, their father William Henry Head, upon his baptism.

During Charles's four years back in Ireland, land sales/purchases increased due to the generous terms of the 1903 Wyndham Act. Tenants on the Derrylahan, Coolross, and Annagh estates met in Rathcabbin in July 1907 to discuss the purchase terms offered them.

The Derrylahan tenants were offered reductions of 3s. 6d. and 4s. 6d. in the £ on second and first term rents, respectively. According to the report in the *Midland Tribune*, some of the Derrylahan tenancies were nonjudicial with very high rents. Considering the reductions offered to be unjust, the Derrylahan tenants counter-offered 6s. and 7s., claiming that some tenants in the neighborhood had got as much as 10s. off.[33]

On September 26, 1908, thirty-nine-year-old Charles Head married twenty-eight-year-old Alice Margery Threlfall, second surviving daughter of Charles Threlfall of Tarporley, Cheshire, and Cadogan Gardens, London. She was an heiress to the Threlfall brewing fortune and the income she brought to the marriage enabled the couple to return Derrylahan to its former condition and live there in considerable comfort. Her brother, Major Charles Morris Threlfall of the 8th Hussars, had married that same year Mabel Anna, a daughter and co-heiress of Benjamin F. Going of Ballyphilip, a deputy lieutenant and JP in Co. Tipperary, who was undoubtedly well known to the Head family. Perhaps Charles met Margery Threlfall at the Threlfall-Going wedding. Their impending marriage, which was described as "arranged," was announced in the *Irish Independent* that July.[34]

Margery accompanied her new husband to Meerut, India, the battery command he had waited for so long.[35] Their first child, Elizabeth (Betty), was born on July 23, 1909 (Margery may have returned to Tilstone Lodge or London for the birth). Charles lauded P Battery as the "best military unit I ever saw," both in its own capacity and the quality of the men and horses, but it also starred "in all the games that soldiers play": rifle-shooting, football (soccer), water polo, and as a formidable competitor in all the mounted sports. He gloried in riding at the head of "a battery of the Horse Artillery in perfect order and at full strength." He remembered decades later that he used to feel as his grandfather may have felt "when he had his 13th Light Dragoons thundering behind him on the plateaux of Spain." He evidently inspired sincere feelings of respect and admiration from his soldiers, according to a letter he received from Battery-Sergeant-Major Bryant of P Battery when he finally decided not to return to India from leave at home in 1910. He still had to serve five more years as a major and then another five years as a colonel in order to qualify for a colonel's pension. But, as he wrote, the pros for retirement outweighed the cons and he looked forward to starting life as a plain country gentleman. Among the pros for retirement was that Margery was expecting another child. Derrylahan had been built by his father as a family house and now it beckoned to him more than ever.

Their children always understood that Charles was not the love of Margery's life. Apparently, she had been engaged to an artistic and poetical young man whom she met or visited in India, where he died. She had also endured the tragic death of three of her sisters after they drank contaminated milk from the local dairy. But life on a remote Irish estate would suit Margery, a shy and retiring but courageous woman who later told one of her daughters that she loathed the coming out balls and other social season events that her very social mother pressed her into in London. Charles, on the other hand, was a convivial and rather selfish man of the world, who had enjoyed his free-ranging bachelor social life. Later, their very different natures would become obvious to all who knew them, but these were happy years, when Margery gave birth to two more tow-headed children, Isabella Grace (Grace), and Michael William Henry (Mike).

As Charles and Margery began family life at Derrylahan, land purchase in Ireland continued at an increasing pace. Parliament enacted the Birrell Act in 1909, which extended the category of congested districts and authorized the compulsory purchase of lands in congested areas. Since it reduced the generous terms of the Wyndham Act and reintroduced payment by land bonds, many landlords raced to benefit from the 1903 terms. Among these, Henry Nugent Head's brother-in-law, Somerset Saunderson, formally initiated the sale of his 10,000-acre County Cavan estate before the cut-off date of November 24, 1908. However, Lord Dunalley, whose ancestors were staunch allies and relatives of the Heads of Derry Castle, failed to act in time. In January 1909, his agent wrote to the estates commissioners claiming that Dunalley was "most anxious the tenants should get" its benefit. Dooley thinks his motives were more self-centered as the commissioners claimed in July that Dunalley was now unwilling to go ahead with negotiations because the sale would not be concluded in time to guarantee him the 12 percent bonus.[36]

Since the passing of the various land acts, as Lord Ashdown claimed in 1906, "a landlord now has only two inducements to remain in Ireland, 1) farming his own land and 2) sport."[37] And, indeed, Charles now settled down to farming and estate management, as well as hunting, shooting, tennis, and polo! "My fireside and occupations grew so satisfying and engrossing," he later wrote, "that I got to dislike going far from home, except for short visits to Dublin." First of all, he had to procure farm machinery: "carts, drays, mowing-machines, binders, hay-making appliances, ploughs, harrows, sowing-machines, chaff-cutting machine, turnip-slicer, oats-crusher, threshing-machine, saw-bench, and a powerful engine to work all the indoor machinery, are indispensable equipment on a fair-sized farm, and a heavy initial strain on resources." Then he had to start from scratch in purchasing cattle, sheep, and horses. In building up a stock of cattle, he bought a few young cows to provide milk for the household and then haunted the local fairs to bargain for further stock. "Coming as I did from the sheltered occupation of the army, it was natural that I was only a child in this strange field of clashing wits, and that many of my first purchases brought me more loss than profit." His earliest mentor in cattle-buying was the local Protestant pastor. They would leave for the country fairs together early in the morning in a dog cart. He described a typical local fair held in the main street of a small town and the exhausting reality of driving the animal purchases to their new home on foot, sometimes arriving late at night. Within a few years, he was able to build up a fine herd of about a hundred short-horn heifers and a Hereford bull. As for tillage, "my neighbour, Lord Rosse, a very keen tillage farmer, kindly gave me much valuable instruction."

The only laborers Charles could find were housed on his estate, where they cultivated potatoes, oats, and mangolds (large beets grown for cattle feed). He managed the men himself. They were hard workers but very quarrelsome so that he often had to break up fights. On one occasion, "the cow-man had had a quarrel with the yard-man, and to vent his wrath pierced the udder of the latter's cow with a pitchfork." On another, "the ploughman reported to me that the herd[sman] was letting out my bull surreptitiously to the cows of some of his friends; and in the subsequent enquiry, I had to get between them to prevent one of them murdering the other."[38] For recreation, Charles played a great deal of polo on an excellent local ground near Birr. Many counties had competitive polo teams, and once a year there were inter-county polo matches on the Phoenix Park ground in Dublin. There was also the major polo tournament at the annual Dublin Horse Show. The day his team beat County Dublin and was presented with the cup was "one of the happiest days of my life," he remembered. "Though there is more sunshine in Ireland, especially in winter, than is generally credited," he wrote, in justifying his devotion to polo, "there are long periods of grey skies and persistent rain, which have a depressing effect on the spirits, and which must be counter-balanced by congenial social intercourse or sporting facilities. Without these antidotes to gloom and depression, an addiction to drink is their usual substitute."[39] He was clearly thinking of one, or even two, of his older brothers.

In 1910, Ethel Alice (Annie), oldest daughter of architect Edward Head, who had grown up with her many siblings in Canada, traveled on the *Lusitania* from New York to spend several weeks in Ireland in order to settle some of her late mother's property and visit relations. Years later, she wrote a full account of the visits she made to her father's and late mother's relations which pointed up the striking difference between the economic circumstances of the remaining Head family landowners and their progeny.[40] She stayed first with her cheerful Aunt Grace O'Reilly and her family, living in somewhat straitened circumstances in their large and very cold house on North Great George's Street, Dublin, and then traveled to her parents' childhood environs in the Irish Midlands.

While staying with one of her father's siblings in Birr, Annie visited the Heads at Derrylahan for a few hours. She was struck by how well kept and furnished the house was and mentioned a large polo field and stables. The 1911 Irish census provides valuable evidence about the comfortable circumstances of the new owners of Derrylahan. There were thirteen people living in the 18-room main house: Charles (42), Margery (30), and their very small daughters,

Betty (20 months old) and Grace (just one month). There were two nurses for the babies, Margaret Hughes (53), Roman Catholic and born in Co. Wexford, and Louise Llewellyn (33), Protestant and born in England, probably Wales. The servants living in the house were nearly all Irish and Catholic, including Winifred Gleeson (23), parlour maid; Annie Imry (40), cook; Agnes Lash (22), housemaid; Ellen Whelan (22), laundry maid; and Fanny Kennedy (16), kitchen maid, and the only one who could speak Irish as well as English. The twenty-year-old groom, William Stanley, was the only Protestant besides the nanny and the Heads.

The houses in which the laborers lived, presumably all built by William Henry Head, were constructed of brick or stone with slate roofs and five or six rooms with three or four windows each. Farm labourer Thomas Bourke (50), originally from Co. Galway, lived in one of them with his wife Mary and three youngest children—three others had obviously grown up and moved away. The groom Ernest Rathwell (29) and his wife Ellen had a one-year-old son, Thomas, at that time, although another had died. Laborer Laurence Connor (60) and his wife Margaret had two school-age sons, as did the gardener Martin Hogan (58), a widower. All were Catholic. There were twenty-two outhouses and farm buildings: three stables, a coach house, harness room, cow house, calf house, dairy, piggery, five fowl houses, boiling house, barn, turf house, potato house, workshop, shed, store, forge, and laundry.[41]

The Derrylahan Heads were descended from the junior branch of the family, as Annie, proud of her descent from the senior Derry Castle line, made a point of noting. But the contrast in financial circumstances was obviously painful to see when she visited nearby Carrig Cottage, where her father and his siblings had grown up. "The place had changed hands several times and was so run down that the Aunts couldn't keep back the tears." Then she traveled by train to spend two weeks with the adult children of Henry Darby Head at Ballyquiveen, south of Nenagh. Their father had been the target of boycotting during the land wars, and it appeared that the estate had never recovered. The four siblings, whose parents were first cousins, included John Prittie Head (Johnny), a "tall, fine-looking, middle-aged man"; his sister Harriette, also "hale and hearty"; and two disabled younger brothers, Tommie, who was not well and deaf, and Eddie, "who never had control of his muscles." Johnny met her at the station and drove her through the countryside and the demesne, "with its masses of rhododendron," to the aging frame house. The room she was shown to was "of heroic proportions," like all the others in the house—she was glad she was there in the summer because it must have been impossible to keep warm. Noting that Harriet had only one maid, Annie rather suspected that even that was because of a visitor being there! Adding to her impressions of severely impoverished gentility was that her relation wore an old-fashioned chatelaine, with innumerable keys. The food was kept carefully locked up and they dined by candlelight.

Annie was shocked at the evidence that these cousins had fallen on hard times. Most of the surrounding places and farms had been sold off "from time to time" and only about 30 acres were left around the house. The surrounding outbuildings were very run down; "A large hothouse in the grounds had lost all its glass and grapevines grew up through the roof, completely untended." They took drives through the beautiful countryside, and Harriette pointed in the direction of Derry Castle, burned down years before. She would have driven Annie there, but Annie suspected it was beyond the failing powers of their single ancient horse. "The only other animal on the place was an enormous cat—and ancient, too."

Annie must have felt somewhat reassured when she spent several weeks with her Aunt Maud Palmer at Glenloe Abbey, a large stone house with gardens running down to the Corrib River near Galway City. Maud's husband was a wealthy grain merchant. "Aunt Maud had plenty of help, cook, maid and groom as well as gardener and a good stable of horses" as Eileen (her daughter, who would marry a future Count de Stacpool) loved to ride. They often motored into the Connemara mountains in Maud's beautiful "Silent Knight" Daimler. "Such quaint cottages we'd pass, with half doors for the hens and pigs; and old women sitting by smoking pipes. Grand big priests' houses, too, and plenty of fat priests about, although the peasants were so poor that they'd go barefoot until they neared town, and then sat down and put their shoes and stockings on."[42]

"The period 1911-13 was a time of great agitation in Irish politics," Charles wrote some thirty years later.[43] In fact, he threw himself into the thick of it, and the establishment honors accorded him after he settled down in Ireland made it quite clear where he stood politically. He was elected a member of the Kildare Street Club in Dublin, "which shared with 'the Castle' all the most virulent opprobrium which Nationalist orators and scribes could express in words." He found it "a delightful old establishment, perhaps the best and most pleasant club in the United Kingdom, but a real Aunt Sally, almost a Lord Clanricarde, for Nationalist Members of Parliament."[44] As Dooley has noted, the Kildare Street Club by the 1880s "was the centre of landlord life in Dublin, all but 10 percent of its 800 or so members coming from landed families. Membership was exclusively male and was dominated by larger landowners."[45] Charles agreed that "Its tone was on the whole governed by the outlook of the Irish nobility and county gentlemen, modified and adjusted to outside opinion by the experience of its many ex-army members, but," as he pointed out, "it actually counted on its roll of membership men of almost every degree of Home Rule proclivity from Sir Horace Plunkett, a strong Imperial Home Ruler, to men in active sympathy with Sinn Fein extremists."[46] On the other hand, according to Mark Bence-Jones, "although the club was meant to be non-political, during the years following the land war it was virtually impossible for an active Home Ruler to become a member."[47] Charles was also appointed a magistrate for Co. Tipperary in 1912, sharing the democratized Bench at two different places with Nationalists "of inferior status." The snobbery he expressed at this point in his memoir is truly astounding, making his assessment of himself as "No Great Shakes" seem hypocritical. It seems that his social discomfort with having "to rub shoulders with the chairmen of country and district councils who were ex-officio J.P.s" was widely shared by other landed gentlemen.[48]

With his mind on larger matters when recalling these increasingly disturbed times decades later, but also characteristically, Charles did not mention important family or local events. On October 15, 1911, his mother, Isabella Head, died at home in the village of Crinkill, on the edge of Birr barracks, of abscess of the gall bladder and exhaustion. Left behind in her house was her daughter

Isabella Dundas, who was apparently estranged from her husband and may have moved to Dublin at that point with her daughter Aileen. The announcement of her funeral reported that all four of her sons and a naval officer brother attended the burial at Clonoghill Cemetery but did not mention her daughters.[49] Her three youngest daughters, Isabella Louise (Bella), Georgiana (Georgie), and Anna Septima (Annie) seem to have lived in Dublin during the last decades of their lives and all are buried in the Protestant section of Dean's Grange Cemetery in suburban Dublin. Isabella E. Head's personal estate, valued at £7,345, was published in March 1912. On April 1, Charles's older brother, Dr. John Head, died age forty-five in Cloughjordan, where he appeared to have moved following his mother's death, perhaps as the result of his alcoholism — although there is no public record of that; in fact he left little trace of his life. It is possible his mother's death "from exhaustion" can be partly attributed to his weaknesses. Charles, who was John's primary beneficiary, was granted administration of his estate of £828. Later that month, as already noted, he was appointed a magistrate for Co. Tipperary and in late June gave an anti-Home Rule speech in Birr that blazoned his passionate Southern Unionist politics and made him ultimately a marked man. Two months later, on September 5, his son and heir, Michael William Henry (Mike), was born at Derrylahan.

It was also a year when Charles brought a legal action against farmer Patrick Meara, who had rented the Heads' 75-acre Ballyduff land for grazing, along with house and offices, since 1892. Under the terms of the land purchase acts, Meara was in the process of purchasing part of the Ballyduff lands from the Dublin solicitor, John A. French, to whom they had been mortgaged by Willie Head. Since Charles had taken up permanent residence at Derrylahan, Meara had blocked a long-established right of way "from plaintiff's house through defendant's land to the county road," a well-constructed avenue built by William Henry before 1883. Years later, the Head daughters recalled frightening confrontations with the Mearas' dog at the gate they had erected during walks with their nursemaid along the avenue. The defendant claimed to be entitled to the right of way under a grant for which he had no documentation. The judge decided that the right of way was included in the conveyance language. Although he granted an injunction to restrain the Mearas from further obstructing the avenue, he fined them just £1, believing that they had not acted "wantonly" but thought they had the right to close the avenue.[50] He and Charles Head may not have known that there had been enduring bad blood between the families since William Henry's agent attempted to evict Patrick Meara's father William O'Meara or Meara for nonpayment of rent in 1872 (see chapter 15).

The renewed impetus for a reintroduction of a Home Rule bill at Westminster after two decades of Conservative rule began with the December 1910 election, when the reduced Liberal majority depended on the Irish vote controlled by John Redmond, lawyer and leader of the Irish Nationalist Party. Prime Minister Herbert H. Asquith promised Redmond that Irish Home Rule would be the highest priority if the Irish MPs supported the budget and the Parliament Act of 1911, which would set clear limits on the delaying power of the conservative House of Lords. This would allow a bill passed three times by the Commons in consecutive sessions to be enacted regardless of the Lords. Since the Irish Nationalists were keeping Asquith in power, they were entitled to seek enactment of a Home Rule bill. The strongly opposed Conservatives had the diehard support of the Protestant Orangemen of Ulster.

The Third Home Rule Bill introduced in April 1912 was intended for all of Ireland and contained no provision for a special status for Ulster. "Ulster had always resisted Home Rule," wrote Charles, "on the grounds that she abhorred the prospect of being ruled by an Irish Nationalist, Roman Catholic government and that such a government would inevitably lead to an Irish Republic, animated by very hostile feelings towards Great Britain."[51] Unionists began preparing to get their way, by force if necessary, and the Nationalists soon emulated them. As leader of the Irish Unionists in Parliament since 1910, Sir Edward Carson threatened a revolt if Home Rule was enacted. Carson, a brilliant Dublin lawyer and Southern Unionist, descended on both sides of his family from Protestant settlers, was elected as an MP for Dublin University in 1892 (and from then on practiced law mainly in London).[52] He was far from the only Southern Unionist who believed passionately that Irishmen would be worse off with Home Rule. Anti-Home Rule meetings were held up and down the country.

In late June 1912, Charles Head proposed a resolution against the Home Rule Bill at a large gathering of King's County Unionists held in Oxmantown Hall, Birr, to protest the bill's threatened passage. The earl of Rosse was in the chair and among those present were Col. Middleton Biddulph, D.L. [of Rathrobbin], Mr. and Miss Darby, Ernest Perry, JP, J. Stoney, JP, Mr. and Mrs. Toler R. Garvey, and Capt. Burdett, all related to or connected with the Head family. Charles Head's resolution stated:

> We, Irishmen, of the King's County, representing many separate interests, and sharing a common desire for the welfare of our country, hereby declare our unalterable determination to uphold the Legislative Union between Great Britain and Ireland. We protest against the Home Rule Bill at present before Parliament upon the following grounds: Because it is a measure for the creation of a separate Irish Executive, which will produce most dangerous confusion, involving a disastrous conflict of interests and classes, and a serious risk of civil war. Because this measure will endanger the commercial relations between Ireland and Great Britain, and will submit Ireland to a double system of taxation, both by the Imperial and by the Irish Parliament, will cause widespread financial disaster, and will be inevitably followed by a complete paralysis of enterprise. Because this measure will imperil personal liberty, freedom of opinion, and the spirit of tolerance in Ireland. Because this measure cannot be final, and instead of effecting a settlement it will pave the way for further efforts towards the complete separation of Ireland from Great Britain. Because the great measures enacted in recent years by the Imperial Parliament have resulted in such industrial, agricultural, and educational progress that our country has been steadily advancing in prosperity, and we view with the greatest alarm an experiment which must destroy the good work already done, and hinder the progress now in operation.

Head's speech, imbued with Carsonite arguments, was much applauded, as reported in the *Dublin Daily Express*. He stressed that the danger confronting them was formidable and immediate, and it was the imperative duty of every person who was not in favor of it to give it strong opposition. It would be better for the country and for all classes, he felt, if those people who were against were more courageous in expressing their views in a serious situation like the present one. There was one argument brought forward by friends and foes alike, he continued, after cheering had died down, "and that was that England was being permeated with Socialist unrest and labour troubles, and that, therefore, they, in Ireland, should cut themselves free from England. Did the people who put forward that argument imagine that Ireland would be free from labour unrest?," he asked, presciently as it happened. "How long would the local Parliament, with its puppet Senate, resist a loud and popular clamour?" After making several other arguments, to continuing applause, he pointed out that "their meeting that afternoon was representative of the professional, business and farming classes in the district, and he would say that they in the King's County were particularly fortunate in their Nationalist neighbours who were men of good conduct and ability (hear, hear). They [the Unionists] wanted to co-operate with friendly Nationalists to promote the prosperity of Ireland, but that work must be carried on under some system of government in which they had confidence, and not a one-sided Parliament," he concluded, followed by more cheering.[53] Beaumont Nesbitt, DL, enthusiastically seconded the resolution, which was also supported by A. W. Samuels, KC.

As part of the tremendous effort to win support for Unionism in mainland Britain, Edward Carson made hundreds of speeches, including one to a great meeting of establishment Unionist supporters at Blenheim Palace on July 27, 1912. On Ulster Day, September 28, 1912, 237,368 men and 234,046 women signed the Ulster Covenant for unaltered preservation of the Union on the basis that "Home Rule would be disastrous to the material well-being of Ulster as well as of the whole of Ireland." The Conservative Party, now led by Bonar Law, supported the Ulster Unionists in their defiance of the will of Parliament. As the Commons debated the Third

Home Rule bill in late 1912 and early 1913, Unionists in the north of Ireland mobilized, with talk of Carson declaring a Provisional Government, the Irish Unionist Alliance, supported by 90,000 Ulster Volunteer Forces (UVF), including many ex-servicemen, built around the Orange Lodges. Increasingly well-armed with smuggled weapons, the UVF prepared to do battle with the British Army if it was ordered to enforce the bill if it passed.

Around this time, Charles traveled to Co. Down at the invitation of a friend to inspect his company of volunteers. "It was quite dark when we went out to his stable-yard and found about a hundred men assembled there," under ex-NCOs of the British Army. Asked to address them, Charles "said a few words addressing the gravity of the situation and their praiseworthy efforts to safeguard their British heritage." Later, he saw another company in which Capt. James Craig, MP for East Down and the architect of Ulster Unionist opposition to the Third Home Rule Bill, was taking a great interest, "one of the few really great men with whom I have come in contact."[54] Craig, son of a whiskey millionaire, was Carson's principal lieutenant, and it was he who had arranged the first big Ulster demonstration of the latest anti-home rule era at his own home outside Belfast on September 23, 1911, before the bill was even introduced.[55]

John Redmond was now forced to take account of a more militant form of Irish nationalism as two more militias were formed to counterbalance the Ulster Volunteers.[56] In November 1913, the Irish Volunteers were established in the South by Eoin MacNeill, a medieval historian and one of the founders of the Gaelic League, as a civil defense force against the threat of Unionist actions. These southern Volunteers were soon infiltrated by extremist Irish Republican Brotherhood (IRB) members. Not to be outdone, the Irish labor movement under John Connolly and Jim Larkin set up its own Irish Citizen Army in order to protect strikers (as Charles Head had predicted, Irish labor began to strike and organize mass protests during 1913). In short, there were five armies in Ireland in early 1914: the UVF, the IRB, the Irish Volunteers, the Irish Citizen Army, and the British Army itself! The Unionist *Irish Times* argued on February 14, 1914 that the exclusion solution (excluding several of the predominantly Protestant Ulster counties from the

Home Rule bill) was impossible—Ulster unionists and nationalists could never agree over the area to be excluded. Exclusion would be "permanently fatal to every Irish hope and every Irish interest...it would condemn our country to an eternity of national weakness, industrial impotence and sectarian strife." Moreover, it involved the sacrifice of the unionists of the south and west and the 'betrayal of loyal friendships."[57]

As the Home Rule bill awaited its third passage through the Commons, the so-called Curragh incident occurred, which "thrilled [Charles] to the marrow," sympathizing as he did with the officers involved. One of those was probably his distant cousin, Major Henry Nugent Head, whose regiment, the 4th (Queen's Own) Hussars, was stationed at the Curragh until the outbreak of WWI. Fifty-seven of the seventy British Army officers based in the Curragh Camp in Co. Kildare, many of them Irish Unionists, led by Brig. Gen. Hubert Gough, announced they would rather be dismissed than obey orders from Westminster in March to deploy troops in Ulster.[58] When the unrest spread to army officers in England, some Cabinet members, against Asquith's wishes, acted to placate them by saying the Government had no intention of using force against Ulster. Asquith fired his War Secretary and took on the role himself. The Home Rule Bill was passed by the Commons on May 25, 1914, by a majority of 77, and, not needing the Lords' consent, it was awaiting royal assent. Most people in Ireland greeted the news that the Home Rule Bill had passed with triumphant celebrations. In late June, an Amending Bill excluding all nine counties of Ulster from Home Rule was introduced in the House of Lords. As the situation in Europe deteriorated, it never came up in the House of Commons. However, Bonar Law and Carson agreed with Asquith that Home Rule should become law together with a Suspensory Act which would prevent it coming into force until a new Amending Bill could be introduced later.

Ulster was now on the brink of civil war. The Irish Unionist Council made it clear that Ulster's nine counties would constitute the territories to be defended, causing deep anxiety to southern Unionists, such as Charles Head, who was an *ex officio* member of the Executive Council of the Irish Unionist Alliance. The Southern Unionists resented the dominance of Ulstermen in the party and feared that the Ulster wing would abandon the south in order to gain a favorable settlement for the north from the British government. Motivated by the landing on April 14, 1914 in Larne, Co. Antrim, of 35,000 rifles and 5 million rounds of ammunition purchased in Imperial Germany for the UVF, the Anglo-Irish spy novelist Erskine Childers landed 1,500 obsolete rifles and 45,000 rounds of ammunition from Germany for the Irish Volunteers on July 26, 1914, aboard his yacht the *Asgard*. What became known as the Howth Gun-running was made in two landings, one on the Wicklow coast in early August and the second at Howth, just north of Dublin, on August 26. Soldiers who had been sent to seize the weapons, were "baited by a hostile crowd" and opened fire "killing three and wounding 38," demonstrating the extreme political tensions.[59] Senior Irish Volunteer Patrick Pearse had commented that: "the only thing more ridiculous than an Ulsterman with a rifle is a Nationalist without one" (they had been forced to drill with wooden rifles and broom handles). The decision to purchase guns was made by a group of mainly upper and upper-middle class Anglo-Irish Home Rulers who lived in London, on the initiative of distinguished consular official Sir Roger Casement, a romantic Protestant Irish nationalist in the 1798 tradition. They raised the necessary funds there and young writer Darrell Figgis volunteered to go at once to buy them. He and Childers went to Hamburg together to make the purchase from a German firm.[60]

The delivery of weapons purchased in Germany by Irish Nationalists further exacerbated already existing tensions, occurring as it did directly after the declaration of war by the five Great European Powers. Following the assassination of the Habsburg heir to the Austro-Hungarian throne, Archduke Franz Ferdinand and his wife, in Sarajevo by Bosnian Serb nationalist Gavrilo Princip on June 28, 1914, the principal European military alliances rumbled gradually into play throughout July with the mobilization of their armies. "Toward the middle of July 1914, on returning to lunch after a round of the farm, thinking only of politics, profit and play," Charles would remember, "I opened the day's *Irish Times* and in it I read the Austrian ultimatum to Serbia. 'That,' I said to my wife, 'means we are going to war, and in a very short time I shall be called out on reserve.'"[61] Charles may have been remarkably prescient or, more likely, writing so many years later, he felt that he knew the war was a certainty at that point. In fact, most in the British government were very reluctant to enter the war on the basis alone of a local dispute between Austro-Hungary and Serbia—until German troops marched into Belgium on August 3. Two days after receiving his notice to mobilize, Charles reported for duty in Dublin. With Redmond's support, Asquith had the Home Rule Bill placed on the statute book, but accompanied by an act suspending it for a year or to the end of the war.

Chapter 18

The Great War: Battlefields, Easter Rising, and Home Fires

If I were fierce, and bald, and short of breath,
I'd live with scarlet Majors at the Base,
And speed glum heroes up the line to death.
You'd see me with my puffy petulant face,
Guzzling and gulping in the best hotel,
Reading the Roll of Honour. 'Poor young chap,'
I'd say—'I used to know his father well.
Yes, we've lost heavily in this last scrap.'
And when the war is done and youth stone dead,
I'd toddle safely home and die—in bed.
—Siegfried Sassoon, "Base Details," March 4, 1917.

…MacDonagh and MacBride
And Connolly and Pearse
Now and in time to be,
Wherever green is worn,
Are changed, changed utterly:
A terrible beauty is born.
—William Butler Yeats, "Easter 1916," September 25, 1916.

In Roy Foster's opinion, the First World War "should be seen as one of the most decisive events in modern Irish history. Politically speaking, it temporarily defused the Ulster situation; it put Home Rule on ice; it altered the conditions of military crisis in Ireland at a stroke; and it created the rationale for an IRB rebellion. Economically, it created a spectacular boost in agricultural prices, and high profits in agriculturally derived industries; though urban workers were less advantaged, and there was much resentment at the imposition of production quotas and the enforcement of tillage rather than pasture farming."[1]

At the outbreak of war in early August 1914, Prime Minister Herbert Asquith moved quickly to appoint the most experienced and decorated officer in the British Army, Irish-born Field Marshall Lord [Herbert] Kitchener as secretary of state for war. The pre-war Regular Army was relatively small and inadequately armed. Presciently, Kitchener was one of the few who foresaw that this war, which most believed would be short, would, in fact, last for at least three years. Thus he used his authority to organize the New Army, the largest volunteer army that Britain had ever seen, and expand the size and purview of Britain's part-time Territorial Force. He also oversaw a significant expansion of materials production to support those who would be fighting. A massive recruitment campaign began, which soon featured a distinctive poster of Kitchener pointing at the reader and declaring, "Your Country Needs You," one of the most enduring images of the war.[2] Fifty thousand Irish regular soldiers and reservists, including Major Charles Head, had been automatically mobilized on August 4. Like Sassoon, Head would come to despise staff officers.

Initially, most Irish people supported the war, regardless of their political affiliation. Large numbers of Irishmen already served in the Regular British Army and Navy. Now, despite having formed an armed militia in defiance of Home Rule, Edward Carson immediately promised Ulster Unionist support for the war effort. On September 3, the strongly Protestant Unionists were granted their own division, the 36th (Ulster) Division, largely recruited from the Ulster Volunteer Force. As the German Army made a swift advance through neutral Catholic Belgium and threatened Paris, Irish Parliamentary Party leader John Redmond felt considerable pressure to demonstrate a similar commitment. On September 20, two days after the Home Rule bill received royal assent, he called on the Irish Volunteers to enlist in existing Irish regiments of the British Army.

Although a large majority of 150,000 followed Redmond, forming the National Volunteers, of whom 25,000 subsequently served in Irish regiments of Kitchener's New Army, the more militant Irish Volunteers, numbering about ten thousand under the leadership of Eoin MacNeill, split with constitutionalist Redmond. This radical fringe of Irish nationalism actively resisted enlistment. Together with the secretive Irish Republican Brotherhood (IRB), they began preparing an armed insurrection against British rule in Ireland entirely paid for by the American Clan na Gael. On the same day in early July that Erskine Childers had sailed to Germany to collect his share of an arms shipment for Howth on the outskirts of Dublin, Sir Roger Casement—a retired British consular officer, celebrated as a pioneer of human rights in the Belgian Congo, whose experiences turned him passionately against imperialism—had sailed to America to procure more arms. There Casement met with John Devoy, head of the secret revolutionary directory of Clan na Gael and began making many useful contacts for raising money and moral support for an Irish insurrection, acting on his long-held conviction that England's difficulties were Ireland's opportunities.

Despite this, a further 100,000 Irishmen, including Protestants and Catholics, who were not members of the National Volunteers, enlisted during the course of the war, responding to recruitment meetings and specially designed posters and, as Belgium was overrun, the call for the "defence of small nations." Forty-four thousand Irishmen enlisted in 1914 and 45,000 in 1915. Irish Nationalists were granted two divisions, the 10th and the 16th, under regular army officers who were sometimes Irish, although predominantly Anglo-Irish Protestants. Irish recruitment was never enough to fill the ranks of these divisions.

Major Charles Head began his war service in Dublin in August 1914, and was engaged first in administration, mostly arranging transportation of horses and troops. This must have been deeply frustrating for a man who preferred action over desk work, particularly since his cavalry officer relatives—his youngest brother Michael, just promoted to major in his regiment, the 5th Dragoon Guards, and his distant cousin, Lt. Col. Henry Nugent Head of the 4th (Queen's Own) Hussars—shipped to France with their regiments that month.[3] Charles applied for and gained a transfer to regimental duty, for which his twenty-year career in the Royal Horse Artillery had more than amply qualified him.

Appointed to a newly formed battery of artillery attached to the 10th (Irish) Division forming at Newbridge in Co. Kildare, Charles remarked that only a small percentage of the men in civilian dress packed into the barracks there were of Irish origin: "They were not so Irish as Mr. Redmond and other politicians claimed. All the support services of the Division...were chiefly English, and Lord Kitchener, weary of waiting for recruits, had filled up the ranks of the Infantry with large blocks of English and others." Near the end of September, they moved to camp "at a cheerless spot known as Donnelly's Hollow on the Curragh." Training there was severely limited by the lack of materials. Charles complained that "The miserable reserve of guns, with which the country had started the greatest conflict in history, had been expended in replacing those lost in the retreat from Mons," Britain's first major action against the Germans.[4]

Training began in earnest after they moved to the barracks at Dundalk on the coast north of Drogheda. Charles described that winter and the following spring, "when the development and training of my young battery entirely engrossed me," as "the hardest-worked time of my life." With the exception of a splendid ex-sergeant of Horse Artillery whom he made his sergeant-major, and two former regular sergeants who became the riding instructor and quartermaster, everyone had to be taught from scratch as "Guns, horses, and equipment dribbled in on us." He rarely left the barracks, except for an occasional weekend visit home.

Early in May 1915, the 10th Division was ordered to move to Basingstoke, England, for final training. Charles, however, was appointed on arrival there "to command a brigade in the Welsh Divisional Artillery, and promoted lieutenant colonel. I left my battery with some regret and proceeded at once to North Wales to take over my new command." This, the 38th Welsh Division, was newly formed at the request of then Chancellor of the Exchequer David Lloyd George, a life-long Welsh nationalist, and Charles had to begin training recruits all over again. "I had about 1,500 men, the greater number of them obviously under-age, and many were boys of fifteen...a good, keen lot of boys, anxious to please and learn." His chief support was an English NCO who acted as adjutant and then took over command of each battery of men until it was trained and organized to a high standard. The weather and the scenery in Snowdonia were glorious that summer and they "marched and counter-marched on the warm sands of the seashore and then cooled off in the sea." Their only artillery was an old gun dug out of an arsenal or museum, and Charles himself was gunnery instructor. After two months, they moved to Winchester for more advanced training where guns, horses, and equipment "flowed in on us freely."

The appalling casualty lists during the first thirteen months of the war overflowed with the names of great Irish regiments, including officers from many Protestant Ascendancy families. "Nearly everyone I know in the army has been killed," lamented Irish scholar and diplomat Douglas Hyde. "...all the gentry have suffered. *Noblesse oblige.*"[5] Irishmen had won seventeen Victoria Crosses, Britain's highest military honor, during thirteen months, which included the inconclusive battles on the Western Front and most of the disastrous Gallipoli Campaign—the Allied attempt to control the sea route from Allied Russia through the enemy-held Dardanelles into the Mediterranean.[6] The first of the three great Irish divisions, the 10th, under the command of Irish General Sir Bryan Mahon, incurred enormous losses from machine gun fire during the landing at Cape Helles and fought with great bravery during the August Gallipoli offensive. Between 2,100 and 2,700 Irishmen were killed in action at Gallipoli.[7] French, Australian and New Zealand divisions also suffered terrible losses there. First Lord of the Admiralty Winston Churchill was blamed for being part of this failed plan to relieve the pressure on the Russians in the Caucasus and subsequently resigned from the government. Since Charles would most likely have been with the 10th Division at Gallipoli if he had not been transferred to the Welsh Division, this might explain why he visited and walked that battlefield in the late 1920s, the subject of his book *A Glance at Gallipoli.*[8]

In June 1915, Prime Minister Asquith, attempting to more successfully prosecute the war, was forced to form a Wartime Coalition Government at Westminster. Despite his vision and hard work to secure war materials, Kitchener was blamed for the chronic shortage of artillery shells that spring and stripped of his control over munitions and strategy. David Lloyd George became Minister for Munitions, a new department, and excelled in this position; however, it was Gen. Sir William Robertson who was given direct access to the Cabinet in Kitchener's place, leaving the Army brass still in control of strategy. Asquith now brought Conservative leader Bonar Law, an English champion of Protestant Ulster, into the cabinet, and Sir Edward Carson was named attorney-general, although he resigned on October 19 because of his dissatisfaction with the conduct of the war. Asquith had also offered a post to John Redmond but he turned it down, feeling that taking a position in the British government would reduce his ability to influence Irish opinion to support a united war effort: his objective was to win united support for Home Rule. Although Redmond blocked Asquith's attempt to appoint one of Carson's most fanatical supporters, J. H. Campbell, as lord chancellor of Ireland—"an antagonist of everything Nationalist Ireland stood for," as the *Manchester Guardian* put it—the threat of conscription began to destroy the Irish Nationalists' trust that Britain would follow through on implementing Home Rule once the war was over.

The British Government and First Secretary for Ireland Augustine Birrell were aware from the outbreak of the war that there was some "hare-brained scheme" afoot involving John Devoy of Clan na Gael in New York and Sir Roger Casement to bring about an Irish rebellion.[9] Messages to that effect had been intercepted between the Germany embassy in Washington and the German government in Berlin. But Birrell refused to give in to the Unionist clamor to have the rebels suppressed. Instead, he followed the advice of members of parliament Redmond and Dillon that the rebels were only a minute proportion of Irish opinion and the only danger lay in making martyrs of them.[10] How right they proved to be. In fact, Roger Casement, who was frankly pro-German, signed an agreement on December 27, 1914, with the German secretary of state at the German foreign office laying down the conditions under which an Irish Brigade was to be raised from Irish prisoners of war held in Germany. He then spent most of 1915 fruitlessly attempting to raise such a brigade in Germany and to acquire the assistance of German officers, reporting by Christmas Eve that he was too sick to do any more there. A few months later, discouraged, depressed, and deeply disillusioned with his idealized Germans, he persuaded them to transport him to Ireland via submarine, hoping he could convince the rebels to postpone the planned rising.

Between May and September that year, the IRB formed a military council whose members took effective control of plans for a projected rebellion. On August 1, 1915, the IRB's most radical leader, the myth-making schoolteacher and poet Patrick Pearse, gave a fiery oration at the massed propagandist funeral of the old Fenian Jeremiah O'Donovan Rossa, who had died in America. Pearse warned Britain that "Ireland unfree shall never be at peace." Sir Matthew Nathan, under-secretary at Dublin Castle, wrote even before the funeral: "I have an uncomfortable feeling that the Nationalists are losing ground to the Sinn Feiners, and that this demonstration is hastening the movement." On September 19, Pearse led some fifteen hundred Irish Volunteers, 600 of them armed, through the streets of Dublin and out into manoeuvers in the countryside. And, in December, beginning to lose trust in the coalition government, the National Party passed a resolution declaring that "any attempt to bring into force a system of compulsory service will meet with our vigorous resistance."[11] The Conscription Act that went through Parliament in January 1916 excluded Ireland, but the threat of its being extended there was always present. That month, James Connolly was encouraged to join the IRB and was voted onto the Military Council, ensuring that the Citizens Army would be involved in the rebellion.

Having put in sterling work training artillery brigades, Lt. Col. Charles Head now realized his lifelong ambition as an army officer to take part in the action for which he had been trained. The Welsh infantry shipped to France early in December 1915 and the artillery brigade followed on Christmas Eve. It was raining and blowing hard and their initial crossing was miserable as most of the men were seasick. That same night, Charles and his brigade left Le Havre in three trains—one for each battery—for "an unknown destination." This turned out to be Lestrem, a village near the front. They could see the "weird German Very lights," or flare guns, going up and down in the east. It was pouring with rain and, when they stepped off their train into three or four inches of mud (shades of horrors to come), they were told that their billet was actually ten or twelve miles further back.

It was nighttime and they were instructed to march in the dark to an area marked on a map by a circle. There Charles would have to find billets for each of his batteries. A guide on a bicycle soon betrayed his limited knowledge of the area, so he was dismissed to bed and they proceeded "by the help of map and matches" to the area where a farm had been marked with a cross as a possible billet. Approaching the front door in pitch dark, Charles nearly fell into the noxious midden (manure) pool and then faced a large, hostile dog whose chain was just long enough to allow Charles to squeeze past him and the pool to the door. After he had knocked for five minutes, a woman came to the door at last and Charles struggled to explain in his very limited French that they were looking for shelter for the night. Having tied their horses to equipment around the farmyard, the exhausted young men were soon fast asleep in a comfortable barn. Charles and his junior officers, however, still had to locate billets for the other batteries. They were now anxious to "get at it," as he put it, but they were held in the reserve lines for seven months.

The 1916 Easter Rising

On April 9, 1916, the German vessel *Libau* set sail from Lubeck, Germany, heading for Tralee, Co. Kerry, on Ireland's southwest coast, with a cargo of 25,000 rifles and about a million rounds of ammunition. En route, the German captain changed the name of the ship to *Aud*, the name of a similar Norwegian vessel, to avoid interception by the British. Three days later, Roger Casement and two other rebels boarded the submarine U-19 at Wilmshaven, Germany, bound for a rendezvous with the *Aud* at Tralee. The *Aud* arrived there on April 20 but, since the local Volunteers were not expecting it until Easter Saturday, the arms were not landed. Early the following morning, Casement and his companions went ashore from the submarine at Banna Strand or Beach in Tralee Bay. Hours later, when Casement—who felt that the Rising should be postponed—was discovered at a local fort, he was arrested by the Royal Irish Constabulary. The *Aud* was captured by the British Navy and forced to sail toward Cork Harbor. At 1 a.m. the following morning, the captain and his crew scuttled the *Aud* to prevent her precious cargo falling into enemy hands, and the weapons intended for the Rising were lost at sea.

At 10 o'clock that night, on hearing about that disaster, Eoin MacNeill, chief of staff of the Irish Volunteers, who felt he had been seriously misled by the radicals, issued the countermanding order in Dublin to stop the Rising that was being planned without his participation. He and another leader, Michael O'Rahilly, business manager of the *Gaelic League* magazine, embarked for the South to deliver that order. In Co. Tipperary, Volunteer commandant Pierce McCann's orders were to link up with the Volunteers in Co. Limerick and "hold the line of the Shannon." However, he immediately obeyed the countermand, as did the Limerick Volunteers. Therefore, in those two counties and throughout the West and Southwest, nothing occurred except for a tentative rising in Galway.[12]

The following morning, Easter Saturday, the Military Council in Dublin put the rising on hold for twenty-four hours while hundreds of copies of "The Proclamation for the Republic" were printed. It was signed by council members Thomas Clarke, Seán MacDermott, Thomas MacDonagh, Patrick Pearse, Eamonn Ceannt, Joseph Plunkett, and James Connolly, several of them poets, all intensely religious, and all young—with one exception. On Easter Sunday, April 23, 1916, John Dillon, who was in Dublin during the parliamentary recess, wrote to Redmond, who had stayed in London: "Dublin is full of the most extraordinary rumours...you must not be surprised if something very unpleasant and mischievous happens this week."[13]

Fearing a British crackdown in the wake of the discovery of the attempt to import weapons and recalling the abidingly inspirational revolutionary figures of Lord Edward Fitzgerald, Robert Emmet and other icons of the 1798 rebellion, the rebel leaders in Dublin went ahead with their plan the next day. At noon on Monday, the 24th, a hundred or so Irish Volunteers and Citizen Army men marched through the city streets—nothing unusual over the past several months—stopped opposite the neoclassical General Post Office in O'Connell Street (Sackville Street at the time), then turned and ran into the building. Within minutes, the men, armed with revolvers, cleared out customers and officials from the building. Two flags, one the traditional green flag with the gold harp, but now inscribed with the words "Irish Republic," the other a new flag, a tricolor of orange, white, and green, were soon flying over the Irish Republic's headquarters.

Sometime later, schoolteacher and self-proclaimed leader Patrick Pearse stood on the steps of the portico and, with rhetoric glorifying blood-sacrifice and mystical Catholicism, proclaimed an Irish Republic. He read the proclamation from the Provisional Government calling on the support of Ireland's "exiled children in America" and "gallant allies in Europe," i.e., the German government, thus dismissing the fact that the flower of Ireland's manhood had been fighting those allies in Europe for the past twenty months. "We declare the right of the people of Ireland to the ownership of Ireland, and to the unfettered control of Irish destinies to be sovereign and indefeasible," it began. "The long usurpation of that right by a foreign people and government has not extinguished the right, nor can it ever be extinguished except by the destruction of the Irish people...we hereby proclaim the Irish Republic as a Sovereign Independent State, and we pledge our lives and the lives of our comrades-in-arms to the cause of its freedom, of its welfare, and of its exaltation among the nations."

Although the Dublin administration was humiliatingly unprepared for insurrection, having assumed that the well-leaked enterprise would be abandoned after the interception of the German arms and capture of Casement, the city swarmed with troops within two days. These included members of six Irish battalions then stationed in Ireland as well as reinforcements from Britain. By that time, the insurgents had occupied and fortified other prominent positions, including the Four Courts building, led by the young Fenian Edward Daly, and—under the leadership of mathematics professor Eámon de Valera—Boland's Flour Mills with outposts commanding the main road into Dublin from the harbor of Kingstown (Dún Laoghaire). Soon innocent citizens were caught in a lethal hailstorm of sniper-fire, machine guns, and field artillery, and eventually a gunboat on the River Liffey. In the midst of this tumult, many people angrily decried the summary execution of pacifist Francis Sheehy Skeffington—who had been apprehended while simply trying to prevent looting—by a firing squad commanded by an Anglo-Irish army officer.

When Pearse surrendered on behalf of the Republican forces on April 29, the toll was sixty-four rebels killed, including Michael O'Rahilly (descendant of legendary Irish poets Aodhagan

O Rathaille and James Clarence Mangan) as he fled the General Post Office, and 132 British Army and Royal Irish Constabulary. At least 230 civilians were killed and more than 600 wounded from sniping and artillery fire, the latter causing devastating damage to shops and houses.[14] The city's center resembled the shelled remains of French towns razed during battles on the Western Front. The reaction of ordinary Dubliners varied between puzzlement and open hostility, since many of them had relatives in the British Army in Europe, innocent lives had been lost, and the center of their city had been traumatically and expensively damaged. Ordinary Dubliners could not get to work and resented the hot-headed rebels' disruption of their livelihoods. In fact, there was little sympathy for the rebels initially; the vast majority of the Irish people found the thought of German support repellent—that is, until the British government decided to make an example of the leaders. On April 30, John Dillon, longtime leader of the more radical wing of the Irish Parliamentary Party, wrote to Redmond in London:

> You should urge strongly on the government the *extreme* unwisdom of any wholesale shooting of prisoners. The wisest course is to execute *no one* for the present. This is the *most urgent* matter of the moment. If there were shootings of prisoners on any large scale the effect on public opinion might be disastrous in the extreme. So *far* feeling of the population in Dublin is against the Sinn Feiners. But a reaction might very easily be created."[15]

Despite Redmond's pleas to Asquith, three of the leaders (Patrick Pearse, Thomas MacDonagh, and Thomas Clarke) were executed in Kilmainham jail at dawn on May 3. Four more executions were carried out the next day (Joseph Plunkett, Edward Daly, Michael O'Hanrahan, and William Pearse, Patrick's younger brother). John MacBride was shot on May 5 and four more on May 8. On May 12, John Connolly and Seán MacDermott were executed despite Dillon's ferocious speech in Parliament the day before: "it is not murderers who are being executed; it is insurgents who have fought a clean fight, however misguided, and it would be a damned good thing for you if your soldiers were able to put up as good a fight as did these men in Dublin."[16] All those executed instantly became martyrs, memorialized by William Butler Yeats in his poem "Easter 1916." Thus the conspirators achieved their aim of reversing the movement toward Anglo-Irish reconciliation.

Although Prime Minister Asquith had tried to stop the continuing executions, "his need to placate the Unionists seemed more urgent to him."[17] The British public and Protestant Ascendancy in Ireland, particularly in Ulster, which was heavily involved in the war effort, felt that the executions were amply justified by the bloodshed and destruction of property the rebels had caused, not to mention the stabbing in the back of loyal Irishmen and British at a dark hour of the war...Constance Markievicz, a republican member of the Anglo-Irish gentry who had married a Polish count, and Éamon de Valera, both prominent figures in the Rising, were both condemned to death but reprieved and sent to prison in England.[18] More than fifteen hundred prisoners were taken across the Irish Sea by May 10, and 1,867 were eventually interned there, either in criminal prisons or at a special camp at Frongoch in Wales where they were further radicalized.

On June 29, a British court in London found Roger Casement guilty of high treason. He tried to claim that he was answerable only to his country, Ireland, but he had accepted a knighthood from King George V in 1911. Casement's fate was sealed when pages from his diary indicating promiscuous homosexuality were circulated, affecting many who were inclined to seek a reprieve. The executions enraged Irish Americans and threatened to jeopardize the desperate need for America to join the Allied forces against Germany. The decision to execute Casement as the rebels' chief contact with Germany delivered an even more serious blow to Anglo-Irish and Anglo-American relations. He was hanged in Pentonville Jail on August 3, becoming the sixteenth martyr of Easter week.[19] Casement's execution on the very day the U.S. government requested that he be granted clemency, especially offended and angered Americans—not just Irish Americans—who were already irritated with Britain over its naval blockade policies, which put a big dent in American trade with neutral European countries.

Between April and November 1916, Ireland was governed under martial law. Asquith sent Gen. Sir John Maxwell to Ireland as "supreme commander of the forces in Ireland." The resignation of Birrell, Nathan, and other senior officials in Dublin Castle incapacitated the civil administration. When Sir Bryan Mahon, former commander of the 10th Division at Gallipoli, succeeded Maxwell, he did his best to restore the balance between the civil and military authorities.[20] Roy Foster has frequently expressed the opinion that, as the British government attempted to "teach a lesson" to would-be rebels, it transformed Sinn Féin into a republican separatist political movement by referring to the insurrection as the "Sinn Féin rebellion."

On June 5, Lord Kitchener was on board *HMS Hampshire* en route to Russia for negotiations when it struck a German mine one and half miles west of the Scottish Orkneys and sank. Kitchener was among the 737 who died. Lloyd George succeeded Kitchener as secretary of state for war. Although he had little control over strategy, he told a journalist in late September that "the fight must be to a finish—to a knockout," thus rejecting President Woodrow Wilson's continuing efforts to mediate. General Haig and his staff spent the first six months of 1916 preparing plans for an immense attempt to penetrate the German line on the Somme, an operation Haig was confident would succeed and hasten an overall Allied victory. This time, the German defensive wire must be cut and the German front-line positions obliterated by artillery fire. Haig thought this could be done by bombarding the enemy trenches for a week, followed by eleven British divisions climbing out of their trenches in attacking waves on a thirteen-mile front. In the event, the bombardment had little effect on the wire. It did, however, alert the Germans to the impending assault.

The War became even darker when, on July 1, 1916, the first day of the Battle of the Somme, the British Army saw the bloodiest day in its history, with 57,470 casualties, about 19,240 killed, and 40,000 taken prisoner. The Germans survived the futile bombardment in their deep dugouts before carrying their machine guns back to the line and mowing down the British and Dominion forces moving toward them through an increasingly hellish No Man's Land. In the first two days of fighting, the 36th (Ulster) Division alone, one of the first units "over the top," lost over a third of its men. Of nine

Victoria Crosses awarded to British forces in the battle, four were given to 36th Division soldiers.

The V.C. was also awarded to Private Martin O'Meara of the 16th Battalion AIF of Australia's 4th Division, for his bravery as a stretcher bearer during four days of heavy fighting (August 9-12) in the Battle of Mouquet Farm—part of the larger Somme Offensive. O'Meara, a member of one of the many branches of a large Lorrha family that is still resident in the parish, was born in 1885 at Lissernane, which may still have been part of William Henry Head's estate at that time. He emigrated to Australia in 1911. The recommendation stated, "For most conspicuous bravery. During four days of very heavy fighting he repeatedly went out and brought in wounded officers and men from 'No Man's Land' under intense artillery and machine gun fire. He also volunteered and carried up ammunition and bombs through a heavy barrage to a portion of the trenches, which was being heavily shelled at the time. He showed throughout an utter contempt of danger, and undoubtedly saved many lives."[21] Gen. William Bernhard Hickie presided at an event, attended by hundreds of people, in the little village of Lorrha to honor and show their pride in O'Meara's bravery, but O'Meara missed it, having had to return to the army. When, eleven months later, O'Meara returned to Lorrha, his reception could not have been colder due to the "dramatic transformation in people's attitudes to the insurrection."[22] Thus began decades of resistance in Ireland to any reference to the participation of Irishmen in WWI.

The British government was all too conscious of Irish discontent and its dangers in wartime, damaging as it was to British prestige in the USA and the Dominions, and under pressure by the Irish Parliamentary Party. With the Battle of the Somme already proving to be a disaster, Secretary of State Lloyd George attempted to negotiate an agreement between Redmond and Carson on Home Rule and the exclusion of six Protestant-majority Ulster counties. However, the Conservatives in Parliament were adamantly against Home Rule, the gentry of the border counties of Cavan, Monaghan, and Donegal were enraged that Carson approved their exclusion from Ulster, and Asquith was in no position to break up his Coalition government as the country's and the government's high hopes for Haig's strategy were dashed. Lloyd George's scheme was rejected by the Irish Parliamentary Party but Ireland's discontent could not be ignored much longer and would be taken up in convention the following year.[23]

Charles Head began his account of the Battle of the Somme and subsequent battles in which he participated with reference to the general he came to deride for his failures of tactical or military expertise and lack of imagination: "When I arrived in France," he wrote, "Sir Douglas Haig had just taken over the command of the army from Sir John French...He [Haig] was a man of terrific will-power and great obstinacy, but had not hitherto shown himself to be enlightened or expert in military science. He was a very reactionary trainer of troops, sternly repressing any tendency of his own arm, the cavalry, to consider dismounted action as an essential part of its training and looking with cold disfavour on all weapons with which he was not familiar."[24] Although Lloyd George soon formed the same opinion of Haig, he had promised the Unionists to retain him and Robertson in command. Neither side proved able to deliver a decisive blow for the next two years. Around 800,000 soldiers from the British Empire were on the Western Front at any one time. One thousand battalions, occupying sectors of the line from the North Sea to the Orne River, operated on a month-long four-stage rotation system, unless an offensive was underway. The 440-mile-long Western Front contained over 6,000 miles of trenches. Each battalion held its sector for about a week before moving back to support lines and then further back to the reserve lines for a week of rest.

Charles Head's Welsh artillery brigade joined the battle on July 7, 1916, coming into action in No Man's Land, facing north to engage the enemy holding the Mametz Wood and Contalmaison. There he saw the British dead lying "in swathes in front and around us, mown down in their ranks by machine-guns from the flanks." The division made excellent progress that day, breaking up the German line as they moved north and destroying many German guns. "Now was the opportunity for a great general," he wrote. On July 14, "the day on which we assaulted the Bazentin villages, was a day of great hopes and promise...The whole British cavalry, we knew, was sitting massed behind us ready for the great opportunity that was surely coming. The trenches were crowded with keen, fit infantrymen, only too willing to play their part, and the enemy seemed to be almost entirely devoid of artillery, and in some confusion." By eight o'clock in the morning, "we had taken the villages with slight loss to ourselves, and then it was as if cease-fire had sounded on a field-day, and the mock battle had abruptly ceased."

When Charles reported the enterprising advance of two infantry battalions and their occupation of the southern edge of High Wood, he was astonished to find that Corps headquarters had no knowledge of it. "Were there no eyes on the battlefield, and was my telephone the only means of communication with the front? From high ground in our possession the whole scene was plainly visible, and hostile fire of any kind was practically negligible." The sole effort of the magnificent cavalry that day, Charles recalled, was their leisurely advance to pick up some German prisoners and escort them back behind their lines. However, one historian of the Battle of Bazentin Ridge saw the actions of the 7th Dragoon Guards and the 2nd Deccan Horse differently, claiming that they charged with their lances against High Wood after taking all day to move forward from their encampment and across the churned battlefield. Having reached High Wood, they killed a number of Germans and took 32 prisoners.

It was reported in the Co. Antrim *Larne Times* of August 26, 1916, that Lt. Col. Charles O. Head, R.A., had been wounded. The report continued: "He is a son of the late Mr. W. H. Head, D.L. Derrylahan Park, Birr. One of his brothers, Capt. W. E. Head, who married the eldest daughter of Mr. Digby Johns, of Rosebrook, Carrick, was formerly in the Antrim Artillery. Another brother, Lieut. Col. M. R. Head, has served with distinction in the present war. Major H. N. [Henry Nugent] Head of Strangford, [Co. Down], is a relative of the officer who has now been wounded." By stressing these connections, the paper seemed to be claiming Charles Head for the Ulster Unionist side and raises the question of who provided these details, and why. Again, when he was awarded the DSO in 1917, it was announced in an Ulster newspaper below the same award to his kinsman Lt. Col. Arthur Head. The nature of Charles's wound is not known but it cannot have been serious since he was soon back on the front lines.

Having suffered severe casualties, the Welsh brigade was subsequently withdrawn from the battle and sent to the Ypres salient where it saw no action during the next year. However, as part of the reorganization of the field artillery, Charles was now given command of the 29th Brigade of the 4th Division, a regular army division which included a number of Irish battalions, including the 1st Bn., the Royal Irish Fusiliers and the 2nd Bn., the Royal Dublin Fusiliers. He considered this a great honor. In September 1916, his new brigade was ordered back to the Somme. "The battlefield was now a dismal sight, villages and woods obliterated, and the whole area covered with shell-holes, water and mud." He doubted if there had ever been more futile operations than those of October and November on the Somme. While the infantry had to struggle over "the wide waste of mud to the miserable trench which was the starting line for their assaults, they had a still worse time getting back again, after leaving many of their number behind them," the survivors being weak and exhausted from their ordeals.

Charles noted that, while the artillery was better off due to their stationary condition, they lost many of their horses in the arduous work of supplying the guns with ammunition: "all ammunition had to be carried on improvised pack-saddles, holding only four rounds each. It took a horse all night to get to the front and back to the wagon-lines...The horse mortality in these two months was a shocking waste of our resources." Why was this wasteful and ineffective battle being prolonged, he wondered? The French on their right were fighting more intelligently and cautiously: "they didn't churn the ground into a quagmire before launching their men at it; and having got it they brought up immediately their labour troops to provide it with cover and connect it by a good road to the rear positions."

As a career regimental officer who had always prided himself on the welfare of the men under his command, Charles was once again appalled at the way they were treated once they received the long-deferred order for their relief from their position just behind the front lines. They were ordered to march twenty-eight miles to a first stopping place on their way to rest billets in the rear. "This was an impossible demand; we were under strength in horses and those we had were weak; the gunners sitting in mud at the gun positions had done no marching for months, so their feet were soft, and they were tired and out of condition." The first two or three miles were through thick, sticky mud, and the road beyond for several miles was badly cut up. They had to carry all their forage and much of their baggage on their gun carriages and wagons, so that the gunners had to walk most of the way.

Forced to point out that this feat was beyond them, their artillery brigadier made their case to the Army Corps which should have been aware of the difficulties and could have assigned brand-new lorries standing idle nearby to take much of the baggage and spare men, thus lightening the load of the already very heavy guns behind the horses. Their remonstrance "was coldly received, and appeared to create offence." After marching for hours on a miserably wet and cold day, they were told grudgingly that they could stop half-way, but no billets could be found for them in an already over-crowded town. The unfortunate troops spent a wretched night in worse accommodation than at the front, and Charles received a reprimand a week later from the Corps commander, among several in response to his report that some of the troops had relieved themselves on the training ground. "I suppose a meek attitude was the right one, but I had to reply that I considered the misplacement of a small quantity of human waste-product to be a small price to pay for defective and unsympathetic staff work." Charles presumed that his kind artillery commander softened his words.[25]

Lloyd George was increasingly frustrated at the limited gains of the Somme offensive and criticized General Haig to General Ferdinand Foch, the French commander, on a visit to the Western Front that September. The British casualty ratios were worse than those of the French, who were more experienced and had more artillery. He proposed sending General Robertson on a mission to Russia (he refused to go) and demanded that more troops be sent to Salonika to help Romania. Robertson eventually threatened to resign, but Lloyd George never succeeded in dislodging either him or Haig.[26] Much of the press still argued that the professional military leadership of Haig and Robertson was preferable to the civilian interference that had led to the disasters at Gallipoli. Lord Northcliffe, owner of *The Times* and a chief propagandist for the war, stormed into Lloyd George's office on October 1. "You can tell him that I hear he has been interfering with Strategy," he said, "and that if he goes on I will break him." Lloyd George had to give his "word of honor" that he had complete confidence in Haig and Robertson.[27]

Asquith's weakness as a planner and organizer was increasingly apparent to senior officials. On December 5, 1916, he was forced to step down, and Lloyd George succeeded him as prime minister. But Asquith's fall split the Liberal Party into two factions, those who supported him and those who supported the coalition government under Lloyd George. Lloyd George now relied on the support of the Conservatives, including press baron Lord Northcliffe. The five-member war cabinet now included three Conservatives: Leader of the House of Lords Lord Curzon, chancellor of the exchequer, House of Commons leader Bonar Law, and Minister without Portfolio Lord Milner. Although Edward Carson was appointed First Lord of the Admiralty, he was excluded from the war cabinet.[28]

Later that month, the new prime minister, as a gesture of good will designed to encourage the Americans to enter the war, released the 560 Irish prisoners who were being held without trial in Britain. Among them was twenty-seven-year-old Michael Collins. He had expressed the opinion that the Easter Rising had been "terribly bungled" and, as leader of the Irish Republican Army, he would become the most effective organizer of armed rebellion in Irish history.[29] In 1917, four members of Sinn Féin were elected to Parliament: Count Plunkett (Joseph's father), Joe McGuinness, Éamon de Valera, and W. T. Cosgrave (the last two while still imprisoned at Frongoch, Wales, both future presidents of the Irish Free State). That April, the U.S. entered the war at last, finally impelled to do so by Germany's resumption of unrestricted submarine warfare and the sinking of several American ships.

In the spring of 1917, the 29th Brigade of the 4th Division was withdrawn from the Somme area and sent north, where it was subsequently engaged in the battle of Arras (April 9-May 16). The field artillery was ordered to bombard the enemy for five days—when two would have been plenty in Charles's opinion. But this time they were supplied with large quantities of high explosive shells of recent manufacture. The opening day of the battle was one of the most successful of the war, when artillery and infantry left a hole in the German defense line. But once again a great opportunity was wasted when the cavalry was brought in, a rare occurrence at this point in the war. They so monopolized the tracks that had been built to cross the shell holes that they impeded passage of the guns and ammunition required to assist the 4th Division. The same afternoon, the cavalry was sent back over those tracks, again completely blocking the tracks for the rest of the day. Their failure to achieve anything of value was due once again, in Charles's opinion, to "the hesitating, blundering management of the authority which controlled their action." Charles concluded, "The battle which had opened on April 9th with a brilliant success ended on May 3rd with little more to show for it than the fruits gathered on its first day..." By 1917, few illusions remained about breaking the line and sending the cavalry through to end the war.

Charles's brigade had a peaceful and pleasant summer following the Battle of Arras in a concealed position, "with bathing and fishing in the Scarpe close at hand, and a good macadamized road right up to it." His headquarters was on the top of a hill in a German dugout which had previously sheltered some senior German army officer. It was forty feet below ground, paneled throughout and with two flights of stairs to the top and a passage in between—spacious enough, in other words, to accommodate his whole staff. At the end of August, they got their call to join the ongoing Battle of Passchendaele (third Battle of Ypres) on the Pilckem Ridge above the Steenbeek river. The 4th Division was ordered to capture a section of the German front line. That August was the wettest in thirty years with only three days in which no rain was recorded; the total rainfall for the month was almost double the normal August average. Much of the battlefield turned into a quagmire in which men and animals sometimes drowned, making movement of men and supplies difficult and severely reducing the accuracy and effectiveness of artillery.

"The 4th Division...did its part valiantly and advanced the line beyond Poelcapelle before it was withdrawn," wrote Charles. "We, the Artillery of the Division, remained in action, a separation which was customary [but] we were nobody's children and were deprived

of the care and sympathy of our own commanders. During this battle we served under at least six different artillery generals." When
asked to move forward to the valley of the Steenbeek, they entered
a month of misery and hardship as the ground now resembled that
of the Somme at its worst. "Digging gun-pits was out of the question, each [of the twenty four] gun[s] stood on a thin crust of earth
covering a bed of ooze, and perforated by innumerable shell-holes
in which the water stood level with the top of the ground. Little
islands of ammunition were dumped round about between the
craters and frequently disappeared into them when their support
gave way." Fortunately, they found a few concrete pillboxes which
provided precarious and crowded shelter to officers and men. The
brigade headquarters was in a pillbox built of reinforced concrete
on a prominent position about five hundred yards behind the guns;
this was not the first time that Charles had cause to admire the materials and labor used by the enemy for their defensive works. This
pillbox was the target of all sorts of guns, but it was only hit once
by a very heavy shell while they occupied it. No lives were lost, but
they did lose all their equipment and rations.

The greatest difficulty was getting damaged guns out of the line
to send them back for repair. One of them was blown into a big
shell-hole and it "took the united strength of the brigade several
days and nights to extract the damaged piece from its miry cavity
and from the many similar holes into which it subsided before it
reached the infirm surface of the road." Then a team of horses succeeded in getting it back to a better road. In the process, however, a
particularly valuable officer, one of Charles's battery commanders,
was killed by a German bomb. Charles was ordered to move the
brigade forward. Since he could not see how this could be done and
none of his superiors would come forward to see for themselves, he
made the decision to stay where they were.

As the scholar Paul Fussell put it in his landmark study of the
cultural and literary impact of the war: "after weeks of frustration,
the [Passchendaele] attack finally (and literally) bogged down in
early November. Lieut. Gen. Sir Lancelot Kiggell, of the staff, 'paid
his first visit to the fighting zone': As his staff car lurched through
the swampland and neared the battleground he became more and
more agitated. Finally he burst into tears and muttered, 'Good God,

did we really send men to fight in that?' The man beside him, who had been through the campaign, replied tonelessly, 'It's worse further up.'" Fussell also noted that novelist Alec Waugh, who also saw action at Passchendaele as a subaltern in a machine-gun company, saw no officers above the rank of lieutenant-colonel at the front.[30]

They all felt greatly relieved when the order came through on about November 6 for them to withdraw "from the squalid misery of the battlefield" and hand over to another brigade. They then played a subsidiary but increasingly important role in the battle of Cambrai (November 20-December 6, 1917), which included the first (temporarily) effective assault by massed tanks. But "The German counter-attack swept our exhausted men off much of the ground they had conquered, leaving us with nothing more to show for our losses and exertions than another of those small salients that cost us so many casualties to hold." Charles was awarded the Distinguished Service Order (DSO) that year, subsequently with bar.[31]

Charles Head was one of those lieutenant-colonels who, in his words, "spent a lot of time, more than most of my rank, I think, in the forefront of the Battles of the Somme, Arras, Passchendaele and on the fringe of Cambrai, and saw there much on which to speculate and reflect." He critiqued the British New Army's conduct of operations in France in the introduction to his book *The Art of Generalship* (1929). He questioned why no rifle or machine gun fire was aimed by the British at the low-flying German planes mercilessly machine-gunning the troops moving along the duckboards, while the Australians fired barrages at them, even managing to bring down the great Baron von Richthofen (aka the Red Baron); why the French were so much better at moving their troops forward while the British troops struggled painfully through the mud; why were so many officers who could have provided valuable leadership at or near the front held back in "five huge Army Staffs, about a dozen unduly inflated Corps staffs, a swarm of minor officials, hosts of experienced officers concerned only with the provision and care of horses which were of little use, over-staffed supply services, etc.... How could such a system produce good results?"[32] He had probably long since read and approved Sassoon's poem about useless staff officers. He believed that, if the British Army had been better directed and organized, with the measure of support it was receiving from the Allies, it would have been able to completely defeat the Germans and end the war in 1917. "There should have been no March 1918, no American intervention to complicate the terms of peace, and, perhaps, no Bolshevik Russia."[33] Noticeably, he did not mention the effect of the war on the Irish rebellion.

Charles was referring to what historian Michael Hopkinson called "the enormous assistance that President Woodrow Wilson gave to Sinn Féin in 1917 and 1918 by propagating the doctrine of self-determination and continually stressing to worldwide audiences the rights of small nations and the evils of imperialism."[34] Charles's own view, expressed in *No Great Shakes*, was that "[s]mall nationalities are an unmitigated nuisance all over the world, and deserve no encouragement. In the interests of the peace and welfare of humanity they should subordinate their nationalist pride to the claims of geography, expediency and common sense, and should place themselves under the protection of their big neighbours, while retaining any local characteristics and privileges that are not injurious to their protectors."[35]

On the eve of the Battle of Pilckem Ridge, Prime Minister Lloyd George called the Irish Convention (July 25, 1917-April 1918) in a final attempt to settle the Irish question without excluding Ulster. He now hoped that, as a result of the Easter Rising, the moderates, both Unionists and Nationalists, were even more anxious for a peaceful settlement. Nationalists formed the majority of the 95 representatives who met at Trinity College under the chairmanship of noted agriculturalist and moderate Nationalist Horace Plunkett, including mayors and chairmen of county councils as well as MPs and peers. Only the Sinn Féin party refused to attend. During this meeting, the Ulster Unionists treated the Southern Unionists in a high-handed manner, excluding them from meetings, with the result that the southerners began to feel more sympathy with the Nationalists. Lord Desart, a leader of the Southern Unionists, put forward a scheme for a wide measure of self-government with safeguards for minorities. It seemed that this might go through, in which case the Southern Unionists had solved the problem of Ulster and Home Rule. Ironically, though, the scheme was thwarted by Horace Plunkett when he postponed discussion until all the committees had reported, giving the extremists on both sides time to have second thoughts. The Nationalists might have stuck with this plan if John Redmond had not died, a bitterly disappointed and saddened man, on March 6. His health had been declining for some time, and nine months earlier, in June 1917, he had received a severe personal blow when his brother Willie died in action at the onset of the Battle of Messines (June 7-14, 1917); Willie's vacant seat in East Clare was won in July by Éamon de Valera, the most senior surviving commandant of the Easter 1916 insurgents.

The Convention ended with the Ulstermen more determined than ever to stay out of a Home Rule Ireland, and with the Southern Unionists having to come to terms with Home Rule. But Irish public opinion had already moved away from Home Rule, to the extreme nationalism of Sinn Féin.[36] Charles Head confirmed that the Irish Southern Unionist population was on the whole quite reconciled to the adoption of Home Rule at that point.[37] However, the conciliatory attitude adopted by Southern Unionists at the Convention led to a split in the Irish Unionist Alliance. Some of the most influential landlord Unionists, such as Lord Desart and other Anglo-Irish peers, formed the breakaway Unionist Anti-Partition League under the leadership of Lord Midleton in January 1919, while hard-liners, such as Lord Farnham (Co. Cavan), Lord Dunalley, E. J. Beaumont-Nesbitt, and J. M. Wilson remained with the IUA.[38]

At a Sinn Féin convention on October 25 and 26, 1917, attended by about two thousand people, including delegates from over a thousand Sinn Féin clubs, the party candidates pledged to abstain from attending parliament at Westminster, having defeated the more moderate Redmondites in the parliamentary by-elections. Sinn Féin announced that their aim was to have Ireland recognized as "an independent Republic" with its own government. Released from prison in June 2017 and elected to parliament in July, Éamon de Valera quickly became the leading figure in the republican ranks, especially in terms of political policy and tactics. When he was elected president of the Sinn Féin movement and the Irish Volunteers on October 25, the civil and military wings of the advanced nationalist movement were brought closer together.

As historian Terence Dooley has noted, "the development of

nationality and of nationalism in Ireland was specifically bound up with the struggle for land that continued to characterize Irish life long after independence, just as it had done for generations before."[39] The mass of peasant proprietors created by the various land acts remained aggrieved. They had not got what they required, enough land to make their holdings economically viable. Raids for arms by independent groups of Volunteers began to be reported early in 1918. In February, de Valera encouraged every Sinn Féin club in Co. Clare, his constituency, to form a company of the Irish Volunteers "to help divide the land evenly." In the western and midland counties, large bodies of landless men "marched to grazing farms and forcibly took possession of as much land as they required," and there was "an upsurge in agrarian crime directed against landowners."[40] In Co. Tipperary, on the initiative of a local Volunteer, Dan Breen, raids on private houses were stepped up. "We generally went at night and asked for the arms," he wrote afterward. "Those who would have liked to refuse knew they dare not. Many others gave them willingly, and some even sent us word to call for them."[41]

At the end of 1917, from Charles's point of view, "the great British army was quite worn out, bereft of all power of attack and but little more of defence...That invaluable weapon, the tank, had been grossly misused and its great potentialities neglected. What general with imagination, armed with this powerful weapon, would have selected the swamps of Flanders for his operations?" After Cambrai (where tanks were first used successfully before the tide of battle turned), he went home on leave and then on an artillery course, rejoining his brigade in January 1918. But, having been through a great deal of hardship and strain and feeling he was getting a bit too old for front line work at forty-eight, he asked his brigadier-general if he could apply for a transfer home. He spent the rest of the war in command of the instructional brigade on Salisbury Plain and received the usual notice of thanks for his services in January 1919.

On March 21, 1918, Germany sought to capitalize on Russia's collapse by launching a major spring offensive on the Western Front with the aim of defeating Britain and France before U.S. forces arrived. They almost completely wiped out the 16th (Irish)

Division and the 36th (Ulster) Division due to Gen. Sir Hubert Gough's inadequate defense preparations. Britain's 5th Army fell back in a confused rout for forty miles. One third of the men were killed; over 6,400 of the 16th and over 6,300 of the 36th, which resulted in the Irish conscription crisis in April. Gough, who was a great favorite of Haig's, was dismissed from command of the 5th Army on April 5 for the failure of his army to hold the line and stem the German advance. Charles Head's friend William Parsons, the 5th earl of Rosse of Birr Castle, who, like Charles, had reentered service (as an officer in the Irish Guards) at the outbreak of war, was mortally wounded in this devastating assault. He died of his wounds on June 10, 1918, aged forty-four, leaving a young son and heir. Some of the other Lorrha, North Tipperary, and Birr Anglo-Irish families with ties to the Heads who provided many officers to the British Army in the War were the Stoneys, the Biddulphs, and the Trenches.

The British Parliament passed the Military Service Act imposing conscription on Ireland on April 18, 1918, provoking an immediate outcry throughout Nationalist Ireland. The Catholic hierarchy denounced the threat in the strongest terms, and members of the Irish Parliamentary Party withdrew from Parliament and returned to Dublin to make common cause with Sinn Féin in the anti-conscription campaign. Influenced by de Valera, Catholic bishops ordered the pledge against conscription to be read at every mass in every parish the following Sunday. The Trades Union Congress in Dublin ordered a complete shutdown to protest conscription. Except in Belfast, everything came to a standstill on April 23. In May, the Dublin Castle administration alleged that a "German Plot" existed between the Sinn Féin movement and the German Empire to start an armed insurrection in Ireland. The alleged but spurious conspiracy, which would have diverted the British war effort, was used to justify the internment of Sinn Féin leaders who were actively opposing attempts to introduce conscription in Ireland. But Irish conscription was spared by the rapid conclusion to the war over the next months. On August 8, the Allies, commanded since May by Marshall Foch, counter-attacked, initiating the Battle of Amiens (August 8-11), and advanced eight miles before German resistance stiffened. Facing concerted Allied attacks all along the Western

Front, including the American-led St. Mihiel Offensive (September 12-15) and the Meuse-Argonne campaign (September 26-November 11), the German forces now began to fall apart. On November 9, the Kaiser having fled, Germany declared itself a republic and two days later signed the armistice.

The war had cost the four nations of the Central Powers three and a half million men. It had cost the thirteen nations of the Allies and the United States (fighting as an associated nation) over five million.[42] Those statistics are, of course, just the generally agreed-upon military dead. Adding in civilians (including passengers on sunk vessels, victims of artillery and air raids, deaths from disease and starvation caused by the British blockade, etc.) pushes the human lives lost in the war up to about forty million, by some estimates. Millions more were maimed, physically and mentally. As the English military thinker John Keegan asked in his conclusion to his history of the war: "Why did a prosperous continent, at the height of its success as a source and agent of global wealth and power and at one of the peaks of its intellectual and cultural achievement, choose to risk all it had won for itself and all it had offered to the world in the lottery of a vicious and local internecine conflict?…and eventually to commit the totality of their young manhood to mutual and essentially pointless slaughter?"[43] My grandfather questioned a great deal but perhaps did not have sufficient separation from the events themselves to question the point of it all, the justification for starting and continuing that terrible war.

Derrylahan in Wartime

In a section of his book on the Great War, Paul Fussell remarks that "what makes experience in the Great War unique and gives it a special freight of irony is the ridiculous proximity of the trenches to home." During "their two-week leaves from the front, the officers rode the same Channel boats they had known in peacetime and the presence of the same porters and stewards ('Nice to serve you again, Sir') provided a ghastly pretence of normality."[44] Much of the poetry and prose by those who experienced "this stinking world of sticky trickling earth" recalls with considerable sentimentality the beautiful untrammeled English countryside. It must have been agonizing to have to leave family and friends and return to the hell that was the Western Front.

Loving Derrylahan as he did (see chapters 16, 17, and 19), Charles might have made every effort to spend his longer leaves there. However, it seems that he rarely returned home to North Tipperary during his active service in France; it was simply too far and perhaps too difficult for a middle-aged soldier who needed to rest above all. His daughter Betty recalled that her father was once staying in a hotel at Bray while on leave from France when it burned down, with the loss of all his uniform, an embarrassment and perhaps an additional disincentive. Instead, Margery, and often the children too, and once or twice even servants from Derrylahan, would travel to London to meet him at her mother's house during his leaves, as their daughters Betty and Grace recalled in their memories of their Derrylahan childhood written forty years after they left for good in 1921. Grace remembered that they would run out into the garden to watch the Zeppelins fly over.

Most of Grace's and Betty's memories of their Arcadian childhood began after their father was recalled into the British Army in 1914. Left to run the farm and household, their mother wore her husband's cap backward as a symbol of his authority when on the farm. Grace dedicated her notes to her mother, "to whom all credit must be given for the way she tackled her life in Ireland...She was often all alone at Derrylahan except for her young children and her wild but devoted Irish servants for months, even years, during World War I." She had been brought up "in the proverbial lap of luxury with everything money and culture could provide, even to two years in a French school where she not only learned French fluently but also German, music and elocution—all attributes most unsuitable for a life of running and even working on a large Irish estate miles from anywhere..."

Betty's notes are the fullest, probably because she was older and closer to her mother. She would have been five at the outbreak of the war. Their brother, Michael (Mike), was born in 1912, so was too young to remember most of the incidents that Betty described. With their mother battling with household and farm work, the children were free to roam. Betty's lively account of how they spent their days outdoors at Derrylahan when they were not confined to the house for lessons with various governesses can be found in chapter 1. She described a lifestyle that the children never forgot—of careless play in the park and the nearby bog and on the farm, together and with local children, their naughtiness, and, unsaid by her, the comfort and security of their privileged circumstances. The girls loved to play in the hayloft, to climb over the wall into the kitchen garden to gorge on fruit, and to climb trees in the pleasure grounds. Betty described haymaking in the summer as "the best time of all" and recalled her love of June when the turf was cut and laid out to dry before being piled in a huge stack in the stable yard, as well as the general merriment when extra labor was brought in for the harvest.

During the war, the acreage of corn was increased—as a result of the government's compulsory tillage order in early 1917—and then a steam threshing machine would come and stay for a few days until the work was done. They had a Model T Ford before the war but gave it up when the chauffeur joined the army and bought a smart new trap and a pony. They traveled in this to Birr six miles away for shopping, to favorite picnic spots, and for all other expeditions. Betty recalled a number of accidents in the trap, particularly when the pony took fright at traffic and either ran away or reared up and broke the shafts.

Betty shared with her father a particular love for the bog, recalling with enthusiasm that she "went there a lot." Among the plants she described was "pretty, multi-colored bog cotton or sphagnum moss." Because the latter was used in hospital dressings during the war, they collected masses of it, laid it out to dry, and then picked it over to get rid of bits of heather, etc. Other war efforts involved weekly sewing parties at various houses, including Derrylahan, to make clothes for refugees: "I don't know what my sewing was like but I always had to do some and can remember making grey flannel dresses at a very early age." Grace also remembered those journeys by pony and trap to sewing parties where she was made to hold bandages as they were rolled while "Mummy entertained the sowers by reciting some lines in French."

Margery Head faced all too frequent problems with the quarrelsome household staff and farm workers during the war. Several of the most trustworthy employees, such as the young Protestant chauffeur and the Catholic gamekeeper, were serving with the Army and had been replaced by some difficult and incompetent characters. One day, the cook had a row with the herd[sman] so he threw the day's precious bucket of milk over her. After the war, two of the men started knifing each other and had to be separated. The Protestant chauffeur, who was back from the war, intervened, the beginning of a long-lasting deadly feud which explained why he decided to move to England with the Heads after the burning.

Both women recalled an occasion when their mother's plans went awry for one of their crossings to England. "The cab we had hired arrived so late that we missed the train and boat," Betty remembered. "When we set out next day we heard that if we had gone as intended we would have been on the Leinster which was sunk that very day by a German submarine!" *RMS Leinster* served as the Kingstown (now Dún Laoghaire) to Holyhead mailboat until it was torpedoed and sunk by the German submarine UB-123 on October 10, 1918, while bound for Holyhead. Five hundred and one people died, the highest ever casualty rate on an Irish-owned ship, of which eleven were from Co. Tipperary and one from Lorrha.[45] No wonder the girls never forgot this near miss.

"Towards the end of the war," remembered Betty, "the I.R.A. became troublesome and twice during the night we were raided for arms. The first time my Mother asked them not to go upstairs as I was ill, so they did not find my father's revolver. They looked in the hall cupboard where the shot guns were kept but did not realize they were in cases so did not take them. In the hall there was an immensely long and quite useless gun that my father had brought back from China and for some reason they took that! It took three men to hold it, resting it on their shoulders and another to fire it. We always hoped to find it thrown away in the bushes but never did...Living so far from help and without a telephone it was nerve-racking for our Mother who never knew when strange men would come at night, and the nearest man was the groom who lived half a mile away in the stable yard. The bachelor gardener had not come then and when he did we thought he belonged to the I.R.A. too." Terror was even visible in daytime when local men were often seen drilling in the park.[46]

This was the situation that Charles Head returned home to in January 1919. Many of his friends and neighbors had been killed or seriously wounded in the war, leaving sad gaps locally. Moreover, the December election had brought stunning results under a new and greatly expanded electorate following passage on February 6, 1918, of the Representation of the People Act, which added all males over twenty without qualification and women over thirty who met some basic property requirements. The Nationalist Home Rule party was decimated, reduced to just six seats, and Sinn Féin won 73 out of 105 seats in Ireland. The Unionists held firm in the north-east with 26 seats, but throughout the rest of the country a major political change had taken place. For the first time in almost seven hundred years of English occupation, a party demanding total sovereign independence for Ireland dominated the political scene and Irish public opinion.[47] Ignoring Westminster, the Sinn Féin members met in Dublin and declared themselves to be the Dáil or Parliament of an independent Irish Republic; a provisional government was set up, led by de Valera with Constance Markiewicz as minister for labour. While it was not recognized by Britain, "it had the legality of being backed by a majority of the elected representatives of the Irish people."[48] On January 31, 1919, *An t'Óglach*, the journal of the Irish Volunteers, ominously declared war on the British Empire.

Chapter 19

"British First, Irish Second":[1]
War of Independence

ANOTHER MANSION BURNED. Derrylahan Reduced to Ashes. Col. Head 'Too Friendly with the English.'
—*King's County Chronicle*, July 7, 1921.

In many ways, the revolutionary period from 1919 to 1923 realized the fears of Irish landlords which had been growing since the land war began some forty years previously. During these years, landlords, largely because of their socio-political, economic and religious backgrounds, were to suffer outrage and intimidation on a scale the like of which their class had not experienced in living memory, not even at the height of the land war in the 1880s…A major feature of this intimidation was the burning of big houses.
—Terence Dooley, *The Decline of the Big House in Ireland*, 191.

"It was a great joy to get home again to the seeming peace and green of Ireland, after the mud and squalor of France and camps in England and take up again the old life interrupted by the war," Charles Head wrote in his 1943 memoir. In the chapter titled "Last Days in Ireland," he recalls being cheered by the abundance of fresh food and the country's booming prosperity. Before long, however, "it became clear that this optimistic view was not justified." Perhaps because he was absent on the European battlefields as Irish popular opinion turned against Britain following the execution of the leaders of the Easter Rising and the failure to implement Home Rule, he seems to have been unaware at the time of the more recent changes in public opinion or chose not to address them at this point in his memoir. Instead, he blamed the growing malaise in the country on farmers who "were nearly content," except for "the lure of acquiring their farms, without paying further instalments of rent." Beyond that he criticized "the large number of young farmers, labourers, and shop-boys, wishing to justify their non-participation in the war [World War I, or the Great War]," who were "ignorant, conceited, and easily manipulated," and therefore dangerous. The manipulators, in his opinion, were "the ferocious, bitter, fanatical haters of England, scheming, plotting, and working ceaselessly, not for the good of Ireland, but for the mortal injury of England." As always an advocate for law and order, he blamed the failure to stand up against these radical forces on the vacillations and incompetence of the British administration at Dublin Castle and on his former allies, the Southern Unionists, who, at the 1917 Irish Convention and since the war, were either "advocating schemes of compromise," or "proving themselves very broken reeds," or had become "unconscious abettors of Sinn Fein."[2]

In his penultimate chapter, "Home Rule," however, Charles noted that:

> The Irish rebellion of 1916 furnished arguments both pro and con Home Rule ...The war-slogans, self-determination and the rights of little nations, further weighted the scales in favour of Home Rule, and, an important factor, the Irish southern Unionist population was on the whole quite reconciled to its [Home Rule's] adoption. Mr. Lloyd George with his Insurance bill and his budget had made more converts to Home Rule than Parnell and Redmond; and the heavy imperial taxation, necessitated by the war, swelled their numbers. So when the war ended some form of Home Rule was inevitable, and the time was ripe for it. A complete change of conditions had taken place since Gladstone's day; the most important one, after perhaps the reconciliation of the Irish Unionists, being that the land question was practically settled.

For Head, it was Sinn Féin's proclamation of an Irish republic and its stubborn refusal "to negotiate on any other terms" that led to the "squalid, horrible struggle [that] ensued."[3]

Terence Dooley strongly disagrees with Head's contention that "the land question was practically settled," arguing in his 'The Land for the People' that, despite the Land Acts, land hunger remained intense in Ireland. Tens of thousands of landless men, the younger sons of farmers, were denied access to landownership by the realities, or accidents, of birth. Many of these were agricultural laborers who became deeply envious of farmers, particularly during the war years from 1914-1918, when their profits grew dramatically as the unprecedented need for agricultural products increased the demand for tillage. Then there were those who had been evicted since the beginning of the Land Wars and considered it to be their right to have their holdings returned. Indeed, the Great War had greatly increased agrarian unrest. The virtual closure of emigration outlets meant that a higher percentage of discontented and under-employed young men were trapped in rural Ireland. In addition, the war virtually halted land purchases after the British Treasury curtailed advances since its priority was to finance the war. Lastly, a considerable number of purchases made under the 1903 and 1909 Land Acts had been delayed due to logistical difficulties.[4]

From Charles's point of view, "the year 1919 was quite comfortable": "we shot in the winter without much interference and talked of reviving the polo club the following year. Farming flourished and the idea of serious political trouble seemed ridiculous." Avid reader of newspapers that he was, this seems like another instance of "convenient amnesia." As he surely knew, a great deal was happening that year beyond his sheltered demesne in the far north of Co. Tipperary that did indeed indicate serious political trouble, some of which may only have become significant in hindsight. As historian Michael Hopkinson has noted, "Of all counties, Tipperary, and particularly south Tipperary, has been most strongly identified with the War of Independence. The fact that the South Tipperary Brigade [of the Irish Republican Army (IRA)] was the first to go to war meant that events there have been better recorded and more graphically described than those in most other places."[5]

January 21, 1919, became significant in Nationalist Irish history for two events, one centered in Dublin, the other in Tipperary. On that date, all the Sinn Féin members elected for Irish constituencies were summoned to meet for the first time in Dublin's Mansion

House to constitute the Dáil Éireann, or national assembly, of the Irish Republic. Those members who were not imprisoned for involvement in the 1918 so-called German Plot attended.[6] Since Éamon de Valera was again in prison, Cathal Brúgha, now minister of defense in the Dáil Éireann government, was in the chair. Among several founding initiatives that day was the reading of Ireland's Declaration of Independence which linked the Irish Republic that was voted for in December 1918 with that "proclaimed in Dublin on Easter Monday, 1916, by the Irish Republican Army, acting on behalf of the Irish people." Thus the failed Easter Rising, led as it was by a few extreme Nationalists and supported by a minority of Irish people at that time, would become the origin myth of the Irish Republic. The Unionists ignored the new assembly, which had no standing in British law and was soon to be proscribed as illegal. Following de Valera's escape from prison on February 3, he attended the Second Dáil in April, was elected president of the nascent government, and set out shortly thereafter on a fundraising scheme in the United States.[7]

The second significant event on January 21 was the notorious ambush of two Royal Irish Constabulary (RIC) officers escorting a load of gelignite to a quarry in Soloheadbeg, South Tipperary. Generally accepted as the beginning of the War of Independence, it resulted in the death of those innocent and locally well-liked policemen, both Catholic and one a widower with four children. The ambush party comprised Irish Volunteers acting on their own initiative, two of whom became notorious. Dan Breen, who grew up in a poor family in Co. Tipperary, was sworn into the Irish Republican Brotherhood in 1912 and the Irish Volunteers in 1914. Seán Treacy, a local man and one of the leaders of the Third Tipperary Brigade of the Irish Republican Army during the Anglo-Irish War, was imprisoned for two years after the Easter Rising. He wrote to his fellow travelers in South Tipperary, "Deport all in favour of the enemy out of the country. Deal sternly with those who try to resist. Maintain the strictest discipline, there must be no running to kiss mothers goodbye." Breen later wrote a self-indulgent memoir, *My Fight for Irish Freedom* (1924), a bible of the traditional nationalist interpretation, in which he argued that the South Tipperary Brigade had shown the way by triggering the move away from the tactics of passive resistance. The Volunteer GHQ in Dublin had not authorized the action, however, and it was widely criticized by the Catholic church and in the press. Breen had initially indicated that the intention was only to capture the explosives and detonators. In other words, as historian Michael Hopkinson has written, it was an operation that went wrong.[8]

On January 24, South Tipperary was placed under martial law. In the meantime, Breen and Treacy hid out with supporters in Counties Clare and Limerick. When they rescued Seán Hogan, one of their colleagues in the South Tipperary Brigade, from a train in Knocklong, Co. Limerick, on May 13, two more RIC officers were killed and Breen and Treacy were wounded. They took shelter briefly that summer in Lorrha parish while recovering, according to local historian Seán Hogan, (apparently no relation to the rescued insurgent).[9] In April 1919, Sinn Féin had made the first attempt to coordinate nationally a campaign of "social ostracisation of people," or specifically the RIC, although not yet of physical violence against them.[10]

The Sinn Féin leaders had high hopes that the Paris Peace Conference would take up their cause. The Dáil chose three envoys, Count Plunket, Arthur Griffith, and Éamon de Valera, to present the Irish case at the conference, but they were never given safe passage to attend. An Irish delegation led by Sean T. O'Kelly, a future president of Ireland, did go to Paris, but was not admitted to the conference.[11] Irish Americans were determined, however, to force the cause. In mid-February, 5,000 nationalist delegates attended the third Irish Race Convention in Philadelphia's mammoth Second Regiment Armory. It was organized by the Friends of Irish Freedom to "listen to two days of oratory on Ireland's sufferings, England's sins, and the hopes that President Woodrow Wilson had aroused." Headline speakers included Cardinal James Gibbons of Baltimore, Cardinal William Henry O'Connell of Boston, Archbishop Dennis Joseph Dougherty of Philadelphia, and the Republican senator for Idaho William Borah. *The Irish Press* of Philadelphia, whose editor and publisher were deeply involved in planning the convention, reported that "one of the most important steps taken by the Irish Race Convention...was its demand that President Wilson secure from the Peace Conference for the envoys chosen by the Dáil

Éireann…the same status and recognition which have been accorded to those of other small nations." The convention would also send delegates to Paris "who will assist the representatives of the Irish Republic in securing for the Irish Government recognition of its sovereign claims."[12]

President Wilson met "extremely reluctantly" in New York with a delegation from the convention on March 4, when he was back in America during a break in the Paris Conference. When the Irish Americans entered his room, "they were so insistent," Wilson said, "that I had hard work keeping my temper." Indeed, there was never any realistic hope that the Irish cause would be heard in Paris. Speaking for the American Commission to Negotiate Peace, its press officer stated that the Irish question was a domestic affair of the British Empire and neither [President Wilson] nor any other foreign leader had any right to interfere or to advocate any policy. The failure in Paris drove Irish Americans to oppose American participation in the new League of Nations, which was fervently supported by Wilson as the best measure against future wars and included in all Allied treaties with nations of the Central Powers.[13] Even Republican Senator Henry Cabot Lodge, arch-opponent of Irish interests in Boston, switched support to the Irish nationalist cause, driven by his well-broadcast detestation of Woodrow Wilson.[14]

The Head family of Derrylahan had begun the year thinking that life would return to normal after the stress of the Great War. However, violence reached North Tipperary on September 2, 1919, when RIC officer Sergeant Philip Brady, a married man with six children and more than twenty-eight years of unblemished service, was assassinated only four days after he arrived from Enniskillen about half a mile from the quiet village of Lorrha, near Derrylahan, to take charge of the small RIC barracks there. Seán Hogan claims that a local IRA leader sought the support of South Tipperary fugitives Dan Breen and Seán Treacy for a plan to attack a police patrol when they stayed in Lorrha that summer.[15] Seamus J. King, a well-known and prolific local historian, has written a full and sympathetic account of Brady's murder, published in a collection of his articles in *Lorrha Miscellany*. According to King, Charles Head was the presiding magistrate at the monthly ordinary court held at Lorrha when he proposed a resolution condemning the murder of Sergeant Brady, which he saw, correctly, as a general conspiracy against the police. The other magistrates agreed with him. At Brady's funeral, the parish priest declared that "Every right thinking man in the church and state condemns this foul crime."[16] The Catholic Church would continue to condemn violent acts committed by both sides throughout the conflict.

Six weeks later, a party of armed and disguised men entered Annaghbeg House near Nenagh demanding arms from the frail seventy-three-year-old owner Anna Minnitt—the last of a long line of Anglo-Irish Protestant landlords in Co. Tipperary—but found only a double-barrel shotgun and a rifle. As previously noted, the Head family was also raided for arms at Derrylahan two or three times toward the end of the Great War before Charles Head returned home. In the Annaghbeg case, eight local men were arrested, but when they appeared in court—as large crowds of supporters gathered outside the court singing nationalist songs—they refused to recognize it, would not take off their caps in the dock, and lit cigarettes. One of the eight had been coerced to testify, but he and his family were boycotted. The boycott dissuaded others from giving evidence before the crown courts, helping to break down the local British judicial system.[17]

The IRA became noticeably more audacious and daring in 1920 by targeting the police and the judicial system. Lloyd George's government introduced the Government of Ireland Bill to the House of Commons on February 25, making provision for two Irish parliaments, one for Northern Ireland (six counties) and one for Southern Ireland (twenty-six counties), each responsible for its own domestic affairs. The last of the Home Rule bills, it was also the first to give form to the partition of Ireland. The Unionist delegates of Monaghan, Cavan and Donegal were bitterly disillusioned with the Ulster Unionist Council's decision to exclude them from partition and the Monaghan delegates resigned.[18] The bill was rejected out of hand by the nationalists and southern Unionists; Lord Farnham of the Cavan Unionists told Edward Carson that they were being handed over to a Dublin parliament.[19] It enraged Sinn Féin and gave the militant IRA led by Michael Collins dominance over the political non-revolutionary element. The country was now committed to a violent rebellion against British rule. On April 4, the IRA raided and burned income tax offices, destroying their records all over Ireland, and reducing the administration to revenues from customs and excise. In the first three months of 1920 alone, the RIC evacuated approximately five hundred police barracks and huts in outlying areas, leaving local residents even more vulnerable. By the end of June, the IRA had destroyed 424 of these abandoned facilities to prevent their future re-occupation, while a further sixteen occupied barracks were destroyed and another twenty-nine damaged.[20]

Among the RIC barracks attacked was that of Borrisokane, a few miles south of Derrylahan. Supplied with arms from Dublin, about two hundred men assaulted the barracks on June 26. After about two hours, when it seemed as if the police inside were on the verge of surrendering, the IRA commander ordered a withdrawal from the burning building, leaving behind two wounded insurgents. The building was so badly damaged that it was evacuated the next day. In the local council elections for the Borrisokane area in May, Rody Cleary had headed the poll for Sinn Féin with 663 votes, and all four candidates elected for the area were members of Sinn Féin.[21] Two of Rody Cleary's nephews, James and Thomas Devaney of Pallas, Toomevara, were active IRA members and were shot dead by Crown forces in separate incidents. As a prominent Sinn Féin councilor and a judge of the local arbitration court, Rody Cleary was himself a target for the Crown forces. He spent much of the latter part of 1920 on the run and was arrested shortly before Christmas. He was detained at the military barracks at Nenagh for a fortnight but was released unharmed.[22]

By the summer of 1920, law-and-order was on the brink of collapse. Summer assizes failed across the South and West; trials by jury could not be held because jurors would not attend. The collapse of the British court system demoralized the RIC, and many officers resigned or retired. By then, Sinn Féin courts were operating all over the country. On July 9, the Nenagh district arbitration court met publicly for the first time in Nenagh Courthouse, the property of the Tipperary County Council, which had come under the control of the Sinn Féin when they swept the local elections in January. This court met numerous times in public before it was suppressed by the military authorities and driven underground for the duration of the War of Independence.[23]

In June 1920, the RIC county inspector painted a dismal picture of the "social war" being waged against them:

> Sinn Fein courts have set aside Petty Sessions courts to a great extent...The Police cannot go on patrol except in considerable force and on the slightest opportunity they are held up. It is difficult for them to get provisions and fuel & light in many places. Their condition of life in barracks with light and air shut out by sand bags, shell boxes and steel shutters is very irksome and disagreeable. At night they cannot sleep during the dark hours apprehending an attack at any time. No one speaks to them in a friendly way. No one will give them any information...Men cannot travel by rail armed, and transfers cannot be carried out by rail, owing to the munition strike...The old form of police control is practically beaten to the ropes and it is as well to recognize the situation.[24]

Coinciding with the Irish War of Independence, major sectarian conflict broke out in Belfast. This was due partly to the IRA killing of a northern RIC police officer in Cork and partly because of competition over jobs due to the high unemployment rate. On July 21, 1920, loyalists marched on the Harland and Wolff shipyards and forced over seven thousand Catholic and left-wing Protestant workers from their jobs. The result was sectarian rioting, loss of life, and both Catholics and Protestants being expelled from their homes. In response, the Dáil imposed a boycott on goods produced in Belfast starting on August 6, but that proved to be ineffective. Further violence in August led to the revival of the Ulster Volunteer Force and recruitment of an auxiliary police force, the Ulster Special Constabulary, for counter-insurgency purposes.

The hawks in the British Coalition Government now prevailed and, on August 9, the Restoration of Order in Ireland Bill received Royal Assent. The bill gave Dublin Castle the power to govern by regulation, to replace the criminal courts with courts martial, to re-place coroners' inquests with military courts of inquiry, and to pun-ish disaffected local governments by withholding their grants of money. While the wave of barrack attacks ended late that summer, they were replaced by ambushes on police and military convoys and patrols. By the end of the year, eight southern counties were officially under martial law and recruitment in England had begun to reinforce the RIC with demobilized and unemployed army and navy war veterans. Most of these recruits were from London and the surrounding area and had urban working-class backgrounds, while the majority of the regular RIC were from farming back-grounds. These special constabulary recruits were nicknamed the Black and Tans due to their mixture of bottle-green RIC pants and army khaki jackets until regular RIC uniforms were made available. At the same time, former army officers, mostly non-commissioned officers (NCOs), were recruited for a new paramilitary Auxiliary Division, whose uniforms were dark blue.[25]

From then on, the humiliated Irish government and the RIC, particularly the Black and Tan element, carried out tougher and vindictive initiatives, raising the level of violence in this national conflict. Most notorious of all were the armored Auxiliary divisions spread out all over the country, led from Dublin headquarters by a newly appointed and highly experienced former artillery officer, Major General—now Police Advisor—Henry H. Tudor. While the British Government claimed that the insurgency was being handled by the police, it was a force now shot through with army veterans, while the actual British Army was officially confined to barracks.

Charles Head in his account of that year appeared at first to have blinkers on about the state of the country. Sounding like an entitled landowner, he noted that "1920 also progressed without much disturbance till the winter, when game-shooting, a trusty barometer of the state of Irish affairs, was found to be a difficult and hardy occupation. Cartridges could then only be obtained by permission of the Dublin police, and had to be taken charge of personally for conveyance where required. Permits were needed for keeping guns. Poaching became rife, and many shooters were forcibly deprived of their guns by armed men." He managed to keep shooting "constantly and without interference" because the commander of the local British troops kept his gun in barracks (Crinkill Barracks in Birr) and would bring it with him when they shot together at a meeting spot generally chosen for them by one of his patrols. "There was undoubtedly some risk attached to this pursuit, either of losing one's gun or of personal unpleasantness or injury," but "without knowledge of our plans any ill-wishers we had could not get together strong, or soon, enough to stop us."[26] It would certainly be held against Head that he was on friendly terms with the British Army officers stationed at Crinkill Barracks.

Charles's continuing account of personal experiences indicates the great inconvenience caused by the innumerable strikes that year. In a lengthy anecdote about his struggle to return home from a trip to England, he must have been referring to the General Strike called on April 12 in support of hunger strikes by prisoners in Dublin's Mountjoy Prison and the fatal shooting of the Sinn Féin mayor of Cork, Tomas MacCurtain, on March 20 by assassins who were almost certainly members of the RIC. The strike had shut down the docks, trams, trains, taxis, and hotels. After people meeting some of the passengers tied the ferry up to the pier at Kingstown (Dún Laoghaire), Charles carried his heavy bag to the rooms of a relative, who then drove him along "weirdly" deserted roads to Dublin. There he managed to get a room at the Kildare Street Club, which "cheerful as usual, felt like a ship in the ocean cut off from contact with the outer world." He then got a ride with a club member driving to his own home in Tipperary. It was an unpleasant journey with men in some villages apparently moving to stop them until the driver put his foot down and sped away. Charles's own car was supposed to meet him at their point of divergence but was not there when they arrived. The owner of the town's hotel grudgingly provided him with a meal, then warmed up a little to the point where they "got into a political discussion, amicable but futile, as all the stock arguments and catchwords which he knew by heart were impervious to my qualifying suggestions." He tried to hire the only available car in that town but was told it was booked to pick up released prisoners in Dublin. His car eventually arrived, having been delayed at various roadblocks.[27]

The war entered its bloodiest phase following the arrest on

August 12, 1920, of the new republican mayor of Cork, playwright, author, and political zealot Terence MacSwiney, who was accused of sedition. On September 20, the IRA ambushed a truck carrying British soldiers in Dublin. Three of the soldiers were killed, the first in the city since the 1916 Easter Rising. Eighteen-year-old Kevin Barry was arrested at the scene, charged with murder and subsequently hanged. The following night, 100 to 150 Black and Tans sacked the coastal town of Balbriggan 34 miles north of Dublin in revenge for the killing of District Inspector Burke and his brother Sergeant Burke earlier in the day. They killed two men, looted and burned four public houses, destroyed a hosiery factory, and damaged or destroyed forty-nine houses. The next day, five RIC men were killed in an ambush at Rineen in Co. Clare. The local resident magistrate (RM) was then kidnapped, shot dead, and his body dumped on a nearby beach. In response, the Black and Tans ran amok, killing six civilians in nearby towns, and burning twenty-six buildings, including two town halls. The catalog of atrocities and reprisals, particularly in the South and Southwest, was beyond calculation, with ordinary Irish people caught and suffering in the middle.

Author and historian Mark Bence-Jones felt that the fearful brutality of the Black and Tan reprisals led directly to the burning of country houses and that September 1920 was the month Anglo-Irish writer Elizabeth Bowen had in mind when she wrote her novel *The Last September*, first published in 1929.[28] At their country estate, Danielstown in County Cork, the protagonists Sir Richard Naylor and his wife, Lady Myra, and their friends maintain a skeptical attitude to the events going on around them but, behind the façade of tennis parties and army camp dances, they all know that the end of British rule in the south of Ireland is approaching and, with it, the demise of a way of life that had survived for centuries. Bowen's own beloved family home, Bowen's Court in Co. Cork, remained untouched throughout "The Troubled Times," as she called them in a later preface about her book. The preface explores the ramifications for witnesses of "Ambushes, arrests, captures and burning, reprisals and counter-reprisals" as "The British patrolled and hunted; the Irish planned, lay in wait, and struck." "I was the child of the house from which Danielstown derives" Bowen concludes, "nevertheless, so often in my mind's eye did I see it [Bowen's Court] burning that the terrible last event in *The Last September* is more real than anything I have lived through."[29]

The Bowens' history in Ireland was similar to the Heads'. One of Bowen's ancestors served with William Henry Head on a grand jury and another married a member of the Derry Castle branch of the Head family. However, Elizabeth Bowen lived chiefly in London with summer visits as a child to Bowen's Court before she inherited the place in 1929, while Charles Head and his family lived year-round at Derrylahan and were inevitably caught up in events. With some misgivings, Charles attended a meeting of magistrates which was convened at the instigation of the nationalist magistrates "to consider, and urge, steps that ought to be taken to restore peace to the country." He was sure that it would be utilized for political propaganda but hoped that "some good might come of it." As he had feared, a great majority of the magistrates failed to appear and "those of Unionist tendencies who did come had no remedial suggestions to offer." The spokesman for a "knot of Nationalist magistrates...read out a long typewritten travesty of modern Irish history," then "called on us to resolve that a single Irish Government, for the whole of Ireland, should be established immediately; that the Lord Mayor of Cork, then hunger-striking in prison, should be released; that the 'pogrom' and 'blood-thirsty vendetta' in Belfast should instantly be suppressed; and that failing the achievement of these three objects within one month, we should all resign our commissions of the Peace." The Belfast vendetta referred to vengeance exacted by Carson's Ulster Volunteers in the North against the minority of Sinn Féiners who lived there. This reflected the Ulster Volunteers' abhorrence of the Dáil's claim to be a Parliament for All Ireland, enflamed and exasperated as they were by accounts of events in the South.[30]

It was a sad irony that in this same courthouse in January 1847, in the depth of the agonies caused by the potato famine, Charles's father, William Henry Head, gave his impassioned speech before a gathering of all parties, both Catholic and Protestant, to consider "the present distressed state of Ireland, and to petition Parliament to adopt speedily such remedial measures as the calamitous condition of the country so imperatively requires." "...I think it peculiarly incumbent on all classes of Irishmen in this country to unite," he began then, to general approval (see chapter 14).

Instead, Ireland was now torn apart and the world was watching. The death of hunger striker Terence MacSwiney in Brixton Prison, London, on October 25 after seventy-three days of suffering, closely followed by the death of another Cork hunger striker and Kevin Barry's execution at Mountjoy Prison just days later, brought public opinion to fever-pitch. Barry's treatment and death attracted great international attention and attempts were made by U.S. and Vatican officials to secure a reprieve. Thirty thousand people filed past MacSwiney's bier in St. George's Church in Southwark, London, and his vast and moving funeral in Cork brought further worldwide attention. Some 75,000 people attended a memorial for MacSwiney at the Polo Grounds in New York City, and MacSwiney's wife and sister traveled to America to testify before a committee in Washington.[31] Sinn Féin leader Arthur Griffith called off the remaining hunger strikes in November.

Despite orders from the Sinn Féin administration that justices of the peace must resign their commissions, many loyalists refused to do so, at great risk to their lives, while others resigned or refrained from actually sitting on the bench. Charles Head was among those who continued to attend petty sessions at the courthouses where he was authorized to sit. These included the burned out Borrisokane courthouse, "a substantial imposing building," where, thinking it was his duty to stick to his post, he sat in its ruins, sometimes with an RM but mostly alone, with a bodyguard of Black and Tans. They heard the most trivial cases since "people were forbidden to bring their disputes to our jurisdiction, but had to submit them to the Sinn Féin courts, which were quite openly established and attended by all the local solicitors."[32] Perhaps to their surprise, many Unionist landowners discovered that, as long as they were allowed to operate, these Sinn Féin courts respected even their own rights of property. The Sinn Féin propaganda sheet, the *Irish Bulletin*, was able to report by the middle of June 1920 that 84 arrests of criminals in twenty-four counties had been made by Republican police in the past thirteen days. At the same time, a Sinn Féin Land Commission held inquiries in the parts of the country worst affected by land hunger and hardship to see what could be done to assist genuine cases.[33]

By now, Black and Tans were vilified in Ireland and liberal England too for their brutality and unrestrained looting. Charles acknowledged their excesses while coming partly to their defense. Ever the loyal army officer, he reminded the readers of his memoir that these ex-soldiers were hailed as heroes in the Great War and were by the time of his writing "highly respected members of the British Legion at Armistice services." But, he continued, "No one can defend—or wants to—some of their earlier actions, which were the acts of a wild lot of undisciplined men, exasperated by incidents and methods to which they were unaccustomed." But he considered that their later, more disciplined, conduct was mild in comparison to methods the police in any other country under similar circumstances would have used.[34] The popular Irish claim made at the time that most of the men serving in the Black and Tans had criminal records and had been recruited straight from British prisons is incorrect as a criminal record would have disqualified anyone from working as a policeman. The vast majority of the men serving in the Black and Tans were veterans of the First World War, including Irishmen, who were having trouble finding jobs, and most of them were driven by economic reasons to join the Temporary Constables.[35]

The Black and Tans were not subject to strict discipline in their first months and, as a result, their deaths at the hands of the IRA in 1920 were often repaid with arbitrary reprisals against the civilian population. In the summer of 1920, the Black and Tans burned and sacked many small towns and villages in Ireland, beginning with Tuam in Co. Galway in July 1920 and also including Trim, Balbriggan, Knockcroghery, Thurles, and Templemore, among many others. In November 1920, the Tans "besieged" Tralee in revenge for the IRA abduction and killing of two local RIC men. They closed all the businesses in the town, let no food in for a week, and shot dead three local civilians. On November 14, the Tans were suspected of abducting and murdering a Roman Catholic priest, Father Michael Griffin, in Galway. His body was found in a bog in Barna a week later. On the night of December 11, 1920, they sacked Cork, destroying a large part of the city center.

Respected author Robert Kee has written of the Black and Tans' actions, "…it is necessary to remember that they were reprisals for things that had been done to the police, and that the majority of the personnel of the RIC remained, to the end, Irish…The increasingly brutal behavior of the police, and the very rough Black and Tan reprisal campaign which was soon to develop, grew out of a situation in which an Irishman could have a shotgun discharged into his knee simply for joining the RIC or be killed while sitting drinking in uniform in a bar, or, having been shot in the back while on routine patrol, be finished off while lying on the ground asking for mercy. The total of RIC deaths for 1920 alone amounted to well over one hundred, with 170 wounded."[36] J. H. Bernard, the former Church of Ireland archbishop of Ireland and then provost of TCD, wrote to a friend, "It is to be regretted that some members of the auxiliary police are desperate men, but they were appointed to do desperate work, and if it were not for their activity in the south and west of Ireland no Protestant could live in security."[37]

By this time, the IRA had established a new style of operation with active service units, or flying columns. It was first put into practice in East Limerick and then enthusiastically adopted by Michael Collins at GHQ in Dublin. As Kee described it, "the flying column was a nucleus of about thirty-five men on full-time active service for specific periods, supplemented where necessary by part-time IRA men who otherwise continued with their normal civilian lives. This now became the chief defensive weapon of the IRA."[38] The IRA guerrillas had the unfair advantage of striking unexpectedly and of being indistinguishable from ordinary civilians and thus able to melt back into the supportive mass of the Irish nationalist population, whereas the RIC and Auxiliaries were all too easily identified and vulnerable in their uniforms.

A tentative suggestion of a peace initiative first reached Lloyd George in October 1920 from a private individual close to Sinn Féin leader Arthur Griffith; however, Lloyd George remained politically dependent on the Conservative, pro-Ulster, and anti-Irish Nationalist elements in his Coalition Government, while the subordinate government in Dublin Castle under Chief-Secretary Sir Hamar Greenwood was militaristic. Then the vague possibility of truce talks receded even further on November 21, when Michael Collins launched the assault that became known later as Bloody Sunday.[39] That morning, the IRA attacked eight addresses in central and south-central Dublin, killing eleven British Army officers and wounding five, one of them fatally. Some of those targeted were intelligence agents. A gun battle ensued between the IRA and Auxiliaries who stumbled across the scene of one assassination. Two Auxiliaries were killed and one IRA man captured. In response to the earlier IRA shootings that morning, police, Auxiliaries, and soldiers raided Croke Park, Dublin's Gaelic Athletic Association football ground, during a football match that afternoon. For reasons unknown, the police opened fire on the crowd, killing fourteen spectators, including a woman, a child, and a Tipperary forward. Tipperary newspapers used the words "Holocaust," "slaughter," and "massacre," to describe what happened in Croke Park.[40]

That evening, Dublin Castle claimed that the raiding party came under fire from rebel gunmen, a claim that was contradicted by the press and, later, by the findings of military courts of inquiry. Those findings were suppressed by the government, but the shootings were generally considered to be a reprisal. Also that evening, two of Michael Collins' most valued Dublin Brigade IRA men and an innocent West of Ireland football fan who had been arrested with them were "shot while trying to escape" Dublin Castle. Three days later, Sinn Féin leaders Arthur Griffith and Eoin MacNeill were arrested by the British in Dublin.

This astounding level of violence moved from Dublin to County Cork three days later when the West Cork Flying Column under Tom Barry, a former British serviceman (Royal Artillery, Charles Head's regiment), ambushed a patrol of Auxiliaries on a lonely site near Kilmichael, killing seventeen of them and severely wounding an eighteenth. On December 10, the British administration responded with a Proclamation of Martial Law in Cork, Kerry, Limerick, and Tipperary. The very next day, the center of Cork city was looted, wrecked, and burned by Crown forces, who prevented firefighters from tackling the blaze in reprisal for an IRA ambush in the city. During that action, the Auxiliaries shot two IRA men dead in their beds. The next ambush occurred at Kilcommon Cross in North Tipperary when four British soldiers were killed and three wounded. During the remainder of that terrible winter, the Government of Ireland Bill was enacted, creating the provinces of Northern Ireland and Southern Ireland, each with its own parliament, Éamon de Valera returned to Dublin from the U.S., and martial law was extended to Counties Clare, Kilkenny, Waterford, and Kilkenny.

In the first three months of 1921, the Dublin Castle administration revealed a change of attitude by dismissing 208 Black and Tans and 59 Auxiliaries as unsuitable and removing more than fifty from the force as a result of prosecutions or sentencing by court martial. The *Freeman's Journal* reckoned that there were 707 civilians killed from all causes between January 1 and July 11, 1921 and 756 wounded. Kee thinks that it would not be an exaggeration to say that well over a hundred of these dead were "spies' shot by the IRA, 73 of them between January 1 and April 1 alone. For instance, on January 28, Mrs. Lindsay, an elderly Unionist woman in West Cork, tipped off British troops about an IRA ambush she had seen being prepared on the Macroom-Cork road. The soldiers killed two IRA men and captured five of them. They were executed later under martial law. The local IRA kidnapped Mrs. Lindsay and her chauffeur-butler, charged them with being spies, and shot them after the IRA men were executed. The IRA reprisals continued the next day with the killing of six unarmed soldiers in the streets of Cork.[41]

As the *Irish Times* wrote in February, it and other daily newspapers had become a nightmare, recording as they did in every edition, callous and brutal individual killings on both sides, a catalog of horrors for which there seemed to be no escape. "The whole country runs with blood," wrote the *Times*. "Unless it is stopped and stopped soon every prospect of political settlement and material prosperity will perish and our children will inherit a wilderness." The bodies of "spies" bore warning messages, such as "Tried by court martial and found guilty—All others beware—IRA" or "Convicted Spy. The penalty for all who associate with Auxiliary Cadets, Black and Tans and RIC—IRA Beware." These "spies" were sometimes British officers or soldiers, but they were more often ordinary Irishmen, laborers or farmers of all ages.[42] In his 1997 book *Crisis and Decline*, TCD historian R. B. McDowell, focusing on loyalist Southern Protestants and a lifelong Unionist himself, listed page after page of atrocities, murders and burnings throughout the twenty-six counties. The incidents were drawn from his close study of the *Irish Times*, the criminal injuries records of the Irish Grants Committee at the Public Record Office in London, and numerous other archival records. He recorded the testimonies of ordinary Unionists—farmers, shopkeepers, policemen, and others—who sought compensation.[43]

Burnings of houses in a tit for tat on both sides were a constant threat. There was no class discrimination among the victims. The loss of a family home was always tragic, whether the residence was modest or grand. Summerhill, the dramatic hilltop Palladian mansion in Co. Meath, was one of the first Big Houses in Ireland to be burned. Its owner, Colonel Rowley, heir to Lord Langfeld, had been living in England since December 1919, so the house was occupied by the butler and a few servants at the time. On the night of February 4, thirty or forty raiders broke down the back door, seized about 30 gallons of petrol, poured it over the floors, and set the house on fire. The servants hid in the grounds, too frightened to call for help until it was too late to save the building and all its contents. Estimated damages were £200,000. Dublin Castle reported that Summerhill was burned to prevent occupation by British forces. An IRA leader said later that its burning was imperative because of its strategic position on high ground overlooking the principal road to the west.[44] Occupation or expected occupation by the Auxiliaries made other houses targets for burning, including Templemore Abbey, southeast of Nenagh—one of the finest houses in Ireland. A company of Auxiliaries had been based there since 1920 and, when they departed the Abbey in May 1921, the local IRA brigade was ordered to burn the house so that it could not be used if British forces were to return.[45]

On the night of March 6-7, 1921, George Clancy, Mayor of Limerick, and Michael O'Callaghan, the former mayor, were shot dead by masked men who burst into their houses, a reprisal apparently triggered by the killing of RIC Sergeant James Maguire the day before. The murderers were almost certainly Black and Tans or Auxiliaries, or both.[46] Charles Head had his first bad experience that month when conveying a party to serve on the Grand Jury at

Nenagh. A huge and beautiful sycamore was cut down at the Derrylahan lodge, damaging the wall. This was despite the presence of a lodge keeper, who was either intimidated or an IRA sympathizer. Charles wrote yet another of his numerous letters to the *Irish Times*, this time arguing that the forces of disorder in Ireland should be suppressed before any political settlement was made.

Under martial law, Irish country life was extremely bleak in the early months of 1921. The boredom was almost as bad as the nightly fear of armed men with petrol cans. Shooting for game, Charles's favorite winter sport, had become virtually impossible since all guns and cartridges had to be surrendered to the military and even landlords could be arrested and fined if they were found to be keeping illicit guns. Curfew started at 8 p.m. and driving more than twenty miles from home was forbidden, if a permit had been granted to drive at all. Even for the privileged few with permits, driving had become a challenge on account of felled trees and trenches dug across the road. As Charles recalled, "Motor-drivers had to drive warily, especially round corners; and everybody carried an equipment of planks, poles and tools. Many bad accidents occurred, and endless inconvenience was caused to everybody…at one time we were cut off from exterior relations for about three days." "Another mischievous nuisance was the raiding of motor-cars," he continued. "Some were stolen, others damaged, more or less seriously, the intention being to prevent their use." The first disabling efforts on his car that spring were inexpert and easily corrected but, about a fortnight later, "the garage was raided again, and the magneto and carburetor" were stolen. He had insured the car against outrage at a premium but it was two or three weeks before the parts arrived from England.[47]

Paradoxically, some continued to quietly discuss peace throughout this final bitter stage of the conflict. In April 1921, Lord Derby, recent British ambassador in Paris, attempted to spur peace moves. He was taken to see de Valera in Dublin, having previously seen Sir James Craig, who had succeeded to the leadership of the Ulster Unionists in the North following the retirement of Edward Carson. There were also rumors of changes at Dublin Castle, including Chief-Secretary Greenwood's transfer back to London. As it turned out, it was the viceroy, Lord French, who departed.

He was replaced by Edmund Talbot, Lord Fitzalan of Derwent, the duke of Norfolk's son and the first Catholic to be appointed to the post. On April 21, Lloyd George defined the British government's attitude in the House of Commons, saying that the government was ready to meet representatives of the Irish people "for the purpose of discussing any proposals which offer the prospect of reconciliation and settlement, subject only to the reservations that the strategic unity of the Empire must be safeguarded, and that Ulster must not be coerced. Every facility of safe conduct for a meeting of members of the Dáil would be granted" with the exception of three or four members accused of serious crime (Collins and Mulcahy, no doubt). The exception of men like Collins was totally unacceptable to the Dáil.[48]

Elections were held in May 1921 for the two new Parliaments for Northern and Southern Ireland created by the 1920 Government of Ireland Act. In fact, no election took place in the twenty-six counties of Southern Ireland. All 124 seats were filled by the Sinn Féiners elected to the First Dáil. Apart from the four TCD seats, to which four Unionists were returned unopposed, no other candidates put themselves forward. The First Dáil became the Second Dáil and, according to historian Hopkinson, "advanced nationalist control was consolidated at the expense of wide-ranging minority opinion." The timetable for the Government of Ireland Act meant that the Southern Parliament had to be established by July 12.[49]

Forty Unionists and twelve Nationalists were returned to the Northern Parliament in a more regular election. The election was effectively a referendum on approval of partition. It is not well known today, however, that the Ulster Unionist leaders had been considering the idea of a united Ireland. In an election speech earlier that month, Craig had pointed out that the Council of Ireland provided automatic machinery for a meeting with de Valera. Three days later, he showed personal courage by entrusting himself to an IRA escort to bring him to a secret meeting place with de Valera to explore the possibility of absolute unity in Ireland. De Valera remained convinced, however, that it was the British government's responsibility to solve the Ulster problem. When the Northern Parliament came into being, de Valera stuck with previously declared policy and declared an economic boycott of Ulster goods.

The partition of Ireland was now a more unalterable fact than it had ever been in the whole previous nine years it had been under consideration. The slight inclination of Ulster Unionists to show some awareness of their weakness compared to the South was further blighted and the continuing violence and daily bloodshed only increased the traditional sectarian embitterment between Protestants and Catholics.[50]

There were two attacks in which Unionist women were murdered during the election month. On May 14, Paddy Ryan of the Tipperary IRA, whose family home had been burned by the British early that year, and a party of IRA assassinated RIC detective inspector Harold Biggs and young Winifred Barrington, the only daughter of Sir Charles and Lady Barrington of Glenstal Castle in Co. Limerick. Winifred, who had served as a nurse in WWI and was very well liked by locals of all classes, was riding in a police car with Biggs, two other women, and an army officer when it was ambushed. The next day, the wife of Captain Blake, another RIC detective inspector, was killed. She and her husband were driving down a country house driveway after a tennis party, along with Margaret Gregory, widowed daughter-in-law of the famous Lady Gregory, and two young army officers. One of the army officers left the car to open the gates and was promptly mown down. Armed and masked men surrounded the car and ordered the women to leave. Mrs. Blake refused to leave her husband and was killed alongside him and the other army officer.[51] Margaret Gregory was the only survivor, due, she was told later, to the love and respect felt for her mother-in-law in Ireland.

Violent action was increasingly centered in Dublin. Michael Collins had formed an Active Service Unit for the city, headed by a special élite known as "The Squad." There were frequent casualties among civilians in the street, including many women and children. Between January 1 and June 4, 1921, there were 147 street attacks on Crown forces in Dublin, resulting in forty-six civilians killed and 163 wounded.[52] On May 25, Dublin IRA units comprising more than a hundred men occupied and burned the beautiful Custom House, one of the jewels of Dublin's Georgian architecture and the center of local government in Ireland (see chapter 10). Records of the Irish Local Government Board and of Customs and Inland Revenue were lost, making the British civil administration in Ireland almost impossible. As the building was burning and before the IRA units evacuated, they were surrounded by several hundred British troops. Five IRA men were killed and between 80 and 130 captured, a disaster for the Dublin IRA. As the old parliamentarian John Dillon wrote the next day, "The whole scene was one of the most...tragic I have ever witnessed. A *lovely* summer afternoon, the crowds of *silent* people, afraid to express any opinion, and the appalling sight of the most beautiful [building] of Ireland [of] our period of greatness, wantonly and deliberately destroyed by the youth of Ireland as the latest and highest expression of idealism and patriotism."[53]

The cycle of violence in 1921 took place against a spring and summer described as "wonderful and unforgettable" according to many accounts, including that of Charles Head at Derrylahan. As Mark Bence-Jones described it, "There was day after day of brilliant sun and from seven in the evening onwards, when motor cars were not allowed on the roads, 'the country seemed to belong to the sheep and lambs and birds.'" But "the burnings and shootings continued, all the more frightful in the glorious weather."[54] Northern Tipperary had been rendered even more vulnerable in May when GHQ in Dublin ordered the complete withdrawal of the Auxiliary Division there to reinforce companies based elsewhere. On one beautiful day, June 3, an attack by an IRA flying column of seventeen men on an RIC and Black and Tan patrol at Kylebeg Cross in Modreeny resulted in the deaths of four RIC men, one of them a Black and Tan from Scotland who had been decorated several times when serving with the Royal Scots Fusiliers in WWI. The patrol of twelve men was cycling from the damaged RIC barracks in Borrisokane to the local petty sessions in Cloughjordan Courthouse where the court was transferred, with Charles Head possibly presiding, although he did not say so. The twelve-man cycle patrol was overtaken by a motorized patrol of sixteen men in cars and a military truck from Roscrea RIC barracks just before the attack, but the IRA decided to attack nonetheless. Besides the dead, fourteen policemen were wounded. An informer was arrested by the IRA but he managed to escape.[55] One of the IRA men was Sean Glennon of Redwood, who commanded six riflemen in the action. As John Glennon, he had distinguished himself in action as a lance corporal in the Irish Guards Machine Gun Battalion in France, joining the IRA on his return home.[56]

On June 6, the British government called off the policy of house-burnings as official reprisals for IRA ambushes. However, IRA headquarters issued a retaliatory general order for the burning of houses of those implicated in RIC/Black and Tan ambushes of IRA people, which officially authorized the burning of houses "belonging to the most active enemies of Ireland" as legitimate targets. A warning was added that "no one shall be regarded as an enemy of Ireland, whether they may be described locally as Unionist, Orangeman, etc. except [when] they are actively anti-Irish in their actions."[57] McDowell made the point that loyalists who were on friendly terms with local police and army officers "must have talked about politics, the conditions of the country and what was happening in the neighborhood...Moreover, keen supporters of Crown authority sometimes gave the authorities specific information concerning IRA activities. Frequently, in fact, the insurgents' plans must have been seriously disrupted as a result of information received from loyalists."[58] As noted by Bence-Jones, "The chance of a house being burnt on the whole bore little relation to the owner's popularity, still less to that of his or her forebears...There may, however, be some significance in the fact that the first batch of houses to suffer in June, the month in which the burnings really started, included Oak Grove in Co. Cork, one of the two family homes of Capt. John Bowen-Colthurst, whose rampages in Dublin during Easter Week 1916 had brought him a spell in Broadmoor, since when he had emigrated to Canada."[59]

Terence Dooley remarked that "the disillusionment which landowners felt with the degree of protection offered to them by the British government diluted their Unionism." He quotes Lord Dunraven's claim in the House of Lords that month: "Outrages and murder are committed, not for any political motives, but purely for personal motives of malice and revenge, hate and spite. There is in Ireland today absolutely no protection whatever for life or property. Honest, decent citizens have no protection and can get no protection from the police and are not allowed to protect themselves."[60]

From the beginning of June until the calling of a truce, thirty-three Big Houses were burned. Big House owners were considered to be anti-Irish, not necessarily because of their actions but because of their cultural and political alienation from the majority of the population of the twenty-six counties. The worst affected county was Co. Cork.[61]

Whatever the reasons, be it fallout from the Modreeny Ambush or the IRA's retaliatory order against those they considered to be "actively anti-Irish in their actions," Col. Charles O. Head was now targeted for execution on his own land on June 18, Waterloo Day, "a glorious day of a beautiful summer." Presumably, following the orders of the IRA adjutant general that April, the conviction and sentence of Charles Head had been ratified by the brigade commander of the district IRA. Head later described the experience:

> I strolled out in the morning, as was my custom, to see the men employed on the place at their various occupations... Sauntering through the covert of young birch, fir, and heather, where the woodcock resorted in winter, how lovely and peaceful the surroundings were! The men were working happily...Then homewards after a delightful walk, pleased with my people, and hoping that the British Government would soon suppress the forces of disorder, and enable us all to enjoy in peace the lovely country in which we lived. That there could be any other solution of our troubles, was, I thought, impossible. Here were an average lot of Irishmen, peaceful and contented, sympathizing, no doubt, more or less, with the racial aspirations of their countrymen, and not much horrified at the methods selected to give them effect, but quite ready to acquiesce in any scheme of government that would protect their lives and liberties. As I approached my house I met one of my men apparently looking for something. Asking him what he was doing, he said he had lost some of the sheep, then coming nearer he whispered, "Did you see them fellows?" "What fellows?" "I don't know who they were, but four of them came into the yard just after you had left it and asked for you. They were masked. One of them had a gun, and the others pistols, and they put

us up against the wall and searched us, then followed you down to the bog." This was rather a shock to my pleasant meditations; the murder of gentlemen in their houses, as reprisals for the execution of rebels, had just come in vogue, and it looked as if I had been selected for this distinction. Getting into my house, I procured a revolver from its hiding-place in the attics. I would have preferred my gun, but it was in the barracks at Birr. My gamekeeper then arrived and filled in the blanks of the story for me. It seemed that, from his cottage, he saw me leave the yard on my way to the bog, then, having business at the house, he went up in that direction, his way leading through a shrubbery past the yard. As he was passing it, he was surprised to see four armed and masked men, half-concealed in some laurels adjoining the carriage-drive. At that moment my car came out of the yard on its way to the forge, and the gamekeeper saw the men at once put up their weapons and aim at the driver, but lower them again without firing. He evidently wasn't the man they wanted, nor was the car their objective. The keeper then, all the time concealed by the shrubbery, saw them go into the yard. After an interval they came out again and took the path I had taken towards the bog, about ten minutes after me. In the bog wood he lost sight of them, but saw them later emerge from it and apparently go over to question the haymaker, and then enter a small plantation near the carriage-drive. Here they seemed to stop. So he came in to report their movements. It was difficult not to shudder at the reflection of these cold-blooded murderers tracking my footsteps in the glorious sunshine, and at the thought that only my impulse to see the water-hole had prevented my returning by the path used in going, and so, alone and unarmed, meeting these worthies face to face in a place most suitably fitted for their designs. It was full of deep holes overgrown with heather, where I could have been comfortably stowed away, without trace, if that unnecessary condition was required. The turf-cutters would have heard the shots with their ears, without those usually acute organs conveying the sound to their minds, or any mention of the strange deafness which had suddenly afflicted them. However, reflections were useless, something had to be done. With my wife and the gamekeeper the situation was discussed calmly. One revolver was an insufficient armament for offence or defence, so flight seemed the only alternative. I changed my clothes and put a few necessary articles in my pockets. As already mentioned, my car had gone to the forge for the adjustment of the new parts, so my decision was to make for it, hoping to find it in running order, and by its means find safety in the Birr military barracks, six miles distant. While my wife went out by the front door and down the front drive on a bicycle, acting as a flank-guard, the keeper and I got out by the garden door, and thus into a large wood at the back of the house, through which we circuitously made our way towards the forge. Joining my wife before reaching the entrance gate, we dismissed the keeper, and reached the forge without incident. My wife then returned home with the motor-driver, a dismal prospect requiring considerable nerve and courage to face it; but two of the children were there, and of course all our possessions, which we wished to save. The car was reported ready, but, in fact was barely able to move, as the timing-gear was not yet properly adjusted. It crawled along the road to Birr till it came to rest pathetically in a badly filled-in trench intersecting the road. Unable alone to get it out of this, and the road being curiously bare of traffic, considering it was market day, I went to the nearest house and found a hulking young labourer in it, who not very readily came out to assist me. Together we levered the car out, after which it completed the journey to the barracks without incident. The vicinity of Birr was a safe region, as there were troops and police there, which made it objectionable to gunmen. So I was not confined to barracks but moved about the town at will. My wife with a farm-horse brought in consignments of clothing and plate for safe custody, and we arranged with the local furniture dealer to send for some of our furniture for warehousing. Her situation in the lonely house without a car was a cruel one. But she hoped by staying there to save the house from destruction and the place from robbery. I paid a surprise visit home on the day but one following my flight, and harangued the men there, telling them I relied on their protecting my property, but that under no circumstances would I voluntarily part with my land. This I thought necessary, as the labourers on some estates were reported to be preparing to eject the owners, and divide up the land among themselves. They all expressed regret at the events of the day before yesterday, and denied having seen anything of the intruders, which of course was untrue, as each party of them in turn was visited. As suspicious-looking people and one of the well-known local Sinn Feiners had been seen on the previous day, Sunday, near the gate lodge, and on the road to church, it seemed advisable to go away for a while and await the suppression of the prevailing state of murder and crime, leaving my wife to follow as soon as she could make any arrangements for the security of our property that were possible. So I left for England a few days later."[62]

Three days after the failed attempt to shoot Charles Head, a band of IRA kidnapped seventy-year-old Lord Bandon of Castle Bernard in the village of Bandon, Co. Cork, and set fire to the castle. Fifteen other country houses around Bandon went up in flames. The following day, King George V and Queen Mary arrived in Belfast on the royal yacht accompanied by four battleships and eight destroyers. King George gave a speech at the opening of the Belfast parliament, calling on "all Irishmen to pause, to stretch out the hand of forbearance and conciliation, to forgive and forget, and to join in making for the land they love a new era of peace, contentment and good will."[63] On June 25, Lloyd George sent de Valera a letter inviting him to discuss peace terms in London. Before accepting, de Valera conferred with his own colleagues and four leaders of the Southern loyalists in meetings that took place in Dublin's Mansion House. The loyalists were pleased to find de Valera and Arthur Griffith helpful, particularly when they agreed to various safeguards for the Protestant and loyalist minority. The Sinn Féin leaders also agreed to release Lord Bandon as assurance of their good faith effort to secure a truce which was to precede a London peace conference. On July 8, Lord Midleton, acting as an intermediary between Sinn Féin and the British Government, was able to arrange a truce, which was to come into force on July 11.[64] Sir James Craig, on the other hand, was negotiating with Lloyd George for the *status quo* in Northern Ireland and refused to attend the truce conference.[65] De Valera had also indicated he was willing to meet in London following a truce but only if Sir James was *not* present.

Despite the ongoing political negotiations, the violence continued, and it came closer and closer to Margery Head and her children at Derrylahan. My grandmother must have been only too aware that failure to execute her husband would be followed by further actions, however much the couple seems to have deluded themselves otherwise. And, indeed, as they nervously awaited the truce "which was," as Kee put it, "to end all aggressive acts and provocative displays of force by either side," the family would soon be caught up in a spate of retribution by the local IRA, whose members were often seen drilling in the parkland.[66]

It is not known if Margery Head was informed of an act of extreme violence that occurred at Coolacrease, near Cadamstown, Kinnity, Co. Offaly, on June 30 (members of the Drought family, relations of the Heads, still lived in Kinnity at that time). Richard and Abraham Pearson, the twenty-four- and nineteen-year-old sons of a Nonconformist farming family, were turning hay on their land there with a family friend, William Stanley, when they were surrounded by thirty or so armed and masked men who ordered them to go to the farmhouse. William Stanley managed to run away and spent some terrifying days on the run, but the IRA men ordered the brothers' mother, three sisters, youngest brother, and visiting female cousins out of the house and began to set fire to it. In the meantime, they lined Richard and Abraham up against a wall, read them a death sentence, and shot them, allegedly in front of their family. The mortally wounded brothers were transported by the RIC to the military infirmary at Crinkill Barracks in Birr, where Richard died two hours later and Abraham died early the following morning.

William Stanley's son Alan wrote an account of the murder, as he understood it, in his 2005 self-published book *I Met Murder on the Way—The Story of the Pearsons of Coolacrease,* which became the basis for a documentary aired twice on RTÉ, the national broadcasting network. The documentary brought a firestorm of criticism and countless lengthy articles disputing the book and documentary and offering additional archival information. These included another book, *Coolacrease: the true story of the Pearson executions,* written by four local historians and launched at the premises of the Offaly Historical and Archaeological Society in Tullamore in November 2008. The authors refuted Stanley's claim that the shooting was the result of sectarian land-grabbing and argued that it was in fact the ordered execution of "spies" and enemy combatants. The authors alleged that three Pearson brothers had killed or wounded one or two IRA men manning a roadblock next to their land earlier that month, resulting in damaging arrests of local IRA men by the RIC. One of those brothers was away from home overnight with his father at a Christian conference so escaped death. Taken together, these accusatory or defensive writings, several of them amounting to diatribes, demonstrate that the War of Independence, like so much of Irish history, was still being fought on the eve of its centenary.[67]

The same night, June 30, that the Pearson brothers were shot and the Pearson farmhouse burned, there was an attempt to burn the Birr Courthouse. Apparently, there had been a meeting of the local IRA Brigade in Tullamore the night before when the decision was made to execute a number of perceived Loyalist "spies" and/or burn their houses. During the night of July 1 and 2, as described in the opening chapter of this book, a gang of about twenty armed and masked young men hammered on the door of Derrylahan, waking up Margery Head, her children, and the women servants. They ordered them all out of the house before splashing gasoline over everything. The children were held under armed guard on the driveway. Margery pleaded with the leader to save the house, even offering to purchase it for a high price, with no effect whatsoever. The men decamped when the house was ablaze, leaving the exhausted little family, dressed only in their night clothes, to find their way to sanctuary in Birr. A few days later, the family and their Protestant chauffeur, another William Stanley, joined Charles Head at the home of Margery's brother in Shropshire, England.

Operations by the Crown forces virtually ceased from the time of the truce agreement on July 8 at the Dublin Mansion House, but IRA activity continued up to the very last minute. On that same day, two "spies" were shot dead, one near Cashel and another near Tullamore. The latter bore the slogan "sooner or later we get them. Beware of the IRA." Four unarmed soldiers were kidnapped in the streets of Cork on the night of Sunday, July 10, and three of them were found blindfolded and shot dead in a field the next morning. But as soon as the truce came into force on July 11, there was suddenly a total cessation of killing.[68] It has been estimated that just over 2,100 people were killed in Ireland between January 1917 and December 1921, compared to the 35,000 Irishmen killed between 1914 and 1918 in the course of the Great War, and 20,000 Irish people killed by the Spanish flu epidemic of 1918-19.[69] The only mention of the burning of Derrylahan House in the *Nenagh Guardian*, which had long reported on events involving the Head family, was a report of the quarterly meeting of the Borrisokane Council. Under "Malicious Injuries" was listed "The burning of Derrylahan House, £50,000."[70]

Chapter 20

Irish Civil War: A Country Torn Apart

If the Irish Protestants were in truth a garrison, they were a garrison in peculiar and difficult circumstances. Though almost perpetually under siege, they had neither means nor authority to organize their own defence. They must work always under orders from a remote headquarters, where strategy and tactics were liable to frequent fluctuations... They had no power to come to terms on their own behalf; but they lived in constant fear that terms would be arranged behind their backs; that...sooner or later, the whole fortress would be abandoned and they themselves left to their own fate.
—J. C. Beckett, *The Anglo-Irish Tradition*, 1976.

I never expected to see the day when ships would sail away to England with the Auxiliaries and the Black and Tans— the RIC and the British soldiery...Dublin Castle itself – that dread Bastille of Ireland—formally surrendered into my hands by the lord lieutenant.
—Michael Collins.[1]

While Margery Head and two of her three children (the oldest daughter was away at boarding school) recovered at a relative's house in Birr from the shock of the nighttime burning of their home, she made plans to leave Ireland for good. It must have occurred to her as they crossed on the ferry from Kingstown (Dún Laoghaire) to Holyhead, Wales, that it was less than three years since they had narrowly escaped the fate of drowning following the torpedoing by a German U-boat of another of those ferries—and not much less than that since her husband had returned from service in the Great War. Although she had lived in Ireland for less than fourteen years since her marriage in 1908, she had thrown herself into life as a gentleman farmer's wife, holding the fort for Charles during his four-year absence. Her two younger children were born at Derrylahan just before the war, while their father's ancestral roots there went back almost three centuries, a birthright that seemed of little consequence to the unleashed forces of Irish nationalism. But, as the next few years would show, any suspicion that a family had benefitted from the seventeenth-century Cromwellian land redistribution scheme could result in the burning of the Big House that symbolized that reviled Protestant conquest. Moreover, an owner's commitment to the British Union provided an excuse to return that land to the Catholic small farmers and laborers who hungered for it. Charles Head came to believe that it was a blessing that they had been forced to leave Ireland before the anarchy of the short-lived Irish Civil War when another 199 big houses were burned in the Twenty-Six Counties of the newly independent south, forty-eight of those houses in counties Tipperary and Cork.

The truce that was to end all aggressive acts and provocative displays of force by either side in the Anglo-Irish War came into force at noon on July 11, 1921, just nine days after Derrylahan was consumed by flames. Although sporadic killings had continued until the night before the truce, there was indeed an immediate end to the violence at that point. However, in Belfast there was a major flare-up in the sectarian violence that had begun there in 1920. The day before the truce, gun battles raged along the sectarian "boundary" between the Falls and the Shankill roads in day-long violence known at the time as "Belfast's Bloody Sunday," with significant loss of life and the destruction of 161 houses. There were two further spikes in violence in Belfast that year.

Now the leaders of the far-from-united Sinn Féin party had to face the British government across the negotiating table. Seeing himself once again as the political strategist and conciliator, Éamon de Valera almost immediately took personal control. However, his Sinn Féin party had no political control over the Volunteers, the military side of Irish republicanism—the secretive Irish Republican

Brotherhood in particular—that had grown powerful under the leadership of Michael Collins. It was Collins, not the ministers of Sinn Féin or its absentee president de Valera, who were prominent during the Anglo-Irish War. That caused considerable jealousy, distrust, and disagreement among the Irish leadership as they turned to forging a treaty with Great Britain.

Negotiations, which began almost immediately following the military truce, went through many complex stages, including de Valera's visit to London with other Sinn Féin leaders in July, during which he had private "verbal sparring sessions" with the prime minister.[2] On July 20, Britain offered limited Dominion status for the Twenty-Six Counties of nationalist Ireland— with the fundamental reservation that the six Ulster Unionist counties would remain under a Parliament of Northern Ireland and as part of the United Kingdom. At de Valera's recommendation, the Dáil unanimously rejected the British proposals. There was then a prolonged correspondence between de Valera and Lloyd George until eventually it was agreed to go ahead with a conference in London "with a view to ascertaining how the association of Ireland with the community of nations known as the British Empire can best be reconciled with Irish national aspirations." Meanwhile, de Valera and his colleagues had begun to formulate the proposition that an independent Ireland could be associated with the British Empire through a "treaty of free association."

The first session of the conference began on October 11. De Valera remained in Dublin, apparently because he did not want to leave the provisional government in the hands of his more radical deputy ministers, Cathal Brúgha and Austin Stack, who both refused to go to London. As the best political strategist on the Irish side, de Valera's absence has been seen as a fundamental mistake and possibly a major factor in the subsequent Irish civil war. While his choice of delegates was meant to preserve unity in nationalist ranks, it only compounded already existing tensions. The Irish mission was led by the moderate Arthur Griffith, who had been appointed minister for foreign affairs that August. Although he had the relevant experience and negotiating skills, his bad health caused him to virtually hand over leadership to Michael Collins. Collins himself admitted that he lacked the necessary temperament and negotiating skills and he seemed to believe that he and Griffith had been put forward as scapegoats. The five-man delegation also included liberal landlord Robert Barton and two lawyers, with Erskine Childers serving as secretary. The British had the advantage of the brilliant negotiating minds of Lloyd George, Lord Birkenhead, and Winston Churchill.

Over the next weeks, the Irishmen and the Englishmen debated two vital questions: unity and status. Should Ireland be partitioned or not and what would be the nature of Ireland's association with the Crown and the British Empire? The Irish delegates were prepared to offer the six Ulster counties a generous autonomy so long as it was exercised in an all-Ireland parliament under the aegis of the Dublin parliament, not Westminster. Above all, they stood firmly against allegiance to the Crown. Sir James Craig, now premier of Ulster, was not present at the negotiations and was just as firm in his refusal to submit to Irish unity. On November 25, Griffith, Collins, and Barton crossed to Dublin to consult with de Valera and returned still adamant in their refusal to swear allegiance to the King. All the delegates felt, correctly, that Childers was communicating with de Valera about developments behind their backs.

Following a dramatic ultimatum from Lloyd George, possibly a bluff, that the alternative to a treaty was "immediate and terrible war," Griffith and Collins and the other delegates all signed what became known as the Anglo-Irish Treaty in London early in the morning of December 6, 1921, having been persuaded that there was no time to refer it back to the Dublin cabinet for approval first. Collins, who did not believe Ireland could win a renewed war with Britain, remarked to F. E. Smith upon signing the Treaty, "I may have signed my actual death warrant." By the Treaty's articles, the Irish Free State was established as a dominion within the British Commonwealth based on the Canadian model; members of its parliament were to swear to be "faithful" to the British monarchy; and a Council of Ireland would enable the governments in Belfast and Dublin to discuss matters of common interest, including "safeguards for minorities in Northern Ireland." Lloyd George managed to convince Griffith and Collins into thinking that his idea of a Boundary Commission would transfer large Catholic areas of the six Northern counties to the nationalist South, something that never happened. He also convinced them that Craig had agreed to his aims to modify the border through a Boundary Commission (see chapter 21). But the partition of Ireland was not the main bone of contention; it was the fact, utterly obnoxious to the republicans, that the British monarch would remain head of state.[3]

De Valera read a summary of the treaty for the first time on December 7. The following evening, he issued a proclamation declaring that the terms were in violent conflict with the wishes of the majority "as expressed freely in successive elections during the past three years." He continued, "I feel it my duty to inform you immediately that I cannot recommend the acceptance of this Treaty either to Dáil Éireann or to the country. In this attitude I am supported by the Ministers for Home Affairs [Stack] and Defence [Brúgha]." Griffith issued a statement the next day: "I believe that this treaty will lay the foundations of peace and friendship between the two nations. What I have signed I will stand by in the belief that the end of the conflict is at hand."[4]

Charles Head wrote about the Treaty:

Ulster had considerable reason in regarding the treaty with dismay and resentment. She had quite recently been given her own Parliament for six counties, which had been opened by the King in person, and was duly working. She was no party to the conference with Sinn Fein, and was not consulted about any of the articles of the treaty, but she woke up one morning and found that she had been handed over to the rule of Dublin, which was what she had taken infinite pains to avoid, and that, though a loophole of escape was provided for her, it was coupled with a condition which might make the duration of her liberty so short as to be valueless. The whole of Ireland was included in the treaty, but Ulster was given an option of contracting out of its provisions on certain conditions, the one most serious for her being that the delimitation of her boundary would have to be submitted to a Commission for decision. Having thought she had her six counties, she now had a vista of harrowing anxiety as to how much territory would eventually be allowed her; and her people on the border were plunged into a state of uncertainty and alarm. It was not a creditable performance on the part of the British Government, and one that was by no means necessitated by the situation."[5]

When it came to the twenty-six counties, most loyalists had serious misgivings about a Treaty that set up an Irish Free State under the same conditions applying to Canada and Australia, feeling that the Treaty contained few of the safeguards for the loyalist minority in the South to which de Valera and Griffith had agreed in negotiations with Lord Midleton and his colleagues before the truce. Other loyalists were simply appalled. Lady Alice Howard wrote in her diary on December 10: "The Government have given over everything to the rebels and they are to govern Ireland entirely. Too dreadful—with only a nominal oath of allegiance to the King—Such a dreadful year of rebellion and murder—and now England has cast us off and given us to the murderers," she wrote on the last day of 1921. Field Marshall Sir Henry Wilson, an intransigent Unionist and an advisor to the Ulster leaders, shared her opinion: "The agreement is a complete surrender. 1. A farcical oath of allegiance. 2. Withdrawal of our troops. 3. A rebel army, etc., etc.," concluding "The British Empire is doomed."[6]

In the opinion of historian Michael Hopkinson, the signing of the Anglo-Irish treaty was "the decisive event which led to the Civil War. No document could have more effectively brought out into the open the divisions in the philosophy and leadership of the Sinn Féin movement."[7] From December 14, 1921 to January 6, 1922, there was a heated debate in the Dáil over ratification. Arthur Griffith and Michael Collins—the latter was backed by the powerful IRB—persuaded a majority to vote for the Treaty, with Collins arguing that it gave "not the ultimate freedom that all nations aspire and develop to, but the freedom to achieve it." De Valera argued that the Treaty would keep British authority the master in Ireland: "You have an oath to the Irish Constitution which will have the King of Great Britain as Head of Ireland. You will swear allegiance to that Constitution and to that King." Erskine Childers and Austin Stack were equally uncompromising in their arguments against the treaty.[8] Cathal Brúgha turned the issue into a vote on Collins' popularity, which probably swung the majority against his own side.

The vote on January 7 was 64 for and 57 against the Treaty. Unable to accept ratification, de Valera resigned as president and he and his supporters withdrew from the Dáil, which then elected Griffith as president of the Provisional Government of the Free State and Collins as chairman and finance minister. De Valera became the figurehead for the majority of the IRA who were anti-Treaty.

For almost six months between the truce and the Treaty of December 1921, the republican courts and police had functioned alongside the Crown courts and the RIC. However, once the Treaty was signed, the RIC was concentrated in the Dublin area in preparation for disbandment as the withdrawal of the British Army from the major garrison at Dublin began, waking people up to the vast change that was taking place. Shocked loyalists watched the familiar legal and political framework being swept away. The Castle was now one of the symbols of the centuries of British rule. While there was still a governor, he was now Irish. There was, nonetheless, administrative continuity from British rule since most of the civil service remained unchanged. The long standoff that followed the signing of the treaty gave invaluable time to the Provisional Government under Michael Collins to set up a new National Army with the aid of the British government, undermining the initial numerical superiority of the anti-Treaty forces, or Irregulars. To replace the RIC, recruitment and training began of a new civic guard which, however, was to prove totally inadequate in the face of challenges to law and order during the civil war.

Despite the meeting of former southern Unionists on January 19, 1922, in which they declared loyalty to the Free State, numerous Unionist landlords decided to leave Ireland altogether, with no desire to return. Many were being subjected to continuous agrarian aggression, including threats, raids, and rustling of their cattle. In March, Lord Bandon went to England to recover from his kidnapping ordeal, writing that "no protection was afforded to human life, and many of the exiles would not dare run the risk of placing themselves against the power of criminals who desire to injure them." He was referring to the final months of the Anglo-Irish War, but the situation was about to become even more terrifying for landlords. While the Provisional Government struggled to exercise undisputed authority throughout the country, a number of IRA units were defiant, believing that, as a citizens' army, they had a duty not only to defend the country but to defend its political independence.

Violence in Belfast peaked in the first half of 1922 after the Anglo-Irish Treaty confirmed the partition of Ireland. Michael Collins sent arms and aid to the northern IRA, aiming to try and defend the Catholic population there and attempting to destabilize Northern Ireland. However, despite his previous determination to prevent partition, Collins made a pact with Sir James Craig on March 30, with encouragement from Churchill, to abandon the southern campaign against the border and lift the boycott of Northern Irish goods that began in August 1920. In return, Craig agreed that Roman Catholics would be included in the northern constabulary.[9] But the pact broke down when neither Craig nor Collins could defend their respective minorities and violence resumed. On May 22, the IRA assassinated Unionist politician William Twaddell in Belfast. Immediately after, under the new Civil Authorities (Special Powers) Act passed in Northern Ireland, 350 IRA men were arrested and imprisoned without trial in Belfast, crippling the IRA organization there. Several thousand Catholics fled Belfast during the violence that followed, seeking refuge in Dublin and outside of Belfast. An estimated total of 465 people died in Belfast during the conflict of 1920-22.[10] Most of the guerillas, or Iregulars, who opposed the Anglo-Irish Treaty picked up where they had left off six months earlier, pursuing the same imagined enemies, ex-soldiers and policemen as well as Protestants. Anyone suspected of collaborating with the enemy was in danger. This drive for revenge was fueled by anger at the anti-Catholic violence in the North, heavily publicized in southern newspapers. The Belfast boycott was reapplied, mainly against Protestant traders, and Protestant houses were seized throughout the south, ostensibly to provide shelter for northern refugees.[11]

In April 1922, the Irregulars, already in control of the counties south of a line between Limerick and Waterford (which they referred to as the Munster Republic), occupied the Four Courts and other buildings in Dublin as their headquarters. Despite increasingly frantic attempts to bring the two sides together, talks on army and political unification broke down over Collins' insistence that there must be an election on the Treaty issue. At a mid-April meeting of the IRB's Supreme Council, Liam Lynch, who still hoped for a compromise with Free Staters, laid down hardline minimum terms, insisting on the Republic and an independent Army Executive, that the IRA do all the necessary policing, and there should be no election until the British threat of war was removed. In his new role as national unifier, Collins had proceeded to draft a constitution for the Free State that would be republican enough to reconcile the anti-Treaty party, an action that would be certain to outrage the British.[12]

Crinkill Barracks, Birr, where officers of the British regiments stationed there had provided support and social life to two generations of the Derrylahan Heads and whose proud red-jacketed soldiers had inspired Charles Head to choose the army for his career, was handed over to Lorrha native Capt. Felix Cronin of the new Irish National army on February 13, 1922. The British Army had ordered the disbandment of its last occupying British regiment, the Prince of Wales Leinster Regiment, the month before and it soon marched out of the barracks, leaving behind all the cutlery, linen, pianos, and furniture.[13] By May 1922 all British police and military forces had left southern Ireland with the exception of the Dublin garrison.[14] Acknowledging that fact, Collins argued that "the one thing for us to do now is to consolidate the position, having in view the unity of Ireland [including the North]," warning that it would be easy enough for the British to return "if we start slaughtering each other."

Pleased with Collins' speech, de Valera closeted with him to attempt some form of compromise. He proposed "external association" with the British Empire, leaving Ireland's foreign policy in her own hands and a republican constitution with no mention of the British monarch. On May 20, the two men signed a pact to fight the 1922 general election together and form a coalition government afterward, which Collins' biographer called "a complete give-away of the Treaty position." It was agreed that the just completed Free State constitution would be published on the eve of an election in mid-June. Collins scribbled a note on the compromise: "Above all Ulster." Winston Churchill, then secretary of state for the colonies, responded to the pact by refusing to hand over any more arms to the Provisional Army and halting the evacuation of British troops. He had already insisted that the Provisional Government send him a draft of the constitution before its confirmation so that he could be sure it adhered to the terms of the Treaty.

All the British government's worst fears were confirmed by the constitution. Lloyd George told Griffith and Collins on May 27 that their constitution was a republican one with "a thin veneer," a "complete evasion" of the Treaty. During his two meetings with Griffith and Collins in London, Lloyd George insisted that the Crown must have genuine authority, while Conservative leader Austen Chamberlain affirmed that the Provisional Government had to choose between appeasement of de Valera and support for the Treaty. As Griffith and Collins sat in the Strangers Gallery, Churchill told the House of Commons that an Irish Republic could not be tolerated and that, in its event, the Government intended "to hold Dublin as one of the preliminary essential steps to military operations." When Lloyd George insisted on June 1 that the proposed Irish constitution must agree with the Anglo-Irish Treaty, Griffith and Collins both agreed. Collins returned to Dublin, but Griffith stayed on to supervise the detailed work of amending the constitution. Nonetheless, the amended constitution remained essentially republican, putting the emphasis far more on Irish internal authority than the role of the British Crown.

Collins called off the pact with de Valera on the eve of the election and the constitution he proposed, as altered by Griffith and others, was published on election morning, June 16. Ninety-four of 128 Dáil members elected that day were pro-Treaty, demonstrating the popular realization of the need for stable government and the acceptance of realistic compromise. Thus the election results played an important role in legitimizing the Treaty and the status of the Provisional Government. But, just as the British Government concluded that it was time for the Provisional Government to assert its authority, a dramatic event typical of the countless turning points in Irish history occurred in London.

On June 22, two London-based IRA men, both Irish veterans of the Great War, assassinated former Chief of the Imperial Defense Force Field Marshall Sir Henry Wilson as he stepped from a taxi in front of his house in Eaton Square. Wilson, an advocate of British reconquest of Ireland, was chief security advisor to the Northern Ireland Government, which was wary of the threat from the pro- or anti-Treaty forces in the south. He was also elected as Unionist MP for Co. Down. Subsequent testimony seems to indicate that the order came from Collins himself, and it is possible that both he and those leading the Irregulars occupying the Four Courts building were involved in the planning. However, rather than damage Collins' relationship with the British Government and his colleagues in the Provisional Government, the assassins were persuaded to take the responsibility on themselves as they faced execution. Henry Wilson's boyhood home, Currygrane, the Co. Longford mansion of Wilson's older brother, the prominent Unionist James M. Wilson, was burned in retaliation for the execution of Wilson's assassins. J. M. Wilson had been forced to flee Ireland due to agrarian intimidation at Currygrane early that year; according to Sir Edward Carson, he was "now living in humble lodgings in an English village, shattered in health and broken in spirit."[15]

The day after Wilson's assassination, the British conference of ministers decided on a policy of retaliation in the form of a military operation to end the Four Courts occupation. Fortunately, the order was withdrawn at the eleventh hour, and British naval vessels, already on their way to Kingstown, were ordered to turn back. Instead, under pressure from the British authorities, the Provisional Government decided to launch its own attack on the Four Courts, which Collins agreed to with extreme reluctance. Liam Lynch joined the garrison there when it was attacked by the newly formed National Army, resuming the position of chief of staff of the Irregulars. After three days and nights of heavy shelling using artillery that the National Army borrowed from the remaining British garrison, the Irregulars surrendered. The Four Courts buildings remained relatively intact, but during the battle a massive explosion destroyed the Irish Public Record Office, incinerating the majority of the precious documents of seven hundred years of Irish history.[16] As Free State forces cleared the surrounding streets of Republican fighters, destroying what was left of Sackville Street (now O'Connell Street) after the Easter Rising. Cathal Brúgha, who had been appointed commandant of the Republican forces there, was mortally wounded during this fighting.

During July and August, the Free State Army sent units by sea to the South and West and gradually cleared the Republicans out of Waterford, Limerick, Cork, and other places. When war broke out, Southern Tipperary's main towns of Tipperary, Clonmel, and Carrick-on-Suir were in anti-Treaty hands and had to be wrested from the Irregulars in sharp fighting. Likewise, there was fierce fighting in Nenagh, including the destruction of its workhouse. People who happened to be behind the Republican lines were completely cut off from the outside world, with no telephones, telegrams, or mails, and no road or railway communications owing to the destruction of bridges.

The Midland town of Birr, where relatives and friends of the Head family still lived, was cut off for some weeks in July when it was held by Republican forces. At that time, fifteen-year-old Lord Rosse and the rest of his family were away from Birr Castle. The family's agent Toler Garvey, who was also agent to Charles Head, organized a Citizens' Committee to regulate food supplies and generally safeguard the interests of the townspeople. When the Free State troops were approaching, Garvey heard that the Republicans intended to burn the Castle before they evacuated the town. During the night of July 13, a small band of Irregulars took control of Crinkill Barracks, set fire to it, and completely destroyed it, apparently planning to burn Birr Castle the same night. Fortunately, the Castle was spared. Garvey wrote on July 22, "The place is now occupied by Government troops and I can feel easy once again as to its safety." Nevertheless, after the Free State troops—who now occupied part of the Castle itself as well as the stable yard—executed three young Republican prisoners in the Castle grounds on January 26, 1923, Garvey "wrote at once on behalf of the Trustees protesting against this having been done in private grounds and requesting that the bodies be re-interred elsewhere."[17] On the eightieth anniversary of this reprisal execution, a memorial was erected on the north wall of the Castle gatehouse.

While the Free State forces were occupied in clearing the towns of militant Republicans, those who lived in rural areas had little or no protection. In large tracts of the country, IRA military factions and local agrarian organizations could do what they wanted. Landed classes and loyalists in general were subjected to increasingly vicious intimidation. As early as June 10, 1922, the bishop of Killaloe reported that, in the Templederry, Silvermines, and Ballinaclough districts of North Tipperary, south of Nenagh, there was "scarcely a Protestant family in the district which has escaped molestation... houses have been burned. Cattle have been driven off farms. Protestant families have been warned to leave the neighbourhood. Altogether a state of terrorism exists." Predators were coming down from the hills, he said.[18] Most of these Protestant families had been encouraged to settle on the land granted to Cromwellian officers, such as the Pritties and the Otways. Large landowners among the Southern Unionists suffered most, since their estates and houses were extremely vulnerable targets. They were attacked on both nationalist and social protest grounds. As one historian put it more recently, "To be Protestant in Munster, during the Civil War, was to be labelled "privileged", "British" and to be tarred with bad memories of, and assumptions about, the old regime—it was to be deemed less Irish than the majority of the Free State."[19] It should be remembered that, before the 1650s, two-thirds of the land was in Catholic hands, by the end of that decade only one tenth, creating a long-festering resentment of the grantees.

Three mansions or castles in the Nenagh area that were owned by families connected to the Heads since the Cromwellian Protestant land grants were burned and looted during the summer of 1922. The first was Leap Castle located close to the Co. Tipperary border of Co. Offaly, about four miles north of Roscrea, and southeast of Birr. Formerly a stronghold of the O'Carrolls of Ely, it was awarded to the first Jonathan Darby, a Cromwellian officer, in 1659 and, following a brief return to O'Carroll ownership in the seventeenth century, it had remained in the hands of the Darby family. The Darbys were connected by two marriages with members of the Head family.[20] According to their granddaughter, Marigold Freeman-Attwood, author of the excellent *Leap and Its Castle*, the latest Jonathan Darby and his wife Mildred (née Dill) had left Leap in March 1922 for their own safety after sixteen break-ins and several threatening letters, leaving the property in the charge of their steward and gardener. Freeman-Attwood gathered different accounts of the actual burning and looting of the Castle, which occurred over two nights. It appeared from these that a number of locals, even small tenant farmers, were involved in destroying the massive castle walls with bombs and gasoline.

As a result of the burning and subsequent looting, Milly Darby, a Gothic novelist and poet, lost all her unpublished manuscripts and most of her clothes and jewelry. As she wrote to a friend later, "Absolutely no home to go to if 'times' grow safer, no stock, no farming machines, barns, stables, no anything left!" Between the destruction during the assault on the Four Courts in Dublin and Jonathan's home office, all land and estate papers were lost. A perpetrator who survived into old age admitted that he was a member of the IRA but claimed he had twice saved Jonathan Darby's life before the burning. Apparently locals had feared being evicted if the estate was sold, but it was also probable that they had their eyes on the 3,000 acres that might be divided between them if the landlord left. As the Darbys' granddaughter concluded, "Lust by the Irish for Irish soil was the prime motive for the wanton destruction of Leap, and in the last analysis we can discount my grandfather's unpopularity for ruining him."[21]

Next was the burning on August 2 of Kilboy House, the mansion that was built five miles south of Nenagh during the lifetime of the fifth Henry Prittie and first Lord Dunalley (1743-1801) on the lands that were awarded to his ancestor, the Cromwellian officer Col. Henry Prittie. Michael Head of Waterford had been a trustee for the Prittie family's land grant in Co. Tipperary in the seventeenth century, and the families became more closely allied with the marriage of that Michael's great-grandson, another Michael, with Margaret Prittie in 1761, sister of that first Baron Dunalley. The couple had thirteen children, three sons and ten daughters (see chapters 10, 11). The Dunalleys' extensive land holdings (more than 21,000 acres in the early 1920s) abutted William Henry Head's far more modest Modreeny estate near Cloughjordan in the nineteenth century, and Head leased Dunalley land for his lucrative cattle raising.

Beginning in November 1921, Kilboy House and its farm were raided and looted multiple times and silver plate, jewelry, household items, cattle, sheep, and farm implements were stolen. Four herds of cattle were driven from the lands at Silvermines into a river with a total loss to the estate of £3,000, 779 trees were maliciously damaged, and 400 yards of fencing was stolen. As a consequence of the withdrawal of protection from outlying districts, Nenagh itself and the entire area were greatly disturbed by violence and intimidation, while "assaults on the roads paralysed travel, in every parish around Tipperary."[22] The local creamery had been destroyed by the Black and Tans in November 1920. Since it was practically the town's only industry and employed four hundred locals, there was an alarming scarcity of milk in the town and rampant unemployment. The Nenagh Urban Council requested exemption from the ban on markets and fairs so that country people could bring in their produce for sale, and also requested an increase in its grant from the Dáil.

The elderly Dunalleys, both of whom were apparently held in high regard, had decided to leave for England (Lady Dunalley was English) after they were shot at while engaged in conversation on the front steps of the imposing Kilboy House by a marksman concealed in nearby bushes, the latest of several shots aimed at Lord Dunalley. On July 29, 1922, about a month after the Dunalleys' departure, a party of armed men, well known in the area, banged on the door at about midnight and demanded beds for the night. After locking up the few resident servants, they proceeded to ransack the house. Four nights later, at about 2 a.m., the same or another party of men impatiently smashed the door down after receiving no response from the terrified occupants, and entered the house. They gathered Protestant steward Samuel Doupe, his wife, and some of the servants into Doupe's quarters and set the main part of the vast Georgian mansion alight with the usual gallons of gasoline. The house burned all that night and the next day as floor after floor collapsed, taking with them art treasures, valuable furniture, and most of the family's archival papers.

When the raiders left, the staff manned the water hoses in a desperate effort to staunch the fire and saved what they could, including two pianos and some furniture. However, the night after the burning, while the shell of the mansion was still smoldering, the raiders returned to loot and smash the cellars, conservatory, garden, out-offices, and farmyard, burn the outhouses to the ground (including the buildings housing the rescued furniture), and steal the rest of the farm machinery and twenty-eight sheep. Samuel

Doupe, whose life was threatened repeatedly, wrote to Dunalley, "Such wanton destruction was never witnessed." He also made a passionate plea for someone to come and help him. Although Doupe reported to the brigadier at the local barracks every day, he received no assistance from the Free State troops there. Later, Dunalley heard "on excellent authority" that the furniture saved by the servants "was stolen and is now in many of the houses round about." Without witnesses willing to testify and failing to get any help from the troops, Doupe was powerless to prevent such blatant robberies, threats, and intimidations. Whatever Doupe managed to save, he deposited in the bank in Nenagh for Lord Dunalley, but the servants and estate workers who valiantly hauled items out of the burning house had little idea of comparative value when choosing what to save. On August 14, the houses of the Dunalleys' guardsman, yardsman, and herdsmen were burned, leaving them homeless, destitute, and under orders from the raiders to leave the estate in three days. On August 19, Doupe provided a list of additional livestock that had been stolen or sold.

At last, as the *Tipperary Star* reported on August 26, Free State troops swooped down on Kilboy and arrested a number of men who had loaded their carts with all kinds of estate property. Six men were charged in a special court. According to Doupe, this belated action followed an angry phone call from Michael Collins a few days earlier to the brigadier at Nenagh Barracks giving him hell for failing to provide assistance to anyone and allowing the whole county to fall into desolation. However, when a friend of the Dunalleys went to Kilboy to assess the damage on their behalf in mid-September, he saw no one in charge and people brazenly carrying away timber from the storehouse. "Things are very disturbed here," he reported, "we have no railway, post or telegraph service. The whole thing would make a grown man cry."[23] In November, the admirable Doupe left with his family for new employment on an estate in Northern Ireland.

As Teresa Byrne has noted, the motives behind the burning of Kilboy House and others are complicated. The owners of Kilboy represented the Crown, Dunalley himself had been lord-lieutenant of Co. Tipperary and most of the males in the family had served in the King or Queen's army. His son, Capt. Francis Reginal Dennis

Prittie, had fought and died in the Great War in 1914, the family had played a prominent part in Irish administration, and the British forces had used three of his houses as barracks for the RIC. There were also a number of local ancestral grievances handed down from generation to generation.[24]

Castle Otway, which was the seat of the Otway family in the eighteenth and nineteenth centuries, was burned on the same day as Kilboy House, reputedly by the Irregulars. The headline in the *Nenagh Guardian* of August 6 was "Local mansions gutted, Kilboy and Castleotway in ruins."[25] Castle Otway was built of stone by Col. Thomas Otway in 1770 on a hill on the outskirts of Templederry, nine miles south of Nenagh up against the ruins of Cloghane Castle, which was rebuilt in the nineteenth century as a huge tower house. The land had been granted to Cromwellian officer Capt. John Otway and confirmed by King Charles II in 1685. Like the other Cromwellian officers granted land, the Otways increased their landholding by purchasing soldiers' debentures for land. The other Otway property, Lissenhall, was sold through the Encumbered Estates Court in 1853. This was also burned, most probably by Irregulars or "land grabbers." The Otways were related to the Heads through the Pritties and the Tolers. Capt. John Head of Ashley Park served with Lt. James Otway in Col. Daniel Toler's Volunteer regiment in the late eighteenth century (the Toler family's mansion in County Offaly would meet the same fate as these others in March 1923). John's son Col. Michael Head of the 13th Light Dragoons served alongside Lt. Col. Loftus Otway, a younger son of the Castle Otway family, in the Peninsular War (both would become generals). By that time, the Otways were resident in England.[26]

Lord Dunalley's equally elderly friend and neighbor Cosby G. Trench of Sopwell Hall, Cloughjordan wrote to him on August 14 from the safety of his London home, enclosing a statement describing the atrocities committed at Sopwell Hall on July 29 in his absence. While acknowledging that these were relatively insignificant compared to the Dunalleys' huge losses, he wanted his friend to know about the sexual assault that had been perpetrated on his two Protestant servant girls. The horrors began when five armed men demanded beds, looted the house, "filled themselves with drink" in the cellar, and then separated the three women servants "in their night attire" from the two men in the house. They did not molest the Catholic girl but "did their best to outrage" the Protestant girls, leaving them bruised and exhausted, only stopping when they were offered money. The housekeeper and Catholic maid both testified about the targeted assault in court and identified two of the defendants. All five men were from the parish, knew the girls from local dances, and were strongly condemned for their behavior by local priests and the press. Three of the men were sentenced by the Dublin court to penal servitude for ten years and a fourth for five years.[27]

The Biggs-Atkinsons, owners since 1825 of Ashley Park, the former home of the junior branch of the Head family, were luckier. Capt. Biggs-Atkinson's Dodge car and a bicycle were taken by armed men on May 6, 1922, before the outbreak of the Civil War. The following January 23, four armed men entered Ashley Park House and threatened to burn it down if they were not given arms and money. They did not carry out their threat but left with items of clothing and jewelry.[28]

The Free State Government was dealt a double blow in August, first with the death following a brain hemorrhage of President Arthur Griffith and then, a week later, on August 22, the assassination of Michael Collins when his convoy was ambushed by a small party of the Cork No. 2 Brigade of the Republican IRA in the remote western Cork valley of Béal na mBláth. William Cosgrave replaced Collins as chairman of the Provisional Government and Kevin O'Higgins became vice-president of the Executive Council and minister for justice, while former IRA chief of staff Richard Mulcahy moved into the leadership breach in the Free State Army. Although they commanded authority, none of these men had Collins' charisma or achieved his popularity with ordinary people. Some 500,000 people, almost a fifth of the population of the country at the time, attended his funeral ceremony in Dublin's Pro-Cathedral or lined the streets, among them foreign and Irish dignitaries.

When the Third Dáil met on September 5, circulars to the press ordered that the government should be referred to as "The National Government" and not the "Provisional Government." The constitution was passed that day and subsequently enacted on October

25. The Free State's military leadership, convinced that they were in a war for their very survival, now insisted on a tougher policy against widespread guerrilla warfare and introduced the harsh Public Safety Act on September 27, 1922.[29] It set up military courts whose powers included execution of anyone found bearing arms or aiding and abetting attacks on government forces. The Catholic bishops gave powerful support to the government's authority in their joint pastoral of October 10, denouncing Republican opposition: "They carry on what they call a war, but which, in the absence of any legitimate authority to justify it, is morally only a system of murder and assassination of the national forces—for it must not be forgotten that killing in an unjust war is as much murder before God as if there were no war." De Valera regarded the pastoral as a personal affront.[30]

Lloyd George's Coalition Government fell on October 19, 1922, when Conservatives rejected the prime minister's call for war with Turkey, one of the Central Powers defeated in the Great War, after the Turks had pushed Greek armies out and were threatening British troops in the Allied occupied territories of Turkey. The Conservative party voted 187 to 87 to end the Coalition and fight the election as "an independent party." Lloyd George resigned the next day. Conservative discontent with the Irish settlement contributed to his overthrow and, despite his reputation as a war leader, he never again held office. The partition of Ireland had been forced on him by the Unionists in his Coalition government.

Meanwhile, Ireland's Free State government was tightening its grip on dissidents. Under the harsh Public Safety Act, it executed five Republican prisoners on November 17. A week later, Erskine Childers, who had been arrested carrying a small automatic that Michael Collins had given him, was executed. Following that, Liam Lynch retaliated with a letter to the Speaker of the Dáil Powers Resolution threatening "very drastic measures" against those who had voted for the Special Powers Act, and then contributed to the increasing bitterness of the war by issuing "orders of frightfulness" against the Provisional Government. This General Order sanctioned the killing of Free State members of the Dáil and senators, as well as certain judges and newspaper editors, in reprisal for the Free State's killing of captured republicans, although there was little appetite for putting these reprisals against old comrades into effect. That order was acted on by the Dublin No. 1 Brigade when it killed a former member of parliament. The next morning, four of the Republican prisoners in Mountjoy Jail who had been captured during the Four Courts attack were executed, probably at Richard Mulcahy's initiative. One of them, Liam Mellows, wrote in his last letter: "I shall die for Ireland—for the Republic, for that glorious cause that has been sanctified by the blood of countless martyrs throughout the ages...before long all Irishmen...will be united against Imperialist England—the common enemy of Ireland and of the world." There was a shocked reaction in England and Ireland to the reprisal executions of untried and unconvicted men. This led to a cycle of atrocities on both sides, including the Free State's official execution of seventy-seven republican prisoners and "unofficial" killing of roughly 150 other captured republicans. Lynch's men for their part launched a concerted reprisal campaign against the homes of Free State members of the Dáil. Anti-Treaty fighters burned W. T. Cosgrave's family home and shot one of his uncles dead. Likewise, they burned Kevin O'Higgins' family home in Stradbally, Co. Laois and murdered his father.

When the Irish Free State came into existence on December 6, the six counties of Northern Ireland promptly exercised their right to opt out of the jurisdiction of the new twenty-six county Free State. In a national gesture of good will on that day, W. T. Cosgrave, the newly elected President of the Executive Council, persuaded twenty former Irish Unionists and centrists to support the Free State government by agreeing to be nominated to the Senate which met on December 11. Between January and March 1923, many of the mansions of these ex-Unionist senators became the most prominent of the Irregulars' targets. The grandest of these was probably Palmerstown in Co. Kildare, completed for the earl of Mayo in 1874 for nearly £25,000 (the cost of building such houses today could be £30 million).

The Mayos were finishing dinner when a party of armed men burst through the back door and told Lord Mayo they were going to burn his house in reprisal for the execution of six anti-Treatyites at the Curragh army barracks; another man asked Lady Mayo if her husband was a member of the Senate, which he was. The earl asked for time to remove his paintings but was given just fifteen minutes so that only three of the most valuable paintings, the silver plate, and a few items belonging to the housekeeper were removed. As usual, gasoline saturated the carpets and floors of the main reception rooms, and the massive house was ablaze all night as floor after floor collapsed. As with Derrylahan, however, the outhouses and the servants' quarters remained unscathed. When Lord Mayo was asked if he would now leave Ireland, he replied, "I will not be driven from my own country." Palmerstown was rebuilt more or less as it was.[31]

Among the other newly appointed senators whose houses were burned were former chair of the 1917-1918 Irish Convention Sir Horace Plunkett; former British Army general Sir Bryan Mahon (who had commanded divisions in Gallipoli and France); barrister and pro-Home Ruler Sir John Keane, Cappoquin, Co. Waterford; and the 5th earl of Desart, a Unionist delegate to the Irish Convention and lord-lieutenant of Co. Kilkenny from 1920 until lord lieutenancies were abolished in 1922. Lord Desart lost everything of value when the eighteenth-century Irish Palladian Desart Court in Co. Kilkenny was burned by raiders from Co. Tipperary, and he was only the brother-in-law of a senator. Heartbroken at the loss of his beautiful house and its valuable contents, seventy-four-year-old Lord Desart subsequently left Ireland, although the house was rebuilt by his niece in 1926. While the elderly Horace Plunkett also moved to England, the Mahons refused to be driven out following the burning of Mullaboden in Co. Kildare. Free State senator Sir Thomas Esmonde's ancestral seat, Ballynastragh in Co. Wexford, was burned on March 9 despite the fact that Esmonde had been a Nationalist MP for North Wexford from 1900 to 1918 and was the first chairman of the Wexford County Council in 1899. At first, Esmonde was philosophical about his loss. "The only reason for such an act is that I am a senator of the Free State, and, of course, I am in no worse a position than anybody else." He became more bitter and despondent as the realization of what he had lost sank in, particularly the loss of his library which had contained a wealth of archival material.[32]

Two of the last of the Big Houses to be burned in King's County as the Civil War fizzled out in April 1923 were Durrow Abbey and Rathrobbin, both with connections to the Heads. Durrow Abbey House was built in the mid-1830s by William Henry Head's cousin Hector Toler, 2nd earl of Norbury, although he had not yet moved into it when he was assassinated on his land in January 1839 (see chapter 13). Lord Norbury's heir, the 3rd earl, chose to leave Ireland for England with his family at that point, but Otway Scarlett Graham Toler, a Norbury descendant, owned and occupied Durrow Abbey when it was burned. Rathrobbin, the Tudor Revival mansion built by Lt. Col. Middleton Westenra Biddulph to replace the family's former house, was burned on April 23, 1923.[33] The Biddulphs had left that year for London due to Col. Biddulph's ill health.

As long as Lynch continued to lead the Irregulars, guerrilla warfare would continue. In March 1923, the Anti-Treaty IRA Army Executive met in a remote location in the Nore Valley of the Comeragh Mountains in Co. Waterford. When several members of the executive proposed ending the civil war, Lynch opposed them and narrowly carried a vote to continue the war. The following month, on April 10, a Free State Army unit was seen approaching Lynch's secret headquarters in the Knockmealdown Mountains between Co. Waterford and Co. Tipperary. Lynch and six companions tried to evade them and ran into another unit of fifty soldiers approaching from the opposite direction. Lynch was hit by rifle fire, and the Free State soldiers who captured him thought at first he was Éamon de Valera. "I am Liam Lynch," he told them, "Chief of Staff of the Irish Republican Army. Get me a priest and doctor. I'm dying." He died later that evening at the hospital at Clonmel. He was found to be carrying documents that appeared to be calling for the end of the war.

Lynch's successor, Frank Aiken, called for a unilateral cease fire on April 30 (he was much closer to de Valera ideologically and personally than Lynch had been). In April, the pro-Treaty Sinn Féin members organized a new political party called Cumann na nGaedheal with W. T. Cosgrave as leader. De Valera said that the oath to the British monarchy was the only barrier to Republican participation in the Dáil and, on May 24, Aiken ordered the Republicans to dump their arms. Since there was no negotiated peace, the Civil

War was never officially ended but the depth of the divisions left a lasting legacy of bitterness on the Irish political scene and in personal relations. As historian Robert Kee saw it, "For all the corpses and all the burned houses the worst casualty of the Civil War from the point of view of the ideals of nationalism was the cause of One-Ireland." Kevin O'Higgins commented bitterly, "Generally we preferred to practice upon ourselves worse brotherly indignities than the British had practiced on us since Cromwell and Mountjoy and now we wonder why the Orangemen are not hopping like so many fleas across the Border in their anxiety to come within our fold and jurisdiction." The Free State had lost three outstanding leaders, Michael Collins, Arthur Griffiths, and Cathal Brúgha and 927 others dead.

Chapter 21

Compensation Struggles and Enforced Land Purchase

> That was the end of my Irish life; my home was in ruins, my land, after a long process of proving my undisputed title to it—a source of much profit to the lawyers—was compulsorily acquired at an arbitrary price for distribution among claimants…
> —Lt. Col. Charles O. Head, *No Great Shakes.*

Whatever allegations may have been made against him—outspoken Loyalist and Unionist (he was an *ex officio* member of the Executive Committee of the Irish Unionist Alliance); British army officer and veteran of imperialist wars; suspected of collaborating with or informing the British forces during the War of Independence; Protestant descendant of Cromwellian land grantees; his letters to the Press—all of which he acknowledged in his memoir—Charles Head was certain that the real target during the War of Independence was not him but his excellent farming land.[1] There was a widespread belief in rural Ireland that removal of a large landowner and his family would increase the likelihood that the land would be awarded to the local people who farmed it. Following the local IRA's failed attempt to assassinate him on that land on June 18, 1921, he returned to Derrylahan briefly two days later to tell his men that he relied on them to protect his property and that he would never give it up voluntarily.[2] Instead, with the house gone, he was to struggle for compensation for the house and a fair sale of the land and farm buildings and equipment for several years.

There were just two mentions of the burning of Derrylahan in the Irish press. First was the brief report in the *King's County Chronicle* of July 7. Then, on July 16, the *Nenagh Guardian*, the landlord friendly newspaper which had long reported on events involving the Head family, now simply listed under "Malicious Injuries" from the quarterly meeting of the Borrisokane Council, "The burning of Derrylahan House, £50,000."[3] That Charles Head had managed to obtain a decree for that amount just two weeks after the burning seems unlikely, especially given his absence from Ireland. He had been in England for a month, staying with his brother-in-law in Shropshire, where his family had recently joined him.

The owners or representatives of big houses burned before the truce on July 11, 1921 initially lodged claims for compensation under the terms of the 1898 Local Government (Ireland) Act and the Criminal Injuries (Ireland) Acts of 1919 and 1920. The 1898 Act allowed application to be made against the council of the county in which the house was located or against that council and the council of any neighboring county or counties. When increased claims made during 1920 resulted in an increased burden on ratepayers, there was a further change of terms under the 1920 Act. According to this act, if the county council made representation to the lord-lieutenant that the amount of compensation could not be raised by means of a rate in one year "without imposing an excessive burden on the ratepayer," the lord-lieutenant could direct that it be paid in installments over a maximum of five years. The whole process became complicated when Nationalist-dominated county councils refused to appear as defendants so that decrees or awards for damage to or loss of big houses that were made by county court judges were uncontested. Then county council members refused *en bloc* to pay the sums decreed, not wanting to be viewed as taxing relatively impoverished ratepayers to rebuild landlords' houses. In any event, they were virtually impossible to collect from ratepayers who were furious at being made responsible for compensating landlords.[4]

As a justice of the peace who had continued sitting at Crown petty sessions in the burned out Borrisokane courthouse "out of duty," as he described it, until forced to leave Ireland, Charles Head can hardly have expected a hearing from the town's opposition council. According to the *Nationalist* (Clonmel) newspaper of October 5, 1921, his claim was referred next to the British Government-controlled Nenagh quarter sessions, where Head's family had a long history of service and participation. Col. Head now claimed a more realistic sum of £32,000 for the burning of the Derrylahan mansion and its contents and was awarded £27,120. Mrs. Head was awarded £426 for loss of personal chattels in the fire (all her clothes and, presumably, jewelry).[5] The £50,000 originally applied for was no doubt an opening gambit; all applicants overstated losses, well knowing that the amount actually awarded to them would be reduced. Unfortunately for the Heads and for all landlord victims of house burnings, the Sinn Féin-dominated Dáil government, and the North Tipperary county council which at the time was controlled by Sinn Féin, would not have recognized the quarter sessions as legitimate, since British control of that body was only to last until the Anglo-Irish Treaty became law.

The experiences of the owners of three other houses of the approximately seventy-six burned during the War of Independence might already have warned Charles Head that the Sinn Féin-controlled county councils were strongly disinclined to award compensation to former landlords. Hermitage in Castle Connell, Co. Limerick, was the principal seat of the Massy family, to which two of Head's ancestors were linked by marriage. Other Heads had lived in Castle Connell for a time in the mid-1800s. Thus, the Heads were familiar with the Massy family and their large Georgian house, spectacularly located overlooking the Falls of Doonass on the River Shannon. Hermitage was burned to the ground in the early hours of June 16, 1920. Frank Tracy has described its fate and the subsequent struggle for compensation in his tragic tale of the last of the Baron Massys in Ireland in his book *If Those Trees Could Speak*.[6] By this time the Massys had fallen on hard times, due mostly to the spendthrift ways of the 6th baron Massy. The mansion had been empty since his death in 1915 and the contents were sold in a huge auction in January 1916 to pay the family's debts.

Hermitage was probably burned because of a local rumor that it was going to be used to billet British troops. Since her husband, the 7th baron, was "taking shelter in drink," as author Tracy delicately put it, his dauntless wife, Lady Ellen Ida Massy, submitted a claim for malicious damages of £70,000 to the Limerick and Clare county councils. At a subsequent hearing, she obtained a decree for £28,500 and £609 for legal costs against those councils, each of which was liable for half of the award. But Lady Massy was unable to obtain payment from either of those Sinn Féin-dominated councils. She died in 1923 at the age of fifty-eight. Her financial settlements on her husband and children depended on the investment of compensation for the burning of Hermitage. Since this was never paid, the family was left with no source of income and banks were disinclined to help following the death of the only financial realist in the family. Her oldest son became known as "the penniless peer."

Perhaps the most devastating loss during the War of Independence, because it was deemed to be an architectural treasure, was Summerhill House in Co. Meath, the 6th baron Langford's imposing one hundred-room mansion. Built in 1731 on top of a hill and dominating the landscape, it was destroyed by the IRA on February 4, 1921 after months of agrarian agitation. The original claim for compensation by Col. William Rowley, who succeeded his nephew as Lord Langford in September 1922, was made to the Trim Quarter Sessions for £100,000 for the house and £30,000 for the contents. That September, the judge awarded only £65,000 for the house and £11,000 for the contents under the Criminal Injuries Act which was "to be raised off the County Meath at large." But, as in other cases where settlements were awarded by the British-administered courts, this settlement, too, was not actually paid due to the unsettled state of the country.[7]

As for Lord Bandon, who was kidnapped in the wake of the burning of Castle Bernard in Co. Cork on June 21, 1921 (see chapter 19), he made an initial claim for the castle of £100,000 but the judge awarded only £62,000. Lady Bandon claimed £70,000 for the contents but was awarded only £14,000.[8] These claims must not have been paid since Lord Bandon subsequently transferred his claim to the first of several compensation commissions set up by the British and Irish governments.

An uneasy peace followed the Truce of July 11, 1921 but, in January 1922, British and Irish ministers reached a working agreement on setting up the Irish Free State Constitution. Article 3 stated that "fair compensation should be paid for criminal injuries inflicted during the conflict." To address the principle of compensation, the Compensation (Ireland) Commission was established jointly by the two governments to consider claims of damage or injury incurred between January 21, 1919 and July 11, 1921—each side was to pay for the losses it had inflicted. The British and Irish governments compensated their own "supporters" and split the cost "where the injured person was a neutral in the Anglo-Irish conflict."[9] Since the commission sat in Ireland from May 1922 under the initial presidency of Lord Shaw of Dumfermline, it became known as the Shaw Commission. Compensations it recommended were to be "in full substitution for all rights" under previous proceedings but the onus now fell upon the state rather than local authorities to honor compensation awards.[10]

Further complicating the claims of Big House owners, there had been a flood of as many as twenty thousand people onto British shores during the spring of 1922 following the withdrawal from Ireland of British ex-servicemen, of the disbanded Royal Irish Constabulary, and of civilians believed to have been loyal to the British regime in Ireland, some with their entire families. The British government gave them refugee status through its Irish Distress Committee. Renamed the Irish Grants Committee (IGC), this body first sat in May 1922 to investigate applications for the relief of the refugees' immediate necessities until they either found work in Britain or were able to return to Ireland. With a budget of £10,000, it made circa £17,000 in grants and loans but, as soon as the Free State Government was elected that June, civil war broke out between the Free State army and the Republicans or Irregulars over the terms of the Treaty; thus providing joint action on compensation was seriously delayed until fighting was suspended.[11] In a House of Lords debate in July, Lord Carson referred to the "outrages" committed against "those who have been loyal to this country," and were "absolutely helpless" due to the "utter want of protection." The marquis of Salisbury said that Ireland was now left with "no proper provision of courts, or of law, recognized by the Provisional Government, or of armed forces or police forces."[12]

On October 9, 1922, under the headline "REBELS' CAMPAIGN OF DESTRUCTION," *The Times* of London announced the organization by the Shaw Commission of a general meeting to be held in London on October 24 "of compensation claimants and refugees who have been deprived of their homes and belongings." The meeting was to "decide upon a policy to be adopted with a view to putting forward the claims for obtaining justice and payment of compensations due." The article then listed some of the mansions in Ireland that had been destroyed or severely damaged up to that point along with their furniture and contents, for which most of their owners had previously been denied compensation. These ranged from the very grand establishments of aristocrats, such as Summerhill, Templemore Abbey, Castle Bernard, Moydrum Castle, and Hermitage, to the big houses of gentry, including "Col. Head, Derrylahan, Co. Tipperary," all burned in the War of Independence.

Big House owners were not happy with the ground rules laid down for the Shaw Commission. Since it was felt that many earlier claims had been inflated, the commission had to decide what reasonable compensation should be awarded for malicious damage to person and property in cases where no decree or award had been obtained or where the case had been undefended. The commission tended to reduce awards previously made after both governments came to realize the amount that would be necessary to meet claims. Compensation claims could not be made for looting or theft by soldiers or civilians, for losses sustained from the commandeering of big houses, or for losses sustained from the billeting of soldiers in them. There could be no compensation for the loss of money, jewelry or chattels if it could not be proved they had been taken by an unlawful association. Compensation for buildings should be based on market value and since many of them were huge and out of date and there had been a dramatic fall in values, there seemed to be little incentive to underwrite restoration to their former size.[13]

With the Civil War still unresolved, the conservative and landlord-sympathetic London *Morning Post* declared that the work of the Shaw Commission was "unsatisfactory" and that Loyalists were being coerced into accepting severely reduced amounts "through the fear of suffering a total loss unless they agreed with their adversary quickly."[14] The sums eventually awarded to all sectors, but particularly to big house owners, fell far short of the sums claimed for damages. In October 1922, Lord Shaw had estimated that the total number of claims would be in the region of 30,000 and that £20 million would be needed to meet them. By March 1926, when the commission had finished its work, it had dealt with a total of 40,700 claims for £19.1 million but had made awards in only 17,800 cases paying £7.04 million.

Col. Rowley was living in Middlesex and was personally not interested in rebuilding Summerhill. Before making a decision, he wrote asking the opinion of several cousins with some legal interest in the property after that of his heir, a nephew in New Zealand. One responded, "I, personally, have no wish to reside in that unfortunate country." His sister wrote from Nottinghamshire, "Nothing would induce me to live in Ireland if I was paid to do so, a country of murderers." This was before the Shaw Commission reduced the award for the house from £65,000 to £16,775, of which £12,000 had to be spent on building a new house in the demesne. If no building was constructed, then the award sank to an insulting £2,000. After an appeal was made in Parliament, the award for the house was raised to £27,500 with no obligation to build. The total, with contents, was £43,500 which was paid early in 1924, three years after the first claim was made, and invested in gilt-edged stocks.[15]

As for Derrylahan, the unpaid Nenagh quarter sessions award of £32,000 was probably used as a basis for the application to the Shaw Commission. Head family lore indicated that Charles Head eventually received just £5,000 in compensation for a house that had cost *his* father £15,000 to build in 1862. However, an announcement headlined "Birr and Other Injury Claims" in the *King's County/Offaly Chronicle* of August 2, 1923, listed the award of £10,500 for the destruction of Derrylahan House ahead of a long list of lesser awardees, the closest being £5,000 for T. Mylotte's Moorrock in Birr. Where the sums were listed in brackets, they were stipulated for reconstruction of the properties, in this case for Catholic-owned properties in area towns, several of them in Nenagh.[16]

As the Shaw Commission was working its way through pre-Truce compensation claims, a whole new crop of large claims resulted from the destruction in the South and West as the army of the newly elected Free State Government battled the anti-Treaty Irregulars. The Dáil Éireann had begun addressing the issue before the Civil War ended with a November 1, 1922 resolution that the Free State Government would proceed with compensation legislation in due course. Claims could be made in the interim. With the Civil War ended, the government was ready to resume its obligations to victims. Under the Damage to Property (Compensation) Act of 1923 enacted by the Dáil, applications for compensation for "loss, destruction, or damage" were to be made by a standard form to the county and Dublin authorities. The judge at the local sessions assessed the claim and made a "decree," a figure deemed appropriate for compensation, which was then considered by the State Solicitor and reported to the Ministry of Finance. The Ministry paid the decreed award, although with some adjustments or conditions."[17]

What sort of conditions might be applied? The Act stipulated that judges could consider "the steps taken or which might reasonably have been taken" by the owner of the property to prevent the injury. If it was determined that insufficient precautions were taken—a considerable challenge for owners who were absent from their properties when the arson occurred—the award could be reduced. While the affected land owners might claim the malicious intent of the arsonists, the Free State Government, which could not afford large payments, countered large claims by collecting "supporting evidence" from witnesses and associates of the victim about the suspected perpetrators.[18] This supporting evidence was ominous for the 199 owners of big houses burned during the Civil War since Nationalist county councils would look no more favorably on huge claims than they had under the 1919 and 1920 Acts.[19]

The supporters of Anglo-Irish loyalists in Britain stridently criticized the Free State's post-Civil War compensation legislation, especially the 1923 act. The London-based lobbying group, the Irish Claims Compensation Association (ICCA), passed resolutions calling on the British government to fulfill its obligations to pay loyalists what the Free State had failed to pay and called for a commission to adjudicate post-truce claimants. The London-based relief organization, the Southern Irish Loyalist Relief Association (SILRA), headed by influential Conservative politicians, was responsible for sending many cases to the Irish Grants Committee. Although the IGC claimed that cases under the act were being dealt with in a satisfactory manner, in 1924 its second interim report referred to the "peculiar provisions which excluded so many different categories of damage."[20] Speaking in the House of Lords on July 15, 1925, Labour peer Lord Arnold reminded Conservatives that Ireland could not afford to award any more, praised both governments for their generosity, and made the important point that the Damage to Property Act referred "to all cases and a great majority of the cases are not loyalists at all."[21] President of the Irish Executive Council W. T. Cosgrave emphatically rejected the idea of establishing a committee charged with seeking to investigate cases already decided by Irish judges, while L. S. Amery, the British colonial secretary, aware of the Free State Government's sensitivity towards any allegations of discrimination against certain sections of the Irish community, quickly responded that any such committee would be set up to examine British obligations only.[22]

The claims for Big Houses burned during the Civil War included several owned by relatives of the Heads in counties Tipperary and Offaly: Kilboy, Castle Otway, and Woodrooffe (Tipperary) and Leap Castle and Durrow Abbey (King's/Offaly). At the hearing on the destruction of Leap Castle at Birr quarter sessions in June 1924, Jonathan Darby claimed £28,000 but was awarded only £4,100. His counsel argued that his client had "suffered at the hand of tyranny."[23] Darby's case for reparations was then heard at the quarter sessions at Tullamore, presided over by a high court judge, where he did even worse. Having sued for £35,000, he was awarded just £3,900 for the castle and £3,050 for the contents.[24] He had no interest in rebuilding on the original site of Leap Castle; in due course a large bungalow was built for the Darbys on the shores of Lough Derg at Dromomore.

Lord Dunalley insured Kilboy House for £20,000. However, his solicitors informed him in 1924 that "the Northern Assurance Company would not pay out...on the grounds that it [the property's destruction] was due to civil disturbance." His compensation claim to the Free State Government under the Damage to Property (Compensation) Act for both the house and its contents, £75,508, was more than three times the amount the house itself was insured for. Yet he was awarded only £17,395 for the building and £9,534 for the furniture. He claimed £18,403 for the destruction of the outhouses and was awarded just £5,105. A reinstatement clause attached to the award required that Dunalley rebuild the house. Because he owed previously unpaid income tax, rates, and land purchase annuities, however, he was informed by the Ministry of Finance that it was "retaining the actual sums awarded as against arrears of rates due." Even without this setback, his solicitors claimed the award was "quite inadequate to rebuild the old structure." Dunalley was thus forced to rebuild on a reduced scale, without the top storey and with the cellars sealed up. His claim for farm equipment and much else looted was dismissed by the county judge on the basis that it was due to larceny and not malicious injury, his solicitor being unable to prove that these things were taken by the Irregulars. The Irish Claims Compensation Association considered that he and other Irish Loyalists were treated infamously and were willing to use Dunalley's case for propaganda purposes.[25]

Robert Otway-Ruthven and Otway Graham-Toler struggled to receive compensation for Castle Otway and Durrow Abbey respectively. Castle Otway, which was burned on September 9, 1922, was never rebuilt and remains a ruin today. Durrow Abbey, which had undergone extensive renovations before World War I, including the addition of expensive antiques and an impressive library with many rare manuscripts, was burned late in the Civil War.[26] Graham-Toler was able to rebuild after marrying an heiress.

Most of the great houses were burned in the early months of 1923, when Anti-Treaty fighters, or Irregulars, targeted the properties of former Loyalists who had agreed to serve in the Free State Senate. Once again, it was difficult to receive compensation. For example, the 7th earl of Mayo was awarded just £15,000 by the Free State for Palmerstown in Co. Kildare, which made it necessary to rebuild without a third story.[27] Lord Desart was awarded £19,000 for Desart Court, Co. Kilkenny, of which £12,000 was conditional on it being rebuilt. He was too old to undertake the rebuilding so his niece rebuilt it and lived there for a while. It was torn down in 1957. Sir Thomas Esmonde made a claim for £77,500 for Ballynastragh, Co. Wexford. After his case was heard in February 1925, he was awarded £44,800, 60 percent of his original claim. Having rebuilt the house on a much-reduced scale, he remained extremely embittered that he received no sympathy from the new government he had agreed to serve.[28]

The first IGC appeared to have outrun its mandate. However, a second, reformed IGC under the chairmanship of Lord Dunedin was established in 1926. Arguing that the recompense sought and deserved by loyalists was not forthcoming from Free State judges or ministers and it was thus the duty of the British government to award its supporters, both the SILRA and the ICCA immediately began to apply pressure on the new committee. They submitted thirty-three "typical" cases which they divided into three classes: those who had received inequitable compensation under the Damage to Property Act; those whose claims for compensation had been upheld but who had not yet been paid; and those who did not fall within the scope of the act. The second category included pre-truce as well as post-truce cases which had not yet been paid by the Free State. However, the consensus now seemed to be that the Shaw Commission had been generally successful, thus the pre-truce cases were never as controversial as post-truce ones. The lobbying organizations attached a long list of promises and pledges made to loyalists in 1922 by British leaders such as Winston Churchill, Lord Birkenhead, and Lord Arnold as well as a memo signed by future Free State president W.T. Cosgrave during the War of Independence warning that all who had received decrees by enemy courts would be "dealt with accordingly."[29]

The Irish Land Commission

As the back and forth continued on compensation claims, the Free State Government made it clear who would own land in independent Ireland when it legislated for the compulsory purchase of the remaining tenanted lands in the hands of landlords and for the redistribution of other untenanted lands among farmers. Farmers had been identified as "the nation-forming class," the class for whom and by whom the Irish state was created and consolidated. In his landmark study, "The Land for the People", Terence Dooley argues, "It would be difficult to exaggerate the extent to which the redistribution of lands was seen by nationalist contemporaries to be restitution for perceived historical wrongs; time and again in the Dáil public representatives associated redistribution with 'reversing Cromwell's policy.'"[30] The Dáil wasted no time in passing the Irish Free Land Act of 1923 soon after the Irregulars laid down their arms. From this point, all Irish landowners with substantial land holdings (including Charles Head) were apprehensive that the Land Commission might descend on them and acquire a considerable part of their property for redistribution. The Act converted rents into direct payments to the Land Commission, pending compulsory transfer of ownership of remaining tenanted land, and abolished the Congested Districts Board, giving the Land Commission wide powers for the compulsory acquisition of remaining untenanted land anywhere in the state deemed necessary for the relief of congestion, as well as responsibility for redistribution. Dooley has described this act as "one of the most important pieces of legislation passed by an independent Irish government, and probably the most important piece of social legislation."[31]

While Minister for Agriculture Patrick Hogan had administrative control over the Commission, there were certain matters excepted from his brief. Most importantly, four senior land commissioners, all of whom were appointed by the government, determined the persons from whom land was to be acquired, the actual lands that were to be acquired, the price to be paid for them or the price at which they were to be sold, and, finally, the persons to be selected as recipients.[32] Since landlords had to prove title to their estates and the Land Commission had to be assured of a title's authenticity, each record file came to include an originating application recording the name of the vendor, the location and nature of tenure of the property, an abstract of title giving details of the title and details of how the estate came to be in the hands of the landlord, as well as deeds and wills presented by the landlord to the Land Commission as evidence. Charles Head reported in his memoir that he endured a long struggle proving his title to Derrylahan to the exacting Land Commissioners, accruing considerable legal costs in the process. The documents he provided to prove his title, including earlier land sales resulting from the nineteenth-century Land Acts, some deeds, and his father's will, are stored with 11 million others in the Land Commission archives in a purpose-built archive in an industrial estate in Portlaoise, where they remain inaccessible to researchers.[33]

Members of the inspectorate staff were probably the most important part of the Commission, certainly in regard to acquisition and division. When a land purchase scheme was decided upon by the commissioners, an inspector was sent to the area to value the lands for acquisition, building his aggregate price field by field, which, in the case of untenanted lands, meant coming to a price that would be fair both to the owner as vendor and the Land Commission as purchaser. It was not always easy to reconcile the two interests. Nor was it easy to carry out the other practical tasks, such as providing access to all lands and ensuring water supplies for each farm. All eligible applicants living within a mile of an estate to be divided were supposed to be interviewed by an inspector to ascertain the size of their families, their competence to farm the land, and whether they had access to the necessary capital, including manpower, to sustain an allotment. For nearly every parcel of land there could be at least ten and perhaps up to one hundred applicants. The order of priority in the final hierarchy, as specified in the 1923 Land Act, was local "Congests" (those living in over-populated areas with holdings too small to be economical), migrants, ex-employees, evicted tenants and their representatives, and the landless. Potential allottees were, it seems, often more revealing about neighbors who were in competition with them than they were about themselves: one land commissioner claimed that "when the inspector is going his rounds at this work he inevitably hears the whole truth, for the competition for land is so keen that each applicant will see to it that his neighbor will not get away with his particular story." The inspector carefully recorded his allotment scheme on a map and sent it to headquarters, along with a schedule giving the name, address and reference number of each proposed allottee. It was not unknown for inspectors to receive death threats from disgruntled applicants for land.[34]

Where state acquisition and distribution of private land was compulsory, as it was for the property of Charles Head, the Land Commission published a provisional list of the land and a certificate that the land was required for the statutory purposes of the Commission in the *Iris Oifigiúil*, the official organ of the Irish government, formerly the *Dublin Gazette*. The owner then had one month to lodge an objection, which was heard in the Land Commission Court by two of the commissioners. Their decision was subject only to an appeal to the judicial commissioner. If a price could not be agreed upon, a notice fixing the price was published in the *Iris* and

served on the owner, followed by arrangements for taking possession. The Land Commission accountant placed the purchase money to the credit of the estate; inspectors then arranged to let the
lands until such time as a scheme for the disposal/division of the
estate could be arranged.[35]

There are apt examples of what undoubtedly transpired with
Derrylahan. Jonathan Darby's land at Leap Castle was also subjected to compulsory purchase and then sold to the tenant farmers.
According to the Land Commission records that were somehow
provided to the Darbys' granddaughter, 3,288 acres changed hands
and Darby was paid approximately £31,546 in Land Bonds, which
were paid out at 4.5 percent per year.[36] The Land Commission offered Lord Dunalley £16,000 for his lands at various locations (but
by no means all of them), including £500 for timber, payable in
Land Bonds. He was, however, expected to clear all arrears of rates
up to the closing of the sale: £5,000 of the £16,000 was transferred to
the Provincial Bank and Dunalley was informed that "the bank can
sell these bonds in order to produce whatever sum is required for
income tax." A powerful man with a long history in Ireland, Dunalley pursued every possible avenue for compensation and was able
to return to his much reduced estate and rebuilt house.

Charles Head was more fortunate than a significant number of the
other former landlords who left Ireland and were to live in reduced
circumstances in English villages or in unfamiliar countries. His
wife's healthy income from the Threlfall brewery and other investments ensured that the Head family enjoyed a comfortable if rather
conventional life in rural Shropshire away from the dangers, complexities, and colorful people of the beautiful but troubled island his
family had lived in for three hundred years.[37] Sometime after leaving Ireland, Charles and Margery Head purchased Hinton Hall, a
sixty-acre property near Shrewsbury. There the Head children, Betty, Grace, and Mike, grew up while their father, ever sociable and
active, enjoyed English county life, tried some local charity work
without much enthusiasm, was an avid and skilled lawn tennis and
bridge player, participated enthusiastically in gamebird shooting
("the main attraction of Shropshire"), found great satisfaction in
writing books, and made several visits to Ireland to see old friends.

Because his always reserved wife preferred to avoid social life, he was often accompanied by a more socially sophisticated widowed friend—a bridge player, of course!

From this peaceful sanctuary, Charles Head was evidently pressing ahead with attempts to sell his interest in the Derrylahan land before the Land Commission issued him with a compulsory order. The only evidence of his struggle for compensation or sale of Derrylahan that survived a fire that consumed the contents of his study late in his life was a November 1924 letter from his agent, Toler R. Garvey. Garvey referred to his covert attempt to sell Charles's "interest" in the property and some farm equipment to a local farmer, James Delahunt. Head would have had to clear the income tax but Delahunt had the funds to pay the rates. James Delahunt was probably the son of Michael Delahunt who was a tenant of Willie Head, one of six when a deed was drawn up in 1891 placing the running of the bankrupt estate in Toler Garvey's hands (see chapter 16). By the time Charles Head purchased the remaining 803 acres of Derrylahan and the mansion house in 1901, there was just one tenant left. Garvey stressed that the matter had to be handled in great secrecy, no less because Head was already represented by another local man. If any word were to leak out of the would-be purchaser's identity, the sale would be off, no doubt due to intense and jealous local competition for the land. These local negotiations must have foundered in distrust because, as Charles Head reported, the estate was compulsorily bought by the Irish Land Commission and redistributed to locals with a fine war (of Independence) record.

Although Charles remained certain that preference was given to IRA members, the historical record tells a different story. The first significant debate on providing land for the IRA took place in the Dáil on March 1, 1922, before the Civil War broke out in earnest. David Kent, a Sinn Féin member for Cork, introduced a motion: "That it be decreed [by Dáil Éireann] that all lands which were in the occupation of enemy forces in Ireland and which have now been evacuated, except those that may be retained as necessary training grounds for the IRA, be divided up into economic holdings and distributed among landless men; and that preference be given to those men, or dependents of those men, who have been active members of the IRA prior to the Truce, July 1921." But Kent's proposal was never implemented, largely because of the outbreak of the Civil War the following month. When Agriculture Minister Patrick Hogan formulated the terms of the 1923 Land Act and set out the hierarchy of allottees to whom land was to be given, there was no mention of the IRA.[38]

Less than a year after the evidence that Head was attempting to sell his property privately, an order appeared in the October 20, 1925 issue of *Iris Oifigiúil* announcing that the "Estate of Colonel Charles Octavius Head, owner," including its 807 acres and sporting rights in Walshpark and a further 10 acres in Ross, would be vested in the Irish Land Commission within two months. Unfortunately, the agreed price was either not published or that entry was not included in the index. In the issue of June 8, 1926, it was announced that Charles Head had agreed to sell his estate for fee simple in return for the Land Commission's agreement that no further title search would be sought, and that, provided no further problem arose, it would distribute the purchase money within fourteen days.[39] In the end, it was those already farming uneconomic holdings, including Jim Delahunt, who won out. That is confirmed with the names and addresses of the local men and one woman who were awarded parts of the Derrylahan lands, a list provided by a Lorrha descendant of one of them.[40] Another descendant provided me with an annotated ordnance survey map showing the boundaries of farms awarded to his ancestor and two other local farmers.

But it was impossible to satisfy everyone. The *Irish Times* of March 27, 1927 reported a serious revival of agrarian disturbance in Co. Tipperary "where exciting scenes were witnessed yesterday." The Free State Land Commission had recently acquired 3,000 acres of the Loran estate midway between Roscrea and Templemore. Deciding to distribute the land among landless men, it allotted certain holdings on the estate to half a dozen families from other parts of Tipperary, "to the intense annoyance of the local inhabitants, who demanded that they alone should share the distributed lands." When the new tenants of the farms arrived at their holdings, the local people organized a large demonstration. From booing and insulting remarks, their indignation quickly turned into rage, and they drove the unfortunate people roughly from their farms.

A police force rushed to the scene "in Motor-Lorries," and sixteen of the rioters were arrested and driven to Limerick for trial.

This revival of trouble on the land had been expected in Ireland for some time, reported the *Times*. The new land act was designed specifically to redress the grievances of the landless men and Congests, those from overly populated areas, but the wide powers given to the Land Commission took no account of the fierce local jealousies which had been a dangerous feature of the Irish land problem. Importing strangers into any new agricultural area would always be attended by grave risks in Ireland and the outrage on the Loran estate was symptomatic of the attitude of the very people the Land Commission was trying to help. Without some transfer of Congests from one area to another, nothing could be done to relieve the acute land hunger which prevailed throughout Southern Ireland. While memories of the old land war remained, the newspaper concluded, "the best efforts of legislation to solve the problem will be liable to shipwreck."[41] Jack Pardy from Galway was one of those allotted land at Derrylahan and was probably a Congest.[42]

Progress on land transfers was slow and the improvement of material conditions of life for many ordinary people was also slow. From 1923 to March 31, 1932, the Land Commission acquired and distributed some 330,825 acres among 15,687 allottees (an average of just under 20 acres each, a standard holding at the time). But the practical reality was now obvious. There was not enough land in Ireland to satisfy all the landless or low-income landholders in the country.[43]

The Boundary Commission

The other vital issue that the new Free State government had to confront as soon as possible was the boundary with Northern Ireland. This would have been of considerable interest to Charles Head and to his distant cousin Henry Nugent Head in Co. Down, both Ulster Unionists in their sympathies, although Head, as a southern Unionist, had good reason to be angry with the Ulster Unionists who had abandoned them to pursue their own interests.

The Westminster government had already defined the territorial limits of Northern and Southern Ireland with passage of the Government of Ireland Act in December 1920. The following December 1921, the Boundary Commission clause was arbitrarily decided in the Anglo-Irish Treaty which defined its function as being to determine the border "in accordance with the wishes of the inhabitants, so far as may be compatible with economic and geographic conditions." Charles Head expressed his contempt for the way Ulster was treated by the British government. He likened it to a father saying to his daughter, "It is quite true, my dear, that I gave you an establishment of your own, but now I'm very hard pressed by my creditors so I have married you without consent to this nice young man. I know you don't like him, so I have managed with much difficulty to get a clause inserted in our marriage settlement to enable you to divorce him after a short trial if you wish to do so, and in the meantime you are under no compulsion to consummate the union, but in the event of divorce you may have to forfeit a substantial portion of the property settled on you. I'm sure you will find him a most indulgent husband, and you'll be doing me a good turn, if you will accept him."[44]

Following Michael Collins' assassination in late August 1922, the Free State Government quietly dropped his militant policies against Northern Ireland and decided to wait for the results of the Boundary Commission proposed in the Treaty. However, with the military campaign receding, Ulster Unionists became more bullish and pressured the Northern Ireland government to resist the establishment of the Boundary Commission. The Free State Government contributed to the hardening attitudes toward partition by erecting customs posts on the southern side of the border in April 1923. Then a Labour government in Britain was elected in December, with the likelihood that they would welcome serious territorial change through a Boundary Commission.[45]

Kevin O'Higgins, vice president of the Executive Council and minister of justice of the Free State Government from 1922 until his assassination in 1927, put his faith in the boundary clause. Action was delayed, however, until October 24, 1924, partly due to the ill health of Sir James Craig, first prime minister of Northern Ireland, as well as the resistance and filibustering of the Belfast government.[46] Many in the Catholic nationalist-dominated southern and western edges of Northern Ireland expected that, if the border were to be redrawn "in accordance with the wishes of the inhabitants," they would be transferred to the Free State. But the Boundary Commission consisted of two British representatives with unionist sympathies and one Irish nominee, the minister for education in the Free State. The British commissioners put greater emphasis on the second part of Article 12 which stated that any changes in the border had to be compatible with "economic and geographic conditions" and judged that their role was "not to reconstitute the two territories but to settle a boundary between them." The Northern Ireland government came down in favor of non-cooperation with the three-man commission.

After holding their first meetings on November 5-6, the commission members gathered evidence until the summer of 1925, in the process making several visits to Northern Ireland and to the border counties. Their final report recommended very minor changes, with part of south Armagh and south Down and strips of Tyrone and Fermanagh going to the Free State and a portion of Co. Donegal going over to Northern Ireland. This would have transferred 31,000 Northern citizens to the Free State and 7,500 southern citizens to Northern Ireland, a very minor adjustment (except perhaps to the people being transferred). The British commissioners kept the Unionist leadership, including the now retired Edward Carson, abreast of their plans. Carson was delighted to hear that Northern Ireland was keeping the nationalist-majority towns of Newry and Londonderry and all the other major towns in the six-county area.

When this final report was leaked to the conservative *Morning Post* in November 1925, it helped to create a firestorm in Dublin and was highly embarrassing for the Free State government: the relatively insignificant transfers of land and people it recommended be transferred between North and South shocked the Nationalists, who had expected substantial territorial gains. The Free State government managed to have the proposals buried (the report was never published) and gave up any claim to Northern territory in return for being forgiven its share of Britain's Imperial War Debt while accepting liability for "notorious damage" since January 21, 1919. The tripartite agreement between the governments of the United Kingdom, the Irish Free State, and Northern Ireland revoked the powers of the Boundary Commission, and the border stayed as it had been since 1922. The territory of Northern Ireland was confirmed, and Dublin recognized the status of Northern Ireland as part of the United Kingdom.[47] This greatly enhanced the powers of Craig's administration since he had vindicated his battle cry of "not an inch" and overturned the central legal mechanism for the reunification of the island.[48] Charles Head concluded his father and daughter analogy, "Ulster claimed her divorce and then by almost a miracle succeeded in retaining all the property originally settled on her. This was the end of the Union...[49]"

After four days of intense debate in the Dáil, the boundary agreement was approved on December 10, 1925, by 71 to 20. The Irish Senate approved the agreement by 27 votes to 19. But the agreement was a political compromise and the contested border has remained the subject of bitter and sometimes violent contention and confrontation ever since. A border designed to satisfy one minority created another equally aggrieved one, and resentments over this issue were never resolved.

Following the boundary settlement, James Craig was prepared to pursue friendly relations with the South but Éamon de Valera returned to the political stage at that point, breaking with the rump of Sinn Féin/IRA and founding a new party, Fianna Fáil. He intended to return to the Dáil but there was still the barrier of the oath of allegiance to the British Crown, obligatory for new Dáil members. At his first press conference, de Valera made his priorities clear: political independence, language revival, land reform, and an end to partition. Everything changed with the murder of Kevin O'Higgins, a *bête noir* for republicans, by a group of IRA without IRA authority. The Government passed emergency legislation enforcing acceptance of the Oath, de Valera gave way, and Fianna Fáil finally took their seats, winning the 1932 election over Cumann na nGaedheal decisively. De Valera took office as King George VI's "last Irish Prime Minister."

Although he never lost interest in Irish matters, Charles Head turned his attention to the profession for which he was trained, writing three books of military history, all published in the 1930s. For the first, *A Glance at Gallipoli* (1931), he traveled to Turkey's Gallipoli Peninsula on the Simplon Orient Express in May 1930 to spend a few days viewing the scene of that World War I action that was so disastrous for the Allied army. As he noted judiciously in his preface, "I have read much of the writing, British and German, bearing on the subject; and with such local knowledge as I gained, added to some considerable study of military history and strategy, I have attempted to present a miniature picture of the Dardanelles operations in a true perspective. And also, perhaps over-ambitiously or gratuitously, I have been actuated by a desire to draw attention to some faults and weaknesses in our military methods, which were national rather than peculiar to the military system, and which were only developed recently by a false estimate of modern conditions. They militated seriously against the many other excellent factors of potentiality which we had at command, and only require recognition to be eradicated or deprived of their harmfulness."[50]

Abidingly critical of senior British military leadership as he experienced it directly during World War I, he was no doubt drawn to critiquing this "particularly bad example of inept military management" because, had he not been transferred to another division, he might have been there with the 10th Irish Division and would, in any case, have had many friends and acquaintances involved in the catastrophic slaughter. He began with a colorful description of his journey to Constantinople, exhibiting a talent for description that would show itself again in his memoir: "There are few railway journeys in the world that can provide more comfort, interest and variety than the one from Calais to Constantinople." The scenery he passed through recalled for him the great and grim battles of history, particularly of the Great War. He was particularly taken with the peaceful pastoral scenery of "Jugo-Slavia or Bosnia," the scene of horrendous ethnic massacres sixty years later, and then the rich, undulating plain of historic Thrace (split today between southeastern Bulgaria, northeastern Greece, and the European part of Turkey).

Arriving at the station in Istanbul, as he spelled it, he was met by "a little figure, five feet two inches in height, erect and military in bearing, in well-worn European costume: 'Are you Mr. Head? I'm Cook's agent, and I'm going with you to Gallipoli tomorrow.'" His card revealed him to be Mehmed Wassif Bey, ex-naval officer and the doyen or chief of the local corps of guides, an admirable man, full of colorful stories about the Gallipoli tragedy, and the only English-speaker that Charles would hear over the week that he spent walking the battlefields. His critique of the ill-considered strategies that led to a horrific death toll on both sides received a good deal of notice, both critical and approving.[51] He followed with two books exploring his views on the best and worse of military leadership, *The Art of Generalship* (n.d.), and *Napoleon and Wellington* (1939).

The Head children began settling into their adult lives in the early 1930s. Betty and Grace were married and the first grandchildren were born in 1934. Twenty-one-year-old Michael William Henry Head was among the gentlemen cadets from the Royal Military Academy, Woolwich, who was commissioned as a 2nd Lieut. in the Royal Artillery in February 1933.[52]

That year, the Derrylahan Heads' very distant cousins, two brothers who were descended from the Ulster Heads, "The Senior Branch of the Heads of Derry Castle," whose mother was the daughter of Col. Edward Saunderson of Co. Cavan, of Irish Unionist Parliamentary Party fame, married into wealthy American families—a more recent example of the Head family's tendency to make financially advantageous marriages, if they could. Edward Saunderson Nugent Head married the widowed Marie Windrim, daughter of Stanley Griswold Flagg of Philadelphia, Pennsylvania. She was eighteen years older and they had no children together. They subsequently owned or rented the large Georgian Leixlip House in Co. Kildare, now the Leixlip Hotel, and were highly social in Anglo-Irish society. Henry William ("Bunny") Head, MC (1918), 4th Queens Own Hussars, married Ruth, daughter of Sebastian Spering Kresge of Mountainhome, Pennsylvania, the founder of the Kresge department stores.[53] They had two sons, one of whom, Edward Barry Nugent-Head (Barry Head), was a longtime writer and producer for Mr. Rogers (of the Neighborhood, the popular and long-lasting children's television program). I met that charming and talented man once when he arrived bearing two carrier bags of framed family photographs. He said he had no idea who any of them were. In retirement, he was an amateur playwright and artist in his home studios in Sag Harbor, New York, and increasingly in

Oaxaca, Mexico, where he died in 2016. That American line of the Heads continues with his two sons and their families and one of my two sons, Colin Day, and his family. Our older son, Gordon Day, returned to his parents' roots in the U.K., where he lives with his family. My brother, Patrick Head, has three children, one of whom, his son Luke, will carry the name forward.

Charles Head's last visit to Ireland and the ruins of Derrylahan was in 1937, after having "made several expeditions to Ireland to see old friends there, and how the country was getting on under its new system of government." He detected a great improvement in the towns, especially Dublin, and "the Irish main roads were in excellent order but curiously devoid of traffic." But he was saddened to see the sorry state of "his old place," Derrylahan. His nostalgia for Ireland as he had known it weeps off the pages of his unpublished essay "Ould Ireland," along with a fair amount of bigotry:

> It was a picture of dilapidation and neglect. The house was a heap of rubble covered with briars, except for the kitchen-yard end of it, which had been converted into a labourer's residence. Horses and cattle had browsed on the shrubs that used to adorn the pleasure-ground. Of the carriage drives which my father and I had tended with much care, one was closed, the other was a country lane bordered by shabby wire fences. Many conspicuous trees had disappeared, but there had not been a wholesale cutting of timber, which was now the property of the Irish Government.[54] The demesne had been divided into seven or eight small farms, two of them sharing the estate farm-buildings, the others without farm appurtenances of any kind. The tenants of these unfurnished allotments could do nothing better with them than sub-let them to their better-equipped neighbours and sit in them as caretakers and labourers. All of them, except the more fortunate pair who had got the farm-buildings, were in a state of abject poverty. Their so-called freedom had only meant a change of masters, which they did not greatly appreciate.

Epilogue

...in common with most ex-colonial countries, the concomitant of nationalist polarization was a need to assert a separate identity, by social and cultural engineering if need be. In the Irish case, it was important to stress the supposed message of Irish history—which involved a necessary degree of deliberate amnesia.
—Roy Foster, *Modern Ireland* (1988).

The collapse of the world of the Anglo-Irish of Head's stamp was not confined to one country. Even if there had been no political change in Ireland things would never have been the same as in the days when the Mall in Birr was 'Quality Street' in an Irish setting, and the peasants knew their place.
—Terence de Vere White, "The Unknown Unionist," in *The Anglo-Irish* (1976).

In the summer of 1970, my father, the last of the Anglo-Irish Michael Heads of Ireland, made a nostalgic visit to his roots. Terminally ill with cancer, he stopped first in Waterford, where the first Michael Head launched the family fortunes in the seventeenth century. In North Tipperary, he examined the ruins and former demesne of Derrylahan Park where he was born nearly fifty-eight years before. In Dublin, he and my mother visited the last of his Irish aunts, Georgiana (Georgie) Head, in a nursing home. Two years later, at age 103, Georgie died, and so the central chapters of the three-hundred-year story of the Heads of Dublin, Waterford, and Derry Castle, Ashley Park, Modreeny, Ballyquiveen, and Derrylahan in Co. Tipperary drew to a circular and unheralded end.

I began this book by saying that it was my father's stories about his Irish childhood at Derrylahan that remained with me and fueled my curiosity about the very different world he described. Unfortunately, he left nothing in writing about his life, which was full of incident and achievement. We were close and I loved his quick wit: no one else has succeeded in making me laugh to tears. He was a strong man, an engineer officer in the Royal Artillery who rose to be a decorated staff officer and brigadier and a former successful amateur sports car racing driver, with a sentimental streak that kept him emotionally connected to his childhood. He told *me* his Irish stories while the stories he told my brother were about aspects of his active adult life. Of the many letters he must have written to me when I was away from home, I preserved only the long letter he wrote in August 1970, less than a month before he died, in which he described that last trip to his roots at Derrylahan:

> I managed to trace from the foundations the location of all the downstairs rooms in the house. The scullery & laundry end is still standing but is derelict & unoccupied. The stable block is still in existence & used by the inhabitant of the former groom's cottage as farm buildings. Of course, everything looked much smaller than I remembered (I was 9 when we left) excepting the Wall garden which is still intact & is truly enormous—I should think 3-4 acres. The trees in the Pleasure ground are still magnificent although some of them are dying off chiefly because a herd of cows is chewing the bark.

He noticed that a number of those cows were Herefords and probably descendants of his father's pedigree herd. Later, at a pub in Birr, he got talking to an amusing old man, who remembered Derrylahan very well and said: "Sure, your father had a bad deal when he got turned out of there." Knowing the Irish, my father joked that this same man nearly 50 years before had probably poured the first can of petrol inside the house and lit the match! The old man mentioned Lord Rosse's gamekeeper was somewhere in the pub and that he might have known Colonel Head. As soon as the gamekeeper joined them, he said "Your father had a twisted stock on his shotgun because he shot with his left eye. What a memory after 50 years!" Sadly, my father's description of Modreeny Church—where his great-grandfather, Gen. Michael Head, and oldest uncle, Willie Head, were buried—as being immaculately kept up inside and out "by an active and inspiring cleric" was no longer true when my husband and I visited in 2005. Today, it can only be described as a "sad church" since it is largely in ruins. As for Derrylahan, the specimen trees planted by the Heads were nearly all gone and very little remained of the foundations. I was told that the monks from Mount Saint Joseph Abbey in Roscrea carried away the cut stone to build a chapel. I never checked the veracity of this report but, having seen it myself, it does seem that the tall, elegant spire of the chapel there is built of a finer stone than the abbey itself. More likely is an eye witness report that the stone was carried away by truck to build the Catholic Church in Portumna, Co. Galway.

During the many years I spent researching this book, I was able to analyze my grandfather's memories in the context of Anglo-Irish history as taught and written today. While my grandfather Charles Head was right to allege in 1943 that Irish schoolchildren were taught a nationalist history that demonized landlords and the British and made heroes of insurgents against British rule, his own overview of Irish history was equally biased—in other words, collective "convenient amnesia." Head's heroes were the Unionists from 1800 on, Pitt, Castlereagh, Wellington, Salisbury, and Carson. If my ancestor had the advantages that I have had from an abundance of sources and newer histories, would he have been able to modify his opinions? Would he have accepted, rather than denied, that it was the system that was wrong or, as Terence de Vere White correctly defined it, "historically calamitous"?[1] How might he have reacted to my research that some of our ancestors, from the seventeenth century on, were supporters of the Stuarts, Catholic emancipation, and the abolition of tithes? While he gave a pass to his ultra conservative great-uncle John Toler, Lord Norbury as "not as bad as he has been painted," two others he was proud to claim as direct ancestors (Edward Ravenscroft and David La Touche) have been judged by today's standards of political correctness, the first for making his fortune as a director of the East India Company, the second for owning slaves in the Caribbean. Finally, how might this staunch Unionist have reacted to a granddaughter with decidedly liberal views, angered by nationalist-fueled Brexit and the threat it poses to peace, union, and shared economies and opportunities as they relate to Northern Ireland and the Republic of Ireland?

Understanding the forces ranged against Charles Head, and thousands of others like him, has not dulled my sympathy for his losses. One knowledgeable source, a descendant of a prolific local Catholic family, told me that Head might have been left alone, as were certain other local landed families, if he had avoided taking sides, but he realized there would be no future for him as a farmer in Ireland, even if he had been able to hold onto his land. Stripped of the majority of their land by the Irish Land Commission, the ever-declining minority of the former Protestant landed class who remained struggled to maintain their large houses and support their families with farming on the land that remained to them. An outside income therefore became essential. Despite initial efforts to keep Anglo-Irish Protestants in the government, however, there were few opportunities for most of them in political or public life in republican Catholic Ireland, although the civil service continued along established lines and was open to Protestants. While the days of the landlords were over, Protestants continued to hold positions of influence out of proportion to their numbers in banking, insurance, shipping, and the professions generally, and the Anglo-Irish, like William Henry Head in the nineteenth century, continued to play an important role in the valuable livestock industry.

Charles Head witnessed the results of entrenched Catholic and republican leadership in the South and Protestant and Unionist leadership in the North during the final three decades of his life (he died in 1952). In the year that he visited his former property in 1937, Éamon de Valera, independent Ireland's prime minister, proposed a new Irish Constitution, claiming sovereignty over the entire island as their national territory—but with legal jurisdiction only over Irish Free State territory. Two years earlier, he stated "Ireland remains a Catholic nation." Indeed, 93 percent of the population was Catholic and Catholicism dictated societal rules. He also altered the Senate's powers and constitution. James Craig, longtime Unionist prime minister of Northern Ireland, famously and casually observed in the 1930s that, if the South was a Catholic State for a Catholic people, the regime he presided over was a Protestant parliament for a Protestant people. The Unionist treatment of the Catholic minority in Northern Ireland as second-class citizens was a prime reason for the terrifying violence there in the second half of the twentieth century.

As a retired army officer abidingly interested in military strategy and with a son in active service in the British army, my grandfather railed in his 1943 autobiography against the British Government's pre-World War II decision to concede to Éire the three deep-water ports it had retained under the 1921 Anglo-Irish Agreement, in exchange for an end to the Trade War of 1932-1938—as long as the Irish guaranteed that the British could use those ports in times of war.[2] The importance of those ports to British interests stemmed from World War I, when German U-Boats roamed the waters near the Irish coasts (most famously sinking there the passenger liner *RMS Lusitania*), and the very real concern, given the growing militancy of Hitler's Germany, that another war might occur. By September 1939, this had indeed become the case. In 1940, German Luftwaffe and U-Boats were again sinking hundreds of essential merchant ships in the waters surrounding the U-Boat-blockaded British Isles.

In power at the outbreak of what the Irish called "the Emergency," Fianna Fáil declared a pro-British neutrality. Despite his party's official stance, de Valera appeared to believe that the Axis powers would win the war, and a dissident Sinn Féin group drifted into an alliance with Germany, acting yet again on the traditional Irish belief that "England's difficulty is Ireland's opportunity." Determined to uphold Ireland's neutrality, de Valera refused to allow British access to the deep-water ports and ordered the execution of IRA leader Patrick McGrath and a younger associate for subversion. Northern Ireland, as part of the United Kingdom, saved the day by opening its ports to British naval ships and making Belfast, of *Titanic* fame, a base for the repair and refitting of heavily damaged British and American ships.[3]

Following the 1948 election, in which de Valera, having failed to find answers to partition and republican status, lost the outright majority he had enjoyed since 1933, John Costello of Fine Gael became the compromise taoiseach. With the Republic of Ireland Act of 1948, the coalition government declared that Ireland could be officially described as a republic, ending its membership in the British Commonwealth. The partitioning of India into India and Pakistan as a condition of Indian independence the year before resulted in violent clashes between Hindus, Sikhs, and Muslims. Charles Head had comforted himself in his 1943 autobiography, "Though the flag is lowered in Dublin, it still flutters in Delhi, where it is not yet too late to nail it to the mast." Not for much longer, although he would have appreciated India's decision to remain in the Commonwealth of Nations. Realists in Ireland, however, knew very well that to reopen the issue of the partitioning of Ireland was fraught. Of far greater importance at that time were the economy and emigration. Independent Ireland had avoided the devastation of World War II but it did not enjoy the benefits of the postwar boom, despite receiving $150 million from the Marshall Plan. The economy in the postwar years was stagnant and depressed and emigration reached massive levels again in the 1950s, as the Irish reached out for brighter prospects elsewhere. Between 1951 and 1961 approximately 412,000 men and women, mostly between the ages of fifteen and thirty-four, emigrated from the twenty-six counties of the Republic of Ireland. Young Irish men and women were unwilling any longer to endure unemployment or commit to the drudgery and cold reality of life on small working farms.[4]

The problem of Irish partition literally exploded in the late 1960s. The "Troubles" in Northern Ireland began with peaceful civil rights demonstrations by Catholics—of which the most radical leaders were often young men and women influenced by the civil rights movement in the United States. But protests organized by the Northern Ireland Civil Rights Association (NICRA) met with a furious and violent response by Protestant loyalists and the overwhelmingly Protestant police force, the Royal Ulster Constabulary. When broadcast on the Republic's state television channel, the RUC's assault on unarmed civil rights protesters on October 5, 1968 at a march in Derry outraged many throughout the nation.[5] Concerted loyalist attacks on Catholic areas of Belfast and Derry the following August caused the situation to spiral out of the Unionist government's control. This, in turn, moved the British Government to launch Operation Banner, the deployment of troops in the area. At the same time, resurgent Protestant paramilitary forces were now facing a revitalized IRA, which argued that continued British rule over Northern Ireland imperiled the Catholic minority population and the solution must be British withdrawal and Irish re-unification. "Bloody Sunday," the killing of thirteen unarmed civil rights marchers by British paratroopers in Derry in January 1972, generated international sympathy for the Provisional IRA. The IRA then carried out retaliatory bombing, in Belfast (particularly on Bloody Friday, in July) and England.

During that most violent year, 496 people were killed and the parliament of Northern Ireland at Stormont, Belfast, was suspended. It was formally abolished the following year and Northern Ireland came under the direct rule of Westminster. In 1985, the governments of Ireland and the U.K. signed the Anglo-Irish Agreement, recognizing the need for continuing efforts to reconcile, and to acknowledge the rights of the two major traditions in Ireland. Article 1 stated that the future constitutional position of Northern Ireland would be a matter for the people of Northern Ireland. Despite this agreement, the violence and the death toll continued. It was the first of a series of British and Irish initiatives that culminated in the Good Friday Agreement of 1998.

Looking back on all I have absorbed about Ireland, Co. Tipperary, and the men and women of the Republic with whom I have come into contact while researching this history, I am struck by the contrast between the warm and generous people who have been unstinting in their responses to my calls for help with my research, and the visceral hatred, violence, and shameful deceit of those who adopted radical anti-British, anti-landlord or religious sectarian ideology (the latter including Protestants in the North). I was carried back to my grandfather's lucky escape from IRA assassins in June 1921 while reading the shocking details of the Northern Ireland Troubles in journalist Patrick Radden Keefe's 2019 book *Say Nothing*. Keefe focused on the "disappearing" in December 1972 of Jean McConville, a Protestant widow and mother of ten Catholic children, most of whom witnessed the brutality of her capture in their public housing apartment in heavily Catholic West Belfast.

McConville was accused of comforting a young British soldier lying gravely wounded outside her door. The following morning, the soldier was gone but the family found the words BRIT LOVER daubed across their door, always a "poisonous allegation," as Keefe described it. In his 1943 memoir, my grandfather had speculated that, if he himself had been murdered, his body would have been dumped into the peat bog on his land. McConville's body was discovered eventually in 2003 buried in a beach near Carlingford in Co. Louth, just south of the border, but bodies thrown into bogs during various conflicts continue to reemerge.[6]

The partitioning of Ireland was not completely resolved by the Good Friday Agreement of 1998 adjudicated by the U.K., the U.S.A., and both parts of Ireland. Key architects of the agreement included Senator George Mitchell, President Bill Clinton, Prime Minister Tony Blair, Bertie Ahern, taoiseach of the Republic of Ireland, and John Hume, leader of the Social Democratic and Labour Party of Northern Ireland. It was forcefully opposed by the Rev. Ian Paisley of the Protestant Democratic Unionist Party. John Hume, the longtime peace activist inspired by Mahatma Gandhi and Martin Luther King, who persuaded Gerry Adams of Sinn Féin to join the peace process, was awarded the 1998 Nobel Peace Prize along with David Trimble, then leader of the Ulster Unionist Party. While the Agreement acknowledged nationalism and unionism as "equally legitimate political aspirations," included provisions for future referenda on reunification, and subdued the violence, it did not resolve the underlying sectarian, social, and economic conflict.

The Irish Republic and the U.K. had joined the European Economic Union (EEC) in 1973. As a result of EU membership, Ireland would become a far more influential, modern, expansive, and confident country, and relations between the Republic and the U.K. greatly improved following the 1998 Agreement. Nearly a century after partition, however, in June 2016, England and Wales voted to leave the European Union, successor to the EEC—while the majority of those voting in Northern Ireland and Scotland voted for the U.K. to remain. Following its landslide majority in the December 2019 election, including Prime Minister Boris Johnson's pledge to "get Brexit done," the U.K. government formally left the EU on January 31, 2020. On a more regional scale, the most salient and enduring consequence of Brexit may be the breakup of the United Kingdom, while fears of turmoil and violence over the border between the Republic of Ireland, which remains in the EU, and British Northern Ireland, which does not, could reignite the opposing forces. Sinn Féin members of Oireachtas, the Southern Ireland parliament, continue to argue for reunification, while hardline Unionist Protestants are equally adamant in refusing to consider the idea. The severe economic damage caused by the coronavirus pandemic has brought a new reality, making the renewal of the mutually beneficial relationship with the U.K. a priority for the Irish Republic given their joint stewardship of the Good Friday Agreement, people-to-people relationships, and the Ireland-Great Britain economic and trading relationship worth approximately €85 billion per annum before the 2020-2021 pandemic. In the meantime, Scotland is more determined to demand another referendum for independence with the intention of rejoining the EU. And so Charles Head, considered to be "too friendly with the English" by the IRA in 1921, might be shocked to see that the quandary caused by partition continues and that Brexit poses a real and present threat to the British Union that he staunchly defended.

Following independence in 1921, the landed families of the Irish Midlands, whose lives and experiences are described in my book, were often excluded from or vilified by the nationalist history taught in Christian Schools overseas, if not directly run by the socially dominant Roman Catholic Church. But, as the Irish educational system began to loosen its shackles from Catholic control in the late 1960s, educators were able to open the horizon to a full accounting of Irish history and broader access to university education. A new generation of Irish historians, often dubbed and reviled as "revisionist" by nationalists, started to describe a more nuanced history. Roy Foster's still influential *Modern Ireland* (1988) was the first of the inclusive histories of Ireland, in all its complexity. Beginning in the late 1950s and in the face of threats by developers, Desmond Guinness restarted the defunct Irish Georgian Society and launched the purchase and restoration of the gravely dilapidated but still magnificent Castletown House in Co. Kildare and surviving Georgian architecture in Dublin. Conservation efforts like these inspired a number of books about the Big Houses and the "twilight of the Ascendancy," mostly written by descendants of the Irish Ascendancy aristocracy and generally initially published in London.[7]

Although the conservation initiatives were dismissed by critics at the time as elitist, the study of Irish country houses and the Anglo-Irish landed class is a popular topic today for new research by academic and local historians. Terence Dooley of Maynooth University, and director of the Centre for the Study of Historic Houses and Estates, specializes in the history of Irish country houses and the landed class, land and politics in independent Ireland, and local history.[8] He and his students are transforming those fields. I could not have written this book when first researching the Head family twenty years ago due to limited source material for a study of less known landlord families and my original focus on my Anglo-Irish ancestors. However, with the efforts of Foster and Dooley and many other historians writing a more complete history of Ireland, by period and in full, the power of the Internet and online ancestral databases such as Findmypast.com for historical and genealogical research, and the digitization of Irish newspapers for subject searching, my dogged quest was given the boost it needed.[9]

As a descendant of the Anglo-Irish tribe living in America, it struck me that Irish American Catholics often are more stridently nationalistic than those remaining in Ireland. Their antipathy to the British government and the Anglo-Irish landed class that they insist caused their ancestors to leave their homeland has drowned out voices of those descended from the Anglo-Irish Protestant Ascendancy. Many seem disinclined to open their minds or mouths to a more nuanced history. As the Irish historian J. C. Beckett wrote, there is no sound reason to regard the Anglo-Irish as less than truly Irish: "All Irish people are descended from invaders, conquerors and settlers; and no layer of settlement has any exclusive claim to be regarded as 'the Irish people.'"[10] Of the approximately 35 million Americans who currently claim Irish descent, how many of them have kept quiet about their Anglo-Irish origins, intimidated by the current assault on landlordism, racism, colonialism, and imperialism? A number of friends and colleagues felt liberated after hearing about my project to admit that they too are descended from the forgotten Anglo-Irish tribe, and to feel some pride in their historical contributions to Ireland, while still acknowledging faults. What is incontrovertible is that America proved to be the land of opportunity for both traditions. Ideally, it should also be a locus for tolerance, understanding, and prosperity—the only viable basis for an eventual reunification of Ireland.

Finally, my father's exhortation to me not long before he died to "never forget who you are!" has remained a challenge and a spur to me to understand what he meant.

25.   Family group following the September 26, 1908 wedding of Major Charles O. Head and Alice Margaret (Margery) Threlfall. The groom stands at the center with his bride seated to his right. Conspicuously missing is his mother, Isabella Biddulph Head, but his sister Isabella Dundas and niece Aileen are present. Behind the groom is his new brother-in-law, Major Charles Morris Threlfall of the 8th Hussars, who had recently married Mabel Anna, a daughter and co-heiress of Benjamin F. Going of Ballyphilip, a deputy lieutenant and JP in Co. Tipperary.
Head family.

26.   Margery Head and Betty, 1909.
Head Family.

27.   The Call to Arms: Irishmen don't you hear it?
Poster, chromolithograph, Dublin, 1915.
Prints & Photographs Division, Library of Congress.

28. Lt. Col. Charles O. Head, R.A., ca. 1916.
In 1917, Colonel Head was awarded the Distinguished Service Order (DSO), subsequently with bar, for his frontline artillery leadership in such major WWI battles as the Somme and Paschendaele.
Photograph from Colonel Head's autobiography *No Great Shakes*.

29.   The Head children of Derrylahan, Grace (b. 1911), Mike (b. 1912) and Betty (b. 1909), photographed during their 1915 visit to their Threlfall grandparents in London.
Head family.

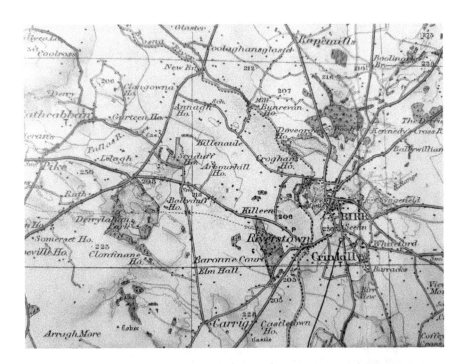

30. A half-inch Ordnance Survey map, 1911-1918, of the area surround-
ing Birr, showing the border between King's County (Offaly) and North
Tipperary and the relative locations of Crinkill Barracks and Derrylahan
Park. It was used by the 7th Battalion of the North Tipperary No. 1 Brigade
of the IRA in 1921.
From *An Atlas of Birr* by John Feehan and Alison Rosse (Dublin: University
College, 2000), photographed by David Broderick for his lecture presen-
tation "Bringing Matters to a Head."

31. A squad of the Lorrha IRA in the townland of Ballyquirke, Lorrha, in
1921. They appear to be armed with WWI rifles.
The Lamp. Lorrha and Dorrha Historical Society. Courtesy of David Broderick.

32. Michael Collins (center), Harry Boland, and Éamon de Valera in conversation prior to the signing of the Anglo-Irish Treaty in December 1921. Collins helped negotiate the Treaty, which he signed. However, his close friend Boland and Sinn Féin leader de Valera were opposed to it, siding with the anti-Treaty IRA during the Irish Civil War, June 1922-May 1923. De Luan/Alamy Stock Photo.

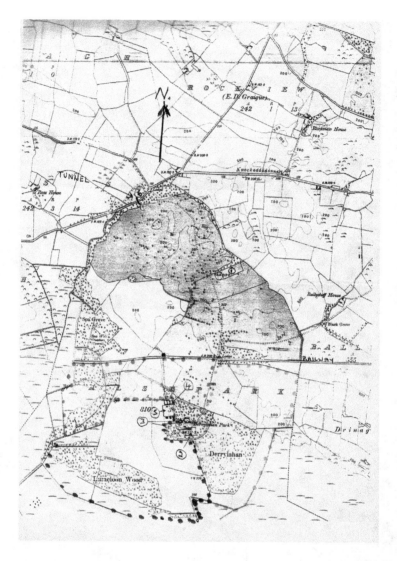

33. Copy of a 1903 Ordnance Survey map of the Derrylahan Park lands annotated by a descendant of one of the awardees to show the division by the Irish Land Commission of the three farms closest to the burned-out house — Monteith, Duffy and Delahunt — and surviving servants' quarters and farm buildings. The former railroad line that briefly ran through the middle of the property was dismantled in the 1870s and all but the cutting was removed by local farmers.
Courtesy of Noel Monteith.

34. The former lodge and gateposts at Derrylahan are the only structures that remain from all those built for William Henry Head in the early 1860s. The lodge is still occupied.
Photograph by David Broderick, 2021.

Notes

Introduction

1 R. F. Foster, *The Irish Story: Telling Tales and Making It Up in Ireland* (Oxford University Press, 2002). Foster was the Carroll Professor of Irish History from 1991 to 2016 at Hertford, College, Oxford, and is the author of many volumes and a manual of Irish history as well as a two-volume biography of William Butler Yeats. He was born in Waterford to a Protestant family and educated in Ireland.

2 Charles Octavius Head, *No Great Shakes: An Autobiography* (London: Robert Hale Ltd., 1943). Cited as COH from here on.

3 Terence de Vere White, *The Anglo-Irish: The men & women who were involved in a confluence of cultures that spanned 200 years* (London: Gollancz, 1972), 257.

4 Foster, 41.

5 "Tipperary history is deficient in critical analyses of landlord society. Published works have concentrated on the great confiscations of the seventeenth century and retrospective reconstructions of the lost Gaelic world of families such as the O'Carrolls, O'Kennedys and O'Dwyers. Planter families have been perceived as transient custodians of unjustly acquired territory and have been dismissed from the pages of Tipperary history. The literature from the Big House is sparse and fragmentary and few scions of Tipperary gentry have cast a critical eye on their place. Theirs was a wider canvas." William Nolan, "Patterns of Living in County Tipperary from 1770-1850," in *Tipperary History and Society* (1985), 292-293.

6 Daniel Grace, *Portrait of a Parish: Monsea & Killodiernan, Co. Tipperary* (Nenagh, Co. Tipperary: Relay Books, 1996), 152.

7 With the exception of Henry Head in Ulster, where some of his descendants would figure in a wider history, this book largely focuses on the branches of the extraordinarily numerous Head family which remained in Northern Tipperary.

Chapter 1

1   Elizabeth Bowen, "The Big House" in Hermione Lee, editor, *The Mulberry Tree* (1986), 26.
2   COH, 218-222.
3   If this was true, my grandfather did not record it, unless it was with the indirect "before they found another roof to shelter them."
4   This was mostly during the brief and relatively untroubled period of rural prosperity between the Irish potato famine and the Land Wars of the 1880s.
5   Demesne was the land held by the manorial lord and not set out to tenants. Joseph Byrne, *Byrne's Dictionary of Irish Local History from earliest times to c.1900* (Cork: Mercier Press, 2004), 97.
6   The estate's land was later noted as 803 acres.

Chapter 2

1   The nomenclature Old English, first employed by New English poet and planter Edmund Spenser in 1596 in his *View of the Present State of Ireland*, came into common currency in the seventeenth century, particularly in Ireland. Nicholas Canny, "Identity Formation in Ireland: The Emergence of the Anglo-Irish," Canny and Anthony Pagden, editors, *The Colonial Identity in the Atlantic World, 1500-1800* (Princeton University Press, 1995), 160. Other important sources for this chapter were Canny's *Making Ireland British 1580-1650* (Oxford University Press, 2001) and James Stevens Curl, *The Londonderry Plantation 1609-1914* (Chichester, Sussex: Phillimore & Co. Ltd., 1986).
2   Canny, "Identity Formation," 161.
3   Munster settler Edmund Spenser attacked the Old English as uncivilized in his 1596 pamphlet (see note 1).
4   TCD's fourth provost, William Bedell (1627-29) attempted to ensure that its students could learn Irish but, after his brief tenure, Trinity returned to its Anglocentric ways. "Trinity College, Dublin," *Oxford Companion to Irish History* (Oxford University Press, 2004), 581-582.
5   Curl, 19.
6   "Ulster plantation," *Oxford Companion*, 591-592. "Timeline for the Plantation of Ulster" http://www.rvgsociety.org/pdf/TimelineForThePlantationOfUlster.pdf says that by 1630 there were approximately 14,500 British settlers in Ulster, a majority of them Scots.

Chapter 3

1   Jane H. Ohlmeyer, Introduction. A failed revolution? in Ohlmeyer, editor, *Ireland from Independence to Occupation 1641-1660* (Cambridge University Press: 1995), 23.
2   Some historians point out that the leaders of these rebellions had originally benefitted from the plantation and, besides religious freedom, they sought improvements in property rights.
3   J. C. Beckett, *The Making of Modern Ireland 1603-1923* (London: Faber and Faber, 1966), 83.
4   Modern historians estimate the number massacred in Ireland in 1641 at between 2,000 and 12,000.
5   The 1641 Depositions consist of The Deposition Books (TCD MSS 809-39), which include the Ulster Deposition Books by county (832-839). Trinity College Library, Dublin: http://1641.tcd.ie/about.php . Nicholas Canny made heavy use of these depositions for his *Making Ireland British 1580-1650*.
6   ibid.
7   My research indicates that John Head, one of the brothers who were progenitors of the family in Ireland, was probably born around 1639 and his brother Michael around 1642, most likely to an Englishman already resident in Ireland, possibly in Co. Tipperary.
8   My principal source for the remarkable life of Robert Phair, spelled Phaire in this case, is W. H. Welpy's 4-part study, "Colonel Robert Phaire, 'Regicide,' his ancestors, history, and descendants," in *Notes and Queries*, Feb. 17 and 24, Mar. 3 and 10, 1923. Welpy had the full range of historical documents available before the tragic destruction of essential documents at the Irish Public Record Office in 1922, which has since posed an extraordinary challenge to historians and genealogists. For instance, Welpy said that about 60 manuscript volumes titled Commonwealth Books teemed with references to Phair.
9   Canny, *Making Ireland British*, 525, 527-528.
10   See Karl S. Bottigheimer, *English Money and Irish Land: The 'Adventurers' in the Cromwellian Settlement of Ireland* (Oxford: Clarendon Press, 1971), Appendix A, 193. There was also a Major William Wade who, in 1660-1661, was one of the Limerick poll tax collectors, possibly his father's namesake and brother of Capt. Samuel Wade. http://www.celticcousins.net/ireland/polltax.htm
11   Tom Reilly in his *Cromwell: An Honourable Enemy* (Dingle, Co. Kerry: Brandon, 1999), 20-21, asserts that "Phelim O'Neill and his savage mob were well matched in excessive cruelties by Sir Charles Coote, an officer in the Royal army, who was also responsible for cold-blooded

slaughter. Coote's instructions were to wage war on the Catholic rebels, and he departed from the gates of Dublin with this in mind. He soon plunged himself into a bloody campaign, slaughtering all the Irish Catholics he could find, irrespective of sex or age, armed or unarmed." These accusations were made by several witnesses in the 1641 Depositions.

12 Reilly, 25; "Owen Roe O'Neill," in *Oxford Companion*, 432.
13 The First Ormond Peace was a treaty concluded with Viscount Muskerry and the Anglo-Irish lords to allow the Irish Army to cross over to England to fight for King Charles in return for limited toleration for the Catholic faith in Ireland. The peace was denounced by Archbishop Rinuccini at a synod of Catholic clergy in Waterford in August 1646. The treaty was consequently a dead letter. "Ormond peace," *Oxford Companion*, 439.
14 Reilly, 25.
15 Welpy, 143.
16 C. V. Wedgwood, *A Coffin for King Charles: The Trial and Execution of Charles I* (Oxford: The Akadine Press, 2001), 201-204.
17 Antonia Fraser, *Cromwell: The Lord Protector* (New York: Alfred A. Knopf, 1973), 290.
18 Wedgwood, 204-223.

Chapter 4

1 From "House of Commons Journal Volume 6: 10 May 1649," *Journal of the House of Commons*, vol. 6, 1648-1651 (1802), 206-07. http://www.british-history.ac.uk/report.asp?compid=256562
2 Fraser, 326.
3 ibid., 326-327.
4 Tom Reilly, *Cromwell: An Honourable Enemy: The untold story of the Cromwellian invasion of Ireland* (Dingle, Co. Kerry: Brandon, 1999), 64-65.
5 Fraser, 332-337.
6 Beckett, 101-102. Revisionist historians like Tom Reilly and Jason McElligott agree with this assessment. In his pamphlet-length *Cromwell our chief of Enemies* (Dundalk: Dundalgan Press, 1994), McGelligot, who became keeper of Marsh's Library in Dublin, attempted "to illustrate the way in which Cromwell's campaign in Ireland has been used for political purposes in nationalist Ireland over the last 150 years," preface.
7 John Morrill, "The Drogheda Massacre in Cromwellian Context," in Edwards, Lenihan, Tait, editors, *The Age of Actrocity* (Dublin: Four Courts Press, 2007), 257.

8   Fraser, 357.
9   ibid., 341.
10   ibid., 341-347; Reilly, chapter 3.
11   Reilly, 207-208. Broghill subsequently became a close friend of Cromwell.
12   ibid., 210.
13   Barbara A. Phayre, *Cromwell's Legacy: The Phayre Family in Ireland* (Sandford Publishing, 2001), 17-18.
14   Fraser, 149.
15   ibid., 671.
16   Phayre, 18.
17   Reilly, 247. According to Fraser, 152, Cromwell was evidently much taken with the beauty of the Tipperary plains and set aside a good deal of that part of the country for himself.
18   Fraser, 352, 353.
19   Under the terms of the surrender, Hugh Dubh O'Neill was to be executed but the Parliamentarian, Gen. Edmund Ludlow, did not carry out the sentence and O'Neill was sent to imprisonment in the Tower of London. The Spanish ambassador intervened on the basis that O'Neill was a Spanish citizen and he was subsequently released into Spanish custody on the condition that he not serve in campaigns against English forces. O'Neill died in Spain in 1660 after Charles II refused to return his family's ancestral lands to him and make him the earl of Tyrone.
20   T. C. Barnard, *Cromwellian Ireland: English Government and Reform in Ireland 1649-1660* (Oxford: Clarendon Press, 2000), 55.
21   Phayre, 18-20; "The Cromwellian regime of the 1650s dispatched several thousand prisoners of war, priests, vagrants, and other dangerous persons to servitude in the West Indies." *Oxford Companion*, 549.
22   Aidan Clarke, *Prelude to Restoration in Ireland* (Cambridge University Press, 1999), 5.
23   "Cromwellian land settlement," *Oxford Companion*, 135-136. Prendergast, a Catholic of Norman descent in Co. Tipperary, succeeded his father and grandfather as agent to Lord Clifden's estates.
24   The Civil Survey for Co.Tipperary has been published.
25   Thomas P. Power, *Land, Politics and Society in Eighteenth-Century Tipperary* (Oxford: Clarendon Press, 1993), 67-68.
26   These hills became an important source of slate from the mid-1700s on, when quarrying brought considerable profits to two generations of Derry Castle Heads.
27   I have been greatly assisted in my efforts to understand the extent and condition of the lands granted to Samuel Wade through the work of

several local historians in North Tipperary: Daniel Grace, Kevin M. and Kevin A. Griffin, and Nancy Murphy. Daniel Grace, *Portrait of a Parish*, Nancy Murphy, *A Trip through Tipperary Lakeside from Nenagh to Ballina-Killaloe and from Nenagh to Portumna by the River Shannon's Lough Derg scenic routes* (Nenagh: Relay Books, 1977), and Kevin M. Griffin and Kevin A. Griffin, *Ballina/Boher Parish: Our History and Traditions* (Ballina, Co. Tipperary: Ballina Killaloe Print, 2000).

28   Griffin, 82, 91, 93-95, 97.
29   ibid., 96. By the time the Hearth Money taxes were levied by Charles II on the homeowners of Ireland for the purpose of "establishing an additional revenue upon His Majesty...for the better support of his and their crown and dignity," most of the Irish appear from the records to have returned to their homes and Sam Wade had a tenuous hold on his property. According to Nancy Murphy, Wade was one of the "most humble and obliged servants" who signed an address presented to Ireland's lord-lieutenant James Butler, the first duke of Ormond, in March 1670, indicating that he had taken up residence and was anxious to have his lands made secure by Royal approval following the restoration of Charles II (see chapter 5).
30   Grace, 52. Elizabeth Butler's manors at Nenagh and Dromineer were leased to Cromwellian officers Col. Daniel Abbott and Capt. John Parker. When the duke of Ormond recovered Nenagh after the restoration in 1660, Abbott was ejected from the property but Capt. Parker was allowed to continue to occupy Dromineer. Grace, 58.
31   Barnard, 39.
32   Beckett, 220.
33   Another John Head would become dean of Killaloe in 1830.
34   Barnard, 121.
35   ibid., 120, 124-5.
36   *Byrne's*, 314-315.
37   Reilly, 262.
38   Barnard, 132-133.

Chapter 5

1   Séamus Pender,"City of Drogheda and Liberties Thereof," in Pender, editor, *A Census of Ireland, circa 1659* (Dublin: The Stationery Office, 1939), 474.
2   Clarke, 119, 123.
3   Beckett, 116; Clarke, 157.
4   "At General Assembly, held at ye Tholsell of Drogheda, the xxvth day of ffebruary, 1659." The year was a misprint. In *Council Book of the Cor-*

poration of Drogheda, Vol. 1., from the year 1649 to 1734, edited by the
Rev. T. Gogarty, C.M. (Drogheda: Drogheda Independent, 1915), 4-9.
There were 55 signatories this time.

5   Byrne's, 79.
6   Welpy, March 3, 1923, 164.
7   Beckett, 117.
8   Phayre, 25.
9   Wedgewood, 253.
10 Welpy, 165.
11 Beckett, 117.
12 In 1922, Leap Castle would be torched, another property belonging to
    the wider kin of the Head family that would suffer that fate.
13 ibid, 120.
14 In Pepper's 1665 claim, he listed John Head once again for £41.07.00
    as well as a Toby Higgins for £16.12.08 and Ensign Thomas Evelyn for
    £20.09.07. He did not give John Head a rank. Pepper Family Papers,
    Ballygarth, Meath. National Archives of Ireland. NAI 999/521.
15 The Peppers of Lissanisky, parish of Ballymackey, Co. Tipperary,
    were a branch of the Pepper family of Ballygarth, Co. Meath. Lambert
    Pepper married Jane Otway in 1730. Their son Simon lived at Lissani-
    skey in 1814 and had ten sons. Several members of this prolific family
    served in the Irish Volunteers with members of the Head family (see
    chapter 10). The Peppers held land in the parish of Ballymackey from
    the Hon. O. F. G. Toler at the time of Griffiths Valuation. Landed Es-
    tates Database, NUI Galway.
16 The 1662 Hearth Tax Act levied a tax of two shillings on every hearth,
    fireplace or chimney imposed at the restoration "for the purpose of
    establishing an additional revenue upon His Majesty...for the better
    support of his and their crown and dignity." Thos. Laffan, *Tipperary
    Families: Being the Hearth Money Records for 1665-6-7* (Dublin, 1911, 53
    [Head], 57 [sadleir], 183 [Head again]. After being governor of Gal-
    way and then Waterford, Sadleir was cashiered on the Restoration
    and arrested by the earl of Cork on suspicion of being implicated in
    the 1662 anti-royalist plot before becoming sheriff of Co. Tipperary.
    Dermot Gleeson, *The Last Lords of Ormond* (London, 1938), 163-164.
17 Grace, 81.
18 Welpy, Mar. 3, 1923, 166. The Muggletonians, named after Lodowicke
    Muggleton, was a small, rigidly unitarian Protestant Christian move-
    ment which began in 1651 when two London tailors, Muggleton and
    John Reeve, announced they were the last prophets foretold in the
    biblical Book of Revelation. The group grew out of the Ranters and
    in opposition to the Quakers. Muggletonian beliefs include a hostility

to philosophical reason, a scriptural understanding of how the universe works, and a belief that God appeared directly on this earth as Christ Jesus. Muggletonians avoided all forms of worship or preaching and, in the past, met only for discussion and socializing amongst members. The movement was egalitarian, apolitical, and pacifist, and resolutely avoided evangelism. Members attained a degree of public notoriety by cursing those who reviled their faith. The Muggletonian sect survived until 1846. See Douglas G. Greene, "Muggletonians and Quakers: A Study in the Interaction of Seventeenth-Century Dissent," *Albion: A Quarterly Journal Concerned with British Studies*, Vol. 15, No. 2 (Summer 1983), 102-22.

Chapter 6

1   Julian C. Walton, "Church, Crown and Corporation in Waterford City, 1520-1620," in William Nolan and Thomas P. Power, editors, *Waterford: History & Society* (Dublin: Geography Publications, 1992), 193-195.
2   Killoteran, Kilbarry, Killculliheen, Ballinakill, Newtown, Ballytruckle and Grange.
3   Thos. P. Power, "Electoral Politics in Waterford City, 1692-1832," in *Waterford*, 227-228.
4   Kerby A. Miller et al, editors, *Irish Immigrants in the Land of Canaan: Letters and Memoirs from Colonial and Revolutionary America, 1675-1815* (Oxford University Press, 2003), 18, note 64. The Cleagh Keating church in the parish of Modreeny, N. Tipperary, was apparently an offshoot of Waterford's congregation. Its congregation of Welsh Baptists emigrated to Cohansey, NJ, in 1683, and founded the Baptist church there. The official name of the Baptist church and settlement at Cleagh Keating was Ormond.
5   Barnard, 103.
6   Colonel Sadleir and his officers were given land grants in Cos. Tipperary and Waterford. John P. Prendergast, *The Cromwellian Settlement of Ireland* (first published in London, 1865. This edition London: Constable, 1996), 64, 92. Sadleir's personal grant was for 5,509 acres. His lands of Ballingarry and Kilmalagha became Sopwell Hall. As a sheriff of Co. Tipperary, he was responsible for assessing and collecting the hearth taxes of 1665-67 (see chapter 5).
7   Rev. James Graves, "The Ancient Fabric, Plate, and Furniture of the Cathedral of Christ Church, Waterford," *Transactions of the Kilkenny Archaeological Society*, Vol. 2, No. 1 (1852), 75-83.
8   See John J. Webb, *The guilds of Dublin* (Dublin, 1929) and *Municipal*

government in Ireland: medieval and modern (Dublin, 1929) and *Byrne's*, 143-144.

9   One of the best-known silversmiths in seventeenth-century Waterford was Edward Russell. In 1666-67, he was commissioned to produce the dies for new copper penny tokens. He was made a freeman of the city on September 1, 1674, and the Russell Chalice he made for the refurbishing of the now Protestant Christ Church Cathedral is one of the many items he is known to have produced.

10 Séamus Pender, editor, *Council Books of the Corporation of Waterford, 1662-1700* (Dublin: Stationery Office for the Irish Manuscripts Commission, 1964). This is a compilation of the surviving accounts of the proceedings of the Waterford city council in the seventeenth century: 1656-7; 1662-3; 1669-88; 1690-1700. It is the primary source of information about the civic and business activities of Capt. Michael Head and, to a lesser extent, of his oldest son, John Head. George Hunt was a member of the Hammermen guild in Waterford and might have been the father or older brother of Michael Head's second wife, Elizabeth Hunt. Waterford 2, 1662. Cited as Waterford from here on

11 Peter Elmer, *The Miraculous Conformist: Valentine Greatrakes* (Oxford University Press, 2013), 46, 51, 55-57.

12 Waterford, 38, Nov. 26; 42, Dec. 3, 1662; Downey, 153.

13 Waterford, 72, Dec. 30, 1662; 88 and 94, Jan. 6, 1663; Downey, 152.

14 Waterford, 306, April 8, 1663; 312, April 22.

15 Downey, 180.

16 Waterford, 420, Feb. 26; 422, Mar. 3; 424, Mar. 8, 1669; Downey, 67-69.

17 Downey, 177.

18 Sir William Petty estimated that in 1672 there were 800,000 Catholics and 300,000 Protestants in Ireland. Half of the Protestants were in the cities, leaving only about 50,000 in the countryside. J. G. Simms, *Jacobite Ireland, 1685-91* (Dublin: Four Courts Press, 2000), 8.

19 Two other Catholic merchants, Martin Walsh and Dominick Sinnott, petitioned for the right by birth to the corporation's freedom "according to his majesties proclamation." They were ordered to produce certified proof from the town clerk at the next sitting. Waterford 679, October 2, 1672.

20 Sir Thomas Dancer, an alderman and Mayor of Waterford city, was created a baronet in 1662. In 1668 he was granted 1,180 acres in the barony of Lower Ormond, County Tipperary. His grandson, also named Thomas, was high sheriff of Co. Tipperary in 1741 but died without male heirs. He was succeeded by his grand nephew Sir Amyrald Dancer.

21 According to the 1672 Rules, orders, and directions made and estab-

lished by the lord- lieutenant and council for "better regulating the several cities, walled towns, and corporations of Cork, Waterford, Kinsale, Youghal…all elections of mayor, sheriffs, recorder, and town clerk must be presented to the lord-lieutenant and privy council for approval, and each person elected to any of these offices must take the oath of supremacy, the oath of allegiance, the oath usually taken on assuming the particular office, and the oath of abhorrence (also known as the oath against taking arms, or the small oath)." Waterford 817, September 23, 1672.

22 *Byrne's*, 291.
23 Downey, 183.
24 Waterford, 1161, September 26, 1676.
25 Downey, 172.
26 Gleeson, 107.
27 From a deed relating to Ashley Park, certified July 13, 1824. Ex Biggs-Atkinson Papers, Ashley Park, Nenagh, Co. Tipperary. Copies of these deeds were given to me by local historian Danny Grace, whose ancestors owned the Rathone lands before the Cromwellian land grants. Grace has informed me that the Rathone lands had belonged to Tyone Abbey but were granted to a Grace on the dissolution of the monasteries.
28 Ormonde MSS, ii (1899), 256; Downey, 172-3.
29 Tim Harris, *Restoration: Charles II and his Kingdoms* (London: Penguin Books Ltd., 2005), 102, 138.
30 Downey, 184-186.
31 Waterford, 1395, July 30, 1680, 190-191; 1407 and 1415, Sept. 9 and 23, 193-199; 1426, September 29, 200-203. Page numbers are given here to indicate the extent and duration of this scandal.
32 Waterford, 1515, April 18, 1682, 220-221.
33 "Cattle Acts," *Oxford Companion*, 83.
34 Downey, 173. A revealing entry for December 1681 in the Corporation records illustrates the extent of these activities. The council listed the amounts that the sheriff receiver was expected to collect for goods lying on the quay: "For every punchion or hogshead of tallow, lying above forty-eight houres on any part of the Key, belonging to a freeman or forreynor, sixpence sterling; for every barrel of tallow, threepence; for every cask of butter, three halfpence; for every barrell of beef, pork, and mutton, which may require time for rebaleing, hooping, and pickleing, which shall bee on the Key above four dayes and four nights, to pay threepence per barrel; for every tierce of salmon that shalbee on the Key above four dayes and four nights, fourpence sterling; for every barrel of herrings lying above four dayes and four

nights, threepence sterling; for every pack of frize, leather, or skins lying above four and twenty houres, twopence sterling; for every thousand of pype, hogshead, or barrel staves lying above two days, to pay twelve pence sterling; for every thusand of hoopes, lathes, and slates lying above three dayes, eightpence sterling. Of all which the master porter is from time to time to give account to the sherif receiver or to the mayor and council, whereof he may not fail, and hereof to give notice forthwith to all persons concerned or to bee concerned." Waterford, 1498, December 12, 1681.

35   Waterford, 1569, March 5, 1682. See chapter 8 for a discussion of the dire consequences of John Head's severe losses at sea.
36   Waterford, 1605, Dec. 15, 1683.

Chapter 7

1   Waterford, 1644; 1651, Nov. 21, 1684. Freedom of the city was also awarded to David Lloyd, merchant, and Capt. Thomas Power.
2   On 2 November 1689, William II created Richard Coote (1636-1701) earl of Bellomont for his loyalty and granted him over 77,000 acres of forfeited Irish lands. The land grant was highly controversial in Parliament and was eventually rescinded by William. Coote was also rewarded with the governorship of County Leitrim. He ended his life as a governor of three New England colonies. See Frederick De Peyster, *The Life and Administration of Richard, Earl of Bellomont, Governor of the Provinces of New York, Massachusetts and New Hampshire, from 1697 to 1701* (New York: New York Historical Society, 1879). The Head family would have many more contacts with the Coote family over the next 250 years.
3   Waterford, 1660, Jan. 13, 1685.
4   Tim Harris, *Revolution: The Great Crisis of the British Monarchy, 1685-1720* (London: Penguin Books, 2006), 41-43. James later regretted he had used the word *preserve* and wished he had said "he never would endeavour to *alter* the established religion."
5   Henry Prittie Deed of Conveyance, Feb. 9, 1685. Dunalley Papers, Ms29806, folder 20, National Library of Ireland.
6   Harris, *Revolution*, 103-5. Talbot had been with the royalist garrison at Drogheda in 1649, was seriously wounded, and became an embittered enemy of Cromwell.
7   Waterford, 1666, March 4, 1685.
8   Herman Murtagh, "Jacobite Waterford," in John Kirwan, editor, *Kilkenny: Studies in Honour of Margaret M. Phelan* (Kilkenny: The Kilkenny Archaeological Society, 1997), 88.

9   Harris, *Revolution*, 112.
10   Waterford, 1689 and 1690, June 22, 1685. Before long, the tithes for all these parishes would be let to Michael Head.
11   Harris, 186.
12   Beckett, 140. Capt. Richard Coote (see chapter opening) was probably one of these dismissed officers.
13   Waterford, 1743, Aug. 23, 1686; 1745, Sept. 4, 1686; 1746, Sept. 10, 1686
14   Waterford, 1751, Oct. 21, 1686; 1753, November 10, 1685; 1755, November 23, 1686. For instance, Mayor Goodrick, who had been elected to a second term, and the sheriff receiver were forced to order sixty barrels of coal for the guards' fires, to be stored in and delivered from Alderman Denis's cellar.
15   Harris, *Revolution*, 124.
16   The Waterford Corporation called him "his exellenties the lord-lieutenant of Ireland" when ordering that "bells and bonefires" be made to honor his arrival at Dublin. Waterford 1763, February 10, 1687.
17   Simms, 35.
18   Waterford, 1765, February 22; 1773, April 1, 1687.
19   ibid., 1775, April 2; 1777, April 6, 1687.
20   Pender, Waterford, xiv; Simms, 35.
21   Waterford, 1796, June 29, 1687. Lloyd had been elected freeman of the city just three years earlier by Mayor Michael Head.
22   Waterford, 1809, Jan. 14; 1811, Jan. 19; 1815, Jan. 24, 1688. The last of these parish lands had once belonged to the abbess and community of Kilculliheen, a religious house dissolved by order of Henry VIII. They were then awarded to the Fitzgerald family.
23   Waterford, 1822, Mar. 17, 1688. As Pender announced in the printed edition of the surviving Waterford Council Books, "The administration of municipal affairs was taken over at this point by the corporation constituted according to the provisions of James II's charter of 1688. As the volume in which the proceedings of this newly-constituted corporation were recorded is now missing, we are left without any knowledge of the details of the municipal administration of Waterford during the period from March 1688 to July 1690," 282.
24   Murtagh, 92. Source: Walter Harris, *The history of the life and reign of William-Henry, prince of Nassau, etc.* (Dublin, 1749), appendix x, xv.
25   Harris, 433.
26   Beckett, 143.
27   Murtagh, 89.
28   Simms, 88.
29   Murtagh, 89. "New interest" purchasers were Catholics who had purchased lands from the 1660s, the titles to which were based on the Res-

toration land settlement. Unlike the majority of their co-religionists, they were lukewarm about attempts to repeal the settlement because they feared the loss of their newly acquired estates. Byrne's, 206-7.

30   ibid., 94, Appendix 3. Source: Harris, *William-Henry, prince of Nassau* (Dublin, 1749), appendix, xliv. Waterford Alderman Joseph Ivie, who *was* attainted, would acquire extensive lands in Co. Tipperary. Power, 80.

31   John D'Alton, editor, *King James's Irish Army List* (Dublin, 1855), 29, 33. Internet access to Boston College volume via Hathi Trust. Dublin City was assessed £5,000 for the three months while King's County was assessed £860.

32   Murtagh, Appendix, 94-95, Appendix 6, 96. Both from "Irish Jacobites," in J. G. Simms, editor, *Anal. Hib.*, no. 22, 1960, 54, 62-3; ibid., 89-135.

33   Harris, 447. According to the entry on the Prittie (Dunalley) family in *Dictionary of Peerage and Baronetage of Ireland*, "After the Battle of the Boyne, Henry Prittie [grandson of the original Cromwellian grantee] sustained a siege of 21 days in his Castle of Dunalley, against the disbanded soldiers of the Royal Army (James II) but the besiegers at length entering, Mr. P was flung headlong from the top of the castle, but miraculously escaped unhurt."

34   ibid., 156.

35   Harris, 447.

36   Murtagh, 90-91.

37   ibid., 91.

38   Waterford, 1866, November 18, 1690.

39   Beckett, 148.

Chapter 8

1   Waterford, 1906, June 18, 1692; 1935, March 27, 1693.

2   Bruce Elliott, "The Protestants of North Tipperary," Chapter 2, *Irish Migrants in the Canadas: A New Approach* (Montreal and Kingston: McGill-Queen's University Press, 2004), 16. One of the lesser officers was Capt. Samuel Wade, whose daughter's inheritance of his Cromwellian land grant passed to her husband John Head upon their marriage in 1696.

3   *Waterford*, 371. According to Samuel Lewis, *A Topographical Dictionary of Ireland* (London: S. Lewis, 1837), Portnescully was a parish in the barony of Iverk, Co. Kilkenny, 3 miles northwest from Waterford on the River Suir. It was a vicarage in the diocese of Ossery. The rectory was impropriate in (controlled by) the corporation of Waterford. The

tithes then amounted to £200, of which £125 was payable to the lessee of the impropriators, and the remainder to the vicar.

4   *Waterford*, 370.

5   Murtagh, 92.

6   Leghorn or Livorno, located just south of Pisa, received the status of a free port in 1675 and was an important connecting point between the Mediterranean, North Sea ports and the Near East.

7   Aldermen Christmas, Seay, Lloyd, and Abraham Smith and councilmen Ben Lambe and Eyres.

8   Waterford, 1993, March 29, 1694.

9   ibid., 2014, January 28, 1695.

10 Harris, 462.

11 Waterford, 2033, July 11, 1695; Thomas P. Power, "Electoral Politics in Waterford City, 1692-1832," in *Waterford*, 229-230.

12 Both Michael and John Head were absent from the council meeting on August 28 which leads me to guess that this was due to John's wedding. My grandfather, Charles O. Head, speculated in his 1943 memoir that the marriage occurred in Limerick since John Head had penetrated that far. I have found no evidence of this, beyond his later shipping activities in Limerick harbor. I think it is unlikely since he became mayor of Waterford in 1700 and the little that remains of his correspondence gives his home address as Woodstowne near Waterford harbor where the River Suir widens into its estuary.

13 Power, 119-121.

14 Waterford, 2112, April 18, 1698; Waterford, 2141, February 24, 1699: "Also that they [the sheriffs] discourse Alderman John Head about his building on the Kea, and report the method next sitting."

15 Caleb Wade: Waterford, 2090, June 29, 1697, and 2146, June 29, 1699; 2127, August 27, 1698.

16 See http://www.igp-web.com/IGPArchives/ire/tipperary/land/claims-tipp-1700.txt Toler's debts by bond of £136 and £500 suggest the risks of land claims and dealing at this point in Co. Tipperary. The latter was due to John Connor according to a judgment in the Court of Exchequer in 1679, but was assigned to Toler by deed on April 23, 1700.

17 Since the Corporation of Waterford records were lost from the point when John Head was sworn in as mayor, there is no way of knowing whether his disastrous losses happened during the year he was in office and whether or not he was an effective mayor. All related letters and the 7-page legal case of Elnathan Lumm against John Head are held in the Lumm Papers at the National Library of Ireland, Ms 8361.

18 Lease made between John and Elizabeth Head and Elnathan Lumm, August 27, 1702. [No. 272]; there is a copy of this lease dated Octo-

ber 22, 1702 in the Lumm Papers, D6644, National Library of Ireland (NLI).

19 Caleb Wade, Limerick, to Elnathan Lumm, Dublin, March 17, 1703. Lumm Papers, Ms8361, NLI.

20 Edmond Forstall was a Catholic merchant of the family that lived in Gurteen Castle at that time. A Forstall relation became governor of Louisiana.

21 A jointure was an annuity payable to a landlord's widow charged on the rents and profits of the land for her lifetime. 2. An estate settled on a wife to be taken in lieu of dower.The exact wording of the disputed 1692 indenture for the marital support of Elizabeth Wade were that the Rochestown lands in Co. Kilkenny: "should not through any Casualty Reduction or misfortune that as God forbid should happen to the said John during the Coverture in the way of his Trade Commerce or by Risqes Adventures at Sea or otherwise be disposed of Converted or Extended to any other use than the maintenance & subsistance of his said intended wife that being the principall scope and intent of the said Agreemt and of the settlemt made by the said Micheal bearing Date the day before the Date of these presents of Rochestowne and other Lands and to the end that the sd John Head may be devested of any Power he may otherwise have to Conveigh Grant or incumber by Judgment Statute Recognizance or otherwise the said Lands soe settled or subject the same to Creditors so as his and intended wife and her Children (with which God may bless her) may be frustrated of that Competent maintenance and Subsistance which the Considerable fortune (she by her marryage is to bring to the sd John Head and his family) deserves."

22 In *Road to Divorce: England 1530-1987* (Oxford University Press, 1990), Lawrence Stone explains the political issues involved in efforts toward reform of the divorce law, leading up to the compromised Act of 1857. He writes, "The demand for the placing of a married woman's property under her own control struck at the heart of the economic aspects of a marriage contract, and threatened the strategic manipulation of marriage to advance family property interests. It also created a dual economic interest between husband and wife, which over a century before Hume had declared to be a threat to marital harmony." But, he continues: "In fact, the top 10 percent of society, including almost all those represented in Parliament, were already marrying under the settlement arrangement, by which the wife kept control over her own property through trustees."

23 Sir Theobald (Toby) Butler (1650-1720) was a leading barrister and politician in late seventeenth-century Ireland, who held office as

solicitor-general for Ireland. He is principally remembered for framing the articles of the Treaty of Limerick and for his eloquent plea to the Irish House of Commons against the Popery Act of 1703, which allowed any Protestant son of a Roman Catholic to debar his Catholic brothers from inheriting the family property. He was a much loved "character" in Dublin, and his great popularity shielded him from any harm which he might have suffered from his religious beliefs. Wikipedia.

24 "Palatine jurisdiction," *Oxford Companion*, 447.
25 Elnathan Lumm's will, April 12, 1708. Public Record Office, National Archives, Kew, London.
26 The Registry includes no documents relating to the Lumm and Head dispute which makes the survival of these documents at the National Library of Ireland even more of a miracle.
27 Deed dates April 19, 1709, RD 17.144.8430. Register of Deeds, Dublin.
28 Memorial of will, RD 17.145.8431.1, May 21, 1709. Register of Deeds, Dublin. See also *Vicars Index to Prerogative Wills, 1530-1818* (1897), 22.
29 Indenture of Deed of Settlement Tripartite between Thomas Head of Waterford, Esq., Rebecca Congreve of Waterford, widow, and trustees, re jointures for Mary Congreve (£100 if she should survive him leaving issue and £130 without issue) from the Freehold and Leasehold estate of Thomas Head (Woodstock and Castlemitchell) plus an annuity of £40 following Thomas's death. Rebecca Congreve covenantd to pay Thomas Head £500 following the solemnization of marriage. The witnesses were James Nugent of Waterford, Edward Doyle of Heads Grove, Co. Kilkenny, and James Higgins of Dublin Gent. Register of Deeds. 30.23.16142, April 30, 1711.

Chapter 9

1 Power, 103.
2 ibid, 152-3.
3 These included the Moore, Sadleir, Coote, Langley, Baker, Cleere, Dawson, Dancer, Harrison, and Mathew families.
4 V. T. H. Delany, "The Palatinate Court of the Liberty of Tipperary," in *American Journal of Legal History*, vol.5, 103-104. Unfortunately, all the records were transferred to the Public Record Office in the Four Courts Building in Dublin in 1871 and were incinerated in the 1922 firebombing, thus eliminating any chance of finding records of the Head v. Lumm case, possibly excepting a short calendar of their contents printed in Public Record Office of Ireland, *5 Report of the Deputy Keeper* and *6 Report of the Deputy Keeper*. The suffix Esquire indicated gentleman status.

5   Michael was not the first Head to attend TCD. His second cousin John, grandson of the original Rev. John Head, entered TCD on February 13, 1697/8 and earned a B.A. in 1702. He took holy orders, became a curate in Borrisokane and married Cassandra Meritt of the nearby parish of Finoe in 1709. *Alumni Dublinenses: A Register of the Students, Graduates, Professors, and Provosts ofTrinity College, in the University of Dublin*. Editors George D. Burtchaell and Thomas U. Sadleir (London: Williams and Norgate, 1924).

6   R. F. Foster, *Modern Ireland 1600-1972* (London: Allen Lane The Penguin Press, 1988), 173.

7   ibid., 157.

8   Local historian Daniel Grace was given a large quantity of deeds copied for a title search by a subsequent owner of one of the later Head properties, Ashley Park near Nenagh. He allowed me to copy these deeds which provided the original pathway to the Heads' story. Others were located in the Registry of Deeds and the National Library of Ireland in Dublin.

9   RD 33.432.20798, July 13, 1721. This indenture was "signed and sealed at Headsgrove about 60 miles from Dublin" in the presence of his cousin, the Rev. John Head of Durrow, Co. Tipperary, and Joseph Cooke, a Waterford gentleman.

10   RD 39.127.24529, Dec. 22, 1721.

11   Bentham Abstracts Series X, vol. I, p. 117.

12   RD 49.18.30509, May 21-22, 1725. Grace and Arthur Burdett had a son, George, and he in turn had two sons, Arthur and the Rev. John Burdett, who, in 1802, would marry his second cousin, Margaret Head of Derry Castle.

13   In the summer of 1718, John Head leased a total of 206 acres in the Barony of Owney and Arra, Co. Tipperary to Hercules Rowley and his heirs "for ever" but redeemable on payment of £600 and a further £36 in interest. He also leased 86 acres in the Barony of Lower Ormond, Co. Tipperary, and 144 acres in the town and land of Rochestown, Barony of Idea, Co. Kilkenny, together with all its houses, to Richard Shaw for £400. Likewise, this lease could be broken on payment by Head of £400 to Shaw plus £28 for one year's interest at the rate of 7 percent per year. Register of Deeds Memorial No. 22.97.11498, July 8-9, 1718 and RD Memorial 27.307.17080, August 13-14, 1718.

14   Register of Deeds. Lib 56/P90/No 37084, March 5, 1727.

15   See <https://en.wikipedia.org/wiki/Mary_Delany>. Dawson also composed a Bacchanalian song "Bumpers, 'Squire Jones'" in the 1730s.

16   Arthur Dawson died in 1775 and was succeeded by his nephew, another Arthur.

17 Otway Toler's heir was Lt. Col., later Gen. Michael Head, who inherited the property of Modreeny. The Otway Toler bible, although badly burned in one of two fires, remains with the general's descendants. Many of the dates entered at the opening of the bible are incorrect.

18 Foster, 184. In April 1767, the Dublin Society, which devoted most of its attention to agriculture, presented Thomas Otway with a silver medal "in testimony…for his laudable improvement of his county—draining, ditching and planting," and he was elected member of the Society.

19 Michael Seymour Dudley Westropp, *Irish Glass: An Account of Glass-making in Ireland from the XVIth Century to the Present Day* (London: Herbert Jenkins Ltd., 1921), 68-69. In 1762, "the glass-house lands" at Gurteen were advertised to be let, but no mention was made of the glasshouse. The lands were still marked "Glass house" on the Ordnance map. In 1783, the celebrated Waterford factory was established, maker of all the old glass in Ireland.

20 Patrick C. Power, *Carrick-on-Suir and Its People* (Carrick-on-Suir: Anna Livia Books for the Carrick Society, 1976), 69.

21 The prerogative will of Mary Head, widow of Michael Head, Derry, Co. Tipperary, was entered in 1760 but was lost in the 1922 firebombing of the Irish Record Office.

22 Cecil Woodham-Smith, *The Great Hunger: Ireland 1845-1849* (London: Penguin Books Ltd., 1991), 28.

23 Charles Octavius Head, *Napoleon and Wellington* (London: Robert Hale Ltd., 1939), vi.

24 *Gentleman's Magazine*, vol. 29, 1759; See <http://en.wikipedia.org/wiki/14th_King's Hussars>

25 J. C. Beckett, *The Anglo-Irish Tradition* (Ithaca, New York: Cornell University Press, 1976), 82.

26 Foster, 185.

27 Particularly resented was the tithe on potatoes, the principal sustenance of the people.

28 Because of charges that Catholic merchants in the ports were supplying funds for the advancement of the Whiteboy activities in Co. Tipperary, attempts were made to get two of those about to be executed to swear against Catholic merchants in Waterford and Cork.

29 T. P. Power, 260, 262-265. Other right-wingers were Richard and William Perry (a Head descendant married a Perry descendant in the late nineteenth century), John Walsh, Thomas Hackett, Richard Moore, and William Chadwick, who themselves or their tenants suffered from Whiteboy outrages or were active in their suppression.

30 T. P. Power, 239.

31 Preliminary agreement to the marriage settlement of Michael Head, Derry, Tipperary, and Margaret, daughter of Henry Prittie, Kilboy, June 16, 1761. Dunalley Papers, Ms 29806, Folder 158. National Library of Ireland (NLI).

32 George Head's father, the Rev. John Head, instituted the vicarage of Ballingarry and Borrisokane through the Board of First Fruits in May 1729 but died the following year. An inventory of the Rev. John Head's goods and effects dated May 12, 1731, turned up in a collection of documents relating to the Protestant Diocese of Killaloe and is now in the British Museum. This showed him to be a man of some substance, owning stock valued at more than £40, corn and potatoes at £18, ready money of £10, and debts owed to him of £296. His household goods valued at £30 included feather beds, 18 chairs, pewter, Delftware, and glasses, as well as two beds and bedclothes for servants. His son George, who entered TCD June 3, 1737 aged 18, was named a scholar in 1740, B.A. 1741 and M.A. 1745. A marriage license bond entered in Killaloe, Co. Clare on January 4, 1760 for his marriage to Sarah White of Greenhall, Co. Tipperary, lists him as gentleman of Kilboy, Co. Tipperary. In a list of County Tipperary freeholders in 1775-76, his address was Ballynahinch, Curraghviller.

33 Head-Prittie marriage settlement, June 27, 1761. Dunalley Papers Ms29,806, Folder 160. NLI. My cousin, Barbara Bowers, and I spent many hours spreading out and weighting down this impressive document on a library table so that we could transcribe it.

34 No documentation of this marriage between these younger members of their respective families has been found.

35 Rathone means "earthen fort," a name derived from several Neolithic ring forts found on the estate.

36 Conveyance Indenture between Thomas Stopford of High Court of Chancery, John Fitzmaurice Esq., of Springfield, Co. Limerick, and Michael Head of Derry over terms of 1728 conveyance and subsequent mortgages, February 25, 1765. Registry of Deeds No. 154,417, Book 238. Reference was frequently made to the tripartite agreement drawn up in 1727 by the Heads' trustees and executors Arthur Dawson and William Sumner of Dublin.

37 Brian Murphy, M.A. thesis, 1997, "The Waterford Catholic Community in the Eighteenth Century." Ironically, a snobbish Head descendant, a sister of my grandfather, was heard to remark that the Heads were never in trade. They would certainly have done better to avoid placing all their bets on Irish land, as this continuing narrative will show.

38 Taylor & Skinner, *Maps and Roads of Ireland*, 1777; W. Wilson, *Post-Chaise*

Companion, 1786. This house, with considerable later embellishments by the family which purchased it in 1825, still stands and is run by its owners as a bed and breakfast and favorite local event space.

39 On February 19, 1773, John E. Head entered into a deed of indemnity with Denis O'Brien "of the City of Dublin Gent" and his brother Michael of Derry for the fee-farm grant of the 140 acres of Drumniscart, part of the Ashley Park estate. For £525, these lands would be transferred from the current tenants to George Jackson and Denis O'Brien. A fee-farm grant was a simple freehold grant to a tenant for an annual fixed rent without any other services, but forever. This was a great advantage to the tenant and was offered by landlords to lure tenants when there was an abundant supply of land and a scarcity of people to till the land. Over the years, as inflation kicked in, the rents became a mere pittance. *Byrne's*, 118.

40 T. P. Power, 97.

41 Foster, 194.

42 Henry and Catherine Prittie's oldest daughter Catherine married Henry Bowen of Bowen's Court, Co. Cork. Bowen was the three times great-uncle of the last owner of Bowen's Court, famed novelist Elizabeth Bowen. Since Henry and Catherine Bowen were childless, the Bowen estate passed to the next oldest brother Robert Bowen.

43 Power, 114-115. Fifteen-year-old Deborah Prittie married Matthew Bunbury of Kilfeakle in September 1755. Although his estate was valued at £2,000 in the Kilboy papers, it was reported in the 1770s that Bunbury "lives most in England, his wife and he live separate and his affairs much embarrassed." Martha Prittie married Thomas Otway of Otway Castle in March 1757 and, following his death without issue in 1786, Thomas Parker of Ballyvally, Co. Clare. Elizabeth Prittie married Peter Holmes of Johnstown Park in January 1765.

44 *Patentee Officers in Ireland 1173-1826, including High Sheriffs, 1661-1684 and 1761-1816* (Dublin: Stationery Office, 1960), 64.

45 Register of Deeds, Book 281, page 466, No. 18743; Journals of the House of Commons of the Parliament of Ireland.

46 Miriam Lambe, *A Tipperary Landed Estate, Castle Otway, Templederry 1750-1853* (Dublin: Irish Academic Press, 1998), 7, from Thomas U. Sadleir, "Manuscripts at Kilboy, Co. Tipperary, in the possession of Lord Dunalley," in *Analecta Hibernia* no. 12 (1943), 113-54.

47 Fortunately for Co. Tipperary, Tenison Groves, a genealogical researcher working in the Public Record Office of Ireland before its destruction in 1922, transcribed some freeholders' registers for the period 1761-1776, and these are available in the National Archives of Ireland and other archives. See Terry Eakin, "An Index to Freeholders'

Registers of County Tipperary 1775-76," in *Directory of Irish Family History Research.* George, John, and Michael Head are listed in this index. www.ancestryireland.com/data/directory/Directory.pdf

48 T. P. Power, 277; "Yearly Estate in County Tipperary, 1775," drawn up from a rare manuscript to survive the burning of Kilboy in 1922. Dunalley Papers, National Library of Ireland.

49 "Lord Norbury," in Jonah Barrington, *Personal Sketches of His Own Times by Sir Jonah Barrington* (London: Henry Colburn and Richard Bentley, 1830). Project Gutenberg EBook, 2015, 337 passim.

50 I remember the horrified reaction of an archivist in Waterford on my first research trip to Ireland in 2001 when he saw John Toler's name on a preliminary family tree I had made at that time. In his memoir, my grandfather slid by the problem by asserting that he had reason to believe Toler "was not as bad as he was painted" and that "racial and political prejudice took infinite pains to blacken his character, and he took none to preserve its actual hue." COH, 12.

51 In 1768, Holmes had bought out his interest in the town and lands of Nenagh for £12,400, of which £7,000 was through a mortgage. Sadly, Elizabeth Prittie Holmes died that year, perhaps in childbirth, and her husband's estate passed on to a cousin, another Peter Holmes, on his death in 1802. T. P. Power, 96.

52 Rackrenting meant to subject to an excessively high rent. It was a term given currency by Maria Edgeworth's famous novel *Castle Rackrent.*

53 Arthur Young, *A Tour in Ireland with General Observations on the Present State of that Kingdom* (2006 Elibron Classics facsimile of 1780 edition published by T. Cadell, London), Vol. II, 122-24.

54 The Georgian house consisted of three stories over a basement. The façade had a three-bay center between two bow windows, and round-headed windows on either side of the pediment fanlighted doorway in the center of each bow.

55 Young, 18-41.

Chapter 10

1 Power, 273. For rise of the Whiteboys, see chapter 9, 70 passim.

2 The principal volunteer regiments in the south of the county were the Tipperary Volunteers, Clonmel Independents, Cashel Volunteers, Cahir Union, Thurles Union, Drum Division of the Thurles Union, Newport Volunteers, and Fethard Independents. Munster volunteer registry (Dublin, 1782)., See http://www.from-ireland.net/tipperary-munster-volunteer-registry-1782 .

3 W. E. H. Lecky, *A History of Ireland in the Eighteenth Century*, Abridged

and with an introduction by L. P. Curtis, Jr. (Chicago: The University of Chicago Press, 1972), 171.

4   Marianne Elliott, *Partners in Revolution: The United Irishmen and France* (New Haven: Yale University, 1982), 12.

5   Roy Foster, *The Oxford Illustrated History of Ireland* ((Oxford University Press, 1989), 177 passim.

6   "parliaments," *Oxford Companion*, 453.

7   A list of the boroughs with an outline of the electoral system in each was published as an appendix in the *History of the Proceedings of the Volunteer Delegates on the Subject of a Parliamentary Reform*, 1784. Familiar names from Waterford included John Congreve, Esq. and Thomas Christmas Esq. from Co. Waterford and Capt. Henry Alcock and Capt. Bolton from the County of the City of Waterford.

8   *Clonmel Gazette*, Jan.15, 1784.

9   "Catholic Relief Acts," *Oxford Companion*, 82.

10 Lecky, 293.

11 Power, 293-294. See *Faulkner's Dublin Journal*, Dec. 22, 1792, re the Nenagh Address.

12 ibid., 296.

13 For his military triumph at Toulon, Bonaparte was promoted from colonel to brigadier-general on December 22. He was not present at the massacre of royalist prisoners by Convention troops three days earlier since he was on his way to take up his new post in Nice.

14 The letter, dated May 30, 1794, is quoted on pages 18-19 of the official *Historical Record of the Twelfth or the Prince of Wales's Royal Regiment of Lancers*, London, 1842.

15 Marcus Beresford to his father. "John Toler," *Dictionary of National Biography*.

16 Thomas Bartlett and Keith Jeffery, editors., *A Military History of Ireland* (Cambridge University Press, 1996), 268.

17 M. Elliott, 119.

18 James St. Clair-Erskine had been assistant adjutant-general in Ireland in 1782, then adjutant-general in 1793, aide-de-camp to King George III in 1795, and promoted to major-general in 1798, lieut-general 1805, and general 1814. In 1806, he was a member of the special mission to Lisbon, which resulted in Sir Arthur Wellesley being sent to the Peninsular. He succeeded as the 2nd earl of Rosslyn in 1805.

19 Drought Papers, NLI. Deed 2369-2089-246923 registered by John Head and John A. Drought on June 21, 1785.

20 The Leesons' second son, William, became chamberlain and Usher of the Black Rod to the lord-lieutenant of Ireland in 1849, a fractious time to play the courtier.

21 George E. (Ted) Russell and David Lee, "The Freemen of Limerick," in David Lee, *Remembering Limerick: Historical Essays Celebrating the 800th Anniversary of Limerick's First Charter Granted in 1197* (Limerick Civic Trust, 1997), 320. Russell (1912-2004) was five times mayor of Limerick.

22 William J. Hayes, *Tipperary in the Year of Rebellion 1798* (Roscrea, Co. Tipperary: Lisheen Publications, 1998), 9, 11-12. Hayes referenced Arthur Young on his visits twenty years earlier to "some of the outstanding landlord demesnes such as Derry Castle, overlooking Lough Derg," etc., 3.

23 ibid., 13-14.

24 ibid., 17-22.

25 Peter Somerville-Large, *The Irish Country House: A Social History* (London: Sinclair-Stevenson, 1995), 214.

26 Hayes, 28-30.

27 Power, 314.

28 Thomas Bartlett, "Defence, counter-insurgency and rebellion: Ireland, 1793-1803," in *Military History of Ireland*, 277. After the abortive and badly coordinated insurrection of 1798, the Tipperary gentry claimed that ten cartloads of pike heads were seized in the baronies of Upper and Lower Ormond and Owney and Arra.

29 Power, 317; Hayes, 40.

30 Foster, 280. Wolfe Tone was elevated to the pantheon of nationalist heroes set up in 1916 by Patrick Pearse.

31 Richard Lalor Sheil, *Sketches of the Irish Bar with Memoir and Notes*, Vol. 2 (London: FB& Ltd., Forgotten Books), 13-14.

Chapter 11

1 Franklin and Mary Wickmire, *Cornwallis: The Imperial Years* (Chapel Hill: University of North Carolina Press, 1980), 243.

2 "Act of Union," *Oxford Companion*, 595.

3 ibid., 595; D. George Boyce, *Nineteenth Century Ireland: The Search for Stability* (Dublin: Gill & Macmillan, 2005), 21.

4 Patrick M. Geoghegan, *The Irish Act of Union* (New York: St. Martin's Press, 1999), 7.

5 "Act of Union," *Oxford Companion*; Power, 321.

6 ibid., 320-321.

7 ibid., 320. The 1st baron Dunalley died on January 3, 1801, aged just 57, and was succeeded by his son Henry Sadleir Prittie as the 2nd baron Dunalley.

8 Lecky called Lord Clare "an unforgiving and unforgiven opponent of concessions to Catholics," 478.

9   Edward Brynn, *Crown & Castle: British Rule in Ireland 1800-1830* (Toronto: Macmillan Co. of Canada, 1978), 24-25.

10   Marianne Elliott, *Robert Emmet: The Making of a Legend* ((London: Profile Books, 2003), 3. In her introduction, Elliott describes discovering as a postgraduate student in the French Consulate archives, the degree to which Emmet was "a single-minded negotiator…a young man who commanded the respect of a number of hardened senior figures in the French government and military command." This led to her Oxford University doctoral thesis and her 1982 book *Partners in Revolution*.

11   For a discussion of whether Despard was a hero or a villain, see Mike Jay, *The Unfortunate Colonel Despard: The Tragic True Story of the the Last Man Condemned to be Hung, Drawn and Quartered* (London: Bantam Press, 2004).

12   I am indebted to historian and Emmet biographer Patrick M. Geoghegan whose careful and objective study of Robert Emmet and particularly his trial before Lord Norbury was based on new archival material from Ireland, the United Kingdom, France, and the United States and answered many of the questions I had after studying other sources. Geoghegan, *Robert Emmet: A Life* ((Dublin: Gill & Macmillan Ltd., 2002).

13   It should be noted that Sarah Curran's father, John Philpot Curran, one of the most popular Protestant lawyers in Ireland for his liberality, support of Catholic Emancipation, and enlargement of the franchise, had never supported militant republicanism, and was appalled by the murder of his friend and mentor Lord Kilwarden. He was scandalized by his daughter's relationship with Robert Emmet and even handed over the couple's letters to the authorities. He broke off relations with Sarah who lived with friends in Co. Cork until she married a British naval surgeon in 1805. She died three years later after giving birth to a premature son who also died. Elliott, 75, 91-92; Geoghegan, 24-25.

14   Geoghegan, 227.

15   Joseph Campbell, *The hero with a thousand faces* (New York, 1949), 356. As quoted in Geoghegan, 260.

16   There is no authoritative text of Emmet's speech that has been accepted throughout the years. The official version was prepared by William Ridgeway, one of the crown lawyers and a distinguished court reporter, who had been a member of the United Irishmen in the early 1790s. But Ridgeway's account did not include the famous line about Ireland taking her place among the nations of the earth and was dismissed by some of Emmet's friends as government propaganda. R. R. Madden spent a good deal of time sifting through

the various versions produced later by people sympathetic to Emmet and produced a text that he believed was the most accurate account. There were problems with that too but, despite all the controversy, Geoghegan says that they differ so little in substance, the content is virtually identical. Geoghegan, 244-245.

17 M. Elliott, 95.

18 Patrick M. Geoghegan, *King Dan: The Rise of Daniel O'Connell 1775-1829* (Dublin: Gill and Macmillan, 2010), 100.

19 M. Elliott, 154-155.

20 Nevertheless, William St. John Mason referred to Norbury in an 1842 letter to the *Times* as "that scum of humanity." Norbury and his supporters, whoever they were, were long dead by that time. His son, the 2nd earl, was murdered in 1839.

21 M. Elliott, 175. I trace the realities of his fate and that of his son, the 2nd earl of Norbury, in chapters 12 and 13.

22 Michael was stationed with his regiment at Topsham Barracks which was established as an artillery barracks around 1800. The following month, Maj. Gen. James Thewles died suddenly at Exeter. He and Frances had four very young children and she was pregnant with a fifth. Since Gen. Thewles had sold his estate in Ireland, it seems likely that Edward Ravenscroft supported Frances and her five children financially. The third Ravenscroft sister, Anna Maria, married an eccentric naval officer, forty-six-year-old Rear-Adm. Henry Paulet, in 1813. Two years later, he was appointed a Knight Commander of the Order of the Bath and promoted to vice-admiral. They also had five children. George Ravenscroft, Edward's only son, continued the family's East India Company tradition but was murdered by natives in Bingha, Oude. His youngest daughter married Robert, 15th viscount Hereford in 1841. Charles Head claimed incorrectly in his autobiography that it was his mother's sister who had married Hereford.

23 Bushy House became the duke's official residence in 1797 when it was granted to him by his father King George III. There he lived with his irregular wife, the famous actress Mrs. [Dora] Jordan, and their ten children until the couple's relationship came to an end in 1811, when William was persuaded to make an appropriate marriage as the heir apparent to his brother, the prince regent. For an excellent account of this relationship, see Claire Tomalin, *Mrs. Jordan's Profession: The story of a great actress and a future King* (London: Viking, 1994). However, there is no mention of any of the duke's aide-de-camps.

24 Loftus Otway was the fourth of five sons of Cooke and Elizabeth Otway of Castle Otway, County Tipperary. The family had a strong military tradition and Otway joined the 5th Dragoon Guards aged

twenty-one in 1796 as a cornet. He was present at the Battle of Vinegar Hill, the culminating battle of the 1798 uprising, transferred to the 8th Dragoons in 1804, serving for three years in Canada, and then volunteered for service in Portugal and Spain with the 18th Light Dragoons, joining Sir John Moore's forces in Galicia. Evacuated from Corunna in January 1809, his regiment was stationed in England. He returned to Wellesley's army in the Peninsula to command a Portuguese cavalry brigade under Gen. William Beresford.

25 A brevet was a type of military commission conferred especially for outstanding service by which an officer was promoted to a higher rank without the corresponding pay.

26 "13th Light Dragoons: The Peninsular War," The British Empire on-line: https://www.britishempire.co.uk/forces/armyunits/britishcavalry/13thltdragoons1778.htm

27 COH, 12-13.

28 "Campo Mayor: The Great Controversy," in Ian Fletcher, *Galloping at Everything: The British Cavalry in the Peninsular War and at Waterloo 1808-1815: A Reappraisal* (Mechanisburg, PA: Stackpole Books, 1999), Ch. 4, 125-143.

29 C. R. B. Barratt, *History of the 13th Hussars* (London, 1913), I: 130; Fletcher, 129.

30 "The Courier," April 20, 1811.

31 Fletcher, 131; note 13, 141.The paymaster of the 13th Light Dragoons, Gardiner, later purchased Chamorin's brass helmet from Logan and presented it to Colonel Head. Apparently, it was not one of the historic emblems that remained in the Head family, despite William Henry Head's passion for Napoleona.

32 Fletcher, 135.

33 The friendship up to that point was remarked on by Beresford's defender, Maj.-Gen. Sir Benjamin D'Urban in his *Further Strictures on those parts of Col. Napier's History of The Peninsular War which relate to the Military Opinions and Conduct of General Lord Viscount Beresford* (London, 1832), 42. D'Urban, then a brigadier general, was Beresford's quartermaster in the Peninsular Campaign.

34 Barratt, I: 136. Fletcher, 136-137.

35 The officers and men of the 13th Light Dragoons repaid Long's regard for them when they voluntarily subscribed to the purchase of a set of silver plate for him when Beresford replaced him in command of his brigade.

36 COH, 16; John Phillippart, *The Royal Military Calendar: containing the services of every general officer in the British Army from the date of their commission* (A. J. Valpi, 1815). Philippart was an industrious compiler

of many books of reference relating to the army. From October 1812 to September 1814 he owned and edited a journal called *The Military Panorama*.

37 General Lord Viscount Beresford, G.C.B., *Refutation of Colonel Napier's Justification of His Third Volume* (London: John Murray, 1834), 44-47, 158.

38 William Napier, *History of the War in the Peninsula*, III, 500-2; COH, 14; Sir John Fortescue, *History of the British Army* (London, 1899), VIII: 132-5.

39 Sir Charles Oman, *A History of the Peninsular War*, vol. IV: December 1810 to December 1811 (Oxford: Clarendon Press, 1902). Fletcher notes that, "by their defeat of the 26th Dragoons during the mêlée before the pursuit, the 13th had set the tone for the entire cavalry war in southern Spain." Fletcher, 138.

40 My brother has noted the irony that he, his son, and our father were all in Beresford House at Wellington College.

Chapter 12

1 Mary Butler, only daughter of William Butler Esq., of Limerick, had married Frederick Forbes, third son of George, 5th earl of Granard, in 1796. Forbes died in February 1817 having had no children with Mary. *Debrett's Genealogical Peerage of Great Britain and Ireland*, 1840-1847.

2 Ulster Ancestry, 1720-1846. Copy of the marriage register for the Parish of Portpatrick, Wigtownshire, Scotland, containing entries relevant to persons who came from Ireland. Perhaps both of them were divorced.

3 "Biggs v. Head, May 8, 1837" in *Reports of Cases in Chancery, Argued and Determined in the Rolls of Court. During the Time of the Rt. Hon. Sir Michael O'Loghlen* (1841), 349.

4 Samuel de la Cherois Crommelin was a descendant of a French Huguenot who was commissioned in 1698 to form a royal corporation to organize the flax and linen tradition in Co. Down for manufacture and export.

5 Lord Dunalley was embarrassed by his younger brother's opposition to the Tory government and tried to persuade the Castle that this resulted from his marriage to a daughter of George Ponsonby, the Irish chancellor. The Ponsonby family was known for its liberal politics. Dunalley was certain that his brother's politics had damaged his prospects for a representative peerage. Indeed, the Hon. Francis A. Prittie continued to vote silently for Catholic relief and parliamentary and sinecure reform. The History of Parliament Online: https://

www.historyofparliamentonline.org/volume/1790-1820/member/
prittie-hon-francis-aldborough-1779-1853.

6   *Dublin Evening Post*, Sept. 1, 1807.

7   ibid.

8   *Clonmel Herald*, Jan. 20, 1808. The noblemen included Headfort, Dorchester, Ormonde and Ossory, Mountcashel, Landaf, Donoughmore, and Lismore. Noticeably absent, however, were Dunalley and Norbury.

9   Griffin, 107

10 Power, 323.

11 Ever since the 1701 Act of Settlement, the Protestant Church of England was the established church in England. As the *ex officio* supreme governor of the Church of England, the monarch swears an oath at coronation to "maintain and preserve inviolably the settlement of the Church of England...as by law established in England." The 1800 Act of Union established the Protestant Episcopal Church of Ireland which would not be separated from the Church of England and disestablished until 1869 (see chapter 15).

12 Galen Broeker, *Rural Disorder and Police Reform in Ireland, 1812-26* (London: Routledge Kean Paul, 1970), 46.

13 ibid., 47, 42.

14 ibid., 74, 89-90.

15 Somerville-Large, 224-225.

16 Bruce Elliott, 36; Paul Bew, *Ireland: The Politics of Enmity, 1789-2006* (Oxford University Press, 2007), 92-93.

17 McGrath in Nolan, *Tipperary*, 272. Tithing potatoes was largely limited to the six counties of Munster and some adjacent parts of Leinster.

18 Deed of settlement, 1815. John Head then listed the next in line for his capital if both Maria and Catherine died: £1,000 to Letitia Drought, his oldest daughter, and the remaining £1,500 to "Michael Head Esquire son of said John Head and to his heirs Executors Administrators or Assigns for ever."

19 Rockview was given by Maria Head to her daughter upon her marriage. In 1876, George Guy Atkinson, who purchased Ashley Park from Gen. Michael Head, purchased Rockview's 32 acres for £300.

20 Daniel Grace, whose ancestors of Anglo-Norman or Old English stock once owned Rathone, renamed Ashley Park by John Head, was entrusted with the Biggs-Atkinson Papers by the current owners of Ashley Park, including copies of many Head family deeds relating to the property, which he generously allowed me to copy. Grace has written that John Head was several thousand pounds in debt but left only "one old carriage and some trifling articles not amounting in value to the sum of twenty pounds, which Maria Head, his widow, defrayed

towards payment of his funeral expenses," a quote that he says came from the final decree for sale of Ashley Park. Grace, 114.

21 *Dublin Evening Post*, October 9, 1819. In addition to the 900 acres of arable land in the Barony of Lower Ormond, the Waterford acres included the 480 acres of Farnoge, otherwise Toryhill, in Co. Kilkenny, four miles from Waterford, which had been let for £240 a year on a 31-year lease due to expire in two years; the lands of Lisdogan in Co. Waterford, also four miles from Waterford City and on a yearly let for three lives (limited to a specific line of heirs) since 1791; and the interest in the lease of the lands of Milford, Co.Waterford, "for lives renewable for ever." "entail" and "life tenancy," *Byrne's*, 112, 183-4.

22 *Dublin Evening Post*, Oct. 17, 1818.

23 The former regent succeeded his father George III in January 1820 and was crowned on July 19, 1821.

24 Boyce, 44.

25 Broeker, 138.

26 Bew, 105. It should be noted that the Spout in Nenagh, an elaborate well that long supplied the town's water, was erected by "the unparalleled benevolence of the English nation to the poor of Ireland at a season of extreme distress. AD 1822." Information from Daniel Grace.

27 It is not known how much M. P. Head spent on his new mansion but, for example, the earl of Kingston spent £220,000 on the building of Mitchelstown Castle during the 1820s. Terence Dooley, *Sources for the History of Landed Estates in Ireland*, edited by MaryAnn Lyons (Dublin: Irish Academic Press, 2000), 6.

28 McGrath in Nolan, *Tipperary*, 273.

29 Bruce Elliott, 34-35.

30 Geoghegan, *King Dan*, 64.

31 "John Toler," in John Gorton, *A general biographical dictionary*, vol. 2, part 3 (London: Hart and Clarke, 1828).

32 Moira Lysaght, "Norbury, 'The Hanging Judge' (1745-1831)," *Dublin Historical Record*, Vol. 30, No. 2 (March 1977), 58-65. Accessed through JSTOR #30087176. North Tipperary local historian John Flannery has found much to soften the almost universal indictment of Toler. Toler was known for his generosity and the granting of pardons when he sensed wrongful convictions. More substantively, Flannery found citations for Harvard Law School's publications of two or three of Toler's law cases but did not provide them to this writer.

33 According to LibraryIreland.com's article on Toler, however, his resignation came as a direct result of O'Connell's petition.

34 James S. Donnelly, Jr., *Captain Rock: The Irish Agrarian Rebellion of 1821-1824* (Madison, Wisconsin: The University of Wisconsin Press, 2009), 31.

35 Anon., *Old Bailey Solicitor* (n.p., [1822]), 16-17.
36 Donnelly, 37-38, 117. Also assassinated were a German Palatine who had been persuaded by Hoskins to come to the Courtenay estate "to establish a colony of Protestants," and Major Richard Going, the former repressive and sectarian head of the police in Co. Limerick. James Bridgeman, aged twenty-two, was hanged in 1824 for the murder of landlord Richard Going and was implicated in two other murders. Donnelly, jr., 48-51.
37 Donnelly, jr., 72-73.
38 ibid., 103.
39 *Dublin Evening Post*, Jan. 25, 1822.
40 Lady Spencer to her husband, May 13, 1822; www.historyofparliamentonline.prittie.
41 Virginia Crossman, "The army and law and order in the nineteenth century," Bartlett & Jeffery, 368-369.
42 *Clonmel Herald*, Aug. [16?], 1823.
43 *Dublin Evening Mail*, Mar. 24, 1824.
44 McGrath in Nolan, 273.
45 Maria gave the couple the house and land of Rockview acquired for her by her late husband. In August 1841, an act of ejectment to recover the lands of Rockview was brought by the plaintiff, John Kirwan, who claimed that the lands, formerly "part of the property of the late General Head," became entitled to him when his mother-in-law Miss [Mrs.] Head gave him a life interest in the land during the course of his marriage to her daughter. *Tipperary Free Press*, Aug. 18, 1841, 2.
46 *Dublin Evening Post*, June 12, 17, 22, and 29, 1824. Otherwise described as Rathone, the lands included Knockoland, 291 ½ acres, Drumniscart 5 acres, Ballythomas 8 acres, Clashitone 35 acres in the Barony of Lower Ormond and the lands of Newtown and Ballyrusheen West 221 acres in the Barony of Owney and Arra.
47 Memorial of Register of Deeds, 802.276.5 41411, August 27, 1824. According to the memorial, of the sum paid into the Bank of Ireland, nominal amounts were payable to Maj. Gen. Michael Head of Modreeny House and his wife, Elizabeth Head; the Hon. Eyre and Phoebe Massey and their only child Phoebe; Arthur Burdett and Nathaniel Eyre Robbins, trustees in the marriage settlement of the Hon. Eyre Massey; Maria Head of Hardwick Place, in Co. Dublin, widow and personal representative of the late John Head of Ashley Park; Robert Nesbitt, surviving trustee of the April 27, 1815 deed; Stephen and Catherine Cassan; John and Letitia Drought; and a mysterious Elizabeth Head, otherwise Brien.

48 O'Donnell, 50.
49 Resolutions of the magistrates at Cashel, Oct. 20, 1827. McGrath, 276 and 461, n. 184.
50 Sir Robert Peel to Lord Francis Leveson-Gower, August 14, 1829. McGrath in Nolan, *Tipperary*,276.
51 Death notices in *Dublin Evening Post*, Dec. 18, 1827; *Waterford Mail*, Dec. 22, 1827; *Oxford University and City Herald*, Dec. 29, 1827; and *Gentleman's Magazine*, March 1828.
52 Last Will & Testament of Michael Head of Ashley Park, Co. Tipperary, May 22, 1869. National Archives, Kew, U.K., Prob 11/1755/362. After a long widowhood, Elizabeth died in 1864 and was buried next to her husband.
53 *The Letters of King George IV, 1812-1830*, Vol. I, 234-235.
54 McGrath in Nolan, 264.
55 *Declaration of the undersigned Protestants in Favour of A Final and Conciliatory Adjustment of the Catholic Question* (Dublin: Alexander Thom, 1829).
56 See chapter 10 for Catholic relief acts of 1792 and 1793; "Catholic Emancipation," *Byrne's, 54.*

Chapter 13

1 Lysaght, 64. This delightful story must nevertheless be apocryphal since John Creighton, 1st earl Erne of Crom Castle, Co. Fermanagh, died on September 1, 1828.
2 *Dublin Evening Packet*, Jan. 17 and 24, 1829 and Jan. 24, 1832.
3 Griffin, 117-119.
4 Two earlier bishops of Killaloe, Edward Worth (1660-1669) and Charles Carr (1716-1739) were central, along with two Henry Pritties, to the Heads' ability to hold on to the Derry lands in earlier troubled times (see chapters 5 to 8).
5 Donald Harman Akenson, *The Church of Ireland: Ecclesiastical Reform and Revolution, 1800-1885* (New Haven: Yale University Press, 1971), 43, 56.
6 The Irish Church Act, 1869, disassociated the Anglican Church of Ireland from the state and repealed the law that required tithes to be paid to it. It also ceased to send representatives to the House of Lords (see chapter 15).
7 See chapter 10.
8 According to Terence Dooley, as many as 1,322 estates with a combined rental of £904,000 were also controlled by the courts of chancery and exchequer. Dooley, *Sources*, 7.

9   Memorial of Indented Deed of Conveyance at High Court of Chancery, July 2, 1828. Register of Deeds 1833.10.277.

10 These newly released lands were advertised to be let for seven years multiple times from November 1829 to 1831 in the *Dublin Evening Packet*.

11 Until I found the marriage announcements of all four women in *Gentleman's Quarterly*, I had thought their brother Michael was the only child (he is described as such in the last Head entry in the 1958 edition of *Burke's*, "HEAD *formerly of DERRYLAHAN PARK*," where my father, then Col. Michael William Henry Head, O.B.E., of Hinton Hall, Shrewsbury, is listed at the head of an otherwise mostly complete family line, and my younger brother is listed ahead of me — primogeniture endured! The only daughter not mentioned in the deed of sale for Ashley Park was Mary Despard, most likely because she had died. Her widower, Francis Green Despard, though, would be the plaintiff against Maria Head in later actions against Gen. Michael Head, handled after the general's death by his son William Henry Head.

12 *The Pilot*, Nov. 4, 1833; *Drogheda Journal*, Nov. 5; and *Warder and Dublin Weekly Mail*, Nov. 6.

13 Edward Ravenscroft granted annuities to his sister and brother and his residuary estate to his "beloved wife Emma Ravenscroft." The will continued, "Whereas it was my intention to have given to my two daughters Elizabeth Head and Frances Thewles the sums of [illegible, several?] thousand pounds each," the payment would not be made until after his wife's death. Having settled a larger sum on his youngest daughter, Lady Maria Paulet, he intended to invest this illegible amount for his older daughters in parliamentary stocks, thus increasing the amount eventually due to them. Emma Ravenscroft lived another twenty years. Last Will and Testament of Edward Ravenscroft of Portland Place, London, proved March 5, 1829. Prob 11/1753/195, National Archives. Kew, London.

14 The Purdons of Tinerana were descended from James Purdon, originally from Cumberland, who settled in Co. Louth during the reign of Henry VIII. His descendant, George Purdon, the first who lived at Tinerana, served as high sheriff of the county in 1663. The Purdons continued to serve as high sheriffs and MPs for the county in the seventeenth and eighteenth centuries. By the 1840s, the Tinerana estate comprised 5,554 acres with 2,966 inhabitants. The Purdons were very active in Limerick City where they owned considerable properties.

15 Most of the details of Simon and Henrietta's long love affair come from testimonies in a high-profile breach of promise suit her brother brought on her behalf in Dublin's court of common pleas in June 1837.

16 McGrath, in Nolan, 257.

17 Broeker, 206.

18 I am grateful for this information to Stephen McCormac whose ground-breaking research in the records of tithe defaulters held by the National Archives was published as "The Tithe War; reports by Church of Ireland Clergymen to Dublin Castle," *18th-19th Century History*, Features, Issue 4 (July-August 2005), Vol. 13. Consulted online on 2/14/2018 at <http:/www.historyireland.com/18th-19th-century-history-the-tithe-wars-reports-by-church-of-ireland-clergymen-to-dublin-castle>

19 Boyce, 70, note 16.

20 Bruce Elliott, 102-103. The Rev. William Homan reported in the 1836 parochial returns for the region that, within the last three years, "about 200 Protestants" had left his parish and these were "generally in comfortable circumstances, and industrious persons."

21 I am grateful for this information from the following website on Richard Ponsonby: <http://fredrickhervey4thearlofbristol.blogspot.com/2013/01/richard-ponsonby-1772-1853-bishop-of.html

22 Akenson, 186.

23 Louisa Ponsonby brought a respectable dowry of £3,000, although, according to the marriage settlement, it formed part of an £8,000 jointure which would provide for her and her children if her husband predeceased her. Simon George Purdon agreed to provide £5,000 "for the issue of the marriage." Registry of Deeds, August 11, 1836, No. 1836015240.

24 "County Tipperary Assizes, Crown Court, Monday," *Tipperary Free Press*, July 20, 1836; *Waterford Chronicle*, July 23, 1836.

25 The Master of the Rolls in the nineteenth century acted as deputy to the lord chancellor of Ireland, with full powers to hear any lawsuit brought to the court of chancery. Perhaps O'Loghlen chose to preside over the Heads' suit because of M. P. Head's reputation as a champion of tithe reform and Catholic emancipation. O'Loghlen had previously served as solicitor-general and attorney-general for Ireland and had been greatly helped in his early career by his friendship with Daniel O'Connell.

26 Anthony Parker of Castlelough, Michael Prittie Head's neighbor, great friend, and trustee died on May 4, 1837 aged sixty-eight. He was buried in the same Castletown churchyard as M. P. Head. The church is in ruins but Head's tomb with its inscription to him and his late daughter Maria has been restored. Anthony Parker was succeeded at Castlelough by his brother, the Rev. Standish Grady Parker, who continued staunch support of his increasingly tragic neighbors.

27 "Biggs v. Head and Others, May 3, 1837" in *Reports of Cases in Chancery, Argued and Determined in the Rolls of Court, During the Time of the Rt. Hon. Sir Michael O'Loghlen* (A. Millliken, 1841), 349. The aggrieved creditor was probably Edward Biggs of Castle Biggs on Lough Derg who claimed that M. P. Head had owed him a bond of £3,000 since 1817 and who was now claiming considerable interest on the original debt.

28 "Rolls Court—Yesterday. Biggs v Head," *Dublin Morning Register*, May 9, 1837; "Retainer of a Solicitor: The acceptance of a retainer involves the utmost good faith towards the client and the solicitor cannot act for any opposing interest, nor disclose, after ceasing to act for a client, information acquired while so acting, *Biggs v. Head* (1837), etc.," *The Queensland Statutes*, Vol. 4, Canals to Elections, 278, Costs.

29 This was just six days before King William IV died in his sleep and was succeeded by his niece Victoria. At that point, of course, all king's counselors became queen's counselers.

30 Charles Grey, 2nd earl Grey, brother-in-law of the bishop of Derry, was long out of power and retired at the time of Henrietta's suit. He was the Whig prime minister from November 1830 to July 1834 and the longtime leader of multiple reform movements, most notably the Reform Act of 1832.

31 My principal source up to this point was the lengthy account of the trial in the June 21, 1837 edition of the *Clonmel Advertiser* which I double-checked with the equally thorough account in the *Freeman's Journal* of June 15, 3-4. I am also grateful to Tim Boland for one or two facts previously unknown to me in his article "A most distressing breach of promise case" which he sent me for fact-checking before it was published in *Tipperary Historical Journal*, 2017, 42-49.

32 He was referring to Viscount Melbourne's second Whig government, 1835-1841.

33 A Supplement to the *Weekly Waterford Chronicle*, June 24, 1837, 5, reported that the defense counsel made a good argument for Purdon, hinting at money-grubbing, questionable taste in releasing the letters, and asked why Henrietta's sisters were not called as witnesses.

34 Maria Luddy, *Matters of deceit: Breach of promise to marry cases in nineteenth- and twentieth-century Limerick* (Dublin: Maria Luddy and Four Courts Press, 2011), 41.

35 The *Suffolk Chronicle*, June 24, 1837, 4.

36 Henry Parsons was listed as a magistrate for Co. Tipperary in 1862 but no address was given. In 1870, a Mrs. Henrietta Parsons was living in Castleconnell, Co. Limerick, listed under Gentry in *Slater's Royal National Commercial Directory of Ireland*.

37 Bew, 147.
38 Ireland, Outrage Reports 1836-1840, Oct. 9, 1838. At the July 1838 summer assizes at Clonmel, William Henry Head was on the grand jury that sat in judgment of 43 prisoners accused of murder and 15 for aiding murder. *Dublin Evening Packet*, July 21, 1838, 3. In 1839, Dean John Head and his wife were both attacked, the former while visiting his daughter and the latter while traveling home to Ballinaclough when six men attacked her carriage. She was unhurt. *Nenagh Guardian Index*, 1839. The July 1839 summer assizes for the North Riding of Co. Tipperary were held on premises in Nenagh for the first time (the new courthouse was not completed until 1843). W. H. Head was among the magistrates sworn onto the grand jury.
39 McGrath, 277.
40 Earl of Glengall to Lord Charlemont, 1838-1839, quoted in Bew, 148. For confirmation of this view, see two articles by Daniel Grace, "The Threatening Notice in Pre-Famine County Tipperary," and "Homicide in Pre-Famine County Tipperary," published respectively in *Tipperary Historical Journal*, 2009, 47-70, and 2013, 158-182.
41 *Nenagh Guardian*, Aug. 11, 1838. Maynooth College is a Catholic seminary founded in 1795 with the aid of a government building grant of £8,000 and an annual subvention for a similar amount for many years. Government support for the institution derived from its concern to eradicate the practice of Irish student-priests traveling to European seminaries for their education. It was hoped that training priests at home would halt the spread of European ideas and give the government a small measure of influence over the Catholic church in Ireland. "Maynooth College," *Oxford Companion*, 194.
42 *Nenagh Guardian*, Oct. 24, 1838. Lord Bloomfield was the friend of Michael Prittie Head who informed him that Simon George Purdon was engaged to another woman. He had been a British Army officer in the Royal Artillery, retired as a major-general, and then spent several turbulent years in the close entourage of King George IV. He was ennobled in the Irish peerage in 1825 and then commanded the Royal Military Academy at Woolwich before retiring to his estate at Moneygall, King's County (Offaly). George Garvey was land agent to Bloomfield, the Earl of Rosse, and the 2nd earl of Norbury.
43 Daniel Grace, *The Great Famine in Nenagh Poor Law Union, Co. Tipperary* (Nenagh: Relay Books, 2000), 19.
44 *Nenagh Guardian*, March 30, 1850, 5.
45 Boyce, 75. This Thomas Meagher was the father of the future revolutionary Thomas Frances Meagher.
46 *Nenagh Guardian*, Aug. 1 and 18, 1838.

47 As reported by Lord Oxmantown in his speech to the magistrates of King's County, Jan. 10, 1839.

48 Ciarán Reilly, *The Irish Land Agent, 1830-60: The Case of King's County* (Dublin: Four Courts Press, 2014), 75-76. Reilly makes a convincing argument that Garvey was the intended victim.

49 *The Spectator* (London), Jan. 12, 1839.

50 *Leinster Express*, Jan. 19, 1839, 5. The full-page supplement describing this meeting included an illustration of Lord Norbury's demesne.

51 Various letters of apology were received, including from the Hon. Francis A. Prittie, younger brother of Lord Dunalley and high sheriff of Co.Tipperary, who was attending the Special Commission at Clonmel, and John-Head Drought, "due to a domestic calamity." This was the accidental death of his sister who was staying with him when the Big Wind caused the chimney to fall into her bedchamber.

52 O'Connell insisted that the Precursor Society, which was launched in Dublin on August 18, 1838, was the reverse of a Repeal society. The aim of the society, he said, was to secure serious reforms in Ireland and thus make the Repeal unnecessary. His objects of reform were partisan judges, jury-packing, "the odious tithe system," municipal reform, an extension of the franchise, and an end to "Orange domination." Patrick M. Geoghegan, *Liberator: The Life and Death of Daniel O'Connell 1830-1847* (Dublin: Gill Books, 2012), 106.

53 http://www.historyhome.co.uk/people/drummo-t.htm

Chapter 14

1 "Repeal Movement," James S. Donnelly, Jr., editor, *Encyclopedia of Irish History and Culture* (Detroit: Thomson Gale, 2004), 624.

2 The Young Irelanders was a romantic nationalist group of journalists active between 1842 and 1848 and comprised mainly of middle-class graduates of TCD, from both Catholic and Protestant backgrounds. They focused on *The Nation* newspaper. Although they were fully involved in the repeal movement, they rejected Daniel O'Connell's pragmatic approach. Their movement, but not their longer-term influence, ended with the abject failure of the rebellion of 1848. *Oxford Companion*, 633-4.

3 *The Nation* and *Nenagh Guardian*, both May 27, 1845.

4 There can be no denying that Irish peerages and other perks were awarded to many Tipperary landowners who supported union in 1800, see chapter 11.

5 *Nenagh Guardian*, ibid.

6 Father Mathew's movement enrolled some 3 million people, or more

than half of the adult population of Ireland, and is credited with a reduction in Irish crime figures of the era. Twenty thousand persons were said to have taken the temperance pledge at Nenagh in one day and this was undoubtedly behind the uncharacteristically trouble-free "monster meeting" nearby, and at others.

7   Those in attendance must have thought the estate was sold to Mr. Guinness for £70,000, but several Irish newspapers reported that Mr. Guinness was actually in private treaty for the estate. *Limerick Chronicle, Saunders's News Letter and Daily Advertiser*, and *Dublin Morning Register*.

8   Grace, 37-39.

9   *Nenagh Guardian*, Aug. 7, 18, 1841. The Captain was, of course, a reference to "Captain Rock" (See chapter 12). Thirty-two-year-old William Henry Head had his own brush with the law in 1840 when he was accused of shooting a ten-year-old child who was gathering brambles and rotten sticks on his property. The shooting was clearly accidental (he had no idea he had shot anyone until he came across the girl), the wound was slight, and Head immediately called his own doctor to attend to her. Nevertheless, he was arraigned in criminal court in Clonmel, where he was eloquently defended by counsel, and acquitted by the jury. Reported in *Clonmel Herald*, March 28, 1840 and *Tipperary Free Press*, May 25, 1840.

10   *Dublin Evening Mail*, March 14, 1842 and the *Statesman and Dublin Christian Record*, March 18, 1842.

11   *Tipperary Free Press*, April 27, 1842.

12   "Perjury," *Tipperary Free Press*, March 25, 1843, 2.

13   *Byrne's*, 239-240.

14   Grace, 23-24.

15   Daniel O'Connell to P. V. FitzPatrick re the Devon Commission, December 13, 1843. Daniel Grace has countered that tenant farmers did give evidence, although fewer than the landlords and usually the better-off and most articulate farmers. E-mail communication with the author, 2/27/21.

16   Grace, 4, 6; Bruce Elliott, 45, 48. In this case, the reason was the assistance that Grace gave Elliott in his research into North Tipperary Protestant landowners.

17   Elliott, 43-45.

18   James Donnelly would call 8 pence a day literally a starvation wage for the typical laboring family two years later, in the winter of 1846. James S. Donnelly, Jr., *The Great Irish Potato Famine* (Stroud, UK: The History Press, 2010), 77.

19   "William Henry Head, esq., landed proprietor and magistrate,"

Agrarian Outrages. Devon Commission. Report from her Majesty's Commissioners of Inquiry into the State of the Law and Practices in Respect of the Occupation of Land in Ireland, 1845, 635-636.

20 Donnelly, Jr., *Famine*, 2.

21 Grace, e-mail communication with the author, 2/27/21.

22 Woodham-Smith, 21.

23 *Tipperary Free Press*, Feb. 15, 1845.

24 *Nenagh Guardian*, Aug. 17, 1844.

25 *Tipperary Vindicator*, April 9, 1845, 1.

26 The church is in ruins but has received some preservation in recent years. Head's tomb has been restored but its inscription does not include Mary's name.

27 *The Cork Examiner*, Jan. 9, 1846.

28 "Testimony of Francis Spaight," Devon Commission, 1845.

29 *Nenagh Guardian*, as abridged for the *Freeman's Journal*, Sept. 22, 1842, 3. *The Parliamentary Gazetteer of Ireland for 1844-45* (Dublin, London and Edinburgh, 1846) and *Slater's Directory of Munster*, 1846, still described Derry-castle as belonging to Mr. Head: and mention the celebrated slate quarries above the beautiful demesne, "which have been so long in successful operation." *Slater's* also reported that the Imperial Co. Slate Quarry was producing more than 15,000 tons of slate annually and employed about 500 men. Courtesy of Clare Library.

30 *Limerick Chronicle*, Aug. 13, 1845.

31 Compensation for improvements had been one of the recommendations made by the Devon Commission.

32 *Nenagh Guardian*, Aug. 9 and 13, 1845.

33 *King's County Chronicle*, Oct. 22, 1845.

34 *Nenagh Guardian*, as subsequently reported in *King's County Chronicle*, Oct. 22, 1845; *Nenagh Guardian*, Oct. 22, 1845, 3; Grace, 42 (National Archives/RLFC2).

35 *Nenagh Guardian*, Nov. 3, 1845; "Address to the British Public from the Magistrates of the North Riding of Co. Tipperary," *Belfast Commercial Chronicle*, Dec. 6, 1845. This important notice was also printed in *Tipperary Vindicator, Dublin Evening Mail, Northern Whig, Freeman's Journal, Cork Examiner*, and *Dublin Weekly Register* on Dec. 6 or 5.

36 Somerville-Large, 274.

37 *The Princeton History of Modern Ireland* (Princeton, 2016), 410, claims this was done in secret. Grace explains that this was simply to ensure that U.S. merchants did not exploit the price if they knew it was a government purchase. Communication to the author, 2/27/21.

38 Woodham-Smith, in particular, vilified Trevelyan who, according to Irish historian F.S. L. Lyons, was of less importance than the economic

doctrine of *laissez faire*. While Lyons praised Woodham-Smith's unparalleled descriptions of "the horrors of starvation and disease, of eviction, of the emigrant ships, of arrival in Canada or the United States, of the terrible slums on both sides of the Atlantic," his stinging criticisms of her focus on narrative and description over analysis were widely shared by other members of the Dublin historical establishment. Donnelly, Jr., 15-16.

39 Grace, 76-77. William Henry Head would purchase the bankrupt Walsh Park from Jonathan Walsh's son in 1860 (see chapter 15).
40 ibid., map opposite p. 50.
41 Grace, 74. National Archives, Distress Papers, 1846, D379; Relief Commission Papers, RLFC3/1/1680; Distress Papers, D434.
42 Grace, 64.
43 ibid.
44 ibid., 62-63.
45 *Tipperary Vindicator*, Aug. 8, 1846.
46 Grace, 45. One stone equals 14 lbs.
47 *Nenagh Guardian*, Sept. 23, 1846.
48 See "Randolph Routh," *Dictionary of Canadian Biography* online.
49 Donnelly, Jr., 69.
50 Grace, 198.
51 *Tipperary Vindicator*, Dec. 12, 1846.
52 *Tipperary Vindicator*, Jan. 9, 1847.
53 Christine Kinealy, *Charity and the Great Hunger in Ireland* (London: Bloomsbury, 2013), 27-28.
54 The Dublin gathering was a prelude to a new political departure. In its immediate aftermath, eighty-three Irish peers and MPs, including the O'Connellites, agreed to act in unison as an Irish parliamentary party with the object of pressing on the government the proposals adopted at the Dublin meeting. Donnelly, Jr., 195.
55 Head was referring to John Hampden (ca. 1595-1643), an English politician and cousin to Oliver Cromwell who was one of the leading parliamentarians involved in challenging the authority of King Charles I in the run-up to the English Civil War. He became a national figure when he stood trial in 1637 for his refusal to be taxed for ship money and was one of the Five Members whose attempted unconstitutional arrest by the King in England's House of Commons in 1642 sparked the Civil War.
56 Conacre was the system whereby poor people rented land from large farmers to sow a crop of potatoes, usually let in quarter-acre units in N. Tipperary. Grace, 34.
57 "North Tipperary has Pronounced—Great Meeting of the Land

Owners, Clergy, and Gentry at Nenagh," *King's County Chronicle*, Jan. 27, 1847, 1. The 3rd viscount Hawarden of Dundrum, Co. Tipperary served in the House of Lords as an Irish representative peer from 1836 to 1850. Henry Labouchere was a prominent English Whig and Liberal politician who served in Lord John Russell's cabinet as secretary for Ireland June 1846-July 1847 and then as President of the Board of Trade until Lord Russell's government fell in 1852.

58 "Imperial Parliament House of Lords, Tues." *King's County Chronicle*, Jan. 27, 1847.

59 Donnelly, Jr., 92-93.

60 Grace, 84, 89. *Nenagh Guardian*, March 20 and April 24, 1847.

61 *Nenagh Guardian*, April 14, 1847 and *Leinster Express*, April 17, 1847; *Nenagh Guardian*, June 30, 1847, *Dublin Evening Mail*, June 28, *Dublin Weekly Register*, July 3, *The Pilot*, Dublin, July 2.

62 Woodham-Smith, 204.

63 Report of the Select Committee of the House of Lords on Colonization from Ireland, British Parliamentary Papers, 1847 (737), Vol. VI. Evidence of Mr. Francis Spaight, 333-336, 338-340.

64 Griffin,128.

65 Spaight testimony. The *Tipperary Vindicator* suggested a rather different story, reporting that a Hanora Magrath had returned home and attempted to reclaim her holding. Spaight had her hauled before the Nenagh magistrates where she was fined 5 pounds or two months imprisonment in default.

66 Woodham-Smith, 218-25, 230-1, 234, 237; John Kelly, *The Graves are Walking: The Great Famine and the Saga of the Irish People* (New York: Henry Holt & Co., 2012), 274-279.

67 Sir William Henry Gregory, husband of Lady Gregory of future cultural nationalism fame and later governor of Ceylon, who was about to inherit an estate in Co. Galway from his father, won support for this clause. In fact, he would gamble away a large part of his inheritance on horse racing before the famine was over.

68 Grace, 117.

69 Father Spain, the Birr parish priest, formerly PP for Lorrha, wrote a letter describing this horror to *The Dublin Evening Post*, Oct. 14, 1847.

70 Gerard O'Meara, 363.

71 John Mitchel, *The Last Conquest of Ireland (Perhaps)* (1860), 115.

72 *Nenagh Guardian*, Nov. 1, 1847.

73 "From our correspondent, Dublin," *London Times*, Nov. 1, 1847.

74 Donnelly, jr., 27-28, 141-143. Donnelly cites Donal Kerr's judgment in his 1994 *A nation of beggars?* that this episode contributed significantly to the growing alienation between Irish Catholic priests and hierarchy and the British government and public opinion.

75 Michael Head's testimony at the first of the trials for "Attempt to Murder Mr. Bayly" before a special commission at Clonmel, Jan. 31, 1848. *Dublin Evening Mail*, Jan. 31, 1848, 4-5.
76 *Tipperary Vindicator*, Nov. 17, 1847.
77 Board of Guardians Minute Books 129/A/4, Dec. 16, 1847. Thurles Public Library.
78 I am grateful once again to Daniel Grace for his comprehensive and affecting description of the assassination attempt on Richard Uniacke Bayly and the complexities of bringing the perpetrators to justice. It was published as "The Shooting of Richard U. Bayly near Nenagh, Co. Tipperary, in 1847" in *Cloughjordan Heritage*, Vol. V, 2001, 14-23. In addition to newspaper reports of the attack, the arrests, the trials, and the executions, another important source was the large file on Richard Bayly in Outrage Reports 1849 (Tipperary), 27/1688 and others at the National Archives.
79 In May 1848, the Rev. William S. Balch, a Universalist minister, arrived by ship in Co. Cork. Horrified by the terrible suffering he witnessed of the starving peasantry in Cos. Cork and Tipperary, he published an impassioned indictment of the entire land system in Ireland in his *Ireland as I saw it: The Character, Conditions, and Prospects of the People,* published in New York in 1850.
80 Grace, 137, 139.
81 *Illustrated London News*, Dec. 22, 1849.

Chapter 15

1 Succession to an entailed estate is limited to a specific line of heirs so that it cannot be sold or passed on to anyone else.
2 Dooley, *Sources*, 7.
3 James. S. Donnelly, Jr., *Landlord and tenant in nineteenth-century Ireland* (Dublin: Gill and Macmillan, 1973), 49.
4 "The principal division of the fine estate of Redwood in the co. of Tipperary (late Major Bloomfield) has been purchased under the Incumbered Estates Court by William Henry Head, Modreeny House, Esq." *Cork Examiner*, Jan. 30, 1852, and also *Dublin Evening Mail, Dublin Evening Post*, and *Tipperary Free Press*. Major John Bloomfield was identified as the owner of Redwood in Griffith Valuation. He must have been related to Lt.-Gen. Benjamin Bloomfield, 1st baron Bloomfield, who died in 1846. Lord Bloomfield was a contemporary and friend of Michael Prittie Head of Derry Castle.
5 Last Will and Testament, Edward Ravenscroft of Portland Place, London, Proved March 5,1829. National Archives, Kew, Prob 11/1753/195

6   Landed Estates website. Estate: Purdon, and *Limerick and Clare Examiner*, Nov. 26, 1853. A Mr. McDermott purchased the property in trust for over £12,000. Evidently, Dean Head did not allow his brother's humiliation by S. G. Purdon in 1836 to influence the family relationship with the Purdons.

7   "The Head family of Ballinaclough: Where love and respect gave way to Boycott and Eviction," in *Mining the Past 2015/15*, Silvermines Historical Society, 22-26 (see chapter 16)

8   Mary Cecelia Lyons, *Illustrated Incumbered Estates Ireland, 1850-1905* (Co. Clare: Ballinakella Press, 1993), 81-82. This fine book of lithographic and other illustrations material in the Incumbered Estates Rentals, is dedicated to her late friend Professor A. J. Otway of Trinity College Dublin, the last of the Otway line. Otway Castle was burned in 1922.

9   Ironically, the infamous charge of the Light Brigade, a tragic farce which resulted in devastatingly high losses to British cavalry against Russians during the Battle of Balaclava, included William Henry's father's old regiment, the 13th Light Dragoons. See Cecil Woodham-Smith's account in *The Reason Why: The Story of the Fatal Charge of the Light Brigade*.

10   *Limerick and Clare Examiner*, Oct. 26, 1853.

11   *Dublin and Daily Express*, Aug. 11, *Cork Examiner* and *Warder & Dublin Mail*, Aug. 14, 1858. The Borrisokane lands were purchased in trust by a Mr. Lloyd, possibly for David Clarke.

12   He was a descendant of the large Welsh Catholic family that came to Ireland with the Norman invasion in the twelfth century. Walshes formerly owned vast tracts of Irish land in several counties, particularly Kilkenny and Waterford, until the arrival of Cromwell whose armies "methodically removed all vestiges of the Walsh landholders" in the mid-seventeenth century: http://homepages.rootsweb.com/~walsh/folklore.html. Retrieved 7/5/18.

13   *Dublin Evening Mail*, Jan. 4, 1860, and *Belfast Mercury*, Jan. 7, 1860.

14   Terence Dooley, *The Decline of the Big House in Ireland: A Study of Irish landed families, 1860-1960* (Dublin: Wolfhound Press, 2001), 70. Nicola Jennings, an expert genealogist living in Dublin who, like this author, is a descendant of Isabella's father Nicholas Biddulph, has made an exhaustive study of the individuals in the many branches of her family, including women like the Biddulph sisters, on her blog "Family History," <carrigoran.blogspot.com> I am most grateful for the scans she made for this book of Isabella Biddulph and five of her children from an album in her possession.

15   COH, 18.

16 *King's County Chronicle*, June 3, 1863, 3.
17 "This Week a Century Ago," *Nenagh Guardian*, Oct. 10, 1964, 9. It is possible that Head's friend, the Hon. Crosby Trench of nearby Sopwell Hall, was influenced by Head to remodel his eighteenth-century house with fine quality materials, including crisp cut limestone details of particular note, according to the National Inventory of Architectural Heritage. This house and its cut-stone outbuildings, two gate lodges, and other impressive features, still stands, unlike Derrylahan Park, where only the original gate lodge remains occupied.
18 *King's County Chronicle*, March 20, 1867.
19 "Desirable Farm," *King's County Chronicle*, March 12, 1862, 4.
20 Landed Estates Court Rentals 1850-1885, Feb. 4, 1865. Findmypast. com.
21 *The Evening Freeman*, Oct. 29, 1862.
22 Clive A. Spinage, *Cattle Plague: A History* (Springer Science & Business Media, 2003). Cattle plague was the second disease, after smallpox, to be eradicated by vaccination.
23 *Freeman's Journal*, June 8, 1866, 3.
24 The name derives from the ancient Irish Fenians, a professional military corps that roamed over ancient Ireland (ca. 3rd century) in the service of the high kings. Fenian Movement. Encyclopedia.com. Accessed 8/30/18.
25 *Tyrone Constitution*, March 15, 1867, as reported in the *Limerick Chronicle*.
26 "Malicious Demolition of a House," *Nenagh Guardian*, July 7, 1866.
27 *Allnut's Irish Land Schedule*, June 7, 1869, 3.
28 "In the Landed Estates Court, Ireland." Prospectus for Head Estate Sale at Modreeny, June 29, 1869, Tipperary Studies. W. H. Head sent this prospectus to his friend Henry Trench of Cargort Park, Roscrea.
29 *Saunders's News-Letter*, June 30, 1869, 1, and *Tipperary Free Press*, July 2, 1869, 3. "Property Owners County Tipperary 1870" listed George Whitfield as the new owner of Modreeny's 443 acres, whereas it still listed William Spaight's Derry Castle as the full 4,597 acres.
30 Unfortunately, Charlie Swan, the great equestrian and eventer who became a successful trainer, retired from training at Modreeny in the face of a ruinous tax bill but still lives at Modreeny.
31 Maynooth College was established in 1795 as an appeasing token to Catholics in the wake of the French Revolution.
32 W. E. Vaughan, *Landlords and Tenants in Mid-Victorian Ireland* (Oxford University Press, 1994), 220.
33 "The Church: Killaloe Diocesan Meeting," *King's County Chronicle*, Aug. 16, 1871, 2 and "Diocesan Synod of Killaloe," *King's County Chronicle*, Sept. 13, 1871, 1.

34 COH, 230-231.

35 COH, ibid.

36 From Canon Leslie's typescript lists of Deans of Killaloe, provided by Dr. Susan Hood of the Representative Church Body Library, 121.

37 "Funeral of the late Dean Head, D.D.," *Nenagh Guardian*, June 28, 1871.

38 Henry Haswell Head (1820-1910) was the first member of the Head family to attend university in England, rather than Trinity College, Dublin. He graduated in 1843 with an MD in medicine from the University of Edinburgh with a thesis *On the Extent to Which Several Forms of Mental Alienation Affect Man's Freedom of Action*. The following year, he gained the Fellowship of the Royal College of Surgeons in Ireland. He was admitted a licentiate of the Irish College of Physicians in 1864, receiving his fellowship two years later, and was elected president in 1878. He practiced in Dublin as a consulting physician to the Adelaide Hospital. Royal College of Physicians of Ireland Heritage Center. H. H. Head's second wife and mother of his seven children was a member of the very ancient Anglo-Norman Nugent family of Portaferry House, Co. Down, further cementing the family of the acknowledged senior representatives of the Heads of Derry Castle with the leading landed families in Ulster.

39 COH, 19.

40 "The Killaloe Fishery Case," *King's County Chronicle*, July 27, 1870, 2; Dooley, *Decline*, 182. The portico of the house was salvaged and now fronts Parteen House near Limerick. Nancy Murphy, 35.

41 "Wilful Trespass," *Nenagh Guardian*, May 29, 1872, 3.

42 Vaughan, 14-15, 166-167.

43 *Dublin Daily Express*, March 31, 1873, p.3

44 Vaughan, 143, 146, 150-151.

45 *Nenagh Guardian*, April 17, 1872.

46 *Nenagh Guardian*, Sept. 22, 1875, 2. "Alleged Agrarian Outrage," *The Irishman*, Sept. 25, 1875, p.3; "Alleged Threatening an Agent," *Freeman's Journal*, Sept. 30, 1875, p. 3. Ciarán O'Reilly asserts that this was the first attempt on a land agent's life in the Parsonstown (Birr) area since the Famine and before the Land War. His source was *Times*, Oct. 1, 1875. O'Reilly, 144.

47 *Dublin Weekly Nation*, Dec. 28, 1878, 8.

48 COH, 19.

49 Demesne was the land held by the manorial lord and not set out to tenants. *Byrne's*, 97.

50 COH, 22-26.

51 Brian De Breffny, editor, *The Irish World: The Art and Culture of the Irish People* (New York: Harrison House/Harry N. Abrams, Inc., 1986), 193.

.Chapter 16

1   De Breffny, 193.
2   Davitt visited the U.S. after his release from prison, where he was "deeply influenced by Henry George's ideas about the relationship between land monopoly and poverty." *Encyclopedia Britannica.*
3   Historian Kevin H. Flynn made this claim in his article "Parnell, The Rebel Prince," *History Today*, vol. 55, no. 4, April 2005.
4   Somerville-Large, 310.
5   "Boycott," Wikipedia, sourced from Joyce Marlow, *Captain Boycott and the Irish* (Ireland: History Books, 1973). In his unfinished novel, *The Landleaguers* (1883), Anthony Trollope combined a virtually documentary record of the devastating boycotting techniques waged on a Co. Galway landlord by the Land League with an imaginative sub-plot.
6   Dooley, *Sources*, 10, quoting W. E. Vaughan.
7   Tim Boland, who published his article in the newsletter of the Silvermines Historical Society, 2015-2016, also wrote the article on Henrietta Head's breach of promise suit (see chapter 13).
8   Roy Foster points out that, even though the Griffith's valuation was taken by tenants as the standard, it was actually "pitched well below a realistic level; it was calculated when prices were abnormally low, and had never been intended as a rental guide." Foster, *Modern Ireland*, 380; Dooley explains that "comparisons of contemporary rents with Griffith's valuation was a tactical ploy exploited by the Land League as rents that had risen in the period could be deemed to be rack-rents when compared to the old valuation." Dooley, *Decline*, 91.
9   COH, 28.
10 Terence Dooley, Introduction, *'The Land for the People': The Land Question in Independent Ireland* (Dublin: University College Press, 2004), 8. According to Dooley, "275,525 tenants with an aggregated rental of £5,883,904 entered the land courts to have their rents fixed during the first statutory term after 1881. . . Soon after its establishment, the Land Commission was also developed by law into a land purchase agency charged with facilitating the transfer of agricultural holdings from landlords to tenants." 9.
11 "Spoliation of Landlords," *The Nenagh Guardian*, Nov. 23, 1881, 2.
12 Grace, *Monsea-Killodiernan*, 160-161,
13 Alvin Jackson, *Home Rule: An Irish History 1900-2000* (London: Phoenix, 2004), 51.
14 "'No Rent' Manifestoes," *Dublin Daily Express*, April 19, 1882, 3.
15 *Tipperary Advocate*, May 6, 1882, 157.
16 Boyce, 183; Jackson, *Home Rule*, 53.

17 Boyce, 185.

18 Dooley, *Decline*, 68.

19 William Edward Head to Isabella Louisa Head, Derrylahan, "midwinter," possibly 1883 or 1884. This was found in "Aunt Bella's box," which was handed down to her niece Isabella Grace and her grandniece Victoria Isabella. I am grateful to my cousin Victoria Wilson for bringing this and other handwritten written items in the box to my attention.

20 Willie's appointment was announced in the *Dublin Daily Express*, May 9, 1885, 6.

21 "Marriages: Head and Johns. August 17, at St. Nicholas Church, Carrickfergus, by the Rev. Ribton McCracken, AM, curate of Christ Church, Belfast, assisted by the Rev. George Chamberlain, AM, rector of Carrickfergus." *Dublin Daily Express*, Aug. 19, 1886, 1.

22 *Freeman's Journal*, Oct. 4, 1881, 2; Sept. 12, 1882, 2; and *Dublin Daily Express*, Jan. 12, 1883, 1.

23 COH, 30-31. Charles's brother John Henry earned a Bachelor of Medicine and Bachelor of Surgery at TCD, the entry-level professional medical degree in the U.K. and Ireland where the M.D. is a postgraduate research degree in medicine. He returned home and was living in Cloughjordan, Co. Tipperary, at the time of his early death in 1912. He was always referred to as "Dr. John" by the family, but otherwise his life story is a mystery.

24 In 2019, the empty and vandalized Tinerana House was found to be harboring an outpost of a drug operation with a fine crop of marijuana plants. *Clare Herald*, May 31, 20-19; *Irish Examiner*, June 2, 2019.

25 Irish Land Commission

26 This was the analysis of Michael Morris, Irish lord chief justice, in the wake of Parnell's put down of one of his chief lieutenants. Bew, 346.

27 Boyce, 190-191.

28 Irish Unionists believed that full political integration with Great Britain, as brought about by the 1801 Act of Union, was preferable to a flawed or unattainable legislative independence. "unionism," *Oxford Companion*, 596.

29 Jackson, *Home Rule*, 73.

30 Having fought for the parliamentary cause, Robert Saunderson was granted over 10,200 acres of what had previously been O'Reilly territory in Co. Cavan in 1654. The O'Reillys had fought for the Catholic Confederation in the 1640s and were expropriated under the Cromwellian land settlement. Capt. James OReilly, a loyal Jacobite, rose to pre-eminence under the patronage of Tyrconnell, and sat as MP for Cavan in the "patriot parliament" of 1689. His planter rival, Col.

Robert Saunderson, refused to acknowledge the authority of James, and attempted to flee to England. He was one of the 2,400 Protestant refugees attainted by the patriot parliament in the summer of 1689. But the Saunderson family was restored to the Cavan estate, and to political authority with the fall of the Jacobite cause. Alvin Jackson, *Colonel Edward Saunderson: Land and Loyalty in Victorian Ireland* (Oxford: Clarendon Press, 1995), 12-13. In 1900, at the Church of the Holy Redeemer, Cheyne Row, Chelsea, London, Grace Head of Carrig married Michael O'Reilly, a Dublin solicitor and direct descendant of the O'Reillys of Cavan. Their second son, also Michael O'Reilly, would become chief of police in Waterford. Source: Maureen "Betty" Perry's family materials, in possession of the author.

31 De Breffny, 195-196.
32 Jackson, *Saunderson*, 243.
33 Patrick Buckland, *Irish Unionism, 1885-1923: A documentary history* (Belfast: Her Majesty's Stationery Office, 1973), xi-xii.
34 Dooley, *Decline*, 101, 102.
35 The Plan of Campaign was conceived by another Parnellite MP, Timothy Healy, and devised and organized by Timothy Harrington, secretary of the Irish National League, William O'Brien, and John Dillon.
36 F. S. L. Lyons, "Parnellism and Crime, 1887-90," *Transactions of the Royal Historical Society* 27 (1974), 123-40.
37 "Coercive Acts," *Oxford Companion*, 108.
38 "Congested Districts Board," *Oxford Companion*, 117; *Byrne's*, 76; Dooley, *Land*, 26.
39 Isabella Head was staying with her sick mother, Isabella Biddulph, who died on December 29, 1886—which may place this letter of "Wednesday 19th" ten days earlier.
40 COH, 26.
41 Dooley, *Sources*, 11.
42 The first mortgage between Willie and Thomas Joyce was made on April 22, 1891 to secure £1,027.15.0 and further advances with interest at the rate of 60 percent per annum. Joyce assigned that mortgage to Dublin solicitor John Alexander French. On October 23 that year, an indenture was made between Joyce, William E. Head, and French "in consideration of £2,682.15.10 then due for advances and of the further sum of £796.14.6 due for interest," for a mortgage debt total of £3,479.10.4 (the equivalent of $487,000 today). This debt was assigned to J. A. French and Willie could pay that back at 7 percent which French would accept in lieu of the interest reserved by the April 22 indenture.
43 Toler Garvey was also agent to the earl of Rosse which explains why

this comprehensive receivership deed is in the Armory Archives at Birr Castle. I copied it there by hand in 2007 with the gracious permission of Lord and Lady Rosse.

44 The deed refers to the terms of the December 1859 marriage settlement between Willie's parents, by which his father had named Francis Edward Biddulph and John Massy, a cousin since deceased, as trustees for his estate (Modreeny at that point) so that Isabella might receive £400 annual jointure if she survived him. A second deed, in 1869, presumably following the sale of his Modreeny estate, devised all his real and freehold lands of Derrylahan and its built properties to the same trustees to hold in trust for his eldest son (then aged five), also for the jointure payments to Isabella. This was repeated in William Henry Head's will, dated February 18, 1886.

45 *Report from the Select Committee on Money Lending, etc.,* in *Parliamentary Papers, 1850-1908,* vol. 10, 1898, and information kindly supplied by Biddulph's great-granddaughter, Nicola Jennings. Several high-profile lawsuits were brought against Thomas Joyce in the 1890s. In one of them, the bankrupt Henry Walter Smith had mortgaged all the lands that he expected to inherit from his father in Co. Meath to Thomas Joyce at the exorbitant rate of 60 percent. The plaintiff had left the army in 1889 and moved to Dublin where, lacking employment, he was "entering a career of dissipation." Joyce's argument in court was that the plaintiff was "reckless and improvident," and "ready to accept loans from anyone who would supply the means of pursuing the evil career on which he had entered." Smith was now an outcast from his family, and "an absconding debtor," who had escaped to Bechuanaland where he joined the police force. "Kevans v. Joyce," *The Irish Reports, Containing Cases Argued and Determined in the Court of Appeal, etc.,* vol. 1, 1896, 442-493.

46 These split loyalties were the meat of the dinner party conversation in James Joyce's *Portrait of the Artist.* I am grateful to Anne Burnham for this reference.

47 Bence-Jones, 72

48 His kinsman, the Hon. Cosby G. Trench, received just 462 votes to the anti-Parnellite nationalist P. J. O'Brien's 4,064 for Tipperary North.

49 Grace and Robert had four sons. Their oldest son, Major John Robert Perceval-Maxwell (1896–1963), was a member of both the Northern Ireland House and Senate, and very active in Northern Ireland political and cultural life. There are 700 letters between Grace, Robert, and their sons John and Richard while the latter served in WWI archived at PRONI. Richard was killed in action in 1918.

50 During my visit to the area in October 2001, I learned a good deal

about this family from Maureen Grace "Betty" Perry (the Perrys were another long-established Anglo-Irish family in Co. Tipperary). Her mother Grace (Gracie) Head was the youngest daughter and her father was Dublin solicitor Michael O'Reilly of the ancient Irish Gaelic family of Co. Cavan. Betty gave me a cache of material, including her mother's girlhood diary, a joyous chronicle of fun with the exception of her disappointment when she failed to make the grade with nursing training in London and the death of her mother.

51 The cousin was a son of Dean John Head's youngest sister Louisa who had married barrister Thomas Forde of Seaforde, Co. Down. Of their many children, their marine architect son and his wife, with whom Annie stayed in London, apparently had seventeen daughters! His firm was Forde Marine Architecture.

52 When Gracie's second son, Michael O'Reilly, became chief of police in Waterford, he told a local newspaper that he was descended from Michael Head, mayor of Waterford in 1684.

53 Jackson, 95.

54 Born in Co. Galway, John F. Finerty (1846-1908), a staunch supporter of Irish independence, had a distinguished career in Chicago journalism and was a one-term Democratic Congressman.

55 Jackson, 101-102.

56 Robert Kee, *The Green Flag: A History of Irish Nationalism* (London: Penguin Books, 2000 edition), 431.

57 "To be let together or in divisions...", *King's County Chronicle*, Nov. 11, 1897; "Subscriber has been instructed by T. R. Garvey, Esq., J.P., Receiver...", *Midland Tribune*, April 1998.

58 Bence-Jones, 79.

Chapter 17

1 The Manchester Martyrs were three members of the Irish Republican Brotherhood, or Fenians, who murdered a Manchester City police officer in the course of attempting to rescue two arrested leaders of the Brotherhood. They were executed on November 23, 1867 in front of a crowd of 8-10,000. They are memorialized in Manchester and Ireland as inspirational heroes to many.

2 "Diamond Jubilee – Birr," and "The Editor's Chair," *Midland Tribune*, June 26 and July 3, 1897.

3 "Parsonstown Horticultural Show," *Midland Tribune*, Aug. 21, 1897.

4 "The Royal Visit to the Shannon," *Midland Tribune*, Sep. 4, 1897.

5 Although women were included in the household suffrage, they were forbidden from serving as councilors, with the exception of certain women in certain elections.

6   I am grateful to Donal A. Murphy for his excellent book on the first county council elections in North Tipperary, *Blazing tar barrels and standing orders: Tipperary North's First County and District Councils, 1899-1902* (Nenagh, Co. Tipperary: Relay, 1999).

7   Murphy, 28-29.

8   ibid., 45-46.

9   ibid., 48, 61, 78.

10   *Londonderry Sentinel*, Oct. 12, 1899, 6. It is interesting that this scandal was reported in an Ulster newspaper.

11   Murphy, 107.

12   Kee, 449.

13   In 1901, Bellary was the seventh largest town in Madras Presidency, and one of the chief military stations in southern India, garrisoned by British and native Indian troops under the British Indian Government.

14   COH, 96. Characteristically, Charles Head made no mention in his memoir of his cavalry officer brother Michael Ravenscroft's presence in those battles, for which MRH would receive the South Africa Medal, beyond the comment that seemed to refer to his brothers, that those men who moved away from home generally did better than those who stayed.

15   Today Umballa is called Ambala. Ambala separates the Ganges river network from the Indus river network and is surrounded by two rivers—Ghaggar and Tangri—to the north and to the south. Located in the state of Haryana, on the border with the state of Punjab, it has a large Indian Army and Indian Air Force presence.

16   Identified by the German authorities as a strategically important port, Qingdao was administered by the Imperial Department of the Navy (*Reichsmarineamt*) rather than the Imperial Colonial Office (*Reichskolonialamt*). The growing Imperial German Navy based their Far East Squadron there, allowing the warships to conduct operations throughout the western Pacific.

17   The port of Weihaiwei was the base for the Beiyang Fleet (Northern Seas Fleet) during the Qing dynasty. Together with Lüshunkou (Port Arthur) it controlled the entrance to the Gulf of Zhili and, thus, the seaward approaches to Beijing. In 1895, the Japanese captured it in the Battle of Weihaiwei, the last major battle of the First Sino-Japanese War. The Japanese withdrew in 1898. After the Russian Empire leased Port Arthur from China for 25 years in March 1898, the United Kingdom pressured the Chinese government into leasing Weihaiwei, with the terms of the treaty stating that it would remain in force for as long as the Russians were allowed to occupy Port Arthur.

18   The Hai River (lit."Sea River"), formerly known as the Peiho, Pei He

or Pei Ho ("White River"), connects Beijing to Tianjin and the Bohai Sea.

19   Charles wrote very little about his experiences in Japan, claiming that he saw nothing that could not be found in guidebooks. However, he must have felt at home as he hiked through countryside which he felt resembled the south-west of Ireland. On one of those walks, he was reminded that this was in fact a very different culture as he found himself looking into a bathhouse exposed to the public road where the sexes bathed together in the nude, separated only by a stick across the water. This made "a striking contrast to Ireland, where even husband and wife, though voluminously clad, used to have to do their sea-bathing separately." COH, 106-107.

20   The adoptive family lived in Weston-super-Mare, not far from Bristol, as Nicola Jennings was told. It is possible that the connection was made by Georgie's oldest sister, Elizabeth (Bessie) Bennett, whose clergyman husband served a church there for several years in the 1880s. According to the 1911 Irish Census, Georgie was living with Elizabeth Marshall, a widow from King's County and perhaps Emma's mother, in Co. Kildare.

21   "In the High Court of Justice in Ireland, Chancery Division—Land Judges, dated April 26, 1901," *Nenagh Guardian*, May 1, 1901, 2. Toler Garvey had been discharged from his duties as receiver to the Ballyduff lands on December 12, 1900 after Isabella Head's petition to sell those lands had been dismissed. On October 31, 1904, Willie Head conveyed his equity of redemption in Ballyduff and other lands to John A. French.

22   Register of Deeds, 1902.36.168

23   COH, 136.

24   Resolution of the Irish Landowners Convention, October 1902.

25   William E. Head was listed in the "Prison Ennis General Register Ennis" in 1900, and then in the 1901 census for Ennis No. 4 Urban by his initials only, along with other Ennis Reformatory inmates, as "Gentleman-Landowner," his offence given as "false pretences," and his sentence as 3 years. On March 3, 1903, he was reregistered as "prisoner" for "False Pretences and being a Habitual Drunkard." Irish Prison Registers 1790-1924. Findmypast.com; Clare County Library.

26   William E. Head in "History of Inmates Before and After Treatment in the Reformatory," Ennis State Inebriate Reformatory. Irish Prison Registers 1790-1924. Findmypast.com.

27   Conor Reidy, *Criminal Irish Drunkards: The Inebriate Reformatory System 1900-1920* (Dublin: The History Press, 2014), 21.

28   ibid., 56, 59.

29 "History of Inmates," Ennis Reformatory. Irish Prison Registers 1790-
1924.

30 COH, 118-125. Many years later, this battery, the 7th, was captured
by the Ottoman Army in the surrender at Kut Al Amara on April 29,
1916. Historian Christopher Catherwood has called the siege "the
worst defeat of the Allies in World War I. Charles Head would walk
the Gallipoli battlefields twice when researching his book *A Glance at
Gallipoli.*

31 The Champions Cup had been presented by Capt. John G. H. Beresford, 7th Hussars, a member of the aristocratic Waterford family, to
the Rand Polo Club in Johannesburg in 1899. Lord John Graham Hope
Horsley de la Poer Beresford (1866-1944), who succeeded his brother as 5th Baron Decies, was an international polo player who won
the Gold Medal for polo in the 1900 Summer Olympics. Horace A.
Laffage, *The Polo Encyclopedia*, 2nd edition. The seventeenth-century
ancestors of the de la Poer Beresford family were well known to the
Heads during their two generations in Waterford.

32 COH, 129-130.

33 *Midland Tribune*, July 20, 1907.

34 *Irish Independent*, July 3, 1908.

35 Famous for being the starting point of the 1857 rebellion against the
British East India Company, Meerut is in the western part of the state
of Uttar Pradesh.

36 Historian Alvin Jackson discovered that the capital received by Somerset Saunderson from the sale of his 10,000 acres in Co. Cavan was
"converted into an extensive colonial share portfolio" and that "only
in Ireland did Somerset resist investment." Dooley, *Decline*, 114 and
120.

37 ibid., 118.

38 COH, 143. Under the Land Acts, Charles would receive a loan for £200
for land improvement from the Office of Public Works in August 1913.
General Advertiser for Dublin, and all Ireland, Aug. 16, 1913.

39 COH's memories of turning to farming and the sporting and social
amusements and limited civic responsibilities available to Irish landowners before WWI are found in his chapter VIII, 134-154.

40 Betty Perry gave me a copy of Annie's typed account of that trip,
which includes the Head genealogy sent to her father in 1924 by a
cousin.

41 Census of Ireland, 1911.

42 Ethel (Annie) Head was an independent, single woman, perhaps a
teacher. She drew up this account of her 1910-1911 trip to Ireland at
her home in Stamford, Connecticut, in March 1952 and sent it to all

her family members in Canada and the U.S. One of them gave a copy to Betty Perry and she gave it to me.

43 COH, 145.

44 The definition of "Aunt Sally" is a person or thing that is subjected to much criticism, especially one set up as an easy target for it, e.g., "today's landowner is everyone's Aunt Sally." Hubert de Burgh, 2nd marquess of Clanricarde (1832-1916) was considered to be one of the more notorious and despised of the absentee Anglo-Irish landlords. He lived in London and never visited his 52,000-acre estate in Co. Galway, ordering wholesale evictions of his tenants during the land wars and sending some 75 of them who resisted to prison.

45 Dooley, Decline, 62.

46 An Imperial Home Ruler was one who advocated a separate bicameral parliament for Ireland, charged with responsibility for Ireland's internal affairs, while Westminster would retain control of such areas as imperial and foreign affairs, armed forces, currency, security, and major taxation. "Home rule," Oxford Companion, 257-258.

47 Bence-Jones, 55.

48 R. B. McDowell, Crisis & Decline: The Fate of the Southern Unionists (Dublin: The Lilliput Press, 997), 10.

49 King's County Chronicle, Oct. 19, 1911.

50 See "Head v. Meara. Ross, J., Feb. 20, 27, 1912" in Irish law reports annotated reprint: containing [1894] 1 and 2.1.R, vol. 12, 638-640, by Wm. Green, Incorporated Council of Law Reporting for Ireland.

51 COH, 145.

52 In 1895, Carson was engaged by the marquess of Queensberry (whose son, Sir Alfred Douglas, was Oscar Wilde's young lover) to lead his defense against Oscar Wilde's libel action.

53 "Southern Unionists: King's County Protest against Home Rule," Dublin Daily Express, June 29, 1912, 5.

54 COH, 146-147.

55 Kee, 466-467.

56 Redmond's compromises were "scornfully derided by advanced-nationalist opinion...In 1914, what Redmond and the Irish Parliamentary Party had achieved seemed to radical imagination in Ireland an inadequate structure, flimsily assembled and founded on sand..." Redmond's party "seemed more and more old-hat, collaborationist and unexciting...and wanting on all the issues that inspired the revolutionary generation (Irish language, cultural renewal, economic autarky, separatist traditions, the eradication of 'foreign' influence)," according to R. F. Foster, Vivid Faces: The Revolutionary Generation in Ireland, 1890-1923 (New York: W. W. Norton, 2014), 187.

57 *Irish Times*, Feb. 19, 1914, as quoted in McDowell, 49.
58 Charles Head strongly related to General Gough, with whom he had hunted with the Tipperary Hounds when both were subalterns.
59 "Howth gun-running," *Oxford Companion*, 263-264.
60 Kee, 507-508.
61 COH, 153.

Chapter 18

1 Foster, *Modern Ireland*, 471.
2 The poster was a major influence on American artist James Montgomery Flagg when he used himself as a model for Uncle Sam on the iconic "I Want You..." WWI recruitment poster.
3 Major Michael Ravenscroft Head was one of six officers and four non-commissioned officers and men of the British Army serving in the campaign in France and Flanders who were awarded the Order of Leopold. *Liverpool Echo* and *Birmingham Evening Post*, Oct. 2, 1915. He was also awarded the 1914-15 Star and mentioned in dispatches. The 5th Dragoon Guards spent the greater part of the war in the dismounted role but the last weeks of the war found them in action again on horseback. They captured or killed over 700 German troops when they attacked a troop train at Harbonnières. Col. Nugent Head's regiment, the 4th (Queen's Own) Hussars, came under Gen. Gough's command of the 2nd Cavalry Division in September 1914 and remained on the Western Front for the remainder of the War. Col. Nugent Head was awarded the Military Cross (M.C.) in 1918.
4 COH described his training of artillery brigades before shipping to France, 158-169. His Great War experiences are recounted in chapters X and XI. The Great Retreat, also known as the Retreat from Mons, is the name given to the long withdrawal to the River Marne, in August and September 1914, by the British Expeditionary Force (BEF) and the French Fifth Army, Allied forces on the Western Front, after their defeat by the armies of the German Empire at the Battle of Charleroi (August 21) and the Battle of Mons (August 23).
5 Kee, 525. I have relied heavily on Professor Kee's beautifully objective account of World War I and the 1916 Easter Rising; Hyde quoted in Bence-Jones, 171.
6 The V.C. is the highest and most prestigious award of the British honors system, awarded for gallantry "in the presence of the enemy" to members of any rank in the British Armed Forces.
7 See "Gallipoli—an Irish, as well as an Australian, campaign": https://tintean.org.au/2015/04/06/gallipoli-an-irish-as-well-as-an-australian-campaign/ Checked 8/7/19.

8   COH, *A Glance at Gallipoli* (London: Eyre and Spottiswoode, 1931).

9   Casement was honored in 1905 for the Casement Report on the Congo and knighted in 1911 by King George V for his important investigations of human rights abuses in Peru.

10   Kee, 536-537.

11   ibid., 529, 534-535, 547.

12   Dangerfield, *The Damnable Question: One Hundred and Twenty Years of Anglo-Irish Conflict* (Boston/Toronto: Little, Brown, 1976), 204-205.

13   Kee, 548. Although I have read several fictionalized accounts of the Easter Rising, including Sebastian Barry's moving and bestselling *A Long Long Way*, my principal sources have been Robert Kee's *The Green Flag* and Roy Foster's more recent and extremely comprehensive *Vivid Faces: The Revolutionary Generation in Ireland*.

14   David Fitzpatrick, "Militarism in Ireland, 1900-1922," in Bartlett and Jeffery, *A Military History of Ireland*, 394. Statistics about the losses during or because of the Rising vary. For instance, John Gibney, *A Short History of Ireland 1500-2000* (Yale University, 2017), 193, lists 488 killed in total and 2,600 wounded, while Foster, 243, cites a total of 450 people killed, 2,614 wounded, and 9 missing with a surprisingly high toll of civilians.

15   Kee, 576, 573.

16   Quoted in F. S. L. Lyons, *John Dillon: A Biography* (London: Routledge & Kegan Paul, 1968), 373.

17   Kee, 573-4, 578.

18   Bence-Jones, 178. De Valera was reprieved because he was born in New York and Markievicz because she was a woman.

19   Kee, 586.

20   Fitzpatrick, in *Military History of Ireland*, 395.

21   Gerard O'Meara, *Lorrha People in the Great War* (Gerard O'Meara, 2016), Chapter 5, 193-208. Gerard O'Meara, a native of Lorrha who has a keen interest in local history, discovered a significant number of Lorrha men of other ranks, non-commissioned and officers, who served in the British Army in all the theaters of WWI. This was extraordinary for a parish and a county with a reputation for Republican activism. I owe a large measure of gratitude to Ger for his research and guidance. His chapter on my grandfather, based as it largely is on the latter's memoir and military histories, is by far the longest in his study. Less noted by me when I first read his book was the fact that quite a number of the WWI veterans, who were presumably receiving British pensions, joined or supported the IRA during the War of Independence.

22   Seamus J. King, "All Quiet on the Lorrha Front," *The Lamp*, 2015, 5-6.

King contends that there was virtually no participation by Lorrha people in the 1916 Easter Rising itself.

23   McDowell, 57-60.

24   COH, NGS, 173-4. See also COH's *The Art of Generalship: Four Exponents and One Example* (Aldershot: Gale & Polden, Ltd., Wellington Works, 1929).

25   COH, "Introduction," *Generalship*, 8-10.

26   David R. Woodward, *Field Marshall Sir William Robertson: Chief of the Imperial General Staff in the Great War* (Westport, Connecticut: Praeger, 1998), 62-63.

27   ibid., 64-65, 71-72.

28   Stephen Koss, *Asquith* (London: Hamish Hamilton, 1985), 224.

29   Kee, 594-595. COH agreed with this opinion of Collins.

30   Paul Fussell, *The Great War and Modern Memory* (Oxford University Press, 1977), 84, quoting from Leon Wolf, *In Flanders Fields: The 1917 Campaign*, 228, and Alec Waugh, *The Early Years of Alec Waugh*, 1962, 36. The attribution of the quote to Lt. Gen. Kiggell may have been apocryphal.

31   *Belfast News-Letter*, Jan. 1. 1917. This newspaper first listed the award of the DSO to Charles Head's distant relation, Lt. Col. Arthur Edward Maxwell Head, R.F.A., younger son of Dr. Henry Haswell Head, before noting that the Lt. Colonel's kinsman, "Major (temporary Lieut.-Colonel) Charles O. Head, R.F.A.," had received the same award, an astonishing coincidence. The Distinguished Service Order (DSO) is a military decoration awarded for meritorious or distinguished service by officers of the armed forces during wartime, typically in actual combat. A bar is awarded for an act which would have merited the Order in the first place. The year of conferment is engraved on the reverse of the bar.

32   COH, *Generalship*, 16. O'Meara, 111, quotes from Denis Winter's book *Haig's Command, A Reassessment*, where Winter quotes from COH's *The Art of Generalship*: "In a book which carries the authority of a dedicated professional soldier with experience going back to 1887, Colonel Head highlights the bloated staff levels in the Army and the prodigious energy expended on the huge bureaucracy and the mass of correspondence."

33   COH, *Generalship*, 14-16.

34   Michael Hopkinson, *The Irish War of Independence* (Dublin: Gill & Macmillan, 2004), 20.

35   COH, 239.

36   Bence-Jones, 181-184.

37   COH, NGS, 235.

38 Dooley, *Decline*, 232.
39 Dooley, *Land*, 3.
40 Dooley, *Decline*, 128.
41 Kee, 619.
42 Fussell, 18.
43 John Keegan, *The First World War* (New York: Alfred A. Knopf, 1999), 426.
44 Fussell, 64.
45 Ella De Burgh Dwyer of Ballyquirke, Lorrha, a large landowner, stock raiser, and generous employer, was among those who died. She and an English friend were late for their train and almost missed the boat. Miss Dwyer was buried in the Lorrha churchyard. Capt. Trench of Sopwell, Cloughjordan, whose family is frequently mentioned in this book, lost several members of his family. See O'Meara, 70-78.
46 Martin Needham, a vice commandant of the 4th Battalion, North Tipperary Brigade during the Irish War of Independence, testified to the Irish Bureau of Military History that he joined Felix Cronin's Lorrha company of Irish Volunteers in the summer of 1917 and was sworn-in to the Irish Republican Brotherhood at the Sinn Féin Hall in Lorrha that winter. In the face of the conscription threat, the company comprised 120 men by the end of February 1918. The 45 men who remained with the company after that threat receded remained with the company until the end of the war. Bureau of Military History 1913-21. Martin Needham Witness Statement W.S. 1,323.
47 Kee, 624-625.
48 Bence-Jones, 188.

Chapter 19

1 Charles Head [COH] described himself as "British First, Irish Second," in his 1943 memoir, *No Great Shakes*.
2 With these words, COH was attempting to recall his earliest reaction to the local violence in Lorrha Parish shortly after his return there. COH, 209-211.
3 COH, 235-236.
4 Dooley, *Land*, 31-32.
5 Hopkinson, 115
6 The "German Plot" was the conspiracy alleged in May 1918 by the Dublin Castle administration in Ireland to exist between the Sinn Féin movement and the German Empire to start an armed insurrection in Ireland during World War I. This alleged conspiracy, which would have diverted the British war effort, was used to justify the internment

of Sinn Féin leaders, who were actively opposing attempts to introduce conscription in Ireland (see chapter 18).

7   Kee, 631, and Dangerfield, 302.

8   Hopkinson, 115-116. In recent decades a more nuanced view of Soloheadbeg has developed. This has been reflected in recent annual commemorations at which the police victims were prayed for as well as the Volunteers who took part in the ambush. The State-sponsored centenary commemoration reflected the episode in all its complexity. See "The Irish Times view on Soloheadbeg: a complex legacy," *Irish Times*, Oct. 4, 2019.

9   Seán Hogan, *The Black and Tans in North Tipperary—Policing, Revolution and War 1913-1922* (2013).

10 David Fitzpatrick, *Politics and Irish Life 1913-1921* (Cork University Press, 1998), 10.

11 *Encyclopedia Brittanica* online.

12 *The Irish Free Press*, Philadelphia, March 1, 1919. http://www.markholan.org/archives

13 Congressional opposition to the League was a principal reason the United States eventually entered into separate treaties with the Central Powers.

14 Hopkinson, 166-167

15 Hogan, ibid.

16 Seamus J. King, "The Shooting of Sergeant Brady," first published in *Cois_Deirge*, no. 18, 1986/87, 6-7 https://www.seamusjking.com/sjk-articles/2014/6/24/spanclassposttitlethe-shooting-of-sergeant-bradys-pancois-deirge-no-18-198687-pp-44-53 Two local men were arrested for the crime and went on trial but were found not guilty and released.

17 Grace, *Monsea-Killodiernan*, 279-280.

18 Dooley, 231. Exclusion was justified on the basis of the large, troublesome Nationalist Catholic population in those three counties.

19 McDowell, 73.

20 Dooley, 178.

21 One of them was T. F. O'Meara, who farmed the adjacent land to Derrylahan in Lorrha.

22 Grace, 281, 284-285. Cleary served on the Tipperary County Council for 40 years and was a prominent farmer and stockbreeder.

23 ibid., 283.

24 D. M. Leeson, *The Black & Tans: British Police and Auxiliaries in the Irish War of Independence* (Oxford University Press, 2011), 42.

25 Gibney, 197.

26 COH, 211-212.

27 ibid., 213-214.

28 Bence-Jones,195, 199.
29 Elizabeth Bowen, "Preface to the The Last September" in *Seven Winters: Memories of a Dublin Childhood & Afterthoughts* (New York: Knopf, 1962), 201-204.
30 COH, 216; Kee, 680.
31 Foster, *Vivid Faces*, 275; Hopkinson, 173.
32 COH, 217. According to McDowell, a Co. Tipperary land agent who "sat when no other JP would attend," was murdered in January 1921. McDowell was incorrect when he asserted that a Galway landowner who "'flatly refused' to resign the Commission of the Peace and continued to attend Tuam petty sessions" was the only JP to do so. McDowell, 85.
33 Kee, 678-679.
34 COH, 218.
35 Joost Augusteijn, review of D. M. Leeson's *The Black and Tans* in *The Journal of Modern History*, Vol. 85, No. 4, December 2013, 939.
36 Kee, 672, 686.
37 J. H. Bernard to A. Martin, March 2, 1921. Quoted by McDowell, 80-81.
38 Kee, 688.
39 Another and even more notorious Bloody Sunday occurred on January 30, 1972 in the Bogside of Derry, Northern Ireland during "the Troubles" when British soldiers shot 28 unnamed civilians during a protest march.
40 Diarmaid Ferriter, "Bloody Sunday 1920 changed British attitudes to Ireland." *Irish Times*, Nov. 21, 2020
41 *Freeman's Journal*, July 12, 1921. Kee, 699, McDowell, 93-94.
42 *Irish Times*, Nov. 26, 1920 and Feb. 16, 1921. Kee, 701-703.
43 McDowell, 83-101. Eunan O'Halpin and Daithi O Corrain's *The Dead of the Irish Revolution* (Yale University Press, 2020) provides an infinitely more comprehensive account, record, and analysis of all the deaths arising from the Irish revolution between 1916 and 1921. Of the deaths of all men, women, and children who died during these years, they count 505 in 1916 and 2,344 between 1917 and 1921.
44 Dooley, *Decline*, 172.
45 Templemore Abbey had been in the Carden family since the seventeenth-century Cromwellian settlement. The neo-gothic house was built in the 1860s, replacing one built around 1820: http://greatirishhouses.blogspot.com/2013/03/templemore-abbey-co-tipperary.html
46 According to Leeson, 189, journalist Richard Bennett found convincing evidence forty years later that Clancy and O'Callaghan were killed by Auxiliary George Nathan, who belonged to an organization called "The Dublin Castle Murder Gang" in Dublin.

47 COH, 215.
48 Kee, 712.
49 Hopkinson, 193-194. The date was postponed to July 14 due to the former unfortunately colliding with the anniversary of the Battle of the Boyne.
50 Kee, 715.
51 Bence-Jones, 207-208.
52 Kee, 705.
53 Kee, 706.
54 Bence-Jones, 204-205.
55 There is some discrepancy in the accounts of this ambush between Ernie O'Malley, *Raids and Rallies* (Cork: Mercier Press, 2011. First published in 1982), 134-155, and Hopkinson's brief summary, 121-122.
56 O'Meara, 87-88.
57 General Orders New Series, June 1921. UCD Archives, Mulcahy Papers P7/A/45. Dooley, *Decline*, 183.
58 McDowell, 92.
59 Bence-Jones, 197.
60 Dooley, *Decline*, 233. Quoted in Dunraven, *Past Times and Pastimes*, 202.
61 ibid., 183.
62 COH, 218-222.
63 *Nenagh Guardian*, June 22, 1921. Appendix H. Speech of King George V opening Northern Ireland Parliament, June 22, 1921, Hopkinson, 214.
64 Bence-Jones, 213.
65 Kee, 716.
66 Replacing deference for the old order with defiance was indeed a key part of the IRA campaign of 1916-23. IRA officer Ernie O'Malley believed that physical force could free the Irish of their "slave-mindedness." The physical dismantling of the traditional British power base, the big house, through fire, was the logical development of O'Malley's War of Independence training: in 1918 he "made the men manoeuvre in demesne land to rid them of their inherent respect for the owners. Even yet their fathers touched their hats to the gentry." Gemma Clark, *Everyday Violence in the Irish Civil War* (Cambridge University Press, 2014), 75.
67 Alan Stanley, *I Met Murder on the Way: The Story of the Pearsons of Coolacrease*, self-published by Alan Stanley in 2005. Furious criticism of the book can be followed on Indymedia: http://www.indymedia.ie/article/76350. But that was just the beginning. See Tom Wall, "Getting them Out, Southern Loyalists in the War of Independence," *Dublin Review of Books*, Issue 9, Spring 2009, his review of two Aubane Historical

Society books, *Coolacrease: the true story of the Pearson executions—an incident in the Irish War of Independence* and *Troubled History: Ten Years of Controversy in Irish History—a 10th Anniversary Critique of Peter Hart's The IRA and its Enemies*. Philip O'Conor and Pat Muldowney, and others (the latter a co-author of *Coolacrease*) responded at extraordinary length to Tom Wall's review with "A House Built on Sand, Coolacrease Propaganda Exposed," also in the *Dublin Review of Books*, Issue 109, March 2009: https://www.academia.edu/221018/A_house_built_on_sand_Coolacrease_propaganda_exposed_Dublin_Review_of_Books An excellent article by Ann Marie Hourihane in the *Irish Times* throws wider and more balanced light on reactions to the Coolacrease story: https://www.irishtimes.com/opinion/we-are-still-hiding-from-our-history-ann-marie-hourihane-1.975995

68   Kee, 717.
69   Dangerfield, 199.
70   *Nenagh Guardian*, July 16, 1921, 5.

Chapter 20

1   Michael Collins, "Clearing the road–an essay in practical politics," in William G. Fitzgerald (ed.), *The voice of Ireland* (Dublin, 1923), 42.
2   Hopkinson, *Green against Green: The Irish Civil War* (Dublin: Gill Books, 1988), 24.
3   Gibney, 200-201; Kee, 725-728.
4   Dangerfield, 342.
5   COH, 237.
6   Bence-Jones, 214; Diaries of Lady Alice Howard, National Library of Ireland, MS 3,625; Quoted in Foster, *Modern Ireland*, 507-508. Charles Head was an admirer of Sir Henry Wilson's leadership in WWI, selecting him as the last of four great generals in his *The Art of Generalship: Four Exponents and One Exponent*.
7   Hopkinson, *Green*, 35.
8   Dangerfield, 343.
9   Hopkinson, 82; Bew, 430-434.
10   Hopkinson, 85.
11   Peter Hart, *The I.R.A. at War 1916-1923* (Oxford University Press, 2005), 236-237. A letter was sent to scores, possibly hundreds, of homes by western IRA units accusing Protestants of being in sympathy with the Belfast murders by supporting the union between England and Ireland.
12   Foster, *Modern Ireland*, 508-9; Dangerfield, 349.

13 O'Meara, 356.

14 Lt. Col. Michael Ravenscroft Head resigned from the British Army at this point.

15 Dooley, 233.

16 This devastating loss occurred just three years after a comprehensive two-volume guide to the collections was published. Herbert Wood, *A guide to the records deposited in the Public Record Office of Ireland* (Dublin: H.M. Stationery Office, 1919). Among the records that this author would have relied on were those of the Courts of Chancery, Common Pleas, and Prerogative; Ecclesiastical and testamentary collections of the Prerogative Court, Diocesan Registries, Probate and Matrimonial Division, Parish Registers and Deeds, the extinct jurisdiction of the Palatinate of Tipperary, and the census records of 1821, 1831, 1841, and 1851. The guide can be studied online: http://www.nationalarchives. ie/wp-content/uploads/2019/03/Herbert-Woods-Guide-to-Public-Records_2_Part1.pdf (and Part 2). See also Catriona Crowe (National Archives of Ireland), "Ruin of Public Record Office marked loss of great archive," *Irish Times*, June 30, 2012.

17 O'Meara, 356; Bence-Jones, 225-226.

18 Hart, 237; McDowell, 127, 232.

19 Gemma M. Clark, Queen's College, Oxford, Ph.D thesis, "Fire, boycott, threat and harm: social and political violence within the local community. A study of three Munster counties during the Irish Civil War, 1922-23." 2010. See 2. Arson iii Big houses, 55. Downloaded 8/12/19.

20 John Head of Ashley Park's granddaughter, Elizabeth Drought of Lettybrook, became the second wife of William Henry Darby—who succeeded to Leap Castle in 1834. In 1815, the Rev. John Head, third son of Michael and Margaret Head of Derry Castle, married Susannah Darby, a niece of William Henry Darby. Harriet, the Heads' only daughter among a passel of sons, lived at Leap Castle for a while before her marriage to Richard Uniacke Bayly (see chapter 15).

21 Marigold Freeman-Attwood, *Leap Castle: A place and its people* (Norwich, UK: Michael Russell, 2001), 138-147. Freeman-Attwood was an Oxford-educated veteran of the secret Bletchley Park WWII code-breaking center.

22 The burning of Kilboy was the subject of a comprehensive M.A. thesis under the supervision of historian Terence Dooley: Teresa Byrne, "The burning of Kilboy House, Nenagh, County Tipperary, 2 August 1922," NUI Maynooth, Oct. 2006. She based her account of the raiding, looting, and burning on extensive reports in the *Nenagh Guardian* and Samuel Doope's many letters to Lord Dunalley.

23 William Harkness to Lord Dunalley, Sept. 13, 1922, Dunalley Papers, NLI. Charles Head expressed some admiration for Collins's leadership ability and character in his memoir.

24 Teresa Byrne, 56, 202-205.

25 *Nenagh Guardian*, Aug. 6, 1922.

26 Miriam Lambe made a fine study of this Otway estate between 1750 and 1853 based on incomplete but valuable Otway papers, considering how many other estate papers were lost in the burnings. Miriam Lambe, *A Tipperary Landed Estate: Castle Otway 1750-1853*. Maynooth Studies in Local History (Dublin: Irish Academic Press, 1998).

27 Gemma Clark, 188-190. The men, who wore no uniforms, did not identify themselves as IRA and Clark wondered if they might have been Free State since they were treated leniently by the Free State legal system.

28 Grace, 287.

29 This was a temporary measure, similar to acts passed in 1923, 1924, 1926, etc.

30 Hopkinson, 181-182.

31 Dooley, 30, 175; Bence-Jones, 233, 241.

32 Dooley, 238, 193-194.

33 Rathrobbin was designed by Sir Thomas Drew who was the consulting architect on both St. Patrick's Cathedral and Christ Church Cathedral in Dublin and designed St. Anne's Cathedral in Belfast.

Chapter 21

1 Gerard O'Meara, author of *Lorrha People in the Great War*, who has deep-rooted family connections in Lorrha Parish, told the author that Derrylahan might have been spared if Charles Head had kept his head down, as did most other Anglo-Irish proprietors in that parish.

2 See chapter 19.

3 *Nenagh Guardian*, July 16, 1921, 5.

4 Dooley, 197-198.

5 *Nenagh Guardian*, July 16, 1921. Two servants, Agnes Creighton and J. M. Dundas, were awarded £100 and £8 respectively for their burned possessions

6 Frank Tracy, *If Those Trees Could Speak: The Story of an Ascendancy Family in Ireland* (Frank Tracy and South Dublin Libraries, 2005), 64-67.

7 Bence-Jones, 237; Dooley, 198.

8 ibid., 198.

9 Clark, 23. Establishing the allegiance of the injured party was obviously a challenge and involved a protracted "correspondence" between the

Ministry of Defence, Irish Office, and applicants' solicitors." Niamh Brennan, "A Political Minefield: Southern Loyalists, the Irish Grants Committee and the British Government, 1922-31," *Irish Historical Studies*, Vol. 30, No. 119 (May, 1997), 409-10. Accessed through JSTOR # 30008628..

10 Dooley, 199-200.

11 Brennan, 406-7.; Colonial Office, Irish Distress Committee, The National Archives, Kew. A second Irish Grants Committee reconvened in October 1926 with wider scope than its predecessor since it now laid special emphasis on the plight of loyalists in Southern Ireland who had suffered hardship and loss between July 11, 1921 and May 12, 1923. This later committee sat until 1930.

12 *Parl. Debates*, 1922.

13 McDowell, 139-142.

14 *Morning Post*, April 2, 1923.

15 Bence-Jones, 237-239.

16 *King's County/Offaly Chronicle*, Aug. 2, 1923, 3.

17 Clark, 19.

18 ibid, 20. Clark examined both the IGC records at the National Archives at Kew and the then uncataloged Damage to Property files in the Records of the Ministry of Finance at the National Archives of Ireland, Dublin.

19 Dooley, *Decline*, 201.

20 Brennan, 411.

21 ibid. Hansard 5 (Lords), lxii, 90-126 (July 15, 1925). Ciarán Reilly emphasized that the claims of Big House owners "were small in number compared to the thousands made by farmers, shopkeepers, publicans, and ordinary citizens," and "The fledgling Free State was hampered in its initial growth by the tide of compensation bills," Reilly, "The burning of country houses in Co. Offaly during the revolutionary period, 1920-3," in *The Irish Country House: Its Past, Present and Future*. Eds. Terence Dooley and Christopher Ridgway (Dublin: Four Courts Press, 2015), 131, 132.

22 Brennan, 412.

23 *Midland Tribune*, June 5, 1924. His wife, however, had written to a friend that he was a very militant Orangeman with his own Orange Lodge, the Leap Loyal Independents, and that "Nationalists" of any kind were persona non grata. Freeman-Attwood, 136-137.

24 ibid., 146; *Midland Tribune*, Feb. 14, 1925. In 1974, as descrbed by Freeman-Attwood, the ruined castle was bought and extensively restored and remains in private ownership today.

25 Byrne, 59-66. She cites Compensation Claims Registers (N.A., O.P.W.,

files 2/62/60-9 Munster Registers 1, 2 and 3). Kilboy was demolished in about 1955 and a single-storey Georgian-style house built in its place. When that house was destroyed by fire, Irish billionaire Tony Ryan rebuilt the house based on the original Georgian mansion but that, in turn, was badly damaged by fire in 2005.

26 Reilly, 127-128. Today Durrow Abbey is vacant and deteriorating rapidly.

27 *Leinster Leader*, Dec. 12, 1925. Today Palmerstown House Estates, with its mansion and nine hundred acres, is a choice events and golfing venue.

28 Dooley, *Decline*, 203-204.

29 Brennan, 413. Ballynastragh House is still the home of the Esmonde family.

30 Dooley, *Land*, 2-3.

31 Terence Dooley, "Land and Politics in Independent Ireland, 1923-48: The Case for Reappraisal," *Irish Historical Studies*, 34:175 (2004), 175-97.

32 Dooley, *Land*, 10.

33 Unfortunately, I was not allowed access to these records in 2007 when they were located in Dublin and they remain closed to historians, genealogists, and researchers in their permanent location in Portlaoise, despite countless appeals to the Minister of Agriculture and the matter being raised on a regular basis in the Oireachtas (Irish Parliament). Terence Dooley, *The Big Houses and Landed Estates of Ireland: A Research Guide* (Dublin: Four Courts Press, 2007), 94-95; Fiona Fitzsimons, "Records of the Irish Land Commission," *History Ireland* (Jan-Feb. 2014, vol. 22); Ray Ryan, "Land Commission records are still working documents," *Irish Examiner*, July 10, 2017; Ciaran Moran, "Calls for release of Land Commission records," Feb. 22, 2019, in *Farm Ireland*, April 24, 2019.

34 Dooley, *Land*, 12-13, 66.

35 ibid., 69.

36 Freeman-Attwood, 147. She acknowledged her debt to Noel Guerin for providing the Land Commission statistics. I have been unable to ascertain who Guerin is or was.

37 I was told by my father that Margery Head, my grandmother, also paid annuities to several members of her husband's family who spent the rest of their lives in Ireland. Aunt Grace Dean, when writing to Terence de Vere White, who had mocked my grandfather in an entire chapter based on the latter's memoir in his book *The Anglo-Irish,* informed White that the mortgage on Derrylahan had not been paid off when it was burned. Grace Dean to Terence de Vere White, copy, nd.

38 Dooley, *Land*, 84-85.
39 "Estate of Colonel Charles Octavius Head, Owner, County Tipperary." Record No. S.3732, Irish Land Commission, *Iris Oifigiúl*, Oct. 20, 1925, 1077, and June 8, 1926, 517. A fee simple estate was held by a person in his own right, free from condition of limitation. *Byrne's*, 119.
40 Jim Delahunt of Clonmona, Riverstown, evidently the same James Delahunt who had been in secret negotiation with Charles Head through Toler Garvey—this award evidently increased his existing holding; Peter Monteith from Killeen; "The Gos" Duffy from Sharragh, Rathcabbin; George Ogle (possibly from Clonfert) married to a sister of Long Bill Burke; Paddy Burke of "The Hill," Graigue, Rathcabbin; Paddy Kennedy of Walshpark—one of "The Peeler" Kennedys; Jack Pardy from Galway, possibly an awardee from a congested area; and Mary Barnwell (according to the 1911 Census there was a Barnwell family in Riverstown). Monteith's great-nephew Pat Smyth provided this information to Gerard O'Meara, my frequent informant on the inhabitants of Lorrha Parish.
41 http://www.rootsweb.com/~irltip2/newspapers/times_1927.htm
42 Felim Kennedy, whose father purchased James Delahunt's property in 1963, informed me that the migrants problem continues today. Phone conversation 6/30/20.
43 Dooley, *Land*, 94-95.
44 COH, 237-238.
45 Jackson, *Home Rule*, 244-245.
46 ibid, 245.
47 Bew, 447-448.
48 Jackson, 249
49 COH, 238. He meant a united Ireland.
50 COH, Preface, *Glance at Gallipoli*, 13-14.
51 Reviews and associated cuttings of Gen. Ian Hamilton's response to Head's criticism of his leadership of the Dardanelles Campaign, May 1931, are held in the Hamilton collection at the Liddell Hart Centre for Military Archives, King's College London. Hamilton: 17/52 1929 Oct 1-1932 May 17.
52 *The London Gazette*, Feb. 3, 1933. Six years later, he would be with the British Expeditionary Force trapped and then spectacularly rescued from the beaches of Dunkirk. In November 1942, he married Joan Phillips, daughter of a senior naval engineer officer, a veteran of WWI who was still in active service. I was born a year later, the year *No Great Shakes* was published, and my brother Patrick (future co-founder and technical director of the Williams Formula One team) in 1946.
53 Bunny Head died of a heart attack in New York City in 1964. I saw his

obituary in the *New York Times* when I arrived there that May but it was clearly not the time to contact a branch of the family I had never met, even if I had had the nerve to do so at the age of twenty.

54 Derrylahan had two beautiful oak woods, both of which were eventually cut down. Knigh Wood, owned by the former landlords of Knigh, the Tolers of Beechwood, was sold off to the timber firm of MacAinish. They cut down the wood in the early 1960s and sold off the land. Grace, 6. "In many places, woods were being cut down. Trees were a luxury associated with the old landlord class. At Roxburgh, Lady Gregory's home, everything was felled by 1929 except a few lime trees. At Castle Durrow, 650 acres of oak, beech and ash were cleared to provide land for the surrounding farmers." Valerie Pakenham, *The Big House in Ireland* (London: Cassell Paperbacks, 2000), 178.

Epilogue

1 De Vere White, 248.

2 Irish farmers were badly hit by what became known as the "economic war" between Ireland and Britain from 1932, when Fianna Fáil came into power, until 1938 when it was resolved with the Anglo-Irish Trade Agreement. Fianna Fáil had refused to pay monies owed to the British exchequer under the Land Acts and Britain responded by imposing 20 percent tariffs on a wide range of agricultural products.

3 This too touches on my family history. From late 1943, my maternal grandfather, Capt. O. W. Phillips, RN, was Naval Engineer Officer, Belfast, overseeing the repair and refitting of naval frigates, as well as a number of U.S. fighting ships, in the Pollock Dock adjacent to the famed Harland & Wolff shipyard. Toward the end of his assignment in Belfast, according to my grandfather's memoirs, I made my first trip to Ireland: "In early February 1945, my wife had to undergo a serious operation. My daughter, whose husband, Major Michael Head, R.A., a regular soldier, was fighting in Italy, flew over with her baby daughter, and kept house for me." "The Naval Career and Memoirs of Rear Admiral Owen William Phillips, C.B.E., 1891-1981," typescript, an original copy of which is archived at the Imperial War Museum, London.

4 *Gibney*, 220.

5 Protestants continued to call this city Londonderry, its official name since the 1613 charter establishing the city built by investors from the livery companies of the City of London. The mention of either name at the outbreak of the Troubles acted as a shibboleth used to associate the speaker with one of Northern Ireland's two main communities.

6   Patrick Radden Keefe, *Say Nothing: A True Story of Murder and Memory in Northern Ireland* (New York: Anchor Books, Penguin Random House LLC, 2019). This horrific story should be balanced with *Lethal Allies: British Collusion in Ireland* (Cork: Mercier Press, 2013), by journalist Anne Cadwallader. Cadwallader alleged that members of the Royal Ulster Constabulary (RUC) and Ulster Defence Regiment (UDR) were part of a loyalist gang that killed more than a hundred people, most of them Catholic civilians, in just one small area of Co. Antrim in the 1970s.

7   Bence-Jones, *Twilight of the Ascendancy*, 1987; Peter Somerville-Large, *The Irish Country* House, 1995; and others.

8   Dooley, *Decline*, 2001, and several others.

9   A new Irish owner has restored magnificently the early eighteenth-century Sopwell Hall, mentioned numerous times in this book as the home of the Sadliers first and then the Trenches. Cosby Patrick Trench (1915-1983), the last of his family to own the house, and his wife were much admired and respected locally and nationally for their services to music. The house and its 300-acre estate were offered for sale in 2020 for €8.5 million.

10 Beckett, *Anglo-Irish Tradition*, 148.

Bibliography

Akenson, Donald H., *The Church of Ireland: Ecclesiastical Reform and Revolution, 1800-1885* (New Haven: Yale University Press, 1971)

Andrews, John H., *Shapes of Ireland: Maps and their Makers* (Oxford: Clarendon Press, 1975)

Barnard, T. C., *Cromwellian Ireland: English Government and Reform in Ireland 1649-1660* (New York: Oxford University Press, 2000)

Barnard, Toby, *A New Anatomy of Ireland, The Irish Protestants, 1641-1770* (New Haven: Yale University Press, 2003)

Barnard, Toby, *Making the Grand Figure, Lives and Possessions in Ireland, 1641-1770* (New Haven: Yale University Press, 2004)

Bartlett, Thomas and Keith Jeffery, eds., *A Military History of Ireland* (Cambridge University Press, 1996)

Beaumont, Gustave de, *Ireland: Social, Political, and Religious* (Cambridge, MA: Belknap Press, Harvard, 2006)

Beckett, J. C., *The Anglo-Irish Tradition* (Ithaca, NY: Cornell University Press, 1976)

Beckett, J. C., *The Making of Modern Ireland, 1603-1923* (London: Faber & Faber, 1966)

Bence-Jones, Mark, *Twilight of the ascendancy* (London: Constable, 1987)

Bew, Paul, *Ireland: The Politics of Enmity 1789-2006* (Oxford University Press, 2007)

Bottigheimer, Karl, *English Money and Irish Land* (Oxford: Clarendon Press, 1971)

Bourke, Richard, and Ian McBride, editors, *The Princeton History of Modern Ireland* (Princeton, 2016)

Bowen, Elizabeth, *Bowen's Court & Seven Winters* (London: Vintage, 1999)

Bowen, Elizabeth, *The Last September* (New York: Anchor Books, 2000)

Boyce, D. George, *Nineteenth-Century Ireland: The Search for Stability* (Dublin: Gill & Macmillan, 1990, 2005)

Breen, Dan, *My Fight for Irish Freedom* (Dublin: Anvil Books, 1981)

Broeker, Galen, *Rural Disorder and Police Reform in Ireland, 1812-26* (London: Routledge Kegan Paul, 1970)

Brynn, Edward, *Crown & Castle: British rule in Ireland, 1800-1830* (Dublin: O'Brien Press, 1978)

Byrne, Joseph, *Byrne's Dictionary of Irish Local History from earliest times to c. 1900* (Cork: Mercier Press, 2004)

Buckland, Patrick, *Irish Unionism, 1885-1923: A documentary history* (Belfast: Her Majesty's Stationery Office, 1973)

Burtchaell, George D., and Thomas U. Sadleir, *Alumni Dublinenses: A Register of the Students, Graduates, Professors, and Provosts of Trinity College, in the University of Dublin*. (London: Williams and Norgate, 1924).

Canny, Nicholas, *Making Ireland British, 1580-1650* (Oxford University Press, 2001)

Canny, Nicholas, "Identity formation in Ireland: the emergence of the Anglo-Irish," in N. Canny and A. Pagden, eds., *Colonial identity in the Atlantic World, 1500-1800* (Princeton, 1987)

Clark, Gemma, *Everyday Violence in the Irish Civil War* (Cambridge University Press, 2014)

Clarke, Aidan, *Prelude to Restoration in Ireland: the end of the Commonwealth, 1659-1660* (Cambridge, 1999)

Connolly, S. J., ed., *The Oxford Companion to Irish History* (Oxford University Press, 1998)

Curl, James S., *The Londonderry Plantation, 1609-1914* (Chichester, Sussex: Phillimore Co., 1986)

Dangerfield, George, *The Damnable Question: One Hundred and Twenty Years of Anglo-Irish Conflict* (Boston: Little Brown & Co., 1976)

De Breffny, Brian, ed., *The Irish World: The History of Cultural Achievements of the Irish People* (London: Thames & Hudson, 1977)

Donnelly, James S., Jr., *Captain Rock: The Irish Agrarian Rebellion of 1821-1824* (Madison, Wisc.: Univ. of Wisconsin Press, 2009)

Donnelly, James S., Jr., editor-in-chief, *Encyclopedia of Irish History and Culture* (Thomson Gale, 2004)

Donnelly, James S. Jr., *Landlord and tenant in nineteenth-century Ireland* (Dublin: Gill and Macmillan, 1973)

Donnelly, James S., Jr., *The Great Irish Potato Famine* (Stroud, Gloucestershire: The History Press, 2001)

Dooley, Terence and Christopher Ridgway, editors, *Sources for the History of Landed Estates in* Ireland, ed. MaryAnn Lyons (Maynooth Research Guides for Irish Local History, 2000)

Dooley, Terence, *The Big Houses and Landed Estates of Ireland: A Research Guide* (Dublin: Four Courts Press, 2007)

Dooley, Terence, *The Decline of the Big House in Ireland: A study of Irish landed families, 1860-1960* (Dublin: Wolfhound Press, 2001)

Dooley, Terence and Christopher Ridgway, editors, *The Irish Country House: Its Past, Present and Future* (Dublin: Four Courts Press, 2015)

Dooley, Terence, *'The Land for the People,' The Land Question in Independent Ireland* (University College of Dublin Press, 2004)

Elliott, Bruce, *Irish Migrants in the Canadas* (Montreal: McGill Queens University Press, 1988)

Elliott, Marianne, *Partners in Revolution: The United Irishmen and France* (New Haven: Yale University Press, 1982)

Elliott, Marianne, *Robert Emmet: The Making of a Legend* (London: Profile Books, 2003)

Elliott, Marianne, *Wolf Tone: Prophet of Irish Independence* (New Haven: Yale University Press, 1989)

Fletcher, Ian, *Galloping at Everything; the British Cavalry in the Peninsular War and at Waterloo, 1808-15: A Reappraisal* (Staplehurst, UK: Spellmount, 1999)

Foster, R. F., *Modern Ireland 1606-1972* (London: Allen Lane The Penguin Press, 1988)

Foster, R. F., *The Irish Story: Telling Tales and Making It Up in Ireland* (Oxford University Press, 2002)

Foster, R. F., *The Oxford Illustrated History of Ireland* (Oxford University Press, 1989)

Foster, R. F., *Vivid Faces: The Revolutionary Generation in Ireland, 1890-1923* (New York: W. W. Norton, 2014)

Fraser, Antonia, *Cromwell, the Lord Protector* (New York: Grove Press, 2001)

Fraser, Antonia, *The King and the Catholics: England, Ireland and the Fight for Religious Freedom, 1780-1829* (New York: Doubleday, 2018)

Freeman-Atwood, Marigold, *Leap Castle: A Place and Its People* (Norwich: Michael Russell Publishing, 2001)

Geoghegan, Patrick, *King Dan: The Rise of Daniel O'Connell, 1775-1829* (Dublin: Gill & Macmillan, 2008)

Geoghegan, Patrick M., *Liberator: The Life and Death of Daniel O'Connell 1830-1847*

Geoghegan, Patrick M., *Robert Emmet: A Life* (Dublin: Gill & Macmillan, 2002)

Geoghegan, Patrick M., *The Irish Act of Union* (New York: St. Martin's Press, 1999)

Gibney, John, *A Short History of Ireland, 1500-2000* (Yale University Press, 2017)

Grace, Daniel, *Portrait of a Parish: Monsea & Killodiernan, Co. Tipperary* (Nenagh, Co. Tipperary: Relay Books, 1996)

Grace, Daniel, *The great famine in Nenagh poor law union, Co. Tipperary* (Nenagh: Relay Books, 2000)

Griffin, Kevin M. and Kevin A., *Ballina/Boher Parish: Our History and Traditions* (Ballina, Co. Tipperary: Ballina Killaloe Print, 2000)

Harris, Tim, *Restoration: Charles II and His Kingdoms 1660-1685* (London: Penguin, 2005)

Harris, Tim, *Revolution: The Great Crisis of the British Monarchy 1685-1720* (London: Penguin, 2007)

Hart, Peter, *The I.R.A. at War 1916-1923* (Oxford University Press, 2003)

Hayes, William J., *Tipperary in the Year of Rebellion* (Carrig Hill, Co. Tipperary: Lisheen Publications, 1998)

Head, Charles O., *A Glance at Gallipoli* (London: Eyre & Spottiswoode, 1931)

Head, Charles O., *Napoleon and Wellington* (London: Robert Hale Ltd., nd)

Head, Charles O., *No Great Shakes: An Autobiography* (London: Robert Hale Ltd., 1943)

Head, Charles O., *The Art of Generalship: Four Exponents and One Example* (Aldershot: Gale & Polden Ltd, n.d.)

Hopkinson, Michael, *Green against Green: The Irish Civil War* (Dublin: Gill Books, 1988)

Hopkinson, Michael, *The Irish War of Independence* (Dublin: Gill & Macmillan, 2004)

Jackson, Alvin, *Colonel Edward Saunderson: Land and Loyalty in Victorian Ireland* (Oxford: Clarendon Press, 1995)

Jackson, Alvin, *Home Rule: An Irish History 1800-2000* (London: Phoenix, 2004)

Alvin Jackson, *Ireland 1798-1998: War, Peace and Beyond* (Chichester, West Sussex: Wiley-Blackwell, 2010)

Jay, Mike, *The Unfortunate Colonel Despard: The Tragic True Story of the Last Man Condemned to be Hung, Drawn, and Quartered* (London: Bantam Books, 2004)

Kee, Robert, *The Green Flag: A History of Irish Nationalism* (London: Penguin Books, 2000)

Keegan, John, *The First World War* (New York: Vintage Books, 2000)

Kelly, John, *The Graves are Walking: The Great Famine and the Saga of the Irish People* (New York: Henry Holt & Co., 2012)

Kenyon, John and Jane Ohlmeyer, eds., *The Civil War: A Military History of England, Scotland and Ireland 1628-1660* (Cambridge University Press, 1996)

Lambe, Miriam, *A Tipperary landed estate: Castle Otway, 1750-1853* (Dublin: Irish Academic Press, 1998)

Lecky, W. E. H., *A History of Ireland in the Eighteenth Century, Abridged and with an Introduction by L. P. Curtis, Jr.* (University of Chicago Press, 1972)

Lecky, W. E. H., *A History of Ireland in the Eighteenth Century*, Vol. 3 (Cambridge University Press, 2010)

Leeson, D. M., *The Black & Tans: British Police and Auxiliaries in the Irish War of Independence* (Oxford University Press, 2011)

Loftus, Simon, *The Invention of Memory: An Irish Family Scrapbook, 1560-1934* (London: Daunt Books, 2013)

Lyons, Mary C., *Illustrated Incumbered Estates Ireland 1850-1905* (Whitegate, Co. Clare: Ballinakella Press, 1993)

Magan, William, *The Story of Ireland: A History of an Ancient Family and Their Country* (Shaftesbury, Dorset, 2000; first published as *Umma-More* in 1983)

McDowell, R. B., *Crisis and Decline: The Fate of the Southern Unionists* (Dublin: The Lilliput Press, 2015)

McElligott, Jason, *Cromwell: Our Chief of Enemies* (Dundalk: Dundalgan Press, 1994)

McEneaney, Eamonn, *Discover Waterford* (Dublin: The O'Brien Press, 2001)

Murphy, Donal A., *The Two Tipperarys: the national and local politics, devolution and self-determination, of the unique 1838 division into two ridings, and the aftermath* (Nenagh: Relay Books, 1994)

Murphy, Nancy, *A trip through Tipperary Lakeside: from Nenagh to Ballina-Killaloe* (Nenagh: Relay Books, 1997)

Nolan, William and Timothy P. O'Neill, eds., *Offaly: History and Society* (Dublin: Geography Publications, 1999)

Nolan, William, and T. G. McGrath, eds., *Tipperary: history and society* (Dublin: Geography Publications, 1985)

Nolan, William, and Thomas P. Power, *Waterford history and society: interdisciplinary essays on the History of an Irish County* (Dublin: Geography, 1992)

O'Brien, Conor Cruise, *The Story of Ireland* (New York: Viking, 1972)

O'Donnell, Ruan, *Remember Emmet: Images of the Life and Legacy of Robert Emmet* (Dublin: Wordwell in association with the National Library of Ireland, 2003)

Ó Gráda, Cormac, *Black '47 and Beyond: The Great Irish Famine in History, Economy, and Memory* (Princeton, 1999)

O'Hart, John, *The Irish and Anglo-Irish landed gentry when Cromwell came to Ireland; or, A supplement to Irish pedigrees* (Dublin: M. H. Gill & son, 1884)

Ohlmeyer, Jane H., ed., *Ireland from independence to occupation, 1641-1660* (Cambridge University Press, 1995)

O'Meara, Gerard, *Lorrha People in the Great War* (Cork: Gerard O'Meara, 2016)

Pakenham, Valerie, *The Big House in Ireland* (London: Cassell Paperbacks, 2000)

Pender, Seamus, ed., *Council books of the Corporation of Waterford, 1662-1700, together with nine documents of 1580-82* (Dublin, Stationery Off. For the Irish Manuscripts Commission, 1964)

Penn, William, *My Irish Journal 1669-1670,* editor, Isabel Grubb (London: Longmans, Green & Co., 1952)

Power, Thomas P., *Land, Politics and Society in Eighteenth-Century Tipperary* (Oxford: Clarendon Press, 1993)

Prendergast, J. P., *The Cromwellian Settlement of Ireland* (London: Constable & Co., 1996; first published 1865)

Reidy, Conor, *Criminal Irish Drunkards: The Inebriate Reformatory System 1900-1920* (Dublin: The History Press Ireland, 2014

Reilly, Ciarán, *The Irish Land Agent 1830-60: The Case of King's County* (Reilly and Four Courts Press, 2014)

Reilly, Tom, *Cromwell: An Honourable Enemy: the untold story of the Cromwellian invasion of Ireland* (Dingle, Co. Kerry, Ireland: Brandon, 1999)

Seymour, St. John D., *The Puritans in Ireland, 1647-1661* (Oxford: Clarendon Press,1969)

Sheil, Richard Lalor, "Lord Norbury," in *Sketches of the Irish Bar,* vol. 2 of (Forgotten Books, 2018)

Somerville-Large, Peter, *The Irish Country House: A Social History* (London: Sinclair-Stevenson, 1995)

Stanley, Alan, *I met Murder on the way: The Story of the Pearsons of Coolacrease* (Quinagh, Co. Carlow: Alan Stanley, 2005)

Tillyard, Stella, *Citizen Lord: The Life of Edward Fitzgerald, Irish Revolutionary* (New York: Farrar Straus & Giroux, 1997)

Vaughan, W. E., *Landlords and Tenants in mid-Victorian Ireland* (Oxford: Clarendon Press, 1994)

Wedgwood, C. V., *A Coffin for King Charles: The Trial and Execution of Charles* (Oxford: The Akadine Press, 1964)

Wheeler, James S., *Cromwell in Ireland* (New York: St. Martin's Press, 1999)

White, Terence de Vere, *The Anglo-Irish: The men & women who were involved in a confluence of cultures that spanned 200 years* (London: Gollancz, 1972)

Wolf, Ellen M., *"An Anarchy in the Mind and in the Heart" Narrating Anglo-Ireland* (Lewisburg: Bucknell University Press, 2006)

Woodham Smith, Cecil, *The Great Hunger: Ireland 1845-1849* (London: Penguin Books, 1991)

Wyndham, Andrew Higgins, editor, *Re-imagining Ireland: How a storied island is transforming its politics, economy, religious life, and culture for the twenty-first century* (Charlottesville, Va: University of Virginia Press, 2006)

Young, Arthur, *A Tour in Ireland: with General Observations on the Present State of that Kingdom* (Elibron Classics, 2006), Vols. I and II

Articles and Chapters

Boland, Tim, "A most distressing breach of promise case," *Tipperary Historical Journal*, 2017, 42-49

Boland, Tim, "The Head Family of Ballinaclough: Where love and respect gave way to Boycott and Eviction," in *Mining the Past 2015/16*, Silvermines Historical Society, 22-26

Brennan, Niamh, "A Political Minefield: Southern Loyalists, the Irish Grants Committee and the British Government, 1922-31," *Irish Historical Studies*, Vol. 30, No. 119 (May, 1997), 406-419.

Delany, V. T. H., "The Palatinate Court of the Liberty of Tipperary," in *American Journal of Legal History*, vol. 5, 103-104.

Grace, Daniel, "The Shooting of Richard U. Bayly near Nenagh, Co.Tipperary, in 1847," in *Cloughjordan Heritage*, Vol. V, 2001, 14-23

Daniel Grace, "The Threatening Notice in Pre-Famine County Tipperary," *Tipperary Historical Journal*, 2009, 47-70

Daniel Grace, "Homicide in Pre-Famine County Tipperary," *Tipperary Historical Journal*, 2013, 158-182.

Lysaght, Moira, "Norbury, 'The Hanging Judge' (1745-1831)," *Dublin Historical Record*, Vol. 30, No. 2 (March 1977), 58-65.

Murtagh, Herman, "Jacobite Waterford," in John Kirwan, editor, *Kilkenny: Studies in Honour of Margaret M. Phelan* (Kilkenny: The Kilkenny Archaeological Society, 1997), 88-97.

Welpy, W H, "Colonel Robert Phaire, 'Regicide,' his ancestors, history, and descendants," in *Notes and Queries*, Feb. 17 and 24, Mar. 3 and 10, 1923.

Index